Pearson New International Edition

Introducing Hospitality
Sixth Edition
John R. Walker

Pearson Education Limited
Edinburgh Gate
Harlow
Essex CM20 2JE
England and Associated Companies throughout the world

Visit us on the World Wide Web at: www.pearsoned.co.uk

© Pearson Education Limited 2014

 ISBN 10: 1-292-02006-7
ISBN 13: 978-1-292-02006-8

British Library Cataloguing-in-Publication Data
A catalogue record for this book is available from the British Library

Printed in the United States of America

Table of Contents

Introducing Hospitality

Introducing Hospitality

OBJECTIVES

After reading and studying this text, you should be able to:

- Describe the characteristics of the hospitality industry.

- Explain corporate philosophy.

- Discuss why service has become such an important facet of the hospitality industry.

- Suggest ways to improve service.

Prelude

Hospitality through the Ages[1]

The concept of hospitality is as old as civilization itself. Its development from the ancient custom of breaking bread with a passing stranger to the operations of today's multifaceted hospitality conglomerates makes fascinating reading, and interesting comparisons can be made with today's hospitality management.

The word *hospitality* comes from *hospice,* an old French word meaning "to provide care/shelter for travelers." The most famous hospice is the Hospice de Beaune in the Burgundy region of France, also called the Hotel Dieu or the House of God. It was founded as a charity hospital in 1443 by Nicolas Rolin, the Chancellor of Burgundy, as a refuge for the poor.

The hospital is still functioning, partly because of its role in the wine world. Throughout the centuries, several Burgundian landowners have donated vineyards to the Hospice to help pay for maintaining its costs. Every Fall, the wines from these vineyards—about a hundred acres of vines—are sold at a colorful wine auction on the third Thursday in November, which determines the prices for the next year's Burgundy wines.

Ancient Times

The Sumerians (who lived in what is now Iraq) were the first to record elements of hospitality in about 4,500 years B.C.E. They moved from being hunter-gatherers to growing crops, which, due to surpluses, they were able to trade. More time became available for other activities such as writing, inventing money, creating pottery, making tools, and producing beer, which was probably safer to drink than water! Taverns served several beers, and as with today, provided a place for locals to relax and enjoy each other's company.

Between 4,000 and 2,000 B.C.E., early civilizations in Europe, China, Egypt, and India all had some elements of hospitality offerings, such as taverns and inns along the roadside.

The Hospice de Beaune.

Greece and Rome

Mention of hospitality—in the form of taverns—is found in writings dating back to ancient Greece and Rome, beginning with the Code of Hammurabi (circa 1700 B.C.E.). The Code required owners to report guests who planned crimes in their taverns. The penalty for not doing so was death, making tavern-keeping a hazardous occupation. The death penalty could also be imposed for watering the beer!

Increased travel and trade made some form of overnight accommodations an absolute necessity. Because travel was slow and journeys long and arduous, many travelers depended solely on the hospitality of private citizens.[2] In the Greek and Roman empires, inns and taverns sprang up everywhere. The Romans constructed elaborate and well-appointed inns on all the main roads. They were located about twenty-five miles apart. To ensure that fresh horses were available for officials and couriers of the Roman government, these inns could only be used with special government documents granting permission. By the time Marco Polo traveled to the Far East, there were 10,000 inns, the best of which were in China.[3]

Some wealthy landowners built their own inns on the edges of their estates. These inns were run by household slaves. Nearer the cities, inns and taverns were run by freemen or by retired gladiators who would invest their savings in the "restaurant business" in the same way that so many of today's retired athletes open restaurants. The first "business lunch" is reputed to have been the idea of Seqius Locates, a Roman innkeeper; in 40 B.C.E. Locates devised the idea for ships' brokers, who were often too busy to go home for their midday meals.

Medieval Times

On the European continent, Charlemagne established rest houses for pilgrims in the eighth century; the sole purpose of several orders of knighthood was to protect pilgrims and to provide hospitality for pilgrims on their routes. One such rest house, an abbey at Roncesvalles, advertised services such as a warm welcome at the door, free bread, a barber and a cobbler, cellars full of fruit and almonds, two hospices with beds for the sick, and even a consecrated burial ground.

In 1282, the innkeepers of Florence, Italy, incorporated a guild, or an association for the purpose of business. The inns belonged to the city, which sold three-year leases at auction. They must have been profitable, because by 1290, there were eighty-six innkeepers as members of the guild.

In England, the stagecoach became the favored method of transportation. A journey from London to the city of Bath took three days, with several stopovers at inns or taverns that were also called post houses. Today, the journey from London to Bath takes about one and a half hours by car or train. As travel and travelers increased during the Middle Ages, so did the number of wayside inns in Europe; yet, they were primitive affairs by today's standards. Guests often slept on mattresses in what today would be the inn's lobby. As the quality of the inns improved, more people began to travel. Many of the travelers were wealthy people, accustomed to the good life; their expectations demanded that inns be upgraded.

In the late sixteenth century, a type of eating place for commoners called an *ordinary* began to appear in England. These places were taverns serving a fixed-price, fixed-menu meal at a long common table. Ordinary diners could not be choosy, nor did they often question what they were eating. Frequently, the main dish served was a long-cooked, highly seasoned meat-and-vegetable stew. Culinary expertise was limited by the availability and cost of certain ingredients. Few diners had sound teeth—many had no teeth at all—so the meal had to be able to be gummed as well as being edible. Fresh meat was not always available; spoiled meat was often the rule rather than the exception. Spices helped not only to preserve meat but also to disguise the flavor of gamey or "high" meat.

Coffee Houses

During the sixteenth century, two "exotic" imports began to influence the culinary habits of Western Europe: coffee and tea. These beverages, so integrated into the twenty-first century way of life, were once mere curiosities. Travelers to Constantinople (now Istanbul, Turkey) enjoyed coffee there and brought it back to Europe.

During the seventeenth century, coffeehouses sprang up all over Europe. By 1675, the city-state of Venice had dozens of coffee houses, including the famous Café Florian on the piazza San Marco, still filled to capacity today. The first English coffee house was opened in 1652. Coffee houses, the social and literary centers of their day and the predecessor of today's cafés and coffee shops, served another, even more useful (though less obvious), purpose: They helped to sober up an entire continent.

In a day when water was vile, milk dangerous, and carbonated beverages centuries in the future, alcoholic drinks were the rule, rather than the exception. Adults drank amounts measured in gallons. Queen Elizabeth I's ladies-in-waiting, for instance, were allowed a breakfast allowance of two gallons of ale. Drunkenness was rampant.

The New World

There is some evidence that a tavern was built in Jamestown, Virginia, during the early days of the settlement. It was in Boston where the first ordinary was recorded—Cole's Ordinary—in 1663. After Cole's, the next recorded ordinary was Hudson's House, in 1640.[4] The Dutch built the first known tavern in New York—the Stadt Huys—in 1642. Early colonial American inns and taverns are steeped as much in history as they are in hospitality. The next year, Kreiger's Tavern opened on Bowling Green in New York City. During the American Revolution, this tavern, then called the King's Arms, became the Revolutionary headquarters of British General Gage.

The even more famous Frauncis Tavern was the Revolutionary headquarters of General George Washington and was the place where he made his famous Farewell Address. It is still operating today. As the colonies grew from scattered settlements to towns and cities, more and more travelers appeared, along with more accommodations to serve them. The inn, tavern, or ordinary in the colonies soon became a gathering place for residents, a place where they could catch up

Café Florian, St. Marks Square, Venice, Italy.

on the latest gossip, keep up with current events, hold meetings, and conduct business. The innkeeper was often the most respected member of the community and was always one of its more substantial citizens. The innkeeper usually held some local elected office and sometimes rose much higher than that. John Adams, the second president of the United States, owned and managed his own tavern between 1783 and 1789.

The Revolutionary War did little to change the character of these public places. They maintained their position as social centers, political gathering places, newsrooms, watering holes, and travelers' rests; now, however, these places were going by different names—hotels—that reflected a growing French influence in the new nation.

The French Revolution

The French Revolution took place at approximately the same time as the American colonies were fighting for their independence. Among many other effects, the French Revolution helped to change the course of culinary history. M. Boulanger, "the father of the modern restaurant," sold soups at his all-night tavern on the Rue Bailleul. He called these soups *restorantes* (restoratives), which is the origin of the word *restaurant*. One dish was made of sheep's feet in a white sauce, another was *boulangere* potatoes—a dish in use today—made of sliced potatoes cooked in stock, which was baked in the bread baker's oven after the bread was done.[5]

The French Revolution, 1789–1799, changed the course of culinary history. Because nearly all the best chefs worked for the nobility, who were deposed or literally "lost their heads," the chefs lost their employment. Many chefs immigrated to America, especially to New Orleans, a French enclave in America. Others scattered throughout Europe or immigrated to Quebec, a French-speaking province of Canada. The chefs brought their culinary traditions with them. Soon the plain, hearty fare of the British and the primitive cooking of the Americans were laced with *sauces piquantes* (sauces having a pleasantly sharp taste or appetizing flavor) and *pots au feu* (French beef stew). In 1784, during a five-year period as an envoy to France, Thomas Jefferson acquired a taste for French cuisine. He later persuaded a French chef to come to the White House to lend his expertise. This act stimulated interest in French cuisine and enticed U.S. tavern owners to offer better quality and more interesting food.

Over time, New Orleans was occupied by Britain, Spain, France, and America, and one interesting restaurant there, the Court of the Two Sisters, has the names of prisoners of various wars inscribed on the walls of its entrance.

The Court of the Two Sisters.

The Nineteenth Century

Restaurants continued to flourish in Europe. In 1856, Antoine Carême published *La Cuisine Classique* and other volumes detailing numerous dishes and their sauces. The grande cuisine offered a carte (or list) of suggestions available from the kitchen. This was the beginning of the à la carte menu. In 1898 the Savoy Hotel opened in London. The general manager was the renowned César Ritz (today, the Ritz-Carlton hotels bear his name) and the chef de cuisine was August Escoffier. Between them, they revolutionized hotel restaurants. Escoffier was one of the greatest chefs of all time. He is best known for his classic book *Le Guide Culinaire,* which simplified the extraordinary works of Carême. He also installed the brigade de cuisine system in the kitchen.

Americans used their special brand of ingenuity to create something for everyone. By 1848, a hierarchy of eating places existed in New York City. At the bottom was Sweeney's "sixpenny eating house" on Ann Street, whose proprietor, Daniel Sweeney, achieved questionable fame as the father of the "greasy spoon." Sweeney's less than appetizing fare ("small plate sixpence, large plate shilling") was literally slid down a well-greased counter to his hungry guests, who cared little for the social amenities of dining.

The famous Delmonico's was at the top of the list of American restaurants for a long time. The Delmonico family owned and operated the restaurant from 1827 until 1923, when it closed due to Prohibition, The name *Delmonico's* was synonymous with fine food, exquisitely prepared and impeccably served—the criteria by which all like establishments were judged. Delmonico's served Swiss-French cuisine and became the focal point of American gastronomy (the art of good eating). Delmonico's is also credited with the invention of the bilingual menu, Baked Alaska, Chicken à la King, and Lobster Newberg. The Delmonico steak is named after the restaurant. More and more, eating places in the United States and abroad catered to residents of a town or city and less to travelers; the custom of eating out for its own sake had arrived.

Thirty-five restaurants in New York City have now celebrated their one-hundredth birthdays. One of them, PJ Clarke's established in 1884, is a "real" restaurant-bar that has changed little in its hundred years of operation. On entering, one sees a large mahogany bar, its mirror tarnished by time, the original tin ceiling, and the tile mosaic floor. Memorabilia ranges from celebrity pictures to Jessie, the house fox terrier that customers had stuffed when she died and who now

PJ Clarke's, established in 1884 and still going strong.

stands guard over the ladies' room door. Guests still write down their own checks at lunchtime, on pads with their table numbers on them (this goes back to the days when one of the servers could not read or write and struggled to remember orders).[6]

Many American cities had hotel palaces: Chicago had the Palmer House, New Orleans had the St. Charles, St. Louis had the Planter's Hotel, Boston had The Lenox, and San Antonio had The Menger. As the railroads were able to transport passengers to exotic locations like South Florida, hotels such as The Breakers in Palm Beach were built to accommodate the guests.

The Breakers, Palm Beach, Florida.

The Twentieth Century

In 1921, Walter Anderson and Billy Ingraham began the White Castle hamburger chain. The name White Castle was selected because white stood for purity and castle for strength. The eye-catching restaurants were nothing more than stucco building shells, a griddle, and a few chairs. People came in droves, and within ten years, White Castle had expanded to 115 units.[7]

The Four Seasons restaurant opened in 1959 as the first elegant American restaurant that was not French in style. The Four Seasons was the first restaurant to offer seasonal menus. With its modern architecture and art as a theme, Joe Baum, the developer of this and many other successful restaurants, understood why people go to restaurants—to be together and to connect to one another. It is very important that the restaurant reinforce why guests chose it in the first place. Restaurants exist to create pleasure, and how well a restaurant meets this expectation of pleasure is a measure of its success.[8]

Following World War II, North America took to the road. There was a rapid development of hotels, motels, fast food, and coffee shops. The 1950s and 1960s also saw an incredible growth in air transportation. Cross-continental flights were not only more frequent, but took much less time. Many of the new jets introduced in this period helped develop tourism worldwide. Hotels and restaurant chains sprang up to cater to the needs of the business and leisure traveler as well as city residents.

In the 1980s, hospitality, travel, and tourism continued to increase dramatically. The baby boomers began to exert influence through their buying power. Distant exotic destinations and resorts became even more accessible. The 1990s began with the recession that had started in 1989. The Gulf War continued the downturn that the industry had experienced. As hospitality and tourism companies strived for profitability, they downsized and consolidated. From 1993 until 9/11, the economic recovery proved very strong and hospitality businesses expanded in North America and abroad, particularly in Europe and China.

Welcome to You, the Future Hospitality Industry Leaders!

The hospitality industry is a fascinating, fun, and stimulating one in which to enjoy a career, plus you get compensated quite well and have excellent advancement opportunities. We often hear from industry professionals that it (the industry) gets in your blood—meaning we become one with the hospitality industry. On countless class industry visits, the persons speaking to the class said that they wouldn't change their job—even if they had a chance. Only one speaker said, "You must be nuts if you want to work in this industry"—of course, he was joking! But there are some realities you need to be aware of, and they are discussed in the section titled, "Characteristics of the Hospitality Industry," found later in the text. Many examples exist of people graduating and being offered positions that enable them to gain a good foundation of knowledge and experience in the industry. Possible career paths are illustrated in Figure 1. In most cases, it does not take long for advancement opportunities to come along. Let's begin our journey with a look at *service spirit*, which plays a crucial role in the success of our industry, no matter what your position or title is.

Ever think about why Marriott International is so successful? Well, one of the reasons is given by Jim Collins writing in the foreword to Bill Marriott's book, *The Spirit to Serve: Marriott's Way*. Collins says Marriott has *timeless core values and enduring purpose*, including the belief that its people are number one: "Take care of Marriott people and they will take care of the guests." Also, Marriott's commitment to continuous improvement and good old-fashioned dedication to hard work and having fun while doing it provide a foundation of stability and enduring character. Collins adds that Marriott's core purpose—making people away from home feel that they are among friends and are really wanted—serves as a fixed point of guidance and inspiration.

So, where does *hospitality spirit* fit into all this? It's simple—it begins with each and every time we have a guest encounter. People with a *service spirit* are happy to do something extra to make a guest's experience memorable. The hospitality spirit means that it is our passion to give pleasure to others, or as one human resources director, Charlotte Jordan, calls it, "creating memorable experiences for others and being an ambassador of the world, adding warmth and caring."[9] Every day we encounter guests who rely on us for service, which can make or break their experience. We want to "wow" guests and have them return often with their friends. Yes, we are in the people business, and it's "we the people" who succeed in the hospitality industry when we take pride in the words of the Ritz-Carlton hotel company: We are ladies and gentlemen taking care of ladies and gentlemen.

The **National Restaurant Association (NRA)** forecasts a need for thousands of supervisors and managers for the hospitality and tourism industries. Are you wondering if there's room in this dynamic industry for you? You bet! There's room for everyone. The best advice is to consider what you love to do most and get some experience in that area—to see if you really like it—because our

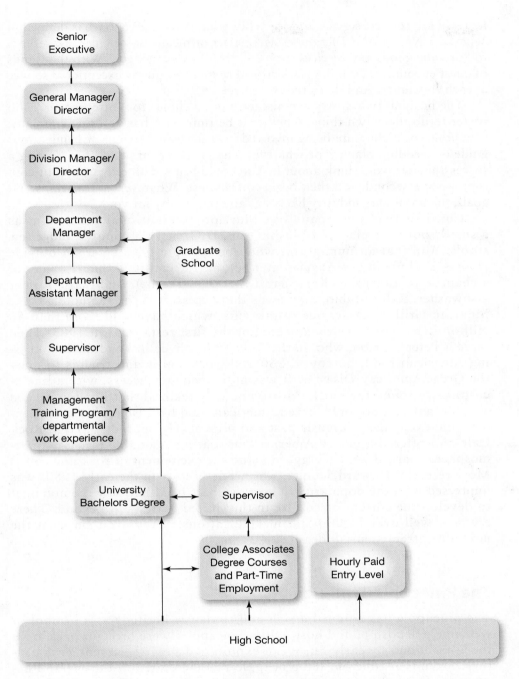

Figure 1 • A Possible Career Path in the Hospitality Industry. Is Education Worth It? You Bet! Just Think—Over a Career, the Difference in Salary between an Associate and a Bachelor's Degree Is $500,000. Yes, That's Half a Million Bucks!

(*Source:* U.S. Census Bureau Average Lifetime Earnings—Different Levels of Education.)

industry has some distinct characteristics. For starters, we are in the business of giving service. When Kurt Wachtveilt, thirty-year veteran general manager of the Oriental Hotel in Bangkok, Thailand—considered by many to be one of the best hotels in the world—was asked, "What is the secret of being the best?"

he replied, "Service, service, service!" But what is service? *Service* is defined in *Webster's New World Dictionary* as "the act or means of serving." To serve is to "provide goods and services for" and "be of assistance to." With thousands of guest encounters each day, it is critical to give our guests exceptional service at each encounter. And that's the challenge!

The hospitality industry can also be a good choice for entrepreneurs who prefer to do their own thing, whether it be running a bar, catering company, restaurant, or night club; being involved in event management; or being a tour guide or wedding planner or whatever. The prospects are good for starting a successful endeavor. Think about it: You could begin with one restaurant concept, open a second, and then begin to franchise. Whatever your dreams and goals, the hospitality industry likely has an opportunity for you.

Consider that a company like Marriott International started out as a small root beer place, in Washington, D.C., with a counter and a few stools. And that an immigrant, who opened up a hot dog stand outside Dodger Stadium in Los Angeles later became the multimillionaire owner of a chain restaurant (Karl Kartcher, owner of Carl's Jr.). And that a former dishwasher, Ralph Rubio, now owns the successful chain of Rubio's Fresh Mexican Grill quick-service restaurants, which have sold more than 50 million fish tacos since the opening of the first restaurant in 1983. Then there is Peter Morton, who, in the early 1970s, lived in London, and, missing American food, borrowed $60,000 from family and friends to open the Great American Disaster. It was an immediate success, with a line of customers around the block. Morton quickly realized that London needed a restaurant that not only served American food but also embodied the energy and excitement of music past and present. He opened the Hard Rock Cafe and offered a hearty American meal at a reasonable price in an atmosphere charged with energy, fun, and the excitement of rock and roll.[10] More recently, Howard Schultz, who while in Italy in the early 1980s was impressed with the popularity of espresso bars in Milan, saw the potential to develop the coffee bar culture in the United States and beyond. There are now well over 16,000 Starbucks locations.[11] Any ideas on what the next hot entrepreneurial idea will be?

The Pineapple Tradition

The pineapple has enjoyed a rich and romantic heritage as a symbol of welcome, friendship, and **hospitality**. Pineapples were brought back from the West Indies by early European explorers during the seventeenth century. From that time on, the pineapple was cultivated in Europe and became the favored fruit to serve to royalty and the elite. The pineapple was later introduced into North America and became a part of North American hospitality as well. Pineapples were displayed at doors or on gateposts, announcing to friends and acquaintances: "The ship is in! Come join us. Food and drink for all!"

Since its introduction, the pineapple has been internationally recognized as a symbol of hospitality and a sign of friendliness, warmth, cheer, graciousness, and conviviality.

The pineapple is the symbol of hospitality.

The Interrelated Nature of Hospitality and Tourism

The hospitality and **tourism** industries are the largest and fastest-growing industry groupings in the world. One of the most exciting aspects of this industry is that it is made up of so many different professions. What picture comes to mind when you think about a career in hospitality and tourism? Do you picture a chef, a general manager, owners of their own businesses, a director of marketing, or an event manager? The possibilities are many and varied, ranging from positions in restaurants, resorts, air and cruise lines, theme parks, attractions, and casinos, to name a few of the several sectors of the hospitality and tourism industries (see Figures 2 and 3).

James Reid, a professor at New York City Technical College, contributed his thoughts to this section. As diverse as the hospitality industry is, there are some powerful and common dynamics, which include the delivery of services and products and the guests' impressions of them. Whether an employee is in direct contact with a guest (**front of the house**) or performing duties behind the scenes (**heart of the house**), the profound and most challenging reality of working in this industry is that hospitality employees have the ability to affect the human experience by creating powerful impressions—even brief moments of truth—that may last a lifetime. (A "moment of truth" is an industry expression used to describe a guest and an associate meeting, as when a guest walks into a restaurant.)

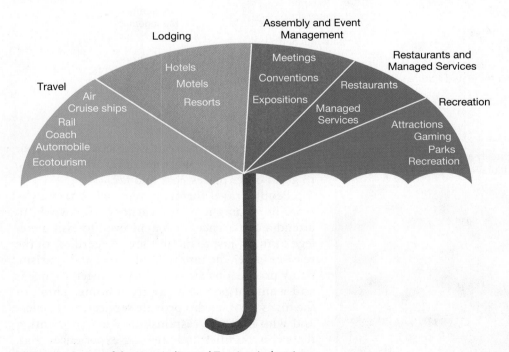

Figure 2 • Scope of the Hospitality and Tourism Industries.

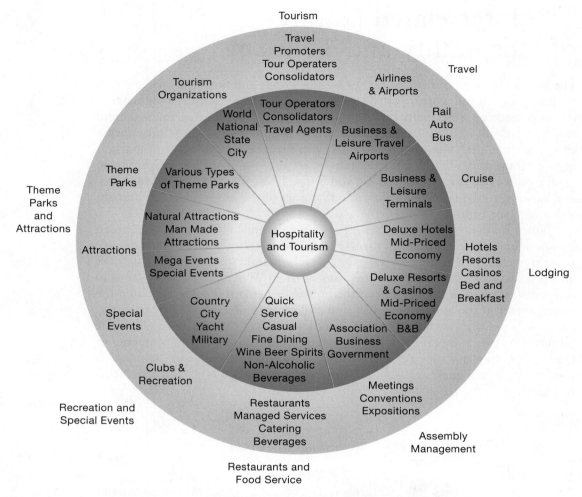

Figure 3 • The Interrelated Nature of Hospitality, Travel, and Tourism.

The interrelated nature of hospitality and tourism means that we would fly here, stay in a restaurant, and eat in a restaurant.

Imagine all the reasons why people leave their homes temporarily (whether alone or with others) to go to other places near and far.

People travel for many reasons. A trip away from home might be for vacation, for work, to attend a conference, or maybe even to visit a college campus, just to name a few. Regardless of the reason, under the umbrella of travel and tourism, many professions are necessary to meet the needs and wants of people away from home. Think of the many people who provide services to travelers and who have the responsibility of representing their communities and creating experiences that, when delivered successfully, are pleasurable and memorable for travelers. These people welcome, inform, comfort, and care for tourists and are collectively a part of a process that can positively affect human lives and well-being.

The hotel business provides career opportunities for many associates who help make reservations and greet, assist, and serve guests in hospitality operations of varied sizes and in locations all over the world. Examples include a husband and wife who operate their own bed and breakfast (B&B) in upstate Vermont. This couple provides the ideal weekend retreat for avid skiers during a frosty February, making their guests want to return year after year. Another ex-

Gramercy Tavern, a Danny Meyer, Union Square Hospitality Group Restaurant.

ample is the hundreds of employees necessary to keep the 5,505-room MGM Grand in full swing 365 days a year! Room attendants, engineers, front-desk agents, food servers, and managers are just a few of the positions that are vital to creating experiences for visitors who come to Las Vegas from around the globe.

The restaurant business is also a vital component under the travel and tourism umbrella. People go to restaurants to fulfill diverse needs and wants. Eating is a biological need that restaurants accommodate, but restaurants and the people who work in them fulfill numerous other human desires, such as the need for socialization and to be entertained.

Gramercy Tavern restaurant in New York City may be the perfect location for a certain group of friends to celebrate a twenty-first birthday. The individual guest who turned twenty-one may remember this fête for a lifetime because the service and food quality were excellent and added value to the experiences for all the celebrants. For this kind of collective and powerful impression to be made, many key players are needed to operate and support the service-delivery system: several front-of-the-house staff members, such as the food servers, bartenders, greeters, managers, and bus attendants; plus the back-of-the-house employees, such as the chefs, dishwashers, food purchaser, and stewards (to name a few). All these people had to coordinate a variety of activities and responsibilities to create this dynamic, successful, and, for the restaurant ownership, profitable event.

In managed services, foodservices are provided for airlines, military facilities, schools, colleges and universities, health care operations, and business and industry. These foodservice operations have the dual challenge of meeting the needs and wants of both the guests and the client (i.e., the institution that hired the foodservices). The employees who are part of foodservices enterprises have responsibilities very much like those of other restaurant operations. The quality of food products delivered in an airline, for example, may be the key to winning passengers back in the future and creating positive word-of-mouth promotion that attracts new customers.

Since history has been recorded, beverages have provided a biological need that has expanded the beverage menu far beyond water alone! Whether it is the cool iced tea garnished with lemon and mint served poolside at a Riviera resort or the champagne toast offered at a fiftieth wedding anniversary party in Boston, beverages play a major role in satisfying people and adding to the many celebrations of life.

As with food products, the creation and delivery systems for beverage products are vital components of the hospitality industry. These operations involve many people who consumers rarely see: the farmer in Napa Valley who tends to the vineyard every day of the year, the coffee bean harvester in Colombia, the sake server in Tokyo, or the orchard owner who crates oranges in Florida. These individuals behind the scenes have diverse and crucial responsibilities so that guests, whether in a resort, an office, a hospital, a college, or a roadside snack bar, can have the quality of products they want.

TECHNOLOGY SPOTLIGHT

The Increasing Importance of Technology to the Hospitality Industry

Cihan Cobanoglu, Ph.D., Dean, School of Hotel and Restaurant Management, University of South Florida, Sarasota-Manatee

Think about the last travel reservation that you made—did you book your travel online? Did you check consumer reviews on the hotel or restaurant? Studies show that as many as 55% of consumers now use the Internet to book their travel, a percentage that vastly changes the landscape of the hospitality industry. In fact, technology could be the thin line between a successful business and bankruptcy for many organizations. In 2011, only four out of every ten restaurants that open will still be operating in three years. One of the main reasons for the high failure rate is the lack of control in a slim profit-margin industry. With technology, hospitality and tourism businesses can attempt to control costs and generate success. Technology used to be accepted as a cost center by hospitality and tourism organizations. However, in today's world, technology is a strategic enabler. Technology has become such a vital tool that it is hard to imagine a hotel, resort, theme park, cruise ship, restaurant, or airline company running without it.

This text tries to show technology applications and uses for each different part of hospitality and tourism business. Consider this: In a typical full-service hotel, there are about 65 different technology applications. This number is around 35 for a limited-service hotel. Hotels are finding new ways to use technology for a strategic advantage. Consider this example: Mandarin Oriental is keeping track of the fruits eaten by the guest. These records are kept in the guest's profile. Next time the guest visits the hotel, when a fruit basket is sent, it is dominated by the fruits that guest likes. This creates a "wow" factor since it is not directly solicited, rather, quietly observed and recorded with the help of proper training and technology.

Similarly, restaurants use more than 30 different technology applications to provide faster, more cost efficient and productive business operations for guests and staff. Airline companies use complex central reservation and yield-management tools. Travel agencies depend on global reservation system networks to operate. Cruise ships employ different technology and navigation systems to operate in an efficient and fast way. Theme parks use different biometric technologies to keep track of their guests and staff members.

The Airline industry became a commodity a long time ago. In the contemporary age, travelers do not necessarily care about which carrier will take them from point A to point B. Price seems to be the most important factor in selecting an air carrier. The hotel industry is showing similar symptoms. In the age where hospitality and tourism products are becoming a commodity, technology is becoming a true differentiator. Hoteliers like in the example of Mandarin Oriental are turning to technology to differentiate themselves so that they do not become a commodity in the eyes of guests. Many studies already showed that high-speed Internet is one of the most important in-room amenities that enable guest satisfaction in a hotel. In this new age of technology, it is very important for hospitality and tourism students to understand all different technology applications out there to be able to compete in a tough market environment.

Characteristics of the Hospitality Industry

Hospitality businesses are open 365 days a year and 24 hours a day. No, we don't have to work all of these days, but we do tend to work longer hours than people in other industries. Those on their way to senior positions in the hospitality industry, and many others for that matter, often work ten hours a day. However, because of managerial burnout, there is a trend in the industry of reducing working hours of managers to fifty hours a week to attract and retain members of Generation X and the Millennial Generation. Evenings and weekends are included in the workweek—so we have to accept that we may be working when others are enjoying leisure time.

The hospitality industry depends heavily on shift work. Early in your career, depending on the department, you will likely work on a particular shift. Basically, there are four shifts, beginning with the morning shift, so you may be getting up as early as 6:00 A.M. to get to the shift that starts at 7:00 A.M. The midshift is usually from 10:00 A.M. to 7:00 P.M.; the evening shift starts at 3:00 P.M. and goes on until 11:00 P.M.; and finally there is the night shift that begins at 11:00 P.M. and lasts until 7:30 A.M. Supervisors and managers often begin at 8:00 A.M. and work until 6:00 or 8:00 P.M. Success does not come easily.

In the hospitality industry, we constantly strive for outstanding **guest satisfaction**, which leads to guest loyalty and, yes, profit. Our services are mostly

intangible, meaning the guest cannot "test drive" a night's stay or "taste the steak" before dining. Our product is for the guest's use only, not for possession. Even more unique, for us to produce our product—hospitality—we must get the guest's input. Imagine General Electric building a refrigerator with the customer in the factory, participating in the actual construction of the product! Seems preposterous, yet we do it every single day, numerous times per day, and in a uniquely different way each time. This is referred to as the **inseparability** of production and consumption of the service product, which presents a special challenge because each guest may have his or her own requests.

The other unique dimension of our industry is the **perishability** of our product. For example, we have 1,400 rooms in inventory—that is, available to sell—but we sell only 1,200 rooms. What do we do with the 200 unsold rooms? Nothing. We have permanently lost 200 room-nights and their revenue. This example illustrates that in the hospitality industries we are in business to make a **return on investment** for owners and/or shareholders and society. People invest money for us to run a business, and they expect a fair return on their investment. Now, the amount that constitutes a fair return can be debated and will depend on the individual business circumstances. The challenge increases when there is an economic downturn or, worse, a recession, such as we have recently experienced. Then, the struggle is to make more money than is spent, known as keeping one's head above water!

▶ Check Your Knowledge

1. List and describe the four shifts in the hospitality industry.
2. Identify and explain two differences between the hospitality business and other business sectors.

Each year, the National Restaurant Association (NRA) invites the best and brightest students from universities and colleges to participate in the annual restaurant show in Chicago. The highlight of the show is the "Salute to Excellence" day when students and faculty attend forums, workshops, and a gala award banquet with industry leaders. Coca-Cola and several other corporations involved in the industry sponsor the event.

During the day, students are invited to write their dreams on a large panel, which is later displayed for all to enjoy. Here are a few of one of the previous year's hopes and dreams:

- To help all people learn and grow (Jason P.)
- To be the best I can (NMC)
- To establish a chain of jazz cafés in six years and go public in ten years (Richard)
- To successfully please my customers (J. Calicendo)
- To be happy and to make others happy, too

- To put smiles on all faces
- To be one of the most creative chefs—I would like to be happy with everything I create
- To make a difference in the lives of people through food! (Mitz Dardony)
- To be successful professionally, socially, and financially (Marcy W.)
- To preserve our natural resources by operating a restaurant called Green (Kimberley Mauren)
- Anything I do I like to do it in such a way that I can always be meaningful to people (Christian Ellis-Schmidt)
- To reach the top because I know there is a lot of space up there (P. W., Lexington College)
- To use the knowledge that I've gained throughout my career and pass it on to others in hopes of touching their lives in a positive way! To smile and to make smiles. (Armey P. DaCalo)
- I want to be prosperous in my desire to achieve more than $. Happiness and peace are the keys to life. (D. McKinney)
- To teach and be as good as those who have taught me (Thomas)

So what are your dreams and goals? Take a moment to think about your personal dreams and goals. Keep them in mind and look back on them often. Be prepared to amend them as you develop your career.

Careers

There are hundreds of career options for you to consider, and it's fine if you are not yet sure which one is for you. In Figure 3 you can see the major hospitality industry segments: lodging, restaurants and foodservice, recreation and special events, assembly management, theme parks and attractions, travel, and tourism. For instance, lodging provides career opportunities for many associates who make reservations, greet, assist, and serve guests in hotels, resorts, and other lodging operations all over the world. Among the many examples are the operators of a B&B in upstate New York who cater to seasonal guests. Another example is the hundreds of employees necessary to keep the City Center in Las Vegas operational.

Figures 4, 5, and 6 show a career ladder for lodging management and food and beverage management and the rooms division in mid-sized and large hotels. Figure 7 shows a career ladder for restaurant management. Information relating to careers comes from the U.S. Census Bureau's statistic of lifetime salaries by education level,[12] which indicates that high school graduates earn $1.2 million, Associate degree holders earn $1.6 million, Bachelor's degree holders earn $2.1 million, and Master's degree holders earn $2.5 million. Now, these numbers are based on 1999 data, so the good news is that they are going to be much higher for you! Speaking of salaries, Figure 8 is a salary guide for hospitality positions.

Figure 4 • Lodging Management Career Ladder.

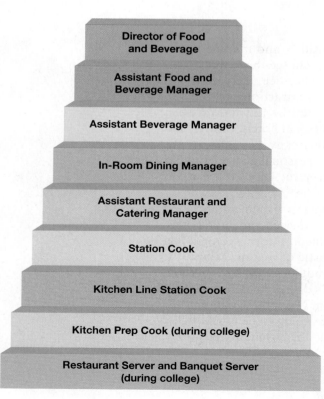

Figure 5 • Lodging Food and Beverage Career Ladder.

Figure 6 • Lodging Rooms Division Career Ladder.

Figure 7 • Restaurant Management Career Ladder.

Hospitality Salaries	
President of a Chain Lodging Company	$250,000–500,000
President of a Chain Restaurant Company	$175,000–450,000
Vice President of a Lodging Company	$150,000–250,000
Hotel/Resort General Manager	$75,000–175,000
Country Club General Manager	$100,000–350,000
Vice President of a Restaurant Company	$75,000–150,000
Restaurant General Manager	$40,000–80,000
Hotel or Resort Rooms Division Director	$50–80,000
Hotel/Resort Human Resources Director	$50,000–80,000
Hotel or Resort Food and Beverage Director	$55,000–100,000
Hotel/Resort Catering Manager	$50,000–90,000
Assistant Restaurant Manager	$25,000–40,000
Hotel Front Office Manager	$30,000–60,000
Hotel/Resort Executive Housekeeper	$30,000–75,000
Hotel/Resort Assistant Food and Beverage Manager	$35,000–60,000
Hotel/Resort Executive Chef	$40,000–90,000
Restaurant Chef	$30,000–80,000
Front Desk Agent	$16,000–25,000
Servers	$20,000–40,000
Cooks	$20,000–30,000

Figure 8 • A Guide to Hospitality Salaries.

Hospitality Industry Philosophy

Current **hospitality industry philosophy** has changed from one of managers' planning, organizing, implementing, and measuring to that of managers' counseling associates, giving them resources, and helping them to think for themselves. The outcome is a more participative management style, which results in associate **empowerment**, increased productivity, and guest and employee satisfaction. For example, Ritz-Carlton associates are empowered to spend up to $2,000 to make a guest completely happy. Imagine a bride-to-be arriving at a hotel and sending her wedding dress to be pressed. Unfortunately, the iron burns the dress. Luckily, the concierge comes to the rescue by taking the bride to a wedding dress store, where they select a gorgeous dress for around $1,800, and the bride is happy because it is a nicer dress than the original. Corporate philosophy has strong links to quality leadership and the **total quality management (TQM)** process. (TQM is discussed in a later section.)

Corporate philosophy embraces the values of the organization, including ethics, morals, fairness, and equality. The new paradigm in corporate American hospitality is the shift in emphasis from the production aspect of our business to the focus on guest-related services. The philosophy of "whatever it takes" is winning over "it's not my job." Innovation and creativity are winning over "that's the way we've always done it." Successful organizations are those that are able to impart corporate philosophies to employees and guests alike. Disney Corporation, as discussed later in the text, is a good example of a corporation that has a permeating corporate philosophy.

Service Philosophy Is a Way of Life

J. W. (Bill) Marriott Jr. is chairman of the board of directors of Marriott International. Marriott's web site defines the "Marriott Way" as "about serving the associates, the guest, and the community." These ideals serve as the cornerstone for all Marriott associates who strive to fulfill the "Spirit to Serve."[16] The values originate from deep inside the people themselves—authentic, bone deep, and passionately held. Marriott's **core values** include the belief that people are number one ("Take care of Marriott people and they'll take good care of Marriott guests"), a commitment to continuous improvement and overcoming adversity, and a good old-fashioned dedication to hard work and having fun while doing it.

Marriott's core values drive the culture. Similarly, regardless of which service organization we work for, our culture influences the way we treat associates, guests, and the community, and that affects the success of everyone. In the words of J. W. Marriott Jr., "Culture is the life-thread and glue that links our past, present, and future."[17]

J.W. (Bill) Marriott Jr.

Sustainable Hospitality

Sustainable development is a holistic concept based on a simple principle. As outlined in the 1987 Brundtland Commission Report titled, "Our Common Future." The Bruntland Commission, formally the World Commission on Environment and Development, was convened by the United Nations to address the growing concern "about the accelerating deterioration of the human environment."[13] The concept of sustainability involves "development that meets the needs of the present without compromising the ability of future generations to meet their own needs."

Sustainability is the ability to achieve continuing economic prosperity while protecting the natural resources of the planet and providing a high quality of life for its people and future generations.[14] Operators of hospitality businesses have generally embraced the concept of sustainable hospitality and are increasingly operationalizing it. As an example in the lodging industry, the Willard InterContinental's Sustainable Development initiative is showing substantial results. The program's chief goals are based on profits, people, and planet. The first goal is to find ways to operate the hotel according to the idea of a "triple bottom line," which embodies profitable operation combined with attention to the people who use and work in the hotel and with a focus on careful stewardship of resources.[15]

▶ Check Your Knowledge

1. Describe Marriott's "Spirit to Serve."
2. What is corporate philosophy?

Success in Service

What must happen to achieve success in service? Given that approximately 70 percent of the U.S. and Canadian economies and an increasing percentage of other countries' are engaged in **service industries**, it is critical to offer guests exceptional service, but what is exceptional service? *Service* is defined in *Webster's New World Dictionary* as "the act or means of serving." To serve is to "provide goods and services for" and "be of assistance to."

This is the *age of service*, and the hospitality industry is getting revamped because guest expectations have increased and the realization is that "*we buy loyalty with service.*"[18] With thousands of guest encounters, or moments of truth, each day, it is critical to incorporate service excellence in each hospitality organization. Some corporations adopt the expression, "If you're not serving the guest, you had better be serving someone who is." This is the essence of teamwork: Someone in the **back of the house** also called the **heart of the house** is serving someone in the **front of the house**, who is serving the guest.

A guest is anyone who receives or benefits from the output of someone's work. The external guest is the guest most people think of in the traditional sense. The satisfaction of external guests ultimately measures a company's success, because they are the people who are willing to pay for its services. The internal guests are the people inside a company who receive or benefit from the output of work done by others in the company, for example, the server or busser preparing the restaurant to serve lunch has been "served" by the dishwasher, who has prepared clean plates, knives, forks, spoons, and glassware.

For success in service, we need to do the following:

1. Focus on the guest.
2. Understand the role of the guest-contact employee.
3. Weave a service culture into education and training systems.
4. Emphasize high-touch as well as high-tech.
5. Thrive on change—constantly improve the guest experience.

As hospitality professionals, we need to recognize a variety of guest-related situations and act to relieve them or avoid them. Imagine how an associate can win points by showing empathy—that is, putting him- or herself in someone else's shoes—in the following situation: A party of two ladies arrives for lunch one cool January day at an upscale Florida water-front hotel. They decide it would be nice to have lunch on the terrace. A server from the adjacent lounge notices the guests, and upon learning of their request to have lunch on the terrace, quickly lays up a table for them, brings them hot tea, takes their order, and then goes to the laundry to have two blankets put in the dryer for a couple of minutes to take out to the ladies to keep them warm. Little did the server realize who the guests were—travel writers for the *New York Times* who described their outstanding experience in an article that brought praise to the hotel and its service.

Another key objective in the service equation is to encourage guest loyalty. We not only need to keep guests happy during their stay but also to keep them

INTRODUCING J. W. (BILL) MARRIOTT JR.

Chairman and Chief Executive Officer, Marriott International

Bill Marriott is the son of J. W. Marriott, founder of Marriott International, a company that began as a nine-stool root beer stand in Washington, D.C., in 1927. Bill was an Eagle Scout and recipient of the Distinguished Eagle Scout Award who, during and after high school, worked various positions in his parents' Hot Shoppes restaurant chain. He graduated from the University of Utah with a Bachelor of Science degree in finance and served as an officer in the Navy before joining the Marriott Corporation in 1956.

Bill Marriott has had an enormous influence on the hospitality industry with years of dedicated service. He is an example of the Spirit to Serve, the title of his well-worth-reading book. Under Marriott's lead, Marriott International has grown from a family restaurant business to a global lodging company of over 3,000 managed and franchised properties of 18 brands, ranging from economy limited-service brands up to full-service luxury hotels and resorts, as well as executive apartments, conference centers, and golf courses in 67 countries and territories.[19]

Mr. Marriott continues his father's tradition of visiting two to three hundred hotels a year. He is passionate about quality and service and can quickly tell how good a general manager (GM) is by the reaction of associates to him or her when the GM is walking the halls of the property. If the associates smile and greet the GM with a cheerful good morning, he knows he has a great GM, but if the associates look down and don't say anything, he knows that there is a problem.

Bill Marriott also cares passionately about Marriott associates by giving them the best possible working conditions, competitive wages and salaries, and excellent benefits. Marriott also provides outstanding training programs to help associates do a great job and to retain the best associates. One of the often used quotes from Mr. Marriott is, "I want our associates to know that there really is a guy named Marriott who cares about them."[20] A central part of Marriott's core values is that attention to detail, quite simply, leads to high customer satisfaction, to repeat business—and to good profits and attractive returns for stockholders and property owners.[21]

returning—with their friends, we hope! It costs several times more to attract new guests than it does to retain existing ones. Imagine how much more profitable a hospitality business would be if it could retain just 10 percent of its guests as loyal guests. Losing a guest equates to losing much more than one sale; it has the potential to be a loss of a lifetime guest. Consider a $40 restaurant dinner for two people. If the guests return twice a month over several years—say, ten—the amount they have contributed to the restaurant quickly becomes huge ($9,600). If they bring their friends, this amount is even higher. Can you remember your worst service experience? Also, can you remember your best service experience?

We know that service is a complex yet critical component of the hospitality industry. In their book, *Service America!*, Albrecht and Zemke suggest two basic kinds of service: "Help me!" and "Fix it."[22] "Help me!" refers to guests' regular and special needs, such as, "Help me find the function room" or, "Help me to get a reservation at the best restaurant in town." "Fix it" refers to services such as, "Please fix my toilet; it won't flush" or, "Please fix the TV so that we can watch the World Series."

Moments of Truth

"Moments of truth" is a term coined by Jan Carlson. When Carlson became president of Scandinavian Airline System (SAS), it was ranked at the bottom of the European airline market. He quickly realized that he had to spend a lot of time on the front line coaching SAS associates in how to handle guest encounters, or as he called them, "moments of truth." As a result of his efforts, SAS was soon ranked at the top of the European airlines for service. Service commitment is a total organizational approach that makes the quality of service, as perceived by the customer, the number one driving force for the operation of the business.[23]

FOCUS ON SERVICE

Hospitality Is Offering a Cup of Kindness

William B. Martin, Cal Tech–Monterey Bay

Customer service is a central focus of hospitality. It is what hospitality is all about—what we do. If you are interested in a hospitality career, it is important to understand and learn as much as possible about customer service and particularly how to be successful at it. Your success will come from a complete understanding of hospitality.

Let's begin by exploring why we provide hospitality. Why are hospitality businesses in business? What is the primary purpose of a foodservice operation? A lodging establishment? A travel- or tourism-related business? Is it just for the money? Many of you might answer an easy yes to this question. But as you will see, hospitality is much more than just about money. Money is important, but it is important as a means and as a necessary ingredient to help us get to where we want to go. Money is not the primary reason for hospitality. Then what is the primary purpose of hospitality?

Our job, first and foremost, is to enhance the lives of those people (guests, customers, passengers, etc.) to whom we are dedicated to serve. Yes, it is that simple (and complex at the same time). Our job is to make the lives of others better in a small way or big way; it makes no difference. Whatever it is, we are out to make people's lives on this planet a little bit better, or maybe even a lot better. This is our purpose. It is where we find meaning. We in the hospitality industry are about enhancing the lives of others—period. Ultimately, that is what makes it all worthwhile.

With that said, where does customer service fit in? Good question. If you are a sharp student, you've already got it. You can readily see that if the purpose of hospitality is to enhance the lives of others, the way we do that is through service. And what is service? It is how we go about treating our guests—how we make (or fail to make) their lives better by how we treat them. And we can go a long way toward treating them well by simply offering them a cup of kindness.

What does this mean? What does it take to be kind? What do we have to do? How do we enhance the lives of others through kindness? We begin by *understanding* what it is that they need. The problem is that all of our guests come to us with many needs. Some we can meet, some we can't. But of all the needs they come with, four of them are specifically hospitality related. If you can work toward helping them satisfy these needs, you can go a long way toward making their lives better through kindness. Quality customer service demands that service providers understand what it is that customers want. Kindness, after all, comes through understanding. Kindness is demonstrated by making everyone feel *welcome*.

Quality customer service requires that we make all guests feel *comfortable*—that we provide the assurance that they will be taken care of, and follow through. They don't need to worry; they are in good hands. In short, when we can do this we are filling their cups with more kindness. Whether they deserve it or not, they should be made to feel important. Why? Because, we all have a *need to feel important*. This is a part of our job. Moreover, it is another important way we can show kindness to our guests.

We need to stay focused on the primary purposes of hospitality. We need to understand the power of kindness and the importance of satisfying the four basic customer service needs of our guests. In the final analysis, hospitality and customer service success are found in our ability to enhance the lives of others through how we treat them—with a little cup of kindness.

Every hospitality organization has thousands of moments of truth every day. This leads to tremendous challenges in maintaining the expected levels of service. Let's look at just some of the moments of truth in a restaurant dining experience[24]:

1. Guest calls the restaurant for a table reservation.
2. Guest tries to find the restaurant.
3. Guest parks.
4. Guest is welcomed.
5. Guest is informed that the table is not ready.
6. Guest either waits or goes to the lounge for a cocktail.
7. Guest tries to attract the bartender's attention for a cocktail because there are no seats available.
8. Guest is called over a loudspeaker or paged.
9. Guest is seated at the table.
10. Server takes order.
11. Server brings beverages or food.
12. Server clears food or beverages.
13. Server brings check.
14. Guest pays for meal.
15. Guest departs restaurant.

From your own experiences, you can imagine just how many moments of truth there are in a restaurant dining experience.

▶ Check Your Knowledge

1. What is the purpose of a mission statement?
2. Why is service so important?
3. What is a moment of truth?

The Focus on Service

Giving great service is a very difficult task; few businesses give enough priority to training associates in how to provide service. We suffer from an overreliance on technology so that service providers are often not motivated to give great service. For example, when checking a guest into the hotel, the front-desk associate may greet the guest but then look down at the computer for the remainder of the service encounter, even when asking for the guest's name. Or consider the reservations associate who says nothing when asked for a specific type of guest room because he is waiting for the computer to indicate availability.

To help improve service in the hospitality industry, the Educational Foundation of the NRA, one of the hospitality industry's leading associations, developed a number of great programs that will enhance your professional development. Further information may be obtained from the NRA's web site (**www.restaurant.org**).

Among the various programs and courses is one titled Foodservice Leadership. Effective leaders are those who make things happen because they have developed the knowledge, skills, and attitude required to get the most out of the people in their operation. Leadership involves change; in fact, change is the one thing we can be sure of in the coming years. Our guests are constantly changing; so is technology, product availability, and, of course, our competition.

The American Hotel & Lodging Association (AH&LA) offers a great variety of information on service-related topics including **best practices**, which give details of the most effective techniques in lodging operations. One area of interest is the Green Resource, where innovative means of going green are shared to improve the carbon footprint and the "bottom line."[25]

One way in which leaders involve employees in the process of improving guest service is through TQM and empowerment.

Service and Total Quality Management

The increasingly open and fiercely competitive marketplace is exerting enormous pressure on service industries to deliver superior service. Inspired by rising guest expectations and competitive necessity, many hospitality companies have jumped on the service quality bandwagon. W. Edwards Deming is credited with launching the Total Quality movement. He was best known for his work in Japan, where in the 1950s and onward, the quality of Japanese products was not good. He taught top Japanese management how to improve design—through the use of statistical methods he reduced the number of defects—and thus service, product quality, testing, and sales. Dr. Deming made a significant contribution to the improvement of Japanese products.[26]

The Malcolm Baldrige National Quality Award is the highest level of national recognition for quality that a U.S. company can receive. Named after former commerce secretary Malcolm Baldrige, who was a champion of quality movement as a way of improving U.S. commerce, the award promotes an understanding of quality excellence, greater awareness of quality as a critical competitive element, and the sharing of quality information and strategies.

The Ritz-Carlton Hotel Company, the only hospitality company to win two Malcolm Baldrige National Quality Awards, in 1992 and 1999, was founded on principles of excellence in guest service. The essence of this philosophy was refined into a set of core values collectively called the Gold Standards. The credo is printed on a small laminated card that all employees must memorize or carry on their person at all times when on duty. The card lists the three steps of service:

1. A warm and sincere greeting; use the guest name, if and when possible.
2. Anticipation and compliance with guests' needs.
3. Fond farewell; give them a warm good-bye and use their names if and when possible.

The quality movement began at the turn of the century as a means of ensuring consistency among the parts produced in the different plants of a single company so that they could be used interchangeably. In the area of service, TQM is a participatory process that empowers all levels of employees to work in groups to establish guest service expectations and determine the best way to meet or exceed these expectations. Notice that the term *guest* is preferred over the term *customer*. The inference here is that if we treat customers like guests, we are more likely to exceed their expectations. One successful hotelier has insisted for a long time that all employees treat guests as they would like to be treated themselves.

TQM is a continuous process that works best when managers are also good leaders. A successful company will employ leader–managers who create a stimulating work environment in which guests and employees (sometimes called internal guests: One employee serves another employee, who in turn serves a guest) become integral parts of the mission by participating in **goal** and objective setting.

Implementing TQM is exciting because after everyone becomes involved, there is no stopping the creative ways employees will find to solve guest-related problems and improve service. Other benefits include cost reductions and increased guest and employee satisfaction, leading ultimately to increased profits.

The Employee Promise

At the Ritz-Carlton, our Ladies and Gentlemen are the most important resource in our service commitment to our guests.

By applying the principles of trust, honesty, respect, integrity, and commitment, we nurture and maximize talent to the benefit of each individual and the company.

The Ritz-Carlton fosters a work environment where diversity is valued, quality of life is enhanced, individual aspirations are fulfilled, and the Ritz-Carlton mystique is strengthened.

I am proud to be Ritz-Carlton

1. I build strong relationships and create Ritz-Carlton guests for life.
2. I am always responsive to the expressed and unexpressed wishes and need of our guests.
3. I am empowered to create unique, memorable, and personal experiences for our guests.
4. I understand my role in achieving the Key Success Factors, embracing Community Footprints, and creating The Ritz-Carlton Mystique.
5. I continuously seek opportunities to innovate and improve the Ritz-Carlton experience.
6. I own and immediately resolve any guest problems.
7. I create a work environment of teamwork and lateral service so that the needs of our guests and each other are met.
8. I have opportunity to continuously learn and grow.
9. I am involved in the planning of the work that affects me.
10. I am proud of my professional appearance, language, and behavior.
11. I protect the privacy and security of our guests, my fellow employees, and the company's confidential information and assets.
12. I am responsible for uncompromising levels of cleanliness and creating a safe and accident-free environment.

A DAY IN THE LIFE OF RYAN LASHWAY

Assistant Manager, Mar Vista Dockside Restaurant, Longboat Key, Florida

To describe a typical day of work for me at the Mar Vista, I must first tell you a little bit about the restaurant. Located on Sarasota Bay on the north end of Longboat Key in historic Longbeach Village, the Mar Vista has existed for over 60 years. Built in the early 1940s, "The Pub" was originally a bait and tackle shop until the 1950s, when the owners started selling hamburgers and beer to the local fishermen crowd. The Mar Vista operated like this until coming under the ownership of Ed Chiles of the Chiles Group Corporation in 1990. Chiles is the son of former governor of Florida Lawton Chiles and also owns the Beachhouse and Sandbar restaurants on Anna Maria Island. The Mar Vista is an authentic part of Old Florida, and our history and ambiance make it a fun and relaxing place. Our goal at the Mar Vista is to provide our guests with the finest in food and courteous,

(continued)

A DAY IN THE LIFE OF RYAN LASHWAY *(continued)*

prompt service. For further information about the Chiles Group Corporation, visit our web site at **www. groupersandwich.com**.

A typical day for a manager at the Mar Vista goes like this:

8:30 A.M. Arrive and check the premises for any unusual activity. Unlock the doors and turn on all lights and A/C units. Check to see that the overnight cleaning crew has done a thorough job, especially in the kitchen, restrooms, and behind the bars. Then, look at the schedules to see which employees are working on any given day and make ready for the kitchen staff's arrival at 9:00 A.M.

9:00 A.M. Upon arrival, the kitchen staff is entered into our in-house computer system so that their hours for the day will be recorded. Towels and cleaning materials must also be supplied for the entire staff. The restrooms must be checked and stocked with hand towels, liquid soap, and toilet paper. The premises are then walked again and the grounds checked for trash. All windows and mirrors must be cleaned.

10:30 A.M. The wait staff and bar staff arrive. The cash banks for the bar must be counted and paired up for daily use. The safe in the manager's office must then be opened and the money from the previous day made ready for pickup by our financial officer. The kitchen manager must then be met with to discuss the daily specials. Upon agreement of the best use for food items, the specials must then be printed and inserted into the menus.

11:30 A.M. Open for lunch business. Throughout the day, management focuses on customer relations and making sure the restaurant runs smoothly. Incoming paperwork from deliveries for the kitchen and bar must be fully documented, and all incoming orders must be checked in and signed for. Any problems with food orders or guest service must be handled in such a way that the customer is never scorned; return business is the primary focus. In general, the customers are always right, and in this business we must do whatever is necessary to keep them happy.

3:00 P.M. Toward the end of the lunch shift, servers are finishing their daily work and will require checkout forms to do their money drops. Managers must check each server out individually and make sure that all side work is completed and that the restaurant will be ready for the next shift crew arriving at 4:00 P.M. Managers must meet with the kitchen manager again and prepare the dinner specials. The P.M bartender will also be arriving and will require a night bank, while the A.M. bartender will need to be checked out and his or her bank checked for correct money transactions.

5:00 P.M. Dinner begins and the night manager arrives. Discuss the events and highlights of the day with the P.M. manager and notify him or her of any problems.

Then it's off to rest up and prepare to do it again tomorrow!

Top executives and line managers are responsible for the success of the TQM process; when they commit to ownership of the process, it will be successful. Focused commitment is the foundation of a quality service initiative, and leadership is the critical component in promoting commitment. Achieving TQM is a top-down, bottom-up process that must have the active commitment and participation of all employees, from the top executives down to those at the bottom of the corporate ladder. The expression "If you are not serving the guest, then you had better be serving someone who is" still holds true today.

The difference between TQM and quality control (QC) is that QC focuses on error detection, whereas TQM focuses on error prevention. QC is generally based on industrial systems and, because of this, tends to be product oriented rather than service oriented. To the guest, services are experiential; they are felt, lived through, and sensed. The moment of truth is the actual guest contact.

The nature of business has changed. Leaders empower employees who welcome change. Empowerment is a feeling of partnership in which employees feel responsible for their jobs and have a stake in the organization's success. Empowered employees tend to do the following:

- Speak out about their problems and concerns.
- Take responsibility for their actions.
- Consider themselves a network of professionals.
- Accept the authority to make their own decisions when serving guests.

To empower employees, managers must do the following:

1. Take risks.
2. Delegate.
3. Foster a learning environment.
4. Share information and encourage self-expression.
5. Involve employees in defining their own vision.
6. Be thorough and patient with employees.

CORPORATE PROFILE

Marriott International, Inc.[27]

Marriott International is a leading worldwide hospitality company. Its heritage is traced back to a root beer stand opened in Washington, D.C., in 1927 by J. Willard and Alice S. Marriott. Today, Marriott International has more than 3,500 lodging properties in the United States and 67 other countries and territories. Marriott International operates and franchises hotels under the following tiers of brands:

Luxury Tier: Bulgari Hotels and Resorts, a collection of sophisticated, intimate luxury properties tucked away in exclusive destinations

The Ritz-Carlton Hotel Company, LLC: The worldwide symbol for the finest in hotel and resort accommodations, dining, and service. Two-time recipient of the Malcolm Baldrige National Quality Award, offering signature service amenities, fine dining, 24-hour room service, twice-daily housekeeping, fitness centers, business centers, and concierge services.

(continued)

CORPORATE PROFILE *(continued)*

JW Marriott Hotels and Resorts: The most elegant and luxurious Marriott brand, offering business and leisure travelers a deluxe level of comfort and personal service

Autograph Collection: A collection of high-personality, independent hotels, powered by the world-class platforms of Marriott International

Lifestyle/Boutique: EDITION was created in partnership with boutique hotel pioneer Ian Schrager to introduce a new brand with as many as one hundred hotels that have perfected a highly personal, intimate, and rarified experience for each guest.

Renaissance Hotels invite guests to "stay interesting" at distinctive hotels offering unique, locally relevant architecture and design, destination restaurants and bars, and off-the-radar travel experiences worldwide.

- **Signature Brand: Marriott Hotels and Resorts:** The flagship brand of quality-tier, full-service hotels and resorts with features such as fully equipped fitness centers, gift shops, swimming pools, concierge levels, business centers, meeting facilities, and high-speed Internet.

- **Select Service & Extended Stay Brands: Courtyard by Marriott:** A moderately priced lodging brand designed by business travelers for business travelers that has recently increased the number of downtown locations, often through conversions of historical buildings. Features include 80 to 150 guest rooms, high-speed Internet access, restaurants, lounges, meeting spaces, central courtyards, exercise rooms, swimming pools, and 24-hour access to food.

- **SpringHill Suites by Marriott:** A moderately priced, all-suite lodging brand that offers up to 25 percent larger-than-standard hotel rooms. Features include complimentary continental breakfast, self-serve business centers, indoor pools, whirlpool spas, high-speed Internet access, and exercise rooms.

- **Fairfield Inn by Marriott:** A consistent, quality lodging at an affordable price. Features include spacious guest rooms, daily complimentary breakfast, and swimming pools. Future plans call for exercise rooms.

- **Residence Inn by Marriott:** Designed as a home away from home for travelers staying five or more nights, it includes a residential atmosphere with spacious accommodations. Features include complimentary hot breakfasts, evening hospitality hours, swimming pools, sport courts, personalized grocery shopping, guest suites with separate living and sleeping areas, fully equipped kitchens, and work spaces with data ports and voice mail.

- **Towne Place Suites by Marriott:** A midpriced, extended-stay brand that provides all the comforts of home in a residential atmosphere.

- **Marriott Executive Apartments:** A corporate housing brand designed to meet the needs of business executives on an overseas assignment for thirty days or more by offering residential accommodations with hotel-like amenities.

In addition to these brands there are also several Vacation Clubs, which are offered on a fractional ownership basis.

Marriott has been ranked the number-one most admired company in the lodging industry by *Fortune* for the past five years and also one of the "100 Best Companies to Work For" for the past seven years.

► Check Your Knowledge

1. List five attributes, traits, and characteristics of a leader.
2. What is the Malcolm Baldrige National Quality Award?

The Disney Approach to Guest Service

The Disney mission statement is simple: "We create Happiness." The following discussion, adapted from a presentation given by Susan Wilkie to the Pacific chapter of the Council on Hotel Restaurant and Institutional Education (CHRIE) conference outlines Disney's approach to guest service.

When conceiving the idea to build Disneyland, Walt Disney established a simple philosophical approach to his theme park business, based on the tenets of quality, service, and show. The design, layout, characters, and magic of Disneyland grew out of Walt's successful experience in the film industry. With Disneyland, he saw an opportunity to create a whole new form of entertainment: a three-dimensional live show. He wanted Disneyland to be a dynamic, ever-changing experience.

To reinforce the service concept, Disney has *guests*, not *customers*, and *cast members*, not *employees*. These terms set the expectations for how guests will be served and cared for while at the park or resort. This commitment to service means the following:

- Disney clearly understands its product and the meaning of its brand.
- It looks at the business from the guests' perspective.
- It considers creating an exceptional experience for every individual who enters its gates to be its responsibility.

Disney executives say that "our inventory goes home at night." Disney's ability to create a special brand of magic requires the talents of thousands of people fulfilling many different roles. But the heart of it is the frontline cast members. So, what is it that makes the service at Disney so great? The key elements of Disneyland guest services include the following:

- Hiring, developing, and retaining the right people
- Understanding its product and the meaning of the brand
- Communicating the traditions and standards of service to all cast members
- Training leaders to be service coaches
- Measuring guest satisfaction
- Recognizing and rewarding performance

Disney has used profile modeling but says it all comes down to a few simple things:

- Interpersonal relationship–building skills
- Communication
- Friendliness

Disney uses a forty-five-minute team approach to interviewing called *peer interviews*. In one interview, there may be four candidates and one interviewer. The candidates may include a homemaker returning to the workforce, a teacher looking for summer work, a retiree looking for a little extra income, and a teenager looking for a first job. All four candidates are interviewed in the same session. The interviewer is looking for how they individually answer questions but also how well they interact with each other—a good indicator of their future onstage treatment of guests.

The most successful technique used during the forty-five-minutes is to *smile*. The interviewer smiles at the people being interviewed to see if they *return the smiles*. If they don't, it doesn't matter how well they interview—they won't get the job.

On the first day at work, every new Disney cast member participates in a one-day orientation program at the Disney University, "Welcome to Show Business." The main goal of this experience is to learn the Disney approach to helpful, caring, and friendly guest service.

How does this translate into action? When a guest stops a street sweeper to ask where to pick up a parade schedule and the sweeper not only answers the question but recites the parade times from memory, suggests the best viewing spots on the parade route, offers advice on where to get a quick meal before parade time, *and* ends the interaction with a pleasant smile and warm send-off, people can't help but be impressed. It also makes the sweepers feel their jobs are interesting and important—which they are!

I AM YOUR GUEST

We can all find inspiration from these anonymous words about people who make our business possible:

- ✓ *I am your guest.* Satisfy my needs, add personal attention and a friendly touch, and I will become a "walking advertisement" for your products and services. Ignore my needs, show carelessness, inattention, and poor manners, and I will cease to exist as far as you are concerned.
- ✓ *I am sophisticated.* Much more so than I was a few years ago. My needs are more complex. It is more important to me that you appreciate my business; when I buy your products and services, I'm saying you are the best.
- ✓ *I am a perfectionist.* When I am dissatisfied, take heed. The source of my discontent lies in something you or your products have failed to do. Find that source and eliminate it or you will lose my business and that of my friends as well. For when I criticize your products or services, I will talk to anyone who will listen.
- ✓ *I have other choices.* Other businesses continually offer "more for my money." You must prove to me again and again that I have made a wise choice in selecting you and your company above all others.

The Show is why people go to Disneyland. Each land tells a unique story through its theme and attention to detail, and the cast members each play a role in the Show. The most integral component of the training is the traditions and standards of guest service. The first of these is called the *Personal Touch*. The cast members are encouraged to use their own unique style and personality to provide a personal interaction with each guest. One of the primary ways Disney accomplishes this is through name tags. Everyone, regardless of position, goes by his or her first name. This tradition was started by Walt and continues today. It allows cast members to interact on a more personal level with guests. It also assists internally, by creating an informal environment that facilitates the flow of open communication and breaks down some of the traditional barriers.

Cinderella's castle soaring above tourists at Walt Disney World, Orlando, Florida.

Opening Disneyland

Imagine what Walt Disney had to overcome to open Disneyland. Disneyland opened on July 17, 1955, to the predictions that it would be a failure. And, in truth, everything that could go wrong did. Just to give an example, here is what happened on opening day:

- Plumbers went on strike.
- Tickets were duplicated.
- Attractions broke down.
- There was a gas leak in Fantasyland.
- The asphalt on Main Street didn't harden in time, so in the heat of July, horses' hooves and women's high heels stuck in the street.

As Walt once said, "You may not realize it when it happens, but a kick in the teeth might be good for you." Walt had his fair share of challenges, one of which was obtaining financing to develop Disneyland—he had to deal with more than 300 banks.

So what is the Disney service model?

It begins with a smile. This is the universal language of hospitality and service. Guests recognize and appreciate the cast members' warmth and sincerity.

Make eye contact and use body language. This means stance, approach, and gestures. For instance, cast members are trained to use *open* gestures for directions, not pointed fingers, because open palms are friendlier and less directive.

Respect and welcome all guests. This means being friendly, helpful, and going out of the way to *exceed* guests' expectations.

Value the magic. This means that when they're on stage, cast members are totally focused on creating the magic of Disneyland. They don't talk about personal problems or world affairs, and they don't mention that you can find Mickey in more than one place.

Initiate guest contact. Cast members are reminded to initiate guest contact actively. Disney calls this being aggressively friendly. It's not enough to be responsive when approached. Cast members are encouraged to take the first step with guests. They have lots of little tricks for doing this, such as noticing a guest's name on a hat and then using the name in conversation or kneeling to ask a child a question.

Creative service solutions. For example, one Disneyland Hotel cast member recently became aware of a little boy who had come from the Midwest with his parents to enjoy the park and then left early because he was ill. The cast member approached the supervisor with an idea to send the child chicken soup, a character plush toy, and a get-well card from Mickey. The supervisor loved the idea, and all cast members are now allowed to set up these arrangements in similar situations without a supervisor's approval.

End with a "thank you." The phrases cast members use are important in creating a service environment. They do not have a book of accepted phrases; rather, through training and coaching, cast members are encouraged to use their own personality and style to welcome and approach guests, answer questions, anticipate their needs, thank them, and express with sincerity their desire to make the guest's experience exceptional.

Taken individually, these might sound pretty basic. But taken together, they help define and reinforce the Disney culture. After initial cast member training is completed, these concepts must be applied and continually reinforced by leaders who possess strong coaching skills. Disney uses a model called the *Five Steps of Leadership* to lead the cast member performance.

Each step in the leadership model is equally important in meeting service and business goals. Each leader must do the following:

1. Provide clear expectations and standards.
2. Communicate these expectations through demonstration, information, and examples.
3. Hold cast members accountable for their feedback.
4. Coach through honest and direct feedback.
5. Recognize, reward, and celebrate success.

To supplement and reward the leadership team, Disney provides technical training to every new manager and assistant manager. In addition, the management team also participates in classes at the Disney University to learn the culture, values, and the leadership philosophy necessary to be successful in the Disney environment.

Disney measures the systems and reward process by distributing 1,000 surveys to guests as they leave Disneyland and 100 surveys to guests who stayed at each of the Disney hotels. The guests are asked to take the surveys home and mail them back to Disney. In return, their names are entered for a drawing for a family weekend package at the park and hotel.

Feedback from the surveys has been helpful in improving the guest experience. For example, as a result of the surveys, the entertainment division realized that the opportunity to interact with a character was a key driver to guest satisfaction. So, the entertainment team designed a brochure, "The Characters Today," which is distributed at the main entrance daily. This brochure allows guests to maximize their opportunity to see the characters. This initiative has already raised guest satisfaction by ten percentage points.

Cast members are also empowered to make changes to improve service. These measures are supplemented by financial controls and "mystery shoppers" (when people use the services like any other guest, but they are really employed to sample the service and report their findings) that allow Disney to focus resources on increasing guest satisfaction. The reward system does not consist of just the hard reward system we commonly think of, such as bonuses and incentive plans, important though they are. Recognition is not a one-size-fits-all system. Disney has found that noncash recognition is as powerful as, if not more powerful than, a recognition tool in many situations. Some examples follow:

- Disney recognizes milestones of years of service. They use pins and statues and have a formal dinner for cast members and guests to reinforce and celebrate the value of their experience and expertise at serving Disney's guests.

- Throughout the year, Disney hosts special social and recreational events that involve the cast members and their families in the product.

- Disney invites cast members and their families to family film festivals featuring new Disney releases to ensure that they are knowledgeable about the latest Disney products.

- The Disneyland management team hosts the Family Christmas Party in the park after hours. This allows cast members to enjoy shopping, dining, and riding the attractions. Management dresses in costumes and runs the facilities.

Career Paths

Now that we know that the hospitality industries are the largest and arguably the fastest growing in the world, let's explore some of the many **career paths** available to graduates. The concept of career paths describes the career progression available in each segment of the hospitality industry. A career path does not always go in a straight line, as sometimes described in a career ladder. You could liken it to jumping into a swimming pool: You get wet whichever end you jump in and then you might swim over to the other side—but not always in a straight line. It's like that in the hospitality industry, also. We may begin in one area and later find another that is more attractive. Opportunities come our way and we need to be prepared to take advantage of them. To illustrate, take Barbra. A few years ago, she was a hospitality management graduate who was not very outgoing, so she decided to take a position in the hotel accounting office. A few years later, we visited the hotel where she was working, and to our pleasant surprise, we found a smiling Barbra welcoming us as the front office manager. After a few more years, she moved into the food and beverage department and then the marketing department, and is now a general manager.

Progression means that we can advance from one position to another. In the hospitality industry we don't always use straight-line career ladders because we need experience in several areas before becoming, say, a general manager, director of human resources, catering manager, meeting planner, or director of marketing. The path to general manager in a hotel may go through food and beverage, rooms division, marketing, human resources, or finance and accounting, or, more likely, a combination of these, because it is better to have experience in several areas (cross-training). The same is true for restaurants. A graduate with service experience will need to spend some time in the kitchen learning each station and then bartending before becoming an opening or closing assistant or manager, general manager, area manager, regional director, vice president, and president.

Sometimes we want to run before we can walk. We want to progress quickly. But remember to enjoy the journey as much as the destination. If you advance too quickly, you may not be ready for the additional responsibility, and you may not have the skills necessary for the promotion. For instance, you cannot expect to become a director of food and beverage until you really know "food and beverage": this means spending a few years in the kitchen. Otherwise, how can you relate to an executive chef? You have to know how the food should be prepared and served. You have to set the standards—not have them set for you. Be prepared because you never know when an opportunity will present itself.

Career Goals

You may already know that you want to be a director of accounting, an event manager, a director of marketing, or of food and beverage, or a restaurant owner. If you are not sure of which career path to pursue, that's OK. Now is the time to explore the industry to gain the information you need to decide which career path to follow. A great way to do this is through internships and work experience. Some suggest trying a variety of jobs rather than sticking to the same one.

If we follow the interrelated nature of hospitality, travel, and tourism in Figure 2 or 3, we can see some of the numerous career options in various industry segments.

Is the Hospitality Industry for You?

In this text, we described some characteristics of the hospitality industry. Due to the size and scope of the hospitality industry, career prospects are gradually improving. We also know that it is an exciting and dynamic industry with growth potential, especially when the economy is strong. In the hospitality industry we are often working when others are at leisure—think of the evening or weekend shift; however, in some positions and careers, many evenings and weekends can be yours to enjoy as you wish. (Accounting, marketing and sales, human resources, and housekeeper are some examples).

The hospitality industry is a service industry; this means that we take pride in caring about others as well as ourselves. Ensuring that guests receive outstanding service is a goal of hospitality corporations. This is a business that gets into your blood! It is mostly fun, exciting, and seldom dull, and an industry in which almost everyone can succeed. So, what does it take to be successful in the hospitality industry? The personal characteristics, qualities, skills, and abilities you'll need are honesty, hard work, being a team player, being prepared to work long hours spread over various shifts, the ability to cope with stress, good decision-making skills, good communication skills, being dedicated to exceptional service, and having a passion and desire to exceed guest expectations. Leadership, ambition, and the will to succeed are also important and necessary for career success.

Recruiters look for *service-oriented* people, who "walk their talk," meaning they do what they say they're going to do. Good work experience, involvement in on-campus and professional organizations, a positive attitude, a good grade point average—all show a commitment to an individual's studies. Career-minded individuals who have initiative and are prepared to work hard and make a contribution to the company, which has to make a profit, are what companies are looking for.

Self-Assessment and Personal Philosophy

The purpose of completing a self-assessment is to measure our current strengths and weaknesses and to determine what we need to improve on if we are going to reach our goals. Self-assessment helps establish where we are now and shows us the links to where we want to go, our goals. In a self-assessment, we make a list of our positive attributes. For example, we may have experience in a guest-service position; this will be helpful in preparing for supervisory and managerial positions. Other positive attributes include our character and all the other things that recruiters look for, as listed previously.

We also make a list of areas where we might want to make improvements. For example, we may have reached a certain level of culinary expertise, but need more experience and a course in this specialty. Or you may want to improve your Spanish-language skills because you will be working with Spanish-speaking colleagues. Your *philosophy* is your beliefs and the way you treat others and your work. It will determine who you are and what you stand for. You may state that you enjoy giving excellent service by treating others as you would like to be treated and that you believe in honesty and respect.

A great web resource for self-assessment is www.queendom.com; this site provides self-assessment quizzes.

Now Is the Time to Get Involved

For your own enjoyment and personal growth and development, it is very important to get involved with on-campus and professional hospitality and tourism organizations and participate in the organization of events. Recruiters notice the difference between students who have become involved with various organizations and students who have not, and they take that into consideration when assessing candidates for positions with companies. Becoming involved will show your commitment to your chosen career and will lead you to meet interesting peers and industry professionals who can potentially help you along your chosen career path. You will develop leadership and organizational skills that will help you in your career.

Professional Organizations

Professional organizations include becoming a student member of CHRIE (www. chrie.org). You can also access the excellent Webzine *Hosteur*, which is published especially for students; CHRIE offers its members free access. The NRA (www. restaurant.org) is another organization to join. You will likely find several NRA magazines and publications to be very helpful. The NRA and your state restaurant association are affiliated, and both have trade shows; the NRA hosts the Salute to Excellence, a day of activities that culminates with a gala dinner. Only two students from each school are invited to this special event; make sure you're one of them, as it is well worth it. The AH&LA (www.ahla.com) is a good organization to belong to if you are interested in a career in the lodging segment of the industry. Benefits of AH&LA memberships include access to the organization's career center, which is powered by Hcareers.com, the largest online database of career opportunities in the lodging industry; a subscription to *Lodging* magazine, a leading industry publication with news, product information, and current articles on industry-related topics; subscriptions to *Lodging News*, *Lodging Law*, *Lodging H/R* e-newsletters; and use of the AH&LA's information center—helpful for those pesky term papers! And you receive scholarship information, too!

The International Special Events Society (ISES; www.ises.com) includes over 3,000 professionals representing special event producers, from festivals to trade shows. Membership brings together professionals from a variety of special events disciplines. The mission of ISES is to educate, advance, and promote the special events industry and its network of professionals, along with related issues.

The Professional Convention Management Association (PCMA; www.pcma.org) is a great resource for convention management educational offerings and networking opportunities. The National Society of Minorities in Hospitality (NSMH; www.nsmh.org) has a membership of several hundred minority hospitality majors who address diversity and multiculturalism as well as career development via events and programs.

Trends in Hospitality and Tourism

There is a healthy increase in hospitality and tourism not only in North America but around the world. We can identify a number of trends that are having and will continue to have an impact on the hospitality industry. Some, like diversity, have already been realized and are sure to increase in the future. Here, in no particular order, are some of the major trends that hospitality professionals indicate as having an influence on the industry.

- *Globalization.* We have become the global village that was described a few years ago. We may have the opportunity to work or vacation in other countries, and more people than ever travel freely around the world.
- *Safety and security.* Since September 11, 2001, we have all become more conscious of our personal safety and have experienced increased scrutiny at airports and federal and other buildings. But it goes beyond that; terrorists kidnap tourists from their resorts and hold them for ransom, thugs mug them, and others assault them. Security of all types of hospitality and tourism operations is critical, and disaster plans should be made for each kind of threat. Personal safety of guests must be the first priority.
- *Diversity.* The hospitality industry is one of the most diverse of all industries; not only do we have a diverse employee population, but we also have a diverse group of guests. Diversity is increasing as more people with more diverse cultures join the hospitality workforce.
- *Service.* It is no secret that service is at the top of guests' expectations, yet few companies offer exceptional service. World-class service does not just happen; training is important in delivering the service that guests have come to expect.
- *Technology.* Technology is a driving force of change that presents opportunities for greater efficiencies and integration for improved guest service. However, the industry faces great challenges in training employees

to use the new technology and in standardization of software and hardware design. Some hotels have several systems that do not talk to each other, and some reservation systems bounce between 7 and 10 percent of sales nationally.

- *Legal issues.* Lawsuits are not only more frequent, but they cost more if you lose and more to defend. One company spent several million dollars just to defend one case. Government regulations and the complexities of employee relations create increased challenges for hospitality operators.
- *Changing demographics.* The U.S. population is gradually increasing, and the baby boomers are retiring. Many retirees have the time and money to travel and utilize hospitality services.
- *Price–value.* Price and value are important to today's more discerning guests.
- *Social media.* This phenomenon has grown rapidly, allowing people to connect for social and business communications.
- *Sanitation.* Sanitation is critical to the success of any restaurant and foodservice operation. Guests expect to eat healthy foods that have been prepared in a sanitary environment.

CASE STUDY

Being Promoted from Within

One month ago, Tom was promoted from line cook to kitchen manager. It was a significant step up in his life. He felt that his promotion was well deserved, as he had always been a hard worker. Tom never had a second thought about going the extra mile for his employer. He felt that since he had seniority in the kitchen and was friendly with everyone in the back of the house, he would be sure to get the respect he deserved from everyone for whom he had responsibility. About three weeks into his new position, Tom found that this was not the case. Several back-of-the house employees had become careless about their responsibilities after Tom were promoted. They were coming to work late, wearing unlaundered uniforms, and becoming more and more sloppy with their plate presentations. Every day at work, Tom was becoming more frustrated and upset. He knew that the employees were never careless about these matters with their previous supervisor.

Discussion Questions

1. What are some possible reasons for the back-of-the house employees' carelessness?
2. How should Tom assess the current situation?
3. If you were Tom's supervisor, what advice would you have given him before he started his new position?

Career Information

Do you know exactly where you want to be in five or ten years? The best advice is to follow your interests. Do what you love to do and success will soon come. Often, we assess our own character and personality to determine a suitable path. Some opt for the accounting and control side of the tourism business; others, perhaps with more outgoing personalities, vie for sales and marketing; others prefer operations, which could be either in back or in front of the house. Creating your own career path can be an exciting and a challenging task. However, the travel and tourism industry is generally characterized as dynamic, fun, and full of challenges and opportunities. And remember, someone has to run Walt Disney World, Holland American Cruise Lines, Marriot Hotels and Resorts, B&Bs, restaurants, and be the airport manager.

The anticipated growth of tourism over the next few years offers today's students numerous career opportunities in each section of the industry, as well as increasing job stability. However, there are many general things that can be said about a career in the hospitality industry. For example, a regular 8:30 A.M. to 4:30 P.M. job is not the norm; nearly all sectors operate up to 24 hours a day, 365 days a year—including evenings, weekends, and holidays. The good news is that nearly all sectors are experiencing growth and should continue to do so over the next few years.

CASE EXAMPLE

How to Treat Prospective Associates

One of the many jobs I have had through my career was working for the Stamford Marriott, where I experienced firsthand how a world-class human resources (HR) department executed a well-devised HR plan. I should first start by describing this hotel: It is a 500-room hotel that is full service and always busy. We had about twenty-five to thirty employees in the kitchen alone; the banquet and service staff represented another forty people, and there were probably another one hundred people employed as housekeepers, room service, front desk, bellman, maintenance, HR, and management. The Marriott Corporation has very high standards for the employees they hire, and getting a job with Marriott is not as easy as it might appear to be. My first experience with the Marriott was its HR department. I applied to the job from a listing at the school I was attending in Hyde Park, New York. The listing stated they needed a cook to work long weekend hours and they would accept applications Monday through Friday between 2:00 and 4:00 P.M. I chose to go on Tuesday at 2:00 P.M. and leave my application. When I arrived, I was greeted by one of the HR employees, who gave me the application and offered me a soda while I filled out the application. After filling out the paperwork, I handed it to the employee and thought that they would probably contact me if they were interested, but as I turned to leave, the HR employee asked me to stay. Amanda, the HR director, asked me to come into the office for a prescreening, where I was asked questions about prior experience, my education, and my plans for the future. Amanda kept using terms like *team members* and *family*. After a short time, Amanda had the sous chef come down to talk to me, and he asked me questions about my passions and hobbies. I began to feel as if they might hire me, but the sous chef said he needed to send the chef down to talk to me. By now, I had been in the HR office for over an hour. The chef came down and asked me to take a trip up to the restaurant on the top floor. It was empty and it was just the two of us. He began by telling his story about how he made it to where he is today. I began to feel that this was a big decision for the hotel; the entire staff was sizing me up to see if they wanted me to work with them. The chef said he would like to have me on his staff, but there was one more person I would need to talk to. A few minutes later, I was in the office of the hotel manager, feeling very nervous. The hotel manager stood up, introduced himself, and asked me why I chose the Marriott, as if I had this plan all along to work for this corporation. I answered that it was because of the company's excellent reputation. The hotel manager said he thought I would fit in well with his team. After finishing all my interviews, I was escorted back down to Amanda, who finished my paperwork, took me on a tour of the hotel, and introduced me to the entire staff. As I walked through the hotel, there was not one person I passed who did not say hi and introduce themselves.

So why did I walk you through the interview process at the Marriott? I realized after my experience with human resources (HR) that it was their mission to make sure they had the right person for the job. The planning to make sure that every applicant was interviewed by at least three managers and the interest in my future goals and future with the company was very impressive. Amanda was able to free up three very important people and it was with pleasure that those managers interviewed me. I was trained in my job for two weeks before I went solo, and Amanda checked on me three times in my first two weeks. The employees at this Marriott loved their jobs and did not have to be prodded to do what they were supposed to do. We all felt grateful to be working with a company that cared so much about their employees. The quality of work that these employees produced was incredible, and everyone watched everyone else to make sure that the standards stayed high and that guest satisfaction was our main focus.

In the planning stages of this HR department, the long-term or strategic plan was to hire only the right person for each position; they also took extra care in the hiring process to make sure that the person fit the Marriott team. The personnel for that Marriott were chosen by the managers of HR and were handpicked; when they found a person to fit the mold. they took extra time with the applicant to make sure everything lined up. The Marriott used the exemption form of management and were able to use this style because of the quality of the employees they would hire. The job descriptions were clearly defined so that employees knew what their job entailed, and all employees were thoroughly trained.

Having a plan in place allows companies like the Marriott to choose the best people, they become proactive instead of reactive, they are ready to hire a good person because the system is in place to allow the interviews, and the training is in place so the employee does not become frustrated. The HR manager knows that checking on the employee in the first week helps build confidence in the employee that if he or she has problems he or she has somewhere to go. My experience with the Marriott was an experience that I will never forget.

Courtesy of Joseph Moreta.

Summary

1. The hospitality and tourism industries are the largest and fastest-growing industries in the world.
2. Now is a great time to be considering a career in the hospitality and tourism field because thousands of supervising managers are needed for this dynamic industry.
3. Common dynamics include delivery of services and guest impressions of them.
4. Hospitality businesses are open 365 days a year and 24 hours a day and are likely to require shift work.
5. One essential difference between the hospitality business and other businesses is that in hospitality we are selling an intangible and perishable product.
6. Corporate philosophy is changing from managers' planning, organizing, implementing, and so on, to that of managers' counseling associates, giving them resources, and helping them to think for themselves.
7. Corporate philosophy embraces the values of the organization, including ethics, morals, fairness, and equality. The philosophy of "do whatever it takes" is critical for success.
8. Corporate culture refers to the overall style or feel of the company, or how people relate to one another and their jobs.
9. A mission statement is a statement of central purposes, strategies, and values of the company. It should answer the question, "What business are we in?"
10. A goal is a specific target to be met; objectives or tactics are the actions needed to accomplish the goal.
11. Total quality management has helped improve service to guests by empowering employees to give service that exceeds guest expectations.

Key Words and Concepts

corporate philosophy
empowerment
front of the house
goal
guest satisfaction
heart of the house

hospitality
inseparability
intangible
National Restaurant
    Association (NRA)
perishability

total quality management
    (TQM)
tourism
sustainability
return on investment

Review Questions

1. Why is service so critical in the hospitality and tourism industries?
2. Describe and give an example of the following:
    Mission statement
    Moment of truth
3. What is the Disney service model?
4. Explain why Ritz-Carlton won the Malcolm Baldrige award.

Internet Exercises

1. Organization: **World Travel and Tourism Council**
   Web site: **www.wttc.org**
   Summary: The World Travel and Tourism Council (WTTC) is the global business leaders' forum for travel and tourism. It includes all sectors of industry, including accommodation, catering, entertainment, recreation, transportation, and other travel-related services. Its central goal is to work with governments so that they can realize the full potential economic impact of the world's largest generator of wealth and jobs: travel and tourism.
   (a) Find the latest statistics or figures for the global hospitality and tourism economy.

2. Organization: **Ritz-Carlton Hotels**
   Web site: **www.ritzcarlton.com**
   Summary: The Ritz-Carlton is renowned for its elegance, sumptuous surroundings, and legendary service. With seventy-four hotels in twenty-three countries worldwide, a majority of them award winning, the Ritz-Carlton reflects one hundred years of tradition.
   (a) What is it about Ritz-Carlton that makes it such a great hotel chain?

3. Organization: **Disneyland and Walt Disney World**
   Web site: **disneyland.disney.com** and **disneyworld.disney.com**
   (a) Compare and contrast Disneyland's and Walt Disney World's web sites.

Apply Your Knowledge

1. Write your personal mission statement.

2. Suggest ways to improve service in a hospitality business.

Suggested Activities

1. Where are you going? Take a moment to think about your future career prospects. Where do you want to be in five, ten, or twenty years?
2. Prepare some general hospitality- and career-related questions, and interview two supervisors or managers in the hospitality industry. Share and compare the answers with your class next session.

Endnotes

1. This section draws on: *Hospitality through the Ages.* (Corning, NY: Corning Foodservice Products: Corning Foodservice Products, February 1972), 2–34.
2. William S. Gray and Salvatore C. Liquori, *Hotel and Motel Management and Operation* (Englewood Cliffs, NJ: Prentice Hall, 1980), 4–5, quoted in John R. Walker, *Introduction to Hospitality*, 2nd ed. (Upper Saddle River, NJ: Prentice Hall, 1999), P5.
3. John R. Walker, *Introduction to Hospitality,* 2nd ed. (Upper Saddle River, NJ: Prentice Hall, 1999), P5.
4. Garvin R. Nathan, *Historic Taverns of Boston: 370 Years of Tavern History in One Definitive Guide* (Lincoln, NE: iUniverse, 2006), 3.
5. Linda Glick Conway, ed., *The Professional Chef,* 5th ed. (Hyde Park, NY: The Culinary Institute of America, 1991), 5.
6. Ibid.
7. John Mariani, *America Eats Out* (New York: William Morrow, 1991), 122–124.
8. Martin E. Dorf, *Restaurants That Work* (New York: Whitney Library of Design, 1992), 9.
9. Personal conversation with Charlotte Jordan, May 6, 2007.
10. Nathan Cobb, *Boston Globe Magazine*, June 4, 1989, quoted in John R. Walker, *The Restaurant from Concept to Operation*, 6th ed. (New York: John Wiley and Sons, 2012), 59.
11. Starbucks Coffee Company, *Our Heritage*, www.starbucks.com/about-us/our-heritage (accessed January 14, 2011); and Starbucks Coffee Company, *Company Profile,* http://assets.starbucks.com/assets/company-profile-feb10.pdf (accessed January 18, 2011).
12. Robert Longley, *Lifetime Earnings Soar with Education: Masters Degree Worth $2.5 Million Income Over a Lifetime*, http://usgovinfo.about.com/od/moneymatters/a/edandearnings.htm (accessed February 3, 2011).
13. NGO Committee on Education, United Nations, *Our Common Future, Chairman's Foreword*, http://www.un-documents.net/ocf-cf.htm (accessed February 15, 2011).
14. Sustainable Hospitality Group, *What Is Sustainability?* http://www.sustainablehg.com/sustainable-hospitality-group/sustainability.htm#whatis (accessed February 14, 2011).
15. Hervé Houdré, Center for Hospitality Research, *Sustainable Hospitality: Sustainable Development in the Hotel Industry*, www.hotelschool.cornell.edu/research/chr/pubs/perspective/perspective-14924.html (accessed February 14, 2011).
16. Marriott International, Inc., *Core Values*, www.marriott.com/corporateinfo/culture/coreValues.mi (accessed January 18, 2011).
17. Marriott, *Marriott Culture*, www.marriott.com/corporateinfo/culture/coreCulture.mi (accessed January 18, 2011).
18. Mohamed Gravy, General Manager Holiday Inn Sarasota, address to University of South Florida students, Tampa, Florida, February 8, 2010.
19. Marriott International, Inc., *J.W. Marriott, Jr.*, www.marriott.com/corporateinfo/culture/heritageJWMarriottJR.mi (accessed May 27, 2011).
20. Ibid.
21. JW Marriott Jr and Kathi Ann Brown, *The Spirit to Serve: Marriott's Way* (New York: Harper Collins, 1997), 34.
22. Karl Albrecht and Ron Zemke, *Service America!* (Homewood, IL: Dow Jones-Irwin, 1985), 2.
23. Karl Albrecht, *At America's Service* (New York: Warner Books, 1992), 13.
24. Albrecht, *At America's Service*, 27.
25. American Hotel & Lodging Association, *AH&LA Green Resource Center*, http://www.ahla.com/green.aspx (accessed February 3, 2011).
26. Phil Cohen, "Deming's 14 Points," *HCi*, http://www.hci.com.au/hcisite2/articles/deming.htm (accessed January 14, 2011).
27. Marriott International, Inc., *Brands*, http://www.marriott.com/hotel-development/marriott-brands.mi (accessed August 10, 2011).

Glossary

Corporate philosophy   The core beliefs that drive a company's basic organizational structure.

Empowerment   The act of giving employees the authority, tools, and information they need to do their jobs with greater autonomy.

Front-of-the-house   Comprises all areas with which guests come in contact, including the lobby, corridors, elevators, guest rooms, restaurants and bars, meeting rooms, and restrooms. Also refers to employees who staff these areas.

Goal   A specific result to be achieved; the end result of a plan.

Guest satisfaction   The desired outcome of hospitality services.

Heart of the house   The back of the house.

Hospitality   1. The cordial and generous reception of guests. 2. A wide range of businesses, each of which is dedicated to the service of people away from home.

Inseparability   The interdependence of hospitality services offered.

Intangible   Something that cannot be touched.

National Restaurant Association (NRA)   The association representing restaurant owners and the restaurant industry.

Perishability   The limited lifetime of hospitality products; for example, last night's vacant hotel room cannot be sold today.

Return on Investment (ROI)   An important financial measure that determines how well management uses business assets to produce profit. It measures the efficiency with which financial resources available to a company are employed by management. ROI 5 Annual Profit divided by Average Amount Invested. *See also* ROA.

Total quality management (TQM)   A managerial approach that integrates all of the functions and related processes of a business such that they are all aimed at maximizing guest satisfaction through ongoing improvement.

Tourism   Travel for recreation or the promotion and arrangement of such travel.

Photo Credits

Credits are listed in the order of appearance.

The Hotel Business

From Chapter 2 of *Introduction to Hospitality*, Sixth Edition. John R. Walker. Copyright © 2013 by Pearson Education, Inc. Published by Pearson. All rights reserved.

The Hotel Business

OBJECTIVES

After reading and studying this text, you should be able to:

- Describe hotel ownership and development via hotel franchising and management contracts.

- Classify hotels by type, location, and price.

- Discuss the concept and growth of vacation ownership.

- Name some prestigious and unusual hotels.

A Brief History of Innkeeping in the United States[1]

1634—Samuel Coles Inn opens on Washington Street and is the first tavern in Boston; it is later named the Ships Tavern.

1642—The City Tavern in New York City is built by the the West India Company.

1775—The Green Dragon in Boston becomes the meeting place of American Revolutionaries. Patrick Henry calls the taverns of colonial America the "cradles of liberty."

1790—The first use of the word *hotel* in America is at Carre's Hotel, 24 Broadway, New York City.

1801—The Francis Union Hotel in Philadelphia opens in a former presidential mansion.

1801–1820—Taverns are rechristened as *hotels* following a surge in popularity of all things French.

1824—The Mountain House, the first of the large resort hotels in the Catskills, eventually has 300 rooms and accommodates 500 persons.

1829—The Tremont House in Boston appears. Designed from cellar to eaves to be a hotel, it has three stories and 170 rooms. This hotel is known for several firsts: the first bellboys, the first inside water closets (toilets), the first hotel clerk, the French cuisine on a Yankee menu, the first menu card in this country, the first annunciators in guest rooms, the first room keys given to the guests, and the first guests checked in at a dedicated reception area—previously they checked in at the bar.

1834—The Astor House, New York City's first palatial hotel, has rooms furnished in black walnut and Brussels carpeting.

1846—The first centrally heated hotel, the Eastern Exchange Hotel, opens in Boston.

1848—Safety deposit boxes are provided for guests by the New England Hotel in Boston.

1852—Electric lights dazzle guests for the first time in New York City's Hotel Everett and at Chicago's Palmer House in 1894.

1859—The first passenger elevator goes into operation in the Old Fifth Avenue Hotel; upper rooms are sometimes more expensive than those on lower floors.

1875—The Palace Hotel in San Francisco is billed as the "world's largest hotel"; floor clerks are installed along with four elevators.

1880–1890s—There is a resort boom in Florida, New England, Virginia, Pennsylvania, and Atlantic City.

1887—The Ponce de León Hotel, in St. Augustine, is built; it is the first luxury hotel in Florida.

1888—The Del Coronado Hotel is built; it is the first luxury resort in California.

1892—The Brown Palace Hotel in Denver is built with "gold money" to be as fine as any hotel back east. The Brown Palace focuses on catering to business people and is regarded as one of the first convention hotels.

1908—The Statler Hotel in Buffalo, New York, is established by Elsworth Milton Statler, and is considered by many to be the premier hotelier of all time (his story makes interesting reading—try Googling him). The Statler hotel is the first to introduce keyholes for safety, electric light switches, private baths, ice water, and the delivery of a morning newspaper. The hotel is also constructed so as to have bathrooms backing onto each other; this enables the plumbing to go up or down one shaft along with protected electrical wiring. The Statler Inn at Cornell University is built with money from the Statler foundation.

1919—Conrad Hilton opens the Mobley Hotel in Cisco, Texas.

1920—There are 12 million cars in America, and auto camping becomes a national pastime as cities open up camps for people to stay at.

1922—Cornell University begins a hotel and restaurant program.

1929 to 1945—During the Great Depression and World War II, hotel occupancy drops and several hotels are lost by owners—others just manage to survive.

1946—The Golden Nugget and the Flamingo open in Las Vegas, prompting a boom in hotel construction that continues to this day.

1950s and 1960s—More interstate highways are constructed and more motels and hotels are established for the ordinary person, not just the rich.

1954—Kemmons Wilson opens the first Holiday Inn.

1966—The ice and vending machines make their debuts in InterContinental hotels.

1967—The Atlanta Hyatt Regency Hotel, designed by John Portman with an atrium and an indoor garden, opens.

1960s—Westin introduces 24-hour room service.

1960s and 1970s—Hotels begin to develop internationally.

1970s—Hotels are hit hard by the energy crisis—there is little development. Cable TV arrives; it later evolves into Internet access.

1975—Hyatt introduces concierge lounges for its VIP guests.

1980s—The electric key card is introduced, and hotels begin to accept major credit cards as payment.

1980s and 1990s—Hotel chains develop more rapidly internationally.

1980s and 1990s—Hotel chains develop hotels in several tiers/price points to appeal to different market segments.

1990s—Voice mail and in-room Internet connections are introduced.

2000s—Boutique hotels come of age, and LEED (Leadership in Energy and Environmental Design) hotels are constructed. Sustainability becomes increasingly more important.

THE AMERICAN HOTEL & LODGING ASSOCIATION

Dedicated to Serving the Interests of Hoteliers

For over one hundred years, the American Hotel & Lodging Association (AH&LA) has been an advocate for all matters relating to lodging. The AH&LA represents 50,800 properties with 4,762,095 guestrooms, $127.2 billion in sales, $53.50 revenue per available room (Rev Par), and an average occupancy rate of 54.7 percent. As a nonprofit trade association, the AH&LA exists to help the lodging industry prosper, with national advocacy on Capitol Hill, public relations and image management, education, research, and information. The AH&LA also has several programs that benefit members, among which are a comprehensive Green Resource Center; diversity programs and advice for helping members improve their diversity initiatives; technology resources and initiatives to help members improve their technology efforts; social media advice, including resources for Facebook, blogs, Twitter, Yelp (the number-one travel application for the iPhone) and Four Square (another way for consumers to write reviews, leave suggestions, and talk about hotels), and LivingSocial, Groupon, Buy With Me, and so on, online resources for leveraging the collective buying power to which more than 20 million people subscribe, with electronic promotions sent daily.

The AH&LA has conventions, the main one being in New York City in November. Additionally, there are state chapters and conventions that are recommended for you to attend as they offer several interesting presentations and discussions on lodging topics.

FOCUS ON DEVELOPMENT

Dr. Chad M. Gruhl, Associate Chair and Associate Professor at Denver State University

Dr. Chad Gruhl is a hotel expert working for such places as the Waldorf Astoria in New York City, Trump Plaza Hotel and Casino in Atlantic City, New Jersey, Hotel InterContinental in Chicago, and Residence Inn by Marriott in three states.

There has been a tremendous amount of development in the hotel industry that has taken place in the past thirty years. The large hotel corporations discovered that if they targeted specific markets, they would be able to increase market share for particular segments. For example, in the early 1980s Marriott International focused primarily on its major hotel chain, full-service Marriott Hotels. Later in the 1980s, Marriott began expanding and developing other concepts in order to capture a larger market share:

1983—Created and opened Courtyard by Marriott (mid-economy segment)

1984—Entered into the timeshare segment of hospitality (now the largest in the world)

1987—Acquired Residence Inn by Marriott (extended-stay segment)

1987—Created the concept of Fairfield by Marriott (economy segment)

1995—Purchased Ritz-Carlton Hotels (high-end segment)

1997—Opened TownePlace Suites (select extended-stay segment), Fairfield Suites (economy segment), and Marriott Executive Residence Brand (residence segment)

1999—Acquires ExecuStay (corporate housing segment)

Today Marriott International flies 18 flags with over $10 billion in sales, 192,000 employees, over 5,000 eating places, and over 3,000 lodging properties in 67 countries and territories in the world.

Do these large companies do it all themselves? Meaning, Do they operate, own, and expand the corporate name all by themselves? The answer is, absolutely not. The largest hotel companies have expanded their companies at very fast rates through franchising. This is one of the primary sources of income for most large hotel and restaurant companies.

For example, to apply for an InterContinental Hotel and Resorts flag (the right to use their name), it costs $500 per room with a $75,000 minimum for the initial cost and application fee. After the hotel opens, it costs 5 percent of revenue for royalty fees and another 3 percent for marketing fees. In other words, it is very expensive to fly a major hotel flag. So why would anyone develop a hotel where they fly another company's flag? The answer is simple: The major hotel companies have very large reservation systems and brand recognition that brings people to that hotel once the hotel opens its doors.

There are eight large corporate hotel companies that fly approximately 75 percent of all U.S. hotels. Behind each large corporation are only a few of the larger flags that they own:

1. **Wyndham Hotels:** Days Inn, Howard Johnson, Ramada, Super 8
2. **Choice Hotels:** Comfort Inns, Quality Inns, Clarion, Econo Lodge
3. **Accor:** Sofitel, Novotel, Mercure, Ibis, Motel 6, Formule 1
4. **InterContinental Hotel Group:** Crowne Plaza, Holiday Inn, Staybridge Suites
5. **Marriott International:** Ritz-Carlton, Renaissance, Courtyard, Fairfield Inns, Residence Inns
6. **Blackstone:** Hilton Hotels, Waldorf Astoria, DoubleTree, Embassy Suites, Hampton Inns
7. **Carlson Hospitality:** Radisson Hotels, Country Inns, Park Inn, TGI Fridays
8. **Starwood:** Sheraton Hotels, Four Points, St. Regis, Le Meridien Hotels, W Hotels, Westin Hotels

There are many development and franchising opportunities in the hotel and restaurant world. You, too, can make your mark on the industry.

Hotel Development and Ownership

Franchising and management contracts are the two main driving forces in the development and operation of the hotel business. After the potential of franchising caught on, there was no stopping American ingenuity. In about a half century, the hotel business was changed forever, and here is how it happened.

Franchising

Franchising in the hospitality industry is a concept that allows a company to expand more rapidly by using other people's money than if it had to acquire its own financing. The company, or franchisor, grants certain rights to the franchise—for example, the rights to use its trademark, signs, proven operating systems, operating procedures and possibly reservations system, marketing know-how, purchasing discounts, and so on—for a fee. In return, the franchisee agrees by signing the franchise contract to operate the restaurant, hotel, or franchised outlet in accordance with the guidelines set by the franchisor. Franchising is a way of doing business that benefits both the franchisor—who wants to expand the business rapidly—and the franchisee—who has financial backing but lacks specific expertise and recognition. Some corporations franchise by individual outlets and others by territory. North America is host to more than 180 hotel brand extensions and franchised hotel brands.

Franchising hotels in the United States began in 1907, when the Ritz Development Company franchised the Ritz-Carlton name in New York City.[2] Howard Johnson began franchising his hotels in 1954—he had since 1927 successfully franchised the "red roof" restaurants. Holiday Inn (now a part of InterContinental Hotels Group [IHG], one of the largest lodging enterprises in the world) also grew by the strategy of franchising: In 1952, Kemmons Wilson, a developer, had a disappointing experience while on a family vacation when he had to pay for an extra room for his children. Therefore, Wilson decided to build a moderately priced family-style hotel.

Each room was comfortably sized and had two double beds; this enabled children to stay for free in their parents' rooms. In the 1950s and early 1960s, as the economy grew, Holiday Inn grew in size and popularity. Holiday Inns eventually added restaurants, meeting rooms, and recreational facilities. They upgraded the furnishings and fixtures in the bedrooms and almost completely abandoned the original concept of being a moderately priced lodging operation.

One of the key factors in the successful development of Holiday Corporation was that it was one of the first companies to enter the midprice range of the market. These inns, or motor hotels, were often located away from the expensive downtown sites, near important freeway intersections and the more reasonably priced suburbs. Another reason for their success was the value they offered: comfort at a reasonable price, avoiding the expensive trimmings of luxury hotels.

At about this time, a new group of budget motels emerged. Motel 6 (so named because the original cost of a room was $6 a night) in California slowly spread across the country, as did Days Inn and others. Cecil B. Day was in the construction business and found Holiday Inns too expensive when traveling on vacation with his family. He bought cheap land and constructed buildings of no more than two stories to keep the costs down. These hotels and motels, primarily for commercial travelers and vacationing families, were located close to major highways and were built to provide low-cost lodging without frills. Some of these buildings were modular constructions. Entire rooms were built elsewhere, transported to the site, and placed side by side.

It was not until the 1960s that Hilton and Sheraton began to franchise their names. Franchising was the primary growth and development strategy of hotels and motels during the 1960s, 1970s, and 1980s. However, franchising presents two major challenges for the franchisor: maintenance of quality standards and avoidance of financial failure on the part of the franchisee.

The colorful lobby of a Hotel Indigo, a franchised InterContinental Hotels Group concept.

It is difficult for the franchise company to state in writing all the contingencies that will ensure that quality standards are met. Recent franchise agreements are more specific in terms of the exterior maintenance and guest service levels. Franchise fees vary according to the agreements worked out between the franchisor and the franchisee; however, an average agreement is based on 3 or 4 percent of room revenue.

The world's leading franchisors of hotels are Wyndham Worldwide with 597,674 rooms in 7,160 hotels; Choice Hotels International, ranked second with 487,410 rooms in 6,000 hotels; and InterContinental Hotels and Resorts with 646,679 rooms in 4,400 hotels.[3]

Franchising provides both benefits and drawbacks to the franchisee and franchisor. The benefits to the franchisee are as follows:

- A set of plans and specifications from which to build
- National advertising
- A centralized reservation system (CRS)
- Participation in volume discounts for purchasing furnishings, fixtures, and equipment
- Listing in the franchisor's directory
- Low fee percentage charged by credit card companies

The drawbacks to the franchisee are as follows:

- Franchisees must pay high fees, both to join and ongoing.
- Central reservations generally produce between 17 and 26 percent of reservations.
- Franchisees must conform to the franchisor's agreement.
- Franchisees must maintain all standards set by the franchisor.

The benefits to the franchise company are as follows:

- Increased market share and recognition
- Up-front fees

The drawbacks to the franchise company are as follows:

- The need to be very careful in the selection of franchisees
- Difficulty in maintaining control of standards

Franchising continues to be a popular form of expansion both in North America and the rest of the world. However, there are always a few properties that lose their right to franchise by not maintaining standards.

Factors propelling franchise growth include the following:

- Fresh looks (curb appeal)
- Location near highways, airports, and suburbs

- Expansion in smaller cities throughout the United States
- New markets located in proximity to golf courses and other attractions
- Foreign expansion and a move to increase brand awareness

Is There a Franchise in Your Future?[4]

Many of you may not realize the pervasiveness of franchised operations in the United States. Predictions are that more than 50 percent of all retail sales in the United States (including restaurants) will soon be transacted through franchised units. Furthermore, franchises are available not only in the hotel, restaurant, travel, and recreation industries, but also in a large variety of other businesses that might interest you. These businesses include automotive tires and parts, retailing of all kinds, mail and copy services, janitorial and decorating services, personnel agencies, and so on. Today, many franchises can be operated from home by those interested in lifestyle changes.

If you end up working for a hospitality-related organization after graduation, chances are that your career will be influenced by franchising. You may work directly for a franchisor (the company that sells a franchised concept to an entrepreneur), whether on the corporate staff (for example, training, franchise consulting) or in an operations position in a franchisor-owned unit. Many franchisors own their own units that they use to test new operational or marketing ideas and to demonstrate the viability of the business to potential franchisees (the entrepreneurs who buy the franchised unit).

Alternatively, you may work for a franchisee. Some franchisees are small businesses, owning only one or a few units. Other franchisees are large corporations, owning hundreds of units and doing hundreds of millions of dollars in sales every year. For instance, RTM, Inc., owns and operates more than 600 Arby's restaurants. Additionally, it owns and franchises two midsized chicken restaurants, Lee's Famous Recipe Chicken and Mrs. Winner's Chicken and Biscuits. Working for a company as large as RTM would be similar to working for a large franchisor.

A third way that franchising may involve you is through ownership. Rather than starting your own independent business after college, you may want to consider buying a franchise. Several advantages can result. First, by working with a larger company you get the benefits of its experience in running the business that you have chosen to enter. Many of the mistakes that a new entrepreneur may make have already been overcome by your franchisor. The company might provide cash flow. The company might also provide other support services at little or no cost, such as marketing and advertising, site selection, construction plans, assistance with financing, and so on. All this assistance leads to a second key reason for buying a franchise—reducing your risk of failure. Franchising is probably less risky than starting your own business from scratch.

Consider the following factors that many franchisors seek. Are you strongly motivated to succeed and do you have a past history of business success, even if it is in a different business? Do you have a significant sum of money as well as access to credit? Are you willing to accept the franchisor's values, philosophy, and ways of doing business, as well as its technical assistance? Do you have the full support of your immediate family as you develop your business? Are you willing to devote substantially all of your working time to the business?

CORPORATE PROFILE

Wyndham Worldwide—A Collection of Hotel Brands

Wyndham Hotels and Resorts, Days Inn, Howard Johnson, Ramada, Knights Inn, Super 8, Trave-lodge, Baymont Inns & Suites, Microtel Inns and Suites, Hawthorn Suites, and Wingate by Wind-ham, totaling 7,160 hotels in 66 countries.[5]

As a franchisor, the company licenses the owners and operators of independent businesses to use Wyndham brand names, without taking on big business risks and expenses. Wyndham does not operate hotels, but instead provides coordination and services that allow franchisees to retain local control of their activities. At the same time, franchisees benefit from the economies of scale of widely promoted brand names and well-established standards of service, national and regional direct marketing, co-marketing programs, and volume purchasing discounts.

All brands share extensive market research, use proprietary reservation systems and a room inventory tracking system, which is extremely technology intensive and eliminates waste. By monitoring quality control and extensively promoting the brand names, Wyndham offers its independent franchise owners franchise fees that are relatively low compared to the increased profitability they gain.

Through franchising, the company limits its own risks and is able to keep overhead costs low. Wyndham also limits the volatility in the business as best as they can because fees come from revenue, not the fran-chisee's profitability. A further advantage of being a franchiser of such dimension is that the company is even more protected from the cyclical nature of the economy than are other franchise ventures.

Wyndham Vacation Ownership is the largest vacation ownership business when measured by the number of vacation ownership interests. Wyndham Vacation Ownership develops, markets, and sells vacation ownership interests and provides consumer financing to owners through its three primary consumer brands: Wyndham Vacation Resorts, WorldMark by Wyndham, and Wyndham Vacation Resorts Asia Pacific.[6]

Wyndham Vacation Ownership has developed or acquired approximately 150 vacation ownership resorts throughout the United States, Canada, Mexico, the Caribbean, and the South Pacific that represent approxi-mately 20,000 individual vacation ownership units and more than 830,000 owners of vacation ownership interests.[7]

Wyndham Exchange and Rentals helps to deliver vacations to more than 3.8 million members in approximately 100 countries. Wyndham provides exclusive access for specified periods to more than 87,000 vacation properties, including vacation ownership condominiums, traditional hotel rooms, villas, cottages, bungalows, campgrounds, city apartments, second homes, fractional resorts, private residence clubs, condominium hotels, and yachts. With a portfolio of more than thirty brands, Wyndham delivers unique vacation experiences to over 4 million leisure-bound families each year.[8]

Wyndham has been named to the Diversity Inc. twenty-five noteworthy companies that are raising diversity management leaders. Wyndham has also been ranked among the best one hundred greatest companies in America by *Newsweek* magazine, who also ranked Wyndham among the top one hundred greenest companies in America.

Franchising does have some disadvantages, as noted by many former franchisees. Your expectations of success may not be met. Perhaps the business did not have the potential that you expected, or perhaps you were not willing to invest the time needed. In a few cases, an overzealous or dishonest franchisor representative has misled franchisees.

As a franchisee, your freedom is somewhat restricted. You must operate within the constraints set out by your franchise agreement and the operational standards manual. Although there may be some room for you to express your creativity and innovation, it is generally limited. This may mean that, over time, the work might become monotonous and unchallenging, yet you have a long-term commitment to the company because of the franchise agreement that you signed. Your failure to consistently follow the franchisor's methods for running the business could result in the termination of your contract and your forced removal from the business.

Finally, the franchisor may not be performing well, thereby hurting your local business. Also, they may allow other franchisees to open units so near to your operation that your business is adversely affected.

Buying a franchise can be a very rewarding business experience in many ways. But like any other business venture, it requires research and a full discussion with family, friends, and business advisors, such as your accountant and attorney. You should carefully weigh whether you are psychologically suited to be a franchisee. Perhaps you perform more effectively in a corporate structure as an employee. Perhaps you are better suited to starting your own business from scratch. A careful analysis can help you make an informed decision. Buying a franchise such as Subway, Cold Stone Creamery, or Sea Master cruises is a lot cheaper—as in a few thousand dollars—compared to $1 million–plus for a hotel or even a McDonald's. A key question to be answered before you buy a franchise is whether you are better suited to being a franchisee or an independent entrepreneur.

Referral Associations

Referral associations offer similar benefits to properties as franchises, albeit at a lower cost. Hotels and motels with a referral association share a CRS and a common image, logo, or advertising slogan. In addition, referrals may offer group-buying discounts to members, as well as management training and continuing education programs. Each independent hotel refers guests to each of the other member hotels. Hotels and motels pay an initial fee to join a referral association. Size and appearance standards are less stringent than those in a franchise agreement; hence, guests may find more variation between the facilities than between franchise members.

Preferred Hotels and Resorts Worldwide is a consortium of 185 independent, luxury hotels and resorts united to compete with the marketing power of chain operations. It promotes the individuality, high standards, hospitality, and luxury of member hotels. It also provides marketing support services and a reservation center.

A hotel lobby.

With the decrease in airline commissions, referral organizations—especially those at the luxury end of the market—are well placed to offer incentives to agents to book clients with the referral group's hotels. An example is awarding trips to the property for every ten rooms booked. Another is when the referral hotels offer, for instance, a 20 percent commission to travel agents during slow periods.

Three luxury Boston-area preferred properties—the Boston Harbor Hotel, the Bostonian Hotel, and the Charles Hotel in Cambridge, Massachusetts— joined together in promoting a St. Patrick's Day weekend package. Preferred Hotels in Texas—the Mansion on Turtle Creek and Hotel Crescent Court in Dallas, La Mansion Del Rio South in San Antonio, and the Washington Hotel in Fort Worth—launched a major, year-long promotion that includes a tie-in with major retail, credit card, and airline partners.

In addition to regional marketing programs, the referral associations that handle reservations for members have joined Galileo International's Inside Availability Service. This gives agents access to actual rates and room availability that are not always available information on the standard central reservation system (CRS) databases.

Leading Hotels of the World (LHW) was set up in 1928 as Luxury Hotels of Europe and Egypt by 38 hotels, including the London Savoy; the Hotel Royal in Evian, France; and the Hotel Negresco in Nice, France—each was interested in improving its marketing. The organization operated by having hotels advise their guests to use the establishments of fellow members. It then opened a New York office to make direct contact with wealthy American and Canadian travelers wishing to visit Europe and Egypt.

LHW, which is controlled by its European members, acts as an important marketing machine for its members, especially now, with offices around the world providing reservations, sales, and promotional services. All the hotels and offices are connected by a central computer reservation system called ResStar. The number of reservations members receive from Leading Hotel members varies from place to place, but with 420 member hotels, it must be beneficial.

Like LHW, Small Luxury Hotels of the World (SLH) is another marketing consortium in which seventy-nine independently owned and managed hotels and resorts are members. For more than thirty-five years, it has sought to market and sell its membership to the travel industry and to provide an inter-hotel networking system for all members. Each hotel is assessed and regularly checked to ensure that it maintains the very highest standards. Figure 1 shows the largest hotel chains in terms of number of rooms, number of countries represented, and total hotels.

Management Contracts

Management contracts have been responsible for the hotel industry's rapid boom since the 1970s. They became popular among hotel corporations because little or no up-front financing or equity is involved. Hotel management companies often form a partnership of convenience with developers and owners who generally do not have the desire or ability to operate the hotel. The management company provides operational expertise, marketing, and sales clout, often in the form of a CRS.

Company	Number of Guest Rooms	Number of Countries	Total Hotels
InterContinental Hotels Group (InterContinental Hotels & Resorts, Crowne Plaza Hotels & Resorts, Hotel Indigo, Holiday Inn Hotels & Resorts, Holiday Inn Express, Staybridge Suites, Candlewood Suites)	646,679	100	4,400
Wyndham Worldwide (Super 8, Days Inn, Ramada, Wyndham Hotels & Resorts, Baymont Inn & Suites, Wingate Inn, Travelodge, Howard Johnson, AmeriHost Inn, Knights Inn, Villager Lodge, Hawthorn Suites, Microtel Inns and Suites)	597,674	66	7,160
Marriott International (Marriott Hotels & Resorts, JW Marriott Hotels & Resorts, Renaissance Hotels & Resorts, Courtyard, Residence Inn, Fairfield Inn, Marriott Conference Centers, TownePlace Suites, SpringHill Suites, Ritz-Carlton	595,461	70	3,500
Hilton Hotels Corporation (Conrad, DoubleTree, Embassy Suites, Hampton Hotels, Hilton, Hilton Garden Inn, Homewood Suites, Scandic, Waldorf Astoria Collection)	585,060	81	3,600
Choice Hotels International (Comfort Inn, Comfort Suites, Quality, Sleep Inn, Clarion, Cambria Suites, MainStay Suites, Econo Lodge, Rodeway Inn, Suburban Extended Stay Hotel, Ascend)	487,410	35	6,000
Accor (Sofitel, Red Roof Inn, Motel 6, Studio 6, Novotel, Suitehotel, Ibis, Etap, Formule 1, Ibis, Orbis, Sofitel, Pullman, M Gallery, All Seasons Hotels)	475,433	90	4,000
Best Western International	308,447	80	4,000
Starwood Hotels & Resorts Worldwide (St. Regis, The Luxury Collection, Sheraton, Westin, Four Points by Sheraton, element, Le Meridien, W Hotels, aloft)	308,447	80	4,000
Carlson Hospitality Worldwide (Regent Hotels & Resorts, Radisson Hotels & Resorts, Park Plaza Hotels & Resorts, Country Inns & Suites by Carlson, Park Inn Hotels)	159,129	77	938
Global Hyatt Corporation (Hyatt Hotels & Resorts, Hyatt Place, Hyatt Summerfield Suites, Park Hyatt, Grand Hyatt, Hyatt Regency)	134,296	45	434

2010 Hotels.

Figure 1 • The Largest Hotel Chains in Terms of Number of Rooms, Number of Countries, and Total Hotels.

Some companies manage a portfolio of properties on a cluster, regional, or national basis. Even if the hotel corporation is involved in the construction of the hotel, ownership generally reverts to a large insurance company or other large corporation. This was the case with the La Jolla, California, Marriott Hotel. Marriott Corporation built the hotel for about $34 million, and then sold it to Paine Webber, a major investment banking firm, for about $52 million on completion. Not a bad return on investment!

The management contract usually allows for the hotel company to manage the property for a period of five, ten, or twenty years. For this, the company receives as a management fee, often a percentage of gross and/or net operating profit, usually about 2 to 4.5 percent of gross revenues. Lower fees in the 2-percent range are more prevalent today, with an increase in the incentive fee based on profitability. Some contracts begin at 2 percent for the first year, increase to 2.5 the second, and to 3.5 the third and for the remainder of the contract.[9]

Hyatt Hotels operates most of its hotels by management contract, rather than owning them all.

Today, many contracts are for a percentage of sales and a percentage of operating profit. This is normally 2 + 2 percent. Increased competition among management companies has decreased the management contract fees in the past few years. In recent years, hotel companies increasingly have opted for management contracts because considerably less capital is tied up in managing as compared with owning properties. This has allowed for a more rapid expansion of both the U.S. and international markets.

Recent management contracts have called for an increase in the equity commitment on the part of the management company. In addition, owners have increased their operational decision-making options to allow them more control over the property. General managers have increased responsibility to owners who also want their share of profit.

Today, hotel management companies exist in an extremely competitive environment. They have discovered that the hotel business, like most others, has changed and they are adapting accordingly. Today's hotel owners are demanding better bottom-line results and reduced fees. Management companies are seeking sustainability and a bigger share of the business. With international expansion, a hotel company entering the market might actively seek a local partner or owner to work within a form of joint venture.

► Check Your Knowledge

1. What main factor changed the nature of the hotel industry? What impact does it have today?

2. In your own words, define *franchising* and *management contracts*.

Real Estate Investment Trust

Real estate investment trusts (REITs) have existed since the 1960s. In those early days, they were mostly mortgage holders. But in the 1980s, they began to own property outright, often focusing on specific sectors such as hotels, office buildings, apartments, malls, and nursing homes. A REIT must have at least 75 percent of its assets in real estate. Today, about 300 REITs, with a combined market value of $70 billion, are publicly traded. Investors like them because they do not pay corporate income tax and instead are required to distribute at least 95 percent of net income to shareholders. In addition, because they trade as stocks, they are much easier to get into or out of than are limited partnerships or the direct ownership of properties. In the hotel industry, REITs are clearly where the action is. As with any investment, the investor is looking for a reasonable return on the investment. Anyone can buy stocks of REITs or other publically traded companies; first, it is wise to ensure that the company is well managed and financially sound before putting any money down. The leading REIT corporations are Patriot American Hospitality, Wyndham Hotels, and Starwood Lodging Trust.

INTRODUCING CONRAD HILTON AND HILTON HOTELS CORPORATION

"King of Innkeepers" and Master of Hotel Finance

Before he was 18, Conrad Hilton had worked as a trader, a clerk, a bellboy, and a pianist. By age 25, he had worked in politics and banking.

In 1919, while visiting Cisco, Texas, Conrad Hilton had intended to take advantage of the oil boom by buying a small bank. Instead, he found bank prices prohibitive and hotels so overbooked he could not find a place to sleep. When one owner in Cisco complained he would like to sell his property in order to take advantage of the oil boom, Hilton struck a deal. He bought the Mobley Hotel with an investment of $5,000. Hilton rented rooms to oil industry prospectors and construction workers. Because of high demand for accommodations and very little supply, Hilton rented rooms in eight-hour shifts, for 300-percent occupancy. On some occasions, he even rented out his own room and slept in a lobby chair.

Because Hilton knew the banking business well and had maintained contacts who would lend him money for down payments on properties, he quickly expanded to seven Texas hotels. Hilton's strategy was to borrow as much money as possible to expand as rapidly as possible. This worked well until the Great Depression of the early 1930s. Hilton was unable to meet the payments on his properties and lost several of them but did not declare bankruptcy.[1]

Hilton, like many great leaders, even during the Depression years had the determination to bounce back. To reduce costs, he borrowed money against his life insurance and even formed an alliance with the National Hotels Corporation.

Hilton's success was attributed to two main strategies: (1) hiring the best managers and letting them have total autonomy and (2) being a careful bargainer who, in later years, was careful not to overextend his finances. Conrad Hilton had begun a successful career in the banking business before he embarked on what was to become one of the most successful hotel careers ever.

Hilton's business and financial acumen is legendary. The *New York Times* described Conrad Hilton as "a master of finance and a cautious bargainer who was careful not to overfinance" and as someone who had "a flawless sense of timing."[2] In 1954, Conrad acquired the Statler Hotel Company for $111 million, which at the time was the world's most expensive real estate transaction.

Hilton was the first person to notice vast lobbies with people sitting in comfortable chairs but not spending any money. So he added the lobby bar as a convenient meeting place and leased out space for gift shops and newsstands. Most of the additional revenue from these operations went directly to the bottom line. Today, Hilton Hotels Corporation includes Conrad Hotels, DoubleTree, Embassy Suites Hotels, Hampton Inn and Hampton Inns & Suites, Hilton Hotels, Hilton Garden Inn, Hilton Grand Vacation, Homewood Suites by Hilton, and the Waldorf Astoria Collection. These brands total thousands of hotels in cities all over the world, and "Be my guest" is still the gracious and warm way guests are received. There are 3,600 Hilton brand hotels today, and they are owned by the Blackstone Group.[3]

[1]Paul R. Dittmer and Gerald G. Griffen, *The Dimensions of the Hospitality Industry: An Introduction* (New York: Van Nostrand Reinhold, 1993), 91–92; and Conrad Hilton, *Be My Guest* (New York: Prentice Hall Press, 1957), 184–199.

[2]Joan Cook, "Conrad Hilton, Founder of Hotel Chain, Dies at 92," *New York Times*, January 5, 1979, sec. 11.

[3]Hilton worldwide, *Home Page*, www.hiltonworldwide.com (accessed February 17, 2011).

Hotel Development

Hotel ownership and development is very **capital intensive**. It takes millions of dollars to develop a property. New hotels are built as a business venture by a developer, and because the developer expects to make a **fair return on the** (substantial) **investment**, a **feasibility study** is done to assess the viability of the project—this is required by lenders. The feasibility study examines the market area's demand and supply, including any potential or real competition in the pipeline. The feasibility study determines the degree to which the proposed hotel project would be financially successful. Revenue projections based on anticipated occupancy, average daily rate, and revenue per available room are presented. The feasibility study also helps determine the type of hotel that would best suit the market and is used by the developer to obtain financing for the project. One of the most important documents is a **Summary Operating Statement**, which details revenues and expenses for a period; an example of a Summary Operating Statement is given in Figure 2. Also of interest is the source and disposition of the industry dollar. An example is given in Figure 3.

In Figure 2, note that close to 70 percent of a hotel's revenue and most of the profit comes from the sale of rooms. About 26 percent of revenue comes from food and beverage sales. In Figure 3 we can see that the average hotel room revenue is slightly different, at 66.6 percent. Each hotel will have a slight variation on these figures according to its own individual circumstances. Note in Figure 3 how high the percentage of wages, salaries, and benefits are at 46.7 percent.

Obviously, there needs to be a gap in the market in which a segment is currently not being served (for example, the hip, lifestyle boutique hotels such as Hotel Indigo), plus, a new hotel is expected to take some business away from existing properties if the room rates are close in price. There are two views on new hotels versus remodeled hotels as far as room rates and profits are concerned. It is often difficult for a

CONSOLIDATED INCOME WITH VARIANCES
For the Twelve Months Ending December 31, 2010

YEAR TO DATE

	ACTUAL	%	BUDGET	%	VARIANCE	PRIOR YEAR	%	VARIANCE
TOTAL ROOMS OCCUPIED	52,985	74.1%	50,784	71.0%	2,201	52,168	72.9%	817
TOTAL ROOMS AVAILABLE	71,540		71,540		0	71,540		0
TOTAL A.D.R	$219.68		$204.21		$15.47	$206.50		$13.18
REVPAR	$162.70		$144.96		$17.74	$150.58		$12.12
DEPARTMENTAL REVENUE								
ROOMS	11,639,641	61.5%	10,370,540	61.3%	1,269,101	10,772,724	61.5%	866,917
FOOD	4,532,944	23.9%	4,226,134	25.0%	306,810	4,253,435	24.3%	279,509
BEVERAGE	1,788,711	9.4%	1,563,904	9.2%	224,807	1,510,419	8.6%	278,292
TELEPHONE	42,877	0.2%	44,148	0.3%	(1,271)	46,914	0.3%	(4,037)
OTHER INCOME	316,945	1.7%	112,760	0.7%	204,185	332,427	1.9%	(15,483)
MINI BAR	75,281	0.4%	76,684	0.5%	(1,403)	76,963	0.4%	(1,683)
PARKING	536,839	2.8%	518,751	3.1%	18,088	531,325	3.0%	5,515
TOTAL REVENUE	18,933,238	100.0%	16,912,921	100.0%	2,020,317	17,524,208	100.0%	1,409,030
DEPARTMENTAL INCOME								
ROOMS	8,865,555	76.2%	7,744,979	74.7%	1,120,576	8,019,679	74.4%	845,876
FOOD	863,133	19.0%	863,366	20.4%	(233)	789,310	18.6%	73,823
BEVERAGE	1,243,380	69.5%	1,077,443	68.9%	165,937	1,027,144	68.0%	216,235
TELEPHONE	(89,252)	−208.2%	(97,428)	−220.7%	8,176	(119,963)	−255.7%	30,712
OTHER INCOME	217,118	68.5%	11,076	9.8%	206,042	227,147	68.3%	(10,028)
MINI BAR	25,401	33.7%	19,063	24.9%	6,338	19,034	24.7%	6,367
PARKING	312,343	58.2%	310,943	59.9%	1,400	401,540	75.6%	(89,197)
TOTAL DEPARTMENTAL INCOME	11,437,678	60.4%	9,929,442	58.7%	1,508,236	10,363,890	59.1%	1,073,788
UNDISTRIBUTED OPERATING EXPENSES								
ADMINISTRATIVE & GENERAL	1,506,103	8.0%	1,364,085	8.1%	142,018	1,466,980	8.4%	39,123
SALES AND MARKETING	1,154,957	6.1%	1,090,337	6.4%	64,620	1,028,346	5.9%	126,612
FRANCHISE FEE	1,011,621	5.3%	919,238	5.4%	92,383	951,431	5.4%	60,191
PROPERTY MAINTENANCE	597,253	3.2%	523,475	3.1%	73,778	552,043	3.2%	45,210
UTILITIES	404,098	2.1%	386,663	2.3%	17,435	391,568	2.2%	12,530
TOTAL UNDISTRIBUTED OPER EXPS	4,674,032	24.7%	4,283,798	25.3%	390,234	4,390,367	25.1%	283,665
GROSS OPERATING PROFIT	6,763,646	35.7%	5,645,644	33.4%	1,118,002	5,973,524	34.1%	790,122
MANAGEMENT FEES	378,665	2.0%	338,336	2.0%	40,329	350,485	2.0%	28,180
INCOME BEFORE FIXED CHARGES	6,384,981	33.7%	5,307,308	31.4%	1,077,673	5,623,039	32.1%	761,942
FIXED CHARGES								
PROPERTY TAXES - PERSONAL	135,223	0.7%	160,848	1.0%	(25,625)	153,082	0.9%	(17,858)
INSURANCE	29,714	0.2%	67,400	0.4%	(37,686)	66,375	0.4%	(36,661)
INTEREST	11,056	0.1%	43,921	0.3%	(32,865)	7,644	0.0%	3,412
BASE RENT	4,829,181	25.5%	4,829,184	28.6%	(3)	4,720,939	26.9%	108,242
PERCENTAGE RENT	810,036	4.3%	153,790	0.9%	656,246	426,217	2.4%	383,819
OWNERS EXPENSES	29,704	0.2%	0	0.0%	29,704	(152,875)	−0.9%	182,580
EXTRAORDINARY EXPENSES	89,431	0.5%	0	0.0%	89,431	0	0.0%	89,431
OUTSIDE ACCOUNTING FEES	17,485	0.1%	18,000	0.1%	(515)	35,803	0.2%	(18,318)

Figure 2 • A Full-Service Hotel Summary Operating Statement.

(PFK Hospitality Research, Sage Hospitality.)

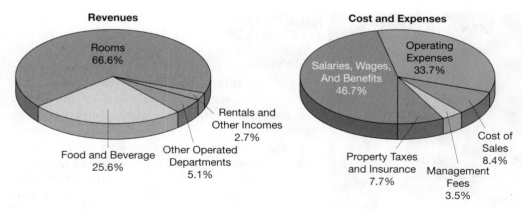

Figure 3 • Source and Disposition of the Industry Dollar.

(Courtesy of PKF Hospitality Consulting.)

new property to make a profit for a few years because of the higher cost of construction and the need to become known and to gain a good market share. On the other hand, a remodeled hotel has the cost of remodeling to pay for plus higher operating costs for energy and maintenance, so the two options tend to cancel each other out.

Today, many larger hotels are developed as part of a mixed-use project. The hotel could be near or next to a convention center, business, or attraction. The hotel may also have a residential component (as in residencies if it's a Ritz Carlton or a condotel) and may include a spa.

Older hotels are generally renovated about every seven years. This is bacause they become dated and would otherwise lose market share, which equals profit. Older hotels have an advantage over new ones—or should have an advantage as a result of positive recognition in the market. Additionally, much or all of their mortgage may be paid off, so their debt service is likely easier on the cash flow than it is for a new hotel. Older hotels may have more charm, but they are more expensive to maintain. Older hotels should also have built up repeat business through guest loyalty, something a new hotel needs to do.

Kimpton hotels have an amazing collection of boutique properties. In 1981, Bill Kimpton pioneered the boutique hotel concept in the United States. His dream was to provide weary travelers with a haven of comfort, service, security, and style. According to Market Metrix Hospitality Index,™ Kimpton has the highest customer satisfaction scores (higher than 93 percent) and emotional attachment scores (89 percent) of any hotel company operating in the United States.[10]

Hotel chains are introducing new brands to their portfolio as they identify market segment needs. Marriott has the Autograph collection of diverse independent hotels—boutique Arts, Iconic historic, Boutique Chic, Luxury Redefined, and Retreat properties.[11] Starwood has almost one hundred Aloft hotels. and Hyatt has introduced Andaz, also a boutique style-hotel which is vibrant yet relaxed, with each hotel reflecting the unique cultural scene and spirit of the surrounding neighborhood.[12]

The Economic Impact of Hotels

Hotels provide substantial **direct** and **indirect economic impact** to the communities in which they are located. For direct impact, consider a hotel that has an average of 240 guests a night who spend $250 at the hotel and in restaurants

Aloft Tempe, Arizona.

and stores in the community. That would mean $240 × $250 × 365 days = $21.9 million a year infused into the local economy.

The indirect impact comes from the ripple effect; this is where money is spent by the employees (wages and salaries) of the hotel in the community. It is also money used by the hotel to purchase all the items to service the guests. Communities also benefit from the Transient Occupancy Tax (TOT), otherwise known as the bed tax. Interestingly, the TOT tax averages 12.62 percent in the United States, or $12.39 a night nationwide.[13] In addition, the hotel and its guests and employees also pay local taxes on the purchases they make. This all adds up to a considerable economic impact. Every dollar collected by a hotel eventually recycles, or multiplies itself, creating many levels of economic activity in communities. This multilevel economic activity generated by a hotel's business is estimated by using economic multipliers for revenues, wages and salaries, and employment. If we take just the revenue impact, we can see that if a hotel's annual sales are $4,250,000 and the revenue multiplier for that area is 1.979, then the total revenue impact for the year would be $8,410,750. If we consider the employment impact, we note that if the example hotel has 160 employees and the employment multiplier for the area is 1.62, then the hotel will generate 259 jobs in the area.[14] Figure 4 illustrates the multiplier effect of hotels.

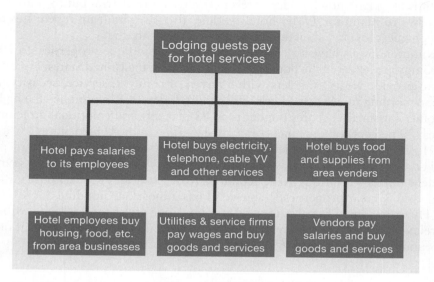

Figure 4 • The Multiplier Effect of Hotel Dollars on a Community.
(Courtesy of the American Hotel and Lodging Association.)

Classification of Hotels

According to the AH&LA, in 2010 the U.S. lodging industry consisted of 50,800 hotels and motels, with a total of 4,762,095 rooms. The average revenue per available room was $53.50 and the average occupancy was 54.7 percent.[15] Unlike many other countries, the United States has no formal government classification of hotels. However, the American Automobile Association (AAA) classifies hotels by diamond award, and the Mobil Travel Guide offers a five-star award.

The AAA has been inspecting and rating the nation's hotels since 1977. About 3 percent of the 59,000 properties inspected annually throughout the United States, Canada, and Mexico earn the five-diamond award, which is the association's highest award for excellence. In 2011, the five-diamond award was bestowed on 179 lodgings in the United States, Canada, the Caribbean and Mexico—an increase of 100 in the last ten years.[16] AAA uses descriptive criteria to evaluate the hotels that it rates (see Figure 5).

- One-diamond properties have simple roadside appeal and the basic lodging needs.
- Two-diamond properties have average roadside appeal, with some landscaping and a noticeable enhancement in interior decor.
- Three diamonds carry a degree of sophistication through higher service and comfort.
- Four diamonds have excellent roadside appeal and service levels that give guests what they need before they even ask for it.
- Five-diamond properties have the highest service levels, sophistication, and offerings.

Hotels may be classified according to location, price, and type of services offered. This allows guests to make a selection on these categories as well as personal criteria. Following is a list of hotel classifications:

City center. Luxury, first-class, midscale, economy, suites

Resort. Luxury, midscale, economy suites, condominium, timeshare, convention

Airport. Luxury, midscale, economy, suites

Freeway. Midscale, economy suites

Casino. Luxury, midscale, economy

Full service.

Convention.

Economy.

Extended stay.

Bed and breakfast.

	◇	◇◇	◇◇◇	◇◇◇◇	◇◇◇◇◇
General	Simple roadside appeal Limited landscaping	Average roadside appeal Some landscaping	Very good roadside appeal Attractive landscaping	Excellent roadside appeal Professionally planned landscaping	Outstanding roadside appeal Professional landscaping with a variety of foliage and stunning architecture
Lobby	Adequate size with registration, front desk, limited seating, and budget art, if any	Medium size with registration, front desk, limited seating, carpeted floors, budget art, and some plants	Spacious with front desk, carpeted seating area arranged in conversation groupings, good-quality framed art, live plants, luggage carts, and bellstation	Spacious or consistent with historical attributes; registration and front desk above average with solid wood or marble; ample seating area with conversation groupings and upscale appointments including tile, carpet, or wood floors; impressive lighting fixtures; upscale framed art and art objects; abundant live plants; background music; separate check-in/-out; bellstation	Comfortably spacious or consistent with historical attributes; registration desk and front desk above average; ample seating with conversation groupings and upscale appointments; impressive lighting fixtures; variety of fine art; abundant plants and fresh floral arrangements; background music; separate check-in/-out; bellstation that may be part of concierge area; concierge desk
Guestrooms	May not reflect current industry standards	Generally reflect current industry standards	Reflect current industry standards	Reflect current industry standards and provide upscale appearance	Reflect current standards and provide luxury appearance
Service	Basic attentive service	More attentive service	Upgraded service levels	High service levels and hospitality	Guests are pampered by flawless service executed by professional staff

Figure 5 ● Summary of AAA Diamond Rating Guidelines.

(Reprinted from http://www.aaasouth.com/travel/diamond/diamond_ratings.aspx?Link_Source=diamond&From_Page=AAA.com&zip=32836, by permission of AAA.)

Alternatively, the hotel industry may be segmented according to price. Figure 6 gives an example of a national or major regional brand-name hotel chain in each segment.

City Center Hotels

City center hotels, by virtue of their location, meet the needs of the traveling public for business or leisure reasons. These hotels could be luxury, midscale, business, suites, economy, or residential. They offer a range of accommodations and services. Luxury hotels offer the ultimate in decor, butler service, concierge and special concierge floors, secretarial services, the latest Wi-Fi or in-room technology, computers, fax machines, beauty salons, health spas, 24-hour room

Economy $49–$69	Midprice $69–$125	Upscale $125–$225	Luxury $150–$450	All-Suites $109–$225
Holiday Inn Express	Holiday Inn Fairfield Inn		Crowne Plaza Hotel InterContinental	
Fairfield Inn	Courtyard Inn Residence Inn	Courtyard Inn Marriott Residence Inn	Marriott Marquis Ritz-Carlton	Marriott Suites
Days Inn		Omni	Renaissance	
EconoLodge	Radisson Inn	Radisson		Radisson Suites
Ramada Limited	Ramada Inn	Ramada		Ramada Suites
	Sheraton Inn Four Points	Sheraton	Sheraton Grande	Sheraton Suites
Sleep Inn	American Inn	Hyatt	Grand Hyatt Hyatt Regency Hyatt Park	Hyatt Suites
Comfort Inn	Quality Inn Wingate	Clarion Hotels		Quality Suites Comfort Suites
Extended Stay America	Hilton Inn	Hilton	Hilton Towers	Hilton Suites
Thrift Lodge	DoubleTree Club	DoubleTree		DoubleTree Suites
Travelodge Hotels	Travelodge Hotels	Forte Hotels	Forte Hotels	
Motel 6	Country Inn & Suites	Westin	Westin	Spring Hill Suites
Super 8	La Quinta			
	Red Roof Inn			Homewood Suites by Hilton
	Best Western			Hampton Suites
	Hampton Inn			Embassy Suites

Note: Some brands' price ranges may overlap because of location and seasonal pricing.

Figure 6 • Hotels by Price Segment.

service, swimming pools, tennis courts, valet service, ticket office, airline office, car rental, and doctor/nurse on duty or on call.

Generally, they offer a signature restaurant, coffee shop, or an equivalent recognized name restaurant; a lounge; a named bar; meeting and convention rooms; a ballroom; and possibly a fancy night spot. The Drake Hotel in Chicago is an example of a city center luxury hotel. An example of a midpriced hotel in New York City is the Ramada Hotel; an economy hotel is the Day's Inn; a suites property is the Embassy Suites.

Resort Hotels

Resort hotels came of age with the advent of rail travel. Increasingly, city dwellers and others had the urge to vacation in locations they found appealing. Traveling to these often more exotic locations became a part of the pleasure experience. In the late 1800s, luxury resort hotels were developed to accommodate the clientele that the railways brought. Such hotels include the famous Greenbrier at White Sulphur Springs, West Virginia; the Hotel del Coronado near San Diego, California; the Breakers in Florida; and the Homestead at Hot Springs, Virginia.

The leisure and pleasure travelers of those days were drawn by resorts, beaches, or spectacular mountain scenery. At first, many of these grand resorts were seasonal. However, as automobile and air travel made even the remote resorts more accessible and an increasing number of people could afford to visit, many resorts became year-round properties.

Resort communities sprang up in the sunshine belt from Palm Springs to Palm Beach. Some resorts focus on major sporting activities such as skiing, golf, or fishing; others offer family vacations. Further improvements in both air and automobile travel brought exotic locations within the reach of the population.

The Main Lodge at Copper Mountain Ski Resort in Copper Mountain, Colorado.

Europe, the Caribbean, and Mexico became more accessible. As the years passed, some of the resorts suffered because the public's vacation plans changed.

The traditional family month-long resort vacation gave way to shorter, more frequent getaways of four to seven days. The regular resort visitors became older; in general, the younger guests preferred the mobility of the automobile and the more informal atmosphere provided by the newer and more informal resorts.

Hyatt hotels have organized a program consisting of a variety of activities for children, thereby giving parents an opportunity either to enjoy some free time on their own or join their children in fun activities. Many resort hotels began to attract conventions, conferences, and meetings so that they could maintain or increase occupancy, particularly during the low and shoulder seasons.

Guests go to resorts for leisure and recreation. They want a good climate—summer or winter—in which they can relax or engage in recreational activities. Because of the remoteness of many resorts, guests are a kind of "captured clientele," who may be on the property for days at a time. This presents resort managers with some unique operating challenges. Another operating challenge concerns seasonality: Some resorts either do not operate year-round or have periods of very low occupancy. Both present challenges in attracting, training, and retaining competent staff.

Many guests travel considerable distances to resorts. Consequently, they tend to stay longer than they do at transient hotels. This presents a challenge to the food and beverage manager to provide quality menus that are varied and are presented and served in an attractive, attentive manner. To achieve this, resorts often use a cyclical menu that repeats itself every fourteen to twenty-one days. Also, they provide a wide variety and number of dishes to stimulate interest. Menus are now more health conscious—lighter and low in saturated fats, cholesterol, salt, and calories.

The food needs to be presented in a variety of ways. Buffets are popular because they give guests the opportunity to make choices from a display of foods. Barbecues, display cooking, poolside dining, specialty restaurants, and reciprocal dining arrangements with nearby hotels give guests even more options.

With increased global competition, not only from other resorts but also from cruise lines, resort managers are challenged to both attract guests and to turn those guests into repeat business, which traditionally has been the foundation of resort viability.

To increase occupancies, resorts have diversified their marketing mix to include conventions, business meetings, sales meetings, incentive groups, sporting events, additional sporting and recreational facilities, spas, adventure tourism, ecotourism, and more.

Because guests are cocooned in the resort, they expect to be pampered. This requires an attentive, well-trained staff; hiring, training, and retaining a competent staff present a challenge in some remote areas and in developing countries.

There are a number of benefits to operating resorts. The guests are much more relaxed in comparison to those at transient hotels, and the resorts are located in scenically beautiful areas. This frequently enables staff to enjoy a better quality of life than do their transient hotel counterparts. Returning guests tend to treat associates like friends. This adds to the overall party-like atmosphere, which is prevalent at many of the established resorts.

INTRODUCING VALERIE FERGUSON

Regional Vice President of Loews Hotels, Past Chair of the American Hotel & Lodging Association and Regional Vice President of Loews Hotels

To most, "making it big" seems like a regular statement and a task easily achieved. To Valerie Ferguson, well, it comes with a lot of work, dedication, and heart. She speaks often about seizing opportunities and adding self-interest to what you do for your career.

For this African American woman, life wasn't always easy. As the managing director of Loews Philadelphia Hotel and regional vice president of Loews Hotels, she has a lot to say about what got her where she is now.

One of her most important role models was her father, Sam Ferguson. She says, "My father and I had a great relationship in which he supported me, but in which he never put any images in front of me about what I should shoot for."

After high school, Valerie applied to and was accepted at the University of San Francisco, where she earned a degree in government. Eventually realizing that law wasn't where her heart was, she decided to move out to Atlanta where she got a job as a nighttime desk clerk at the Hyatt Regency. She fell in love with the hotel industry and saw it as a challenge. Soon enough, though, she realized that the challenges she was really facing were issues of race and gender. She explains, "I was raw in my approach to the business world, but I soon came to realize that it takes more than working hard. To succeed, a person must be able to proclaim his or her goals."

Her success comes from being out there and connecting with people and society. Valerie is past chair of the American Hotel & Lodging Association (AH&LA) board and still serves on the Diversity Committee. She is also past associate director of the National Restaurant Association. She is a director on the boards of the Pennsylvania Travel Council, Philadelphia Workforce Investment, Communities in Schools, and the Educational Institute.

Valerie was nominated general manager of the year for the Hyatt Hotels Corporation. Through the years, she has managed several hotels for Hyatt and Ritz-Carlton. Her outstanding work and devotion to the hospitality and lodging industry have not gone unrewarded. She was named one of the Top 100 Black Women in Corporate America by *Ebony* magazine. She was named one of the Top 100 Black Women of Influence by the Atlanta Business League Pioneers. She was also named one of the 100 Most Influential Women in Travel by *Travel Agent* magazine. Other honorary awards for her work in the lodging industry were the 1998 National Association for the Advancement of Colored People (NAACP) Southeast Region Trailblazer Award for Business, the Martin Luther King Jr. Drum Major for Justice Award from Coretta Scott King and the Women of the Southern Christian Leadership Conference (SCLC). Ed Rabin, executive vice president of Hyatt and an early Ferguson mentor, says, "From the get-go, she demonstrated an ability and willingness to understand and learn the business and win over guests, colleagues, and peers in the process."

When Loews was being opened, Valerie was thrilled with the adventure of being with a still-growing company. President and CEO of Loews Jonathan Tisch became a close friend as they served together on the board of the American Hotel and Lodging Association (AH&LA). In 1994, Valerie ran for a seat on the AH&LA's executive committee and eventually succeeded Tisch as chair. She was the first African American and second woman to serve as AH&LA chair.

She comments on the hospitality industry: "The hospitality industry is one of the last vestiges of the American dream, where you can enter from very humble beginnings and end up a success." The great relationship she has with people has been a great contribution to her well-deserved success.

Ferguson has come a long way in her career. She is proud of what she is doing and doesn't believe that she has stopped climbing the ladder of success. She is fighting to make other women and minority members realize that there is a whole world of opportunities out there and they should set their goals high. She believes that equality of opportunity "should not come as the result of a mandate of the federal government or as the result of pressure from groups outside this industry. The impetus for change must come from within the hearts and souls of each of us."

Sources: *Lodging* 23, no. 5 (January 1998); Loews Hotels and Resorts, *Welcome to Loews Hotels*, www.loewshotels.com accessed (October 26, 2011); American Hotel & Lodging Association, *Officers: valerie Ferguson*, ww.ahma.com/about/officers/ferguson.htm (accessed May 14, 2005; site now discontinued); www.findarticles.com/cf_0_/mv0VOU/1998_July_30/50216477/pl/article.jhtml; Robert A. Nozar, "Newsmaker Interview: Valerie Ferguson," *Hotel & Motel Management*, November 1998, www.hotel-online.com/Neo/SpecialReports1998/Nov98_Ferguson.html (accessed October 26, 2011).

Airport Hotels

Many airport hotels enjoy high occupancy because of the large number of travelers arriving and departing from major airports. The guest mix in airport hotels consists of business, group, and leisure travelers. Passengers with early or late flights may stay over at the airport hotel, whereas others rest while waiting for connecting flights.

Airport hotels are generally in the 200- to 600-room size and are full service. To care for the needs of guests who may still feel as if they are in different time zones, room service and restaurant hours may be extended or even offered around the clock. More moderately priced hotels have vending machines.

As competition at airport hotels intensified, some added meeting space to cater to businesspeople who want to fly in, meet, and fly out. Here, the airport hotel has the advantage of saving the guests from having to go downtown. Almost all airport hotels provide courtesy van transportation to and from the airport.

Convenient locations, economical prices, and easy and less costly transportation costs to and from the airport are some reasons why airport hotels are becoming intelligent choices for business travelers. Airport hotels can mean a bargain for groups, especially considering that the transportation to the hotel and back from the airport is usually free or is very inexpensive, says Brian Booth, director of sales and marketing at the Dallas Hyatt Regency Airport Hotel. One of the most conveniently located hotels in the country is the Miami International Airport Hotel, which is located within the airport itself.

Freeway Hotels and Motels

Freeway hotels and motels came into prominence, with the help of the Interstate Highway Act, in the 1950s and 1960s. They are smaller than most hotels—usually fewer than fifty rooms—and are frequently mom-and-pop establishments or franchised (such as Motel 6). As Americans took to the open road, they needed a convenient place to stay that was reasonably priced with few frills. Guests could simply drive up, park outside the office, register, rent a room, and park outside the room. Over the years, more facilities were added: lounges, restaurants, pools, vending machines, game rooms, and satellite TV.

Motels are often clustered near freeway off ramps on the outskirts of towns and cities. Today, some are made of modular construction and have as few as eleven employees per hundred rooms. These savings in land, construction, and operating costs are passed on to the guest in the form of lower rates.

Casino Hotels

The casino hotel industry is now coming into the financial mainstream, to the point that, as a significant segment of the entertainment industry, it is reshaping the U.S. economy. The entertainment and recreation sector has become a very important engine for U.S. economic growth, providing a boost to consumer spending, and thus creating tremendous prosperity for the industry. One of the fastest-growing sectors of the entertainment field is gaming.

The gaming business is strictly for adults; in addition to gaming, a multinational fine cuisine for dining, health spas for relaxation, dance clubs, and dazzling shows are available. Casino hotels are now marketing themselves as business hotels. They include in their rooms work space, Wi-Fi, a fax, a copier, and computer data ports. Other amenities include a full-service business center, travel bureau, and room service. Larger casino hotels also attract conventions, which represent a lucrative business. There are now more than 150 hotels in Native American tribal land. They cater to an increasing number of guests who want to stay and be entertained as well as gamble.

Convention Hotels

Convention hotels provide facilities and meet the needs of groups attending and holding conventions. Apart from this segment of the market, convention hotels also attract seasonal leisure travelers. Typically, these hotels exceed 500 guest rooms and include larger public areas to accommodate hundreds of people at any given time. Convention hotels have many banquet areas within and around the hotel complex. These hotels have a high percentage of double occupancies, and rooms have double queen-sized beds. Convention hotels may also offer a concierge floor to cater to individual guest needs. Round-the-clock room service, an in-house laundry, a business center, a travel desk, and an airport shuttle service are other amenities found in convention hotels.

The Universal Portofino Bay Hotel in Orlando, Florida, is a popular convention hotel modeled after Portofino, Italy.

Full-Service Hotels

Another way to classify hotels is by the degree of service offered: full-service, economy, extended-stay, and all-suite hotels. Full-service hotels offer a wide range of facilities, services, and amenities, including many that were mentioned under the luxury hotel category: multiple food and beverage outlets including bars, lounges, and restaurants; both formal and casual dining; and meeting, convention, and catering services. Business features might include a business center, secretarial services, fax, in-room computer hookups, and so on.

Most of the major North American cities have hotel chain representation, such as Four Seasons, Hilton, InterContinental, Choice, Hyatt, Marriott, Omni, Wyndham, Radisson, Loews, and Starwood. Each of these chains has a portfolio of brands in different market segment: deluxe, such as Marriott's Ritz-Carlton and the JW Marriott; luxury, such as Renaissance; luxury boutique, such as Edition and Autograph, a collection of high-personality independent hotels.

Economy/Budget Hotels

After enjoying a wave of growth for most of the last twenty years, the economy hotel segment may be close to the saturation point. There are about 25,000 properties in this segment with many market categories. The economic law of supply and demand rules: If an area has too many similar properties, then price wars usually break out as they try to attract guests. Some will attempt to differentiate themselves and stress value rather than discounting. This adds to the fascination of the business.

An economy or budget hotel offers clean, reasonably sized and furnished rooms without the frills of full-service hotels. Popular brands in this market sector are Hampton Inn, Fairfield Inn, Holiday Inn Express, Best Western, Travelodge, Motel 6, Microtel, Days Inn, Choice's Sleep Inn, Roadway Inn and Econo Lodge, Wingate, Super 8, Baymont Inn, and Country Inn. These properties do not have restaurants or offer substantial food and beverages, but they do offer guests a continental breakfast in the lounge or lobby.

These chains became popular by focusing on selling beds, not meals or meetings. This enabled them to offer rates about 30 percent lower than the midpriced hotels can. Economy properties, which represent about 15 percent of total hotel rooms, have experienced tremendous growth.

Boutique Hotels

Boutique hotels offer a different lodging experience compared to mid- to large chain hotels. Boutique hotels have a unique architecture, style, decor, and size. They are smaller than their chain competitors, with about 25 to 125 rooms and a high level of personal service. Some examples of boutique hotels are the trendy South Beach retro types, Kimpton Hotels, Joie de Vivre

La Quinta Inn.

A DAY IN THE LIFE OF SEAN BAKEWELL

Guest Services Supervisor, Palmer House Hilton, Chicago

The Palmer House has 1,639 rooms and is considered North America's longest continuously run hotel. It was built in 1871 and two weeks later burned to the ground in the Great Chicago Fire. It was rebuilt and was considered the world's only fireproof hotel in 1875. The hotel has many unique features, such as prohibition-era tunnels in the basement leading to the Chicago river, many original Tiffany decorative pieces, and a score of celebrities past and present who have entertained in our famed Empire room. The hotel has an art deco–style design and is truly unique.

As a Guest Services Supervisor, I primarily oversee the bell desk. I supervise around thirty employees–both the doormen and bellmen. Our bellmen must follow Hilton Hotel's standards; these include welcoming each guest to the hotel, offering luggage assistance, using the guest's name if possible, escorting guests to their rooms, pointing out key amenities in the room, offering to fill the ice bucket, asking the guests to please call the bell desk if they require anything during their stay, and inviting the guests back to stay with us again.

Besides maintaining and upholding the Hilton standards for bellmen and doormen, there are other responsibilities of the position. I do the payroll for the department. This involves monitoring time-clock punches and ensuring each employee has taken a lunch break. Many groups that stay in the hotel desire that we deliver items to guests staying in their group block. These items can include gift bags, gift baskets, newsletters, newspapers, and wedding gift bags. There are charges for these services, and each bellmen gets paid per item they deliver. It's my responsibility that the bellmen receive the materials, the correct rooming lists for such groups, and the correct amount of money for delivering these items. We call these distributions. Some bellmen can earn an extra thousand dollars a month doing these distributions.

The bellmen and doormen are both union positions. It is my responsibility to make sure that the hotel is living up to their side of the union contract. This affects disciplinary actions, payroll, and scheduling. Another aspect of my job is to handle guest concerns. This involves talking to upset guests and finding ways to satisfy their concerns. Examples include broken luggage, wrong luggage being delivered to the room, and poor attitude from the staff.

I have worked for Hilton for over three years. I started as a Guest Service Agent, which is essentially a front desk agent. After two years of being a Guest Service Agent, I was promoted to the supervisory position. I majored in hospitality business at Michigan State University. My best advice to any hospitality student is simply to start working and gain experience.

Hotels, Edition from Marriott, and the avant-garde hotel George in Washington, D.C.

A good example of a chain boutique hotel is Hotel Indigo, an InterContinental Hotels Group. Hotel Indigo provides an oasis where guests can escape the hectic pace of travel and think more clearly, work more productively, rest more refreshingly. It offers an environment that doesn't just shelter guests, but inspires and reenergizes them. That's the idea behind Hotel Indigo.[17]

Extended-Stay Hotels and All-Suites
Extended-Stay Hotels

Some hotels cater to guests who stay for an extended period. They do, of course, take guests for a shorter time when space is available; however, the majority of guests are long term. Guests take advantage of a reduction in room rates based on the length of their stay. The mix of guests is mainly business and professional/technical guests, or relocating families.

Candlewood Suites, Extended Stay America, Homestead Studio Suites, Hawthorn Suites, Baymont Inns and Suites, Residence Inns, and Homewood Suites are popular brands in this segment of the lodging industry. These properties offer full kitchen facilities and shopping services or a convenience store on the premises. Complimentary continental breakfast and evening cocktails are served in the lobby. Some properties offer a business center and recreational facilities.

All-suites extended-stay hotels typically offer approximately 25 percent more space for the same amount of money as the regular hotel in the same price range. The additional space is usually in the form of a lounge and possibly a kitchenette area.

Residence Inn is a market leader in the extended-stay segment of the lodging industry.

Embassy Suites, owned and operated by Hilton Hotels Corporation; Residence Inns, Fairfield Suites, and Town-Place Suites, all by Marriott; Extended Stay America; Homewood Suites; and Guest Quarters are among the popular brands in the all-suites, extended-stay segment of the lodging industry. Several of the major hotel chains have all-suites extended-stay subsidiaries, including Radisson, Choice Hotels (which dominate the economy all-suites segment with Comfort and Quality Suites), Sheraton Suites, Hilton Suites, Homegate Studios, and Suites by Wyndham Hotels. These properties provide a closer-to-home feeling for guests who may be relocating or attending seminars or who are on work-related projects that necessitate a stay of greater than about five days.

There are now almost 2,500 all-suites extended-stay properties. Many of these properties have business centers and offer services such as grocery shopping and laundry/dry cleaning. The designers of extended-stay properties realize that guests prefer a homelike atmosphere. Accordingly, many properties are built to encourage a community feeling, which allows guests to interact informally.

Condotels and Mixed-Use Hotels

As the word suggests, a condotel is a combination of a hotel and condominium. Developers build a hotel and sell it as condo units, which the owners can pool for use as hotel rooms and suites. The hotel operating company gets a cut of the money from renting the units and so does the owner. The owner of the condo unit may have exclusive right to the use of the unit for a fixed period of time (usually one month); other than that, the hotel operating company knows that it can rent out the condos.

Some new hotels are developed as mixed-use properties, meaning that a hotel may also have "residences"—real condos that people use, so they are not for renting like condotel—along with amenities such as a spa and sports facilities. Mixed-use hotels can also be a part of a major urban or resort development, which may include office buildings, convention centers, sporting facilities, or shopping malls.

A Bed and Breakfast in Yorkshire, England.

Bed and Breakfast Inns

Bed and breakfast inns, or B&Bs as they are familiarly known, offer an alternative lodging experience to the normal hotel or motel. According to *TravelASSIST* magazine, B&B is a concept that began in Europe and started as overnight lodging in a private home. A true B&B is an accommodation with the owner, who lives on the premises or nearby, providing a clean, attractive accommodation and breakfast, usually a memorable one. The host also offers to help the guest with directions, restaurants, and suggestions for local entertainment or sightseeing.

There are many different styles of B&Bs with prices ranging from about $30 to $300 or more per night. B&Bs may be quaint cottages with white picket fences leading to gingerbread houses, tiny and homey, with two or three rooms available. On the other hand, some are sprawling, ranch-style homes in the Rockies; multistoried town homes in large cities; farms; adobe villas; log cabins; lighthouses; and many stately mansions. The variety is part of the thrill, romance, and charm of the B&B experience.[18]

There are an estimated 25,000 bed and breakfast places in the United States alone. B&Bs have flourished for many reasons. Business travelers are growing weary of the complexities of the check-in/checkout processes at some commercial hotels. With the escalation of transient rates at hotels, an opportunity has been created to serve a more price-sensitive segment of travelers. Also, many leisure travelers are looking for accommodation somewhere between a large, formal hotel and staying with friends. The B&Bs offer a homelike atmosphere. They are aptly called "a home away from home." Community breakfasts with other lodgers and hosts enhance this feeling. Each B&B is as unique as its owner. Décor varies according to the region of location and the unique taste of its owner. The owner of the bed and breakfast often provides all the necessary labor, but some employ full- or part-time help.

▶ Check Your Knowledge

1. What characteristics do the following hotel segments encompass?
   a. City center hotels
   b. Resort hotels
   c. Airport hotels
   d. Freeway hotels and motels

e. Full-service hotels

f. Economy/budget hotels

g. Extended-stay hotels

h. Bed and breakfast inns

Best, Biggest, and Most Unusual Hotels and Chains

So, which is the best hotel in the world? The answer may depend on whether you watch the Travel Channel or read polls taken by a business investment or travel magazine. Magazines like *Travel + Leisure* and web sites like Trip Advisor invite readers to vote for their favorite hotels and then they publish the list, so it's more of a popularity poll. However, the results are interesting and are not split into several categories: best in Asia, best in the Caribbean, best romantic, best city, and so on. One recent list had the Golden Well, Prague, Czech Republic, as number one, whereas another had Oberoi Vanyavilas, Rajasthan, India. High on the list was the Fairmont Mara Safari Club, Masai Mara, Kenya, and the Earth Lodge at Sabi Sabi Private Game Reserve, Kruger National Park, Southern Africa. The Oriental Hotel in Bangkok, Thailand, has been rated number one in the world; so, too, has the Regent of Hong Kong, the Mandarin Oriental of Hong Kong, and the Connaught of London. Each "list" picks other hotels. The largest hotel in the world is the Izmailovo Hotel in Moscow with 7,500 rooms, followed by the 7,372-room MGM Grand in Las Vegas and the Venetian Hotel, also in Las Vegas, which has 7,117 rooms.

The Best Hotel Chains

The Ritz-Carlton and the Four Seasons are generally rated the highest-quality large chain hotels. The Ritz-Carlton Hotel Company has received all the major awards the hospitality industry and leading consumer organizations can bestow. It has received the Malcolm Baldrige National Quality Award from the United States Department of Commerce—the first and only hotel company to win the award and the first and only service company to win the award two times, in 1999 and 1992. Ritz-Carlton has long been recognized as the best luxury hotel chain in the industry. Amanresorts has been awarded the Zagat best hotel group in the world, and Rosewood Hotels and Resorts have several outstanding properties.

A bedroom in an ice hotel.

TECHNOLOGY SPOTLIGHT

The Use of Technology in Property Management

Cihan Cobanoglu, Ph.D., Dean, School of Hotel and Restaurant Management, University of South Florida, Sarasota-Manatee

Technology has become an inseparable part of the hotel business. In a typical full-service hotel, there are about sixty-five different technology applications. This number is around thirty-five for a limited-service hotel. The use of technology starts even before a guest checks in to a hotel. More than half of the hotel guests book their hotel rooms electronically. This means that guests use either direct or indirect reservation/distribution channels. Direct reservation/distribution channels include walk-in, phone call to the hotel, hotel's web site, and hotel chain's web site (central reservation system). Indirect reservation/distribution channels include online travel agencies such as Expedia.com, Travelocity.com, Orbitz.com, and opaque travel agencies where the consumer does not know the brand of the hotel until after the purchase is completed. These opaque online travel agencies include priceline.com and Hotwire.com. A distribution/reservation system typically performs the following basic functions: (1) selling individual reservations, (2) selling group reservations, (3) displaying room availability and guest lists, (4) tracking advance deposits, (5) tracking travel agent bookings and commissions, and (6) generating confirmation letters and e-mails and various reports.

Each hotel has a property management system (PMS). The functions of the PMS are enabling guest reservations, enabling guest check-in/out, enabling staff to maintain guest facilities, keeping accounting for a guest's financial transactions, and tracking guest activities. The PMS is often interfaced to central reservation systems and global reservation systems. This way, when a guest makes a reservation from a hotel chain's web site such as Hilton.com or Marriott.com, the reservation is automatically transferred to the hotel's property reservation system. This interface allows the hotel to control the room inventory on a real-time basis and to manage the revenue management process efficiently. The revenue management module of the PMS also uses advanced technology systems. Hotels use the revenue management system to calculate the rates, rooms, and restrictions on sales in order to best maximize the return. These systems measure constrained and unconstrained demand along with pace to gauge which restrictions—for example, length of stay, nonrefundable rate, or close to arrival. Revenue management teams in the hotel industry have evolved tremendously over the last ten years, and in this global economy, targeting the right distribution channels, controlling costs, and having the right market mix plays an important role in yield management. Yield management in hotels is selling rooms and services at the right price, at the right time, to the right people.

The use of technology continues after the reservation. When the guest checks in, the reservation details are found in the PMS and an electronic key card is cut. The guest can use this electronic card to access his or her room and other general areas of the hotel such as fitness room, pool area, and concierge club.

The Most Unusual Hotels

Among the world's most unusual hotels are ones like the Treetops Hotel in one of Kenya's wild animal parks—literally in the treetops. The uniqueness of the hotel is that it is built on the tops of trees overlooking a wild animal watering hole in the park.

Another magnificent spectacle is the Ice Hotel, situated on the shores of the Torne River in the old village of Jukkasjäsvi in Swedish Lapland. The Ice Hotel is built from scratch on an annual basis with a completely new design, new suites, new departments, even the "Absolut Ice Bar," a bar carved in ice with ice glasses and ice plates. The Ice Hotel can accommodate more than one hundred guests, with each room having its own distinct style. The hotel also has an ice chapel, an ice art exhibition hall, and, believe it or not, a cinema.

Australia boasts an underwater hotel at the Great Barrier Reef, where guests have wonderful underwater views from their rooms.

Japan has several unusual hotels. One is a cocoon-like hotel, called Capsule Hotel, in which guests do not have a room as such. Instead, they have a space of about 4 feet by 7 feet. In this space is a bed and a television—which guests almost have to operate with their toes! Such hotels are popular with people who get caught up in the obligatory late-night drinking with the boss and with visiting professors, and who find them the only affordable place to stay in expensive Tokyo.

The highest hotel in the world, in terms of altitude, is nestled in the Himalayan mountain range at an altitude of 13,000 feet. Weather permitting, there is a marvelous view of Mount Everest. As many as 80 percent of the guests suffer from nausea, headaches, or sleeplessness caused by the altitude. No wonder the hottest-selling item on the room-service menu is oxygen—at $1 a minute.

Vacation Ownership

From its beginnings in the French Alps in the late 1960s, **vacation ownership** has become the fastest-growing segment of the U.S. travel and tourism industry, increasing in popularity at the rate of about 15 percent each year.

Vacation ownership offers consumers the opportunity to purchase fully furnished vacation accommodations in a variety of forms, such as weekly intervals or in points-based systems, for a percentage of the cost of ownership. For a one-time purchase price and payment of a yearly maintenance fee, purchasers own their vacation either in perpetuity (forever) or for a predetermined number of years. Owners share both the use and cost of upkeep of their unit and the common grounds of the resort property. Vacation ownership purchases are typically financed through consumer loans of five to ten years duration, with terms dependent on the purchase price and the amount of the buyer's down payment. The average cost of a vacation ownership is $14,800–$18,500.[19]

Vacation clubs, or point-based programs, provide the flexible use of accommodations in multiple resort locations. With these products, club members purchase points that represent either a travel-and-use membership or a deed real estate product. These points are then used like money to purchase accommodations during a season, for a set number of

Marquis Villas timeshare condos, Palm Springs, California.

days at a participating resort. The number of points needed to access the resort accommodation varies by the members' demand for unit size, season, resort location, and amenities.

Henry Silverman, formerly of Avis Budget–which owns the Indianapolis, Indiana–based Resort Condominiums International (RCI)–said that a timeshare is really a two-bedroom suite that is owned, rather than a hotel room that is rented for a transient night. A vacation club, on the other hand, is a "travel-and-use" product. Consumers do not buy a fixed week, unit size, season, resort, or number of days to vacation each year. Instead, they purchase points that represent currency, which is used to access the club's vacation benefits. An important advantage to this is the product's flexibility, especially when tied to a point system. Disney Vacation Club is one major company that uses a point system. General manager Mark Pacala states, "The flexibility of choosing among several different vacation experiences is what sets the Disney Vacation Club apart from many similar plans. The vacation points system allows members to select the type of vacation best suited to their needs, particularly as those needs change from year to year." Each year, members choose how to use their vacation points, either for one long vacation or for a series of short getaways.[20]

The World Tourism Organization has called timeshares one of the fastest-growing sectors of the travel and tourism industry. Hospitality companies are adding brand power to the concept with corporations such as Marriott Vacation Club International, the Walt Disney Company, Hilton Hotels, Hyatt Hotels, Choice Hotels, InterContinental, and even the Ritz-Carlton and Four Seasons participating in an industry that has grown rapidly in recent years. Still, only about 4 percent of all U.S. households hold vacation ownership. RCI estimates that the figure could rise to 10 percent within the next decade for households with incomes of more than $75,000. It is not surprising that hotel companies have found this to be a lucrative business.

RCI, the largest vacation ownership exchange (that allows members to exchange vacations with other locations), has more than 2.8 million member families living in 200 countries. There are 3,700 participating resorts, and members can exchange vacation intervals for vacations at any participating resort, and to date, RCI has arranged exchange vacations for more than 54 million people.[21] Vacation ownership is popular at U.S. resorts from Key West in Florida to Kona in Hawaii and from New York City and Las Vegas to Colorado ski resorts.

Interval World is a vacation exchange network made up of more than 2,000 resorts and more than 1.6 million member families worldwide. Interval does not own or manage any of the resorts, but rather provides members— vacation owners from around the world—with a variety of exchange services to enhance their vacation experiences. Members can exchange a stay at their home resort for a stay at one of the timeshares supported by Interval World.

By locking in the purchase price of accommodations, vacation ownership helps ensure future vacations at today's prices at luxurious resorts with amenities, service, and ambience that rival any of the world's top-rated vacation destinations. Through vacation exchange programs, timeshare owners can travel to other popular destinations around the world. With unparalleled flexibility and fully equipped condominiums that offer the best in holiday luxury, vacation ownership puts consumers in the driver's seat, allowing them to plan and enjoy vacations that suit their lifestyle.

Timeshare resort developers today include many of the world's leading hoteliers, publicly held corporations, and independent companies. Properties that combine vacation ownership resorts with hotels, adventure resorts, and gaming resorts are among the emerging timeshare trends. The reasons for purchasing most frequently cited by current timeshare owners are the high standards of quality accommodations and service at the resorts where they own and exchange, the flexibility offered through the vacation exchange opportunities, and the cost effectiveness of vacation ownership. Nearly one-third of vacation owners purchase additional intervals after experiencing ownership. This trend is even stronger among long-time owners: More than 40 percent of those who have owned for eight years or longer have purchased additional intervals within the timeshare.

Travel the World through Exchange Vacations

Vacation ownership offers unparalleled flexibility and the opportunity for affordable worldwide travel through vacation ownership exchange. Through the international vacation exchange networks, owners can trade their timeshare intervals for vacation time at comparable resorts around the world. Most resorts are affiliated with an exchange company that administers the exchange service for its members. Typically, the exchange company directly solicits annual membership. Owners individually elect to become members of the affiliated exchange company. To exchange, the owner places his or her interval into the exchange company's pool of resorts and weeks available for exchange and, in turn, chooses an available resort and week from that pool. The exchange company charges an exchange fee, in addition to an annual membership fee, to complete an exchange. Exchange companies and resorts frequently offer their members the additional benefit of saving or banking vacation time in a reserve program for use in a different year.

International Perspective

We are all part of a huge global economy that is splintered into massive trading blocks, such as the European Union (EU) and the North American Free Trade Agreement (NAFTA) among Canada, the United States, and Mexico, with a total population of 441 million consumers.[22]

The EU, with a population of more than 501 million people in twenty-seven nations, is an economic union that has removed national boundaries and restrictions not only on trade but also on the movement of capital and labor.[23] The synergy developed between these twenty-seven member nations is beneficial to all and is a form of self-perpetuating development. As travel, tourism, commerce, and industry have increased within the European Economic Community (EEC), which could soon expand by another five nations, and more in the future, so has the need for hotel accommodations.

In the Middle East, in countries like Dubai and Abu Dhabi, United Arab Emirates, several very impressive hotels

Burj Al Arab hotel, Dubai, United Arab Emirates.

and resorts have been added as part of a strategy to encourage more tourism to and within the region and the world. Once the airport is capable of handling several international flights daily, then soon hotels are built to cater to the traveler's needs. Now, these cities are gateways to the region and host international conferences.

NAFTA will likely be a similar catalyst for hotel development in response to increased trade and tourism among the three countries involved. But Argentina, Brazil, Chile, and Venezuela may also join an expanded NAFTA, which would become known as the Americas Trading Bloc.

It is easy to understand the international development of hotels given the increase in international tourism trade and commerce. The growth in tourism in Pacific Rim countries is expected to continue at the same rate as in recent years. Several resorts have been developed in Indonesia, Malaysia, Thailand, and Vietnam, and China and India have both seen hotel growth. Further international hotel development opportunities exist in Eastern Europe, Russia, and the other republics of the former Soviet Union, where some companies have changed their growth strategy from building new hotels to acquiring and renovating existing properties.

In Asia, Hong Kong's growth has been encouraged by booming economies throughout Southeast Asia and the kind of tax system for which supply-siders hunger. The Hong Kong government levies a flat 16.5 percent corporate tax, a 15 percent individual income tax, and no tax on capital gains or dividends. Several hotel corporations have their headquarters in Hong Kong. Among them are Mandarin Oriental, Peninsula, and Shangri-La, all world-renowned for their five-star status. They are based in Hong Kong because of low corporate taxation and the ability to bring in senior expatriate executives with minimal bureaucratic difficulty.[24]

In developing countries, once political stability has been sustained, hotel development quickly follows as part of an overall economic and social progression. An example of this is the former Eastern European countries and former Soviet republics that for the past few years have offered development opportunities for hotel corporations.

Raffles Singapore, a world-famous classic hotel.

Sustainable or Green Lodging

Today, of necessity, developers are more environmentally conscious because it can cost far more not only to build a lodging facility but also to run it if it is not sustainable. By using local materials, a new hotel or resort can save money on the cost of materials plus the cost of transporting those materials from a distance, or even importing them. Given the weak U.S. dollar, it increases costs if materials must be imported.

The cost of energy has increased so much in recent years that lodging construction now incorporates ways of using natural lighting and building energy-efficient buildings. Energy-efficient buildings require far less air-conditioning than do conventional buildings because they use materials such as darkened glass and lower-wattage lighting that produces lower temperatures.

How can hotels, motels, lodges, and resorts become more sustainable? Reducing and eliminating waste can produce the biggest positive environmental impact. This can be accomplished through a number of practices, including sustainable lighting and water conservation. A property with 300 guest rooms can spend $300,000 per year on electricity and $50,000 on natural gas, and another $60,000 annually on water and sewer.[25]

Lighting can account for 30 to 40 percent of commercial electricity consumption. This can be reduced by the following strategies:

- Use lighting only when necessary—employ motion detectors.
- Use energy-efficient fixtures and lamps.
- Use low-wattage lighting for signs and décor.
- Avoid over-lighting wherever possible.

Water conservation is another method that can greatly reduce waste. Today, many hotels are replacing showerheads, toilets, and faucets with low-flow water devices. Low-flow showerheads can save 10 gallons of water every five minutes of showering. That means a savings of over $3,000 annually if one hundred people shower each day, and water and sewer costs are one cent per gallon.[26] Other water conservation methods include only washing full loads of dishes and laundry, serving drinking water by request only, asking guests to consider reusing towels, and restricting lawn watering.

Fairmont Hotels and Resorts[27] are among the leading sustainable lodging companies whose projects fall into three key areas: (1) minimizing the company's impact on the environment by making ongoing operational improvements, mainly in waste management and energy and water conservation; (2) working at a corporate level to foster high-profile partnerships and accreditations that help promote environmental issues and to share its stewardship message; and (3) to follow best practices, which include working at individual properties to develop innovative ways to reduce the carbon footprint of hotels.

Career Information

A variety of career options are directly and indirectly related to hotel development and classification. Some examples include working in the corporate office to develop hotels or searching out locations, negotiating the deals, and/or organizing the construction or alterations. This involves knowledge of operations plus expertise in marketing, feasibility studies, finance, and planning.

Similarly, consulting firms like PKF have interesting positions for consultants who provide specialized services in feasibility studies, marketing, human resources, and accounting and finance due diligence (a check to ensure that the cost of purchasing a property is reasonable and that all systems are in working order). Working for a consulting firm usually requires a master's degree plus operational experience in an area of specialty. AAA and Mobil both have inspectors who check hotel standards. Inspectors are required to travel and write detailed reports on the properties at which they stay.

Good advice comes from Jim McManemon, general manager of the Ritz-Carlton, Sarasota, Florida: "It is important to have a love of people, as there is so much interaction with them. I also suggest working in the industry to gain experience. Actually, it is a good idea to work in various departments while going to school so you can either join a management-training program or take a supervisory or assistant management position upon graduation. Work hard, be a leader, and set an example for the people working with you."[28]

Go to the university relations web site for Wyndham Hotels and scroll down to see what advice is given: www.wyndhamworldwide.com/careers/university.html.

Trends in Hotel Development

- *Capacity control.* Refers to who will control the sale of inventories of hotel rooms, airline seats, auto rentals, and tickets to attractions. Presently, owners of these assets are in control of their sale and distribution, but increasingly control is falling into the hands of those who own and manage global reservation systems and/or negotiate for large buying groups. Factors involved in the outcome will be telecommunications, software, available satellite capacity, governmental regulations, limited capital, and the travel distribution network.

- *Safety and security.* Important aspects of safety and security are terrorism, the growing disparity between the haves and have-nots in the world, diminishing financial resources, infrastructure problems, health issues, the stability of governments, and personal security.

- *Assets and capital.* The issues concerning assets and capital are rationing of private capital and rationing of funds deployed by governments.

- *Technology.* An example of the growing use of *expert systems* (a basic form of artificial intelligence) would be making standard operating procedures available online, twenty-four hours a day, and establishing yield management systems designed to make pricing decisions. Other examples include increasing numbers of smart hotel room and communications ports to make virtual office environments for business travelers and the impact of technology on the structure of corporate offices and individual hotels.

- *New management.* The complex forces of capacity control, safety and security, capital movement, and technology issues will require a future management cadre that is able to adapt to rapid-paced change across all the traditional functions of management.

- *Globalization.* A number of U.S. and Canadian chains have developed and are continuing to develop hotels around the world. International companies are also investing in the North American hotel industry.

- *Consolidation.* As the industry matures, corporations are either acquiring or merging with each other.

- *Diversification within segments of the lodging industry.* The economy segment now has low-, medium-, and high-end properties. The extended-stay market has a similar spread of properties, as do all the other hotel classifications.

CASE STUDY

In recent years, several new lodging brands have been introduced by leading hotel chains to the market. Among the names of these brands are DoubleTree, Candlewood Suites, Homewood Suites, Mainstay, Spring Hill Suites, and so on. In addition, there is Hyatt, which recently purchased AmeriSuites, which it has renovated and now calls Hyatt Place.

A hot trend in lodging development is condo hotels, called condotels. With condotels, a developer can more quickly raise the funds necessary from investors than from other traditional sources such as banks and finance houses. As a result, it makes sense for developers to encourage investors by offering an arrangement for owners to have exclusive use of the unit for a fixed number of days a year (typically 30–60 days) and for the hotel company to rent out the units/rooms for the remainder of the year. The cost of development is high and ranges from an average of $800 to $900 per square foot up to a high of $1,400. Projects such as the Residences at MGM Grand Las Vegas, which sold more than $1 billion, or the Hard Rock Hotel and Casino, also in Las Vegas, which launched 1,300 units in less than ten weeks, are amazing. Other areas of the United States are good existing or potential markets for condotel development.

Despite the rave reviews on Wall Street for condotels, there are some unresolved issues. With time, who will develop and pay for the replacement of furniture fixtures and equipment (FF&E)? What are the association dues and what form will the relationship take between owners, the developer, and the hotel company? There are the additional complexities for the hotel operator—such as space for meetings, restaurants, and recreation—and how many rooms will be available on any given night. Yet, the payoffs for both individual investors–owners and hotel operating companies—are good to great. With 78 million baby boomers ready to retire, the prospects look very good to all concerned.

Discussion Questions

1. So what is in a name? Is Hyatt right to use the name Hyatt Place?

2. Is InterContinental or Hilton wrong not to include their name, as in Hilton Hampton Inn or Hampton Inn by Hilton? What is your opinion?

3. Which other areas of the United States are good potential locations for condotels and why?

4. Will condotels split into various segments like other lodging properties have?

- *Rapid growth in vacation ownership.* Vacation ownership is the fastest-growing segment of the lodging industry and is likely to continue growing as the baby boomers enter their fifties and sixties.
- *An increase in the number of spas and the treatments offered.* Wellness and the road to nirvana are in increasing demand as guests seek release from the stresses of a fast-paced lifestyle.
- *Gaming.* An increasing number of hotels are coming online that are related to the gaming industry.
- *Mixed-use properties.* An increasing number of hotels are being developed as multiuse properties, meaning hotels with residences (condominiums), spas, and recreational facilities.
- *Sustainable lodging development.* There is increasing development of lodging facilities with environmentally designs, construction, and operating procedures.

Summary

1. Improved transportation has changed the nature of the hotel industry from small, independently owned inns to big hotel and lodging chains that are operated using concepts such as franchising and management contracts.
2. Hotels can be classified according to location (city center, resort, airport, freeway), types of services offered (casino, convention), and price (luxury, midscale, budget, and economy). Hotels are rated by Mobil and AAA (five-star or five-diamond rankings).
3. Vacation ownership offers consumers the opportunity to purchase fully furnished vacation accommodations, similar to condominiums, sold in a variety of forms, such as weekly intervals or point-based systems, for only a percentage of the cost of full ownership. According to the World Tourism Organization, timeshares are one of the fastest-growing sectors of the travel and tourism industry.
4. Every part of the world offers leisure and business travelers a choice of unusual or conservative accommodations that cater to personal ideas of vacation or business trips.
5. The future of tourism involves international expansion and foreign investment, often in combination with airlines, and with the goal of improving economic conditions in developing countries. It is further influenced by increased globalization, as evidenced by such agreements as NAFTA.

Key Words and Concepts

capital intensive	indirect economic impact	referral associations
fair return on investment	franchising	vacation ownership
feasibility study	management contracts	
direct economic impact	real estate investment trusts (REITs)	

Review Questions

1. What are the advantages of (a) management contracts and (b) franchising? Discuss their impacts on the development of the hotel industry.
2. Explain how hotels cater to the needs of business and leisure travelers in reference to the following concepts: (a) resorts, (b) airport hotels, and (c) vertical integration.
3. Explain what vacation ownership is. What are the different types of timeshare programs available for purchase?

Internet Exercises

1. Organization: **Hilton Hotels**
   Web site: **www.hiltonworldwide.com**
   Summary: Hilton Hotels Corporation and Hilton International have a worldwide alliance to market Hilton. Hilton is recognized as one of the world's best-known hotel brands. Collectively, Hilton offers more than 3,600 hotels in more than 66 countries, truly a major player in the hospitality industry.
   (a) What are the different hotel brands that can be franchised through Hilton Hotels Corporation?
   (b) What are your views on Hilton's portfolio and franchising options? click on "Hilton Worldwide Brands."

2. Organization: *Hotels* **Magazine**
   Web site: **www.hotelsmag.com**
   Summary: *Hotels* magazine is a publication that offers vast amounts of information on the hospitality industry with up-to-date industry news, corporate trends, and nationwide developments.
   (a) What are some of the top headlines currently being reported in the industry?
   (b) Click on "Print Magazine Archives," click on the icon for the October 2010 edition, and then go to page 22 of the online magazine. Browse through the corporate rankings and industry leaders. List the top five hotel corporations and note how many rooms each one has.

Apply Your Knowledge

1. From a career perspective, what are the advantages and disadvantages of each type of hotel?
2. If you were going into the lodging sector, which type of property would you prefer to work at and why?

Suggested Activities

1. Identify which kind of hotel you would like to work at and give reasons why.

Endnotes

1. http://www.bostonhistorycollaborative.org/ BostonFamilyHistory/ancestors/english/eng_1650.html (accessed February 16, 2011); Donald E. Lundberg, *The Hotel and Restaurant Business*, 6th ed. (New York: Van Nostrand Reinhold, 1994), 28–29; John Caprarella, et al.: *The History of Lodging: The Hotel in America*, 2002.

2. New York Architecture, *The Plaza Hotel*, www. nyc-architecture.com/MID/MID056.htm (accessed October 26, 2011).

3. Source company web sites and "HOTELS' 325," *Hotels*, October 2010, www.marketingandtechnology.com/repository/ webFeatures/HOTELS/2010giants.pdf (accessed February 23, 2011).

4. This section is courtesy of Robert Kok, Professor, Johnson and Wales University.

5. Wyndham Worldwide, *Wyndham Hotel Group*, www.wyndhamworldwide.com/about/wyndham_ hotel_group.cfm (accessed February 22, 2011).

6. WorldMark by Wyndham, *About Wyndham*, www.worldmarkbywyndham.com/about/ (accessed February 22, 2011).

7. Ibid.

8. Wyndham Worldwide, *Wyndham Exchange & Rentals*, www.wyndhamworldwide.com/about/wyndham_ exchange_and_rentals.cfm (accessed February 22, 2011).

9. Personal conversation with Bruce Goodwin, President of Goodwin and Associates hotel consultants, May 4, 2011.

10. Kimpton Hotels & Restaurants, *About Us*, www. kimptonhotels.com/about-us/about-us.aspx (accessed February 22, 2011).

11. Marriott International, Inc., *Our Brands: Autograph Collection*, www.marriott.com/corporateinfo/glance.mi#brand4 (accessed February 18, 2011).

12. Hyatt Corporation, *Our Brands: Andaz*, www.hyatt.com/hyatt/about/our-brands/andaz.jsp (accessed February 18, 2011).

13. American Hotel & Lodging Association, *Press Release: 2008 Study on Hotel Room Taxes Quantifies Economic Impact*, www.ahla.com/pressrelease.aspx?id= 22524 (accessed on February 24, 2011).

14. Adapted from the American Hotel & Lodging Association's Economic Impact of Hotels and Motels.

15. American Hotel & Lodging Association, *AH&LA Lodging Industry Profile (LIP) Archive: 2010*, www.ahla.com/content.aspx?id=30505 (accessed February 18, 2011).

16. Barbara De Lollis, "AAA Announces Five Diamond Hotels for 2011," *USA Today Travel*, http://travel.usatoday.com/hotels/post/2011/01/aaa- five-diamond-awards-hotels-restaurants/138554/1 (accessed February 18, 2011).

17. InterContinental Hotels Group, *Hotel Indigo: Our Story*, www.ichotelsgroup.com/h/d/in/1/en/c/2/content/dec/ teaser/in/1/en/lp/read_our_story.html (accessed October 26, 2011).

18. "What Is a Bed and Breakfast Inn?" *TravelASSIST*, January 1996, www.travelassist.com/mag/a88.html (accessed October 26, 2011).

19. Great Escapes, *Home Page*, www.greatescapesonline.com/Visitor/Ownership.aspx (accessed February 19, 2011); Resort Condominiums International, *About Us*, www.rci.com/RCI/prelogin/ aboutUs.do (accessed February 19, 2011).

20. Lynn Sheldon, "Timeshare Concept Adopted by Hotel Industry," *Rhode Island Roads*, www.riroads.com/archive/timesharehotels.htm (accessed October 26, 2011).

21. Resort Condominiums International, *RCI Milestones*, www.rci.com/RCI/RCIW/RCIW_index? body=RCIW_Milestone&action=aboutrci (accessed October 26, 2011).

22. NAFTANOW.org, *Fast Facts: North American Free Trade Agreement*, www.naftanow.org/facts/default_en.asp (accessed February 24, 2011).

23. Matej Hruska, "EU Population Tops 500 Million," *Bloomberg Businessweek*, July 29, 2010, www.businessweek.com/globalbiz/content/jul2010/gb20100729_623637.htm (accessed on February 24, 2011).
24. Personal conversation with Leonard Gordon, March 15, 2006.
25. N.C. Division of Pollution Prevention and Environmental Assistance (DPPEA), *Hotel/Motel Waste Reduction: Facilities Management*, www.p2pays.org/ref/14/13910.pdf (retrieved February 24, 2011).
26. Ibid.
27. Fairmont Hotels & Resorts, Green Partnership Program, www.fairmont.com/EN_FA/AboutFairmont/environment/GreenPartnershipProgram/ (accessed February 25, 2011).
28. Personal interview with Jim McManemon, General Manager, Ritz-Carlton, Sarasota, Florida, and Chris Bryant, Guest Services Manager, Grand Hyatt, Tampa Bay, Florida, February 26, 2011.

Glossary

Capital intensive   Something requiring a lot of capital.
Fair return on investment   A reasonable return for the amount invested.
Franchising   A concept that allows a company to expand quickly by allowing qualified people to use the systems, marketing, and purchasing power of the franchiser.
Indirect economic impact   An economic impact that is not direct.
Management contract   A written agreement between an owner and an operator of a hotel or motor inn by which the owner employs the operator as an agent (employee) to assume full responsibility for operating and managing the property.

Real Estate Investment Trust (RIET)   A method that enables small investors to combine their funds and protects them from the double taxation levied against an ordinary corporation or trust; designed to facilitate investment in real estate in much the same way a mutual fund facilitates investment in securities.
Referral associations   Associations that refer guests to other participating members.
Vacation ownership   Offers consumers the opportunity to purchase fully furnished vacation accommodations in a variety of forms, such as weekly intervals or points in point-based systems, for a percentage of the cost of full ownership.

Photo Credits

Credits are listed in the order of appearance.

Jerryway/Dreamstime.com
Chad M. Gruhl
Hotel Indigo
Demetrio Carrasco/DK Images
McKibbon Hotel Management, Inc.
David Zanzinger/Alamy
akg-images/Newscom
Starwood Hotels and Resorts Worldwide
Wesley Hitt/Creative Eye/MIRA.com

Valerie Ferguson
Magnus Rew/DK Images
Paul Franklin/DK Images
Sean Bakewell
Marriott International
Emma Lee/Life File/Photodisc/Getty Images
Michael Newman/PhotoEdit
Eye Ubiquitous/Alamy
Simon Bracken/DK Images

Food and Beverage Operations

From Chapter 4 of *Introduction to Hospitality,* Sixth Edition. John R. Walker. Copyright © 2013 by Pearson Education, Inc. Published by Pearson. All rights reserved.

Food and Beverage Operations

OBJECTIVES

After reading and studying this chapter, you should be able to:

- Describe the duties and responsibilities of a food and beverage director and other key department heads.

- Describe a typical food and beverage director's day.

- State the functions and responsibilities of the food and beverage departments.

- Perform computations using key food and beverage operating ratios.

Food and Beverage Management

In the hospitality industry, the food and beverage division is led by the **director of food and beverage**. He or she reports to the general manager and is responsible for the efficient and effective operation of the following departments:

- Kitchen/Catering/Banquet
- Restaurants/Room Service/Minibars
- Lounges/Bars/Stewarding

Figure 1 illustrates a food and beverage organization chart.

The position description for a director of food and beverage is both a job description and a specification of the requirements an individual needs to do the job. In recent years, the skills needed by a food and beverage director have grown enormously, as shown by the following list of responsibilities:

- Exceeding guests' expectations in food and beverage offerings and service
- Leadership
- Identifying trends
- Finding and keeping outstanding employees
- Training
- Motivation
- Budgeting
- Cost control

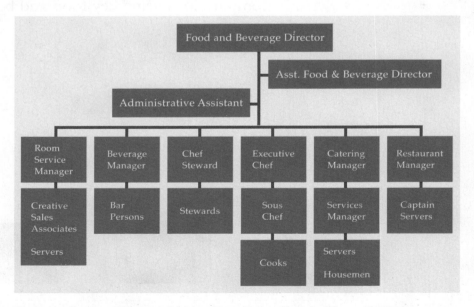

Figure 1 • Food and Beverage Division Organization Chart for a Large Hotel.

- Finding profit from all outlets
- Having a detailed working knowledge of the front-of-the-house operations

These challenges are set against a background of stagnant or declining occupancies and the consequent drop in room sales. Therefore, greater emphasis has been placed on making food and beverage sales profitable. Traditionally, only about 20 percent of the hotel's operating profit comes from the food and beverage divisions. In contrast, an acceptable profit margin from a hotel's food and beverage division is generally considered to be 25 to 30 percent. This figure can vary according to the type of hotel. For example, according to Pannell Kerr Forster, an industry consulting firm, all-suite properties achieve a 7 percent food and beverage profit (probably because of the complimentary meals and drinks offered to guests).

A typical food and beverage director's day might look like the following:

8:30 A.M.	Check messages and read logs from outlets and security. Tour outlets, especially the family restaurant (a quick inspection).
	Check the breakfast buffet, reservations, and the shift manager.
	Check daily specials.
	Check room service.
	Check breakfast service and staffing.
	Meet the executive chef and purchasing director.
	Meet executive steward's office to ensure that all equipment is ready.
	Meet banquet service office to check on daily events and coffee break sequence.
10:00 A.M.	Work on current projects: new summer menu, pool outlet opening, conversion of a current restaurant with a new concept, remodeling of ballroom foyer, installation of new walk-in freezer, and analysis of current profit-and-loss (P&L) statements. Plan weekly food and beverage department meetings.
11:45 A.M.	Visit kitchen to observe lunch service and check the "12:00 line," including banquets.
	Confer with executive chef.
	Check restaurants and banquet luncheon service.
1:00 P.M.	Have working lunch in employee cafeteria with executive chef, director of purchasing, or director of catering.
1:30 P.M.	Meet with human resources to discuss current incidents.
2:30 P.M.	Check messages and return calls. Telemarket to attract catering and convention business.
	Conduct hotel daily menu meeting.
3:00 P.M.	Go to special projects/meetings.
5:30 P.M.	Tour cocktail lounges.

	Check for staffing.
	Review any current promotions.
	Check entertainment lineup.
6:00 P.M.	Check special food and beverage requests/requirements of any VIPs staying at the hotel.
	Tour kitchen.
	Review and taste.
8:00 P.M.	Review dinner specials.
	Check the restaurant and lounges.

A food and beverage director's typical day starts at 8:00 A.M. and ends at 8:00 P.M., unless early or very late events are scheduled, in which case the working day is even longer. Usually, the food and beverage director works Monday through Saturday. If there are special events on Sunday, then he or she works on Sunday and takes Monday off. In a typical week, Saturdays are used to catch up on reading or specific projects.

The director of food and beverage eats in his or her restaurants at least twice a week for dinner and at least once a week for breakfast and lunch. Bars are generally visited with clients, at least twice per week. The director sees salespersons regularly because they are good sources of information about what is going on in the industry and they can introduce leads for business. The director attends staff meetings, food and beverage meetings, executive committee meetings, interdepartmental meetings, credit meetings, and P&L statement meetings.

To become a food and beverage director takes several years of experience and dedication. One of the best routes is to gain work experience or to participate in an internship in several food and beverage departments while attending college. This experience should include full-time, practical kitchen work for at least one to two years to master the core concepts, followed by varying periods of a few months in purchasing, stores, cost control, stewarding, and room service. Stewarding is responsible for back-of-the-house areas such as dishwashing and issuing and inventorying china, glassware, and cutlery. Stewarding duties include maintaining cleanliness in all areas. Additionally, a year spent in each of the following work situations is helpful: restaurants, catering, and bars. After these departmental experiences, and once you master the core competencies, you can likely serve as a department manager, preferably in a different hotel from the one in which the departmental experience was gained. This prevents the awkwardness of being manager of a department in which the person was once an employee and also offers the employee the opportunity to learn different things at different properties.

▶ Check Your Knowledge

1. What are the skills and responsibilities of a food and beverage director?
2. Describe a food and beverage director's day.

INTRODUCING GEORGE GOLDHOFF

Vice President of Food and Beverage, Beau Rivage Resort and Casino, Biloxi, Mississippi

Being hired as the pot washer for the Old Homestead Country Kitchen at the early age of fifteen hardly seemed to herald the beginnings of an auspicious career in the hospitality industry. But to George Goldhoff, with his high energy and natural leadership skills, he had found the perfect environment in which to excel. The sense of family and camaraderie between the staff members and the interaction with guests, mixed with the intensity of performance and deadlines, have never lost their appeal. Excellence in service would become his lifelong pursuit.

Fast-forward twenty years. As director of food and beverage at Bellagio of MGM/Mirage, Inc., in Las Vegas, George was responsible for the quality assurance, personnel development, and financial performance of seventeen restaurants and ten bars, with 3,000 employees and more than $200 million in revenues. His responsibilities may have increased since his pot washer days, but the core message in his service training remains intact: sincerity toward the guest and anticipation of guest needs. His approach to service is simple: Greet all guests with a smile, make sure they are comfortable, offer them something to eat and drink. These service basics, simple instructions given to him as a five-year-old by his parents, have stayed with him. Playing host at one of his parents' dinner parties, he learned early the power of a sincere smile and the rewarding experience of pleasing others. Little did he or his parents intuit that one day his child's play would evolve into a rewarding career in hospitality.

As one of the original members of the opening team for the Bellagio, George drew from his extensive and varied food and beverage background to make the Bellagio's opening a success. In 1983 George graduated from Schenectady County Community College as a dean's list student and recipient of an athletic scholarship award. He continued on to the University of Massachusetts where he earned his B.S. degree in hotel, restaurant, and travel administration. His acceptance to these two institutions, after having dropped out of high school, instilled in George the self-confidence in his abilities and the technical skills necessary to achieve his goals. For a young man without a high school diploma who was often characterized as wild and rebellious, it was a revelation, an awakening to his potentials and the realization that he could accomplish great things. His introduction to corporate culture was as an assistant front office manager and Hyatt corporate trainee in Savannah, Georgia.

Upon completion of his training, he moved to beautiful Tahoe in 1988, where he was able to combine his love for restaurants and sports. An all-around athlete, adhering to the work hard, play hard principle, he pursued speed skiing competitions at the highest levels. He stayed on as general manager of Rosie's Café for two and a half years. However, growing tired of the small town confines of Tahoe City and with the singular challenges of Rosie's Café becoming undemanding, George acted on a friend's advice, contacted a mutual friend, and took a job on a 750-foot merchant ship. For the next six months George sailed around the world cooking breakfast, lunch, and dinner for a crew of twelve, while visiting ports in Gibraltar, Malta, Egypt, the United Arab Emirates, Kuwait, and Saudi Arabia. In 1990, aspiring to be a major player not just in skiing, but in the restaurant arena as well, he sought grander, more sophisticated restaurants to manage.

George's ambitions led him to the Plaza Hotel in New York, where he started as an assistant beverage director. George immersed himself in his new position with his usual high-voltage energy and infectious enthusiasm, earning him nicknames such as the Golden Boy and Mr. Hollywood. It did not take long for George to be recognized for his positive attitude and management abilities. Within six months, he was promoted to manager of the stately Oak Room, the youngest manager in the restaurant's ninety-year history. Within a two-year period, he was promoted to managing four of the Plaza Hotel's five à la carte restaurants.

Holding to his personal belief that "you are the company you keep," he has always endeavored to associate with the highest quality restaurateurs and organizations. In 1993, he realized one of his dreams—the

(continued)

opportunity to work with the legendary Joe Baum—managing the famous Rainbow Room in Rockefeller Center. His commitment to service, the evident pride he takes in his work, and his high standard of ethics earned George praise from Joe Baum as being his best maître d' ever. Such a high compliment could have gone to his head. However, George is not one to sit back and take it easy. Instead, he set even higher standards and focused his energies on new goals. He quotes his old boss and industry idol Joe Baum as saying, "Values and standards are those you make for yourself. You don't have to be as good as the other guy. You have to be better—a lot better."

Against the advice of well-meaning family and peers, he left the Rainbow Room in 1997 to enroll in the MBA program at Columbia University. This was no easy decision, considering George was happily married at this point, with one child and another on the way. However, he has never been afraid to take risks, and is not one to fear taking on new challenges. In fact, his adventurous and go-getter nature revels in change. With the same self-confidence, resourcefulness, and ability to focus on multiple tasks he, not surprisingly, took first place in Columbia's Business Plan competition and was the recipient of the prestigious Eugene Lang Entrepreneurial Initiative Fund. Armed with his MBA degree and newly acquired business skills, he was ready for his next adventure.

Even before he had graduated, he was tapped by Stephen Rushmore, founder and president of Hospitality Valuation Services, to work with him as a consultant and valuation analyst. Here he was afforded the opportunity to incorporate his academic learning, fresh ideas, and extensive hotel background into his work. He created the 1996 Hotel Valuation Index (HVS), which was later published in the *Cornell Quarterly*. Ever the entrepreneur, he left HVS in 1997 to establish his own venture, The Irish Coast, Inc., creating and implementing the Guinness Irish pub concept. He jumped into the task of perfecting the Irish pub ambience of warmth, comfort, and congeniality, the heart of hospitality. Hence, it was only a matter of time before he would find himself in Las Vegas, the "Hospitality Capital of the World." In 1998, he signed on with Mirage Resorts to open the ultimate luxury resort and casino, Bellagio.

For George, it's all about service. Excellence in customer satisfaction and a genuine concern for his staff and coworkers have been his guiding principles. Characterized by colleagues as a dreamer, he has the rare ability to communicate his vision and to motivate and inspire others into executing that vision, making it a reality. The ability to instill in those around him the desire to strive beyond and stretch past their comfort zones is just one of his leadership characteristics. His motivational secret is to "constantly remind the staff that their job is precious, even if they've been doing it year after year." He maintains that the key to service is to "know one's job and to remember that a little kindness goes a long way to making people happy. A guest always knows if someone doesn't care."

In addition to starting up and overseeing the entire food and beverage operations for the hotel, he was chosen to represent Mirage Resorts in Focus Las Vegas, a leadership development program of the Las Vegas Chamber of Commerce. Making a difference in others' lives has always been one of the appealing factors of being in the hospitality field. He has always felt personally rewarded when he can give back to others, such as promoting a new busperson, building up someone else's self-esteem, watching people gain confidence in themselves and take pride in their work. He concedes he did not reach his position on his own, but with the assistance of many caring mentors. Always mindful and appreciative of those who have helped him throughout his career, he enjoys helping others discover their own potential. He considers human relations to be one of his strengths and regards staff development to be one of his greatest priorities as a leader. Empowering frontline employees is essential to maintaining a restaurant's competitive edge: "Give them the tools and let them do the job."

George has great expectations for himself and those around him and is not afraid of hard work. In fact, he works with a passion. The long hours and the intensity do not faze him. His adaptability to different situations, his ability to relate to a variety of personalities and temperaments, and his keen sense of humor serve him well both in front and back of the house. With his winning smile and straightforward demeanor, he sets his sights on a promising future and the many adventures ahead.

Kitchen

A hotel kitchen is under the charge of the **executive chef** or chef in smaller and medium-sized properties. This person, in turn, is responsible to the director of food and beverage for the efficient and effective operation of kitchen food production. The desired outcome is to exceed guests' expectations in the quality and quantity of food, its presentation, taste, and portion size, and to ensure that hot food is served hot and cold food is served cold. The executive chef operates the kitchen in accordance with company policy and strives to achieve desired financial results.

Some executive chefs are now called **kitchen managers**; they even serve as food and beverage directors in midsized and smaller hotels. This trend toward "right-sizing," observed in other industries, euphemistically refers to restructuring organizations to retain the most essential employees. Usually, this means cutting labor costs by consolidating job functions. For example, Michael Hammer is executive chef and food and beverage director at the 440-room Hilton La Jolla in Torrey Pines, California. Mike is typical of the new breed of executive chefs: His philosophy is to train his sous chefs, *sous* being a French word meaning "under," to make many of the operating decisions. He delegates ordering, hiring, and firing decisions; sous chefs are the ones most in control of the production and the people who work on their teams. By delegating more of the operating decisions, he is developing the chefs de partie (or stations chefs) and empowering them to make their own decisions. As he puts it, "No decision is wrong—but in case it is unwise, we will talk about it later."

The executive chef of a very large hotel manages the kitchen and may not do much cooking.

Mike spends time maintaining morale, a vital part of a manager's responsibilities. The kitchen staff is under a great deal of pressure and frequently works against the clock. Careful cooperation and coordination are the keys to success. He explains that he does not want his associates to "play the tuba"—he wants them to conduct the orchestra. He does not hold food and beverage department meetings; instead he meets with groups of employees frequently, and problems are handled as they occur. Controls are maintained with the help of software that costs their standard recipes, establishes **perpetual inventories**, and calculates potential food cost per outlet. Today, executive chefs and food and beverage directors look past food cost to the actual profit contribution of an item. For example, if a pasta dish costs $3.25 and sells for $12.95, the contribution margin is $9.70. Today, there are software programs such as ChefTec that offer software solutions for purchasing, ordering, inventory control, and recipe and menu costing; ChefTec Plus offers perpetual inventory, sales analysis, theoretical inventory reports, and multiple profit centers.

Controlling costs is an essential part of food and beverage operations and, because labor costs represent the most significant variable costs, staffing becomes an important factor in the day-to-day running of the food and beverage locations. Labor cost benchmarks are measured by covers-per-person-hour. For example, in stewarding, it should take no more than one person per hour to clean 37.1 covers. Mike and his team of outlet managers face interesting challenges, such as staffing for the peaks and valleys of guest needs at breakfast. Many guests want breakfast during the peak time of 7:00 to 8:30 A.M., requiring organization to get the right people in the right place at the right time to ensure that meals are prepared properly and served in a timely manner.

At the Hilton La Jolla–Torrey Pines, Executive Chef Hammer's day goes something like the following:

1. Arrive between 6:00 and 7:00 A.M. and walk through the food and beverage department with the night cleaners.
2. Check to make sure the compactor is working and the area is clean.
3. Check that all employees are on duty.
4. Ask people what kind of challenges they will face today.
5. Sample as many dishes as possible, checking for taste, consistency, feel, smell, and overall quality.
6. Check walk-ins.
7. Recheck once or twice a day to see where the department stands production-wise—this helps reduce or eliminate overtime.
8. Approve schedules for food and beverage outlet.
9. Keep a daily update of food and beverage revenues and costs.
10. Forecast the next day's, week's, and month's business based on updated information.
11. Check on final numbers for catering functions.

Financial results are generally expressed in ratios, such as **food cost percentage**—the cost of food divided by the amount of food sales. A simple example is the sale of a hamburger for $1.00. If the cost of the food is $0.30, then the food cost percentage is 30 percent, which is about average for many hotels. The average might be reduced to 27 percent in hotels that do a lot of catering. As discussed later in this section, in determining the food and beverage department's profit and loss, executive chefs and food and beverage directors must consider not only the food cost percentage, but also the **contribution margin** of menu items. The contribution margin is the amount contributed by a menu item toward overhead expenses and is the difference between the cost of preparing the item and its selling price.

Another important cost ratio for the kitchen is labor cost. The **labor cost percentage** may vary depending on the amount of convenience foods purchased versus those made from scratch (raw ingredients). In a kitchen, the labor cost percentage may be expressed as a **food sales percentage**. For example, if food sales total $1,000 and labor costs total $250, then labor costs may be expressed as a percentage of food sales by the following formula:

$$\frac{\text{Labor Cost}}{\text{Food Sales}}, \quad \text{therefore} \quad \frac{\$250}{\$1,000} = 25\% \text{ labor cost}$$

Labor management is controlled with the aid of programs such as TimePro from Commeg Systems. TimePro is a time, attendance, and scheduling package that provides an analytical tool for managers and saves time on forecasting and scheduling.

CORPORATE PROFILE

Marilyn Carlson, CEO of Carlson Companies

Based in Minneapolis, Carlson's brands and services employ about 170,000 people in nearly 150 countries and territories. Led by Chairperson and Chief Executive Officer Marilyn Carlson Nelson, Carlson Companies continues to build on a cornerstone set by her father, Curt Carlson, nearly 70 years ago: developing long-lasting relationships with clients.

The history of Carlson Companies is one of the classic business success stories in the American free-enterprise system. Starting in 1938 with merely an idea and $55 of borrowed capital, entrepreneur Curtis L. Carlson founded the Gold Bond Stamp Company in his home city of Minneapolis, Minnesota. His trading stamp concept, designed to stimulate sales and loyalty for food stores and other merchants, proved to be right for the times and swept the nation in a wave of dramatic growth.

Through the years, Carlson diversified into hotels, travel, and other related businesses. In the 1960s, Carlson and several other partners collectively bought an interest in the original Radisson Hotel in downtown Minneapolis. Eventually, Carlson became sole owner of the hotel brand and expanded it around the globe.

Among the names in the Carlson family of brands and services are Radisson Hotels & Resorts, Park Plaza Hotels & Resorts, Country Inn & Suites by Carlson, Park Inn hotels, T.G.I. Friday's, and Carlson Wagonlit Travel.

Carlson Hospitality Worldwide encompasses 1,085 hotels in 77 countries, 900 restaurants in 60 countries, and is the world's leading travel management company. Under the banner of Ambition 2015, Carlson has established the following ambitions for its brands:

By 2015 we want our brands to be the leading brand in their segment.

We want to become the number-one hospitality company to work for.

We want to become the number-one hospitality company to invest with.

For Carlson hotels, the Ambition 2015 strategy entails growing the hotel portfolio by at least 50 percent to reach 1,500 hotels in operation by 2015. The hotel strategy is centered around five major themes[1]:

Establish a clear, compelling position for each brand.

Operationalize the brand promises.

Accelerate development.

Win the revenue battle.

Build a global team and organization.

For the restaurant brand T.G.I. Friday's, the Ambition 2015 is focused on driving the growth of this iconic brand. It has three major priorities[2]:

Boost same store sales at existing domestic stores.

Pressure domestic development in a targeted fashion.

Accelerate international growth.

In addition to global business success, Carlson Companies is also recognized as a top employer. Both *Fortune* and *Working Mother* magazines have rated the company as one of their "100 Best Places to Work in America."

A Pastry Chef.

An executive chef has one or more **sous chefs**. Because so much of the executive chef's time is spent on administration, sous chefs are often responsible for the day-to-day running of each shift. Depending on size, a kitchen may have several sous chefs: one or more for days, one for evenings, and another for banquets.

Under the sous chefs is the **chef tournant**. This person rotates through the various stations to relieve the **station chef** heads. These stations are organized according to production tasks, based on the classic "brigade" introduced by Escoffier. The **brigade** includes the following:

Sauce chef, who prepares sauces, stews, sautés, hot hors d'oeuvres

Roast chef, who roasts, broils, grills, and braises meats

Fish chef, who cooks fish dishes

Soup chef, who prepares all soups

Cold larder/pantry chef, who prepares all cold foods: salads, cold hors d'oeuvres, buffet food, and dressings

Banquet chef, who is responsible for all banquet food

Pastry chef, who prepares all hot and cold dessert items

Vegetable chef, who prepares vegetables (this person may be the fry cook and soup cook in some smaller kitchens)

Soup, cold larder, banquets, pastry, and vegetable chefs' positions may be combined in smaller kitchens.

▶ Check Your Knowledge

1. What is a food cost percentage and how is it calculated?
2. What is a contribution margin?
3. How is labor cost percentage calculated?

A DAY IN THE LIFE OF JIM GEMIGNANI

Executive Chef, Marriott Hotel

Jim Gemignani is executive chef at the 1,500-room Marriott Hotel in San Francisco. Chef Jim, as his associates call him, is responsible for the quality of food, guest, and associate satisfaction and for financial satisfaction in terms of results. With more than 200 associates in eight departments, Chef Jim has an interesting challenge. He makes time to be innovative by researching food trends and comparative shopping. Currently, American cuisine is in, as are freestanding restaurants in hotels. An ongoing part of American cuisine is the healthy food that Chef Jim says has not yet found a niche.

Hotels are building identity into their restaurants by branding or creating their own brand name. Marriott, for example, has Pizza Hut pizzas on the room service menu. Marriott hotels have created their own tiers of restaurants. JW's is the formal restaurant, Tuscany's is a northern Italian–themed restaurant, the American Grill has replaced the old coffee shop, and Kimoko is a Japanese restaurant. As a company, Marriott decided to go nationwide with the first three of these concepts. This has simplified menus and improved food quality and presentation, and yet regional specials allow for individual creativity on the part of the chef.

When asked about his personal philosophy, Chef Jim says that in this day and age, one needs to embrace change and build teams; the guest is an important part of the team. Chef Jim's biggest challenge is keeping guests and associates happy. He is also director of food service outlets, which now gives him a front-of-the-house perspective. Among his greatest accomplishments are seeing his associates develop—twenty are now executive chefs—retaining 96 percent of his opening team, and being voted Chef of the Year by the San Francisco Chef's Association.

Chef Jim's advice: "It's tough not to have a formal education, but remember that you need a combination of 'hands-on' and formal training. If you're going to be a leader, you must start at the bottom and work your way up; otherwise, you will become a superior and not know how to relate to your associates."

Food Operations

A hotel may have several restaurants or no restaurant at all; the number and type of restaurants varies as well. A major chain hotel generally has two restaurants: a signature or upscale formal restaurant and a casual coffee shop–type restaurant. These restaurants cater to both hotel guests and to the general public. In recent years, because of increased guest expectations, hotels have placed greater emphasis on food and beverage preparation and service. As a result, there is an increasing need for professionalism on the part of hotel personnel.

Hotel restaurants are run by **restaurant managers** in much the same way as other restaurants. **Restaurant managers** are generally responsible for the following:

- Exceeding guest service expectations
- Hiring, training, and developing employees
- Setting and maintaining quality standards
- Marketing
- Banquets
- Coffee service
- In-room dining, minibars, or the cocktail lounge
- Presenting annual, monthly, and weekly forecasts and budgets to the food and beverage director

Some restaurant managers work on an incentive plan with quarterly performance bonuses. Hotel restaurants present the manager with some interesting challenges because hotel guests are not always predictable. Sometimes they will use the hotel restaurants, and other times they will dine out. If they dine in or out to an extent beyond the forecasted number of guests, problems can arise. Too many guests for the restaurants results in delays and poor service. Too few

The Gelato Cafe, an Italian style cafe in the Bellagio Hotel.

guests means that employees are underutilized, which can increase labor costs unless employees are sent home early. A restaurant manager keeps a diary of the number of guests served by the restaurant on the same night the previous week, month, and year.

The number (house count) and type of hotel guest (e.g., the number of conference attendees who may have separate dining arrangements) should also be considered in estimating the number of expected restaurant guests for any meal. This figure is known as the **capture rate**, which, when coupled with historic and banquet activity and hotel occupancy, will be the restaurant's basis for forecasting the number of expected guests.

Most hotels find it difficult to coax hotel guests into the restaurants. However, many continuously try to convert foodservice from a necessary amenity to a profit center. The Royal Sonesta in New Orleans offers restaurant coupons worth $5 to its guests and guests of nearby hotels. Another successful strategy, adopted by the Plaza Athénée in New York, is to show guests the restaurants and explain the cuisine before they go to their rooms. This has prompted more guests to dine in the restaurant during their stay. At some hotels, the restaurants self-promote by having cooking demonstrations in the lobby: The "on-site" chefs offer free samples to hotel guests. Progressive hotels, such as the Kimco Hotel in San Francisco, ensure that the hotel restaurants look like freestanding restaurants with separate entrances.

FOCUS ON LODGING

Gracious Hospitality

Catherine Rabb, Johnson and Wales University

I find great pleasure in seeing a well-managed hotel handling full occupancy, special events, and busy dining rooms with seemingly effortless grace. How welcoming it is for the traveler or for the guest at a special event to be served by professionals who embody the true spirit of gracious hospitality.

What the guest doesn't see is the complex network of interlocking relationships and intensive training necessary behind the scenes to make each day successful at any hotel. It has been said that hotels need to be like ducks—appearing to glide effortlessly along the surface, while paddling like the devil underneath! Every person in our operation is a critical component of our business. We sell food and beverages in a variety of ways, but in hospitality operations, the interaction with the guest becomes part of the product, with no room for returns if service is defective. We are only as good as our last meal, our last event, or our last contact with a guest. Service itself *is* the product.

As you will learn in this chapter, many different departments and people with diverse skills must work together efficiently. Hotels of different sizes and styles exist, so some operations need more people, and some need less; but for all hotels a dedication to providing the best available services and products is critical. This diverse group of people must work together to create a service product whose appearance is seamless. The coordination of people, talents, schedules, and needs is a complex ballet of intricate steps choreographed to create a seamless whole. A successful operation needs the talents of every member of the staff and welcomes the varied skills, energies, and ideas that their team brings to the table. Everyone, from the newest part-time employee to the manager, needs to be at the top of his or her game to reach the goal of service excellence.

The term *multitasking* has perhaps been overused in recent years; however, nowhere is the term better suited than to describe the routine tasks done by so many industry professionals. Whether we are chefs, bartenders, stewards, catering managers, or food and beverage directors, we all need a wide variety of skills and abilities to be successful in this challenging industry. We need the technical skills necessary to do the job: correct service techniques, food preparation skills, the ability to mix a perfect drink, or to set a room properly for a special event. We must also possess the ability to interact with our team members, each of whom is responsible for a different set of tasks performed under pressure. It is critical that we understand and master the fact that our business must make a profit, and we work hard to blend effective budgets and cost controls with our service goals. We continuously provide extensive, thorough, effective, and ongoing training for ourselves and our staff so that our team is knowledgeable, trained, and empowered to act in the best interest of the guest and, ultimately, our operation. Our knowledge of the legalities of operating a business must be extensive so that our operations and our staff are protected. We are competitive because our market is changing and challenging, and we continually strive to position our businesses to be competitive. We must be strong because the physical demands of the business can be demanding, and we must be self-aware, for doing a challenging job well means that we are able to take care of ourselves and our lives outside the hotel. We lead by example to inspire our teammates to do the very best job they can, whatever the circumstances. Terrific service requires terrific people who possess the ability to integrate these characteristics into every workday.

What type of people are drawn to this business? People who love a challenge. People who enjoy other people. People who love their work and take pride in their ability to create a beautiful banquet, a perfect soup, or a well-designed training program. People with a work ethic, honesty, and integrity that make them an example to others. People who love to learn. People who enjoy the fact that every day is different and brings different challenges. Perhaps someone like you!

Bars

Hotel bars allow guests to relax while sipping a cocktail after a hectic day. This opportunity to socialize for business or pleasure is advantageous for both guests and the hotel. Because the profit percentage on all beverages is higher than it is on food items, bars are an important revenue source for the food and beverage departments. The cycle of beverages from ordering, receiving, storing, issuing, bar stocking, serving, and guest billing is complex, but, unlike restaurant meals, a beverage can be held over if not sold. An example of a world-famous hotel bar is the King Cole Bar in the St. Regis Hotel in New York City. This bar has been a favored New York "watering hole" of the rich and famous for many years. The talking point of the bar is a painted mural of Old King Cole, the nursery rhyme character.

Bars are run by bar managers. The responsibilities of a bar manager include the following:

- Supervising the ordering process and storage of wines
- Preparing a wine list
- Overseeing the staff
- Maintaining cost control
- Assisting guests with their wine selection
- Proper service of wine
- Knowledge of beers and liquors and their service

Bar efficiency is measured by the **pour/cost percentage**. Pour cost is obtained by dividing the cost of depleted inventory by sales over a period of time. Food and beverage directors expect a pour cost of between 16 and 24 percent. Generally, operations with lower pour costs have more sophisticated control systems and a higher-volume catering operation. An example of this is an automatic system that dispenses the exact amount of beverage requested via a pouring gun, which is fed by a tube from a beverage store. These systems are expensive, but they save money for volume operations by being less prone to pilferage, overpouring, or other tricks of the trade. Their greatest savings comes in the form of reduced labor costs; fewer bartenders are needed to make the same amount of drinks. However, the barperson may still hand pour premium brands for show.

Hotel bars are susceptible to the same problems as other bars. The director of food and beverage must set strict policy and procedure guidelines and see to it that they are followed. In today's litigious society, the onus is on the operator to install and ensure **responsible alcoholic beverage service**, and all beverage service staff should receive training in this important area because it might limit the bar's liability. (The National Restaurant Association offers Serve Safe alcohol.) If a guest becomes intoxicated and is still served alcohol or a minor is served alcohol and is involved in an accident involving someone else, then the server of the beverage, the barperson, and the manager may be liable for the injuries sustained by the person who was harmed, the third party.

Another risk bars encounter is **pilferage**. Employees have been known to steal or tamper with liquor. They could, for example, dilute drinks with water or colored liquids, sell the additional liquor, and pocket the money. There are several other ways to defraud a bar. One of the better known ways is to overcharge guests for beverages. Another is to underpour, which gives guests less for their money. Some bartenders overpour measures to receive larger tips. The best way to prevent these occurrences is to have a good control system, which should include **shoppers**—people who are paid to use the bar like regular guests, except they are closely watching the operation.

In a large hotel there are several kinds of bars:

Lobby bar. This convenient meeting place was popularized when Conrad Hilton wanted to generate revenue out of his vast hotel lobby. Lobby bars, when well managed, are a good source of income.

Restaurant bar. Traditionally, this bar is away from the hubbub of the lobby and offers a holding area for the hotel's signature restaurant.

A server carries Singapore Slings in the Long Bar at Raffles Hotel Singapore.

Service bar. In some of the very large hotels, restaurants and room service have a separate backstage bar. Otherwise, both the restaurant and room service are serviced by one of the regular beverage outlets, such as the restaurant bar.

Catering and banquet bar. This bar is used specifically to service all the catering and banquet needs of the hotel. These bars can stretch any operator to the limit. Frequently, several cash bars must be set up at a variety of locations; if cash wines are involved with dinner, it becomes a race to get the wine to the guest before the meal, preferably before the appetizer. Because of the difficulties involved in servicing a large number of guests, most hotels encourage inclusive wine and beverage functions, in which the guests pay a little more for tickets that include a predetermined amount of beverage service. Banquet bars require careful inventory control. The bottles should be checked immediately after the function, and, if the bar is very busy, the bar manager should pull the money just before the bar closes. The breakdown of function bars should be done on the spot if possible to help prevent pilferage.

The banquet bar needs to stock not only large quantities of the popular wines, spirits, and beers, but also a selection of premium spirits and after-dinner liqueurs. These are used in the ballroom and private dining rooms, in particular.

Pool bars. Pool bars are popular at resort hotels where guests can enjoy a variety of exotic cocktails poolside. Resort hotels that cater to conventions often put on theme parties one night of the convention to allow delegates to kick back. Popular themes that are catered around the pool might be a Hawaiian luau, a Caribbean reggae night, a Mexican fiesta, or Country and Western events. Left to the imagination, one could conceive of a number of theme events.

Minibars. Minibars or honor bars are small, refrigerated bars in guest rooms. They offer the convenience of having beverages available at all times. For security, they have a separate key, which may be either included in the room key envelope at check-in or withheld, according to the guest's preference. Minibars are typically checked and replenished on a daily basis. Charges for items used are automatically added to the guest folio.

Night clubs. Some hotels offer guests evening entertainment and dancing. Whether formal or informal, these food and beverage outlets offer a full beverage service. Live entertainment is very expensive. Many hotels are switching to operations with a DJ or where the bar itself is the entertainment (e.g., sports bar). Directors of food and beverage are now negotiating more with live bands, offering them a base pay (below union scale) and a percentage of a cover charge.

Sports bars. Sports bars have become popular in hotels. Almost everyone identifies with a sporting theme, which makes for a relaxed atmosphere that complements contemporary lifestyles. Many sports bars have a variety of games such as pool, football, bar basketball, and so on, which, together with satellite-televised sporting events, contribute to the atmosphere.

Casino bars. Casino bars and beverage service are there to keep people gambling by offering low-cost or free drinks. Some have lavish entertainment and light food offerings, which entice guests to enjoy the gaming experience, even when sustaining heavy losses.

Different types of bars produce revenue according to their location in the hotel and the kind of hotel in which they are located. Nightclubs, sports bars, and the banqueting department see bulk consumption of alcoholic beverages, and restaurant bars usually see more alcohol consumption than minibars and lounge bars.

▶ Check Your Knowledge

1. What departments does the food and beverage director oversee?

2. What are the responsibilities of a food and beverage director on a day-to-day basis?

3. Explain how the pour/cost percentage is used in a bar to measure efficiency.

Stewarding Department

The **chief steward** is responsible to the director of food and beverage for the following functions:

- Cleanliness of the back of the house (all the areas of the backstage that hotel guests do not see)
- Maintaining clean glassware, china, and cutlery for the food and beverage outlets
- Maintaining strict inventory control and monthly stock check
- Maintenance of dishwashing machines

- Inventory of chemical stock
- Sanitation of kitchen, banquet aisles, storerooms, walk-ins/freezers, and all equipment
- Pest control and coordination with exterminating company
- Forecasting labor and cleaning supplies

A chief steward checking the inventory.

In some hotels, the steward's department is responsible for keeping the kitchen(s) clean. This is generally done at night to prevent disruption of the food production operation. A more limited cleaning is done in the afternoon between the lunch and dinner services. The chief steward's job can be an enormous and thankless task. In hotels, this involves cleaning up after several hundred people three times a day. Just trying to keep track of everything can be a headache. Some hotels have different patterns of glasses, china, and cutlery for each outlet. The casual dining room frequently has an informal theme, catering and banqueting a more formal one, and the signature restaurant, very formal place settings. It is difficult to ensure that all the pieces are returned to the correct places. It is also difficult to prevent both guests and employees from taking souvenirs. Strict inventory control and constant vigilance help keep pilferage to a minimum.

TECHNOLOGY SPOTLIGHT

Cihan Cobanoglu, Ph.D., Dean, School of Hotel and Restaurant Management, University of South Florida, Sarasota-Manatee

Full-service hotels have several food and beverage operations. These may include breakfast, lunch, and dinner restaurants; lobby, pool, fitness club, spa, and snack bars; a night club and discothèque; and banquet/event rooms. In addition, hotels may have outlets such as gift shop. All of these transactions are managed by point-of-sale (POS) systems. A POS system can enhance decision-making, operational control, guest services, and revenues. A POS system is a network of cashier and server terminals that typically handles food and beverage orders, transmission of orders to the kitchen and bar, guest-check settlement, timekeeping, and interactive charge posting to guest folios. POS information can also be imported to accounting and food-cost/inventory software packages. A variety of reports can be generated, including open check (list of outstanding checks), cashier, voids/comps, sales analysis, menu mix, server sales summary, tip, labor cost, and so forth. Sophisticated POS systems can generate as many as 200 management reports. The advantages of using a POS system in a food and beverage operations include the following:

1. **Elimination of arithmetic errors:** A POS system may eliminate manual arithmetic calculations, therefore increasing guest satisfaction and tips. A study concluded that restaurants using handwritten checks have lower tipping and a substantial loss of potential revenue.

(continued)

2. **Improved guest check control:** In an industry where the failure rate among restaurants is about 60% within the first three years, controlling costs and revenue is critical. A POS system allows for all transactions to be recorded, allowing less room for fraud. Failure to audit missing checks and to reconcile guest check sales with cash register readings often results in a lower sales volume and higher cost ratios. With a POS system, a server must place the order through a server terminal for it to be printed in the kitchen or bar. This ensures the recording of all sales and provides line cooks with legible orders. It also electronically tracks open checks, settled checks, voids, comps, discounts, and sales for each server, as well as employee meals.

3. **Increased average guest check:** Since orders are transmitted to the kitchen printer, travel time to the kitchen is reduced. This allows more time for suggestive selling and servicing guests. Also, a POS system provides a detailed summary for each server, listing average guest check, items sold, and total sales. This information can be used for job evaluations, motivational programs (for example, wine contest), and assessing merchandising skills (for example, average guest check and item sales) and server efficiency (for example, sales per hour).

4. **Faster reaction to trends:** A POS system can provide a wealth of information on a real-time basis. Most POS systems can easily track sales and cost information by time period (for example, hourly, daily, weekly), employee, meal period, register, outlet, table, and menu item. This allows a restaurant operator to quickly spot and react to problematic areas affecting profitability, such as a declining average guest check during lunch, excessive labor hours in the kitchen, a changing menu mix, or sluggish liquor sales.

5. **Reduced labor costs and greater operational efficiency:** An efficient POS system should be able to increase operational efficiency, therefore allowing staff members to have higher levels of productivity. In the long term, this may result in reduced labor costs.

In addition to the POS system, some of the applications for a restaurant include table management systems, home delivery, frequent-dining and gift card programs, inventory control systems, and menu management systems.

Catering Department

Throughout the world's cultural and social evolution, numerous references have been made to the breaking of bread together. Feasts or banquets are one way to show one's hospitality. Frequently, hosts attempted to outdo one another with the extravagance of their feasts. Today, occasions for celebrations, banquets, and catering include the following:

- State banquets, when countries' leaders honor visiting royalty and heads of state
- National days
- Embassy receptions and banquets
- Business and association conventions and banquets
- Gala charity balls
- Company dinner dances
- Weddings

The term *catering* has a broader scope than does *banquet*. **Banquet** refers to groups of people who eat together at one time and in one place. **Catering** includes a variety of occasions when people may eat at varying times. However, the terms are often used interchangeably.

For example, catering departments in large, city-center hotels may service the following events in just one day:

- A Fortune 500 company's annual shareholders' meeting
- An international loan-signing ceremony
- A fashion show
- A convention
- Several sales and board meetings
- Private luncheons and dinner parties
- A wedding or two

Naturally each of these requires different and special treatment. Hotels in smaller cities may cater the local chamber of commerce meeting, a high school prom, a local company party, a regional sales meeting, a professional workshop, and a small exhibition.

Catering may be subdivided into on-premise and off-premise. In off-premise catering, the event is catered away from the hotel. The food may be prepared either in the hotel or at the event. The organization chart in Figure 2 shows how the catering department is organized. The dotted lines show cooperative reporting relationships, and continuous lines show a direct reporting relationship. For example, the banquet chef reports directly to the executive chef, but must cooperate with the director of catering and the catering service manager.

The **director of catering** (**DOC**) is responsible to the food and beverage director for selling and servicing, catering, banquets, meetings, and exhibitions in a way that exceeds guests' expectations and produces reasonable profit. The director of catering has a close working relationship with the rooms division manager because the catering department often brings conventions, which require rooms, to the hotel. There is also a close working relationship with the executive chef. The chef plans the banqueting menus, but the catering manager must ensure that they are suitable for the clientele and practical from a service point of view. Sometimes they work together in developing a selection of menus that will meet all the requirements, including cost and price.

The director of catering must be able to do the following:

1. Sell conventions, banquets, and functions.
2. Lead a team of employees.
3. Together with input from team members, make up departmental goals and objectives.
4. Set individual and department sales and cost budgets.

A caterer oversees an event.

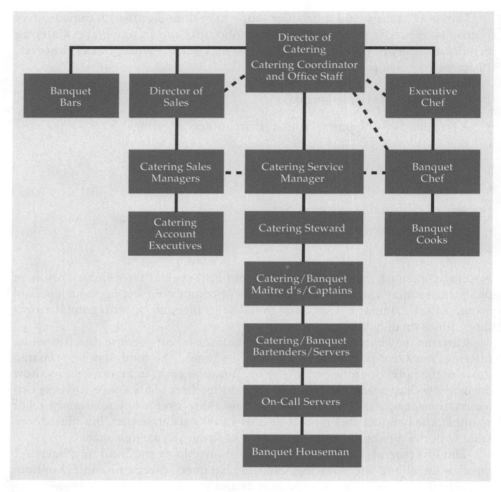

Figure 2 • Organization of the Catering Department.

5. Set service standards.
6. Ensure that the catering department is properly maintained.
7. Be extremely creative and knowledgeable about food, wine, and service.
8. Be very well versed in the likes, dislikes, and dietary restrictions of various ethnic groups, especially Jewish, Middle Eastern, and European.

Position Profile

The director of catering is required to have a variety of skills and abilities, including the following:

- A thorough knowledge of food and beverage management, including food preparation and service
- Ability to sell conventions, functions, and banquets
- Ability to produce a profit
- Ability to develop individual and department sales and cost budgets

Leadership

- Lead a team of employees.
- Set departmental mission, goals, and objectives.
- Train the department members in all facets of operations.
- Set service standards.
- Ensure that the catering department is properly maintained.

The catering department is extremely complex and demanding; the tempo is fast and the challenge to be innovative is always present. The director of catering in a large city hotel should, over the years, build up a client list and an intimate knowledge of the trade shows, exhibitions, various companies, groups, associations, and social, military, education, religious, and fraternal market (SMERF) organizations. This knowledge and these contacts are essential to the director of catering's success, as is the selection of the team members.

The main sales function of the department is conducted by the director of catering (DOC) and catering sales managers (CSMs). Their jobs are to optimize guest satisfaction and revenue by selling the most lucrative functions and exceeding guests' food and beverage and service expectations.

The DOC and catering sales managers obtain business leads from a variety of sources, including the following:

Hotel's director of sales. He or she is a good source of event bookings because he or she is selling rooms, and catering is often required by meetings and conventions.

General managers. These are good sources of leads because they are very involved in the community.

Corporate office sales department. If, for example, a convention were held on the East Coast one year at a Marriott hotel, and by tradition the association goes to the West Coast the following year, the Marriott hotel in the chosen city can contact the client or meeting planner. Some organizations have a selection of cities and hotels bid for major conventions. This ensures a competitive rate quote for accommodations and services.

Convention and visitors bureau. Here is another good source of leads because its main purpose is to seek out potential groups and organizations to visit that city. To be fair to all the hotels, they publish a list of clients and brief details of their requirements, which the hotel catering sales department may follow up on.

Reading the event board of competitive hotels. The event board is generally located in the lobby of the hotel and is frequently read by the competition. The CSM then calls the organizer of the event to solicit the business the next time.

Rollovers. Some organizations, especially local ones, prefer to stay in the same location. If this represents good business for the hotel, then the DOC and GM try to persuade the decision makers to use the same hotel again.

Cold calls. During periods of relative quiet, CSMs call potential clients to inquire if they are planning any events in the next few months. The point is to entice the client to view the hotel and the catering facilities. It is amazing how much information is freely given over the telephone.

The most frequent catering events in hotels are the following:

- Meetings
- Conventions
- Dinners
- Luncheons
- Weddings

For meetings, a variety of room setups are available, depending on a client's needs. The most frequently selected meeting room setups are as follows:

Theater style. Rows of chairs are placed with a center group of chairs and two aisles. Figure 3 shows a **theater-style room seating** setup with equipment centered on an audiovisual platform. Sometimes multimedia presentations, requiring more space for reverse-image projections, reduce the room's seating capacity.

Classroom style. As the name suggests, tables, usually slim 18-inch ones, are used because meeting participants need space to take notes. **Classroom-style seating** usually takes about three times as much space as theater style and takes more time and labor to set up and break down. Figure 4 shows a classroom-style setup.

Horseshoe style. **Horseshoe-style room seating** (Figure 5) is frequently used when interaction is sought among the delegates, such as training sessions and workshops. The presenter or trainer stands at the open end of the horseshoe with a black or white board, flip chart, overhead projector, and video monitor and projector.

Dinner style. Dinners are generally catered at round tables of eight or ten persons for large parties and on boardroom-style tables for smaller numbers. Of course, there are variations of the **dinner-style room seating** setup (see Figure 6).

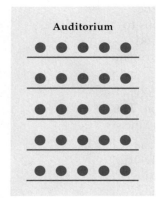

Figure 3 • Theater-Style Seating.

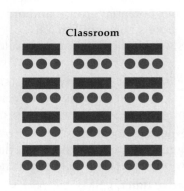

Figure 4 • Classroom-Style Seating.

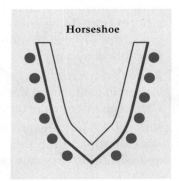

Figure 5 • Horseshoe-Style Seating.

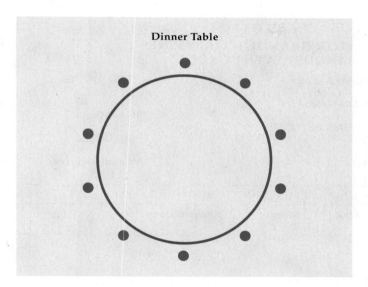

Figure 6 • Dinner-Style Seating.

Catering Event Order

A **catering event order (CEO)**, which may also be called a **banquet event order (BEO)**, is prepared/completed for each function to inform not only the client but also the hotel personnel about essential information (what needs to happen and when) to ensure a successful event.

The CEO is prepared based on correspondence with the client and notes taken during the property visits. Figure 7 shows a CEO and lists the room's layout and decor, times of arrival, if there are any VIPs and what special attention is required for them, bar times, types of beverages and service, cash or credit bar, time of meal service, the menu, wines, and service details. The catering manager or director confirms the details with the client. Usually, two copies are sent, one for the client to sign and return and one for the client to keep.

An accompanying letter thanks the client for selecting the hotel and explains the importance of the function to the hotel. The letter also mentions the guaranteed-number policy. This is the number of guests the hotel will prepare to serve and will charge accordingly. The guaranteed number is given about seven days prior to the event. This safeguards the hotel from preparing for 350 people and having only 200 show up. The client, naturally, does not want to pay for an extra 150 people—hence, the importance of a close working relationship with the client. Contracts for larger functions call for the client to notify the hotel of any changes to the anticipated number of guests in increments of ten or twenty.

Experienced catering directors ensure that there will be no surprises for either the function organizer or the hotel. This is done by calling to check on how the function planning is going. One mistake catering directors sometimes make is accepting a final guest count without inquiring as to how that figure was determined. This emphasizes the fact that the catering director should

SHERATON GRANDE TORREY PINES
BANQUET EVENT ORDER

POST AS:	WELCOME BREAKFAST	CHERI WALTER
EVENT NAME:	MEETING	
GROUP:	CROCKER AND ASSOCIATES	
ADDRESS:	41 MAIN ST	BILLING:
	BOWLING GREEN, OHIO 43218	
PHONE:	(619) 635-4627	DIRECT BILL
FAX:	(619) 635-4528	
GROUP CONTACT:	Dr. Ken Crocker	Amount Received:
ON-SITE-CONTACT:	same	

DAY	DATE	TIME	FUNCTION	ROOM	EXP	GTE	SET	RENT
Fri	January 25, 2013	7:30 AM – 12:00 PM	Meeting	Palm Garden	50			250.00

BAR SET UP:

N/A

WINE:

FLORAL:

MENU:

MUSIC:

7:30 AM CONTINENTAL BREAKFAST

Freshly Squeezed Orange Juice, Grapefruit Juice, and
  Tomato Juice
Assortment of Bagels, Muffins, and Mini Brioche
Cream Cheese, Butter, and Preserves
Display of Sliced Seasonal Fruits
Individual Fruit Yogurt
Coffee, Tea, and Decaffeinated Coffee

PRICE:_____

AUDIO VISUAL:
–OVERHEAD PROJECTOR/SCREEN
–FLIPCHART/MARKERS
–VCR/MONITORS

PARKING:

HOSTING PARKING, PLEASE PROVIDE VOUCHERS

11:00 AM BREAK

Refresh Beverages as needed

LINEN:
HOUSE

SETUP:
–CLASSROOM-STYLE SEATING
–HEAD TABLE FOR 2 PEOPLE
–APPROPRIATE COFFEE BREAK SETUP
–(1) 6' TABLE FOR REGISTRATION AT ENTRANCE
    WITH 2 CHAIRS, 1 WASTEBASKET

All food and beverage prices are subject to an 18% service charge and 7% state tax. Guarantee figures, cancellations, changes must be given 72 hours prior or the number of guests expected will be considered the guarantee. To confirm the above arrangements, this contract must be signed and returned.

ENGAGOR SIGNATURE _____   DATE _____

BEO # 003069

Figure 7 • Catering Event Order.

(Courtesy of Sheraton Grande Torrey Pines.)

be a consultant to the client. Depending on the function, the conversion from invitations to guests is about 50 percent. Some hotels have a policy of preparing for about 3 to 5 percent more than the anticipated or guaranteed number. Fortunately, most events have a prior history. The organization may have been at a similar hotel in the same city or across the country. In either case, the catering director or manager will be able to receive helpful information from the catering director of the hotel where the organization's function was held previously.

The director of catering holds a daily or weekly meeting with key individuals who will be responsible for upcoming events. Those in attendance should be the following:

Director of catering

Executive chef and/or banquet chef

Beverage manager or catering bar manager

Catering managers

Catering coordinator

Director of purchasing

Chief steward

Audiovisual representative

The purpose of this meeting is to avoid any problems and to be sure that all key staff know and understand the details of the event and any special needs of the client.

Catering Coordinator

The **catering coordinator** has an exacting job in managing the office and controlling the "bible," or function diary, now on computer. He or she must see that the contracts are correctly prepared and must check on numerous last-minute details, such as whether flowers and menu cards have arrived.

Web-enabled technology tools such as Newmarket International's Delphi System (which is used at more than 4,000 properties) is a leader in delivering group, sales, catering, and banquet software for global travel and entertainment groups. One of the latest hotels to adopt the Delphi System is the Wynn Las Vegas, which installed the sales and catering systems Delphi Diagrams, MeetingBroker, and e-Proposal. The Delphi System can keep inventory current in real time because of its ability to interface with the property management system. The suite of Delphi products allows function space to be clearly and concisely managed, which increases guest satisfaction and profitability.

An elegant banquet room at a hotel.

A DAY IN THE LIFE OF JAMES McMANEMON

Food and Beverage Manager, Hyatt Regency

Friday—Start of a Busy Weekend

6:30 A.M.–8:00 A.M. (opening manager) When I arrive to work in the morning, the first thing I do is walk through the restaurant to ensure prompt opening. I make sure tables are properly set, the carpet is clean, lighting is set correctly, and that nothing is missing or broken. I check for all the little things that may seem trivial to the untrained eye but that don't go overlooked by our more observant guests. I call this "aesthetic detailing."

Next, I walk through the breakfast buffet to make sure it's fully stocked and meets corporate standards. We offer an array of breakfast items, including scrambled eggs, bacon and sausage, herbed potatoes, pancakes, homemade granola, steel cut oatmeal, fresh sliced fruit, an assortment of delicious cheeses, freshly baked pastries, and smoked salmon with all the fixings to load up your favorite bagel. The buffet comes with juice, coffee, or tea to drink. On average, approximately 60% of our breakfast guests choose the buffet every morning, many of whom have opted to include the buffet package in their daily room rate. This is a popular option for families on vacation, large groups with an appetite, and the typical business traveler who needs something quick in the morning.

Afterwards, I make my way over to the coffee bar to check that the barista is set up and ready to go for the coffee rush. We proudly brew Starbucks coffee, and offer all of their specialty coffees. Espresso, latte, Americano, macchiato—you name it and we'll make it. I will spend the next fifteen minutes talking to guests and conducting quality checks at each table to ensure that all of our guests' needs are being fulfilled and that they are enjoying their dining experience.

8:00 A.M.–8:30 A.M. Morning meeting for Operations Managers. At this time, the managers of each operation in the hotel meet in the General Manager's office to recap the previous day's business, as well as to discuss activity in each department for the current day. This meeting will include the Food and Beverage Manager, Banquets Manager, Housekeeping Manager, Front Office Manager, Sales and Catering Manager, Executive Chef, and General Manager.

I will routinely discuss amenities that need to be sent up to guests' rooms that day, groups in-house that we will see in one of the food and beverage outlets, reservations and parties we are expecting in the restaurant, and anything else that is relevant to the day's business. It just so happens that today the restaurant will be hosting a four-course dinner for thirty people, carefully crafted and paired with unique wines by our executive chef. I will receive the list of each course and will be in charge of creating a menu template and printing special menus for the event.

8:30 A.M.–11:00 A.M. Balance managing the breakfast shift with preparation paperwork. Besides creating the menu for the four-course dinner this evening, I must update each employee's clocks in and out from the previous day for payroll at the end of the week, purchase inventory that we will need for one of the outlets, and check and respond to any e-mails from fellow employees, potential clients, and so on.

11:00 A.M.–12:00 P.M.. Once breakfast ends at 11 A.M., I will conduct a post-shift with my employees (servers, room service attendants, barista), in which I discuss how I felt the breakfast shift went that morning, along with anything else they would need to know for the upcoming lunch shift that day. I will make sure that side-work is completed in a timely manner and that room service has walked all of the floors in the hotel and picked up trays from breakfast. I will also meet with the incoming bartenders who are about to start their shift for the day. I am in charge of managing a lobby bar, a poolside bar, and a boathouse bar.

12:00 P.M.–2:00 P.M. Manage the lunch shift. This will entail expediting food on the line, once again talking with guests and conducting quality checks, assisting bartenders when one of the bars gets busy, and checking in on each of the various outlets from time to time.

2:00 P.M.–4:00 P.M. Complete any unfinished paperwork, and put the finishing touches on the four-course menu we will host this evening. Here is an idea of what we will be serving tonight:

First course: Lemon verbena smoked scallops with a cantaloupe caviar, micro mint leaves, and black lava sea salt, paired with the Four Vines "Naked" Chardonnay from Santa Barbara, California. This wine is "naked" in the sense that it's aged in stainless steel barrels and has never seen a splinter of oak. This is a very crisp wine with flavors of fresh tree fruits and hints of citrus.

Second course: Watermelon steak crusted with a warm and smoky spice blend, wild arugula, Humboldt fog cheese, and aged balsamic, paired with the Montes "Cherub" Rose of Syrah from Colchagua Valley, Chile. This is a cool and refreshing dry blush wine with a peppery aftertaste.

Third course: Espresso braised short rib with forest mushroom polenta and burnt leek chocolate pesto, paired with the Cinnabar "Mercury Rising" Meritage from Paso Robles, California. This is a bold and rounded red wine that combines Cabernet Sauvignon, Cabernet Franc, Merlot, and Petit Verdot.

Fourth course: Cinnamon plum tea panna cotta with amarena cherries, paired with the Bonterra Muscat from Lake County, California. This wine serves as the perfect accompaniment to the thick panna cotta and rich, syrupy cherries.

After the menu has been created and printed, I will show the servers how the restaurant should be set for this event. There should be a different glass for each wine, forks and knives for each course, and a spoon for dessert. The table decorum should be elegant but simple. We don't want to overwhelm our guests with gaudy decorations; the food and wine will speak for itself. This is how we make an impression.

4:00 P.M.–10:00 P.M. (closing manager) Manage the dinner rush. You must be the director of your employees. In addition to the party of thirty, there will be plenty of other guests in the restaurant for dinner this evening who will expect to receive a wonderful dining experience. We are likely to see some heavy action in the lobby bar, boathouse bar, and room service departments as well. The manager must balance the activity in each of these outlets to ensure a smooth and successful operation. This is like playing a game of chess. You know who all your players are (bartenders, servers, bussers, greeter, room service attendants), and you must use them as necessary to maintain a steady flow of business in order to provide quality service. This is the challenge in managing multiple food and beverage outlets, but it is also where the excitement lies.

10:00 P.M.–12:00 A.M. Once the dinner rush is over and the bars have died down, it's time to walk through each of the outlets and make sure they are properly set for the following morning, then finish the closing paperwork and call it a day. Although one manager does not typically stick around from sunrise until midnight, it has been known to happen on occasion. This is an industry that requires sacrifice of your time, and sometimes your patience. Describing a day in the life of a food and beverage manager is somewhat challenging, because each day is so different . . . and that's what I love about it.

Catering Services Manager

The **catering services manager** (CSM) has the enormous responsibility of delivering higher-than-expected service levels to guests. The CSM is in charge of the function from the time the client is introduced to the CSM by the director of catering or catering manager. This job is very demanding because several functions always occur simultaneously. Timing and logistics are crucial to the success of the operation. Frequently, there are only a few minutes between the end of a day meeting and the beginning of the reception for a dinner dance.

The CSM must be liked and respected by guests and at the same time be a superb organizer and supervisor. This calls for a person of outstanding character and leadership—management skills that are essential for success. The CSM has several important duties and responsibilities, including the following:

- Directing the service of all functions
- Supervising the catering housepersons in setting up the room
- Scheduling the banquet captains and approving the staffing levels for all events
- Cooperating with the banquet chef to check menus and service arrangements
- Checking that the client is satisfied with the room setup, food, beverages, and service
- Checking last-minute details
- Making out client bills immediately after the function
- Adhering to all hotel policies and procedures that pertain to the catering department, including responsible alcoholic beverage service and adherence to fire code regulations
- Calculating and distributing the gratuity and service charges for the service personnel
- Coordinating the special requirements with the DOC and catering coordinator

▶ Check Your Knowledge

1. What is the difference between banquets and catering?
2. What does SMERF stand for?
3. Where do the director of catering and the catering sales manager obtain their information?
4. What are the various styles used when setting up a meeting room? Give examples of when each style might be used.

Room Service/In-Room Dining

The term **room service** has for some time referred to all service to hotel guest rooms. Recently, some hotels have changed the name of room service to *in-room dining* to present the service as more upscale. The intention is to bring the dining experience to the room with quality food and beverage service.

A survey of members of the American Hotel & Lodging Association showed that 56 percent of all properties offer room service and that 75 percent of airport properties provide room service. Generally, the larger the hotel and the higher the room rate, the more likely it is that a hotel will offer room service.

Economy and several midpriced hotels avoid the costs of operating room service by having vending machines on each floor and food items such as pizza or Chinese food delivered by local restaurants. Conversely, some hotels prepare menus and lower price structures that do not identify the hotel as the provider of the food. As a result, the guests may have the impression that they are ordering from an "outside" operation when they are in fact ordering from room service.

The level of service and menu prices will vary from hotel to hotel. The Hilton at Torrey Pines, California, has butler service for all guest rooms without additional charge.

A few years ago, room service was thought of as a necessary evil, something that guests expected, but which did not produce profit for the hotel. Financial pressures have forced food and beverage directors to have this department also contribute to the bottom line. The room service manager has a difficult challenge running this department, which is generally in operation between sixteen and twenty-four hours a day. Tremendous effectiveness is required to make this department profitable. Nevertheless, it can be done. Some of the challenges in operating room service are as follows:

Delivering orders on time—this is especially important for breakfast, which is by far the most popular room service meal

Making room service a profitable food and beverage department

Avoiding complaints of excessive charges for room service orders

There are many other challenges in room service operation. One is forecasting demand. Room service managers analyze the front-desk forecast, which gives details of the house count and guest mix—convention, group, and others for the next two weeks. The food and beverage forecast will indicate the number of covers expected for breakfast, lunch, and dinner. The convention résumés will show where the convention delegates

Customer service at a South Seas tropical resort.

123

are having their various meals. For example, the number of in-house delegates attending a convention breakfast can substantially reduce the number of room service breakfast orders.

Experience enables the manager to check if a large number of guests are from different time zones, such as the West or East Coasts or overseas. These guests have a tendency to get up either much earlier or much later than the average guest. This could throw room service demands off balance. Demand also fluctuates between weekdays and weekends; for example, city hotels may cater to business travelers, who tend to require service at about the same time. However, on weekends, city hotels may attract families, who will order room service at various times.

To avoid problems with late delivery of orders, a growing number of hotels have dedicated elevators to be used only by room service during peak periods. At the 565-room Stouffer Riviera Chicago, director of food and beverage Bill Webb has a solution: Rapid action teams (RAT) are designated food and beverage managers and assistants who can be called on when room service orders are heavy.

Westin Hotels recently introduced Service Express, an innovation that allows a customer to address all needs (room service, housekeeping, laundry, and other services) with a single call. In addition, new properties are designed with the room service kitchen adjacent to the main kitchen so that a greater variety of items can be offered.

Meeting the challenge of speedy and accurate communication is imperative to a successful room service operation. This begins with timely scheduling and ends with happy guests. In between is a constant flow of information that is communicated by the guest, the order taker, the cook, and the server.

Another challenge is to have well-trained and competent employees in the room service department. From the tone of voice of the order taker and the courteous manner with which the order is taken to the panache of the server for the VIP dinners, training makes the difference between ordinary service and outstanding service. With training, which includes menu tasting with wine and suggestive selling, an order taker becomes a room service salesperson. This person is now able to suggest cocktails or wine to complement the entree and can entice the guest with tempting desserts. The outcome of this is to increase the average guest check. Training also helps the setup and service personnel hone their skills to enable them to become productive employees who are proud of their work.

Sustainable Food and Beverage Operations

Practicing sustainable food and beverage operations can and does lead to a better bottom line. When operators save water and electricity, recycle, and purchase local produce, they help lessen the footprint of the operation. Guests are increasingly aware of the importance of sustainable operations of a food and beverage facility. They are pleased to see the greening of food and beverage operations and the use of local natural products, which helps reduce the cost of transportation and adds local flavor.

Michelle Leroux, director of sales and marketing at the Delta Chelsea Hotel in Toronto, has noticed a shift in the booking inquiries: "It isn't so much that having a 'green' or 'sustainable' meeting package sells additional pieces of business—it is more along the line that certain groups will not book at your hotel if you can't demonstrate knowledge and experience with sustainable meetings."[3]

According to Brita Moosmann, a consultant,[4] the best way to start the process of making food and beverage more sustainable and profitable is to conduct a comprehensive audit or evaluation of your food and beverage operation in order to provide a baseline in terms of energy efficiency and carbon footprint; they should be part of an overriding strategy that will provide an in-depth analysis of the organization's sustainable position. This evaluation also should measure the impact of the various elements on the organization's stakeholders and have a total quality approach regarding customer satisfaction. It is also advisable to obtain feedback to understand what is important to the local community.

Trends in Lodging Food and Beverage Operations

- Hotels are using branded restaurants instead of operating their own restaurants.
- Hotels are opting not to offer food and beverage outlets. These are usually smaller to midsized properties that may have restaurants on the same lot nearby.
- Restaurants and beverage outlets are being made more casual.
- Restaurants are being developed or remodeled with a theme. For example, one major hotel chain has adopted a northern Italian theme in all its restaurants.
- Menus are being standardized for all hotel restaurants in a chain.
- Many hotels are converting one of the beverage outlets into a sports-themed bar.
- Technology is being used to enhance guest services and control costs in all areas of a hotel, including guest ordering and payment, food production, refrigeration, marketing, management control, and communication.
- More low-fat and low-carb items are being added to menus.

CASE STUDY

Ensuring Guest Satisfaction

The Sunnyvale Hotel is operated by a major hotel management corporation. To ensure guest satisfaction, 300 survey forms each containing sixty-five questions are mailed to guests each month. Usually, about seventy of the forms are returned. The hotel company categorizes the guest satisfaction scores obtained into colored zones, with green being the best, then clear and yellow, and red being the worst. Scores can be compared with those of equivalent hotels.

The most recent survey indicated a significant decline for the Sea Grill Restaurant, with scores in the red zone. Guests' concerns were in the following areas: hostess attentiveness, spread of service, and quality of food.

On investigation, the director of food and beverage also realized that the name of the restaurant, Sea Grill, was not appropriate for the type of restaurant being operated. When asked, some guests commented that "it's a bit odd to eat breakfast in a fish place."

Discussion Question

1. What would you do, as director of food and beverage, to get the guest satisfaction scores back into the clear or green zones?

CASE STUDY

Friday Evening at the Grand Hotel's Casual Restaurant

Karla Gomez is the supervisor at the Grand Hotel's casual restaurant. Karla's responsibilities include overseeing five servers and two bussers, seating guests, and taking reservations. One Friday evening, the restaurant was very busy—all twenty tables were occupied, there was a substantial wait list, and there were people on standby. The service bar was almost full of guests, and most of the seated guests in the dining area had finished their entrées or were just beginning their desserts. They were not leaving, however, in part because of cold, rainy weather outside. The guests did not seem to be in a rush to leave the restaurant, but several of the guests waiting for tables were complaining about the long wait.

Discussion Question

1. What can Karla do to solve the problem?

Summary

1. The food and beverage department division is led by the director of food and beverage, who is responsible for the efficient operation of kitchen, catering, restaurants, bars, and room service; in addition, the director has to keep up with trends and preplan for special events.

2. A hotel kitchen is the responsibility of the executive chef, who is in charge of the quality and quantity of food, organization of the kitchen and his or her sous chefs, administrative duties, and careful calculation of financial results.

3. A hotel usually has a formal and a casual restaurant, which are either directly connected to the hotel or operated separately.

4. Bars are an important revenue source for a hotel, but they must adhere to strict guidelines to be profitable. Commensurate with its size, a hotel might have several kinds of bars, such as a lobby bar, a restaurant bar, a minibar, or even a night club.

5. The chief steward has the often unrewarded job of cleaning the kitchen, cutlery, plates, glasses, and backstage of the hotel and is in charge of pest control and inventory.

6. Catering is subdivided into on-premise and off-premise occasions, which may include meetings, conventions, dinners, luncheons, and weddings. According to the occasion, the type of service and room setup may vary. Catering involves careful planning and the interaction and cooperation of many people.

7. Room service offers the convenience of dining in the room, with quality food and beverage service, at a price acceptable to both the guest and the hotel.

Key Words and Concepts

banquet
banquet event order (BEO)
brigade
capture rate
catering
catering coordinator
catering event order (CEO)
catering services manager (CSM)
chef tournant
chief steward
classroom-style seating
contribution margin
dinner-style room seating
director of catering (DOC)
director of food and beverage
executive chef

food cost percentage
food sales percentage
horseshoe-style room seating
kitchen manager
labor cost percentage
perpetual inventory
pilferage
pour/cost percentage
responsible alcoholic beverage service
restaurant manager
room service
shopper
sous chef
station chef
theater-style room seating

Review Questions

1. Briefly describe the challenges a food and beverage director faces on a daily basis.
2. List the measures used to determine the food and beverage department's profit and loss.

3. Explain the problems a hotel faces in making the following departments profitable: restaurants, bars, and room service.
4. Explain the importance of the catering department for a hotel and list the responsibilities of a catering sales manager.

Internet Exercises

1. Organization: **Foodservice**
   Web site: **www.foodservice.com**
   Summary: Foodservice.com is a web site that focuses on the foodservice industry. It has links to employment, industry resources, foodservice, technology innovations, and much more.
   (a) Click the "Forums and Chat" icon. Go to the "Chef and Cooks Corner," and look at some of the latest posts. Bring your favorite one to the table (discuss in class).
   (b) Look at the most current articles on the food safety forum. What are the major concerns being addressed?

2. Organization: **National Restaurant Association**
   Web site: **www.restaurant.org**
   Summary: The National Restaurant Association is an organization devoted to representing, educating, and promoting the restaurant/hospitality industry.
   (a) Look under the "Education & Networking" tab. What does it mean to be "FMP Certified" and what are the eligibility requirements?
   (b) What are some of the upcoming events and what do they have to offer?

Apply Your Knowledge

1. If a casual dining restaurant in a four-star hotel forecasts 100 covers, how many servers, bussers, hosts, and assistant managers would you schedule on that particular day? Calculate the labor cost of these associates for that day if the manager(s) work from 1:00 P.M. to 11:00 P.M., the server(s) work from 4:00 P.M. to 11:00 P.M., the busser(s) work from 4:30 P.M. to 11:30 P.M., and the host(s) works from 4:00 P.M. to 11:00 P.M. Use minimum wage of $5.75 for calculations. Use the rate of $12 per hour for the assistant manager(s) and $6.50 for hosts.

2. Kitchen labor costs are an important ratio used to determine the efficiency of the food and beverage department. The labor cost for a banquet meal is $126.45 and the revenue for the banquet is $505.80. What is the labor cost percentage?

Suggested Activities

1. Contact a bar manager in your area. Discuss with him or her how to monitor pilferage and overpouring. Ask what the expected and actual pouring cost percentages are and how the manager deals with any variances.

2. Visit a hotel restaurant in your area. Make a note of how busy the establishment is. Does it seem to be staffed with the appropriate number of employees? Are guests being served in a timely manner? Think about why this specific restaurant may be overly crowded or overly vacant. What could or should be done differently? What seems to be working well?

Endnotes

1. Carlson, *Ambition 2015*, www.carlson.com/our-company/ambition-2015.php (accessed January 17, 2011).
2. Ibid.
3. Brita Moosmann, *Sustainable F&B Operations Can Create Valuable Profit Partner* http://www.hotelnewsnow.com/Articles.aspx/2235/Sustainable-FB-operations-can-create-valuable-profit-partner (accessed March 9, 2011).
4. Ibid.

Beverages

Beverages

After reading and studying this text, you should be able to:

- List and describe the main grape varieties.
- Suggest appropriate pairings of wine with food.
- Identify the various types of beer.
- List the types of spirits and their main ingredients.
- Explain a restaurant's liability in terms of serving alcoholic beverages.

This text offers an overview of alcoholic and nonalcoholic beverages in the hospitality industry. Be sure that you realize the utmost importance of responsible beverage consumption and service. Arrange for a designated driver if you intend to have a drink. If you do drink alcoholic beverages, then stay with the same drink—don't mix them (two different types are grape and grain—that is, wine and spirits). That's when trouble really begins and hangovers are bad. Remember that moderation is the key to enjoying beverages, whether at a get-together with friends at a local restaurant or on a getaway for spring break. Examine the tragic alcohol-related auto and other accidents that too many people are involved in each year. Enjoy, but do not overindulge.

Serving beverages is traditional throughout the world. According to his or her culture, a person might welcome a visitor with coffee or tea—or bourbon. Beverages are generally categorized into two main groups: alcoholic and nonalcoholic. **Alcoholic beverages** *are further categorized as wines, beer, and spirits. Figure 1 shows these three categories.*

Wines

Wine is the fermented juice of freshly gathered ripe grapes. Wine may also be made from other sugar-containing fruits, such as blackberries, cherries, or elderberries. In this text, however, we will confine our discussion to grape wines. Wine may be classified first by color: red, white, or rose. Wines are further classified as light beverage wines, still wines, sparkling wines, fortified wines, and aromatic wines.

Light Beverage Wines

White, red, or rose table wines are "still" light beverage wines; such still table wines may come from a variety of growing regions around the world. In the United States, the premium wines are named after the grape variety, such

Wine	Beer	Spirits
Still	Top fermenting	Grapes/fruit
Natural	Lager	Grains
Fortified	Bottom fermenting	Cactus
Aromatic	Ale	Sugar cane/molasses
Sparkling	Stout	
	Lager	
	Pilsner	
	Porter	

Figure 1 • Alcoholic Beverages.

as chardonnay and cabernet sauvignon. This proved so successful that Europeans are now also naming their wines after the grape variety and their region of origin, such as Pouilly Fuisse and Chablis.

Sparkling Wines

Champagne, sparkling white wine, and sparkling rose wine are called the **sparkling wines**. Sparkling wines sparkle because they contain carbon dioxide. The carbon dioxide may be either naturally produced or mechanically infused into the wine. The best-known sparkling wine is champagne, which has become synonymous with celebrations and happiness.

Champagne became the drink of fashion in France and England in the seventeenth century. Originating in the Champagne region of France, the wine owed its unique sparkling quality to a second fermentation—originally unintentional—in the bottle itself. This process became known as *methode champenoise*.

The Benedictine monk Dom Perignon (1638–1715) was the cellar master for the Abbaye Hautvilliers and an exceptional wine connoisseur. He was the first to experiment with blending different wines to achieve the so-called *cuvee* (the basis of champagne production). He also revolutionized wine by retaining the resulting carbon dioxide in the bottles. Dom Perignon's methods were refined throughout the centuries and led to the modern method used in champagne production.

Champagne may, by law, only come from the Champagne region of France. Sparkling wines from other countries have *methode champenoise* written on their labels to designate that a similar method was used to make that particular sparkling wine.

Figure 2 explains how to handle and serve champagne.

Bottles of champagne. Remember not to point the cork at anyone when opening the bottle; point it at the ceiling. In fact, a napkin should be placed over the cork, which is then held there while the bottle is gently twisted open. Champagne is served chilled in fluted glasses, which help the bouquet and effervescence last longer.

▶ Check Your Knowledge

1. Why is champagne served in fluted glasses?

2. How are alcoholic beverages categorized?

3. Why should you avoid mixing grape (wine) and grain (spirits) drinks?

4. Where should you point the cork of a champagne bottle when opening it?

Champagne should be stored horizontally at a temperature between fifty and fifty-five degrees Fahrenheit. However, it should be served at a temperature between forty-three and forty-seven degrees Fahrenheit. This is best achieved by placing the bottle in an ice bucket.

When serving champagne, there are some recommended steps to take to achieve the best results, as listed below.

1. If the bottle is presented in a champagne cooler, it should be placed upright in the cooler, with fine ice tightly packed around the bottle.
2. The bottle should be wrapped in a cloth napkin. Remove the foil or metal capsule to a point just below the wire, which holds the cork securely.
3. Hold the bottle firmly in one hand at a forty-five degree angle. Unwind and remove the wiring. With a clean napkin, wipe the neck of the bottle and around the cork.
4. With the other hand, grasp the cork so that it will not fly out. Twist the bottle and ease the cork out.
5. When the cork is out, retain the bottle at an angle for about five seconds. The gas will rush out and carry with it some of the champagne if the bottle is held upright.
6. Champagne should be served in two motions: pour until the froth almost reaches the brim of the glass. Stop and wait for the foam to subside. Then finish filling the glass to about three-quarters full.

Figure 2 • Handling and Serving Champagne.

Fortified Wines

Sherries, ports, Madeira, and Marsala are **fortified wines**, meaning that they have had brandy or wine alcohol added to them. The brandy or wine alcohol imparts a unique taste and increases the alcohol content to about 20 percent. Most fortified wines are sweeter than regular wines. Each of the groups of fortified wines has several subgroups with myriad tastes and aromas.

Aromatic Wines

Aromatized wines are fortified and flavored with herbs, roots, flowers, and barks. These wines may be sweet or dry. Aromatic wines are also known as aperitifs, which generally are consumed before meals as digestive stimulants. Among the better-known brands of aperitif wines are Dubonnet Red (sweet), Dubonnet White (dry), vermouth red (sweet), vermouth white (dry), Byrrh (sweet), Lillet (sweet), Punt e Mes (dry), St. Raphael Red (sweet), and St. Raphael White (dry).

The History of Wine

Wine has been produced for centuries. The ancient Egyptians and Babylonians recorded using the fermentation process. The very first records about winemaking date back about 7,000 years. The Greeks received the vine from the Egyptians, and later the Romans contributed to the popularization of wine in Europe by planting vines in the territories they conquered.

The wine produced during these times was not the cabernet or chardonnay of today. The wines of yesteryear were drunk when they were young and likely to be highly acidic and crude. To help offset these deficiencies, people added different spices and honey,

Sherry can be dry (fino), medium, or sweet. Pictured here are bottles of dry sherry with a glass. The lighter the color, the drier the sherry.

which made the wine at least palatable. To this day, some Greek and German wines have flavoring added.

The making of good wine is dependent on the quality of the grape variety, type of soil, climate, preparation of vineyards, and method of winemaking. Thousands of grape varieties exist, thriving in a variety of soil and climatic conditions. Different plants thrive on clay, chalky, gravelly, or sandy soil. The most important winemaking grape variety is the *Vitis vinifera*, which yields cabernet sauvignon, gamay, pinot noir, pinot chardonnay, and riesling.

Making Wine

Wine is made in six steps: crushing, fermenting, racking, maturing, filtering, and bottling. Grapes are harvested in the autumn, after they have been scientifically tested for maturity, acidity, and sugar concentration. The freshly harvested grapes are taken to pressing houses, where the grapes are destemmed and crushed. The juice that is extracted from the grapes is called **must**.

The second step of the process is **fermentation** of the must, a natural phenomenon caused by yeasts on the skin of the grapes. Additional yeasts are added either environmentally or by formula. When exposed to air in the proper environment, the yeast multiplies. Yeast converts the sugar in the grapes to ethyl alcohol, until little or no sugar remains in the wine. The degree of sweetness or dryness in the wine can be controlled at the end of the fermentation process by adding alcohol, removing the yeast by filtration, or adding sulphur dioxide.

Red wine gains its color during the fermentation process from the coloring pigments of the red grape skins, which are put back into the must.

After fermentation has ceased, the wine is transferred to racking containers, where it settles before being poured into oak barrels or large stainless steel containers for the maturing process. Some of the better wines are aged in oak barrels, from which they acquire additional flavor and character during the barrel aging. Throughout the aging process, red wine extracts tannin from the wood, which gives longevity to the wine. Some white wine and most red wine are barrel-aged for periods ranging from months to more than two years. White wines that are kept in stainless steel containers are crisp, with a youthful flavor; they are bottled after a few months for immediate consumption.

After maturing, the wine is filtered to help stabilize it and remove any solid particles still in the wine. This process is called **fining**. The wine is then **clarified** by adding either egg white or bentonite, which sinks to the bottom of the vat. The wine then is bottled.

Port wines are generally red, fortified, and sweet. Vintage port is the most prized by port lovers. Port is typically served with cheese and biscuits at the end of a meal.

White grapes make white wines; the main white grapes are chardonnay, sauvignon blanc, riesling, pinot blanc, and gewürztraminer.

Red grapes make red wine; the main red grapes are cabernet sauvignon, merlot, merlot/cabernet sauvignon, pinot noir, and Shiraz.

Sniffing the bouquet of the wine.

Fine **vintage** wines are best drunk at their peak, which may be a few years—or decades—away. Red wines generally take a few more years to reach their peak than do white wines. In Europe, where the climate is more variable, the good years are rated as vintage. The judgment of experts determines the relative merits of each wine-growing district and awards merit points on a scale of 1 to 10.

Matching Wine with Food

The combination of food and wine is one of life's great pleasures. We eat every day, so a gourmet will seek out not only exotic foods and vintage wines, but also simple food that is well prepared and accompanied by an unpretentious, yet quality, wine.

Over the years, traditions have developed a how-to approach to the marrying of wines and food. Generally, the following traditions apply:

- White wine is best served with white meat (chicken, pork, or veal), shellfish, and fish.
- Red wine is best served with red meat (beef, lamb, duck, or game).
- The heavier the food, the heavier and more robust the wine should be.
- Champagne can be served throughout the meal.
- Port and red wine go well with cheese.
- Dessert wines best complement desserts and fresh fruits that are not highly acidic.
- When a dish is cooked with wine, it is best served with that wine.
- Regional food is best complemented by wines of the region.
- Wines should never accompany salads with vinegar dressings, or curries; the tastes will clash or be overpowering.
- Sweet wines should be served with foods that are not too sweet.

Figure 3 matches some of the better-known varietal wines with food.

Food and wine are described by texture and flavor. Textures are the qualities in food and wine that we feel in the mouth, such as softness, smoothness, roundness, richness, thickness, thinness, creaminess, chewiness, oiliness, harshness, silkiness, coarseness, and so on. Textures correspond to sensations of touch and temperature, which can be easy to identify—for example, hot, cold, rough, smooth, thick, or thin. Regarding the marrying of food and wine, light food with light wine is always a reliable combination. Rich food with rich wine can be wonderful as long as the match is not too rich. The two most important qualities to consider when choosing the appropriate wine are richness and lightness.

Flavors are food and wine elements perceived by the olfactory nerve as fruity, minty, herbal, nutty, cheesy, smoky, flowery, earthy, and so on. A person often determines flavors by using the nose as well as the tongue. The combination of texture and flavor is what makes food and wine a pleasure to enjoy; a good match between the food and wine can make occasions even more memorable. Figure 4 suggests the steps to be taken in **wine tasting**.

FOCUS ON WINES

Wine and Food Pairing

Jay R. Schrock, University of South Florida

The combination of food and wine is as old as the making of wine. It is truly one of the great pleasures in life. Food and wine are natural accompaniments and enhance the flavor and enjoyment of each other. The flavor of a wine consumed by itself will taste different than when it is imbibed with food. Much of the wine taste experience is actually perceived from the nose; hence, you will hear that "the wine has a good nose." In fact, wine experts, called *sommeliers*, say that 80 percent of the taste comes from the nose. The nose is where the flavors such as nuts, oak, fruits, herbs, spices, and all the other words used to describe wine come from. To improve the smell and taste of wine, we often decant it and serve it in stemware with large openings. The wine taster often swirls the wine to increase the aromas entering the nose.

Over the years, traditions have developed as to how to approach **wine and food pairing**. Remember, these are traditions and that food and wine pairing is a highly subjective and an inexact process. The traditional rules basically state that red wines are served with red meat and white wines are served with fish and poultry. These rules are still generally valid, but they don't take into consideration the complexity of today's multiethnic fusion cuisines, with their wide range of flavors and the corresponding wide range of wines from around the world that are now readily available to everyone. Today, you are more likely to hear of food and wine pairing suggestions, rather than the hard and fast traditional rules of the past. The new tradition has begun:

1. When serving more than one wine at a meal, it's best to serve lighter wines before full-bodied ones. The drier wines should be served before sweeter wines. The exception is if a sweet-flavored food is served early in the meal. Serve wines with lower alcohol content before wines with higher alcohol content.

2. Pair light-bodied wines with lighter food and fuller-bodied wines with heaver, richer, or more flavorful foods. This is a restatement of the old red wine with red meat and white wine with fish and chicken suggestion.

3. Match flavors. A pinot noir goes well with duck, prosciutto, and mushrooms and a gewürztraminer is a well-suited accompaniment for ham, sausage, curry, and Thai and Indian food. Beware of pairing a wine with food that is sweeter than the wine. Most people agree that chocolate is the one exception. It seems to go with almost anything.

4. Delicately flavored foods that are poached or steamed should be paired with delicate wines.

5. Match regional wines with regional foods; they have been developed together and have a natural affinity for each other. The red sauces of Tuscany and the Chianti wines of the Tuscany region in Italy are an unbeatable combination.

6. Soft cheese such as Camembert and Brie pair well with a variety of red wine, including cabernet sauvignon, zinfandel, and red burgundy. Cabernet sauvignon also goes well with sharp, aged cheddar cheese. Pungent and intensely flavored cheeses, such as a blue cheese, are better with the sweeter eiswein (or icewine) or late-harvest dessert wines. Sheep and goat cheeses pair well with dry white wines, while red wine with fruit flavors goes best with milder cheeses.

Many of your restaurant guests may want to have wine with their dinner but are intimidated by the process or are afraid of the price. Set your guests' minds at ease when they are ordering wine. The know-it-all attitude will not work here; you are not trying to sell a used car or life insurance. You are trying to improve your guests' experience, the check average, and your tip. Make an honest suggestion, and try to explain the differences in wine choices. If guests are pondering two wines by the glass, do not just suggest the more expensive one; bring two glasses and let them taste. They will decide for themselves.

WINE	SMELL AND TASTE ASSOCIATED WITH WINE	FOOD PAIRING
Gewürztraminer (Alsace in France)	grapefruit, apple, nectarine, peach, nutmeg, clove, cinnamon	Thai, Indian, Tex-Mex, Szechwan, ham, sausage, curry, garlic
Chardonnay Chablis (Burgundy in France)	citrus fruit, apple, pear, pineapple, other tropical fruit	pork, salmon, chicken, pheasant, rabbit
Sauvignon Blanc Sancerre (Loire in France)	citrus fruit, gooseberry, bell pepper, black pepper, green olives, herbs	goat cheese, oysters, fish, chicken, pork, garlic
Pinot Blanc	citrus fruit, apple, pear, melon	shrimp, shellfish, fish, chicken
Pinot Noir Cote d' Or (Burgundy in France)	strawberry, cherry, raspberry, clove, mint, vanilla, cinnamon	duck, chicken, turkey, mushrooms, grilled meats, fish and vegetables, pork
Merlot Gamay (Beaujolais in France)	cherry, raspberry, plum, pepper, herbs, mint	beef, lamb, duck, barbecued meats, pork ribs
Cabernet Sauvignon Medoc (Bordeaux in France)	cherry, plum, pepper, bell pepper, herbs, mint, tea, chocolate	beef, lamb, braised, barbecued and grilled meats, aged cheddar, chocolate
Late harvest white wines	citrus fruit, apple, pear, apricot, peach, mango, honey	custard, vanilla, ginger, carrot cake, cheesecake, cream puffs, apricot cobbler

Figure 3 • Matching Wine with Food.

(Courtesy of Jay R. Schrock.)

Many restaurants have introduced wine tastings as special marketing events to promote the restaurant itself, or a particular type or label of wine. Wine tasting is more than just a process—it is an artful ritual. Wine offers a threefold sensory appeal: color, aroma, and taste. Wine tasting, thus, consists of three essential steps.

1. Hold the glass to the light. The color of the wine gives the first indication of the wine's body. The deeper the color, the fuller the wine will be. Generally, wines should be clear and brilliant.
2. Smell the wine. Hold the glass between the middle and the ring finger in a "cup-like" fashion and gently roll the glass. This will bring the aroma and the bouquet of the wine to the edge of the glass. The bouquet should be pleasant. This will tell much about what the taste will be.
3. Finally, taste the wine by rolling the wine around the mouth and by sucking in a little air—this helps release the complexities of the flavors.

Figure 4 • Wine Tasting.

▶ Check Your Knowledge

1. What are the names of the main white and red grape varieties used to make wine?

2. Cabernet sauvignon is best served with _____.

3. Chardonnay is best served with _____.

4. Why does a wine taster swirl the wine around the glass before tasting it?

5. What is the general guideline for serving wine with food?

Major Wine-Growing Regions

Europe

Germany, Italy, Spain, Portugal, and France are the main European wine-producing countries. Germany is noted for the outstanding Riesling wines from the Rhine and Moselle river valleys. Italy produces the world-famous Chianti. Spain makes good wine, but is best known for making sherry. Portugal also makes good wine, but is better known for its port.

France is the most notable of the European countries, producing not only the finest wines but also champagne and cognac. The two most famous wine-producing areas in France are the Bordeaux and Burgundy regions. The vineyards, villages, and towns are steeped in the history of centuries devoted to the production of the finest quality wines. They represent some of the most beautiful countryside in Europe and are well worth visiting.

In France, wine is named after the village in which the wine is produced. In recent years, the name of the grape variety has also been used. The name of the wine grower is also important; because the quality may vary, reputation understandably is very important. A vineyard might also include a chateau in which wine is made.

Within the Bordeaux region, wine growing is divided into five major districts: Medoc, Graves, St. Emilion, Pomerol, and Sauternes. The wine from each district has its own characteristics.

There are several other well-known wine-producing regions of France, such as the Loire Valley, Alsace, and Côtes du Rhône. French people regard wine as an important part of their culture and heritage.

United States and Canada

In California, viticulture began in 1769 when Junipero Serra, a Spanish friar, began to produce wine for the missions he started. At one time, the French considered California wines to be inferior. However, California is blessed with a near-perfect climate and excellent vine-growing soil. In the United States, the name of the grape variety is used to name the wine, not the village or chateau as used by the French. The better-known varietal white wines in the United States are chardonnay, sauvignon blanc, riesling, and chenin blanc; varietal red wines are cabernet sauvignon, pinot noir, merlot, Syrah, and zinfandel.

California viticulture areas are generally divided into three regions:

1. North and central coastal region
2. Great central valley region
3. Southern California region

The north and central coastal region produces the best wines in California. A high degree of use of mechanical methods allows for efficient, large-scale production of quality wines. The two best-known areas within this region are the

A Napa Valley vineyard.

Napa and Sonoma Valleys. The wines of the Napa and Sonoma Valleys resemble those of Bordeaux and Burgundy. In recent years, the wines from the Napa and Sonoma Valleys have rivaled and even exceeded the French and other European wines. The chardonnays and cabernets are particularly outstanding.

The Napa and Sonoma Valleys are the symbols as well as the centers of the top-quality wine industry in California.

Several other states and Canadian provinces provide quality wines. New York, Oregon, and Washington are the other major U.S. wine-producing states. In Canada, the best wineries are in British Columbia's Okanagan Valley and southern Ontario's Niagara peninsula. Both of these regions produce excellent wines.

Australia

Australia has been producing wines for about 150 years, but it is only in the last half-century that these wines have achieved the prominence and recognition they rightly deserve. Australian winemakers traveled to Europe and California to perfect the winemaking craft. Unlike France, with many rigid laws controlling wine growth and production, Australian winemakers use high technology

INTRODUCING ROBERT MONDAVI

Founder of Robert Mondavi Winery

Since its founding in 1966, the Robert Mondavi Winery has established itself as one of the world's top wineries. Robert Mondavi, who recently passed away, was active as wine's foremost spokesperson, having greatly contributed to the wine industry throughout his successful life.

Robert Mondavi was born in 1913 to an Italian couple who had emigrated from the Marche region of Italy in 1910. His father, Cesare, became involved in shipping California wine grapes to fellow Italians. Extremely pleased with California, Cesare Mondavi decided to move to the Napa Valley and set up a firm that shipped fruit east. Robert Mondavi grew up among wines and vines and remained in his father's business.

Robert began by improving the family enterprise, adding to it the management, production, and marketing skills he learned at Stanford University, from which he graduated in 1936. Robert acknowledged the great business potential of the Napa Valley in the broader context of the California wine industry. What the firm needed was to be upgraded with innovations in technology to keep up with the changes in the overall business environment.

Mondavi had an ambitious dream that was realized when the Charles Krug Winery was offered for sale in 1943. The facility was purchased, and Robert knew that the strategy for success included well-planned marketing as well as the crucial winemaking expertise that the family already had.

Mondavi understood also the importance of the introduction of innovative processes that could place the winery in a competitive position. From the 1950s to the 1960s, he performed many experiments and introduced pivotal innovations. For example, Robert popularized new styles of wine, such as the chenin blanc, which was previously known as white pinot and was not doing well in the market. Mondavi changed the fermentation, turning it into a sweeter, more delicious wine. The name was also changed, and sales increased fourfold the following year.

Similarly, he noticed that the sauvignon blanc was a slow-selling wine. He began producing it in a drier style, called it fumé blanc, and turned it into an immediate success. Although the winery's operations were successful, Mondavi was still looking for a missing link in the chain. A trip to Europe, designed to study the finest wineries' techniques, convinced him to adopt a new, smaller type of barrel to age the wine, which he believed added a "wonderful dimension to the finished product."

In 1966, Robert Mondavi opened the Robert Mondavi Winery, which represented the fulfillment of the family's vision to build a facility that would allow them to produce truly world-class wines. In fact, since its establishment, the winery has led the industry, standing as an example of continuous research and innovation in winemaking, as well as a "monument to persistence in the pursuit of excellence."

Throughout the years of operation, the original vision remained constant: to produce the best wines that were the perfect accompaniments to food and to provide the public with proper education about the product. The Robert Mondavi Winery sponsors several educational programs, such as seminars on viticulture, a totally comprehensive tour program in the Napa Valley, and the great chefs program.

The Robert Mondavi Corporation was acquired by Constellation Brands in 2004, a leading international producer and marketer of beverages, selling nearly 90 million cases annually.

to produce excellent wines, many of which are blended to offer the best characteristics of each wine.

Australia has about sixty wine-growing regions, with diverse climates and soil types, mostly in the southeastern part of the continent, in New South Wales, Victoria, and South Australia, all within easy reach of the major cities of Sidney, Melbourne, and Adelaide. There are about 1,120 wineries in Australia. One of the larger and more popular wineries is Lindemans, which regularly receives accolades for its consistent quality and value. The leading red wines are cabernet sauvignon, cabernet-shiraz blends, cabernet-merlot blends, merlot, and shiraz. The leading white wines are chardonnay, semillon, sauvignon blanc, and semillon chardonnay. Among the better-known wine-growing areas is Hunter Valley in New South Wales, which produces semillon. When mature, this wine has a honey, nut, and butter flavor. The chardonnay is complex with a peaches-and-cream character. In recent years, Australian wines have shown exceptional quality and value, leading to increased sales in Europe, the United States, and Asia.

Wine also is produced in many other temperate parts of the world, most notably New Zealand, Chile, Argentina, and South Africa.

How to Read a Wine Label

Labeling requirements vary significantly from country to country. The local laws at the point of sale govern specific information that is required to be on the label where the wine is marketed, rather than where it is produced. This requirement often results in two different wine labels for the same wine. Then, if the wine is marketed where it was produced, it will have one wine label; if the wine is to be exported, it may have another version of the first wine label to meet the requirements of local laws. After the label is designed, it must be approved by the same government agency that controls wine production in that country, as well as the various government agencies that control the import and sale of the wine.[1]

In the United States, we label wines by their varietal grape and include the name of their region on the label. In Europe, wines tend to be labeled regionally rather than by varietal. The wine label on the front of the bottle generally has five headings:

1. The name of the vineyard
2. The grape variety
3. The growing area
4. The vintage
5. The producer

Wine labels are helpful in telling you a lot about what is in the bottle. Most wine bottles have two labels applied to each bottle. The front label is meant to attract your attention, while the back label may be used to provoke your senses. As an example, the label may state: "A wonderful aperitif, this smooth, elegant, wonderfully fruity wine . . . " The label may also include serving suggestions for pairing with food. These statements are not governed by law.[2]

Wine and Health

A glass of wine may be beneficial to health. This perspective was featured in the CBS news magazine program *60 Minutes*, which focused on a phenomenon called the French paradox. The French eat 30 percent more fat than Americans do, smoke more, and exercise less, yet they suffer fewer heart attacks—about one-third as many as Americans. Ironically, the French drink more wine than people of any other nationality—about 75 liters per person a year. Research indicates that wine attacks platelets, which are the smallest of the blood cells that cause the blood to clot, preventing excess bleeding. However, platelets also cling to the rough, fatty deposits on arterial walls, clogging and finally blocking arteries and causing heart attacks. Wine's flushing effect removes platelets from the artery wall. After the *60 Minutes* program was broadcast, sales of wine, particularly red wine, in the United States increased dramatically.

Sustainable Wine Production[3]

Environmentally and socially responsible grape growing and winemaking is not new, but what was once labeled a trend is now becoming an industry standard. Organic is a term given to environmentally friendly methods that use no chemicals or pesticides. Sustainability is defined as a holistic approach to growing and food production that respects the environment, the ecosystem, and even society.

The California Association of Wine Grape Growers has prepared a "Code of Sustainable Winegrowing Practices"; this is a 490-page voluntary self-assessment workbook covering everything from pest management to wine quality to water conservation to environmental stewardship. This tool allows growers and vintners to gauge how they are doing, and then to design and implement their own action plans.

A good example of sustainable winemaking is the Viansa Winery in California. It has long boasted a natural antipest team of bats, barn owls, and insectaries to keep its bug populations under control. The winery uses organic fungicide and has eliminated all herbicides.

Beer

Beer is a brewed and fermented beverage made from malted barley and other starchy cereals and flavored with hops. *Beer* is a generic term for a variety of mash-based, yeast-fermented brewed malt beverages that have an alcohol content mostly between 3.8 and 8 percent.[4] The term **beer** includes the following:

- Lager, the beverage that is normally referred to as beer, is a clear light-bodied, refreshing beer.

- Ale is fuller bodied and bitterer than lager.

- Stout is a dark ale with a sweet, strong, malt flavor.

- Pilsner is not really a beer. The term *pilsner* means that the beer is made in the style of the famous beer brewed in Pilsen, Czech Republic.

The Brewing Process

Beer is brewed from water, **malt, yeast,** and **hops**. The brewing process begins with water, an important ingredient in the making of beer. The mineral content and purity of the water largely determine the quality of the final product. Water accounts for 85 to 89 percent of the finished beer.

Next, grain is added in the form of malt, which is barley that has been ground to a coarse grit. The grain is germinated, producing an enzyme that converts starch into fermentable sugar.

The yeast is the fermenting agent. Breweries typically have their own cultured yeasts, which to a large extent determine the type and taste of the beer.

Mashing is the term for grinding the malt and screening out any bits of dirt. The malt then goes through a hopper into a mash tub, which is a large stainless steel or copper container. Here the water and grains are mixed and heated.

The liquid is now called **wort** and is filtered through a mash filter or lauter tub. This liquid then flows into a brewing kettle, where hops are added and the mixture is boiled for several hours. After the brewing operation, the hop wort is filtered through the hop separator or hop jack. The filtered liquid then is pumped through a wort cooler and into a fermenting vat where pure-culture yeast is added for fermentation.[5] The brew is aged for a few days prior to being barreled for draught beer or pasteurized for bottled or canned beer.

Today, marketing and distribution partnerships promote an even greater choice of beers for consumers. Among those available from Anheuser-Busch distributors are Löwenbräu and Beck's from Germany; Stella Artois and Hoegaarden from the Netherlands; Staropramen and Czechvar from the Czech Republic; Harbin from China;

In the process of making beer, hops are added to the wort in the brew kettle.

and Landshark from Florida. Other interesting beverages include Michelob Ultra Dragon Fruit Peach, Michelob Ultra Fruit Pomegranate Raspberry, and Michelob Ultra Fruit Live Cactus.

Organic and Craft Beers, Microbreweries, and Brewpubs

The U.S. Department of Agriculture (USDA) established the National Organic Program in 1997, opening the door for organic beer. The guidelines for organic beer are the same as for all organic foods: The ingredients must be grown without toxic and persistent pesticides or synthetic fertilizers and in soil that has been free from such chemicals for at least three years. No genetically modified ingredients can be used in the brewing process. Studies show that organic farming reduces erosion and ground-water pollution and that it significantly reduces negative impacts on wildlife.[6]

The organic requirements lend themselves well to smaller breweries. An American craft brewery is a small, independent, and traditional brewery.[7] Craft beer showcases the different areas of the country and their seemingly distinct styles of beer and craft beer scenes. You can get an India Pale Ale (IPA) from anywhere, but there's a reason people will refer to a super hoppy, dry IPA as a "west coast IPA." Also, a lot of craft breweries only distribute in a small- to medium-sized area.[8] As craft brewers have come of age, little did the world know that their full-flavored craft beers would generate such passion and excitement.

Today is a great time to be a beer lover, and as a nation, we now have more beer styles and beer brands to choose from than any other market in the world.[9] Traditionally, a brewer has either an all-malt flagship (the beer that represents the greatest volume sold among that brewer's brands) or has at least 50% of its volume represented by either all-malt beers or by beers that use adjuncts to enhance rather than lighten flavor.[10]

The Brewers Association describes a microbrewery as a brewery that produces a limited amount (less than 15,000 barrels) of beer a year. A brewpub brews and sells beer on the premises and may also be known as a microbrewery if the production has a significant distribution beyond the premises.[11]

Sustainable Brewing

Breweries use a lot of resources yet have the potential to significantly reduce their environmental footprint. Here is how some brewers are reducing their footprint:[12]

- Efficient brewhouse: The brewery is as sustainable and efficient as possible, starting with the parts of the building that were reclaimed and recycled when the Full Sail brewery first opened in the old Diamond Fruit cannery in Oregon. Full Sail utilizes measures such as energy-efficient lighting and air compressors, and compresses the work week into four very productive days, which helps reduce water and energy consumption by 20 percent.

- Sustainable brew process: Pure water literally flows from the peaks that surround the brewery, so Full Sail takes care to conserve this precious resource. While average breweries consume six to eight gallons of water for every gallon of beer produced, Full Sail has reduced its consumption to a mere 3.45 gallons, and operates its own on-site wastewater treatment facility. Local farms supply the other essential ingredients for award-winning brews: 85 percent of hops and 95 percent of barley come straight from Northwest farms.

- Reduce-Reuse-Recycle: Full Sail uses 100 percent recycled paperboard on all its packaging (and was one of the first in the industry to commit to long-term purchasing of recycled paper products). Everything from office paper to glass to stretch wrap to wooden pallets is recycled. Even dairy cows are beneficiaries of brewery waste: 4,160 tons of spent grain and 1,248 tons of spent yeast are sent back to farmers every year to use as feed for cows.

- Community-wide practices: Full Sail purchases 140 blocks of Pacific Power Blue Sky renewable energy per month. This practice results in the reduction of 168 tons of carbon dioxide emissions, the equivalent of planting 33,000 trees. Full Sail also supports over 300 events and charities each year, with a focus on those in Oregon. Employees at the company have inspired environmental change among other businesses in the Hood River area as well. Full Sail was a founding member of the Hood River Chamber of Commerce's "Green Smart" program, an initiative that helps businesses and organizations within the Hood River watershed increase their productivity and profitability by improving resource efficiency and by reducing waste and pollution.

As the push for sustainability gains momentum, one only need to look down at the pint or mug he or she is holding to see how breweries are joining the growing green movement! Beer is the third most-consumed beverage in the world behind water and tea. Upon surveying a number of breweries, and sustainable brewing documents, BlueMap Inc. has determined 10 green steps every brewery should consider.[13]

Utilize Biochar Processing to Re-Use Spent Grains

Processing spent grains through pyrolisis (a process that burns grains to create Biochar, a valuable soil amendment), is a carbon-negative process: it creates heat and syngas while sequestering carbon. By doing so, pyrolisis decreases a brewery's carbon footprint.

Implement Water Use Reduction Measures

Water is one of the largest inputs in brewing. A brewery can conserve water by reducing lost steam, increasing the efficiency of wort production, increasing the life of water in boiler systems, and altogether preventing waste.

Implement Variable-Speed Fans or Motors

Many brewery processes have variable loads that are more efficiently served by variable-speed motors, fans, and drives. Where applicable, an upgrade in a brewery's fans and motors can offer substantial savings and have favorable pay back periods. Savings are only observed if loads vary.

Ensure a Regular Maintenance Regime

A regular maintenance regimen is a great way to cut down on energy inefficiencies. Regularly scheduled maintenance allows breweries to catch problems sooner and address them before excess energy is wasted. Also, keeping a system tuned up means that motors and pumps run at optimum speeds, controls are set properly, and control systems are turned on.

Capture Methane at On-Site Water Treatment Facilities

For breweries that process wastewater on-site, methane capture is a great way to regain value from a waste stream. Currently, closed systems and pond cover methane capture exist. These systems purify and burn methane onsite, which typically offsets the brewery's fuel costs while cutting costs.

Recapture CO_2 during Fermentation

Fermentation releases CO_2. Savvy breweries can capture this CO_2 and use it (instead of purchased CO_2) in the bottling process to carbonate their beer. This reduces both CO_2 released to the air and CO_2 purchasing costs.

Optimize Thermal Resources within the Brewing Process

Much of the brewing process consists of thermal processes: boiling and cooling liquids. Auditing the entire process can reveal ways to capture thermal resources and apply them to other brewing processes, thereby reducing energy and fuel costs of heating and cooling.

Implement Alternatives to Diatomaceous Earth (DE) Filtering

Though DE is a long-standing industry standard as a filter medium, health risks associated with DE (and potential problems regulating its use and disposal) are prompting some to seek alternatives. Where applicable, sheet filtering, cross flow filtration systems, and DE recycling systems can be used to avoid some of these flaws.

Optimize Refrigeration, Lighting, Construction, and Other Building Controls

Sustainable building is potentially one of the largest opportunities for a brewery to reduce energy consumption and curtail demand spikes (thereby minimizing fines). Management systems can be installed to green the lighting of spaces, maximize building functions, optimize chill systems, and stagger cooling loads.

Utilize Renewable Energy Technologies

Beer is made with hops, grain, water and yeast. What could be a more natural way to complement these natural ingredients than using sun or wind to power the beer brewing process? Renewable energy sources include geothermal, syngas, or biogas. When sized correctly, these technologies greatly reduce purchased electricity and fuel and can have very attractive payback periods.

By considering these 10 recommendations, the third-largest beverage industry in the world can reduce its overall ecological impact while in many cases save money.

Further examples of breweries around the country that are finding creative ways to reduce their carbon footprint are by installing wind and solar power. Colorado's New Belgium Brewery has an 870 panel solar array from which it gets 13 percent of its energy needs; Odell Brewing Company gets 39 percent of its energy needs.[14]

INTRODUCING ROB WESTFALL

Bar Manager, The Speakeasy, Siesta Key, Florida

The Speakeasy has been a staple in Siesta Key's Village for over ten years. Known for its exceptional variety of live music, it is also a place where locals feel right at home. The Speakeasy features ice-cold air conditioning in a polished, clean environment. Located at the back of the room is our pool table with plenty of space to allow for professional play. Specialty drinks are another draw for patrons at The Speakeasy. Our menu is loaded with innovative cocktails that are tough to find in another establishment. Along with our extensive list of wines by the glass, we also offer many premium single-malt scotches, cognacs, and bourbons and a host of fine liqueurs. The Speakeasy is owned and operated by Café Gardens, which also owns the Daiquiri Deck located directly next door.

A typical day for a manager at The Speakeasy goes like this:

9:45 A.M. Arrive for manager meeting at the Daiquiri Deck. All Daiquiri Deck managers, the owners, and myself are present at this meeting. The meeting consists of a variety of issues. Typically, the first order of business is reviewing the numbers from the previous week. Numbers like net sales, cost of labor, cost of goods, and promotional costs are discussed. Additionally, budgets are a major concern every week. Budgets are set based on sales projections from the previous year and are very important to the success of the business. Next, we discuss any issues from the previous week. In the bar business, an "issue" could be just about anything from fights to vandalism. We find it extremely important to discuss all of these issues so that the management team is all on the same page.

11:00 A.M. Mondays are very important in the bar business. Inventory must be taken to ensure that costs are in line, and that you know what product you need. First, I take an inventory of all beverage products at The Speakeasy. Liquor, beer, wine, cigarettes, cigars, and mixers are all items that must be counted.

12:00 P.M. Upon completion of the inventory, it is time to put your orders together for the week. Knowing your usage is extremely important when placing an order. Buying in bulk is always superior to simply filling holes from week to week. Simply, it allows you more buying power and, essentially, more free goods.

1:00 P.M. Confirm band schedule. Booking bands and maintaining an entertainment schedule can sometimes be one of the most frustrating areas of the bar business. However, it can also be the most rewarding. The experience you gain from working with so many different types of entertainment is difficult to replace. The majority of bands show up on time and treat their job professionally, but there are a significant amount of them that do not. I call my bands to confirm their schedule on a weekly basis for this very reason.

2:00 P.M. Typically, there is always some bar maintenance that needs to be addressed. I always take a walk around and check everything out to make sure that everything is working property.

3:00 P.M. Work on any upcoming promotions and ensure their success. Spirit tastings, holidays, full-moon parties, and private parties are examples of these types of events.

4:00 P.M. Send memo to corporate office regarding what checks need to be written for entertainment that week. Ensure that each band has proper paperwork filled out for tax purposes.

5:00 P.M. Every day the staff needs to be reminded to step it up. Motivation comes from the top down. The bar business is a stage, and the bartenders are on a stage. The staff will typically need to be reminded of this on a consistent basis. Open lines of communication are very important and allow you to apply constructive criticism or accolades, as they are appropriate.

6:00 P.M. It's time to have a drink.

That's the management side of the bar. The nighttime is another animal entirely!

Spirits

A **spirit** or **liquor** is made from a liquid that has been fermented and distilled. Consequently, a spirit has a high percentage of alcohol, gauged in the United States by its proof content. **Proof** is equal to twice the percentage of alcohol in the beverage; therefore, a spirit that is 80 proof is 40 percent alcohol. Spirits traditionally are enjoyed before or after a meal, rather than with the meal. Many spirits can be consumed straight, or neat (without ice or other ingredients), or they may be enjoyed with water, soda water, juices, or cocktail mixes.

Fermentation of spirits takes place by the action of yeast on sugar-containing substances, such as grain or fruit. Distilled drinks are made from a fermented liquid that has been put through a distillation process.

Whiskies

Among the better-known spirits is whisky, which is a generic name for the spirit first distilled in Scotland and Ireland centuries ago. The word *whisky* comes from the Celtic word *visgebaugh*, meaning "water of life." Whisky is made from a fermented mash of grain to which malt, in the form of barley, is added. The barley contains an enzyme called diastase that converts starch to sugars. After fermentation, the liquid is distilled. Spirits naturally are white or pale in color, but raw whisky is stored in oak barrels that have been charred (burnt). This gives whisky its caramel color. The whisky is stored for a period of time, up to a maximum of twelve to fifteen years. However, several good whiskies reach the market after three to five years.

Most whiskies are blended to produce a flavor and quality that is characteristic of the brand. Not surprisingly, the blending process at each distillery is a closely guarded secret. There are four distinct whisky types that have gained worldwide acknowledgment throughout the centuries: Scotch whisky, Irish whisky, bourbon whisky, and Canadian whisky.

Scotch Whisky

Scotch whisky, or scotch, has been distilled in Scotland for centuries and has been a distinctive part of the Scots' way of life. From its origins in remote and romantic Highland glens, Scotch whisky has become a popular and international drink, its flavor appreciated throughout the world. Scotch became popular in the United States during the days of **Prohibition** (1919 to 1933) when it was smuggled into the country from Canada. It is produced like other whiskies, except that the malt is dried in special kilns that give it a smoky flavor. To be legally called Scotch whisky, the spirit must conform to the standards of the Scotch Whisky Act; only whisky made with this process can be called Scotch whisky. Some of the better-known quality-blended Scotch whiskies are Chivas Regal and Johnnie Walker Black, Gold, and Blue Labels.

A single malt Scotch whisky is the product of one specific distillery and has not been mixed with whisky from any other distilleries. Some whisky aficionados prefer a single malt Scotch, from which there are several brands to chose.

Irish Whiskey

Irish whiskey is spelled with an *e* and is produced from malted or unmalted barley, corn, rye, and other grains. The malt is not dried like it is in the production of Scotch whisky, which gives Irish whiskey a milder character, yet an excellent flavor. Two well-known Irish whiskies are Old Bushmill's Black Bush and Jameson's 12 Year Old Special Reserve.

Bourbon Whisky

Liquor was introduced in America by the first settlers, who used it as a medicine. Bourbon has a peculiar history. In colonial times in New England, rum was the most popular distilled spirit. After the break with Britain, settlers of Scottish and Irish background predominated. They were mostly grain farmers and distillers, producing whisky for barter. When George Washington levied a tax on this whisky, the farmers moved south and continued their whisky production. However, the rye crop failed, so they decided to mix corn, particularly abundant in Kentucky, with the remaining rye. The result was delightful. This experiment occurred in Bourbon County—hence the name of the new product.

Checking the color of Johnnie Walker Scotch that is maturing in barrels.

Bourbon whisky is produced mainly from corn; other grains are also used, but they are of secondary importance. The distillation processes are similar to those of other types of whisky. Charred barrels provide bourbon with its distinctive taste. It is curious to note that barrels can only be used once in the United States to age liquor. Aging, therefore, occurs in new barrels after each distillation process. Bourbon may be aged up to six years to improve its mellowness. Among the better-known bourbon whiskies are Jack Daniels, Maker's Mark, and George Dickel.

Canadian Whisky

Like bourbon, Canadian whisky is produced mainly from corn. It is characterized by a delicate flavor that nonetheless pleases the palate. Canadian whisky must be at least four years old before it can be bottled and marketed. It is distilled at 70 to 90 percent alcohol by volume. Among the better-known Canadian whiskies are Seagram's and Canadian Club.

White Spirits

Gin, rum, vodka, and tequila are the most common of the spirits that are called **white spirits**. Gin, first known as Geneva, is a neutral spirit made from juniper berries. Although gin originated in Holland, it was in London that the word *Geneva* was shortened to gin, and almost anything was used to make it. Often gin was made in the bathtub in the morning and sold in hole-in-the-wall dram shops all over London at night. Obviously, the quality left a lot to be desired, but the poor drank it to the point of national disaster.[15] Gin also was widely produced in the United States during Prohibition. In fact, the habit of mixing something else with it led to the creation of the cocktail. Over the years, gin became the foundation of many popular cocktails (for example, martini, gin and tonic, gin and juice, and Tom Collins).

Rum can be light or dark in color. Light rum is distilled from the fermented juice of sugarcane, and dark rum is distilled from molasses. Rum comes mainly from the Caribbean islands of Barbados (Mount Gay), Puerto Rico (Bacardi), and Jamaica (Myers). Rums are mostly used in mixed frozen and specialty drinks such as rum and Coke, rum punches, daiquiris, and piña coladas.

Tequila is distilled from the *Agave tequilana* (a type of cactus), which is called *mezcal* in Mexico. Official Mexican regulations require that tequila be made in the area around the town of Tequila because the soil contains volcanic ash, which is especially suitable for growing the blue agave cactus. Tequila may be white, silver, or golden in color. The white is shipped unaged, silver is aged up to three years, and golden is aged in oak from two to four years. Tequila is mainly used in the popular margarita cocktail or in the tequila sunrise (made popular in a song by the Eagles rock group).

Vodka can be made from many sources, including barley, corn, wheat, rye, or potatoes. Because it lacks color, odor, and flavor, vodka generally is combined with juices or other mixers whose flavors predominate. To offer consumers more choices, vodka producers have popularized flavored vodkas with lemon, pepper, vanilla, raspberry, peach, pears, and mango, among others. Brand names of vodka producers are Absolut from Sweden, Stolichnaya (or Stoli for short) from Russia, Grey Goose from France, Tru Organic from the United Sates, and Van Gogh from the Netherlands.

Other Spirits

Brandy is distilled from wine in a fashion similar to that of other spirits. American brandy comes primarily from California, where it is made in column stills and aged in white-oak barrels for at least two years. The best-known American brandies are made by Christian Brothers and Ernest and Julio Gallo. Their brandies are smooth and fruity with a touch of sweetness. The best brandies are served as after-dinner drinks, and ordinary brandies are used in the well for mixed drinks.

A glass of cognac.

Cognac is regarded by connoisseurs as the best brandy in the world. It is made only in the Cognac region of France, where the chalky soil and humid climate combine with special distillation techniques to produce the finest brandy. Only brandy from this region may be called cognac. Most cognac is aged in oak casks from two to four years or more. Because cognacs are blends of brandies of various ages, no age is allowed on the label; instead, letters signify the relative age and quality.

Brandies labeled as *VSOP* must be aged at least four years. All others must be aged in wood at least five years. Five years, then, is the age of the youngest cognac in a blend; usually, several others of older age are added to lend taste, bouquet, and finesse. About 75 percent of the cognac shipped to Canada and the United States is produced by four companies: Courvoisier, Hennessy, Martell, and Remy Martin.

Cocktails

The first cocktails originated in England during the Victorian era, but it wasn't until the 1920s and 1930s that cocktails became popular.

Cocktails are usually drinks made by mixing two or more ingredients (wines, liquors, fruit juices), resulting in a blend that is pleasant to the palate, with no single ingredient overpowering the others. Cocktails are mixed by stirring, shaking, or blending. The mixing technique is particularly important to achieve the perfect cocktail. Cocktails are commonly divided into two categories according to volume: short drinks (up to 3.5 ounces) and tall drinks (generally up to 8.5 ounces).

The secret of a good cocktail lies in several factors:

- The balance of the ingredients. No single ingredient should overpower the others.
- The quality of the ingredients. As a general rule, cocktails should be made from a maximum of three ingredients.
- The skill of the bartender. The bartender's experience, knowledge, and inspiration are key factors in making a perfect cocktail.

A good bartender should understand the effect and the "timing" of a cocktail. It is not a coincidence that many cocktails are categorized by when they are best served. There are aperitifs, digestifs, corpse-revivers, pick-me-ups, and so on. Cocktails can stimulate an appetite or provide the perfect conclusion to a fine meal.

▶ Check Your Knowledge

1. Describe the different types of beer.
2. Describe the various spirits.

A martini cocktail served in a martini glass.

Nonalcoholic Beverages

Nonalcoholic beverages are increasing in popularity. In the 1990s and 2000s, a radical shift has occurred from the free-love 1960s and the singles bars of the 1970s and early 1980s. People are, in general, more cautious about the consumption of alcohol. Lifestyles have become healthier, and organizations such as Mothers Against Drunk Driving (MADD) have raised the social conscience about responsible alcohol consumption. Overall consumption of alcohol has decreased in recent years, with spirits declining the most.

In recent years, several new beverages have been added to the nonalcoholic beverage list. From Goji juice to passion fruit green tea, the nonalcoholic beverage world has been innovative in creating flavored teas and coffees and an ever-increasing variety of juices to satisfy all our tastes.

Nonalcoholic Beer

Guinness, Anheuser-Busch, and Miller, along with many other brewers, have developed beer products that have the same appearance as regular beer but that have a lower calorie content and approximately 95 to 99 percent of the alcohol removed, either after processing or after fermentation. The taste, therefore, is somewhat different from regular beer.

Coffee

Coffee is the drink of the present. People who used to frequent bars are now patronizing coffeehouses. Sales of specialty coffees exceed $4 billion a year. The Specialty Coffee Association of America estimates that there are more than 17,400 coffee cafés nationwide.[16]

Coffee first came from Ethiopia and Mocha, which is in the Yemen Republic. Legends say that Kaldi, a young Abyssinian goatherd, accustomed to his sleepy goats, noticed that after chewing certain berries, the goats began to prance about excitedly. He tried the berries himself, forgot his troubles, lost his heavy heart, and became the happiest person in "happy Arabia." A monk from a nearby monastery surprised Kaldi in this state, decided to try the berries too, and invited the brothers to join him. They all felt more alert that night during prayers![17]

In the Middle Ages, coffee found its way to Europe via Turkey but not without some objections. In Italy, priests appealed to Pope Clement VIII to have the use of coffee forbidden among Christians. Satan, they said, had forbidden his followers, the infidel Moslems, the use of wine because it was used in the Holy Communion and had given them instead his "hellish black brew." Apparently, the pope liked the drink, for he blessed it on the spot, after which coffee quickly became the social beverage of Europe's middle and upper classes.[18]

In 1637, the first European coffeehouse opened in England; within thirty years, coffeehouses had replaced taverns as the island's social, commercial, and political melting pots.[19] The coffeehouses were nicknamed *penny universities*, where any topic could be discussed and learned for the price of a pot of coffee.

The men of the period not only discussed business but actually conducted business. Banks, newspapers, and the Lloyd's of London Insurance Company began at Edward Lloyd's coffeehouse.

Coffeehouses were also popular in Europe. In Paris, Café Procope, which opened in 1689 and still operates today, has been the meeting place of many a famous artist and philosopher, including Rousseau and Voltaire (who are reputed to have drunk forty cups of coffee a day).

The Dutch introduced coffee to the United States during the colonial period. Coffeehouses soon became the haunts of the revolutionary activists plotting against King George of England and his tea tax. John Adams and Paul Revere planned the Boston Tea Party and the fight for freedom at a coffeehouse. This helped establish coffee as the traditional democratic drink of Americans.

Brazil produces more than 30 percent of the world's coffee, most of which goes into canned and instant coffee. Coffee connoisseurs recommend beans by name, such as arabica and robusta beans. In Indonesia, coffee is named for the island on which it grows; the best is from Java and is rich and spicy with a full-bodied flavor. Yemen, the country in which coffee was discovered, names its best coffee for the port of Mocha. Its fragrant, creamy brew has a rich, almost chocolaty aftertaste. Coffee beans are frequently blended by the merchants who roast them; one of the best blends, mocha java, is the result of blending these two fine coffees.

Coffee may be roasted from light to dark according to preference. Light roasts are generally used in canned and institutional roasts, and medium is the all-purpose roast most people prefer. Medium beans are medium brown in color, and their surface is dry. Although this brew may have snappy, acidic qualities, its flavor tends to be flat. Full, high, or Viennese roast is the roast preferred by specialty stores, where balance is achieved between sweetness and sharpness. Dark roasts have a fancy, rich flavor, with espresso the darkest of all roasts. Its almost-black beans have shiny, oily surfaces. All the acidic qualities and specific coffee flavor are gone from espresso, but its pungent flavor is a favorite of espresso lovers.

Decaffeinating coffee removes the caffeine with either a solvent or water process. In contrast, many specialty coffees have things added. Among the better-known specialty coffees are café au lait or caffè latte. In these cases, milk is steamed until it becomes frothy and is poured into the cup together with the coffee. A cappuccino is made with espresso, hot milk, and milk foam, which may then be sprinkled with powdered chocolate and cinnamon.[20]

Tea

Tea is a beverage made by steeping in boiling water the leaves of the tea plant, an evergreen shrub, or small tree, native to Asia. Tea is consumed as either a hot or cold beverage by approximately half of the world's population, yet it is second to coffee in commercial importance because most of the world's tea crop is consumed in the tea-growing regions. Tea leaves contain 1 to 3 percent caffeine. This means that weight for weight, tea leaves have more than twice as much caffeine as coffee beans. However, a cup of coffee generally has more caffeine than a cup of tea because one pound of tea leaves makes 250 to 300 cups of tea, whereas one pound of coffee beans makes only 40 cups of coffee.

CORPORATE PROFILE

Starbucks Coffee Company

Operations

Starbucks Coffee Company (named after the first mate in Herman Melville's *Moby-Dick*) is the leading retailer, roaster, and brand of specialty coffee in North America. More than 7 million people visit Starbucks stores each week. In addition to its more than 17,000 retail locations, the company supplies fine dining, foodservice, travel, and hotel accounts with coffee and coffee-making equipment and operates a national mail-order division.

Locations and Alliances

Starbucks currently has 17,018 stores in fifty U.S. states and in fifty countries.[21] Starbucks has strategic alliances with United Airlines and is now the exclusive supplier of coffee on every United flight.

In addition, Specialty Sales and Marketing supplies Starbucks coffee to the health care, business and industry, college and university, and hotel and resort segments of the foodservice industry; to many fine restaurants throughout North America; and to companies such as Costco, Nordstrom, Starwood, Barnes and Noble, Hilton Hotels, Sodexho, ARAMARK, Compass, Wyndham, Borders, Radisson, Sysco, Safeway, Albertson's, Kraft Foods, Pepsico, and Marriott International.

Product Line

Starbucks roasts more than thirty varieties of the world's finest arabica coffee beans. The company's retail locations also feature a variety of espresso beverages and locally made fresh pastries. Starbucks specialty merchandise includes Starbucks private-label espresso makers, mugs, plunger pots, grinders, storage jars, water filters, thermal carafes, and coffee makers. An extensive selection of packaged goods, including unique confections, gift baskets, and coffee-related items, are available in stores and online.

Starbucks introduced Frappuccino blended beverages, a line of low-fat, creamy, iced coffee drinks. This product launch was the most successful in Starbucks history. The company also has a bottled version of Frappuccino, which is currently available in grocery stores and in many Starbucks retail locations.

A long-term joint venture between Starbucks Coffee and Breyer's Grand Ice Cream dishes up a premium line of coffee ice creams, with national distribution of several different flavors to leading grocery stores. Starbucks has become the number-one brand of coffee ice cream in the United States. Currently, ice cream lovers can choose from eight delectable flavors or two ice cream bars.

Community Involvement

Starbucks contributes to a variety of organizations that benefit AIDS research, child welfare, environmental awareness, literacy, and the arts. The company encourages its partners (employees) to take an active role in their own neighborhoods.

Starbucks fulfills its corporate social responsibility mission by reducing its environmental footprint on the planet. The company addresses three high-impact areas: sourcing of coffee, tea, and paper; transportation of people and products; and design and operations (energy, water, waste reduction, and recycling). Starbucks has developed relations with organizations that support the people and places that grow its coffee and tea, such as Conservation International, CARE, Save the Children, and the African Wildlife Foundation. Additionally, Starbucks has entered into a partnership with the U.S. Agency for International Development (USAID) and Conservation International to improve the livelihoods of small-scale coffee farmers through private sector approaches within the coffee industry that are environmentally sensitive, socially responsible, and economically viable. In 2005, Starbucks received the World Environment Center's Gold Medal for International Corporate Achievement in Sustainable Development.

Starbucks has received numerous awards for quality innovation, service, and giving.

The following list shows where the different types of tea originate:

China—oolong, orange pekoe

India—Darjeeling, Assams (also known as English breakfast tea), Dooars

Indonesia—Java, Sumatra

Carbonated Soft Drinks and Energy Drinks

Coca-Cola and Pepsi have long dominated the carbonated soft drink market. In the early 1970s, Diet Coke and Diet Pepsi were introduced and quickly gained popularity. The diet colas now command about a 10-percent market share. Caffeine-free colas offer an alternative, but they have not, as yet, become as popular as diet colas.

Energy drinks are beverages that are designed to give the consumer a burst of energy by using a combination of methylaxanthines (including caffeine), B vitamins, and exotic herbal ingredients. Energy drinks commonly include caffeine, guarana (extracts from the guarana plant), taurine, various forms of ginseng, maltodextrin, inositol, carnitine, creatine, glucuronolactone, and ginkgo biloba. Some contain high levels of sugar, while most brands also offer an artificially sweetened version. Red Bull is an example of a popular energy drink that originated in Thailand and that has a Japanese heritage. It was adapted to Australian tastes and in only a few years has become popular around the world. The claims are that Red Bull vitalizes the body and mind by supplying tired minds and exhausted bodies with vital substances that have been lost, while reducing harmful substances. It purports to provide immediate energy and vitamins to the consumer. Red Bull has a large market share in more than 100 countries.

Sales of energy drinks and shots are soaring, even as there are growing health concerns given the popularity of the high-caffeine drinks among young people. The dollar value of energy-drink sales rose 13.3 percent last year, thanks in part to a "significant boost" from energy-shot sales at convenience stores, according to a report from the market research firm SymphonyIRI Group.[22] American Beverage Association science chief Maureen Storey says energy drinks are no worse than coffee. A 16-ounce cup of Starbucks' Pike Place coffee, for instance, has 330 mg of caffeine. That size of latte has 160 mg—the same as a 16-ounce can of the energy drink Monster Energy, which bills

A juice bar.

itself as "a killer energy brew" that "you can really pound down." The federal Food and Drug Administration limits caffeine in soft drinks to 71 mg for 12 ounces but doesn't regulate the caffeine in energy drinks, coffee, or tea.[23]

Juices

Popular juice flavors include orange, cranberry, grapefruit, mango, papaya, and apple. Nonalcoholic versions of popular cocktails made with juices have been popular for years and are known as virgin cocktails.

Juice bars have established themselves as places for quick, healthy drinks. Lately, "smart drinks" that are supposed to boost energy and improve concentration have become popular. The smart drinks are made up of a blend of juices, herbs, amino acids, caffeine, and sugar and are sold under names such as Energy Plasma Blast and IQ Booster.

Other drinks have jumped on the healthy drink bandwagon, playing on the consumer's desire to drink something refreshing, light, and healthful. Often, these drinks are fruit flavored, giving the consumer the impression of drinking something healthier than sugar-filled sodas. Unfortunately, these drinks usually just add the flavor of the fruit and rarely have any nutritional value.

In addition, some drinks are created by mixing different fruit flavors to arrive at new, exotic flavors such as Passion-Kiwi-Strawberry and Mango-Banana Delight. Some examples of such drinks are Snapple and Tropicana Twister.

Sports enthusiasts also find drinks that professional athletes use and advertise available in stores. These specially formulated isotonic beverages are intended to help the body regain the vital fluids and minerals that are lost during heavy physical exertion. The National Football League sponsors Gatorade and encourages its use among its athletes. The appeal of being able to drink what the professionals drink is undoubtedly one of the major reasons for the success of Gatorade's sales and marketing. Other brands of isotonic beverages include Powerade and All Sport, which is sponsored by the National Collegiate Athletics Association.

Bottled Water

Bottled water was popular in Europe years ago when it was not safe to drink tap water. In North America, the increased popularity of bottled water has coincided with the trend toward healthier lifestyles.

In the 1980s, it was chic to be seen drinking Perrier (a sparkling water) or some other imported bottled water. Perrier, which comes from France, lost market share a few years ago when an employee tampered with the product.

Now the market leader is Evian (a spring water), which is also French. Domestic bottled water is as good as imported and is now available in various flavors that offer the consumer a greater selection.

Bottled waters are available as sparkling, mineral, and spring waters. Bottled water is a refreshing, clean-tasting, low-calorie beverage that will likely increase in popularity as a beverage on its own or to accompany another beverage such as wine or whisky.

Bars and Beverage Operations

From an operating perspective, bar and beverage management follows much the same sequence as does food management, as shown in the following list:

- Forecasting
- Determining what to order
- Selecting the supplier
- Placing the order
- Receiving the order
- Storing
- Issuing
- Serving
- Accounting
- Controlling

Bar Setup

Whether a bar is part of a larger operation (restaurant) or a business in its own right, the physical setup of the bar is critical to its overall effectiveness. There is a need to design the area in such a way that it not only is pleasing to the eye but it also is conducive to a smooth and efficient operation. This means that bar stations—where drinks are filled—are located in strategic spots, and that each station has everything it needs to respond to most, if not all, requests. All well liquors should be easily accessible, with popular call brands not too far out of reach. The brands that are less likely to be ordered (and more likely to be high priced) can be farther away from the stations. The most obvious place for the high-priced, premium brands is the back bar, a place of high visibility. Anyone sitting at the bar will be looking directly at the back bar, giving the customers a chance to view the bar's choices.

As for beer coolers, their location depends on the relative importance of beer to the establishment. In many places, beer is kept in coolers under the bar or below the back bar, and sample bottles or signs are displayed for customers. However, in many places, beer is the biggest seller, and bars may offer numerous brands from around the world. In such places, other setups may be used, such as standup coolers with glass doors so that customers can easily see all the varieties available. This is also true for draft beers.

Inventory Control

The beverage profitability of an organization is not a matter of luck. Profits result largely from the implementation and use of effective **inventory controls** by management and employees. Training is also important to ensure that employees treat inventory as cash and that they handle it as if it were their own money. Management's example will be followed by employees. If employees sense a lax management style, they may be tempted to steal. No control system can guarantee the prevention of theft completely. However, the better the control system, the less likely it is that there will be a loss.[24]

To operate profitably, a beverage operation manager needs to establish what the expected results will be. For example, if a bottle of gin contains twenty-five 1-ounce measures, it would be reasonable to expect twenty-five times the selling price in revenue. When this is multiplied for each bottle, the total revenue can be determined and compared to the actual revenue.

One of the critical areas of bar management is the design, installation, and implementation of a system to control possible theft of the bar's beverage inventory. Theft may occur in a number of ways, including the following:

- Giving away drinks
- Overpouring alcohol
- Mischarging for drinks
- Selling a call liquor at a well price
- Outright stealing of bar beverages by employees

As is the case with food operations, anticipated profit margin is based on the ratio of sales generated to related beverage costs. Bar management must be able to account for any discrepancies between expected and actual profit margins.

All inventory control systems require an actual physical count of the existing inventory, which may be done on a weekly or monthly basis, depending on the needs of management. This physical count is based on units. For liquor and wine, the unit is a bottle, either 0.750 or 1.0 liter; for bottled beer, the unit is a case of twenty-four bottles; for draft beer, the unit is one keg. The results of the most current physical count are then compared to the prior period's physical count to determine the actual amount of beverage inventory consumed during the period. This physical amount is translated into a cost or dollar figure by multiplying the amount consumed for each item by its respective cost per unit. The total cost for all beverages consumed is compared to the sales generated to result in a profit margin, which is then compared to the expected margin.

Management should design forms that can be used to account for all types of liquor, beer, and wine available at the bar. The listing of the items should follow their actual physical setup within the bar to facilitate easy accounting of the inventory. The forms should also have columns where amounts of each inventory item can be noted. A traditional way to account for the amount of liquor in a bottle is by using the "10" count, where the level of each bottle is marked by tenths; thus, a half-full bottle of well vodka would be marked as ".5" on the form. Similarly, for kegs of draft beer, a breakdown of 25, 50, 75, and 100 percent may be used to determine their physical count.

Beverage Management Technology

Technology for beverage management has improved with products from companies such as Scannabar (**www.scanbar.com**), which offer beverage operators a system that accounts for every ounce, with daily, weekly, or monthly results. The ongoing real-time inventory allows viewing results at any time and place, with tamperproof reliability interfaced with major point-of-sale (POS) systems.

The Scannabar liquor module has a bar-coded label on each bottle, making it easy to track bottles from purchase to recycle bin. Each bottle variety has the same scannbar, allowing for easy calibration. The bar-coded ribbon is used as a measuring tool to give accurate results. Inventory taking is done with a portable handheld radio-frequency bar code reader. Once the label is scanned, the level of alcohol in the bottle is recorded and the data are sent from the user's handheld reader to the computer in the office for real-time results.[25]

The wine module keeps control of all wines by region, variety, or vintage. After the wines have been configured within the directory, the procedure is that, when a wine is received, the variety is identified by scanning the bar code already on the bottle or is selected directly from the portable handheld radio-frequency bar code reader. A bar-coded tag is placed around the collar, which creates a unique identity for each bottle. Once the bottle is ready to be served, either at the table or at the bar, the bar-coded tag is removed from the bottle and scanned out of inventory. Scanning the tag around the neck of the bottle accomplishes inventory taking.[26]

The beverage system from AZ Bar America (**www.azbarusa.com**) offers a POS system that runs the operations behind the bar. It rings up the charge as the beverage is being poured while automatically removing the product from inventory.

Instead of holding up bottles and guessing what is left in them or even weighing each bottle at the end of shifts, the AZ2000 controller can at any time give a report of what was sold, who completed the transaction, how the system was used, and what the actual profits are by brand, transaction, or product group. The system can be remotely monitored from home or other location by dialing into the bar location; this is handy for making price changes and monitoring sales activity.

The AZ2000 is the heart of a dispensing system that interfaces with a variety of products: "spouts," a cocktail tower, beer, wine, juice, soft drink machines, and soda guns. The system even runs cocktail programming, so if the bartender does not know what goes into a certain drink, he or she can hit the cocktail button, and the system will tell the bartender what liquor bottle to pick up and will control the recipe pour amounts.[27]

TECHNOLOGY SPOTLIGHT

Using Technology to Control Beverage Costs

Cihan Cobanoglu, Ph.D., Dean, School of Hotel and Restaurant Management, University of South Florida, Sarasota-Manatee

Controlling costs in a food service operation is one of the key elements for being successful. Traditionally, the profit margins in the food service establishments are very slim (about 5 to 8 percent). This requires the restaurant owners and managers to be in control of the food and beverage costs at all times. There are several technology applications that will help food service operations to keep track and control costs. An important part of food service operations is beverage service and sales. Controlling beverage costs differs from controlling food costs. Food costs should be around 28 to 32 percent of the sales price, whereas beverage costs should be between 18 and 22 percent of the sales price. Every reduction in food and beverage cost percentage results in a higher gross profit. Beverage sales (alcoholic and non-alcoholic) are an easy way to increase profitability because the costs are lower and the gross margin is far greater for beverage than for food.

There are several technologies that will help operators to control beverage costs. One of them is AccuBar, which is a sophisticated beverage management program that uses personal digital assistants (PDAs) to scan the bar codes on the labels of liquor, beer, and wine bottles, as well as virtually any other items you may have in inventory. The PDA quickly collects counts to simplify tracking of (1) physical inventory, (2) receiving, (3) perpetual inventory, (4) supplier, (5) ordering, (6) transfers between locations, (7) banquet and event consumption, (8) large wine cellars, (9) requisitions, (10) empties, (11) variances, (12) slow-moving stock, (13) and cost of goods. Once the PDA has collected the data, it syncs with a PC (or wirelessly) to send the encrypted files to AccuBar's back-end software. From there, the user can log in through a secure web site to perform many of AccuBar's functions. Restaurant operators report 50- to 80-percent time savings when using the AccuBar system. That's a key benefit, because often it means the difference between a thorough, insightful inventory and one that has been rushed through after hours. And it can mean one manager efficiently completing the process with time to spare, instead of several burned-out managers having to work late or off hours.

Another way of tracking beverage costs is through a device that controls the dispensing of alcoholic beverages. In this system, each bottle is attached to a dispensing system with different measures of pours. As the bartender pours in to a glass, each pour is registered, therefore allowing full control of the beverage sales and keeping inventory. The disadvantage of this system is the low speed of service in a busy bar environment.

A new generation of beverage-dispensing control systems is the radio-frequency identification (RFID)–based systems. In this system, an RFID spout is assigned to each bottle in the bar, and every drink dispensed is automatically tracked in real time. Beverage Tracker by Capton (**www.beveragetracker.com**) uses RFID–enabled free-pour spouts, allowing bartenders to pour liquor without adjusting normal bar operations. Each spout contains an RFID microchip that wirelessly transmits pour data via radio frequency to a receiver. Every RFID microchip has a unique serial code, so each spout can be tracked individually. Beverage Tracker spouts are completely self-contained and hold the battery, electronics, transmitter, and microchip. They are water resistant and impact resistant so they can be cleaned like any other pour spout. They fit all major brands of liquor and are completely reprogrammable through a simple software update. Every event, including pours, placement on bottle, and placement off bottle, is date and time stamped and transmitted in real time. Beverage Tracker spouts transmit on a low-range AM spectrum (433 megahertz). With this system, the management can know the perpetual inventory (total inventory—all sales) at a given time.

Personnel Procedures

Another key component of internal control is having procedures in place for screening and hiring bar personnel. Employees must be experienced in bartending and cocktail serving and also must be honest because they have access to the bar's beverage inventory and its cash.

Bar managers may also implement several other procedures to control inventory and reduce the likelihood of employee theft. One popular method is the use of *spotters*, who are hired to act like typical bar customers, but who are actually observing the bartenders and/or cocktailers for inappropriate behavior, such as not taking money from customers or overpouring. Another method for checking bar personnel is to perform a bank switch in the middle of the shift. In some cases, employees steal from the company by taking money from customers without ringing it up on the register. They keep the extra money in the cash drawer until the end of the shift when they are cashing out, at which point they retrieve the stolen funds. To do a bank switch, the manager must "z-out" a bartender's cash register, take the cash drawer, and replace it with a new bank. The manager then counts the money in the drawer, subtracts the starting bank, and compares that figure to the one on the register's tape. If there is a significant surplus of funds, it is highly likely that the employee is stealing. If there is less than what is indicated on the tape, the employee may be honest but careless when giving change or hitting the buttons on the register. Either way, there is a potential for loss.

Restaurant and Hotel Bars

In restaurants, the bar is often used as a holding area to allow guests to enjoy a cocktail or aperitif before sitting down to dinner. This allows the restaurant to space out the guests' orders so that the kitchen can cope more effectively; it also increases beverage sales. The profit margin from beverages is higher than the food profit margin.

In some restaurants, the bar is the focal point or main feature. Guests feel drawn to having a beverage because the atmosphere and layout of the restaurant encourages them to have a drink. Beverages generally account for about 25 to 30 percent of total sales. Many restaurants used to have a higher percentage of beverage sales, but the trend toward responsible consumption of alcoholic beverages has influenced people to decrease their consumption.

Bars carry a range of each spirit, beginning with the *well* package. The well package is the least expensive pouring brand that the bar uses when guests simply ask for a "scotch and water." The *call* package is the group of spirits that the bar offers to guests who are likely to ask for a particular name brand. For example, guests may call for Johnnie Walker Red Label. An example of a premium scotch is Johnnie Walker Black Label, and a super premium scotch is Chivas Regal.

The Banyan Court bar at the Moana Hotel is a perfect venue for a "sundowner."

A popular method of costing each of the spirits poured is to calculate cost according to the following example:

A premium brand of vodka such as Grey Goose costs $32.00 per liter and yields twenty-five $1^{1}/_{4}$-oz shots that each sell for $5.50. Therefore, the bottle brings in $137.50. The profit margins produced by bars may be categorized as follows:

Liquor Pouring Cost % (approx.)	12
Beer	25
Wine	38

When combined, the sales mix may have an average pouring cost of 16 to 20 percent.

Most bars operate on some form of par stock level, which means that for every spirit bottle in use, there is a minimum par stock level of one, two, or more bottles available as a backup. As soon as the stock level falls to a level below the par level, more is automatically purchased.

Nightclubs

Nightclubs have long been a popular place to go to get away from the stresses of everyday life. From the small club in a suburban neighborhood to the world-famous clubs of New York, Las Vegas, and Miami's South Beach, all clubs have one thing in common: People frequent them to kick back, relax, and, more often than not, enjoy a wild night of dancing and partying with friends and strangers alike.

Like restaurant ownership, starting up a nightclub is a very risky business. But with the right education and proper planning, nightclub ownership can be a very profitable endeavor. As with most businesses in the hospitality industry, many believe that experience is more important than education and that you can learn as you go. However, when embarking on a journey as involved as owning a nightclub, a person with a degree and a high level of education is well ahead of the game.

The ability to read the market is key in developing a nightclub. When investing anywhere from $300,000 to $1 million in start-up costs, it is of utmost importance to be sure that the right spot is chosen and that a relevant market is within reach. Great nightclubs result from an accurate and calculated read of a marketplace, not by virtue of good luck. In fact, the number-one cause of early nightclub failure stems from an inaccurate read on the marketplace. For example, if an entrepreneur is interested in opening up a country line-dancing nightclub in an urban neighborhood, he or she may want to do extensive market research to be sure that members of the community even like country music.

When considering the prospect of a new nightclub, it is important to invest considerable time in the study of demographics, market attitude, and social dynamics of the proposed target. Many people tend to come up with a concept they are dead set on pursuing without really digging into the market. One should take all markets into account, even if the other markets may not seem relevant at the time. In the future, it may be these same markets that are being divided to come to the newer clubs that have just opened.

A new and exciting concept is a highly important factor in creating a nightclub. Some people feel that if one nightclub is doing well down the street, they will open the same type and be equally successful. This is not true. Variety is one of the keys to successful business. By offering patrons a fresh new opportunity, one can draw clientele away from the old clubs and into the new club.

Budgeting is another big factor in developing a nightclub. Although such an undertaking can be very costly, cutting corners in building and design will only hurt the business later. It is better to spend the money now and do it right than to have to spend more money for repairs later. Creating a budget should include all aspects of the operation, including, but not limited to, food and beverage, staffing and labor, licenses, building ramifications, décor, lighting, and entertainment.

Be sure to know all the legal issues that come with running a nightclub. For example, many laws exist on the sale and distribution of alcohol. In many instances, if a problem occurs involving a patron who was last drinking at the club, the problem can be considered the fault of the operation's management. Lawsuits can arise fairly easily, and it is highly important to be aware of such possibilities.

Nightclubs can be great experiences for both the patrons and the owner because revenues can be very high. However, it is important to remember the risks involved and work to minimize them.

Although this is only a brief discussion of the creation of a nightclub, the points given are quite important to successful operation. As with all business endeavors, the more one knows about the industry with which he or she is getting involved, the better off the business will be. For more information regarding the nightclub industry, go to **www.nightclub.com** or **www.nightclubbiz.com**.

Brewpubs and Microbreweries

Brewpubs are a combination brewery and pub or restaurant that brews its own fresh beer onsite to meet the taste of local customers. Microbreweries are craft breweries that produce up to 15,000 barrels (or 30,000 kegs) of beer a year. The North American microbrewery industry trend revived the concept of small breweries serving fresh, all-malt beer. Although regional breweries, microbreweries, and brewpubs account for only a small part of the North American brewing industry in terms of total beer production (less than 5 percent), they have a potentially large growth rate. One reason for the success of microbreweries and brewpubs is the wide variety of styles and flavors of beer they produce. On one hand, this educates the public about beer styles that have been out of production for decades and, on the other hand, helps brewpubs and restaurants meet the individual tastes and preferences of their local clientele.

Starting a brewpub is a fairly expensive venture. Although brewing systems come in a wide range of configurations, the cost of the equipment ranges from $200,000 to $800,000. Costs are affected by factors such as annual production capacity, beer types, and packaging. The investment in microbreweries and brewpubs is well justified by the enormous potential for returns. Microbreweries can produce a wide variety of ales, lagers, and other beers, the quality of which depends largely on the quality of the raw materials and the skill of the brewer. There are several regional brewpub restaurants of note, including Rock Bottom, which built its foundation on a tradition of fresh handcrafted beers and a diverse menu. It promotes itself as a place to gather with friends, drink the best beer around, enjoy a great meal, and share good times. John Harvard's has a famous selection of ales and lagers that are brewed on the premises according to the old English recipes brought to America in 1637 by John Harvard, after whom Harvard University is named. Gordon Biersch has several excellent brewery restaurants also offering handcrafted ales and beers along with a varied menu.

Sports Bars

Sports bars have always been popular but have become more so with the decline of disco and singles bars. They are places where people relax in the sporting atmosphere, so bar/restaurants such as Trophies in San Diego or Characters at Marriott hotels have become popular "watering holes." Satellite TV coverage of the top sporting events helps sports bars to draw crowds. Sports bars have evolved over the years into much more than corner bars featuring the game of the week. In the past, sports bars were frequented by die-hard sports fans and were rarely visited by other clientele. Today, the sports bar is more of an entertainment concept and is geared toward a more diverse base of patrons.

Sports bars were originally no more than a gathering spot for local sports fans when the home team played on TV. Now, such places have been transformed into mega-sports adventures, featuring musical entertainment, interactive games, and hundreds of TVs tuned in to just about every sport imaginable. "There are no more watering holes," says Zach Strauss, general manager of Sluggers World Class Sports Bar in Chicago. "Things have changed. People are more health conscious; nobody really drinks, drinks, drinks anymore. . . . You have to offer more than booze. People expect sports bars to have more personality, better food, and better service."[28]

Today's sports bars are attracting a much more diverse clientele. Now, more women and families are frequenting these venues, which provide a new prospect for revenue for bar owners. Scott Estes, founding partner of Lee Roy Selmon's restaurant in Tampa, Florida, has recognized that women are an increasing revenue force in the industry and has made adjustments to his restaurant to be sure to capitalize on this rapidly expanding market. Sports bars are also making changes in their establishments to become more family oriented. Lee Roy Selmon's main dining room, for example, is a TV-free environment. Many families go into sports bars and

New York Yankees fans celebrate in a sports bar.

request a room with no TVs, so, recognizing that, an increasing number of owners have chosen to set aside a special place where families can eat uninterrupted by the noise of TV.

Another method of attracting bar patrons on slower nights is to offer games and family-friendly menus. Frankie's Food, Sports, and Spirits in Atlanta attracts families by hosting a sports-trivia game for teens. For the younger crowd, the restaurant provides a kids' menu every day and serves each pint-sized meal on upside-down Frisbees, which children can take home as souvenirs. Sports bars have also become the latest version of the traditional arcade. Many bars offer interactive video games where friends and families can compete against one another. Virtual reality games such as Indy 500 and other sports games are available at many establishments. Some venues have even gone a step farther and offer batting cages, bowling alleys, and basketball courts for their patrons to enjoy.

Another aspect of the sports bar that has changed drastically is the menu. Sports bars have a reputation for serving spicy chicken wings, hamburgers, and other typical bar fare. But just as sports bars have evolved in their entertainment offerings, so too have their menus. People's tastes have changed, causing sports bars to offer a more diverse menu. Today, guests can dine on a variety of foods, from filet mignon, to fresh fish, to gourmet sandwiches and pizza. Now people frequent sports bars as much for the great meal they will have as for the entertainment. In the past, sports bars usually had a few TVs that showcased games that would appeal to the area and big games such as the Super Bowl. The sudden increase in technology and TV programming available has made game viewing very different. The popularity of satellites and digital receivers has allowed bars to tune in to virtually dozens of events at any given time. Bars now have hundreds of TVs, and fans can watch games featuring every sport, team, and level of play around the world at any time of the day or night.

Burbank, California–based ESPN Zone has about 200 TVs in each of its locations so that fans can catch all the action. A handful of TVs are placed in the restaurant's bathrooms because The evolution of sports bars has turned the smoky corner bar into an exciting dining and sports experience. Customers who once rarely frequented the establishments, such as women and families, are now some of the biggest patrons, increasing both attendance and revenue at sports bars.

Coffee Shops

Another fairly recent trend in the beverage industry in the United States and Canada is the establishment of coffeehouses, or coffee shops. Coffeehouses originally were created based on the model of Italian bars, which reflected the deeply rooted espresso tradition in Italy. The winning concept of Italian bars lies in the ambiance they create, which is suitable for conversation of a personal, social, and business nature. A talk over a cup of coffee with soft background music and maybe a pastry is a typical scenario for Italians. Much of the same concept was re-created in the United States and Canada, where there was a niche in the beverage industry that was yet to be acknowledged and filled. The original concept was modified, however, to include a much wider variety of beverages and styles of coffee to meet the tastes of North American consumers. Consequently, the typical espresso/cappuccino offered by Italian bars has been expanded in North America to include items such as iced mocha, iced cappuccino, and so forth.

Students as well as businesspeople find coffeehouses a place to relax, discuss, socialize, and study. The success of coffeehouses is reflected in the establishment of chains such as Starbucks, as well as family-owned, independent shops.

Wireless cafés are a recent trend in the coffeehouse sector. Wireless cafés offer the use of computers, with Internet capability, for about $6 per hour. Guests can enjoy coffee, snacks, or even a meal while online. Reasonable rates allow regular guests to have e-mail addresses.

▶ Check Your Knowledge

1. Describe the bar setup.
2. How is inventory control conducted?
3. What is the average beverage pouring cost percentage?
4. What is a trend in sports bars?

Liquor Liability and the Law

Owners, managers, bartenders, and servers may be liable under the law if they serve alcohol to minors or to persons who are intoxicated. The extent of the liability can be very severe. The legislation that governs the sale of alcoholic beverages is called **dram shop legislation**. The dram shop laws, or civil damage acts, were enacted in the 1850s and dictated that owners and operators of drinking establishments are liable for injuries caused by intoxicated customers.

Some states have reverted back to the eighteenth-century common law, removing liability from vendors except in cases involving minors. Nonetheless, most people recognize that as a society we are faced with major problems of underage drinking and drunk driving.

To combat underage drinking in restaurants, bars, and lounges, a major brewery distributed a booklet showing the authentic design and layout of each state's driver's licenses. Trade associations such as the National Restaurant Association and the American Hotel & Lodging Association, together with major corporations, have produced a number of preventive measures and programs aimed at responsible alcohol beverage service. The major thrust of these initiatives is awareness programs and mandatory training programs, such as Serve Safe for Alcohol, that promote responsible alcohol service. Serve Safe for Alcohol is sponsored by the National Restaurant Association and is a certification program that teaches participants about alcohol and its effects on people, the common signs of intoxication, and how to help customers avoid drinking too much.

Other programs for responsible alcohol service and consumption include designated drivers, who only drink nonalcoholic beverages to ensure that they can drive friends home safely. Some operators give free nonalcoholic beverages to the designated driver as a courtesy.

One positive outcome of the responsible alcohol service programs for operators is a reduction in the insurance premiums and legal fees for beverage establishments, which had skyrocketed in previous years.

Trends in the Beverage Industry

- The comeback of cocktails
- Designer bottled water
- Microbreweries
- More wine consumption
- Increase in coffeehouses and coffee intake
- Increased awareness and action to avoid irresponsible alcoholic beverage consumption
- An increase in beverages to attract more female participation.
- An increase in the number and variety of "energy drinks"

CASE STUDY

Hiring Bar Personnel

As bar manager of a popular local night club, it is your responsibility to interview and hire all bar personnel. One of your friends asks you for a job as a bartender. Because he has experience, you decide to help him out and give him a regular shift. During the next few weeks, you notice that the overall sales for his shifts are down slightly from previous weeks when other bartenders worked that shift. You suspect he may be stealing from you.

Discussion Questions

1. What are your alternatives for determining whether your friend is, in fact, stealing?
2. If you determine that he has been stealing, how do you handle it?

CASE STUDY

Java Coffee House

Michelle Wong is manager of the Java Coffee House at a busy location on Union Street in San Francisco. Michelle says that there are several challenges in operating a busy coffeehouse, such as training staff to handle unusual circumstances. For example, one guest consumed a cup of coffee and ate two-thirds of a piece of cake and then said he didn't like the cake, so didn't want to pay for his order.

Another problem is suppliers who quote good prices to get her business and then, two weeks later, raise the price of some of the items.

Michelle says that the young employees she has at the Java Coffee House are her greatest challenge of all. According to Michelle, there are four kinds of employees—those who are lazy; those who are good but not responsible; those who steal; and those who are great and are no trouble.

Discussion Questions

1. What are some suggestions for training staff to handle unusual circumstances?
2. How do you ensure that suppliers are delivering the product at the price quoted?
3. What do you do with lazy employees?
4. What do you do with irresponsible employees?
5. How do you deal with employees who steal?

Summary

1. Beverages are categorized into alcoholic and nonalcoholic beverages. Alcoholic beverages are further categorized into spirits, wines, and beer.
2. Wine is the fermented juice of ripe grapes. It is classified as red, white, and rose, and we distinguish between light beverage wines, sparkling wines, and aromatic wines.
3. The six steps in making wine are crushing, fermenting, racking, maturing, filtering, and boiling. France, Germany, Italy, Spain, and Portugal are the main European wine-producing areas, and California is the main American wine-producing area.
4. Beer is a brewed and fermented beverage made from malt. Different types of beer include ale, stout, lager, and pilsner.
5. Spirits have a high percentage of alcohol and are served before or after a meal. Fermentation and distillation are parts of their processing. The most popular white spirits are rum, gin, vodka, and tequila.
6. Today people have become more health conscious about consumption of alcohol; nonalcoholic beverages such as coffee, tea, soft drinks, juices, and bottled water are increasing in popularity.
7. Beverages make up 20 to 30 percent of total sales in a restaurant, but managers are liable if they serve alcohol to minors. Programs such as designated driver and Serve Save for Alcohol and the serving of virgin cocktails have increased.

Key Words and Concepts

alcoholic beverage
beer
brandy
champagne
cognac
dram shop legislation
fermentation
fining
fortified wines
hops
inventory control
liquor
malt
mashing

must
nonalcoholic beverage
Prohibition
proof
sparkling wine
spirit
vintage
white spirits
wine
wine and food pairing
wine tasting
wort
yeast

Review Questions

1. What is the difference between fortified and aromatic wines? In what combination is it suggested to serve food and wine and why?
2. Describe the brewing process of beer. What is the difference between a stout and a pilsner?
3. Name and describe the main types of spirits.
4. Why have nonalcoholic drinks increased in popularity, and what difficulties do bar managers face when serving alcohol?
5. Describe the origin of coffee.
6. Describe the proper procedure for handling and serving champagne.
7. Describe the origin of cocktails. What constitutes a cocktail?
8. Describe a typical bar setup.

Internet Exercises

1. Organization: **Clos Du Bois**
   Web site: **www.closdubois.com**
   Summary: Clos Du Bois is one of America's well-known and loved wineries and is a premier producer of wines from Sonoma County in California. The winery was started in 1974 and since then has acquired many more vineyards and a name for itself. It now sells about a million cases of premium wine annually.

   (a) look at the suggested food and wine pairings. What can you serve with the Clos Du Bois North Coast sauvignon blanc? Compare it to what you already know about what to eat with sauvignon blanc.
   (b) The Clos Du Bois has been named Wine of the Year for nine years by *Wine & Spirits*. What is it about this wine that makes it so different from others?

2. Organization: **Siebel Institute of Technology**
   Web site: **www.siebelinstitute.com**
   Summary: Siebel Institute of Technology is recognized for its training and educational programs in brewing technology.

   (a) What are some of the services that the Siebel Institute of Technology offers its students?
   (b) List the career path options available through Siebel Institute of Technology.

Apply Your Knowledge

1. In groups, do a blindfold taste test with cans of Coke and Pepsi. See if your group can identify which is which and who likes Coke or Pepsi the most.
2. Complete a class survey of preference for Coke or Pepsi and share the results with your classmates.
3. Request a local wine representative to demonstrate the correct way of opening and serving a bottle of nonalcoholic wine. Then practice opening a bottle yourself.
4. What type of wine would be recommended with the following:
   (a) Pork
   (b) Cheese
   (c) Lamb
   (d) Chocolate cake
   (e) Chicken

Suggested Activities

1. Search the Internet for underage drinking statistics and related highway deaths in your state.
2. Mothers Against Drunk Driving (MADD) is a nonprofit organization working to stop drunk drivers and support victims of drunk drivers. Find out what impact MADD has had on society.
3. Create an outline for a sports bar concept.

Endnotes

1. Personal correspondence with Jay R. Schrock, Dean, School of Hotel and Restaurant Management, University of South Florida, March 26, 2011.
2. *Ibid.*
3. This section draws on Sarah Berkley, "Organic and Sustainable Wine Production Expanding Rapidly in California," Organic Consumers Association, http://www.organicconsumers.org/organic/wine012104.cfm, retrieved March 12, 2010.
4. Budweiser Brewing Company presentation, University of South Florida, Tampa, Florida, September 7, 2004.
5. *Ibid.*
6. Hottinger, Greg, "Organic Beer," O'Mama Report, Organic Trade Association, www.theorganicreport.com/pages/605_organic_beer.cfm.
7. Craft Beer, *Small, Independent Traditional* www.craftbeer.com/pages/beerology/small-independent-traditional (accessed March 21, 2011).
8. Drink Craft Beer, *Home Page*, www.drinkcraftbeer.com/ (accessed March 21, 2011).
9. Craft Beer, *Small, Independent Traditional* www.craftbeer.com/pages/beerology/small-independent-traditional (accessed March 21, 2011).

10. *Ibid.*
11. Brewers Association, *Home Page,* www.brewersassociation.org (accessed March 21, 2011).
12. Walker_ExpHosp_Chapter10cb[1].doc http://thefullpint.com/beer-news/oregon-honors-full-sail-brewing-for-sustainability, retrieved March 14, 2010.
13. Josh Amaris, "10 Steps toward Sustainability Every Brewery Should Consider," www.bluemapinc.com/articles/article_12_brewing.html and www.checkthemarkets.com/index.php?option=com_content& task=view&id=688&Itemid=98, retrieved March 15, 2010.
14. http://biggreenboulder.com/energy/sustainable http://biggreenboulder.com/energy/sustainable-brewing-in-colorado-not-done-impressing-you-yet/, retrieved March 15, 2010.
15. C. Katsigiris and M. Porter, *The Bar and Beverage Book*, 3rd ed. (New York: John Wiley and Sons, 2002), 139.
16. Personal correspondence with Susan Davis of the Specialty Coffee Association of America, August 26, 2005.
17. Ancora Coffee Roasters, "A Goat and a King: Coffee's Colorful History," *Coffee Class: History*, www.ancoracoffee.com/Class/History_Of_Coffee.aspx (accessed March 21, 2011).
18. Ancora Coffee Roasters, "Coffee's Trek across the World," *Coffee Class: History*, www.ancoracoffee.com/Class/History_Of_Coffee.aspx (accessed March 21, 2011).
19. The Bean Shop, *History of Coffee*, www.thebeanshop.com/beanshop/default.asp?p=31. (accessed March 21, 2011).
21. Starbucks, *Starbucks Company Profile*, July 2011, http://assets.starbucks.com/assets/aboutuscompanyprofileq3201172811final.pdf (accessed November 3, 2001).
22. "Energy drink sales up despite health concerns," *Chicago Sun Times*, March 18, 2011, www.suntimes.com/lifestyles/health/4385825-423/energy-drink-sales-up-despite-health-concerns.html?print=true (accessed November 4, 2011).
23. *Ibid.*
24. Marnie Roberts, "Take me out to the sports bar," *Restaurants USA*, August 2011, www.restaurant.org/tools/magazines/rusa/magArchive/year/article/?ArticleID=515 (accessed March 19, 2011).
25. Scannabar, *Liquor Inventory Software*, (accessed March 19, 2011).
26. Scannabar, *Wine Inventory Software*, http://en.scannabar.com/products/wine-inventory/ (accessed March 19, 2011).
27. www.azbaramerica.com retrieved March 19, 2011.
28. Personal conversation with Zach Strauss, General Manager of Sluggers World Class Sports Bar in Chicago, May 4, 2007.

Glossary

Champagne   Sparkling wine made in the Champagne district of France.

Dram shop legislation   Laws and procedures that govern the legal operation of establishments that sell measured alcoholic beverages.

Fermentation   The chemical process in which yeast acts on sugar or sugar-containing substances, such as grain or fruit, to produce alcohol and carbon dioxide.

Fining   The process by which wine that has matured is filtered to help stabilize it and remove any solid particles still in the wine.

Fortified wine   Wine to which brandy or other spirits have been added to stop further fermentation or to raise its alcoholic content.

Hops   The dried, conical fruit of a special vine that imparts bitterness to beer.

Inventory control   A method for keeping track of all resources required to produce a product.

Malt   Germinated barley.

Mashing   In the making of beer, the process of grinding the malt and screening out bits of dirt.

Must   A mixture of grape pulp, skins, seeds, and stems.

Proof   A figure representing liquor's alcohol content.

Sparkling wine   Wine containing carbon dioxide, which provides effervescence when the wine is poured.

Spirits   Distilled drinks.

Vintage   The year in which a wine's grapes were harvested.

White spirits   Gin, rum, vodka, and tequila.

Wine   Fermented juice of grapes or other fruits.

Wort   In the making of beer, the liquid obtained after the mashing process.

Photo Credits

Credits are listed in the order of appearance.

Chris Howey/Shutterstock
bogdanhoda/Shutterstock
Linda Whitwam/Dorling Kindersley;
    Ian O'Leary/Dorling Kindersley
Ian O'Leary/Dorling Kindersley; Kzenon/
    Fotolia LLC
Jay R. Schrock
The Robert Mondavi Family of Wineries;
    Andy Z./Shutterstock

Chris Laurens/Alamy
Rob Westfall
Monty Rakusen Cultura/Newscom
Jules Selmes and Debi Treloar/DK Images
Stockbyte/Getty Images
Starbucks Coffee Company
Amy Etra/PhotoEdit
Rob Reichenfeld/DK Images

The Restaurant Business

From Chapter 6 of *Introduction to Hospitality*, Sixth Edition. John R. Walker. Copyright © 2013 by Pearson Education, Inc. Published by Pearson. All rights reserved.

The Restaurant Business

OBJECTIVES

After reading and studying this chapter, you should be able to:

- Describe the different characteristics of chain and independent restaurants.

- Identify some of the top chain and independent restaurants.

- List the classifications of restaurants.

- Differentiate characteristics of chain and independent restaurants.

The Restaurant Business

Restaurants are a vital part of our everyday lifestyles; because we are a society on the go, we patronize them several times a week to socialize, as well as to eat and drink. Restaurants offer a place to relax and enjoy the company of family, friends, colleagues, and business associates and to restore our energy level before heading off to the next class or engagement. Actually, the word *restaurant* derives from the word *restore*. Today, there are more than 960,000 restaurants in the United States, with sales of $604 billion and 12.8 million employees (marking the restaurant business as the largest employer apart from the government!). The restaurant industry's share of the food dollar has risen to 47.5 percent. On a typical day, more than 130 million people in the United States are guests in restaurants and foodservice operations.[1]

As a society we spend an increasing amount, approaching 50 percent, of our food dollar away from home. Restaurants are a multibillion-dollar industry that provides employment and contributes to the nation's social and economic well-being. No discussion of restaurants can continue without talking about the main ingredient: food. So, let's take a brief look at our culinary heritage.

Classical Cuisine

North America gained most of its culinary legacy from France. Two main events were responsible for our culinary legacy coming from France. First was the French Revolution in 1793, which caused the best French chefs of the day to lose their employment because their bosses lost their heads! Many chefs came to North America as a result, bringing with them their culinary talents. The second event was when Thomas Jefferson, who in 1784 spent five years as envoy to France, brought a French chef to the White House when he became president. This act stimulated interest in French cuisine and enticed U.S. tavern owners to offer better quality and more interesting food.

No mention of classical cuisine can be made without talking about the two main initiators: Marie-Antoine Carême (1784–1833), who is credited as the founder of classical cuisine, and Auguste Escoffier, who is profiled later in this chapter. Carême was abandoned on the streets of Paris as a child, and then worked his way up from cook's helper to become the chef to the Prince de Talleyrand and the Prince Regent of England. He also served as head chef to the future King George IV of England, Tsar Alexander of Russia, and Baron de Rothschild. His goal was to achieve "lightness," "grace," "order," and "perspicuity" of food. Carême dedicated his career to refining and organizing culinary techniques. His many books contain the first really systematic account of cooking principles, recipes, and menu making.[2]

The other great contributor to classical cuisine, Auguste Escoffier (1846–1935), unlike Carême, never worked in an aristocratic household. Instead, he held forth in the finest hotels of the time: the Place Vendome in Paris and the Savoy and Carlton hotels in London. Escoffier is noted for his many contributions to cuisine, including simplifying the Grand Cuisine of Carême by reducing the number of flavors and garnishes and even simplifying the number of sauces to five "mother" or leading sauces. Escoffier brought simplicity and harmony to the Grand Cuisine. His many cookbooks are still in use today: *La Guide Culinaire* (1903) is a collection of more than 5,000 classic cuisine recipes;

in *Le Liver des Menus* (1912), he compares a great meal with a symphony; and *Ma Cuisine* (1934) contains more than 2,000 timeless recipes. All of his books emphasize the importance of mastering the techniques of cooking.[3]

This is an exciting time to be involved in the culinary arts and restaurant industry. Not only are new restaurant concepts and themes to fit a variety of tastes and budgets appearing on the scene, the culinary arts are being developed by several creative and talented chefs. It is important to realize that in this industry, we are never far from food. So, let's take a look at the recent development of **culinary arts**.

The main "ingredient" in a restaurant is cuisine, and one of the main foundations of classical French cooking, on which much of American cuisine is based, is the five **mother sauces:** bechamel, velouté, espagnole, tomato, and hollandaise. These elaborate sauces were essential accompaniments for the various dishes on the menu. Until about 1900, all menus were written in French—some still are—and regardless of whether a person was dining in a good hotel or restaurant in London or Lisbon, the intention was that the dish should be prepared in the same manner and taste similar to the French version. The travelers of the day either spoke French or had a knowledge of menu French.

Classical French cuisine was popular until the late 1960s and early 1970s, when **nouvelle cuisine** became popular. Nouvelle cuisine is a lighter cuisine than the classical French and is based on simpler preparations—with the aid of processors, blenders, and juicers—using more natural flavors and ingredients. Instead of thickening a sauce with a flour-based **roux**, a **purée** of vegetables could be used instead. Fresh is in, and this includes herbs for flavor. Nouvelle cuisine combines classical techniques and principles with modern technology and scientific research. "Simpler, quicker" quickly became more stylish, with plate presentation becoming a part of the chef's art. North American cooking had arrived. The bounties of Canada and the United States provided the basis for regional cuisine to flourish nationally. **Fusion**, the blending of flavors and techniques from two cuisines, became popular. For example, New England and Italian or Californian and Asian cuisines can be blended. For example, a Japanese recipe might be blended with a Mexican one to create a new hybrid recipe.

Many great chefs have influenced our recent culinary development. Among them are Julia Child, whose television shows did much to take the mystique out of French cooking and encourage a generation of homemakers to elevate their cooking techniques and skills. More recently, Anthony Bourdain on the Travel Channel with his excellent program titled *No Reservations* and Emeril "Bam" Lagasse and Bobby Flay via the Food Network have popularized cooking and the gourmand lifestyle.

Culinary schools have done an excellent job of producing a new generation of chefs who are making significant contributions to the evolving culinary arts. For example, Alice Waters at Chez Panisse, her restaurant in Berkeley, California, is credited with the birth of California cuisine. Waters uses only fresh produce bought from local farmers. Paul Prudhomme is another contemporary chef who has energized many aspiring chefs with his passion for basic cooking, especially cajun style.

Charlie Trotter, chef–owner of Charlie Trotter's in Chicago, who is considered by many to be America's finest chef–owner and king of fusion, said in one of his books:

> *After love there is only cuisine! It's all about excellence, or at least working towards excellence. Early on in your approach to cooking—or in running a restaurant—you have to determine whether or not you are willing to*

commit fully and completely to the idea of the pursuit of excellence. *I have always looked at it this way: if you strive for perfection—an all out assault on total perfection—at the very least you will hit a high level of excellence, and then you might be able to sleep at night. To accomplish something truly significant, excellence has to become a life plan.*[4]

Chef Trotter brings his knowledge and exposure together into a coherent view on what the modern fine-dining experience could be. He says, "I thought the blend of European refinement regarding the pleasures of the table, American ingenuity and energy in operating a small enterprise, Japanese minimalism and poetic elegance in effecting a sensibility, and a modern approach to incorporating health and dietary concerns would encompass a spectrum of elements through which I could express myself fully. Several years later, I find I am even more devoted than ever to this approach."[5]

Food Trends and Practices

As the level of professionalism rises for the chef of the twenty-first century, chefs will need a strong culinary foundation with a structure that includes multiculture cooking skills and strong employability traits, such as passion, dependability, cooperation, and initiative. Additional management skills include strong supervisory training, sense of urgency, accounting skills, sanitation/safety knowledge, nutritional awareness, and marketing/merchandising skills.

Not only are trans fats banned from many cities menus but, according to the National Restaurant Association's research, nearly three out of four Americans say they are trying to eat more healthfully in restaurants than they did two years ago. The **HealthyDiningFinder.com** web site is a great resource for those looking to make smart choices when dining out.[6] Among the early program members are Arby's, P. F. Chang's, Buca di Beppo, Cracker Barrel, Round Table Pizza, El Pollo Loco, and Famous Dave's.

The term *back-to-basic cooking* has been redefined to mean taking classical cooking methods and infusing modern technology and science to create healthy and flavorful dishes. Some examples of this include the following:

- Thickening soups and sauces by processing and using the food item's natural starches instead of traditional thickening methods
- Redefining the basic mother sauces to omit the béchamel and egg-based sauces and add or replace them with coulis, salsas, or chutneys
- Pursuing more cultural culinary infusion to develop bold and aggressive flavors
- Experimenting with sweet and hot flavors
- Taking advantage of the shrinking globe and disappearance of national borders to bring new ideas and flavors to restaurants
- Evaluating recipes and substituting ingredients for better flavor; that is, flavored liquid instead of water, infused oils and vinegars instead of nonflavored oils and vinegars

Charlie Trotter, one of America's finest restaurant chef–owners and king of fusion.

INTRODUCING AUGUSTE ESCOFFIER (1846–1935)

"Emperor of the World's Kitchens"

Auguste Escoffier is considered by many to be the patron saint of the professional cook. Called the "emperor of the world's kitchens," he is considered a reference point and a role model for all chefs. His exceptional culinary career began at the age of thirteen, when he apprenticed in his uncle's restaurant, and he worked until 1920, and retired to die quietly at home in Monaco in 1935. Uneducated, but a patient educator and diligent writer, he was an innovator who remained deeply loyal to the regional and bourgeois roots of French cookery. He exhibited his culinary skills in the dining rooms of the finest hotels in Europe, including the Place Vendome in Paris and the Savoy and Carlton hotels in London.

When the Prince of Wales requested something light but delicious for a late dinner after a night in a Monte Carlo casino, Auguste Escoffier responded with *poularde Derby*, a stuffed chicken served with truffles cooked in champagne, alternating with slices of butter-fried *foie gras*, its sauce basted with the juices from the chicken and truffles. Another interesting anecdote regarding the chef's originality in making sauces tells of a special dinner for the Prince of Wales and Kaiser Wilhelm. Escoffier was asked to create a special dish to honor such an occasion. Struggling with an apparent loss of creativity until the night before the event, the chef finally noticed a sack of overripe mangos, from which he created a sauce that he personally came out from the kitchen to serve. As he placed the plate on the table, he looked at the Kaiser and with a wicked smile said, "*zum Teufel*"—to the devil. Thus was born sauce diable, today a favorite classic sauce. Escoffier's insistence on sauces derived from the cooking of main ingredients was revolutionary at the time and in keeping with his famous instruction: *faités simple*—keep it simple.

In fact, in his search for simplicity, Escoffier reduced the complexity of the work of Carême, the "cook of kings and king of cooks," and aimed at the perfect balance of a few superb ingredients. In *Le Livre des Menus* (1912), Escoffier makes the analogy of a great dinner as a symphony with contrasting movements that should be appropriate to the occasion, the guests, and the season. He was meticulous in his kitchen, yet wildly imaginative in the creation of exquisite dishes. In 1903, Escoffier published *Le Guide Culinaire*, an astounding collection of more than 5,000 classic cuisine recipes and garnishes. Throughout the book, Escoffier emphasizes technique, the importance of a complete understanding of basic cookery principles, and ingredients he considers essential to the creation of great dishes.

Escoffier's refinement of Carême's *grand cuisine* was so remarkable it developed into a new cuisine referred to as *cuisine classique*. His principles have been used by successive generations, most emphatically by the *novelle cuisine* brigade. Francois Fusero, *chef de cuisine* at the Hotel Hermitage, Monte Carlo, and many others, regard Escoffier as their role model.

- Substituting herbs and spices for salt
- Returning to one-pot cooking to capture flavors
- Offering more healthy dining choices in restaurants

Today, being a chef is considered a profession that offers a variety of opportunities in every segment of the hospitality industry and anywhere in the world.

TECHNOLOGY SPOTLIGHT

Weighing Wi-Fi in Restaurants

Cihan Cobanoglu, Ph.D., Dean, School of Hotel and Restaurant Management, University of South Florida, Sarasota-Manatee

Does Wi-Fi, or high-speed Internet access (HSIA), play a significant role in hotel guest satisfaction, and does it have a hand in hotel booking preferences? As per the 2009 Hotel Guest Technology Study, commissioned by the American Hotel & Lodging Association's technology and e-business committee and conducted by the University of Delaware, the answer to that question is a resounding yes. Yet if this question were to be applied to restaurants, would the results be the same? Is Wi-Fi service, whether it is free or comes with a fee, a determinant in customer retention? The University of Delaware conducted a follow-up study to understand the impact of Wi-Fi service in the restaurant environment.

Industry snapshot

Wi-Fi is increasingly becoming a must-have for public places, and consumers are demanding it. Over the past few years, IEEE 802.11 wireless networks have become increasingly deployed over a wide range of environments, with wireless local area networks (LANs) popping up in coffee shops, airports, hospitals, and restaurants. Most restaurants offer Wi-Fi service via the 802.11g standard (at 54 megabits per second) or the 802.11b standard (at 11 megabits per second). A small number of restaurants offer the newest Wi-Fi standard, 802.11n (at 100 megabits per second).

Restaurants that offer Wi-Fi services typically follow one of these three business models:

- For-a-Fee Model: The hot spot is offered by a location owner in partnership with a wireless Internet service provider to generate revenue through paid subscribers.

- Free-of-Charge Model: The hot spot is offered free to the customer with the cost being borne by the location provider.

- Hybrid Model: The hot spot is free to customers who purchase the service in the restaurant (for example, 30 minutes of free Internet for $10 spent in the restaurant). Even though more and more restaurants are offering Wi-Fi to their guests following one of the three business models, there is little research as to its impact on customer retention.

Study results

A survey was sent to roughly 1,000 American consumers, of which 257 people responded. The results showed that (1) Wi-Fi access has become an important amenity in restaurants and cafes in the United States; (2) tech-savvy customers prefer restaurants or cafés with Wi-Fi access; (3) customers prefer the free-of-charge Wi-Fi model over the paid models in restaurants; and (4) a stepwise regression model (a statistical technique used to identify the impact of a variable on other variables) showed that the following are predictors of the likelihood of a customer's return to a restaurant—Wi-Fi service availability, Wi-Fi service quality, the price of Wi-Fi service, the perceived risk of using Wi-Fi service, and the perceived value of Wi-Fi.

This study suggests that there is a positive correlation between Wi-Fi service and customer return visits. This finding makes more sense considering that 70 percent of respondents indicate utilizing a Wi-Fi–enabled device such as a laptop or PDA. Additionally, increasing numbers of consumers own dual-mode cell phones that allow phone conversations to be conducted over a Wi-Fi network for lower or no cost. Given these trends, it is likely that the demand for Wi-Fi access in public places such as restaurants will only increase.

This study also suggests that there is a negative correlation between the cost of Wi-Fi access in restaurants and customers' intentions to return. As the cost of restaurant Wi-Fi access increases, customers are less likely to return to that establishment. To offset this, Wi-Fi service should be offered to customers either free of charge or through a business model where customers are required to make a food or beverage purchase to access the free Wi-Fi service. This way, the cost of the service will be satisfied. The data also shows a positive correlation between perceived value of Wi-Fi and intention to return to a restaurant.

There also is a negative correlation between the perceived risk of using Wi-Fi at a restaurant and a guest's intention to return. There is little that restaurants can offer to address the perceived risk of using Wi-Fi in public networks. Users should be prepared to use their own tools to enable Wi-Fi security, such as secure socket layers and virtual private networks. However, restaurants can offer secure Wi-Fi access to their loyal customers through Wi-Fi protected access, which is an advanced encryption method for Wi-Fi access.

The study results indicate that restaurants could gain a positive return on their Wi-Fi investment. Restaurant owners and operators may do well to review the complete results and evaluate their high-speed Internet offering strategy.

Culinary Practices

In this new millennium, we are seeing culinary education setting the pace for dining exploration.[7] As you prepare for a career in the hospitality industry, you will find it imperative that you develop a strong culinary foundation. Within the structure of this you will need to develop cooking skills, strong employability traits, people skills, menu development skills, nutrition knowledge, sanitation/safety knowledge, accounting skills, and computer skills.

Before you can become a successful chef, you have to be a good cook. To be a good cook, you have to understand the basic techniques and principles of cooking. The art of cooking has not changed much in thousands of years. And, although the concept of cooking has not changed, science and technology have allowed us to improve the methods of food preparation. We still use fire for cooking: Grilling, broiling, and simmering are still popular methods of cooking.

To become a successful chef, you will need to learn all of the basic cooking methods in order to understand flavor profiles. As you look at recipes to cook, try to enhance the basic ingredient list to improve the flavor. As an example, always try to substitute a flavored liquid if water is called for in a recipe. It is also important to understand basic ingredient flavors so that you can improve flavor. The idea behind back-to-basic cooking means you evaluate your recipe and look for flavor improvement with each item.

Employability traits are those skills that focus on attitude, passion, initiative, dedication, sense of urgency, and dependability. These traits are not always traits that can be taught, but a good chef can demonstrate them by example. Most of the employers with job opportunities for students consider these skills to be more important than technical skills. The belief is that if you have strong employability traits, your technical skills will be strong.

One of the most important things to realize about the restaurant industry is that *you can't do it alone.* Each person in your operation has to work together for you to be successful. The most important ingredient in managing people is to *respect them.* Many words can be used to describe a manager (coach, supervisor, boss, mentor), but whatever term is used, you have to be in the game to be effective. Managing a kitchen is like coaching a football team—everyone

INTRODUCING RICHARD MELMAN

Chairman of the Board and Founder, Lettuce Entertain You Enterprises, Inc.

Richard Melman is founder and chairman of Lettuce Entertain You Enterprises, a Chicago-based corporation that owns and licenses seventy restaurants nationwide and in Japan.

The restaurant business has been Melman's life work, beginning with his early days in a family-owned restaurant and later as a teenager working in fast-food eateries and a soda fountain and selling restaurant supplies. After realizing that he wasn't cut out to be a college student and failing to convince his father that he should be made a partner in the family business, Melman met Jerry A. Orzoff, a man who immediately and unconditionally believed in Melman's ability to create and run restaurants. In 1971, the two opened R.J. Grunts, a hip burger joint that soon became one of the hottest restaurants in Chicago. Here, Melman and Orzoff presented food differently and with a sense of humor, creating the youthful and fun restaurant that was a forerunner in the trend toward dining out as entertainment that swept this country in the early 1970s.

Melman and Orzoff continued to develop restaurant concepts together until Orzoff's death in 1981. Through his relationship with Orzoff, Melman formulated a philosophy based on the importance of partners, of sharing responsibilities and profits with them, and of developing and growing together.[1]

To operate so many restaurants well, Lettuce has needed to hire, train, and develop people, and then to keep them happy and focused on excellence. Melman's guiding philosophy is that he is not interested in being the biggest or the best known—only in being the best he can be. He places enormous value on the people who work for Lettuce Entertain You Enterprises and feels tremendous responsibility for their continued success. Today, he has forty working partners, most of whom came up through the organization, and has 5,000 people working for him. Over the years, Melman has stayed close to the guests by using focus groups and frequent-diner programs. The group's training programs are rated among the best in the business, and Melman's management style is clearly influenced by team sports. He says, "There are many similarities between running a restaurant and a team sport. However, it's not a good idea to have ten all-stars; everybody can't bat first. You need people with similar goals—people who want to win and play hard."[2]

Melman's personal life revolves around his family. He and his wife Martha have been married for thirty years and have three children.[3]

[1]Marilyn Alva, "Does He Still Have It?" *Restaurant Business* 93, no. 4 (March 1, 1994), 104–111.
[2]Personal communication with Richard Melman, June 8, 2004.
[3]Lettuce Entertain You Restaurants, *Home Page*, www.leye.com, (accessed November 4, 2011).

must work together to be effective. The difference between a football team and a kitchen is that chefs/managers cannot supervise from the sidelines; they have to be in the game. One of my favorite examples of excellent people management skills is that of the general manager of a hotel who had the ware-washing team report directly to him. When asked why, he indicated that they are the people who know what is being thrown in the garbage, they are the people who know what the customers are not eating, and they are the people most responsible for the sanitation and safety of an operation. There are many components to managing people—training, evaluating, nurturing, delegating, and so on—but the most important is respect.

▶ Check Your Knowledge

1. From what country did North America gain most of its culinary legacy?
2. Define fusion cuisine and give an example.

Developing a Restaurant

Developing a restaurant may be the ultimate entrepreneurial dream. In which other industry can you get into a business like a restaurant for only a few thousand dollars? Of course, you need to have acquired the knowledge and skills along the way by getting experience in the kind of restaurant you intend to open. Yes, independent restaurants are a rush for the owners—they are one of the few places where guests use all of their senses to enjoy the experience. Through taste, sight, smell, hearing, and touch, all employees and guests can savor the food, service, and atmosphere of the restaurant. The successful operation of a restaurant is dependent on a number of factors. Let's examine the factors that make for a successful restaurant development, from the operating philosophy to controls, and all the functions in between.

Operating Philosophy, Mission, Goals, and Objectives

At the heart of an enterprise is the philosophy of the owner. The philosophy represents the way the company does business. It is an expression of the ethics, morals, and values by which the company operates. Many companies have formal mission statements that explain their reason for being in business. Danny Meyer of Union Square Hospitality calls it *"enlightened hospitality*—meaning if your staff is happy your guests will be, too."[8] Meyer gives each of his 450 employees a voucher to dine in one of the restaurants

The Olive Garden, a popular Italian-themed restaurant, is part of Darden Restaurants.

every month. They have to write a report on the experience; Meyer enjoys reading them. Ever the coach and teacher, he says that it's better to have your staff tell you what's wrong than for you to have to tell them. No wonder his restaurants like Union Square Cafe, Gramercy Tavern, Eleven Madison Park, Tabla, Blue Smoke, and others are the top rated in New York.

Restaurant Market

The market is composed of those guests who will patronize the restaurant. A respective restaurant owner will analyze the market to determine whether sufficient demand exists in a particular market niche, such as Italian or Southern cuisine. A **niche** is a marketing term used to describe a specific share or slot of a certain market. A good indication of the size of the market can be ascertained by taking a radius of from one to five miles around the restaurant. The distance will vary according to the type and location of the restaurant. In Manhattan, it may only be a few blocks, whereas in rural West Virginia it may be a few miles. The area that falls within the radius is called the **catchment area**. The demographics of the population within the catchment area is analyzed to reveal age, number of people in various age brackets, sex, ethnicity, religion, income levels, and so on. This information is usually available from the chamber of commerce or data at the local library or real estate offices.

One yardstick used to determine the potential viability of a restaurant is to divide the number of restaurants in the catchment area by the total population. The average number of people per restaurant in the United States is about 500. Perhaps this kind of saturation is one of the reasons for the high failure rate of restaurants. Obviously, each area is different; one location may have several Italian restaurants but no Southern restaurant. Therefore, a Southern restaurant would be unique in the market and, if properly positioned, may have a competitive advantage. If someone in the catchment area wanted to eat Italian food, he or she would have to choose among the various Italian restaurants. In marketing terms, the number of potential guests for the Italian restaurant would be divided by the number of Italian restaurants to determine **fair market share** (the average number of guests that would, if all other things went equal, eat at any one of the Italian restaurants). Figure 1 shows a thousand potential guests. If they all decided to eat Italian in the fair market share scenario, each restaurant would receive 100 guests. In reality, we know this does not happen—for various reasons, one restaurant becomes more popular. The number of guests that this and the other restaurants receive then is called the **actual market share**. Figure 2 shows an example of the actual market share that similar restaurants might receive.

Restaurant Concept

Successful restaurant concepts are created with guests in mind. All too frequently someone thinks it would be a good idea to open up a particular kind of restaurant, only to find there are insufficient guests to make it viable.

For the winners, creating and operating a restaurant business is fun—lots of people coming and going, new faces, old friends. Restaurants provide a social gathering place where employees, guests, and management can get their adrenaline flowing in positive ways. The restaurant business is exciting and

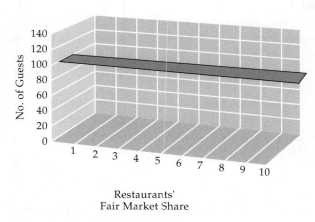

Figure 1 • Fair Market Share.

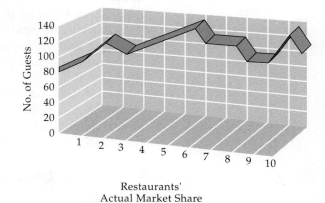

Figure 2 • Actual Market Share.

challenging; with the right location, food, atmosphere, and service it is possible to extract the market and make a good return on investment.

There are several examples of restaurant concepts that have endured over the past few decades. Applebee's, Chart House, Hard Rock Cafe, Olive Garden, Red Lobster, and T.G.I. Friday's are some of the better-known U.S. chain restaurant concepts. Naturally, there are more regional and independent concepts.

The challenge is to create a restaurant concept and bring it into being, a concept that fits a definite market, a concept better suited to its market than that presented by competing restaurants.[9] Every restaurant represents a concept and projects a total impression or an image. The image appeals to a certain market—casual, formal, children, adults, ethnic, and so on. The concept should fit the location and reach out to its target market. A restaurant's concept, location, menu, and decor should intertwine.[10]

In restaurant lingo, professionals sometimes describe restaurants by the net operating percentage that the restaurant makes. T.G.I. Friday's restaurants, for example, are usually described as 20-percent restaurants. A local restaurant may be only a 10-percent restaurant.

For the operation of a restaurant to be successful, the following factors need to be addressed:

- Mission
- Goals
- Objectives
- Market
- Concept
- Location
- Menu planning
- Ambiance
- Lease
- Other occupational costs

The odds in favor of becoming a big restaurant winner are good. Thousands of restaurants do business in the United States. Each year, thousands of new ones open and thousands more close, and many more change ownership. The restaurant business is deceptively easy to enter, but it is deceptively difficult to succeed in it.[11]

Restaurant concept is undoubtedly one of the major components of any successful operation. Some restaurants are looking for a concept; some concepts are searching for a restaurant.

Restaurant Location

The restaurant concept must fit the location, and the location must fit the concept (see Figure 3). The location should appeal to the target market (expected interests). Other things being equal, prime locations cost more, so operators must either charge more for their menu items or drive sufficient volume to keep the rent/lease costs to between 5 and 8 percent of sales.

Key location criteria include the following:

- Demographics—how many people are there in the catchment area?
- The average income of the catchment area population
- Growth or decline of the area
- Zoning, drainage, sewage, and utilities
- Convenience—how easy is it for people to get to the restaurant?
- Visibility—can passersby see the restaurant?
- Accessibility—how accessible is the restaurant?
- Parking—is parking required? If so, how many spaces are needed and what will it cost?

Figure 3 • Concept and Market.
(Reprinted with permission from John R. Walker and Donald E. Lundberg, *The Restaurant from Concept to Operation*, 3rd ed. [New York: John Wiley and Sons, 2001], p. 62.)

- Curbside appeal—how inviting is the restaurant?
- Location—how desirable is the neighborhood?

Several popular types of restaurant locations include the following:

- Stand-alone restaurants
- Cluster or restaurant row
- Shopping mall
- Shopping mall—freestanding
- Downtown
- Suburban

Restaurant Ambiance

The **atmosphere** that a restaurant creates has both immediate conscious and unconscious effects on guests. The immediate conscious effect is how guests react to the **ambiance** on entering the restaurant—or even more importantly as an element in the decision-making process used in selecting a restaurant. Too noisy? Are the tables too close? The subconscious is affected by mood, lighting, furnishings, and music; these play an important role in leaving a subtle impression on guests. Today, atmospherics are part of the theme and have an immediate sensory impact on customers.

Perhaps the most noticeable atmospheric restaurants are those with a theme. The theme will use color, sound, lighting, decor, texture, and visual stimulation to create special effects for patrons. Among restaurants with good atmospherics are Macaroni Grill, Panera Bread, Outback, Hard Rock Cafe, and Chart House.

▶ Check Your Knowledge

1. Imagine you are starting your own restaurant. In the process, you realize you need a mission statement. Write a mission statement for your new restaurant.
2. Define the following terms and briefly describe the role they play:
   a. Market
   b. Concept
   c. Ambiance

Sustainable Restaurants

The average American meal has a shockingly large carbon footprint, usually traveling 1,500 miles to the plate and emitting large amounts of CO_2 in the process, according to the Leopold Center for Sustainable Agriculture. Each meal created produces 275 pounds of waste a day, making restaurants the worst aggressors of greenhouse gas emissions in retail industry, says the

Boston-based Green Restaurant Association [GRA], a nonprofit organization that works to create an ecologically sustainable restaurant industry.[12]

A recent NRA [National Restaurant Association] study shows that utility costs are a big line item for restaurateurs, accounting for a median of between 2.3 percent and 3.6 percent of sales, depending on the type of operation. According to *Zagat's America's Top Restaurants*, 65 percent of surveyors said they would pay more for food that has been sustainably raised or procured. According to National Restaurant Association research, 62 percent of adults said they would likely choose a restaurant based on its environmental friendliness.[13]

Does greenings restaurant sound challenging, time-consuming, and costly? According to the Green Restaurant Association (GRA), it doesn't have to be any of those things. The GRA was founded almost 20 years ago with the mission of creating an ecologically sustainable restaurant industry, and it has the world's largest database of environmental solutions for the restaurant industry.[14] The GRA strives to simplify things because it realizes that restaurateurs have enough on their plates without worrying what kind of paper towel to order, or where they'll get next month's supply of ecofriendly dish soap.[15]

Menu Planning

The menu may be the most important ingredient in a restaurant's success. A restaurant's menu must agree with the concept; the concept must be based on what the guest in the target market expects; and the menu must exceed those expectations. The type of menu will depend on the kind of restaurant being operated.

There are six main types of menus:

A la carte menus. These menus offer items that are individually priced.

Table d'hôte menus. Table d'hôte menus offer a selection of one or more items for each course at a fixed price. This type of menu is used more frequently in hotels and in Europe. The advantage is the perception guests have of receiving good values.

Du jour menus. Du jour menus list the items "of the day."

Tourist menus. These menus are used to attract tourists' attention. They frequently stress value and food that is acceptable to tourists.

California menus. These menus are so named because, in some California restaurants, guests may order any item on the menu at any time of the day.

Cyclical menus. Cyclical menus repeat themselves over a period of time.

A menu generally consists of perhaps six to eight appetizers, two to four soups, a few salads—both as appetizers and entrées—eight to sixteen entrées, and about four to six desserts.

The many considerations in menu planning attest to the complexity of the restaurant business. Considerations include the following:

- Needs and desires of guests
- Capabilities of cooks
- Equipment capacity and layout

- Consistency and availability of menu ingredients
- Price and pricing strategy (cost and profitability)
- Nutritional value
- Accuracy in menu
- Menu analysis (contribution margin)
- Menu design
- Menu engineering
- Chain menus[16]

Needs and Desires of Guests

In planning a menu, the needs and desires of the guests are what is important—not what the owner, chef, or manager thinks. If it is determined that there is a niche in the market for a particular kind of restaurant, then the menu must harmonize with the theme of the restaurant.

The Olive Garden restaurants are a good example of a national chain that has developed rapidly during the past few years. The concept has been positioned and defined as middle of the road with a broad-based appeal. During the concept development phase, several focus groups were asked their opinions on topics from dishes to decor. The result has been extremely successful.

Several other restaurants have become successful by focusing on the needs and desires of the guest. Among them are Hard Rock Cafe, T.G.I. Friday's, Red Lobster, and Applebee's.

Capabilities of Cooks

The capabilities of the cooks must also harmonize with the menu and concept. An appropriate level of expertise must be employed to match the peak demands and culinary expertise expected by the guests. The length and complexity of the menu and the number of guests to be served are both factors in determining the extent of the cooks' capabilities.

The equipment capacity and layout affect the menu and the efficiency with which the cooks can produce the food. Some restaurants have several fried or cold items on the appetizer menu simply to avoid use of the stoves and ovens, which will be needed for the entrées. A similar situation occurs with desserts; by avoiding the use of the equipment needed for the entrées, cooks find it easier to produce the volume of meals required during peak periods.

One of the best examples of effective utilization of menu and equipment is in Chinese restaurants. At the beginning of many Chinese restaurant menus, there are combination dinners. The combination dinners include several courses for a fixed price. Operators of Chinese restaurants explain that about 60 to 70 percent of guests order those combinations. This helps the cooks because they can prepare for the orders and produce the food quickly, which pleases the guests. It would create havoc if everyone ordered à la carte items because the kitchen and the cooks could not handle the volume in this way.

Equipment Capacity and Layout

All restaurant menus should be developed with regard to the capacity and layout of the equipment. Anyone who has worked in a busy kitchen on Friday or Saturday night and been "slammed" will realize that part of the problem may have been too ambitious a menu (too many items requiring extensive preparation and the use of too much equipment).

If the restaurant is already in existence, it may be costly to alter the kitchen. Operators generally find it easier to alter the menu to fit the equipment. The important thing is to match the menu with the equipment and production scheduling. A menu can be created to use some equipment for appetizers; for this one reason, the appetizers selections on the menu often include one or two cold cuts, possibly a couple of salads, but mostly some deep-fried items or soups. This keeps the stove and grill areas free for the entrées. The desserts, if they are not brought in, are mostly made in advance and served cold or heated in the microwave. Other considerations include the projected volume of sales and the speed of service for each menu item.

Most chefs are sufficiently adaptable to be able to prepare quality meals with the equipment provided. Some may prepare a more detailed *mise en place* (everything in place to prepare a menu item), and others will go further to partially cook items so that they can be furnished to order. Of course, there is always the old standby—the daily special—that can take the pressure off the production line.

Consistency and Availability of Menu Ingredients

In the United States, most ingredients are available year-round. However, at certain times of the year, some items become more expensive. This is because they are out of season—in economic terms, the demand exceeds the supply, so the price goes up. An example of this is when a storm in the Gulf of Mexico disrupts the supply of fresh fish and shellfish and causes an increase in price. To offset this kind of situation, some operators print their menus daily. Others may purchase a quantity of frozen items when the prices are low.

FOCUS ON NUTRITION

New Frontiers in Restaurant Dining

Jim Inglis, Professor, Valencia Community College, Orlando, Florida

Over the last several years we have seen a major shift in what dishes restaurants are serving up. The cause for this change? Public interest, some of which is sparked by government legislation and some of which is driven by market or consumer demands. With laws now requiring restaurant chains in some states (soon every state) to disclose calorie counts and other nutritional information, restaurant companies have an opportunity to take advantage of and capitalize on this national movement—and many are.

Health-conscious consumers are demanding that companies change the way they do business; no longer does quantity always trump quality. Chains such as Chipotle, with the slogan "Food with Integrity,"[17] have been successful in marketing the qualities of healthy eating and serving animal products that do not contain growth hormones or antibiotics. Words like *sustainable*, *eco-friendly*, *green*, and *farm-raised* are the new catchphrases.

Some other chain concepts have also set their sights on nutrition by adding menu items with lower total calorie counts, sourcing more locally grown foods, and utilizing healthier cooking methods such as grilling or caramelizing vegetables in dishes rather than adding sugar. In fact, Seasons 52, of Darden Restaurants, "makes a promise that nothing on our menu is over 475 calories."[18] The result, they say, is "great tasting, highly satisfying food that just so happens to be good for you!"[19]

There is also the new push that came from the Obama administration to change the food pyramid, improve our public school meals, and educate children on the benefits of eating healthy and exercising. The USDA's new *My Plate* icon simplifies/replace the old food pyramid and is meant to "help consumers make healthier food choices."[20] It emphasizes the fruit, vegetable, grain, protein, and dairy food groups and clearly shows that half of what you eat every day should be fruits and vegetables. This is something that Americans as a whole are not doing, but Americans are starting to up and demand change.

So what role will the restaurant industry play in this paradigm shift through which the industry is going? This is not a fad or just a trend; I do believe the industry is going to have to embrace the concept of nutritional importance in selecting the items restaurants choose to put on their menus. On my recent visit the National Restaurant Show in Chicago, 2011, there were many examples of gluten-free products, vegan dishes, vegetarian cooking demonstrations, and so forth. We are seeing some innovative restaurant companies already incorporating many of these ideas into their menu concepts to meet the needs of today's consumer. The companies that position themselves correctly, and that can appeal to young and old alike, will be in a position to make substantial revenues, which equals substantial profits.

(Reprinted by permission of Jim Inglis.)

Price and Pricing Strategy

The target market and concept will, to a large extent, determine the menu price ranges. An example might be a neighborhood restaurant where the appetizers are priced from $3.25 and $6.95 and entrées are in the $6.95 and $11.95 price range. The selling price of each item must be acceptable to the market and profitable to the restaurateur. Factors that go into this decision include the following:

- What is the competition charging for a similar item?
- What is the item's food cost?
- What is the cost of labor that goes into the item?
- What other costs must be covered?
- What profit is expected by the operator?
- What is the contribution margin of the item?[21]

Figure 4 illustrates the factors that influence a restaurant's menu prices. There are two main ways to price menus: A comparative approach analyzes the price ranges of the competition and determines the price range for appetizers, entrées, and desserts. The second method is to cost the individual dish item on the menu and multiply it by the ratio amount necessary to achieve the desired food cost percentage. For example, to achieve a 30-percent food cost for

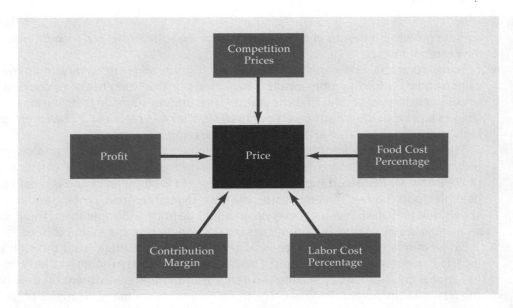

Figure 4 • Factors That Influence a Restaurant's Menu Prices.

an item priced at $6.95 on the menu, the food cost would have to be $2.09. Beverage items are priced the same way. This method will result in the same expected food cost percentage for each item. It would be great if we lived in such a perfect world. The problem is that if some items were priced out according to a 30-percent food cost, they might appear to be overpriced according to customers' perceptions. For example, some of the more expensive meat and fish would price out at $18 to $21, when the restaurant would prefer to keep entrée prices under $15. To balance this, restaurants lower the margin on the more expensive meat and fish items—as long as there are only one or two of them—and raise the price on some of the other items, such as soup, salad, chicken, and pasta. This approach is called the **weighted average**, whereby the factors of food cost percentage, contribution margin, and sales volume are weighted.

Nutritional Value

A more health-conscious customer has promoted most restaurant operators to make changes not only to the menu selections but also to the preparation methods. Restaurant operators are using more chicken, fish, seafood, and pasta items on the menus today compared with a few years ago. Beef is leaner than ever before. All of these items are being prepared in more healthful ways such as broiling, poaching, braising, casseroling, or rotisserieing instead of frying.

Increasingly, restaurants are publishing the nutritional value of their food. McDonald's has taken a leadership role in this. Other restaurants are utilizing a heart-healthy symbol to signify that the menu item is suitable for guests with concerns about heart-healthy eating. Many restaurants are changing the oil they use from oils high in saturated fat, which may be damaging to health, to 100-percent vegetable oil or canola oil, which are lower in saturated fat.

Accuracy in Menu

Laws prohibit misrepresentation of items being sold. In the case of restaurants, the so-called truth-in-menu laws refer to the fact that descriptions on the menu must be accurate. Prime beef must be prime cut, not some other grade; fresh vegetables must be fresh, not frozen; and Maine lobster had better come from Maine. Some restaurants have received sizable fines for violations of accuracy in menu.

Menu Analysis

One of the earliest approaches to menu analysis was developed by Jack Miller. He called the best-selling items *winners*; they not only sold more but were also at a lower food cost percentage. In 1982, Micheal Kasavana and Donald Smith developed menu engineering, in which the best items are called *stars*—those items that have the highest contribution margin and the highest sales. Later, David Paresic suggested that a combination of three variables—**food cost percentage** (percentage of the selling price of an item that must be spent to purchase the raw ingredients), **contribution margin**, and **sales volume**—should be used.

Another key variable in menu analysis is labor costs. A menu item may take several hours to prepare, and it may be difficult to calculate precisely the time a cook spends in preparation of the dish. Operators add the total food and labor costs together to determine prime cost, which should not exceed about 60 to 65 percent of sales. The remaining 35 to 40 percent is for overhead and profit.

Menu Engineering

Menu engineering is a sophisticated approach to setting menu prices and controlling costs. It operates on the principle that the food cost percentage of each menu item is not as important as the total contribution margin of the menu as a whole. Usually this means that the food cost percentage of a menu item could be larger than desired, yet, the total contribution margin of the menu will increase. Through menu engineering, menu items that should be repositioned, dropped, repriced, or simply left alone can be identified.

Menu Design and Layout

Basic menus can be recited by the server. Casual menus are sometimes written on a chalk or similar type board. Quick-service menus are often illuminated above the order counter. More-formal menus are generally single page, or folded with three or more pages. Some describe the restaurant and type of food offered; most have beverage suggestions and a wine selection. The more upscale American-Continental restaurants have a separate wine list.

Some menus are more distinctive than others, with pictures of the items or at least enticing descriptions of the food. Research indicates that there is a focal point at the center of the right-hand page; this is the spot in which to place the star or signature item.[22]

Like a brochure for the hotel, a menu is a sales tool and motivational device. A menu's design can affect what guests order and how much they spend.

The paper, colors, and artwork all play an important role in influencing guest decisions and help to establish a restaurant's image and ambiance.

As you can see, a number of factors make for a successful restaurant. Help is available from the U.S. Small Business Association (**www.sba.gov/category/navigation-structure/counseling-training**), which has several courses and other information for those interested in developing a business plan for a restaurant. Now, let's look at the classifications of restaurants.

Classifications of Restaurants

There is no single definition of the various classifications of restaurants, perhaps because it is an evolving business. Most experts would agree, however, that there are two main categories: **independent restaurants (indies)** and **chain restaurants.** Other categories include designations such as *fine dining, casual dining and dinner house restaurants, family,* and *quick-service restaurants.* Some restaurants may even fall into more than one category—for instance, a restaurant can be both quick service and ethnic, such as Taco Bell.

The National Restaurant Association's figures indicate that Americans are spending a lot of food dollars away from home at various foodservice operations. Americans are eating out up to five times a week—and on special occasions such as birthdays, anniversaries, Mother's Day, and Valentine's Day. The most popular meal eaten away from home is lunch, which brings in approximately 50 percent of fast-food restaurant sales.[23]

Individual restaurants (also called indies) are typically owned by one or more owners, who are usually involved in the day-to-day operation of the business. Even if the owners have more than one store (restaurant-speak for a "restaurant"), each usually functions independently. These restaurants are not affiliated with any national brand or name. They offer the owner independence, creativity, and flexibility, but are generally accompanied by more risk. For example, the restaurant may not be as popular as the owners hoped it would be, the owners lacked the knowledge and expertise necessary for success in the restaurant business, or the owners did not have the cash flow to last several months before a profit could be made. You only have to look around your neighborhood to find examples of restaurants that failed for one reason or another.

Chain restaurants are a group of restaurants, each identical in market, concept, design, service, food, and name. Part of the marketing strategy of a chain restaurant is to remove uncertainty from the dining experience. The same menu, food quality, level of service, and atmosphere can be found in any one of the restaurants, regardless of location. Large companies or entrepreneurs are likely chain restaurant owners. For example, Applebee's is a restaurant chain; some stores are company-owned, but the majority are franchised by territory.

Fine Dining

A **fine-dining restaurant** is one where a good selection of menu items is offered; generally at least fifteen or more different entrées can be cooked to order, with nearly all the food being made on the premises from scratch using raw or fresh ingredients. Full-service restaurants may be formal or casual and may be further categorized by price, decor/atmosphere, level of formality, and menu. Most fine-dining restaurants may be cross-referenced into other categories, as mentioned previously. Many of these restaurants serve **haute cuisine** (pronounced *hote*), which is a French term meaning "elegant dining," or literally "high food." Many of the fine restaurants in the United States are based on French or northern Italian cuisine, which, together with fine Chinese cuisine, are considered by many Western connoisseurs to be the finest in the world.

Most fine-dining restaurants are independently owned and operated by an entrepreneur or a partnership. These restaurants are in almost every city. In recent years, fine dining has become more fun because creative chefs offer guests fine cuisine as an art. At places like Union Square Café and Gramercy Tavern in New York, Danny Meyer is looking for guests who want spectacular meals without the fuss. Many cities have independent fine-dining restaurants that offer fine dining for an occasion—a birthday, an "expense account" (business entertaining), or other celebration.

Marco Maccioni, son of Sirio Maccioni of the famed Le Cirque, says that the sons did not want simply to clone Le Cirque. For the menu, they sought inspiration from Mama's home cooking—pizza, pasta, and comfortable, braised dishes.

Many cities have independent fine-dining restaurants that pursue those who are not content with wings and deep-fried cheese. Chefs are therefore making approachable, yet provocative food; each course is expertly prepared and may be served with wine.

Several types of restaurants are included in the fine-dining segment: various steakhouses; ethnic, celebrity, and theme restaurants. The upscale steakhouses, such as Morton's of Chicago, Ruth's Chris, and Houston's, continue to attract the expense account and "occasion" diners. Naturally, they are located near their guests and in cities with convention centers or attractions that draw big crowds.

Anthony Bourdain, owner and chef of Les Halles Restaurant, sits at one of its tables. Bourdain is the top-selling author of *Kitchen Confidential* and *A Cook's Tour*.

A DAY IN THE LIFE OF MELISSA DOAN-FIEBER

Server, Carrabba's Italian Grill

I started working in the restaurant business as a way to make money while going to school. I thought to myself, "This is a piece of cake." I soon realized that this fast-paced job is hectic and trying. Being a server is like being on center stage waiting for the next performance request. Every guest has their needs and it's up to you to figure out how they want them met. Sound scary? To some it may be; to me, I love it. Every day is something new, someone new, and never a reflection of the day before it. Over the years, I have learned that servers must obtain a few qualities: attentiveness, knowledge, hospitality, and genuine concern. Maintaining these qualities is hard during a busy shift; but in my experience, you can mess up a guest's order, and as long as you acknowledge the problem, seem concerned, and admit you're wrong, the guest will return. Restaurant goers dine out based on a number of reasons, but service is a deciding factor when choosing where to dine.

(continued)

A DAY IN THE LIFE OF MELISSA DOAN-FIEBER (continued)

As a server in a family-friendly fine-dining restaurant, I am never allowed to have a bad day. A typical workday starts before I even leave my house. I have to prepare a presentable uniform and gather all my tools of the trade (tie, wine key, lighter, pens, and server book). My uniform is my first impression and my instant greeting to any guest in the restaurant. Typically, I am scheduled the opening shift, and when I arrive at 3:15 P.M., it is my responsibility to start the shift with the proper amounts of lemons, butters, teas, and garnishes and to bake the bread. Every restaurant is different, but the one I work at schedules two openers and 45 minutes to set up.

Once setup is complete, I focus on making sure I have a clean section. Company policy allows a three-table maximum; this is designed to maintain consistently great service. The doors open at 4:00 P.M., and as the opener, I receive the first two tables. Each table has specific requirements, and it is part of my job to read their needs. Some guests want a quiet meal, while others are looking for entertainment and conversation. Some guests provide more specific instructions, such as allergies, food specifications, or child provisions. The restaurant I serve for is unique in two ways: first, they require their servers to know the ingredients of every item on the menu, and second, they make every item from scratch, allowing the guests to tailor items to their needs. Shortly into the shift, we are all called to the back for a "huddle-up"; here, we learn the soup, fish, and vegetable of the day, as well as the current sales contests. As the shift progresses, the chaos snowballs. Through the course of the night, I can only expect the unexpected. Steaks will be cooked improperly, guests will dislike their food, I will need manager compensations without a manager in sight, and I will always get to the ice bin right as it's emptied. The customer's perception of my service is how I get paid, and as long as I maintain my qualities, the guests will notice. My job is to run my food, meet my table's needs, and do my side work, but my service is the base of my tip.

As the evening winds down, I am cut based on the business of the restaurant. The managers cut the servers that came in first, and this time varies every night. Before I get started on my closing side work, I must finish up my tables and complete my restaurant financials. Ideally, my closing side work should be easy because everyone has running side work that maintains the tasks that need to be completed. Closing side work can consist of cleaning, restocking, and resetting for the following day. Once I am finished, I must get checked out by another server and then I can clock out, expecting a new day tomorrow.

A few ethnic restaurants are considered fine dining—most cities have a sampling of Italian, French, and other European, Latin, and Asian restaurants. Some even have fusion (a blend of two cuisines—for example, Italian and Japanese). Fusion restaurants must pay particular attention when blending two unique ethnic flavors. If successful, the dish could turn out to be the latest craze; if unsuccessful, it could be disastrous!

Celebrity chef–owned fine-dining restaurants of interest include Wolfgang Puck's Spago, in four locations; Chinois in Santa Monica, California; CUT, in four locations; and Wolfgang Puck Pizzeria & Cucina in Las Vegas and Alice Waters's Chez Panisse in Berkeley, California. Both chefs have done much to inspire a new generation of talented chefs. Alice Waters has been a role model for many female chefs and has received numerous awards and published several cookbooks, including one for children.

The level of service in fine-dining restaurants is generally high, with a hostess or host to greet and seat patrons. Captains and food servers advise guests of special items and assist with the description and selection of dishes during order taking. If there is no separate sommelier (wine waiter), the captain or food server may offer a description of the wine that will complement the meal and can assist with the order taking. Some upscale or luxury full-service restaurants have table-side cooking and French service from a gueridon cart (a wheelable cart used to add flair to tableside service; it is also used for flambé dishes). The decor of a full-service restaurant is generally compatible with the overall ambiance and theme that the restaurant is seeking to create. These elements of food, service, and decor create a memorable experience for the restaurant guest.

INTRODUCING SARAH STEGNER

Chef–Owner, Prairie Grass Café

Sarah Stegner opened Prairie Grass Café in Northbrook, Illinois, with her partner, former executive chef George Bumbaris of the Ritz-Carlton Chicago, in 2004. A little history. . .

Stegner, an Evanston, Illinois, native, grew up in a family devoted to food. Her grandmother was a caterer "before women did those kinds of things," and her grandfather was an avid backyard vegetable gardener. The table was the center of the family and was where Stegner's passion for food emerged.

After a year spent studying classical guitar at Northwestern University, Stegner followed her heart and enrolled at the Dumas Pere Cooking School. She graduated with a chef's certificate one year later and was hired as an apprentice at the Ritz-Carlton Chicago.

In 1990, after six years of working in various culinary capacities (including a first job of cleaning fish for twelve hours a day), Stegner was promoted to chef of the Dining Room. She worked for years under the guiding hands of Fernand Gutierrez, former executive chef and director of food and beverage at the Ritz-Carlton Chicago, and current food and beverage director at Four Seasons Mexico City. Since then, Stegner has distinguished herself as one of America's most creative young chefs.

As a result of her talents, she has captured many national honors. Chef Stegner was named Best Chef of the Midwest in 1998 by the prestigious James Beard Foundation and the Dining Room was named one of the top five restaurants in Chicago in 1999 by *Gourmet* magazine, and it received four stars from the *Chicago Tribune*. In addition, it was rated best hotel dining room in Chicago in 1999 by the prestigious Zagat Chicago Restaurant Guide and was named Best Restaurant in Chicago in 1996 by *Gourmet*, one of the top thirteen hotel dining rooms in the United States in 1996 by *Bon Appétit*, and one of the top ten hotel restaurants in the world in 1996 by *Hotels* magazine.

Chef Stegner is recipient of the 1995 Robert Mondavi Culinary Award of Excellence and captured the national title of 1994 Rising Star Chef of the Year in America by the James Beard Foundation. She also holds the title of Prix Culinaire International Pierre Taittinger 1991 U.S. Winner, where she represented the United States in the finals in Paris and was the only female chef present at the global competition.

In recent years, Chef Stegner has enjoyed periodic training in France, under the expertise of Chef Pierre Orsi at his two-star Michelin Pierre Orsi Restaurant in Lyon, France, and with chefs Bertolli and Berard Bessin in Paris.

She also finds time to donate her talents to charitable causes. Six years ago, she founded the Women Chefs of Chicago, comprising the city's top female chefs who donate cuisine for numerous events throughout the city to raise money for charity. Under her direction, The Women Chefs of Chicago have helped raise more than $500,000 for Chicagoland charities in the past few years.

Sarah's support of her state's agriculture is reflected in her food: she uses the finest seasonal produce from Midwest vegetable farmers and cheesemakers. She works with her husband, Rohit Nambiar, who manages the front of house at Prairie Grass Café. Her mother, Elizabeth Stegner, makes the pies served at Prairie Grass Café. Sarah feels right at home in her new restaurant.

Wolfgang Puck and ex-wife Barbra Lazaroff at Spago, known for its innovative cuisine and stunning dining rooms designed by Barbra.

Celebrity Restaurants

Celebrity-owned restaurants have been growing in popularity. Some celebrities, such as Wolfgang Puck, come from a culinary background, whereas others, such as Naomi Campbell, Claudia Schiffer, and Elle Macpherson (owners of the Fashion Café), do not. A number of sports celebrities also have restaurants. Among them are Michael Jordan, Dan Marino, Junior Seau, and Wayne Gretzky. Television and movie stars have also gotten into the act. Oprah Winfrey was part owner of the Eccentric in Chicago for a number of years. She said she bought the restaurant because she liked a sandwich she had there, but was told that the place was closing. So she stepped in and bought it! Matt Damon and Ben Affleck once owned the Continental, and Dustin Hoffman and Henry Winkler were investors in Campanile, a popular Los Angeles restaurant. Dive, in Century City (Los Angeles), was owned by Steven Spielberg; Dan Aykroyd was one of the co-founders of the House of Blues; Robert De Niro, Christopher Walken and others own Ago; Kevin Costner, Robert Wagner, Jack Nicklaus and Fred Couples owned the Clubhouse; and musicians Kenny Rogers and Gloria Estefan are also restaurant owners.

Celebrity restaurants generally have an extra zing to them—a winning combination of design, atmosphere, food, and perhaps the thrill of an occasional visit by the owner(s).

Steak Houses

The steak restaurant segment is quite buoyant despite nutritional concerns about red meat. The upscale steak dinner houses, such as Flemming's of Chicago, Ruth's Chris, and Houston's, continue to attract the expense account and "occasion" diners. Some restaurants are adding additional value-priced items such as chicken and fish to their menus to attract more guests. Steak restaurant operators admit that they are not expecting to see the same customer every week but hopefully every two or three weeks. The Chart House chain is careful to market its menu as including seafood and chicken, but steak is at the heart of the business, with most of its sales from red meat.

Outback Steakhouse, which is profiled in this chapter, owns and operates about a thousand Outback restaurants and about thirty Flemming's Prime Steakhouse and Wine Bars. Other restaurants in this segment include Stewart Anderson's Black Angus, Golden Corral, Western Sizzlin, which all have sales of more than $300 million each. In fact, chains have the biggest share of the segment.

Casual Dining and Dinner House Restaurants

The types of restaurants that can be included in the casual dining restaurants category are as follows:

Midscale casual restaurants. Romano's Macaroni Grill, the Olive Garden
Family restaurants. Cracker Barrel, Coco's Bakery, Bob Evans, Carrows

Ethnic restaurants. Flavor Thai, Cantina Latina, Panda Express
Theme restaurants. Hard Rock Cafe, T.G.I. Friday's, Roy's
Quick-service/fast-food restaurants. McDonald's, Burger King, Pizza Hut, Ponderosa, Popeyes, Subway, Taco Bell

CORPORATE PROFILE

Outback Steakhouse

The founders of Outback Steakhouse have proved that unconventional methods can lead to profitable results. Such methods include opening solely for dinner, sacrificing dining-room seats for back-of-the-house efficiency, limiting servers to three tables each, and handing 10 percent of cash flow to the restaurants' general managers.

March 1988 saw the opening of the first Outback Steakhouse. Outback's founders, Chris Sullivan, Robert Basham, and Senior Vice President Tim Gannon, know plenty about the philosophy "No rules, just right" because they have lived it since day one. Even the timing of their venture to launch a casual steak place came when many pundits were pronouncing red meat consumption dead in the United States.

The chain went public and has since created a track record of strong earnings. It was evident that the three founders were piloting one of the country's hottest restaurant concepts. The trio found themselves with hundreds of restaurants, instead of the five they originally envisioned.

Robert Basham, cofounder, president, and chief operating officer at Outback Steakhouse, was given the Operator of the Year award at the Multi-Unit Foodservice Operators Conference (MUFSO). He helped expand the chain, a pioneer in the steak house sector of the restaurant business, to more than a thousand restaurants with some of the highest sales per unit in the industry despite the fact that they serve only dinner.

Perhaps the strongest indication of what this company is about lies in its corporate structure, or lack thereof. Despite its rapid growth, the company has no public relations department, no human resources department, and no recruiting apparatus. In addition, the Outback Steakhouse headquarters is very different from that of a typical restaurant company. There is no lavish tower—only modest office space in an average suburban complex. Instead of settling into a conservative chair and browsing through a magazine-lined coffee table (as is the case in most reception areas), at Outback you must belly up to an actual bar, brass foot rail and all, to announce your arrival.

Also, Outback's dining experience—large, highly seasoned portions of food for moderate prices—is so in tune with today's dining experience that patrons in many of its restaurants experience hour-long dinner waits seven nights a week. The friendly service is notable, from the host who opens the door and greets guests, to the well-trained servers, who casually sit down next to patrons in the booths and explain the house specialties featured on the menu.

Using such tactics and their "No rules, just right" philosophy, the founders have accomplished two main goals: discipline and solid growth. Good profits and excellent marketing potentials show just how successful the business has become. Outback also owns and operates Bonefish Grill, Flemming's Prime Steakhouse, Carabba's Italian Grill, and Roy's.

Hard Rock Cafe offers first-rate, moderately priced casual American fare with, of course, a side of rock and roll.

As implied, **casual dining** is relaxed and could include restaurants from several classifications: chain or independent, ethnic, or theme. Hard Rock Cafe, T.G.I. Friday's, the Olive Garden, Houston's, Romano's Macaroni Grill, and Red Lobster are good examples of casual dining restaurants.

Houston's is a leader in the casual restaurant segment, with about $5.5 million average per unit sales in its thirty-five restaurants. The menu is limited to about forty items and focuses on American cuisine, with a $16 average per-person ticket for lunch and a cost of $35 to $45 for dinner. While encouraging local individuality in its restaurants and maintaining exceptional executive and unit general manager stability, it succeeds with no franchising and virtually no advertising.

Over the past few years, the trend in **dinner house restaurants** has been toward more casual dining. This trend merely reflects the mode of society. Dinner house restaurants have become fun places to let off steam. A variety of restaurant chains call themselves dinner house restaurants. Some of them could even fit into the theme category.

Many dinner house restaurants have a casual, eclectic decor that may promote a theme. Chart House, for example, is a steak and seafood chain that has a nautical theme. T.G.I. Friday's is an American bistro dinner house with a full menu and a decor of bric-a-brac that contributes to the fun atmosphere. T.G.I. Friday's is a chain that has been in operation for nearly forty years, so the concept has stood the test of time.

Family Restaurants

Family restaurants evolved from the coffee shop style of restaurant. In this segment, most restaurants are individually or family operated. Family restaurants are generally located in or with easy access to the suburbs. Most offer an informal setting with a simple menu and service designed to please all the family. Some of these restaurants offer alcoholic beverages, which mostly consist of beer, wine, and perhaps a cocktail special. Usually, there is a hostess/cashier standing near the entrance to greet and seat guests while food servers take the orders and bring the plated food from the kitchen. Some family restaurants have incorporated salad and dessert bars to offer more variety and increase the average check.

The lines separating the various restaurants and chains in the family segment are blurring as operators upscale their concepts. Flagstar's acquisition of Coco's Bakery and Carrows family restaurant brands has created the high-end niche of family dining—somewhere between traditional coffee shops and the casual dining segment. The value-oriented operator in the family dining segment is Denny's. The more upscale family concepts include Perkins, Marie Callender's, and Cracker Barrel, all of which are sometimes referred to as the "relaxed" segment. These chains tend to have higher check averages than do traditional and value-oriented family chains, and compete not only with them, but also with moderately priced, casual-themed operators, such as Applebee's and T.G.I. Friday's.

Karen Brennan, Synergy Restaurant Consultants, says that people's use of restaurants is very different from five years ago. Consumers are thinking in terms of "meal solutions." The operators in this segment are seeking to capitalize on two trends affecting the industry as a whole: the tendency of families to dine out together more often, and the quest among adults for higher-quality, more flavorful food offerings.

Ethnic Restaurants

The majority of **ethnic restaurants** are independently owned and operated. The owners and their families provide something different for the adventurous diner or a taste of home for those of the same ethnic background as the restaurant. The traditional ethnic restaurants sprang up to cater to the taste of the various immigrant groups—Italian, Chinese, and so on.

Perhaps the fastest growing segment of ethnic restaurants in the United States, popularity wise, is Mexican. Mexican food has a heavy representation in the southwestern states, although, because of near-market saturation, the chains are spreading east. Taco Bell is the Mexican quick-service market leader, with a 60-percent share. This *Fortune 500* company has achieved this incredible result with a value-pricing policy that has increased traffic in all units. There are more than 7,000 units with sales of about $5 billion. Other large Mexican food chains are Del Taco, La Salsa, and El Torito. These Mexican food chains can offer a variety of items on a value menu. Our cities offer a great variety of ethnic restaurants, and their popularity is increasing.

Theme Restaurants

Many **theme restaurants** are a combination of a sophisticated specialty and several other types of restaurants. They generally serve a limited menu but aim to wow the guest by the total experience. Of the many popular theme restaurants, two stand out. The first highlights the nostalgia of the 1950s, as done in the T-Bird and Corvette Diners. These restaurants serve all-American food such as the perennial meatloaf in a fun atmosphere that is a throwback to the seemingly more carefree 1950s. The mostly female food servers appear in short polka-dot skirts with gym shoes and bobby socks.

The second popular theme restaurant is the dinner house category; among some of the better known national and regional chains are T.G.I. Friday's, Houlihan's, and Bennigan's. These are casual, American bistro-type restaurants that combine a lively atmosphere created in part by

Guests being served at a Mexican restaurant.

assorted bric-a-brac that decorate the various ledges and walls. These restaurants have remained popular over the past twenty years. In a prime location, they can do extremely well.

People are attracted to theme restaurants because they offer a total experience and a social meeting place. This is achieved through decoration and atmosphere and allows the restaurant to offer a limited menu that blends with the theme. Throughout the United States and the world, numerous theme restaurants stand out for one reason or another. Among them are decors featuring airplanes, railway, dining cars, rock and roll, 1960s nostalgia, and many others.

Quick-Service/Fast-Food Restaurants

Quick-service restaurants (QSRs) consist of diverse operating facilities whose slogan is "quick food." The following types of operations are included under this category: hamburger, pizza, chicken, pancakes, sandwich shops, and delivery services.

The quick-service sector is the one that really drives the industry. Recently, the home-meal replacement and fast casual concepts have gained momentum (see Figure 5).

Quick-service or fast-food restaurants offer limited menus featuring food such as hamburgers, fries, hot dogs, chicken (in all forms), tacos, burritos, gyros, teriyaki bowls, various finger foods, and other items for the convenience of people on the go. Customers order their food at a counter under a brightly lit menu featuring color photographs of food items. Customers are even encouraged to clear their own trays, which helps reduce costs. The following are examples of the different types of quick-service/fast-food restaurants:

Hamburger. McDonald's, Burger King, Wendy's
Pizza. Pizza Hut, Domino's, Godfather's
Steak. Bonanza, Ponderosa

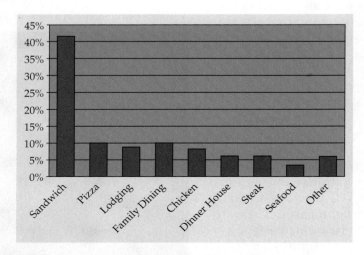

Figure 5 • Approximate Market Share of Restaurant Segments.

Seafood. Long John Silver's

Chicken. KFC, Church's, Zaxby's, Kenny Rogers Roasters, Popeyes

Sandwich. Subway

Mexican. Taco Bell, El Torito

Drive-thru/drive-in/delivery. Sonic, Domino's, Pizza Hut

Quick-service restaurants have increased in popularity because of their location strategies. They are found in very convenient locations in every possible area. Their menus are limited, which makes it easy for customers to make quick decisions on what to eat. The world equates time with money these days, and most people do not want to spend time trying to look through long menus to make an eating decision. These restaurants deliver fast service and usually include self-service facilities, too. Such restaurants also use cheaper, processed ingredients, which allow them to have extremely low, competitive prices. Quick-service restaurants also require minimum use of both skilled and unskilled labor, which increases the profit margins.

In an attempt to raise flat sales figures, more quick-service restaurant (QSR) chains are using cobranding at stores and nontraditional locations, including highway plazas and shopping centers. It is hoped that the traffic-building combos will increase sales among the separate brands, such as Carl's Jr. and Green Burrito. Many QSR chains are targeting international growth, mostly in the larger cities in a variety of countries.

Hamburgers

McDonald's is the giant of the entire quick-service/fast-food segment and serves millions of people daily. McDonald's has 32,478 stores in 117 countries with 400,000 employees and sales of $ 24 billion.[24] This total is amazing because it is more than the next three megachains combined—Burger King, KFC, and Pizza Hut. McDonald's has individual product items other than the traditional burger—for example, chicken McNuggets and burritos as well as salads and fish, which all aim to broaden customer appeal. Customer appeal has also been broadened by the introduction of breakfast and by targeting not only kids but seniors. Innovative menu introductions have helped stimulate an increase in per-store traffic.

In recent years, because traditional markets have become saturated, McDonald's has adopted a strategy of expanding overseas. It is embarking on a rapid expansion in the world's most populous nation, China, with more than 12,000 restaurants nationwide. The reason for this expansion in China is a rapidly developing middle class with a growing appetite for Western culture and food. McDonald's is now in 117 countries and has a potential audience of 3.2 billion people. Of the company's roughly 32,000 restaurants, some 8,600 are outside the United States, serving 47 million people each day.[25]

It is interesting to note that about 50 percent of total profits come from outside of the United States. More than two-thirds of new restaurants added by McDonald's are outside of the United States. McDonald's also seeks out nontraditional locations in the U.S. market, such as on military bases or smaller-sized units in the high-rent districts or gas stations.

McDonald's is taking another step toward being the most convenient food-service operation in the world by striking deals with gasoline companies Chevron, U.S. Petroleum Star Enterprise, and Mobil Oil Corporation to codevelop sites.

It is very difficult to obtain a McDonald's franchise in the United States because they have virtually saturated the primary markets. It often costs between $1 million and $2 million to open a major brand fast-food restaurant. Franchises for lesser-known chains are available for less money (about $35,000) plus the 4 percent of sales royalty fee and 4 percent fee for advertising, but an entrepreneur needs about $125,000 liquid and $400,000 net worth for an upscale, quick-service outlet, not counting land costs.

Each of the major hamburger restaurant chains has a unique positioning strategy to attract their target markets. Burger King hamburgers are flame broiled, and Wendy's uses fresh patties. Some smaller regional chains are succeeding in gaining market share from the big-three burger chains because they provide an excellent burger at a reasonable price. In-N-Out Burger, Sonic, and Rally's are good examples of this.

Pizza

The pizza segment continues to grow, with much of the growth fueled by the convenience of delivery. There are several chains: Pizza Hut, Domino's, Godfather's, Papa John's, and Little Caesar's. Pizza Hut, with 13,200 units,[26] has broken into the delivery part of the business over which, until recently, Domino's had a virtual monopoly. Pizza Hut has now developed systemwide delivery units that also offer two pizzas at a reduced price.

In response to the success of Pizza Hut's Stuffed Crust Pizza, Domino's highlighted its Ultimate Deep Dish Pizza and its Pesto Crust Pizza. It is currently advertising its new artisan pizzas, which are intended to look like bistro-style pizzas, with unusual ingredients such as spinach and feta and salami and roasted vegetables.

Chicken

Chicken has always been popular and is likely to remain so because it is relatively cheap to produce and readily available and adaptable to a variety of preparations. It also is perceived as a healthier alternative to burgers.

KFC, with a worldwide total of more than 15,000 units,[27] dominates the chicken segment. Even though KFC is a market leader, the company continues to explore new ways to get its products to consumers. More units now offer home delivery, and in many cities, KFC is teaming up with sister restaurant Taco Bell, selling products from both chains in one convenient location. KFC continues to build menu variety as it focuses on providing complete meals to families. Amazingly, there are now more than a thousand KFC restaurants in China.

Church's Chicken, with 1700 units, in 22 countries,[28] is the second largest chicken chain. It offers a simple formula consisting of a value menu featuring Southern-style chicken, spicy chicken wings, okra, corn on the cob, coleslaw, biscuits, and other items. Church's focused on becoming a low-cost provider and the fastest to market. To give customers the value they expect day in and day out, it is necessary to have unit economies in order. Systemwide, Church's now registers 34 percent in food costs and 25.9 percent labor costs.[29]

Popeyes is another large chain in the chicken segment, with 1943 units in 44 states and 27 foreign countries. It is owned by AFC, the same parent company as Church's. Popeyes is a New Orleans–inspired "spicy chicken" chain operating more than 2,000 restaurants in the United States and 25 countries.[30]

There are a number of up-and-coming regional chains, such as El Pollo Loco, of Irvine, California. It focuses on a marinated, flame-broiled chicken that is a unique, high-quality product. Kenny Rogers Roasters and Cluckers are also expanding rotisserie chains.

Sandwich Restaurants

Indicative of America's obsession with the quick and convenient, sandwiches have achieved star status. Recently, menu debuts in the sandwich segment have outpaced all others. Classics, such as melts and club sandwiches, have returned with a vengeance—but now there are also wraps and Panini.

A sandwich restaurant is a popular way for a young entrepreneur to enter the restaurant business. The leader in this segment is Subway, which operates more than 34,385 units in ninety-seven countries.[31] Cofounder Fred Deluca parlayed an initial investment of $1,000 into one of the largest and fastest-growing chains in the world. Franchise fees are $12,500, with a second store fee of $2,500.

The Subway strategy is to invest half of the chain's advertising dollars in national advertising. Franchise owners pay 2.5 percent of sales to the marketing fund. As with other chains, Subway is attempting to widen its core eighteen- to thirty-four-year-old customer base by adding Kids' Meals and Fresh Fit Choices aimed at capturing the health-conscious market. Subway has also added a breakfast menu and flatbread to its it bread offerings.

Bakery Café

The bakery café sector is headed up by Panera Bread, a 1,027-unit chain in thirty-eight states, with the mission of "a loaf in every arm" and the goal of making specialty bread broadly available to consumers across the United States. Panera focuses on the art and craft of breadmaking, with made-to-order sandwiches, tossed-to-order salads, and soup served in bread bowls.[32]

Check Your Knowledge

1. Describe the different types of restaurants, and give examples of each. Highlight some of the characteristics that make up the specific restaurant types.

Trends in the Restaurant Business

- *Demographics.* As the baby boomers move into middle age and retirement, a startling statistic is emerging: forty-five- to sixty-four-year-olds (the age group with the highest income) will make up almost one-third of the U.S. population. Simply put, the largest demographic group will have the most money and will offer opportunities for restaurants that meet their needs.

- *Branding.* Restaurant operators are using the power of branding, both in terms of brand-name recognition from a franchising viewpoint and in the products utilized.

- *Alternative outlets.* Restaurants face increased competition from convenience stores ("c-stores") and home meal replacement outlets.

- *Globalization.* Corporations will continue the transnational development of restaurants.

- *Diversification.* Diversification within the various dining segments will continue.

- *Shared locations.* Restaurants will open more twin and multiple locations; restaurants such as Pizza Hut and KFC will share locations.

- *Points of service.* Restaurants will develop more points of service (for example, Taco Bell at gas stations).

- *Las Vegas.* Several restaurants and nightclubs have opened recently, such as the Strip House, CUT, and The Bank; plus, French chef Joel Robuchon at the MGM Grand was recently awarded a coveted three-star rating by the Michelin Guide.

Summary

1. Restaurants offer the possibility of excellent food and social interaction. In general, restaurants strive to surpass an operating philosophy that includes quality food, good value, and gracious service.

2. To succeed, a restaurant needs the right location, food, atmosphere, and service to attract a substantial market. The concept of a restaurant has to fit the market it is trying to attract.

3. The location of a restaurant has to match factors such as convenience, neighborhood, parking, visibility, and demographics. Typical types of locations are downtown, suburban, shopping mall, cluster, or stand-alone.

4. The menu and pricing of a restaurant must match the market the restaurant wants to attract, the capabilities of the cooks, and the existing kitchen equipment.

5. The main categories of restaurants are independent and chain. Further distinctions can be made as follows: fine dining, casual dining and dinner house, family, ethnic, and quick-service/fast-food. In general, most restaurants fall into more than one category.

Key Words and Concepts

actual market share
ambiance
atmosphere
casual dining
catchment area
celebrity-owned restaurant
chain restaurant
contribution margin
culinary arts
dinner house restaurant
ethnic restaurant
fair market share
family restaurant
fine-dining restaurant

food cost percentage
fusion
haute cuisine
independent restaurant (indie)
mother sauces
niche
nouvelle cuisine
purée
quick-service restaurant (QSR)
roux
sales volume
theme restaurant
weighted average

Review Questions

1. Describe the evolution of American culinary arts.
2. What are the five mother sauces?
3. Name some of America's finest chefs.

4. How are restaurants classified?
5. Explain why there is no single definition of the various classifications of restaurants; give examples.

Internet Exercises

1. Organization: **Charlie Trotter**
   Web site: **charlietrotters.com/restaurant**
   Summary: Charlie Trotter is regarded as one of the finest chefs in the world. Chef Trotter's restaurant has received numerous awards, yet chef Trotter is always seeking new opportunities.
   (a) What are Chef Trotter's recent activities?

2. Organization: **Olive Garden Restaurant**
   Web site: **www.olivegarden.com**
   Summary: The Olive Garden is a multiunit chain that primarily serves Italian food. It is currently operated by Darden Restaurants and has about 534 restaurants in the United States and Canada. Olive Garden strives to create a feeling of warmth and caring for every guest, which extends beyond the walls of the

restaurants into the community. Olive Garden participates in civic community service, such as delivering meals during times of crisis, sponsoring charity events, and hosting school tours of the restaurants.

(a) What kind of restaurant does the name Olive Garden represent?
(b) What is the Garden Fare? How is its menu different from the design and layout of the lunch menu?

Apply Your Knowledge

In groups, evaluate a restaurant and write out a list of weaknesses. Then, for each of the weaknesses, decide on which actions you would take to exceed guest expectations.

Suggested Activities

1. Identify a restaurant in your neighborhood and identify its catchment area. How many potential guests live and work in the catchment area?

2. Search the Web for examples of four great restaurant web sites. Compare them and share your findings in class.

Endnotes

1. National Restaurant Association, *About Us*, www.restaurant.org/aboutus/ (accessed March 22, 2011).
2. Sarah R. Labensky and Alan M. Hause, *On Cooking*, 4th ed. (Upper Saddle River, NJ: Prentice Hall, 2007), 6–7.
3. Ibid.
4. Charlie Trotter, *Charlie Trotter* (Berkeley, CA: Ten Speed Press, 1994), 11.
5. Ibid., 12.
6. "NRA Joins Healthy Dining to Promote Healthful Menu Choices," *Fast Casual*, July 18, 2006, www.fastcasual.com/article.php?id=5393 (accessed November 4, 2011).
7. This section is courtesy of Chef Michael Zema, Elgin Community College, Elgin, IL.
8. Danny Meyer, Presentation to the International hotel and Restaurant Show, New York, November 12, 2006.
9. John Walker, *The Restaurant from Concept to Operation*, 6th ed. (Hoboken, NJ: Wiley, 2011), 5.
10. Ibid., 5.
11. Ibid., 5.
12. http://www.restaurantreformer.com/, retrieved March 8, 2010.
13. Ibid.
14. http://www.dinegreen.com/restaurants/standards.asp, retrieved March 8, 2010.
15. Ibid.
16. Ibid., 208.
17. Chipotle, *What Is Food with Integrity?* www.chipotle.com/en-US/fwi/fwi.aspx (accessed November 4, 2011).
18. Seasons 52, *About Our Menu*, www.seasons52.com/menu/about_menu.asp (accessed November 4, 2011).

19. Ibid.
20. U.S. Department of Agriculture, Questions & Answers: MyPyramid Food Guidance System, www.choosemyplate.gov/global_nav/media_questions.html (accessed November 4, 2011).
21. Ibid., 211.
22. Ibid., 230.
23. Personal conversation with Jay R. Schrock, Dean, School of Hotel and Restaurant Management, University of South Florida.
24. Forbes.com, *McDonald's Corporation (NYSE: MCD): At a Glance*, http://finapps.forbes.com/finapps/jsp/finance/compinfo/CIAtAGlance.jsp?tkr=MCD (accessed April 1, 2011).
25. Ibid.
26. Yum! *Brands*, www.yum.com/company/ourbrands.asp (accessed April 1, 2011).
27. Yum! *Financial Data*, www.yum.com/investors/annualreport.asp (accessed April 1, 2011).
28. Church's Chicken, *Company History*, www.churchs.com/company-history.html (accessed April 1, 2011).
29. Ibid.
30. Popeyes Louisiana Kitchen, *Press Release: Popeyes Louisiana Kitchen Opens 2000th Restaurant Globally*, July 15, 2011, popeyes.com/article.php?articleno=MTM0 (accessed November 4, 2011).
31. Subway, *Home Page*, www.subway.com/subwayroot/index.aspx (accessed April 1, 2011).
32. Panera Bread, *Company Overview*, www.panerabread.com/about/company/mgmt.php (accessed April 1, 2011).

Restaurant Operations

From Chapter 7 of *Introduction to Hospitality*, Sixth Edition. John R. Walker. Copyright © 2013 by Pearson Education, Inc. Published by Pearson. All rights reserved.

Restaurant Operations

OBJECTIVES

After reading and studying this chapter, you should be able to:

- Describe restaurant operations for the front of the house.

- Explain how restaurants forecast their business.

- Outline back-of-the-house operations.

- Identify key elements of an income statement.

- Name the key restaurant operating ratios.

- Outline the functional areas and tasks of a restaurant manager's job.

Front of the House

Restaurant operations are generally divided between what is commonly called **front of the house** and **back of the house**. The front of the house includes anyone with guest contact, from the hostess to the busser. The sample organization chart in Figure 1 shows the differences between the front- and back-of-the-house areas.

The restaurant is run by the general manager, or restaurant manager. Depending on the size and sales volume of the restaurant, there may be more managers with special responsibilities, such as kitchen manager, bar manager, and dining room manager. These managers are usually cross-trained to relieve each other.

In the front of the house, restaurant operation begins with creating and maintaining what is called **curbside appeal**, or keeping the restaurant looking attractive and welcoming. Ray Kroc of McDonald's once spent a couple of hours in a good suit with one of his restaurant managers cleaning up the parking lot of one of his restaurants. Word soon got around to the other stores that management begins in the parking lot and ends in the bathrooms. Most restaurant chains have checklists that each manager uses. In the front of the house, the parking lot, including the flower gardens, needs to be maintained in good order. As guests approach the restaurant, hostesses may hold the door open and welcome them to the restaurant. At the 15th Street Fisheries restaurant in Ft. Lauderdale, Florida, hostesses welcome the guests by assuring them that "we're glad you're here!"

Once guests are inside, the **host/hostess**, or as T.G.I. Friday's calls him or her, "smiling people greeter" (SPG), greets the guests appropriately, and, if seating is available, escorts them to a table. If there is a wait, the host/hostess will take the guests' names and ask for their table preference.

Aside from greeting the guests, one critical function of the host/hostess is to rotate arriving guests among the sections or stations. This ensures an even and timely distribution of guests—otherwise one section may get overloaded. Guests are sometimes asked to wait a few minutes even if tables are available. This is done to help spread the kitchen's workload.

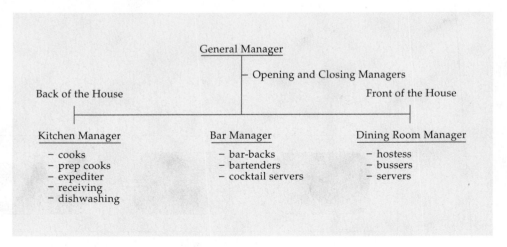

Figure 1 • Restaurant Organization Chart.

The host/hostesses maintain a book, or chart, showing the sections and tables so that they know which tables are occupied. Host/hostesses escort guests to the tables, present menus, and may explain special sales promotions. Some may also remove excess covers from the table.

In some restaurants, servers are allocated a certain number of tables, which may vary depending on the size of the tables and the volume of the restaurant. Usually, five is the maximum. In other restaurants, servers rotate within their section to cover three or four tables.

The server introduces him- or herself, offers a variety of beverages and/or specials, and invites guests to select from the menu. This is known as suggestive selling. The server then takes the entrée orders. Often, when taking orders, the server begins at a designated point and takes the orders clockwise from that point. In this way, the server will automatically know which person is having a particular dish. When the entrées are ready, the server brings them to the table. He or she checks a few minutes later to see if everything is to the guests' liking and perhaps asks if they would like another beverage. Good servers are also encouraged, when possible, to pre-bus tables.

A midtown Manhattan restaurant prepares to welcome guests.

Bussers and servers may clear the entrée plates, while servers suggestively sell desserts by describing, recommending, or showing the desserts. Coffee and after-dinner cocktails are also offered. Suggestions for steps to take in table service are as follows:

1. Greet the guests.
2. Introduce and suggestively sell beverages.
3. Suggest appetizers.
4. Take orders.
5. Check to see that everything is to the guests' liking within two bites of the entrées.
6. Ask if the guests would like another drink.
7. Bring out the dessert tray and suggest after-dinner drinks and coffee.

In addition to the seven steps of the table service, servers are expected to be NCO—neat, clean, and organized—and to help ensure that hot food is served hot and cold food served cold.

For example, during the lunch hour, servers may be scheduled to start at 11:00 A.M. The opening group of two or three people is joined by the closing group of the same number at around 11:45 P.M. If the restaurant is quiet, servers may be phased out early. When the closing group comes in, there is a quick shift meeting, or "alley rally." This provides an opportunity to review recent sales figures, discuss any promotions, and acknowledge any items that are "eighty-sixed"—the restaurant term for a menu item that is not available. Recognition is also given to the servers during the meetings, serving as morale boosters.

Restaurant Forecasting

Most businesses, including restaurants, operate by formulating a budget that projects sales and costs for a year on a weekly and monthly basis. Financial viability is predicted on sales, and sales budgets are forecasts of expected business.

Forecasting restaurant sales has two components: guest counts, or covers, and the average guest check. **Guest counts**, or **covers**, are the number of guests patronizing the restaurant over a given time period—a week, a month, or a year. To forecast the number of guests for a year, the year is divided into thirteen periods: twelve twenty-eight-day and one twenty-nine-day accounting periods. This ensures that accounting procedures are able to compare equal periods rather than months of unequal days. The accounting periods are then broken down into four seven-day weeks. Restaurant forecasting is done by taking into consideration meal period, day of week, special holidays, and previous forecast materializations.

In terms of number of guests, Mondays usually are quiet; business gradually builds to Friday, which is often the busiest day. Friday, Saturday, and Sunday frequently provide up to 50 percent of revenue. This, however, can vary according to type of restaurant and its location.

The **average guest check** is calculated by dividing total sales by the number of guests. Most restaurants keep such figures for each meal. The number of guests forecast for each day is multiplied by the amount of the average food and beverage check for each meal to calculate the total forecast sales. Each day, actual totals are compared with the forecasts. Four weekly forecasts are combined to form one accounting period; the thirteen accounting periods, when totaled, become the annual total.

Restaurant forecasting is used not only to calculate sales projections but also for predicting staffing levels and labor cost percentages. Much depends on the accuracy of forecasting. Once sales figures are determined, all expenditures, fixed and variable, have to be deducted to calculate profit or loss.[1]

Service

More than ever, what American diners really want when they eat out is good service. Unfortunately, all too often, that is not on the menu. With increased competition, however, bad service will not be tolerated in American restaurants. Just as American cuisine came of age in the 1970s and 1980s, service is showing signs of maturing in the twenty-first century.

A new American service has emerged. A less formal—yet professional—approach is preferred by today's restaurant guests. The restaurants' commitment to service is evidenced by the fact that most have increased training for new employees. Servers are not merely order takers; they are the salespeople of the restaurant. A server who is undereducated about the menu can seriously hurt business. One would not be likely to buy a car from a salesperson who knew nothing about the car; likewise, guests feel uneasy ordering from an unknowledgeable server.

FOCUS ON RESTAURANT OPERATIONS

The Manager's Role

John T. Self, California State Polytechnic University, Pomona

It seems like only yesterday that I was walking into my first restaurant as a new manager trainee fresh from college. I found the restaurant industry perfect for me. It had plenty of variety, energy, and opportunity that matched my personality. I loved that I would not have to just sit behind a desk doing one thing every day. As a restaurant manager, your day will include accounting, human resources, marketing, payroll, purchasing, personal counseling, and many more functions that will challenge you.

You will be part of a management team that is the foundation of any restaurant, regardless of whether it is a chain or an independent. Managers have huge a sphere of influence, including customer service, sales, and profitability. You will be part of a management team responsible for a multimillion-dollar operation.

When you first become a manager, it is easy to be overwhelmed. You will probably feel that you will never be able to understand all the moving parts of a restaurant. However, as you grow in your management position, you will not only understand how it all works, you will also understand how you influence each part.

Being a restaurant manager offers the opportunity to grow as an individual because you will deal with so many types of people, including employees, peers, supervisors, vendors, and customers. You will learn how to get your team excited and motivated to share common goals. You will find it very rewarding to teach others about the culture of the business and will have many opportunities to make positive impacts on your staff.

The restaurant industry is the epicenter of the people business and management is at the heart of the restaurant industry. Motivating people, delegating responsibility to people, and leading people is what we are about and what we do.

Whichever company you eventually join, each will present a slightly different environment, career path, hours, days, responsibilities, and opportunities, but they all share food and people as their core.

Restaurants in the United States, Canada, and many other parts of the world all use American service, in which the food is prepared and appealingly placed onto plates in the kitchen, carried into the dining room, and served to guests. This method of service is used because it is quicker and guests receive the food hot as presented by the chef.

At Postrio in San Francisco, servers are invited to attend a one-and-a-half-hour wine class in the restaurant; about three-quarters of the forty-member staff routinely benefit from this additional training. The best employees are also rewarded with monthly prizes and with semiannual and annual prizes, which range from $100 cash, a limousine ride, dinner at Postrio, or a night's lodging at the Prescott Hotel to a week in Hawaii. Servers at other San Francisco restaurants role-play the various elements of service such as greeting and seating guests, suggestive selling, correct methods of service, and guest relations to ensure a positive dining experience. A good food server in a top restaurant in many cities can earn $50,000 or more a year.

A server as a salesperson, explaining a dish on the menu to a guest.

Good servers quickly learn to gauge the guests' satisfaction levels and to be sensitive to guests' needs; for example, they check to ensure guests have everything they need as their entrée is placed before them. Even better, they anticipate guests' needs. For example, if the guest had used the entrée knife to eat the appetizer, a clean one should automatically be placed to the right side of the guest's plate. In other words, the guest should not receive the entrée and then realize he or she needs another knife.

Another example of good service is when the server does not have to ask everyone at the table who is eating what. The server should either remember or do a seating plan so that the correct dishes are automatically placed in front of guests.

Danny Meyer, owner of New York City's celebrated Union Square Cafe and recipient of both the Restaurant of the Year and Outstanding Service Awards from the James Beard Foundation, gives each of the restaurant's employees—from busser to chef—a $600 annual allowance ($50 each a month) to eat in the restaurant and critique the experience.[2]

At the critically acclaimed Inn at Little Washington in Washington, Virginia, servers are required to gauge the mood of every table and jot a number (one to ten) and sometimes a description ("elated," "grumpy," or "edgy") on each ticket. Anything below a seven requires a diagnosis. Servers and kitchen staff work together to try to elevate the number to at least a nine by the time dessert is ordered.

Suggestive Selling

Suggestive selling can be a potent weapon in the effort to increase food and beverage sales. Many restaurateurs cannot think of a better, more effective, and easier way to boost profit margins. Servers report that most guests are not offended or uncomfortable with suggestive selling techniques. In fact, customers may feel special that the server is in tune with their needs and desires. It may be that the server suggests something to the guest that he or she has never considered before. The object here is to turn servers into sellers. Guests will almost certainly be receptive to suggestions from competent servers.

On a hot day, for example, servers can suggest frozen margaritas or daiquiris before going on to describe the drink specials. Likewise, servers who suggest a bottle of fumé blanc to complement a fish dish or a pinot noir or cabernet sauvignon to go with red meat are likely to increase their restaurant's beverage sales.

Upselling takes place when a guest orders a "well" drink like a vodka and tonic. In this case, the server asks if the guests would like a Stoli and tonic. (Stoli is short for Stolichnaya, a popular brand of vodka.)

An example of the benefits of upselling is a server who describes a menu item like this: "Our special tonight is a slow-roasted aged prime Angus beef ribroast, served with roasted potatoes and a medley of fresh vegetables." Now, if this entrée costs $10 more than another beef dish on the menu, and the same thing happens with suggestions for guests to select from fish, seafood, and other meat or vegetarian items, the table's check will increase by $50 to $75. We know that a server receives about 15 percent in tips and does four or five tables that can turn twice each per night. You do the math: 15% of $50 = $7.50; if the server does four tables: $4 \times \$7.50 \times 2 =$ an additional $60 in tips.

Sustainable Restaurant Operations[3]

Sustainability is not just a philosophy about food—it's about people, attitudes, communities, and lifestyles. In the spirit of the theme of this year's International Chefs Congress—"The Responsibility of a Chef"—the ideas below come from chefs across the country. There's an idea to inspire you each day of the next month; even picking one to look into, or act on, per week is a good way to start. Almost everywhere one goes, we hear the same message: small changes and efforts can make a big difference!

1. Go local. It's not possible for everyone all the time. But when it *is* possible, support your local farmers.

2. Take your team to visit a farmer. This is good practice for remembering that each piece of food has a story and a person behind it. (And you can bring back extra produce for a special family meal.)

3. Know your seafood. The criteria for evaluating the sustainability of seafood differ from those for agriculture. Inform yourself using resources like California's Monterey Bay Aquarium's *Seafood Watch Guide,* and demand that your purveyors are informed too. If they can't tell you where a fish is from and how and when it was caught, you probably don't want to be serving it.

4. Not all bottled water is created equal. Some companies are working to reduce and offset their carbon footprint through a number of innovative measures. And some of the biggest names in the restaurant world (like *The French Laundry*) are moving away from water bottled out of house. In-house filtration systems offer a number of options—including in-house sparkling water!

5. Ditch the Styrofoam. Replace cooks' drinking cups with reusable plastic ones, and replace Styrofoam take-out containers with containers made of recycled paper. BioPac packaging is one option.

6. Support organic, biodynamic viniculture. There are incredible, top-rating biodynamic or organic wines from around the world.

7. Support organic bar products. All-natural and organic spirits, beers, and mixers are growing in popularity and availability.

8. Even your kitchen and bar mats can be responsible. Waterhog's EcoLine is made from 100 percent recycled PET postconsumer recycled fiber reclaimed from drink bottles and recycled tires.

9. Devote one morning per quarter or one morning per month to community service. Send staff to a soup kitchen, bring local kids into the kitchen, teach the kitchen staff of the local elementary school a few tricks, or spend a few hours working in the sun at a community garden.

10. The kitchen equipment of the future is green! Major equipment producers, like Hobart and Unified Brands, are developing special initiatives to investigate and develop greener, cleaner, energy-smart machines (that also save you money in the long run).

11. Shut down the computer and POS systems when you leave at night. When the computer system is on, the juice keeps flowing—shutting it down can save significant energy bill dollars over the course of a year.

12. Check the seals on your walk-in. If they're not kept clean and tight, warm air can seep in, making the fridge work harder to stay cool.

13. Compact fluorescent light bulbs (CFLs) use 75 percent less energy than incandescent bulbs. CFLs also last 10 times longer, giving them the environmental *and* economic advantage.

14. Consider wind power. Ask your energy provider about options—ConEd, for example, offers a wind power option. Though it tends to cost 10 percent more than regular energy, there's an incentive to bring the bill down by implementing other energy-saving techniques to offset the higher cost of wind power.

15. Look into solar thermal panels to heat your water. Solar Services, one of the oldest and biggest companies, will walk you through the process—from paperwork to tax credits. With the money saved on a water heater, the system will have paid for itself in two to three years.

16. Green your cleaning routine. Trade astringent, nonbiodegradable, potentially carcinogenic chemical kitchen cleaners for biodegradable, eco-safe products.

17. Use nontoxic pest control. The options are increasing, and even some of the major companies have green options.

18. Consider purchasing locally built furniture. See if there are any artisans in your state working with reclaimed wood (from trees that have fallen naturally because of storms or age).

19. Recycle your fryer oil. Biofuel companies across the country will pick it up and convert it.

20. Grow your own. Consider a roof-top garden or interior/exterior window boxes for small plants and herbs. EarthBoxes are one low-maintenance solution.

21. Cut down on shipping materials. Request that purveyors send goods with the least amount of packing materials possible. Request that Styrofoam packaging not be used.

22. Trade in white toilet paper, c-folds, and restroom paper towels. Instead, use products made of chlorine-free unbleached, recycled paper.

23. Need new toilets? There are a number of water-saving options that save anywhere from half a gallon to more than a gallon per flush. The old-fashioned brick technique is a good start too: place a brick in the tank of your toilet—the space that it takes up is water saved each time the toilet is flushed.

24. Compost garbage. Even high-volume establishments can make this happen. Keep separate cans for all food-based waste, and dump it in a compost bin out back. A common misconception about compost is that it smells bad—this is not true!

25. Recycle! Be strict about kitchen and bar staff recycling glass and plastic receptacles. Recycle cardboard and wood boxes used for produce, and any newspapers or magazines sent to the restaurant.

26. Cut down on linens. Tablecloths and napkins require a large amount of chemical cleaners, bleaches, and starches. Stay away from white, if possible. If it's not imperative, consider eliminating tablecloths all together. Go for soft cloth napkins instead of starched.

27. Ice = water + energy. Don't waste it! Don't automatically refill ice bins—wait until they truly get low, and only add as much as you need to get through the crush. Ice is expensive to produce, both in terms of money and resources.

28. If you're a small restaurant or café, without huge needs or storage space, look into joining (or forming) a local co-op for purchasing green items. Cleaning supplies, paper products, etc are all cheaper in bulk.

29. Educate yourself! From agricultural philosophy to the specifics of restaurant operations, the number of resources for green issues and practices is ever-growing. Pick up *The Omnivore's Dilemma* by Michael Pollan, the Green Restaurant Association's *Dining Green: A Guide to Creating Environmentally Sustainable Restaurants and Kitchens*, and *Sourcing Seafood, a Resource Guide for Chefs* by Seafood Choices Alliance.

30. Last but not least, educate your staff! They need to know *why* you're doing what you're doing, so that they can spread the word—to the diners, and beyond!

▶ Check Your Knowledge

1. What is considered the front of the house?

2. Define curbside appeal.

3. Suggest methods for remembering who ordered what on a table for a large party.

4. Name some of the responsibilities and duties of an assistant restaurant manager.

5. Briefly explain American service.

A popular point-of-sale system.

Front-of-the-House Restaurant Systems

Point-of-Sale Systems

Point-of-sale (POS) systems are very common in restaurants and other foodservice settings, such as stadiums, theme parks, airports, and cruise ships. These systems are used by hotel properties that have food and beverage and retail outlets. They are used to track food and beverage charges and other retail charges that may occur at a hotel or restaurant. A POS system is made up of a number of POS terminals that interface with a remote central processing unit. A POS terminal may be used as an electronic cash register, too.

MICROS, a leading software, hardware, and enterprise systems provider, offers Restaurant 3700, a modular suite of applications that encompasses front-of-the-house, back-of-the-house, and enterprise systems. The popular 3700 POS is a Microsoft Windows–based touch-screen system where client terminals are networked to a central POS server. Transactions are rung at the terminal and posted into the database for later analysis and reporting. The 3700 POS will support a network of kitchen printers so that orders can be presented to line cooks and chefs for food preparation. This POS system also supports use of a wireless personal digital assistant (PDA) as an order-taking device so that servers can take orders directly from the guest tableside. Mobile handheld devices can greatly speed the processing of orders to the kitchen and ultimately increase revenues as a result of faster table turns.

Kitchen Display Systems

Kitchen display systems further enhance the processing of orders to and in the kitchen. Printers in the kitchen may be replaced with video monitors and present orders to kitchen associates along with information on how long orders are taking to be prepared. Orders change color or flash on the monitor, which alerts kitchen associates to orders that are taking too long. Kitchen monitors are widely used in quick-service restaurants but are also gaining momentum in table service restaurants. Kitchen video systems also post order preparation time to a central data base for later reporting and analysis by management to determine how the kitchen is performing.

Guest Services Solutions

Guest services solutions are applications that are designed to help a restaurateur develop a dining relationship with guests. Applications include a frequent-diner management program, delivery management with caller ID interface, and guest-accounts receivable to manage home accounts and gift certificates. All these applications are accessed through the POS system and give restaurateurs the opportunity to offer their guests convenience, while allowing the restaurateurs to track who their best customers are. Guest activity is posted into the central database and management can develop targeted marketing programs based on this information.

▶ Check Your Knowledge

1. What do front-of-the-house systems entail?
2. Briefly define guest services solutions.

Back-of-the-House Restaurant Systems

Back-of-the-house systems are also known as product management systems and include inventory control and food costing, labor management, and financial reporting features. SoftCafe develops software for restaurants and foodservice operations, allowing them to create menus on personal computers. SoftCafe MenuPro creates professional menus at a fraction of the cost of print shop menus, with more than a 150 predesigned menu styles; 1500 images, watermarks, borders, and food illustrations; and more than 100 font types, and a culinary spelling checker.[4]

Restaurant Magic, based in Tampa, Florida, has several excellent restaurant management solutions: Data Central is delivered to a desktop as an enterprise-quality, secure and reliable, centralized business management solution to deliver powerful, user-friendly forms and reports to any Web-connected Windows PC in a restaurant organization. Data Central is a technological breakthrough in centralized application and database management because it is written entirely in the Visual C# language and is deployed as a Microsoft .NET Framework solution. Access to information is specified at the log-in level, and applications, reports, and important data are updated once available to all users automatically.[5] For a restaurant chain such as Outback Steakhouse, "Secure centralized management of enterprise data is more than a best practice, it is a necessity."[6] The benefits of programs such as Data Central are clear: Multistore managers can now view data for the enterprise. Store-level managers can view data for their store or for any group of stores they choose.

Restaurant Magic's Profit and Loss Reporting delivers profit and loss information on demand, consolidating information from purchasing to produce accurate cost of goods sold. All the key data is collected from the POS to track all revenues, forms of payments, and complementary activity (such as data from time clocks in order to collect labor costs) and integrate it with all other data to produce profit and loss (P&L) reporting daily, weekly, and multiperiod. The Profit and Loss Reporting allows a collaborative P&L budgeting system where the store and regional managers work together to build budgets and assess results quickly.[7]

Wireless POS Systems

Peter Perdikakis is the owner of two Skyline Chili fast-casual restaurants in Cincinnati. The restaurants are unusual in that the kitchen is open and visible to diners. Servers used to simply yell the orders across the steam table. Peter says, "You eat off china and have silverware, but it's very fast—typically you get your order about two minutes after it's ordered. Other POS systems slowed this process down because the servers had to go over to a terminal and

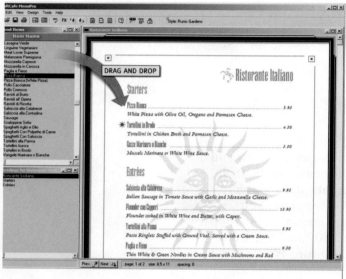

One of the menu-creation programs available from MenuPro.

write down the order," which is why Peter became interested in wireless. When he wanted to expand his operations, he selected a Pocket POS system from PixelPoint, consisting of two primary fixed terminals (one at a drive-through window and one at the checkout station), three handheld units for use on the dining floor, and another fixed unit for the back office.

The PixelPoint wireless POS system allows the servers to use a handheld PDA, which operates on the Windows CE platform, to send orders to the kitchen. Given that wireless POS systems speed up orders, their use in restaurants is likely to increase.

Labor Management

Most front-of-the-house systems have the ability to track employee working time. A back-of-the-house labor management package adds the ability to manage all of a restaurant's payroll and human resource information. A labor management system includes a human resources module to track hiring, employee personal information, vacation, I-9 status, security privileges, tax status, availability, and any other information pertinent to employees working at the restaurant. A labor management system would also include scheduling capability so that managers can create weekly schedules based on forecasted business. Schedules can then be enforced when employees check in and out so that labor costs can be managed.

The labor management package also presents actual work time and pay rates to a payroll processor so that paychecks can be cut and distributed. It also collates tips data and receipt data from the front of the house so that proper tip allocations can be reported according to IRS guidelines.

Financial Reporting

Back-of-the-house and front-of-the-house systems post data into a relational database located on the central server. The restaurant manager uses these data for reporting and decision making. P&L reports, budget variances, end-of-day reports, and other financial reports are generated from the central database. Financial management reporting needs to be flexible so that restaurant operators can manipulate it in ways that are useful to them. It is also important to get reports during the day in real time as the day unfolds so that restaurateurs can make decisions before profit is lost. Some reporting packages provide a graphical representation of the financial data displayed continuously on a monitor so that critical restaurant data is always available. This type of reporting provides restaurants with a real-time "heartbeat" for their operations.

Both back-of-the-house and front-of-the-house systems must be reliably linked so that POS food costs, labor costs, service times, and guest activity can be analyzed on the same reports. Restaurant management can then make critical business decisions armed with all necessary information. Technology is also used to collect data throughout the day for real-time budget control and "on-the-fly" management of labor effectiveness. Budgets are tight, and this is a way for management to watch, in real time, where their labor costs are at all times.

Personal Digital Assistants

Personal digital assistants (PDAs) help hospitality businesses stay effective and efficient by improving time management and helping with faster service. For example, computer systems are used today in restaurants to transmit orders to the kitchen and to retrieve and post guest payments. These actions took extra time in the past, when the computer systems were placed at a distance from the server. PDAs have been created to allow servers to control their business with their fingertips.

One leading software provider to restaurant operators is Restaurant Technology, Inc. (RTI). RTI was founded by two restaurant owners who understand the accounting applications that operate from a central platform known as the Restaurant Financial System. Working together, their accounting programs form an integrated system, with the following modules:

A pocket PC used in restaurants.

- Accounts payable
- Check reconciliation
- Daily store reporting
- General ledger
- Payroll
- Time keeping

PDAs can also be used in the hotel setting. Often, PDAs can be integrated with a property management system (PMS) to give housekeepers real-time information about which rooms need to be cleaned and which rooms are not occupied. In the same way, as housekeepers complete the cleaning of a room, they can send a wireless signal to the front desk to affirm that the room is ready to be occupied.

▶ Check Your Knowledge

1. Explain in what ways advances in technology aid the inventory process in restaurants.

2. What are back-of-the-house systems also known as?

3. What are the benefits of using a PDA?

Back of the House

The back of the house refers to all the areas that guests do not typically come in contact with; it is generally run by the kitchen manager. The back of the house includes purchasing, receiving, storing/issuing, food production, stewarding, budgeting, accounting, and control.

One of the most important aspects to running a successful restaurant is having a strong back-of-the-house operation, particularly in the kitchen. The kitchen is the backbone of every full-service restaurant; thus, it must be well managed and organized. Some of the main considerations in efficiently operating the back of the house include staffing, scheduling, training, food cost analysis, production, management involvement, management follow-up, and employee recognition.

Food Production

Planning, organizing, and producing food of a consistently high quality are no easy tasks. The kitchen manager, cook, or chef begins the production process by determining the expected volume of business for the next few days. The same period's sales from the previous year will give a good indication of the expected volume and the breakdown of the number of sales of each menu item. As described earlier, ordering and receiving will have already been done for the day's production schedule.

The **kitchen manager** checks the head line cook's order, which will bring the prep (preparation) area up to the par stock of prepared items. Most of the prep work is done in the early part of the morning and afternoon. Taking advantage of slower times allows the line cooks to do the final preparation just prior to and during the actual meal service.

The kitchen layout is set up according to the business projected as well as the menu design. Most full-service restaurants have similar layouts and designs for their kitchens. The layout consists of the back door area, walk-ins, the freezer, dry storage, prep line, salad bar, cooking line, expediter, dessert station, and service bar area.

The **cooking line** is the most important part of the kitchen layout. It might consist of a broiler station, window station, fry station, salad station, sauté station, and pizza station—just a few of the intricate parts that go into the setup of the back of the house. The size of the kitchen and its equipment are all designed according to the sales forecast for the restaurant.

The kitchen will also be set up according to what the customers prefer and order most frequently. For example, if guests eat more broiled or sautéed items, the size of the broiler and sauté must be larger to cope with the demand.

Teamwork, a prerequisite for success in all areas of the hospitality and tourism industry, is especially important in the kitchen. Because of the hectic pace, pressure builds, and unless each member of the team excels, the result will be food that is delayed, not up to standard, or both.

Although organization and performance standards are necessary, it is helping each other with the prepping and the cooking that makes for teamwork. "It's just like a relay race; we can't afford to drop the baton," says Amy Lu, kitchen manager of China Coast restaurant in Los Angeles. Teamwork in the back of the house is like an orchestra playing in tune, each player adding to the harmony.

Chefs working together as a team.

Another example of organization and teamwork is T.G.I. Friday's five rules of control for running a kitchen:

1. Order it well.
2. Receive it well.
3. Store it well.
4. Make it to the recipe.
5. Don't let it die in the window.

It is amazing to see a kitchen line being overloaded, yet everyone is gratified when the team succeeds in preparing and serving quality food on time.[8]

A number of chefs are joining the green hospitality movement by encouraging the purchase of sustainable farming produce. More than 20,000 American Culinary Federation members are emphasizing organic and locally grown produce, whole-grain breads, and grass-fed meat products. Sustainable farming is making such a wave in the restaurant industry as a whole that the National Restaurant Association (NRA) began work on a multiyear plan to guide the restaurant and foodservice industry toward environmentally sound practices and to develop policy initiatives focusing on sustainability. The NRA's goal is to identify practices that can reduce costs for restaurants while encouraging the creation and use of sustainable materials and alternative energy sources.[9] As an example of a leadership role in the growth of sustainable food usage is Chipotle Mexican Grill with 1,000 restaurants that sell about 75 million pounds naturally raised meat each year. In addition, a significant portion of the chain's produce is organic. Chipotle's "Food with Integrity" mission is the cornerstone of everything they do.[10]

Kitchen/Food Production

Staffing and Scheduling

Practicing proper staffing is absolutely crucial for the successful running of a kitchen. It is important to have enough employees on the schedule to enable the restaurant, as a whole, to handle the volume on any given shift. Often it is better to overstaff the kitchen, rather than understaff it, for two reasons: First, it is much easier to send an employee home than it is to call someone in. Second, having extra employees on hand allows for cross-training and development, which is becoming a widely used method.

Problems can also be eliminated if a staffing plan is created to set needed levels. These levels should be adjusted according to sales trends on a monthly basis.

Also crucial to the smooth running of the kitchen is having a competent staff. This means putting the best cooks in the appropriate stations on the line, which will assist in the speed of service, the food quality, and the quality of the operations.

Training and Development

Implementing a comprehensive training program is vital in the kitchen because of a high turnover rate. Trainers should, of course, be qualified and experienced in the kitchen. Often, the most competent chefs are used to train new

A DAY IN THE LIFE OF JAMES LORENZ

Kitchen Manager, T.G.I. Friday's, La Jolla, California

7:00 A.M. Arrive. Check the work of cleaning crew (such as clogs in burners, stoves/ovens, etc.) for total cleanliness.

7:15–7:40 A.M. Set production levels for all stations (broiler/hot sauce/expediter, cold sauce, vegetable preparation, baker preparation, line preparation: sauté/noodles, pantry, fry/seafood portioning).

8:00 A.M. The first cooks begin arriving; greet them and allocate production sheets with priority items circled.

9:00 A.M. On a good day, the produce arrives at 9:00 A.M. Check for quality, quantity, and accuracy (making sure the prices match the quotation sheet) and that the produce is stored properly.

9:30–11:00 A.M. Follow up on production. The sauté cook, who is last to come in, arrives. He or she is the closing person for the morning shift.

- Follow up on cleanliness, recipe adherence, production accuracy.
- Check the stations to ensure the storage of prepped items (for example, plastic draining inserts under poultry and seafood), the shelf life of products, and general cleanliness and that what is in the station is prepared correctly (for example, turkey diced to the right size and portioned and dated correctly).

10:45 A.M. Final check of the line and production to ensure readiness. Did everyone prepare enough?

11:00–2:30 P.M. All hands on deck. Jump on the first ticket. Pre-toast buns for burgers and hold in heated drawers. Precook some chicken breasts for salads. Monitor lunch until 2:30 P.M.

- Be responsible for cleanliness.
- Determine who needs to get off the clock.
- Decide what production is left for the remainder of the day.
- Focus on changing over the line, change the food pan inserts (BBQ sauce, etc.).

2:30–3:15 P.M. Complete changeover of the line and check the stocking for the P.M. crew:

- Complete final prep portioning.
- Check the dishwasher area and prep line for cleanliness.
- Check that the product is replaced in the store walk-in or refrigerator.
- Reorganize the produce walk-in. Check the storage of food, labels, and day dots, lids on.
- Thank the A.M. crew and send them home.

4:00–4:15 P.M. Welcome the P.M. crew.

- Place produce order (as a double check, ask the P.M. crew what they might need).

5:00 P.M. Hand over to P.M. manager.

hires. Such trainings are usually done on the job and may include study material. Some restaurants may even require new hires to complete a written test, evaluating the skills acquired through the training process.

Ensuring adequate training is necessary because the success of the business lies in the hands of the trainer and the trainee. If employees are properly trained when they begin their employment, little time and money will need to be spent on correcting errors. Thorough training also helps in retaining employees for longer periods of time.

Training, however, does not stop after the new hire passes a test. Developing the skills of all the employees is critical to the growth and success of the kitchen and, ultimately, the restaurant. A development program may consist of delegating duties or projects to the staff, allowing them to expand their horizons within the kitchen and the restaurant business. Such duties include projections of sales, inventory, ordering, schedule writing, and training.

This will help management get feedback on the running of the kitchen and on how well the development program works in their particular operation. Also, this allows for internal growth and promotion.

Production Procedures

Production in the kitchen is key to the success of a restaurant because it relates directly to the recipes on the menu and how much product is on hand to produce the menu. Thus, controlling the production process is crucial. To undertake such a task, **production control sheets** are created for each station, for example, broiler, sauté, fry, pantry, window, prep, dish, and dessert. With the control sheets, levels are set up for each day according to sales. Figure 2 shows a production sheet for a popular seafood restaurant.

The first step in creating the production sheets is to count the products on hand for each station. After the production levels are determined, the amount of product required to reach the level for each recipe is decided. After these calculations are completed, the sheets are handed to the cooks. It is important to make these calculations before the cooks arrive, considering the amount of prep time that is needed to produce before business is conducted. For instance, if a restaurant is open only for lunch and dinner, enough product should be on hand by 11:00 A.M. to ensure that the cooks are prepared to handle the lunch crowd.

When determining production, par levels should be changed weekly according to sales trends. This will help control and minimize waste levels. Waste is a large contributor to food cost; therefore, the kitchen manager should determine the product levels necessary to make it through only one day. Products have a particular shelf life, and if the kitchen overproduces and does not sell the product within its shelf life, it must be thrown away. More important, this practice allows the freshest product to reach the customers on a daily basis.

After the lunch rush, the kitchen manager checks to see how much product was sold and how much is left for the night shift. (Running out of a product is unacceptable and should not happen. If proper production procedures are followed, a restaurant will not have to eighty-six anything on the menu.) After all production is completed on all stations, the cooks may be checked out. It is essential to check out the cooks and hold them accountable for production

ITEM	PAR	ON HAND	PREP	INITIAL
FRESH CATCH				
Add Island Sauce to any fish				
BBQ Shrimp				
Casino				
Coconut Lobster				
Fried Lobster				
Ritz Crusted				
Seafood Kabob				
Stuffed Salmon				
SNAPPER				
Almondine				
Anna				
Broiled				
Fingers				
Stuffed				
FLOUNDER				
Allmondine				
Fried, Baked				
Stuffed				
GROUPER				
Baked				
Casino				
Coconut				
Coconut				
Floribean				
Fried Nutty				
Mexical				
Nuggets				
Nutty				
Potato Crusted				
Ritz				
Stuffed				
Wisconsin				
Holiday Specials				
DAILY APPETIZERS				
Oysters Maria (3 ea)				
Mozzereal Cheese Sticks (5 ea)				
Jammers, Jalapeno (4ea)				
Jammers, Seafood (10ea)				
Clam Strip Basket (6oz)				
Buffalo Shrimp (5ea)				
BBQ Shrimp (1 Skewer 5 Shrimp)				
Gator Gites (6oz)				

ITEM	PAR	ON HAND	PREP	INITIAL
WRAPS				
Ham or Turkey				
Ham & turkey				
Shrimp Salad				
Chicken Caesar				
Chicken Salad				
BLT Wrap				
DAILY SALADS				
Seafood or Chicken Salad				
Shrimp				
Chicken Mediterrarean				
PIZZA				
Shrimp or B.B.Q. Chicken				
Portabello				
SOUP & SAND				
Clamwich, Mini Grouper				
Crab Cake, Chicken Salad				
EXTRA DAILY SPECIALS				
Monday AUCE Fish				
Tues Lobster				
Wed AUCE Popcorn\Crabby Night				
Thur Prime Rib				
Beef Tips and Noodles				
Chicken Pot Pie				
Salisbury Stk				
Ham & Mac & Cheese				
Chicken Oscar				
Stone Crab Mustard Sauce				
Corn Salsa				
SPECIALS ITEMS FOR CATERING				

Pull From Freezer				
Item	Par	On Hand	Pull	Initial
				08/25/2003
				01/12/04

Figure 2 • A Production Sheet for a Popular Seafood Restaurant.

(*Source:* Anna Maria Oyster Bar, Inc.)

levels. If they are not checked out, they will slide on their production, negatively affecting the restaurant and the customer.

The use of production sheets is critical, as well, in controlling how the cooks use the products because production plays a key role in food cost. Every recipe has a particular "spec" (specification) to follow. When one deviates from the recipe, quality goes down, consistency is lost, and food cost goes up. That is why it is important to follow the recipe at all times.

Management Involvement and Follow-Up

As in any business, management involvement is vital to the success of a restaurant. Management should know firsthand what is going on in the back of the house. It is also important that they be "on the line," assisting the staff in the preparation of the menu and in the other operations of the kitchen, just as they should be helping when things are rushed. When management is visible to the staff, they are prone to do what they need to be doing at all times, and food quality is more apparent and consistent. Managers should constantly be walking and talking food cost, cleanliness, sanitation, and quality. This shows the staff how serious and committed they are to the successful running of the back of the house.

As management spends more time in the kitchen, more knowledge is gained, more confidence is acquired, and more respect is earned. Employee–management interaction produces a sense of stability and a strong work ethic among employees, resulting in higher morale and promoting a positive working environment. To ensure that policies and standards are being upheld, management follow-up should happen on a continual basis. This is especially important when cooks are held accountable to specifications and production and when other staff members are given duties to perform. Without follow-up, the restaurant may fold.

Employee Recognition

Employee recognition is an extremely important aspect of back-of-the-house management. Recognizing employees for their efforts creates a positive work environment that motivates the staff to excel and ultimately to produce consistently better-quality food for the guests.

Recognition can take many different forms, from personally commending a staff person for his or her efforts to recognizing a person in a group setting. By recognizing employees, management can make an immediate impact on the quality of operations. This can be a great tool for building sales, as well as assisting in the overall success of the restaurant.

▶ Check Your Knowledge

1. Explain the following terms: guest counts/covers, product specification, production control sheets.
2. Discuss T.G.I. Friday's five rules for running a kitchen.

TECHNOLOGY SPOTLIGHT

Reversing Restaurant Failure

Cihan Cobanoglu, Ph.D., Dean, School of Hotel and Restaurant Management, University of South Florida, Sarasota-Manatee

In the summer of 2003, American Express aired a commercial with celebrity chef Rocco Di-Spirito purporting that "nine out of ten restaurants fail in the first year." The commercial caught the attention of an associate professor at Ohio State University's hospitality management program, H. G. Parsa. He had heard the statistic before, but, based on his thirteen years of experience in the hospitality industry, was skeptical. In fact, the statistic was somewhat of an urban legend even to American Express. After prodding the credit card company for three months as to the source of its statistic, Parsa received a written response stating that "American Express has not been able to track down a specific data source for the statistic."

In 2005, Parsa co-authored "Why Restaurants Fail," an article published in a Cornell University journal based on a study of restaurant failure. In that study, he found that the restaurant failure rate during the first year is about 30 percent—still a significant number. There are many reasons for restaurant failure: lack of cash flow, poor operational controls, high turnover, poor location, ineffective advertising and sales promotion, and so forth. In markets where net profit margins are slim, as with many quick-service operations, there's even less room for error.

In some cases, an investment in sound technology systems can help boost a restaurant's chances for success and help them avoid becoming a statistic:

- **Cost Control Software:** There are numerous cost control software options available in the market that will enable a chef and managers to make informed decisions about the cost and selling price of their menu items. For example, ChefTec (**www.cheftec.com**) will alert a manager if the cost of a menu item is over a certain price level. This allows for fluctuating inventory items to be kept under control. Additionally, cost control software allows the managers to play "what if" scenarios to determine the best price levels and contribution margins. Similarly, cost control software can alert a chef or manager if an inventory item is approaching the end of its shelf life. If it does, the chef can utilize the item in a special menu, eliminating waste and possibly even boosting sales.

- **Reverse Auction Software:** This solution can be used as a part of a menu engineering or cost control package. Eatec (**www.eatec.com**) and ChefTec both offer this feature, which allows the restaurant manager to determine a maximum price for purchase order items. The system then distributes the purchase order to suppliers electronically, allowing them to reverse bid on items. The software can even select the lowest bids for you. A manager has the freedom to purchase their products from any vendor, regardless of their bids. Of course, logic usually dictates ordering from the lowest cost provider if the qualities are equal. This system is predicted to save restaurants about 4 percent to 9 percent on food costs. In slim margin environments, this could make the difference between success and failure.

- **Point-of-Sale System:** Most restaurants have a point-of-sale system (POS); however, the majority of restaurants use only 20 percent to 30 percent of its features. Consider leveraging data from your POS system to create a menu engineering strategy: Most POS systems will report the menu mix, whereas cost control software will report contribution margins for each menu item. The result is a menu mix analysis that will allow operators to engineer their menus for higher margins. Items can then be identified as one of the four classic menu-engineering examples: "dog" items, which should be replaced; "puzzle" items, which should be repositioned on the menu; "plow horse" items, which should be re-priced; or "star" items, which should be preserved. By re-pricing plow horses and focusing on stars, restaurants can positively affect their bottom lines.

- **Computer-Based Training:** The new generation of POS systems and kitchen display systems can be used as ongoing training devices. The cost of creating these training programs is minimal, with off-the-shelf screen recorder software available from such companies as Camtasia Studio (**www.camtasia.com**) or Adobe Captivate (**www.adobe.com/captivate**). Personalized training tools will ensure high service quality and safety.

- **Other Solutions:** Opportunities for boosting the bottom line are available at nearly every juncture. Restaurants can work to make better use of their web sites (historically among the least effective in the hospitality industry) and can tap such solutions as scheduling software, table management, HACCP (hazard analysis and critical control points) alert systems, and financial management.

INTRODUCING CHRIS DELLA-CRUZ, GENERAL MANAGER OF SUSO RESTAURANT

Expectations of the General Manager

The expectations of the general manager are different in each restaurant; however, there are certain commonalities as well. Some of these commonalities are as follows:

- General managers answer directly to the owner or to regional directors of major corporations.

- General managers are expected to run good numbers for the periods. The numbers analyzed are food cost, labor cost, beverage cost. These areas are controlled to produce sufficient profit for the restaurant.

- General managers promote good morale and teamwork in the restaurant. Having a positive environment in the restaurant is of utmost importance. This will not only keep the employees happy, but it will also contribute to providing better service to the guests.

(continued)

INTRODUCING CHRIS DELLA-CRUZ, GENERAL MANAGER OF SUSO RESTAURANT *(continued)*

Duties and Responsibilities

The general manager of a restaurant is directly in charge of all the operations in the restaurant. General managers are also in charge of the floor managers, kitchen manager, and all the remaining employees in the restaurant.

The general manager should always check on the floor managers to ensure that all policies and regulations are being met. This will keep operations running smoothly.

Another important duty is to organize and control the staffing of the restaurant. The floor managers usually write the employee schedule; however, the general manager is still directly responsible for proper staffing for the period. This will help keep labor costs to about 20 percent of sales. The general manager is also in charge of conducting employee reviews and training.

Qualifications for a General Manager

To be hired as a general manager, the following qualifications are necessary:

- The general manager should be very knowledgeable in the restaurant business.
- He or she should have previously worked all the stations in a restaurant and be very familiar with them.
- The general manager should be able to get along with all people, be fair with all employees, and not discriminate.
- Having a degree is not the most important thing in becoming a general manager. However, a degree is very useful in moving up the ladder in a company to regional manager, regional director, and so on.

Budgeted Costs in a Restaurant

Running a good pace in the restaurant is of absolute importance. Every restaurant has different numbers to make. The following numbers came from Chris's restaurant. These numbers reflect their goals versus actual numbers run for a given week.

	Goal (%)	Actual (%)	Variance (%)
Food Cost	27.0	27.2	+0.2
Labor Cost	19.9	20.8	+0.9
Beverage Cost	19.0	18.2	−0.8

As can be seen, this restaurant did well with the beverage cost; however, the food cost and the labor cost are two areas to focus on for the upcoming week.

Making good percentages for the restaurant is the most important focus simply because this is where the restaurant makes or does not make a profit. When the general manager runs good numbers, then he or she will receive a large bonus check for contributing to the profit of the restaurant. This is why it is so important to focus on these three key areas.

Purchasing

Purchasing for restaurants involves procuring the products and services that the restaurant needs to serve its guests. Restaurant operators set up purchasing systems that determine the following:

- Standards for each item (**product specification**)
- Systems that minimize effort and maximize control of theft and losses from other sources
- The amount of each item that should be on hand (par stock and reorder point)
- Who will do the buying and keep the purchasing system in motion
- Who will do the receiving, storage, and issuing of items[11]

It is desirable for restaurants to establish standards for each product, called a product specification. When ordering meat, for example, the cut, weight, size, percentage of fat content, and number of days aged are all factors that are specified by the purchaser.

Establishing systems that minimize effort and maximize control of theft may be done by computer or manually. However, merely computerizing a system does not make it theft-proof. Instead, employing honest workers is a top priority because temptation is everywhere in the restaurant industry.

An efficient and effective system establishes a stock level that must be on hand at all times. This is called a **par stock**. If the stock on hand falls below a specified reorder point, the computer system automatically reorders a predetermined quantity of the item.

In identifying who will do the buying, it is most important to separate task and responsibility between the person placing the order and the person receiving the goods. This avoids possible theft. The best way to avoid losses is to have the chef prepare the order; the manager or the manager's designee place the order; and a third person, responsible for the stores, receive the goods together with the chef (or the chef's designee).

Commercial (for-profit) restaurant and foodservice operators who are part of a chain may have the menu items and order specifications determined at the corporate office. This saves the unit manager from having to order individually; specialists at the corporate office can not only develop the menu but also the specifications for the ingredients to ensure consistency. Both chain and independent restaurants and foodservice operators use similar prepurchase functions (see Figure 3).

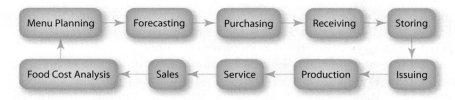

Figure 3 • Food Cost Control Process.

- Plan menus.
- Determine quality and quantity needed to produce menus.
- Determine inventory stock levels.
- Identify items to purchase by subtracting stock levels from the quantity required to produce menus.
- Write specifications and develop market orders for purchases.

Professor Stefanelli at the University of Nevada, Las Vegas, suggests a formal and an informal method of purchasing that includes the following steps[12]:

Formal	*Informal*
Develop purchase order.	Develop purchase order.
Establish bid schedule.	Quote price.
Issue invitation to bid.	Select vendor and place order.
Tabulate and evaluate bids.	
Award contract and issue delivery order.	
Inspect/receive deliveries, inventory stores, and record transactions in inventory.	Receive and inspect deliveries, store, and record transaction.
Evaluate and follow up.	Evaluate and follow up.
Issue food supplies for food production and service.	Issue food supplies for food production and service.

The formal method is generally used by chain restaurant operators and the informal one by independent restaurant operators.

A **purchase order** comes as a result of the product specification. As it sounds, a purchase order is an order to purchase a certain quantity of an item at a specific price. Many restaurants develop purchase orders for items they need on a regular basis. These are then sent to suppliers for quotations, and samples are sent in for product evaluations. For example, canned items have varying amounts of liquid. Typically, it is the drained weight of the product that matters to the restaurant operator. After comparing samples from several vendors, the operator can choose the supplier that best suits the restaurant's needs.

Receiving

When placing an order, the restaurant operator specifies the day and time (for example, Friday, 10:00 A.M. to 12:00 noon) for the delivery to be made. This prevents deliveries from being made at inconvenient times.

Receiving is a point of control in the restaurant operation. The purpose of receiving is to ensure the quantity, quality, and price are exactly as ordered. The quantity and quality relate to the order specification and the standardized recipe. Depending on the restaurant and the type of food and beverage control system, some perishable items are issued directly to the kitchen, and most of the nonperishable items go into storage.

Storing/Issuing

Control of the stores is often a problem. Records must be kept of all items going into and out of the stores. If more than one person has access to the stores, it is difficult to know where to attach responsibility in case of losses.

Items should be issued from the stores only on an authorized requisition signed by the appropriate person. One restaurateur who has been in business for many years issues stores to the kitchen on a daily basis. No inventory is kept in the production area and there is no access to the stores. To some, this may be overdoing control, but it is hard to fault the results: a good food cost percentage. All items that enter the stores should have a date stamp and be rotated using the first in–first out (FIFO) system.

First in–first out (FIFO) is a simple but effective system of ensuring stock rotation. This is achieved by placing the most recent purchases, in rotation, behind previous purchases. Failure to do this can result in spoilage.

Obviously, restaurants should maintain strict controls. Among the better-known controls are taking inventory regularly, calculating food and beverage cost percentages, having receiving done by a person other than the person who orders, using a par-stock reordering system, using one entrance/exit for employees and not permitting employees to bring bags into the restaurant with them, employing a good accountant, and, yes, checking the garbage!

Budgeting

Budgeting costs fall into two categories: fixed and variable. **Fixed costs** are constant regardless of the volume of business. Fixed costs are rent/lease payments, interest, and depreciation. **Variable costs** fluctuate with the volume of business. Variable costs include controllable expenses such as payroll, benefits, direct operating expense, music and entertainment, marketing and promotion, energy and utility, administrative, and repairs and maintenance.

Regardless of sales fluctuations, variable or controllable expenses vary in some controllable proportion to sales. For example, if a restaurant is open on a Monday, it must have a host, server, cook, dishwasher, and so on. The volume of business and sales total may be $750. However, on Friday that sales total might be $2,250 with just a few more staff. The controllable costs increased only slightly in proportion to the sales, and the fixed costs did not change.

Restaurant managers also need to spend time with staff members.

Restaurant Accounting

To operate any business efficiently and effectively, it is necessary to determine the mission, goals, and objectives. One of the most important goals in any enterprise is a fair return on investment, otherwise known as profit. In addition, accounting for the income and expenditures is a necessary part of any business enterprise. The restaurant industry has adopted a uniform system of accounts.

The **uniform system of accounts** for restaurants (USAR) outlines a standard classification and presentation of operating results. The system allows for easy comparison among restaurants because each expense item has the same schedule number.

Balance Sheet

A **balance sheet** for a restaurant, or any business, reflects how the assets and liabilities relate to the owner's equity at a particular moment in time. The balance sheet is mainly used by owners and investors to verify the financial health of the organization. Financial health may be defined in several ways—for example, liquidity, which means having a sufficient amount of cash available to pay bills when they are due, and debt leverage, which is the percentage of a company's assets owned by outside interests (liabilities).

CORPORATE PROFILE

T.G.I. Friday's Restaurant

In the spring of 1965, Alan Stillman, a New York perfume salesman, opened a restaurant located at First Avenue and 63rd Street. The restaurant boasted striped awnings, a blue exterior, and yellow supergraphics reading T.G.I. Friday's. Inside were wooden floors covered with sawdust, Tiffany-style lamps, bentwood chairs, red-and-white tablecloths, and a bar area complete with brass rails and stained glass.

T.G.I. Friday's was an immediate success. The restaurant on Manhattan's Upper East Side became the meeting place for single adults.

In 1971, franchisee Dan Scoggin opened a T.G.I. Friday's in Dallas and in four other sites around the country. The success was instant; thus, began the company that is Friday's today.

By 1975, there were ten T.G.I. Friday's in eight states, but the great success that the company had seen was starting to diminish. Dan Scoggin began a countrywide tour to visit each restaurant; he talked with employees, managers, and customers to isolate the roots of successes and failures. This was the critical turning point for the company. The focus shifted from being just another restaurant chain to giving guests exactly what they wanted. The theories and philosophies Scoggin developed are the principles by which Friday's now does business.

T.G.I. Friday's goal was to create a comfortable, relaxing environment where guests could enjoy food and drink. Stained glass windows, wooden airplane propellers, racing sculls, and metal advertising signs comprised the elegant clutter that greeted guests when they entered a T.G.I. Friday's. Nothing was left to chance. Music, lights, air-conditioning, decor, and housekeeping were all designed to keep guests comfortable. Employees were encouraged to display their own personalities and to treat customers as they would guests in their own homes.

As guests demanded more, T.G.I. Friday's provided more—soon becoming the industry leader in menu and drink selection. The menu expanded from a slate chalkboard to an award-winning collection of items representing every taste and mood.

T.G.I. Friday's also became the industry leader in innovation—creating the now-famous Jack Daniel's Grill. This was the first restaurant chain to offer stone-ground whole-wheat bread, avocados, bean sprouts, and Mexican appetizers across the country. As guests' tastes continued to change, T.G.I. Friday's introduced pasta dishes, brunch items, and fettuccine.

America owes the popularization of frozen and ice cream drinks to T.G.I. Friday's, where smooth, alcoholic, and nonalcoholic drinks were made with fresh fruit, juices, ice cream, and yogurt. These recipes were so precise that T.G.I. Friday's drink glasses were scientifically designed for the correct ratio of each ingredient. These specially designed glasses have since become popular throughout the industry.

Through the years, T.G.I. Friday's success has been phenomenal. T.G.I. Friday's is privately owned by Carlson Companies, Inc., of Minneapolis—one of the largest privately held companies in the country. Today, T.G.I. Friday's has come to be known as a casual restaurant where family and friends meet for great food, fun, and conversation. Everyone looks forward to T.G.I. Friday's!

What does it take to be successful in the restaurant business, and what does it take to be a leader? The answers to these questions are crucial to success as a restaurant company. The essentials of success in business are as follows:

1. Treat everyone with respect for their dignity.
2. Treat all customers as if they are honored guests in your home.
3. Remember that all problems result from either poor hiring, lack of training, unclear performance expectations, or accepting less than excellence.
4. Remember that management tools are methods, not objectives.

As you can see, these are principles to guide decision making as opposed to step-by-step actions. However, if these principles are not followed, then actions have very short-term effects. And if you do choose to follow them, they form a base on which you can easily decide which specific actions are necessary in any given situation.

The basics of leadership are as follows:

1. Hire the right people.
2. Train everyone thoroughly and completely.
3. Be sure that everyone clearly understands the performance expectations.
4. Accept only excellence.

Here are the very basics of how to provide strong, clear leadership. However, once again these are only the minimum requirements, not all the qualities necessary to be a good leader. Individual success and that of a company such as T.G.I. Friday's are predicated on understanding and following the essentials of success in business and the basics of leadership. Whether an hourly employee or a manager, it is critical that each employee manage his or her part of the business using these philosophies.

Restaurants are one of the few, fortunate types of businesses to operate on a cash basis for income receivables. There are no outstanding accounts receivable because all sales are in cash—even credit cards are treated as cash because of their prompt payment. Typically, restaurants invest significant funds in assets, such as equipment, furniture, and building (if they own it). The balance sheet will reflect how much of the cost of these assets has been paid for, and are thus owned by the company (owner's equity), and how much is still due to outsiders (liability). Furthermore, the balance sheet will show the extent to which the company has depreciated these assets, thus providing owners and investors with an indication of potential future costs to repair or replace existing assets.

Operating or Income Statement

From an operational perspective, the most important financial document is the operating statement. Once a sales forecast has been completed, the costs of servicing those sales are budgeted on an income statement. Figure 4 shows an example of an income statement for a hypothetical restaurant.

The **income statement**, which is for a month or a year, begins with the food and beverage sales. From this total, the cost of food and beverage is deducted;

	Budgeted	Actual Amount	Percentage	Variance + (−)	Last Period	Same Period Last Year
Sales						
Food						
Beverage						
Others						
Total sales		____	100			
Cost of Sales						
Food						
Beverage						
Others						
Total cost of sales		____				
Gross profit		____				
Controllable Expenses						
Salaries and wages						
Employee benefits						
Direct operating expenses[a]						
Music and entertainment						
Marketing						
Energy and utility						
Administrative and general						
Repairs and maintenance						
Total controllable expenses		____				
Rent and other occupation costs						
Income before interest, depreciation, and taxes						
Interest						
Depreciation						
Net income before taxes						
Income taxes		____				
Net Income		____				

[a]Telephone, insurance, legal, accounting, paper, glass, china, linens, office supplies, landscaping, cleaning supplies, etc.

Figure 4 • Sample Income Statement.

the remaining total is **gross profit**. To this amount, any other income is added (for example, cigarettes, vending machines, outside catering, and telephone income). The next heading is controllable expenses, which includes salaries, wages, employee benefits, direct operating expenses (telephone, insurance, accounting and legal fees, office supplies, paper, china, glass, cutlery, menus, landscaping, and so on), music and entertainment, marketing, energy and utility, administrative and general, repairs and maintenance. The total of this group is called total controllable expenses. Rent and other occupation costs are then deducted from the total, leaving income before interest, depreciation, and taxes. Interest and depreciation are deducted leaving a total of net income before taxes. From this amount, income taxes are paid, leaving the remainder as net income.

Managing the money to the bottom line requires careful scrutiny of all key results, beginning with the big-ticket controllable items such as labor costs, food costs, and beverages, on down to related controllable items. Additionally, management may wish to compare several income statements representing operations over a number of different periods. The ideal method for comparing is to compute every component of each income statement as a percentage of its total sales. Then, compare one period's percentage to another to determine if any significant trends are developing. For example, a manager could compare labor as a percentage of total sales over several months, or years, to assess the impact of rising labor rates on the bottom line. Notice how Figure 4 has columns for budgeted, actual, percentage of sales, variance (+/−) last period, and same period last year. This really gives management good decision-making information.

Operating Ratios

Operating ratios are industry norms that are applicable to each segment of the industry. Experienced restaurant operators rely on these operating ratios to indicate the restaurant's degree of success. Several ratios are good barometers of a restaurant's degree of success. Among the better known ratios are the following:

- Food cost percentage
- Contribution margin
- Labor cost percentage
- Prime cost
- Beverage cost percentage

Food Cost Percentage

The basic **food cost percentage**, for which the formula is cost/sales × 100, is calculated on a daily, weekly, or monthly basis. The procedure works in the following manner:

1. An inventory is taken of all the food and the purchase price of that food. This is called the *opening inventory*.
2. The purchases are totaled for the period and added to the opening inventory.
3. The closing inventory (the inventory at the close of the week or period for which the food cost percentage is being calculated) and returns, spoilage,

complimentary meals, and transfers to other departments are also deducted from the opening inventory plus purchases.

4. This figure is the cost of goods sold. The cost of goods sold is divided by the total sales. The resulting figure is the food cost percentage.

The following example illustrates the procedure:

Food Sales	$3,000
Opening Inventory	1,000
Add Purchases	500
	1,500
Less Spoilage and Complimentary Meals	–100
Less Closing Inventory	–500
Cost of Goods Sold	$900

$$\frac{\text{Food Cost}(\$900)}{\text{Sales}(\$3,000)} \times 100 = 30\% \text{ Food Cost Percentage}$$

The food cost percentage calculations become slightly more complicated when the cost of staff meals, management meals and entertaining (complimentary meals), and guest food returned are all properly calculated.

Food cost percentage has long been used as a yardstick for measuring the skill of the chef, cooks, and management to achieve a predetermined food cost percentage—usually 28 to 32 percent for a full-service restaurant and a little higher for a high-volume, fast-food restaurant.

Controlling food costs begins with cost-effective purchasing systems, a controlled storage and issuing system, and strict control of the food production and sales. The best way to visualize a food cost control system is to think of the food as money. Consider a $100 bill arriving at the back door: If the wrong people get their hands on that money, it does not reach the guest or the bottom line.

Contribution Margin

More recently, attention has focused not only on the food cost percentage but also on the contribution margin. The **contribution margin** is the amount that a menu item contributes to the gross profit, or the difference between the cost of the item and its sales price. Some menu items contribute more than others; therefore, restaurant operators focus more attention on the items that produce a higher contribution margin. It works like this:

The cost of the chicken dish is $2.00, and its selling price is $9.95, which leaves a contribution margin of $7.95. The fish, which costs a little more at $3.25, sells for $12.75 and leaves a contribution of $9.50. The pasta cost price of $1.50 and selling price of $8.95 leave a contribution margin of $7.45. Under this scenario, it would be better for the restaurant to sell more fish because each plate will yield $1.55 more than if chicken were sold.

Labor Cost Percentage

Labor costs are the highest single cost factor in staffing a restaurant. Fast-food restaurants have the lowest **labor costs percentage** (about 16 to 18 percent), with family and ethnic restaurants at about 22 to 26 percent and upscale full-service restaurants at about 30 to 35 percent.

Labor costs include salaries and wages of employees, employee benefits, and their training. Foodservice is a highly labor-intensive industry, depending on the type of restaurant. Quick-service restaurants have a lower payroll cost primarily because of their limited menu and limited service. Good managers try to manage their labor costs by accurate hiring and scheduling of staff according to the restaurant's cover turnover.

The labor cost is calculated by taking the total cost of labor for a period, say $200,000, and dividing it by the total sales for the same period, $800,000, and multiplying it by 100.

$$\frac{\text{Labor Cost } \$200,000}{\text{Sales} \quad \$800,000} \times 100 = 25\%$$

Prime Cost

Combined food and labor costs are known as **prime cost**. To allow for a reasonable return on investment, prime cost should not go above 60 to 65 percent of sales.

There are various methods of control, beginning with effective scheduling based on the expected volume of business. In reality, because of the high cost of labor, today's restaurateur manages by the minute. Once a rush is over, the effective manager thanks employees for doing a great job and looks forward to seeing them again. This may appear to be micromanagement, but an analysis of restaurant operations does not leave any alternatives.[13]

$$\text{Food cost} + \text{Labor cost percentage} = \text{Prime cost}$$

Beverage Cost Percentage

The **beverage cost percentage** is calculated like the food cost percentage. The method used most often is to first determine the unit cost and then mark up by the required percentage to arrive at the selling price. This is rounded up or down to a convenient figure. The actual beverage cost percentage is then compared with the anticipated cost percentage; any discrepancy is investigated.

The NRA publishes guidelines for restaurant operations. These valuable documents help provide a guide for operators to use when comparing their restaurants with other similar establishments. If the costs go above the budgeted or expected levels, then management must investigate and take corrective action.

Beverage cost is calculated by taking the costs of beverages and dividing it by the total beverage sales and multiplying by 100.

$$\frac{\text{Cost of beverage sales}}{\text{Total beverage sales}} \times 100 \quad \text{For example} \quad \frac{4,250}{19,479} \times 100 = 21.82\%$$

Therefore, if for a casual Italian restaurant, industry comparisons would show the following:

Labor costs at 20 to 24 percent of sales

Food costs at 28 to 32 percent of food sales

Beverage costs at 18 to 24 percent of beverage sales

INTRODUCING RAY KROC

Founder of McDonald's

The world's greatest fast-food success story is undoubtedly McDonald's. Back in the 1950s, Ray Kroc was selling soda fountains. He received an order from Mr. McDonald for two soda fountains. Ray Kroc was so interested in finding out why the McDonald brothers' restaurant needed two machines (everyone else ordered one) that he went out to the restaurant. There he saw the now-familiar golden arches and the hamburger restaurant. Ray persuaded the McDonalds to let him franchise their operation. Billions of burgers later, the reason for the success may be summarized as follows: quality, speed, cleanliness, service, and value. This has been achieved by systemizing the production process and by staying close to the original concept—keeping a limited menu, advertising heavily, being innovative with new menu items, maintaining product quality, and being consistent.

Of all hospitality entrepreneurs, Ray Kroc has been the most successful financially. In 1982, he was senior chairman of the board of McDonald's, an organization intent on covering the earth with hamburgers. Among the remarkable things about Kroc is that it was not until age 52 that he embarked on the royal road to fame and fortune.

The original McDonald's concept was created by two brothers, Richard and Maurice, who had no interest in expanding. The McDonald brothers were content with their profitable yet singular restaurant in San Bernardino, California. However, the golden arches impressed Kroc, as did the cleanliness and simplicity of the operation.

Kroc's organizational skills, perseverance, and incredible aptitude for marketing were his genius. His talent also extended to selecting close associates who were equally dedicated and who added financial, analytical, and managerial skills to the enterprise. Kroc remained the spark plug and master merchandiser until he died in 1984, leaving a multimillion-dollar legacy.

Much of Kroc's $400 million has gone to employees, hospitals, and the Marshall Field Museum. It is distributed through Kroc's own foundation. Most important, Kroc developed several operational guidelines, including the concepts of KISS—keep it simple, stupid—and QSC&V—quality, service, cleanliness, and value. Kroc's "Never Be Idle a Moment" motto was also incorporated into the business.

Enterprises such as McDonald's are not built without ample dedication, and Ray Kroc certainly had a wealth of dedication. Today, an average McDonald's franchise can net more than $1 million annually thanks to Kroc's ingenious marketing strategies. In fact, McDonald's Corporation has become so affluent that it was named *Entrepreneur* magazine's number-one franchise.

Lease and Controllable Expenses

Lease Costs

Successful restaurant operators will ensure that the restaurant's lease does not cost more than 5 to 8 percent of sales. Some chain restaurants will search for months or even years before they find the right location at the right price. Most leases are triple net, which means that the lessee must pay for all alterations, insurance, utilities, and possible commercial fees (e.g., landscaping or parking upkeep, security).

The best lease is for the longest time period with options for renewal and a sublease clause. The sublease clause is important because if the restaurant is not successful, the owner is still liable for paying the lease. With the sublease clause, the owner may sublease the space to another restaurant operator or any other business.

Many leases are quoted at a dollar rate per square foot per month. Depending on the location, rates may range from $2.25 per square foot up to as much as $16 or more per square foot.

Some restaurants pay a combination of a flat amount based on the square footage and a percentage of sales. This helps protect the restaurant operator in the slower months and gives the landlord a bit extra during the good months.

After a lease contract is signed, it is very difficult to renegotiate even a part of it. Only in dire circumstances is it possible to renegotiate lease contracts. The governing factor in determining lease rates is the marketplace. The marketplace is the supply and demand. If there is strong demand for space, then rates will increase. However, with a high vacancy rate, rates will be driven down by the owners in an effort to rent space and gain income.

Controllable Expenses

Controllable expenses are all the expenses over which management and ownership have control. They include salaries and wages (payroll) and related benefits; direct operating expenses such as music and entertainment; marketing, including sales, advertising, public relations, and promotions; heat, light, and power; administrative and general expenses; and repairs and maintenance. The total of all controllable expenses is deducted from the gross profit. Rent and other occupation costs are then deducted to arrive at the income before interest, depreciation, and taxes. Once these are deducted, the **net profit** remains.

Successful restaurant operators are constantly monitoring their controllable expenses. The largest controllable expense is payroll. Because payroll is about 24 to 28 percent of a restaurant's sales, managers constantly monitor their employees, not by the hour but by the minute. Bobby Hays, general manager of the Chart House Restaurant in Cardiff, California, says that he feels the pulse of the restaurant and then begins to send people home. Every dollar that Bobby and managers like him can save goes directly to the bottom line and becomes profit.

The actual sales results are compared with the budgeted amounts—ideally with percentages—and variances are investigated. Most chain restaurant operators monitor the key result areas of sales and labor costs on a daily basis. Food and beverage costs are also monitored closely, generally on a weekly basis.

▶ Check Your Knowledge

1. What is the back of the house?

2. Create a recognition program that would encourage restaurant employees.

3. What is the storing/issuing process? Why is it important?

4. Briefly explain the term *contribution margin*.

Restaurant Manager Job Analysis

The NRA has formulated an analysis of the foodservice manager's job by functional areas and tasks, which follows a natural sequence of functional areas from human resources to sanitation and safety.

Human Resource Management

Recruiting/Training

1. Recruit new employees by seeking referrals.
2. Recruit new employees by advertising.
3. Recruit new employees by seeking help from district manager/supervisors.
4. Interview applicants for employment.

Orientation/Training

1. Conduct on-site orientation for new employees.
2. Explain employee benefits and compensation programs.
3. Plan training programs for employees.
4. Conduct on-site training for employees.
5. Evaluate progress of employees during training.
6. Supervise on-site training of employees that is conducted by another manager, employee leader, trainer, and so on.
7. Conduct payroll signup.
8. Complete reports or other written documentation on successful completion of training by employees.

Scheduling for Shifts

1. Review employee work schedule for shift.
2. Determine staffing needs for each shift.
3. Make work assignments for dining room, kitchen staff, and maintenance person(s).
4. Make changes to employee work schedule.
5. Assign employees to work stations to optimize employee effectiveness.
6. Call in, reassign, or send home employees in reaction to sales and other needs.
7. Approve requests for schedule changes, vacation, days off, and so on.

Supervision and Employee Development

1. Observe employees and give immediate feedback on unsatisfactory employee performance.
2. Observe employees and give immediate feedback on satisfactory employee performance.
3. Discuss unsatisfactory performance with an employee.
4. Develop and deliver incentive for above-satisfactory performance of employees.

5. Observe employee behavior for compliance with safety and security.

6. Counsel employees on work-related problems.

7. Counsel employees on non-work-related problems.

8. Talk with employees who have frequent absences.

9. Observe employees to ensure compliance with fair labor standards and equal opportunity guidelines.

10. Discipline employees by issuing oral and/or written warnings for poor performance.

11. Conduct employee and staff meetings.

12. Identify and develop candidates for management programs.

13. Put results of observation of employee performance in writing.

14. Develop action plans for employees to help them in their performance.

15. Authorize promotion and/or wage increases for staff.

16. Terminate employment of an employee for unsatisfactory performance.

Financial Management

Accounting

1. Authorize payment on vendor invoices.

2. Verify payroll.

3. Count cash drawers.

4. Prepare bank deposits.

5. Assist in establishment audits by management or outside auditors.

6. Balance cash at end of shift.

7. Analyze profit and loss reports for establishment.

Cost Control

1. Discuss factors that affect profitability with district manager/supervisor.

2. Check establishment figures for sales, labor costs, waste, inventory, and so on.

Administrative Management

Scheduling/Coordinating

1. Establish objectives for shift based on needs of establishment.

2. Coordinate work performed by different shifts—for example, cleanup, routine maintenance, and so on.

3. Complete special projects assigned by district manager/supervisor.

4. Complete shift readiness checklist.

Planning

1. Develop and implement action plans to meet financial goals.

2. Attend off-site workshops and training sessions.

Communication

1. Communicate with management team by reading and making entries in daily communication log.
2. Prepare written reports on cleanliness, food quality, personnel, inventory, sales, food waste, labor costs, and so on.
3. Review reports prepared by other establishment managers.
4. Review memos, reports, and letters from company headquarters/main office.
5. Inform district manager/supervisor of problems or developments that affect operation and performance of the establishment.
6. Initiate and answer correspondence with company, vendors, and so on.
7. File correspondence, reports, personnel records, and so on.

Marketing Management

1. Create and execute local establishment marketing activities.
2. Develop opportunities for the establishment to provide community services.
3. Carry out special product promotions.

Operations Management

Facility Maintenance

1. Conduct routine maintenance checks on facility and equipment.
2. Direct routine maintenance checks on facility and equipment.
3. Repair or supervise the repair of equipment.
4. Review establishment evaluations with district manager/supervisor.
5. Authorize the repair of equipment by outside contractor.
6. Recommend upgrades in facility and equipment.

Food and Beverage Operations Management

1. Direct activities for opening establishment.
2. Direct activities for closing establishment.
3. Talk with other managers at beginning and end of shift to relay information about ongoing problems and activities.
4. Count, verify, and report inventory.
5. Receive, inspect, and verify vendor deliveries.
6. Check stock levels and submit orders as necessary.
7. Talk with vendors concerning quality of product delivered.
8. Interview vendors who wish to sell products to establishment.
9. Check finished product quality and act to correct problems.
10. Work as expediter to get meals served effectively.

11. Inspect dining area, kitchen, rest rooms, food lockers, storage, and parking lot.

12. Check daily reports for indications of internal theft.

13. Instruct employees regarding the control of waste, portion sizes, and so on.

14. Prepare forecast for daily or shift food preparation.

Service

1. Receive and record table reservations.

2. Greet familiar customers by name.

3. Seat customers.

4. Talk with customers while they are dining.

5. Monitor service times and procedures in the dining area.

6. Observe customers being served to correct problems.

7. Ask customers about quality of service.

8. Ask customers about quality of the food product.

9. Listen to and resolve customer complaints.

10. Authorize complimentary meals or beverages.

11. Write letters in response to customer complaints.

12. Telephone customers in response to customer complaints.

13. Secure and return items left by customers.

Sanitation and Safety

1. Accompany local officials on health inspections on premise.

2. Administer first aid to employees and customers.

3. Submit accident, incident, and OSHA reports.

4. Report incidents to police.

5. Observe employee behavior and establishment conditions for compliance with safety and security procedures.

Recycling

At the end of the night at most restaurants, leftover food, paper, bottles, and cardboard typically are put in a Dumpster in the back alley, destined for a landfill. Separating garbage is dirty; it requires people and time to do it. But, several operators say making minor changes reduces trash and helps budgets. Zero waste is how Nomad Café in Berkeley, California, prefers to operate its business. It saves more than $10,000 every year by recycling and composting. Making simple changes to its daily routine of throwing out garbage also aided Scoma's in San Francisco. It color-coded the system and got staff into the habit of recycling. Scoma's saves an average of $2,000 per month.[14]

Trends in Restaurant Operations

- More flavorful food
- Increased takeout meals, especially at lunch, and more home meal replacement (for dinner)
- Increased food safety and sanitation
- Guests becoming more sophisticated and needing more things to excite them
- More food court restaurants in malls, movie theater complexes, and colleges and universities where guests line up (similar to a cafeteria), select their food (which a server places on a tray), and pay a cashier
- Steak houses becoming more popular
- With more restaurants in each segment, the segments increasingly split into upper, middle, and lower tiers
- Twin and multi-restaurant locations
- Quick-service restaurants (QSRs) in convenience stores
- The economy beginning to pick up, which is good news for many restaurants, especially fine-dining, high-end steakhouses

CASE STUDY

Short-Staffed in the Kitchen

Sally is the general manager of one of the best restaurants in town, known as The Pub. As usual, at 6:00 P.M. on a Friday night, there is a forty-five-minute wait. The kitchen is overloaded, and they are running behind in check times, the time that elapses between the kitchen getting the order and the guest receiving his or her meal. This is critical, especially if a complaint is received because a guest has waited too long for a meal to be served.

Sally is waiting for her two head line cooks to come in for the closing shift. It is now 6:15 P.M. and she receives phone calls from both of them. Unfortunately, they are both sick with the flu and are not able to come to work.

As she gets off the phone, the hostess tells Sally that a party of fifty is scheduled to arrive at 7:30 P.M. Sally is concerned, knowing that they are currently running a six-person line with only four cooks. The productivity is very high, but they are running extremely long check times. How can Sally handle the situation?

Discussion Questions

1. How would you handle the short-staffing issue?
2. What measures would you take to get the appropriate cooks in to work as soon as possible?
3. What would you do to ensure a smooth, successful transition for the party of fifty?
4. How would you manipulate your floor plan to provide great service for the party of fifty?
5. How would you immediately make an impact on the long check times?
6. What should you do to ensure that all the guests in the restaurant are happy?

CASE STUDY

Shortage in Stock

It is 9:30 Friday morning at The Pub. Product is scheduled to be delivered at 10:00. Sally specifically ordered an exceptional amount of food for the upcoming weekend because she is projecting it to be a busy holiday weekend. Sally receives a phone call at 10:30 from J&G Groceries, stating that they cannot deliver the product until 10:00 A.M. on Saturday morning. She explains to the driver that it is crucial that she receives the product as soon as possible. He apologizes; however, it is impossible to have delivery made until Saturday morning.

By 1:00 P.M., they are beginning to run out of product, including absolute necessities such as steaks, chicken, fish, and produce. The guests are getting frustrated because the staff are beginning to eighty-six a great deal of product. In addition, if they do not begin production for the P.M. shift soon, they will be in deep trouble.

On Friday nights, The Pub does in excess of $12,000 in sales. However, if the problem is not immediately alleviated, the restaurant will lose many guests and a great amount of profits.

Discussion Questions

1. What immediate measures would you take to resolve the problem?
2. How would you produce the appropriate product as soon as possible?
3. Who should you call first, if anyone, to alleviate the problem?
4. What can you do to always have enough product on hand?
5. Is it important to have a backup plan for a situation like this? If so, what would it be?

Summary

1. Most restaurants forecast on a weekly and monthly basis a budget that projects sales and costs for a year in consideration of guest counts and the average guest check.
2. To operate a restaurant, products need to be purchased, received, and properly stored.
3. Food production is determined by the expected business for the next few days. The kitchen layout is designed according to the sales forecasted.
4. Good service is very important. In addition to taking orders, servers act as salespersons for the restaurant.
5. The front of the house deals with the part of the restaurant having direct contact with guests, in other words, what the guests see—grounds maintenance, hosts/hostesses, dining and bar areas, bartenders, bussers, and so on.
6. The back of the house is generally run by the kitchen manager and refers to all areas with which guests usually do not come in contact. This includes purchasing, receiving, storing/issuing, food production, stewarding, budgeting, accounting, and control.

Key Words and Concepts

average guest check
back of the house
balance sheet
beverage cost percentage
budgeting costs
contribution margin
controllable expense
cooking line
covers
curbside appeal
employee recognition
first in–first out (FIFO)
fixed costs
food cost percentage
front of the house
gross profit
guest counts
host/hostess

income statement
kitchen manager
labor costs percentage
net profit
operating ratios
par stock
personal digital assistants (PDAs)
point-of-sale (POS) systems
prime cost
product specification
production control sheets
purchase order
receiving
restaurant forecasting
suggestive selling
uniform system of accounts
variable costs

Review Questions

1. Briefly describe the two components of restaurant forecasting.
2. Explain the key points in purchasing, receiving, and storing.
3. Why is the kitchen layout an important aspect of food production?
4. Explain the purpose of suggestive selling. What characteristics make up a good server?
5. Accounting is important to determine the profitability of a restaurant. Briefly describe the following terms:
     (a) Controllable expenses
     (b) Uniform system of accounts
     (c) Prime cost
6. What is the point-of-sales system, and why is a control system important for a restaurant operation?
7. What are the differences between the back of the house and the front of the house?
8. What steps must one take in preparing production sheets?

Internet Exercises

1. Organization: **National Restaurant Association (NRA)**
   Web site: **www.restaurant.org**
   Summary: The NRA is the business association of the food industry. It consists of 60,000 members and more than 380,000 restaurants. Member restaurants represent table service and quick-service operators, chains, and franchises. The NRA helps international restaurants receive the benefits of the association and gives guidance for success to nonprofit members.

   (a) List the food-borne diseases listed on the NRA site. Find out about each disease and how the National Restaurant Association suggests you can prevent it.

(b) What kinds of careers are available in the restaurant and hospitality industry?

(c) What legal issues does this site advise you on if you want to start your own restaurant?

2. Organization: **Chili's Grill and Bar**
   Web site: **www.chilis.com**
   Summary: Chili's is a fun and exciting place to have burgers, fajitas, margaritas, and chili. Established in 1975 in Dallas, the chain now has more than 1,500 restaurants in the United States and twenty-nine other countries.

   (a) What requirements must you meet to open a Chili's franchise? From what you have learned about the issues involved in starting your own business, how is setting up your own business different from having a franchise?

   (b) What is a "ChiliHead"?

Apply Your Knowledge

In a casual Italian restaurant, sales for the week of September 15 are as follows:

Food sales	$10,000
Beverage sales	$2,500
Total	$12,500

1. If the food cost is 30 percent, how much did the food actually cost?
2. If the beverage cost is 25 percent of beverage sales, how much did the beverages cost?
3. If the total labor cost is 28 percent, how much money does that represent and how much is left over for other costs and profit?

Suggested Activities

1. Divide into groups of two and assign the roles of guest and server. Role-play using the concept of suggestive selling and upselling.

2. Create an income statement for an imaginary restaurant.

Endnotes

1. This section draws from John R. Walker, *The Restaurant from Concept to Operation*, 6th ed. (Hoboken, NJ: John Wiley and Sons, 2011), 86–87.
2. Personal conversation with Danny Meyer, January 14, 2004.
3. This section is adapted from http://www.starchefs.com/features/trends/30_sustainability_tips/index.shtml, retrieved March 10, 2010.
4. SoftCafé, *Make Menus on Your PC—In Minutes*, www.softcafe.com/menupro.htm. (accessed November 6, 2011).
5. Personal correspondence with Magic Software, Tampa, Florida, July 29, 2007.
6. Dusty Williams, Information Technologists," www.restaurantmagic.com/informationTech.php.
7. Data Central, "Welcome to Data Central," www.restaurantmagic.com/home.php (accessed April 2, 2011; site now discontinued).
8. Personal correspondence with James Lorenz, May 16, 2011.
9. Richard Slawsky, "Sustainable Farming Grows on Chefs," *QSR Web*, March 8, 2007, www.qsrweb.com/article.php?id=7025 (accessed November 7, 2011).
10. Chipotle, *2010 Annual Report & Proxy Statement*, http://phx.corporate-ir.net/External.File?item=UGFyZW50SUQ9NDIxMjg4fENoaWxkSUQ9NDM4OTQzfFR5cGU9MQ==&t=1 (accessed November 7, 2011).
11. This section draws from Walker, *Restaurant from Concept to Operation*, 275.
12. Walker, *Restaurant from Concept to Operation*, 275.
13. Personal conversation with Bobby Hays, general manager, Chart House Restaurant, Solana Beach, California, January 2011.
14. Jamie Popp, "Trash Talk," *Restaurants and Institutions* 116 (May 1, 2006): 75.

Rooms Division Operations

From Chapter 3 of *Introduction to Hospitality*, Sixth Edition. John R. Walker. Copyright © 2013 by Pearson Education, Inc. Published by Pearson.

Rooms Division Operations

OBJECTIVES

After reading and studying this text, you should be able to:

- Outline the duties and responsibilities of key executives and department heads.

- Draw an organizational chart of the rooms division of a hotel and identify the executive committee members.

- Describe the main functions of the rooms division departments.

- Describe property management systems and discuss yield management.

- Calculate occupancy percentages, average daily rates, and actual percentage of potential rooms revenue.

- Outline the importance of the reservations and guest services functions.

- List the complexities and challenges of the concierge, housekeeping, and security/loss prevention departments.

This text examines the function of a hotel and the many departments that constitute a hotel. It also helps to explain why and how the departments are interdependent in successfully running a hotel.

The Functions and Departments of a Hotel

The primary function of a hotel is to provide lodging accommodation. A large hotel is run by a general manager and an executive committee that consists of the key executives who head the major departments: rooms division director, food and beverage director, marketing and sales director, human resources director, chief accountant or controller, and chief engineer or facility manager. These executives generally have a regional or corporate counterpart with whom they have a reporting relationship, although the general manager is their immediate superior.

A hotel is made up of several businesses or **revenue centers** and **cost centers**. A few thousand products and services are sold every day. Each area of specialty requires dedication and a quality commitment for each department to get little things right all the time. Furthermore, hotels need the cooperation of a large and diverse group of people to perform well. James McManemon, the general manager (GM) of the elegant Ritz-Carlton Sarasota hotel, calls it "a business of details."[1]

Hotels are places of glamour that may be awe inspiring. Even the experienced hotel person is impressed by the refined dignity of a beautiful hotel like a Ritz-Carlton or the artistic splendor of a Hyatt. The atmosphere of a hotel is stimulating to a hospitality student. Let us step into an imaginary hotel to feel the excitement and become a part of the rush that is similar to show business, for a hotel is live theater and the GM is the director of the cast of players.

Hotels, whether they are chain affiliated or independent properties, exist to serve and enrich society and at the same time make a profit for the owners. Frequently, hotels are just like pieces of property on a Monopoly board. They often make or lose more money with equity appreciation or depreciation than through operations. Hotels have been described as "people palaces." Some are certainly palatial, and others are more functional. Hotels are meant to provide all the comforts of home to those away from home.

The Grand Hall in the Willard InterContinental, Washington, D.C. It was at this hotel that the term *lobbyist* was coined when then-President Grant would retire after dinner to an armchair in the lobby. People would approach him and try to gain his support for their causes.

Management Structure

Management structure differs among larger, midscale, and smaller properties. The midscale and smaller properties are less complex in their management structures than are the larger ones. However, someone must be responsible for each of the key result areas that make the operation successful. For example, a small property may not have a director of human resources, but each department head will have general day-to-day operating responsibilities for the human resources function. The manager has the ultimate responsibility for all human resources decisions. The same scenario is possible with each of the following areas: engineering and maintenance, accounting and finance, marketing and sales, food and beverage management, and so on.

Role of the Hotel General Manager

Hotel general managers have a lot of responsibilities. They must provide owners with a reasonable return on investment, keep guests satisfied and returning, and keep employees happy. This may seem easy, but because there are so many interpersonal transactions and because hotels are open every day, all day, the complexities of operating become challenges that the general manager must face and overcome. The GM not only focuses on leading and operating the hotel departments but also on aspects of the infrastructure, from room atmosphere to security.

Larger hotels can be more impersonal. Here, the general manager may only meet and greet a few VIPs. In the smaller property, it is easier—though no less important—for the GM to become acquainted with guests to ensure that their stay is memorable and to secure their return. One way that experienced GMs can meet guests, even in large hotels, is to be visible in the lobby and food and beverage (F&B) outlets at peak times (checkout, lunch, check-in, and dinner time). Guests like to feel that the GM takes a personal interest in their well-being. Max Blouet, who was general manager of the famous George V Hotel in Paris for more than thirty years, was a master of this art. He was always present at the right moment to meet and greet guests during the lunch hour and at the evening check-in. Great hoteliers always remember they are hosts.

The GM is ultimately responsible for the performance of the hotel and the employees. The GM is the leader of the hotel. As such, she or he is held accountable for the hotel's level of profitability by the corporation or owners.

To be successful, GMs need to have a broad range of personal qualities. Among those most often quoted by GMs are the following:

- Leadership
- Attention to detail
- Follow-through—getting the job done
- People skills
- Patience
- Ability to delegate effectively

A General Manager discussing the "forecast" with a Rooms Division Director.

INTRODUCING CESAR RITZ

Cesar Ritz was a legend in his own time; like so many of the early industry leaders, he began at the bottom and worked his way up through the ranks. In his case, it did not take long to reach the top because he quickly learned the secrets of success in the hotel business. His career began as an apprenticed hotel keeper at the age of fifteen. At nineteen, he was managing a Parisian restaurant. Suddenly, he quit that position to become an assistant waiter at the famous Voisin restaurant. There he learned how to pander to the rich and famous. In fact, he became so adept at taking care of the guests—remembering their likes and dislikes, even their idiosyncrasies—that a guest would ask for him and would only be served by him.

At twenty-two, he became manager of the Grand National Hotel in Lucerne, Switzerland, one of the most luxurious hotels in the world. The hotel was not very successful at the time Ritz became manager, but with his ingenuity and panache, he was able to attract the "in" crowd to complete a turnaround. After eleven seasons, he accepted a bigger challenge, the Savoy Hotel in London, which had only been open a few months and which was not doing well. Cesar Ritz became manager of one of the most famous and luxurious hotels in the world at the age of thirty-eight.

Once again, his flair and ability to influence society quickly made a positive impression on the hotel. To begin with, he made the hotel a cultural center for high society. Together with Escoffier as executive chef, he created a team that produced the finest cuisine in Europe in the most elegant of surroundings. He made evening dress compulsory and introduced orchestras to the restaurants. Cesar Ritz would spare no expense to create the lavish effect he sought. On one occasion, he converted a riverside restaurant into a Venetian waterway, complete with small gondolas and gondoliers singing Italian love songs.[2]

Both Ritz and Escoffier were dismissed from the Savoy in 1897. Ritz was implicated in the disappearance of over 3,400 pounds of wine and spirits.[3] In 1898, Ritz opened the celebrated Hotel Ritz in the Place Vendome, Paris, France. The Hotel Ritz Madrid in Madrid, Spain, opened in 1910, inspired by King Alfonso XIII's desire to build a luxury hotel to rival the Ritz in Paris. Ritz enjoyed a long partnership with Escoffier, the famous French chef and father of modern French cooking.[4]

Ritz considered the handling of people as the most important of all qualities for a hotelier. His imagination and sensitivity to people and their wants contributed to a new standard of hotel keeping. The Ritz name remains synonymous with refined, elegant hotels and service.[5] However, Ritz drove himself to the point of exhaustion, and at age fifty-two, he suffered a nervous breakdown. So, this is a lesson for us not to drive ourselves too much to the point of exhaustion.

A successful GM selects and trains the best people. A former GM of Chicago's Four Seasons Hotel deliberately hired division heads who knew more about what they were hired for than he did. The GM sets the tone—a structure of excellence—and others try to match it. Once the structure is in place, each employee works to define the hotel's commitment to excellence. General managers need to understand, empathize, and allow for the cultures of both guests and employees. Progressive general managers empower associates to do anything legal to delight the guest.

The Executive Committee

The general manager, using input from the **executive committee** (Figure 1), makes all the major decisions affecting the hotel. These executives, who include the directors of human resources, food and beverage, rooms division, marketing and sales, engineering, and accounting, compile the hotel's occupancy forecast together with all revenues and expenses to make up the budget. They generally meet once a week for one or two hours—although the Ritz-Carlton has a daily lineup at 9 A.M.—and might typically cover some of the following topics:

Guest satisfaction

Employee satisfaction

Total quality management

Occupancy forecasts

Sales and marketing plans

Training

Major items of expenditure

Renovations

Ownership relations

Energy conservation

Recycling

New legislation

Profitability

Some GMs rely on input from the executive committee more than others do, depending on their leadership and management style. These senior executives determine the character of the property and decide on the missions, goals,

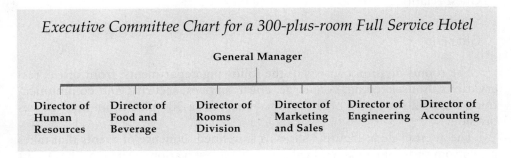

Executive Committee Chart for a 300-plus-room Full Service Hotel

General Manager

| Director of Human Resources | Director of Food and Beverage | Director of Rooms Division | Director of Marketing and Sales | Director of Engineering | Director of Accounting |

Figure 1 • Executive Committee Chart.

and objectives of the hotel. For a chain hotel, this will be in harmony with the corporate mission.

In most hotels, the executive committee is involved with the decisions, but the ultimate responsibility and authority rests with the GM. One major role of the committee is communicator, both up and down the line of authority. This helps build interdepartmental cooperation. Not all lodging operations will have an executive committee—obviously, there is no need for one at a small motel, lodge, or a B&B.

▶ Check Your Knowledge

1. What is the role of the general manager?
2. Who is a member of the executive committee and what topics does this person deal with?

The Departments

In larger hotels, the rooms division has several departments that all work together to please guests. In midsize and smaller properties, those departments may be reduced in size and number, but they still need to serve guests.

Rooms Division

The rooms division director is held responsible by the GM for the efficient and effective leadership and operation of all the rooms division departments. They include concerns such as the following:

Financial responsibility for rooms division

Employee satisfaction goals

Guest satisfaction goals

Guest services

Guest relations

Security

Gift shop

The **rooms division** consists of the following departments: front office, reservations, housekeeping, concierge, guest services, security, and communications. Figure 2 shows the organizational chart for a 300-plus-room hotel rooms division.

The guest cycle in Figure 3 shows a simplified sequence of events that takes place from the moment a guest calls to make a reservation until he or she checks out.

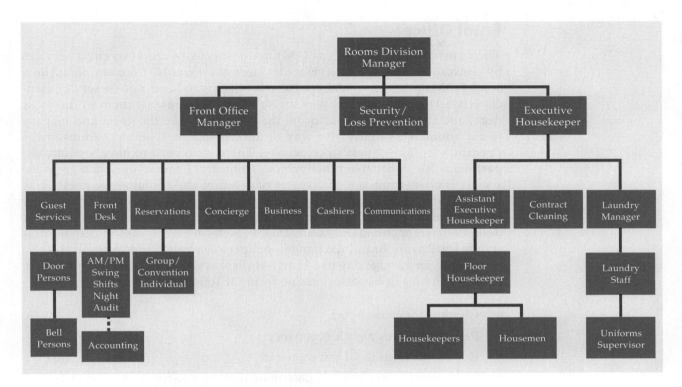

Figure 2 • Rooms Division Organizational Chart.

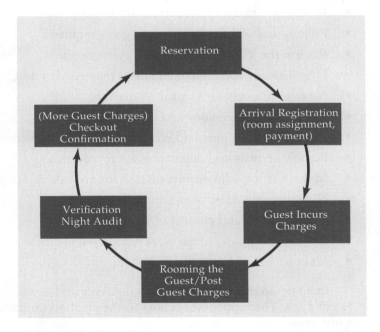

Figure 3 • The Guest Cycle.

Front Office

The front office manager's (FOM) main duty is to enhance guest services by constantly developing services to meet guest needs. An example of how some FOMs practice enhancing guest services is to have a guest service associate (GSA) greet guests as they arrive at the hotel, escort them to the front desk, and then personally allocate the room and take the guest and luggage to the room. This innovative way of developing guest services looks at the operation from the guest's perspective. There is no need to have separate departments for doorperson, bellperson, front desk, and so on. Each guest associate is cross-trained in all aspects of greeting and rooming the guest. This is now being done in smaller and midsized properties as well as at specialty and deluxe properties. Guest service associates are responsible for the front desk, concierge, communications/PBX (The term PBX is still widely used; it stands for Private Brand Exchange), bellpersons, valet, and reservations.

During an average day in a hotel—if there is such a thing—the front office manager and his or her associates perform the following duties:

- Check night clerk report.
- Review previous night's occupancy.
- Review previous night's average rate.
- Look over market mix and determine what rooms to sell at what price.
- Handle checkouts and check-ins.
- Check complimentary rooms.
- Verify group rooms to be picked up for the next thirty days.
- Review arrivals and departures for the day.
- Politely and efficiently attend to guest inquiries.
- Review the VIP list and prepare preregistration.
- Organize any room changes guests may request and follow up.
- Arrange preregistrations for all arrivals.
- Attend rooms divisions and operations meeting.
- Advise housekeeping and room service of flowers/fruit for VIPs.
- Review arrivals and departures for the next day.
- Make staffing adjustments needed for arrivals and departures.
- Note any important things in the log book.
- Check issuing and control of keys.
- Review scheduling (done weekly).
- Meet with lead GSAs (done daily).

In some hotels, the reservations manager and associates report to the director of sales. These positions report to the chief accountant: night auditor, night audit associates, and cashiers.

The front office has been described as the hub or nerve center of the hotel. It is the department that makes a first impression on the guest and one that the guest relies on throughout his or her stay for information and service. Positive first impressions are critical to the successful guest experience. Many guests arrive at the hotel after long, tiring trips. They want to be met by someone with a warm smile and a genuine greeting. If a guest should have a negative experience when checking into a hotel, he or she will be on guard in encounters with each of the other departments. The position description for a guest service agent details the work performed. Position descriptions for the three main functions of the front office are as follows:

1. *To sell rooms.* The hotel departments work like a team in a relay race. Sales or reservations staff make up room sales until the evening before the guest's arrival. At 6:00 P.M., when the reservations office closes, all the expected arrivals and available rooms are then handed over to the front desk P.M. shift. Reservations calls after 6:00 P.M. may either be taken by the front desk staff or the 1–800 number. The front desk team will try to sell out (achieve 100 percent occupancy) by selling the remaining rooms to call-in or walk-in guests—and of course the frantic calls from preferred guests who need a favor!

   Upselling occurs when the guest service agent/front desk clerk suggestively sells the features of a larger room, a higher floor, or perhaps a better view. **Yield management** originated in the airline industry where demand also fluctuates. Basically, a percentage of guests who book and send in a deposit in advance will be able to secure a room at a more reasonable price than can someone booking a room with just three days' notice. The price will be even higher for the booking at three days' notice if demand is good.

   Many other factors influence the hotel's ability to sell out. Chief among these are *demand*—the number of people needing rooms—and *supply*—the number of available rooms. A good example is the New York Hotel Convention. This event takes place in a city that has a high demand for hotel rooms in proportion to its inventory (number of available rooms. Because there is a fairly constant demand for rooms in New York, special events tend to increase demand to a point that forces up **room rates**. (See Figure 4.) Another example comes from the airline industry, which always seems to raise prices at the peak travel times (Thanksgiving, Christmas, Easter, and the summer vacation times). They only offer special fares when school is in session. Revenue management is explained in more detail later in the text.

A front office manager taking care of a guest request.

FOCUS ON ROOMS DIVISION

Rooms Division with Charlie Adams

From the early days of primitive inns to our modern super hotels, like the Izmailovo Hotel with 7,500 rooms in Moscow, employees are the crucial ingredient to a hotel or motel's success. Even with extraordinary advances in technology and the globalization of lodging in the 21st century; lodging remains fundamentally a people business and it is the employees who are responsible for the appearance, image and reputation of a lodging facility.

The rooms division is considered the "center" of hotel activity because it is accountable for revenue, customer service, and departmental forecasting. Room sales are the primary source of income for most hotels and almost 100% of the revenue for many select service or budget hotels. The rooms division has the most guest contacts because it is comprised of reservations, front office, housekeeping and uniformed services. The reservations department provides the needed accurate information for other departments to use to forecast for upcoming events and guest needs; along with scheduling the proper staffing levels in the hotel.

Starting your career in the rooms division of a hotel is an exciting, demanding and rewarding experience. You will be part of a team whose overall responsibility is the well-being of guests and ensuring their expectations are met and they have a memorable experience. As a room division employee you will be part of several interconnected functions which include: front desk, housekeeping, reservations, concierge, guest services, security and communications. The following are some important tips for success in fulfilling the company's promise to each guest:

Front Desk Here is where the first and last impressions are always made! At the front desk it is important to be personable, confident, and patient because your guests will vary in temperament, needs and expectations. Always remember a friendly, calm and positive attitude are your best tools even in trying situations. Multi-tasking becomes an art form at front desk calling on all of your communication, typing and computer skills.

Housekeeping Perception is reality and cleanliness is always at the top of a guest's expectations. In housekeeping it is the attention to details, the eye for the out of place, the worn or frayed that keeps it real for guests. It is a demanding work area with much physical labor that is essential to guest satisfaction. Your work is done mostly behind the curtain, out of guest view, but noticed and appreciated when they enter to fresh towels, a made bed and a flawlessly clean room. This is where you should start your lodging management career because it is the most demanding and least popular department among new hospitality graduates and yet it is the best training ground for early lodging management success!

Reservations How do you convey a smile over the phone? You must as you begin the process of the guest cycle. Reservations calls for total command of the keyboard, awareness of hotel revenue goals , upcoming events, room availability but above all listen, truly **listen**, to the guest so you can match their requests with the hotels services. The promise begins with you and you must never write a check that the front desk can cash at check-in.

Concierge A job that calls for diplomacy, ability to wheel-n-deal and just a touch of magic. Your role is to accommodate the guest needs during their stay. It calls for an encyclopedic memory of restaurants, theater offerings, key points of interest and current city events. The ability to develop a vast network of connections throughout the hospitality community in your area is essential to serve your guests and see to their every wish. Your reward as a successful concierge is that no two days are ever the same and there are always new and different challenges, opportunities and rewards.

Guest Services more commonly referred to as uniformed services; consist of valet, doorperson and bellperson positions. All jobs essential to first and last impressions that set the tone for the quality of service. A congenial disposition that projects a true spirit of helpfulness will disarm any initial guest trepidation. It also calls for thorough comprehension of the hotel, its layout, rooms and amenities. It is work that demands immaculate grooming (especially the uniform), standing for long hours and physical activity. In uniform, you are the hotel to the guest.

Major hotel chains offer a number of different room rates, including the following:

rack rate
corporate
association rate
government
encore
cititravel
entertainment cards
AAA
AARP (American Association of Retired Persons)
wholesale
group rates
promotional special

The rack rate is the rate that is used as a benchmark quotation of a hotel's room rate. Let us assume that the Hotel California had a rack rate of $135. Any discounted rate may be offered at a percentage deduction from the rack rate. An example would be a corporate rate of $110, an association rate of $105, and AARP rate of $95—certain restrictions may apply. Group rates may range from $95 to $125 according to how much the hotel needs the business.

Throughout the world there are three main plans on which room rates are based:

AP/American Plan—room and three meals a day
MAP/Modified American Plan—room plus two meals
EP/European Plan—room only, meals extra

Figure 4 • The Types of Room Rates Offered by Hotels.

2. *To maintain balanced guest accounts.* This begins with advance deposits, opening the guest folio (account), and posting all charges from the various departments. Most hotels have **property management systems (PMSs)** (property management systems are explained in more detail later in the text) and point-of-sale terminals (POS), which are online to the front office.

   This means that guest charges from the various outlets are directly debited to the guest's folio. Payment is either received on guest checkout or transferred to the **city ledger** (a special account for a company that has established credit with the hotel). This means that the account will be sent and paid within a specified time period.

3. *To offer services such as handling mail, faxes, messages, and local and hotel information.* People constantly approach the front desk with questions.

Front desk employees need to be knowledgeable about the various activities in the hotel. The size, layout, and staffing of the front desk will vary with the size of the hotel. The front desk staff size of a busy 800-room city center property will naturally differ from that of a country inn. The front desk is staffed throughout the twenty-four hours by three shifts.

The evening shift duties are the following:

1. Check the log book for special items. (The log book is kept by guest contact; associates at the front office note specific and important guest requests and occurrences such as requests for room switches or baby cribs.)
2. Check on the room status, number of expected checkouts still to leave, and arrivals by double-checking registration cards and the computer so that they can update the forecast of the night's occupancy. This will determine the number of rooms left to sell. Nowadays, this is all part of the capability of the PMS.
3. Handle guest check-ins. This means notifying the appropriate staff of any special requests guests may have made (e.g., nonsmoking room or a long bed for an extra-tall guest).
4. Take reservations for that evening and future reservations after the reservations staff have left for the day.

Night Auditor

A hotel is one of the few businesses that balances its accounts at the end of each business day. Because a hotel is open twenty-four hours every day, it is difficult to stop transactions at any given moment. The **night auditor** waits until the hotel quiets down at about 1:00 A.M., and then begins the task of balancing the guests' accounts receivable. The process of night auditing is as follows:

1. The night audit team runs a preliminary reconciliation report that shows the total revenue generated from room and tax, banquets and catering, food and beverage outlets, and other incidentals (phone, gift shop, etc.).
2. All errors on the report are investigated.
3. All changes are posted and balanced with the preliminary charges.
4. A comparison of charges is carried out, matching preliminary with actual charges.
5. Totals for credit card charges, rooms operations, food and beverages, and incidentals are verified.
6. The team "rolls the date"—they go forward to the next day.

Other duties of the night audit staff include the following:

1. Post any charges that the evening shift was not able to post.
2. Pass discrepancies to shift managers in the morning. The room and tax charges are then posted to each folio and a new balance shown.

3. Run backup reports so that if the computer system fails, the hotel will have up-to-date information to operate a manual system.

4. Reconcile point-of-sale and PMS to guest accounts. If this does not balance, the auditor must balance it by investigating errors or omissions. This is done by checking that every departmental charge shows up on guest folios.

5. Complete and distribute the daily report. This report details the previous day's activities and includes vital information about the performance of the hotel.

6. Determine areas of the hotel where theft could potentially occur.

Larger hotels may have more than one night auditor, but in smaller properties these duties may be combined with night manager, desk, or night watchperson duties.

CORPORATE PROFILE

Hyatt Hotels

When Nicholas Pritzker emigrated with his family from the Ukraine to the United States, he began his career by opening a small law firm. His outstanding management skills led to the expansion of the law firm, turning it into a management company. Pritzker purchased the Hyatt House motel next to the Los Angeles International Airport in 1957.

Today, Hyatt is an international brand of hotels within the Global Hyatt Corporation, a multibillion-dollar hotel management and development company. It is among the leading chains in the hotel industry, with close to 8 percent of the market share.[6] Hyatt has earned worldwide fame as the leader in providing luxury accommodations and high-quality service, targeting especially the business traveler, but strategically differentiating its properties and services to identify and market to a very diverse clientele. This differentiation has resulted in the following types of hotels:

1. *Grand Hyatt* features distinctive luxury hotels in major gateway cities.

2. The *Hyatt Regency Hotels* represent the company's core product. They are usually located in business city centers and are regarded as five-star hotels.

3. *Hyatt Resorts* are vacation retreats. They are located in the world's most desirable leisure destinations, offering the "ultimate escape from everyday stresses."

4. The *Park Hyatt Hotels* are smaller, European-style, luxury hotels. They target the individual traveler who prefers the privacy, personalized service, and discreet elegance of a small European hotel.

(continued)

CORPORATE PROFILE *(continued)*

5. *Hyatt Place* is a lifestyle 125- to 200-room property located in urban, airport, and suburban areas. Signature features include The Gallery, which offers a coffee and wine bar and a 24/7 kitchen where travelers can find freshly prepared food.

6. *Hyatt Vacation Club* offers vacation ownership, vacation rentals, and mini vacations.

7. *Summerfield Suites* is an extended-stay brand of 125- to 200-room all-suite properties that provide the feel of a condominium but with complementary full breakfast and evening social. Locations are urban, airport, and suburban.

8. *Andaz* is a casual, stylish, boutique-style hotel; each hotel reflects the unique cultural scene and spirit of the surrounding neighborhood.

The Hyatt Hotels Corporation is characterized by a decentralized management approach, which gives the individual general manager a great deal of decision-making power, as well as the opportunity to use personal creativity and, therefore, stimulate differentiation and innovation. The development of novel concepts and products is perhaps the key to Hyatt's outstanding success. For example, the opening of the Hyatt Regency Atlanta, Georgia, with its atrium lobby gave the company instant recognition throughout the world. The property's innovative architecture, designed by John Portman, revolutionized the common standards of design and spacing, thus changing the course of the lodging industry.

A further positive aspect of the decentralized management structure is the fact that the individual manager is able to be extremely guest responsive by developing a thorough knowledge of the guests' needs and thereby providing personalized service—fundamental to achieving customer satisfaction. This is, in fact, the ultimate innkeeping purpose, which Hyatt attains at high levels.

The other side of Hyatt's success is the emphasis on human resources management. Employee satisfaction, in fact, is considered to be a prerequisite to external satisfaction. Hyatt devotes enormous attention to employee training and selection. What is most significant, however, is the interaction among top managers and operating employees.

The company operates 453 hotels and resorts in forty-three countries worldwide.

The **daily report** contains key operating ratios such as **room occupancy percentage (ROP)**, which is the number of rooms occupied divided by the number of rooms available:

$$\frac{\text{Rooms Occupied}}{\text{Rooms Available}}$$

Thus, if a hotel has 850 rooms and 622 are occupied, the occupancy percentage is $622 \div 850 = 73$ percent.

The **average daily rate** is calculated by dividing the rooms revenue by the number of rooms sold:

$$\frac{\text{Rooms Revenue}}{\text{Rooms Sold}}$$

If the rooms revenue is $75,884 and the number of rooms sold is 662, then the ADR is $114.63. The ADR is, together with the occupancy percentage, one of the key operating ratios that indicates the hotel's performance. See Figure 5 for an example of a daily report.

Room occupancy percentage (ROP):

If total available rooms are	850
And total rooms occupied are	622

Then:

Occupancy percentage = (622 / 850) × 100 = 73%

Average daily rate:

If rooms revenue is	$75,884
And total number of rooms sold is	622

Then:

$$\text{Average daily rate} = \frac{75,884}{662} = \$114.63$$

A more recently popular ratio to gauge a hotel rooms division's performance is the percentage of potential room's revenue, which is calculated by determining potential rooms revenue and dividing the actual revenue by the potential revenue.

While these figures are of great importance to running a successful hotel, the most important of the lodging ratios is **revenue per available room** (REV PAR), which is discussed in the next section.

Revenue Management

Revenue management is used to maximize room revenue at the hotel. It is based on the economics of supply and demand, which means that prices rise when demand is strong and drop when demand is weak. Naturally, management would like to sell every room at the highest rack rate. However, this is not a reality, and rooms are sold at discounts from the rack rate. An example is the corporate or group rate. In most hotels, only a small percentage of rooms are sold at rack rate. This is because of conventions and group rates and other promotional discounts that are necessary to stimulate demand.

What revenue management does is allocate the right type of room to the right guest at the right price so as to maximize revenue per available room.[7] Thus, the purpose of revenue management is to increase profitability. Generally, the demand for room reservations follows the pattern of group bookings, which are made months or even years in advance of arrival, and individual bookings, which mostly are made a few days before arrival. Figures 6 and 7 show the pattern of individual and group room reservations. Revenue management examines the demand for rooms over a period of a few years and determines the extent of demand for a particular room each night. This includes busy period, slow periods, and holidays. The computer program figures out a model of that

Clarion Hotel Bayview

Daily Management Report Supplement
January 2007

Daily Report
January 2007

Occupancy%	Today	Avg or %	M–T–D Avg or %		Y–T–D Avg or %	
Rack Rooms	9	2.9%	189	3.37	189	3.37
Corporate Rooms	0	0.0%	103	1.83	103	1.83
Group Rooms	274	87.8%	2,379	42.36	2,379	42.36
Leisure Rooms	3	1.0%	395	7.03	395	7.03
Base Rooms	23	7.4%	348	6.14	345	6.14
Government Rooms	2	0.6%	32	.57	32	.57
Wholesale Rooms	1	0.3%	121	2.15	121	2.15
No-Show Rooms		0.0%	0	.00	0	.00
Comp Rooms	0	0.0%	37	.66	37	.66
Total Occ Rooms & Occ %	312	100%	3,601	64.12	3,601	64.12
Rack	$1,011	$112.33	17,207	91.04	17,207	91.04
Corporate	$0	ERR	8,478	82.31	8,478	82.31
Group	$22,510	$82.15	178,066	74.85	178,066	74.85
Leisure	$207	$69.00	24,985	63.25	24,985	63.25
Base	$805	$35.00	12,063	34.97	12,063	34.97
Govt	$141	$70.59	2,379	74.34	2,379	74.34
Wholesale	$43	$43.00	5,201	42.98	5,201	42.98
No-Show/Comp/Allowance	$0		−914	−24.69	−914	−24.69
Total Rev & Avg Rate	$24,717	$79.22	247,466	68.72	247,466	68.72

Hotel Revenue

	Today		M–T–D Avg or %		Y–T–D Avg or %	
Rooms	$24,717		247,466	77.46	247,466	77.46
Food	$1,400		37,983	11.89	37,983	11.89
Beverage	$539		9,679	3.03	9,679	3.03
Telephone	$547		5,849	1.83	5,849	1.83
Parking	$854		11,103	3.48	11,103	3.48
Room Svc II	$70		1,441	.45	1,441	.45
Other Revenue	$1,437		963	1.87	963	1.87
Total Revenue	$29,563		319,484	100.00	319,484	100.00

Figure 5 • A Hotel Daily Report.

Clarion Hotel Bayview

Daily Management Report Supplement
January 2007

Daily Report
January 2007

Cafe 6th & K	Today	Avg or %	M–T–D Avg or %		Y–T–D Avg or %	
Cafe Breakfast Covers	88	57.1%	1,180	47.12	1,180	47.12
Cafe Lunch Covers	43	27.9%	674	26.92	674	26.92
Cafe Dinner Covers	23	14.9%	650	25.96	650	25.96
Total Cafe Covers	154	100.0%	2,504	100.00	2,504	100.00
Cafe Breakfast	$608	$6.91	7,854	6.66	7,854	6.66
Cafe Lunch	$246	$5.72	5,847	8.67	5,847	8.67
Cafe Dinner	$227	$9.86	4,309	6.63	4,309	6.63
Gaslamp Lounge Food			2,431	3.74	2,431	3.74
Total Rev/Avg Check	$1,081	$7.02	20,440	8.16	20,440	8.16
Banquets						
Banquet Breakfast Covers	0	ERR	154	13.24	154	13.24
Banquet Lunch Covers	0	ERR	134	11.52	134	11.52
Banquet Dinner Covers	0	ERR	254	21.84	254	21.84
Banquet Coffee Break Covers	0	ERR	621	53.40	621	53.40
Total Banquet Covers	0	ERR	1,163	100.00	1,163	100.00
Banquet Breakfast	$0	ERR	980	6.36	980	6.36
Banquet Lunch	$0	ERR	2,997	22.36	2,997	22.36
Banquet Dinner	$0	ERR	4,530	17.84	4,530	17.84
Banquet Coffee Break	$0	ERR	1,093	1.76	1,093	1.76
Total Rev/Avg Check	$0	ERR	9,600	8.25	9,600	8.25
Room Service						
Room Service Breakfast Covers	13	40.6%	324	48.00	324	48.00
Room Service Lunch Covers	3	9.4%	53	7.85	53	7.85
Room Service Dinner Covers	16	50.0%	298	44.15	298	44.15
Total Covers	32	100.0%	675	100.00	675	100.00
Room Service Breakfast	$119	$9.13	2,665	8.22	2,665	8.22
Room Service Lunch	$29	$9.77	418	7.89	418	7.89
Room Service Dinner	$171	$10.67	2,907	9.75	2,907	9.75
Total Rev/Avg Check	$319	$9.96	5,990	8.87	5,990	8.87

Figure 5 • A Hotel Daily Report. *(continued)*

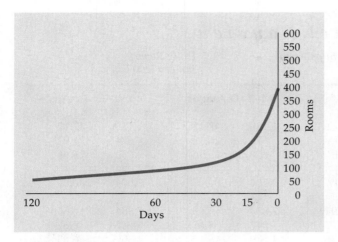

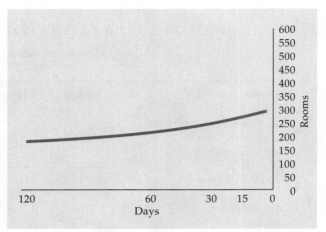

Figure 6 • Individual Room Booking Reservations Curve.

(*Source:* Personal correspondence with Jay R. Schrock, May 18, 2007.)

Figure 7 • Group Booking Curve.

demand, which is then used to guestimate future demand so that management can determine pricing levels to set.

Because group reservations are booked months, even years, in advance, revenue management systems can monitor reservations and, based on previous trends and current demand, determine the number and type of rooms to sell at what price to obtain the maximum revenue.

The curve in Figure 6 indicates the pattern of few reservations being made 120 days prior to arrival. Most of the individual room bookings are made in the last few days before arrival at the hotel. The revenue management program monitors the demand and supply and recommends the number and type of rooms to sell for any given day, and the price for which to sell each room.

With revenue management, not only will the time before arrival be an important consideration in the pricing of guest rooms, but also the type of room to be occupied.

The application of revenue management in hotels is still being refined to take into consideration factors such as multiple nights' reservations and incremental food and beverage revenue. If the guest wants to arrive on a high-demand night and stay through several low-demand nights, what should the charge be?

Revenue management has some disadvantages. For instance, if a businessperson attempts to make a reservation at a hotel three days before arrival and the rate quoted to maximize revenue is considered too high, this person may decide to select another hotel and not even consider the first hotel when making future reservations.

Revenue per available room, or **REV PAR**, was developed by Smith Travel Research. It is calculated by dividing room revenue by the number of rooms available.

For example, if room sales are $50,000 in one day for a hotel with 400 available rooms, then the REV PAR formula is $50,000 divided by 400, or a REV PAR of $125.

Hotels use REV PAR to see how they are doing compared to their competitive set of hotels. Hotel operators use REV PAR as an indicator of a hotel's revenue management program. One of the ways that REV PAR is used is for comparison to other properties in a competitive set on the Smith Travel Star Report.

Smith Travel Report (STR Global) is the publisher of the STAR reports, a benchmarking suite that tracks one hotel's occupancy, average daily rate, and REV PAR against a competitive set of hotels for comparison purposes. The information provided helps identify if a particular property is gaining or losing market share and helps the organization make necessary corrections to its management, marketing, and sales strategies. The STR STAR reports are used extensively in the lodging industry as the best tool for revenue management.[8]

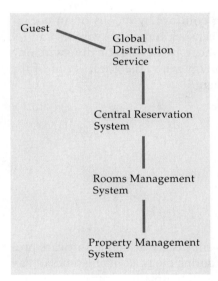

Figure 8 • The Sequence and Relationships of a Hotel Guest Reservation.

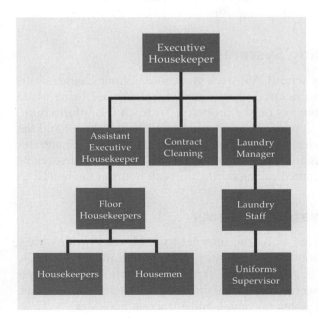

Figure 9 • Housekeeping Department Organization Chart.

▶ Check Your Knowledge

1. What is the rooms division director responsible for?
2. Describe the duties performed by the front office manager (FOM).
3. What is the Rack Rate and what other types of room rates are there?
4. How do you calculate the room occupancy percentage and the average daily rate?

Energy Management Systems

Technology is used to extend guest in-room comfort by means of an energy management system. Passive infrared motion sensors and door switches can reduce energy consumption by 30 percent or more by automatically switching off lights and air-conditioning, thus saving energy when the guest is out of the room. Additional features include the following:

- Room occupancy status reporting
- Automatic lighting control
- Minibar access reporting
- Smoke detector alarm reporting
- Central electronic lock control
- Guest control amenities

Because of increasing energy costs, some operators are installing software programs that will turn off nonessential equipment during the peak billing times of day (utility companies' charges are based on peak usage). Hospitality operators can save money by utilizing this type of energy-saving software to reduce their energy costs.

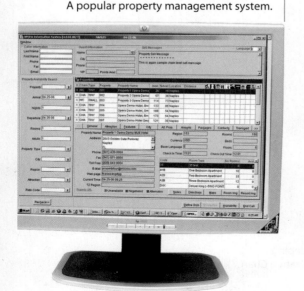

A popular property management system.

Call Accounting Systems

Call accounting systems (CAS) track guest room phone charges. Software packages can be used to monitor where calls are being made and from which phones on the property. To track this information, the CAS must work in conjunction with the PBX (telephone) and the PMS. Call accounting systems today can be used to offer different rates for local guest calls and long-distance guest calls. The CAS can even be used to offer discounted calling during off-peak hours at the hotel.

Guest Reservation Systems

Before hotels started using the Internet to book reservations, they received reservations by letters, telegrams, faxes, and phone calls. Airlines were the first industry to start using **global distribution systems (GDS)** for reservations. Global distribution systems are electronic markets for travel, hotel, car rental, and attraction bookings.

A **central reservation system (CRS)** houses the electronic database in the **central reservation office (CRO)**. Hotels provide rates and availability information to the CRO usually by data communication lines. This automatically updates the CRS so that guests get the best available rate when they book through the central reservation office. Guests instantly receive confirmation of their reservation or cancellation. The hotel benefits from using a central reservation system. With such a system, hotels can avoid overselling rooms by too large a margin. The CRS database can also be used as a chain or individual property marketing tool because guest information can easily be stored. A CRS can also provide yield management information for a hotel. The more flexible a central reservation system is, the more it will help with yield management. For example, when demand is weak for a hotel, rates will need to drop to increase reservations and profitability. When demand is higher, the hotel can sell room rates that are closer to the rack rate (*rack rate* is the highest rate quoted for a guestroom, from which all discounts are offered).

A CRS can be used in several areas of a hotel. If a hotel has a reservations department, the terminals or personal computers in that department can be connected to the central reservation system. It is also important for front desk employees to have access to the CRS so that they know what the hotel has available because they may need to book rooms for walk-ins who don't have reservations. Constant communication back and forth is needed between the central reservation system and the front office and reservations department. Managers who are the decision makers in the hotel will also use the system to forecast and set pricing for rooms and different amenities.

Hotels can use other forms of technology to facilitate reservation systems. Several companies offer an **application service provider (ASP)** environment that can deliver a complete booking system tied to the hotel's inventory in real time via the Web. One operator, Paul Wood of the El Dorado Hotel in Santa Fe, New Mexico, says that he simply went to the ASP web site and put in a promotional corporate rate for the summer, and the same day he started seeing reservations coming in with that code. After a few months, bookings were up 3 percent over the previous year.

Billing Guests

Hospitality businesses today seek to obtain the most high-speed and reliable computer systems they can afford that they can use to bill their guests without delay. Fast access to guests' accounts is required by large hotels because of their high priority of guest satisfaction (no lineups at checkout).

Billing guests has become much easier with the aid of computers. Billing guests can be a long process if information technologies are not used to complete transactions. PMSs aid large hotels to make faster transactions and provide a more efficient service to their guests. These systems help the hospitality associates bill their guests within seconds.

Some hotels utilize software that enables guests to check and approve their bills by using the TV and remote control, thus avoiding the need to line up at the cashier's desk to check out. A copy of the final bill is then mailed to the guest's home address.

Security

Each business in the hospitality industry offers some sort of security for their guests and employees. Peace of mind that the hotel or restaurant is secure is a key factor in increasing guest satisfaction. Security is one of the highest concerns of guests who visit hospitality businesses. Hospitality information technology systems include surveillance systems in which cameras are installed in many different areas of the property to monitor the grounds and help ensure guest safety. These cameras are linked directly to computers, televisions, and digital recorders, which helps security teams keep an eye on the whole property.

Recent technological advances have produced electronic door locking systems, some of which even offer custom configurations of security and safety. Guest room locks are now capable of managing information from both magstripe and smart cards simultaneously. From the hotel's point of view, a main advantage of this kind of key is that the hotel knows who has entered the room and at what time because the system can trace anyone entering the room.

In-room safes can now be operated by key cards. Both systems are an improvement on the old metal keys. Even smarter safes use biometric technology such as the use of thumbprints or retina scans to verify a user's identity.

Guest Comfort and Convenience

Hotels provide guest comfort and convenience to maintain a home-away-from-home feeling for their guests. Hotels receive recognition when they provide many additional in-room services and amenities for their guests, such as dining, television, telephones, Internet connections, minibars, and hygiene products. These amenities help provide a cozy experience for the guest. Many other services can be provided outside of the rooms, such as swimming pools, massages, fine dining, postal services, and meeting space. Other services are provided to suit the demands of all types of guests; a concierge and business center, for example.

Hotels communicate with many entities to provide services for their guests. Some companies offer creative solutions to hotels for enhanced in-room services for guests. Sprint InSite with KoolConnect Interactive Media has created a product that provides many services to the guest from just one supplier. Services include Internet access and e-mail; movies, music, and games on demand; hotel and concierge services; special promotions; advertising; travel planning; feedback from guests; and customer support. All these services aid hotels in fulfilling guest demands. Sprint states, "Build loyalty and promote business retention by enhancing the overall quality-of-visit for your guest."[9] Play Stations and video games are also a part of the technology-based guest amenities.

▶ Check Your Knowledge

1. What functions does the PMS perform?
2. What is revenue management? How is revenue management applied in the hotel industry?

TECHNOLOGY SPOTLIGHT

Hotel Information Technology

Cihan Cobanoglu, Ph.D., Dean, School of Hotel and Restaurant Management, University of South Florida, Sarasota-Manatee

"Home away from home!" This is how we would like to express what hotels means to our guests. For this to happen, we must provide technologies that guests use at home. Of course, the main purpose of the guestroom has never changed: to provide a clean, safe place to spend the night. In 1970, for the first time, hoteliers put ice-cube makers and small refrigerators inside the guestroom. In the beginning, not all rooms had these amenities. Usually, those rooms that had these special amenities were charged more than the other rooms. In 1972, the first models of telephone systems were introduced to the guestroom. In those days, there was only one telephone line for the entire hotel; therefore, guests sometimes waited long hours before they could place a call. In 1975, after color TV was well established in homes, hotels started to offer it. In the beginning, some hotels advertised that they had color TV to differentiate themselves from the competition and charged extra for rooms with TV. In 1980, the Hotel Billing Information System (HOBIC) was introduced. In 1981, it became legal for hotels to profit from phone calls. This is when call-accounting systems exploded in the hotel industry. In 1986, electronic door-keys were introduced, increasing the security and the convenience of guests. Interface between TV systems and property management systems was established in 1990 so that the guests can see their bills through the TV. With that, in 1993, guests were able to check out from their room by using the TV. In 1995, high-speed Internet access was available in hotel rooms. After 2000, hotels started to use voice-over Internet Protocol (IP) phoning systems, high-definition TV, wireless Internet access, interactive entertainment systems, smart-energy management systems, and many other systems.

In today's modern hotel rooms, it is possible to see the following technologies that make the guest stay a more comfortable one: (1) electronic locking system, 2) energy management and climate control systems, 3) fire alarm and security systems, 4) in-room minibars, 5) in-room safe boxes, 6) guestroom phone systems, 7) voice-mail/wake-up systems, 8) in-room entertainment systems, 9) guestroom control panels, and 10) self check-in/check-out systems.

Let's look into the future to see what the guestroom might look like then:

You just booked a hotel room from your smart phone with a voice command. When you go to check in to the hotel, you see that check-in desk is replaced with a "hospitality desk." As soon as you arrive to the hotel, your phone is showing you a map of the hotel rooms, asking you to make a choice. Once you make your choice, your phone becomes your electronic key card. When you wave your phone, the door opens and the 100-percent sustainable room welcomes you with your preferred wall color (thanks to nano-paint) and your favorite song. When you turn on the TV with your voice command, you see your favorite and local TV channels (thanks to Internet TV) and your video library from your home phone. The picture frame shows the pictures from your Facebook page. Your sheets and towels will be changed based on the "green" preferences such as to change the bed sheet and towels every three days and bring the temperature of the room 10 degrees down or up based on the season when you are not in the room. When you need help, you connect to a virtual concierge to get any kind of information about the hotel and the area. The wardrobe door generates power when you open and close the door for lighting. When you use the restroom, the smart toilet checks your health and sends you a digital report to your e-mail. Does this sound like a nice dream? Actually, this is a description of next-generation hotel.

Reservations

The reservations department is headed by the reservations manager who, in many hotels today, is on the same level as the front office manager and reports directly to the director of rooms division or the director of sales. This emphasizes the importance of the sales aspects of reservations and encompasses yield management. Reservations is the first contact for the guest or person making the reservation for the guest. Although the contact may be by telephone, a distinct impression of the hotel is registered with the guest. Because of this, exceptional telephone manners and telemarketing skills are necessary. Because some guests may be shopping for the best value, it is essential to sell the hotel by emphasizing its advantages over the competition.

The reservation department generally works from 8:00 A.M. to 6:00 P.M. Depending on the size of the hotel, several people may be employed in this important department. The desired outcome of the reservations department is to exceed guest expectations when they make reservations. This is achieved by selling all of the hotel rooms for the maximum possible dollars and avoiding possible guest resentment of being overcharged. Reservations originate from a variety of sources:

1. The Internet
2. Corporate/1-800 numbers
3. Travel agents
4. Telephone to the same property
   a. Fax
   b. Letter
   c. Cable
5. Meeting planners
6. Tour operators
7. Referral from another company property
8. Airport telephone
9. Walk-in

Clearly, reservations are of tremendous importance to the hotel because of the potential and actual revenue realized. Many hotel chains have a 1-800 number that a prospective guest may call without charge to make a reservation at any of the company properties in the United States and internationally. The corporate central reservations system allows operators to access the inventory of room availability of each hotel in the chain. Once a reservation has been made, it is immediately deducted from the inventory of rooms for the duration of the guest stay. The central reservations system interfaces with the hotel's inventory and simultaneously allows reservations to be made by the individual hotel reservations personnel. A number of important details need to be recorded when taking reservations.

Confirmed reservations are reservations made with sufficient time for a confirmation slip to be returned to the client by mail or fax. Confirmation is generated by the computer printer and indicates confirmation number, dates of arrival and departure, type of room booked, number of guests, number of beds, type of bed, and any special requests. The guest may bring the confirmation slip to the hotel to verify the booking.

Guaranteed reservations are given when the person making the reservation wishes to ensure that the reservation will be held. This is arranged at the time the reservation is made and generally applies in situations when the guest is expected to arrive late. The hotel takes the credit card number, which guarantees payment of the room, of the person being billed. The hotel agrees to hold the room for late arrival. The importance of guaranteed reservations is that the guest will more likely cancel beforehand if unable to show up, which gives more accurate inventory room count and minimizes no-shows.

Another form of guaranteed reservations is advance deposit/advance payment. In certain situations, for example, during a holiday, to protect itself against having empty rooms (no-shows), the hotel requires that a deposit of either one night or the whole stay be paid in advance of the guest's arrival. This is done by obtaining the guest's credit card number, which may be charged automatically for the first night's accommodation. This discourages no-shows. Corporations that use the hotel frequently may guarantee all of their bookings so as to avoid any problems in the event a guest arrives late, remembering that in cities where the demand is heavy, hotels release any nonguaranteed or nonpaid reservations at 4:00 P.M. or 6:00 P.M. on the evening of the guest's expected arrival.

Communications CBX or PBX

The communications CBX or PBX includes in-house communications; guest communications, such as pagers and radios; voice mail; faxes; messages; and emergency center. Guests often have their first contact with the hotel by telephone. This underlines the importance of prompt and courteous attention to all calls because first impressions last.

The communications department is a vital part of the smooth running of the hotel. It is also a profit center because hotels generally add a 50-percent charge to all long-distance calls placed from guest rooms. Local calls cost about $0.75 to $1.25, plus tax, but many hotels offer local calls for free.

Communications operates twenty-four hours a day; in much the same way as the front office does, having three shifts. It is essential that this department be staffed with people who are trained to be calm under pressure and who follow emergency procedures.

Guest Services/Uniformed Services

Because first impressions are very important to the guest, the guest service or uniformed staff has a special responsibility. The guest service department or **uniformed staff** is headed by a guest services manager who may also happen to be the bell captain. The staff consists of door attendants and bellpersons and the concierge, although in some hotels the concierge reports directly to the front office manager.

Door attendants are the hotel's unofficial greeters. Dressed in impressive uniforms, they greet guests at the hotel front door, assist in opening/closing automobile doors, removing luggage from the trunk, hailing taxis, keeping the hotel entrance clear of vehicles, and giving guests information about the hotel and the local area in a courteous and friendly way. People in this position generally receive many gratuities (tips); in fact, years ago, the position was handed down from father to son or sold for several thousand dollars. Rumor has it that this is one of the most lucrative positions in the hotel, even more lucrative than the general manager's.

A DAY IN THE LIFE OF DENNY BHAKTA

Revenue Manager Hilton Hotels San Diego

Revenue Management is a strategic function in maximizing room revenue (REV PAR) along with growing market share. REV PAR and market share are the two primary barometers used in the industry to grade a Revenue Manager's competency. It is essential for Revenue Managers to have a system in place for daily business reviews to formulate winning strategies. Daily duties include:

1. Analyzing Data: A Revenue Manager must develop a reporting system for daily monitoring. In recent years, the larger hotel brands have developed proprietary Revenue Management systems that provide on-demand reporting of historical data, future position and the ability to apply real time pricing changes to future nights. Understanding past performance can uncover various business trends over high and low demand periods. It is critical to understand the effectiveness of previous pricing strategies to better position the hotel on future nights. The general public can view rates and book rooms up to 365 days into the future. Therefore the Revenue Manager must monitor daily pickup in reservations and regrets for future nights and make necessary adjustments to enhance speed to market. Each hotel will have different booking windows (or lead times) for their Transient & Group business. For example, the San Diego market has a majority of Transient bookings that occur within 120 days to arrival, whereas the Group business is booked many months out, and in some cases several years in advance. The primary booking window must be analyzed on a daily basis and adjusted accordingly. The longer booking windows can be analyzed periodically with the Director of Sales to equip the Sales team with rates to book group business based on the hotel's revenue goals.

2. Mix of Business Assessment: Finding the right balance of Occupancy and ADR could yield the greatest REV PAR and greatly influenced by the mix of business. It is composed of two primary customer segments: Transient (individual travelers for business or leisure) and Groups which are bookings with 10 more rooms per night (i.e. conventions, company meetings, etc). Hotels can differ with mixes of business based on location, number of rooms, and event space. Convention hotels may have a desired mix of 80 percent Group and 20 percent Transient to achieve their optimum point of profit. Whereas small to midsize hotels may have a need for greater Transient business, all of which are key factors in formulating effective pricing strategies. Although the majority of Group business will be booked further in advance, those rates are also determined by the Revenue Manager and Director of Sales based on historical trends and future business needs.

3. Competitor Analysis: It is always valuable to know what the competition is doing. Revenue Management is part science and part craft. With the advancement in technology, companies such as Smith Travel Research and The Rubicon Group have created essential tools that allow hoteliers and Revenue Managers to determine their position in the marketplace. Smith Travel Research produced the STAR report that is routed on a weekly and monthly basis. This report allows a hotel to choose a competitive set, which then compares the hotel's actualized results by segment versus the competitive set, resulting in market share indexes for Occupancy, ADR and REV PAR. Although it is every hotel's goal to capture fair market share (dollar for dollar), it is a greater priority to gain share by outperforming the competition. The Rubicon Group created a "Market Vision" tool that provides the competitors rates and Occupancy levels up to 365 days into the future which can determine peaks and valleys in market demand.

4. Distribution Channels: It is crucial to know where the business is coming from, and how to increase production from the right channels. Most hotel brands have a central reservations systems, which is powered by their website and land based call centers. In addition, there are thousands of travel agencies that book rooms into hotel, which includes: online agencies (i.e. Expedia & Travelocity) and land based agencies (i.e. AAA Travel & American Express Travel). The major agencies will have Regional Market Managers that will supply market share data along with insight on any future developments that could be very beneficial to a hotel's strategy. A great Revenue Manager will establish daily communications with the large agencies to gain knowledge and to leverage hotel placement on their websites. Customers will not book you if they can't find you. The same applies to land based travel agents which are generally serviced by the hotel's Sales & Marketing team, who can be great resources in looking into the future. Greater market intelligence can equate to sound decision making.

5. Pricing Strategies: There is no right and wrong to the number of times rates should be adjusted on any given night. However, a greater understanding of market dynamics will come from a balance of historical knowledge and future market intelligence.

Lastly, the questions will always be asked: could we have done something different to maximize REV PAR? It is the Revenue Manager's responsibility to answer the question with integrity. Successful General Managers will appreciate the honesty and will have greater confidence level in a Revenue Manager that can determine both strengths and weaknesses in their own strategies.

The bellperson's main function is to escort guests and transport luggage to their rooms. Bellpersons also need to be knowledgeable about the local area and all facets of the hotel and its services. Because they have so much guest contact, they need a pleasant, outgoing personality. The bellperson explains the services of the hotel and points out the features of the room (lighting, TV, air-conditioning, telephone, wake-up calls, laundry and valet service, room service and restaurants, and the pool and health spa).

Concierge

The **concierge** is a uniformed employee of the hotel who has her or his own separate desk in the lobby or on special concierge floors. The concierge is a separate department from the front office room clerks and cashiers.

Luxury hotels in most cities have concierges. New York's Plaza Hotel has 800 rooms and a battery of ten concierges who serve under the direction of Thomas P. Wolfe. The concierge assists guests with a broad range of services such as the following:

- Tickets to the hottest shows in town, even for the very evening on the day they are requested. Naturally, the guest pays up to about $150 per ticket.
- A table at a restaurant that has no reservations available.
- Advice on local restaurants, activities, attractions, amenities, and facilities.
- Airline tickets and reconfirmation of flights.
- VIP's messages and special requests, such as shopping.

Less frequent requests are:

- Organize a wedding on two days' notice
- Arrange for a member of the concierge department to go to a consulate or embassy for visas to be stamped in guests' passports
- Handle business affairs

What will a concierge do for a guest? Almost anything, *Condé Nast Traveler* learned from concierges at hotels around the world. Among the more unusual requests were the following:

Concierges assist guests with a variety of services.

1. Some Japanese tourists staying at the Palace Hotel in Madrid decided to bring bullfighting home. Their concierge found bulls for sale, negotiated the bulls' purchase, and had them shipped to Tokyo.

2. After watching a guest pace the lobby, the concierge of a London hotel, now operating the desk at the Dorchester, asked the pacer if he could help. The guest was to be married within the hour, but his best man had been detained. Because he was dressed up anyway, the concierge volunteered to substitute.

3. A guest at the Hotel Plaza Athenee in Paris wanted to prevent her pet from mingling with dogs from the "wrong side" of the boulevard while walking. Madame requested that the concierge buy a house in a decent neighborhood so that her pampered pooch might stroll in its garden unsullied. Although the dog continued to reside at the hotel, Madame's chauffeur shuttled him to the empty house for his daily constitutional.

Concierges serve to elevate a property's marketable value and its image. They provide the special touch services that distinguish a "top property." To make sure they can cater to a guest's precise needs, concierges should make sure that they know precisely what the guest is looking for budget-wise, as well as any other parameters. Concierges must be very attentive and must anticipate guest needs when possible. In this age of highly competitive top-tier properties and well-informed guests, only knowledgeable concierge staff can provide the services to make a guest's stay memorable. As more properties try to demonstrate enhanced value, a concierge amenity takes on added significance.

The concierge needs not only a detailed knowledge of the hotel and its services, but also of the city and even international details. Many concierges speak several languages; most important of all, they must want to help people and have a pleasant, outgoing personality. The concierges' organization, which promotes high professional and ethical standards, is the Union Professionelle des Portiers des Grand Hotels (UPPGH), more commonly called the *Clefs d' Or* (pronounced clays-dor) because of the crossed gold-key insignia concierges usually wear on the lapels of their uniforms.

Housekeeping

The largest department in terms of the number of people employed is housekeeping. Up to 50 percent of the hotel employees may work in this department. Because of the hard work and comparatively low pay, employee turnover is very high in this essential department. The person in charge is the executive housekeeper or director of services. Her or his duties and responsibilities call for exceptional leadership, organization, motivation, and commitment to maintaining high standards. The logistics of servicing large numbers of rooms on a daily basis can be challenging. The importance of the housekeeping department is underlined by guest surveys that consistently rank cleanliness of rooms number one.

The four major areas of responsibilities for the executive housekeeper are as follows:

1. Leadership of people, equipment, and supplies
2. Cleanliness and servicing the guest rooms and public areas
3. Operating the department according to financial guidelines prescribed by the general manager
4. Keeping records

An example of an executive housekeeper's day might be as follows:

7:45 A.M. **Walk the lobby and property with the night cleaners and supervisors**
Check the housekeeping logbook
Check the forecast house count for number of checkouts

A housekeeper checks the linens on her cart. Attention to detail is important in maintaining standards.

Check daily activity reports, stayovers, check-ins, and VIPs
to ensure appropriate standards

Attend housekeepers' meeting

Meet challenges

Train new employees in the procedures

Meet with senior housekeepers/department managers

Conduct productivity checks

Check budget

Approve purchase orders

Check inventories

Conduct room inspections

Review maintenance checks

Interview potential employees

6:00 P.M. Attend to human resource activities, counseling, and
employee development

Perhaps the biggest challenge of an executive housekeeper is the leadership of all the employees in the department. Further, these employees are often of different nationalities. Depending on the size of the hotel, the executive housekeeper is assisted by an assistant executive housekeeper and one or more housekeeping supervisors, who in turn supervise a number of room attendants or housekeeping associates (see Figure 3–9). The assistant executive housekeeper manages the housekeeping office. The first important daily task of this position is to break out the hotel into sections for allocation to the room attendants' schedules.

The rooms of the hotel are listed on the floor master. If the room is vacant, nothing is written next to the room number. If the guest is expected to check out, then SC will be written next to the room number. A stayover will have SS, on hold is AH, out of order is OO, and VIPs are highlighted in colors according to the amenities required.

If 258 rooms are occupied and 10 of these are suites (which count as two rooms), then the total number of rooms to be allocated to room attendants is 268 (minus any no-shows). The remaining total is then divided by 17, which is the number of rooms that each attendant is expected to make up.

Total number of rooms occupied	258
Add 10 for the suites	+10
Less any no-shows	−3
Total number of rooms and suites occupied	= 265
Divided by 17 for the number of rooms that each attendant is expected to make up	17
	265 ÷ 17 = 16

Therefore, sixteen attendants are required for that day.

Figure 10 shows a daily attendant's schedule. To reduce payroll costs and encourage room attendants to become "stars," a number of hotel corporations have empowered the best attendants to check their own rooms. This has reduced the need for supervisors. Notice in Figure 10 how the points are weighted for various items. This is the result of focus groups of hotel guests who explained the things about a room that are important to them. The items with the highest points were the ones that most concerned the guests.

The housekeeping associates clean and service between fifteen and twenty rooms per day, depending on the individual hotel characteristics. Servicing a room takes longer in some older hotels than it does in some of the newer properties. Also, service time depends on the number of checkout rooms versus stayovers because servicing checkouts takes longer. Housekeeping associates begin their day at 8:00 A.M., reporting to the executive or assistant executive housekeeper. They are assigned a block of rooms and given room keys, for which they must sign and then return before going off duty.

The role of the executive housekeeper may vary slightly between the corporate chain and the independent hotel. An example is the purchasing of furnishings and equipment. A large independent hotel relies on the knowledge and experience of the executive housekeeper to make appropriate selections, whereas the chain hotel company has a corporate purchase agent (assisted by a designer) to make many of these decisions.

The executive housekeeper is responsible for a substantial amount of record keeping. In addition to the scheduling and evaluation of employees, an inventory of all guest rooms and public area furnishings must be accurately maintained with the record of refurbishment. Most of the hotel's maintenance work orders are initiated by the housekeepers who report the maintenance work. Many hotels now have a computer linkup between housekeeping and engineering and maintenance to speed the process. Guests expect their rooms to be fully functional, especially at today's prices. Housekeeping maintains a perpetual inventory of guest room amenities, cleaning supplies, and linens.

Amazingly, it took about 2,000 years, but hotels have figured out that guests spend most of their stay on a bed, so they are introducing wonder beds and heavenly beds to allow guests to enjoy sweet dreams—but hopefully not miss that pesky wake-up call. Around the country, guest rooms are getting a makeover that includes new mattresses with devices that allow one side to be set firmer than the other side or on an incline. Other room amenities include new high-definition or plasma TVs, WiFi services, and room cards that activate elevators.

Productivity in the housekeeping department is measured by the person-hours per occupied room. The labor costs per person-hour for a full-service hotel ranges from $2.66 to $5.33, or twenty minutes of labor for every occupied room in the hotel. Another key ratio is the labor cost, which is expected to be 5.1 percent of room sales. Controllable expenses are measured per occupied rooms. These expenses include guest supplies such as soap, shampoo, hand and body lotion, sewing kits, and stationery. Although this will vary according to the type of hotel, the cost should be about $2.00 per room. Cleaning supplies should be approximately $0.50 and linen costs $0.95, including the purchase and laundering of all linen. These budgeted costs are sometimes hard to achieve. The executive housekeeper may be doing a great job controlling costs, but if the sales department discounts rooms, the room sales figures may come in below

Housekeepers Guest Room Self–Inspection Rating
Inspection Codes:

| P – POLISH | R – REPLACE | E – WORK ORDER | S – SOAP SCUM | SM – SMEAR |
| SA – STAIN | H – HAIR | D – DIRT | DU – DUST | M – MISSING |

PART I – GUEST ROOM		S			U	COMMENTS
Entry, door, frame, threshold, latch				1		
Unusual odor OR smoke smell				3		
CLOSET, doors, louvers–containing				1		
Hangers, 8 suits, 4 skirts, 2 bags w/ invoices				2		
Two (2) robes, with info card				2		
Extra TP & FACIAL				1		
One (1) luggage rack				1		
Current rate card				1		
VALET	Shoe Horn & Mitt			2		
DRESSER	LAMP/ SHADE/ BULB			2		
	ICE BUCKET, LID, TRAY			2		
	TWO (2) WINE GLASSES			2		
	Room Service MENU			2		
MINIBAR	TOP, FRONT, 2 Wine glasses/ price list			1		
SAFE	KEY IN SAFE, SIGN			5		
CHECK BEHIND DRESSER				2		
DRAWERS	BIBLE AND BUDDHIST BOOK			1		
	PHONE BOOKS, ATT DIRECTORY			1		
TELEVISION	ON & OFF, CH 19 BEHIND			1		
COFFEE TABLE	REMOTE CONTROL/TEST 1			2		
	T.V. LISTINGS/BOOK MARK			1		
	GLASS TOP/LA JOLLA BOOK			1		
CARPET	VACUUM, SPOTS?			2		
SOFA	UNDER CUSHION/ BEHIND			2		
3 W LAMP	BULB, SHADE, & CORD			1		
WINDOWS	GLASS, DOOR, LATCH—C BAR?			2		
CURTAINS	Pull — check seams			1		
PATIO	2 CHAIRS, TABLE & DECK			3		
DESK	2 CHAIRS, TOP, BASE, & LAMP/SHADE			5		
	GREEN COMPENDIUM			3		
	Waste paper can			1		
BED	Tight, Pillows, bedspread			5		
	Check Under/SHEETS, PILLOWS			3		
HVAC	Control, setting, vent			1		
SIDE TABLES	Lamps & shade			2		
	Telephone, MESSAGE LIGHT			1		
	Clock Radio CORRECT TIME?			1		
MIRRORS	LARGE MIRROR OVER DRESSER			1		
PICTURES	ROOM ART WORK			1		
WALLS	Marks, stains, etc.			3		

Numbers in rating column range from 1 (least important) to 5 (most important).

Figure 10 • Housekeepers Guest Room Self-Inspection Form.

Housekeepers Guest Room Self–Inspection Rating

Inspection Codes:

P – POLISH	R – REPLACE	E – WORK ORDER	S – SOAP SCUM	SM – SMEAR
SA – STAIN	H – HAIR	D – DIRT	DU – DUST	M – MISSING

PART II – BATHROOM		S			U		COMMENTS
BATH TUB/SHOWER							
	GROUT/TILE & EDGE			2			
	ANTISLIP GRIDS			2			
	SIDE WALLS			1			
	SHOWER HEAD			1			
	WALL SOAP DISH			1			
	CONTROL LEVER			1			
	FAUCET			1			
	CLOTHESLINE			1			
	SHOWER ROD, HOOKS			1			
	SHOWER CURTAIN/ LINER			2			
VANITY	TOP, SIDE, & EDGE			1			
	SINK, TWO FAUCETS			3			
	3 GLASSES, COASTERS			2			
	WHITE SOAP DISH			1			
	FACIAL TISSUE & BOX			1			
AMENITY BASKET							
	1 SHAMPOO			1			
	1 CONDITIONER			1			
	1 MOISTURIZER			1			
	2 BOXED SOAP			1			
	1 SHOWER CAP			1			
MIRROR	LARGE & COSMETIC			2			
WALLS, CEILING, & VENT				2			
TOILET	TOP, SEAT, BASE, & LIP			2			
OTHER	TOILET PAPER, fold			1			
	SCALE AND TRASH CAN			2			
	FLOOR, SWEPT AND MOPPED			3			
	TELEPHONE			1			
BATH LINENS, racks							
	THREE (3) WASH CLOTHS			1			
	THREE (3) HAND TOWELS			1			
	THREE (3) BATH TOWELS			1			
	ONE (1) BATH MAT			1			
	ONE (1) BATH RUG			1			
LIGHT SWITCH				1			
DOOR	FULL LENGTH MIRROR			1			
	HANDLE/LOCK			1			
	THRESHOLD			1			
	PAINTED SURFACE			1			

Figure 10 • Housekeepers Guest Room Self-Inspection Form. (*continued*)

A Room at the Mauna Lani Resort on the Kohala Coast ready for guests.

budget. This would have the effect of increasing the costs per occupied room.

Another concern for the executive housekeeper is accident prevention. Insurance costs have skyrocketed in recent years, and employers are struggling to increase both employee and guest safety. It is necessary for accidents to be carefully investigated. Some employees have been known to have an accident at home but go to work and report it as a work-related injury to be covered by workers' compensation. To safeguard themselves to some extent, hotels keep sweep logs of the public areas; in the event that a guest slips and falls, the hotel can show that it does genuinely take preventative measures to protect its guests.

The **Occupational Safety and Health Administration (OSHA)**, whose purpose it is to ensure safe and healthful working conditions, sets mandatory job safety and health standards, conducts compliance inspections, and issues citations when there is noncompliance. Additionally, the U.S. Senate Bill 198, known as the **Employee Right to Know**, has heightened awareness of the storage, handling, and use of dangerous chemicals. Information about the chemicals must be made available to all employees. Great care and extensive training is required to avoid dangerous accidents.

The executive housekeeper must also minimize loss prevention. Strict policies and procedures are necessary to prevent losses from guest rooms. Some hotels require housekeeping associates to sign a form stating that they understand they may not let any guest into any room. Such action would result in immediate termination of employment. Although this may seem drastic, it is the only way to avoid some hotel thefts.

Laundry

Increasingly, hotels are operating their own laundries. This subdepartment generally reports to the executive housekeeper. The modern laundry operates computerized washing/drying machines and large presses. Dry cleaning for both guests and employees is a service that may also come under the laundry department. Hotels are starting to get away from in-house dry cleaning because of environmental concerns.

Sustainable Lodging

Green Hotel Initiatives

The environmentally conscious companies are not only helping to avoid further environmental degradation but are also saving themselves money while being good corporate citizens. Operationally, hotels have been recycling for years and saving water and chemicals by leaving cards in guest rooms saying that sheets will be changed every third day unless otherwise requested. Some hotels move the top sheet down to the bottom on the second or third day. Likewise, a card in the bathroom explains to guests that if they want a towel changed to leave it on the floor. Hotels have been quick to realize that the life of sheets and towels has been greatly extended, thus increasing savings.

The wattage of lighting has been reduced and long-life and florescent bulbs are saving thousands of dollars a year per property. Air-conditioning units can now control the temperature of a room through body-motion sensing devices that even pick up people's breathing. These devices can automatically shut off the air-conditioning unit when guests are out of their rooms. Savings are also being made with low-flow toilets and showerheads that have high-pressure low-volume flows of water.

Ecoefficiency, also generally termed *green*, is based on the concept of creating more goods and services while using fewer resources and creating less waste and pollution. In other words, it means doing more with less. So what does this have to do with your bottom line? Ecoefficiency helps hotels provide better service with fewer resources; reducing the materials and energy-intensity of goods and services lowers the hotel's ecological impact and improves the bottom line. It's a key driver for overall business performance.[10] Figure 11 shows a model for the implementation of sustainable lodging practices.

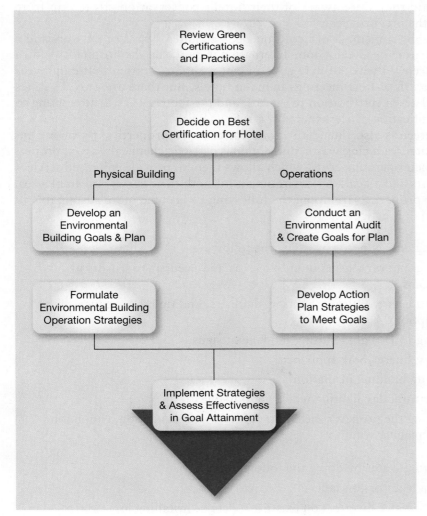

Figure 11 • A Model for the Implementation of Sustainable Lodging Practices.

Triple bottom line, sometimes called the TBL or 3P approach (people, planet, and profits), requires thinking in three dimensions, not one. It takes into account ecological and societal performance in addition to financial. Today, quantifiable environmental impacts include consumption of finite resources, energy usage, water quality and availability, and pollution emitted. Social impacts include community health, employee and guest safety, education quality, and diversity.[11]

Sustainable lodging, also known as green hotels, has become a powerful movement. The American Hotel and Lodging Association (AH&LA) and various state associations are leading the way with operational suggestions for best practices that lead to a green certification. Both corporations and independent properties are increasingly becoming greener in their operating practices. Sustainable Lodging & Restaurant–certified facilities develop goals and identify people in their organizations to find new opportunities to improve their operations through education, employee ideas, and guest feedback.

J.D. Power and Associates' 2009 North America Hotel Guest Satisfaction Index Study, which surveyed over 66,000 guests who stayed in North American hotels between May 2008 and June 2009, found that guests' awareness of their hotel's green programs increased significantly in 2009. Sixty-six percent of guests said they were aware of their hotel's conservation efforts, up from 57 percent the previous year.[12]

Ray Hobbs, a member of EcoRooms & EcoSuites' board of advisors and a certified auditor for Green Globe International, said, "In the hospitality industry, we're seeing a wave of new government mandates stating that employees can only stay in or host meetings in green hotels. But there are only 23 states with official green certification programs, and the industry is still attempting to find the certification process that best serves its needs."[13]

Being green is also financially good for certified properties. By saving energy and water, reducing waste, and eliminating toxic chemicals, green properties lower their operating costs, which allows them to provide enhanced services to their guests and a healthier environment for both their guests and employees. Sustainable properties are doing the following to become more sustainable in their operating practices[14]:

- Reducing energy needs by doing the following:

  Installing motion sensors in public areas and occupancy sensors in guestrooms

  Installing energy-efficient lighting, dimmers, and timers to reduce energy consumption

  Installing LED (light emitting diode) exit signs

  Installing Energy Star appliances

  Increasing building insulation

  Using natural day lighting whenever possible

  Tightening the property shell, with added/better insulation, eliminating leaks, replacing windows

- Conserving water by doing the following:

  Installing aerators on faucets

  Installing water diverters on existing toilets or installing low-flow toilets

Installing low-flow showerheads

Implementing towel and linen reuse programs

Landscaping with native plants

Using timers/moisture sensors in landscape watering

Changing lawn watering to encourage deeper root growth

- Reducing waste by doing the following:

Providing recycling areas for guests and staff

Purchasing postconsumer recycled paper and buying in bulk

Serving meals with cloth napkins and reusable china and dinnerware

Using refillable soap/shampoo dispensers in bathrooms

Recycling usable furniture, etc., at "dump stores" or through charity

Reusing old towels and linens as cleaning rags

Asking vendors to minimize packaging

Recycling cooking grease

Composting food and lawn waste

- Reducing hazardous waste by doing the following:

Properly disposing of fluorescent lighting, computers, and other electronic equipment

Participating in local hazardous waste collection days

Using low VOC (volatile organic compound) paints, carpets, and glues

Using rechargeable batteries

Using energy-efficient shuttle vans

Using environmentally friendly cleaning products

Another hotel company has a plan for its sustainability[15]:
HTI Explore Green Options for Business at the Hutchinson Hotel

Guest Shuttle

Free shuttle service to area attractions is provided; the vehicle is either a hybrid car or a 15-passenger van for bigger groups.

Guest Bicycles

Bicycles are available for guest use in warm weather. Excellent bicycle-route maps are provided for those who want to explore the city on two wheels.

Greening the Guestroom

Guest rooms offer an opportunity for greening. Sustainable hotels do the following[16]:

- Give guests an option to have the towels and linens changed every other day, or less frequently, rather than every day. Surveys have shown that more than 90 percent of guests like the option.

- Encourage staff to close drapes and turn off lights and air conditioning when rooms are unoccupied.

- Install water-efficient fixtures, such as showerheads, aerators, and low-flow toilets in each room.

- Use refillable soap and shampoo dispensers.

- Encourage guests to recycle by providing clearly marked recycling bins for cans, bottles, and newspapers.

- Install energy-efficient lighting fixtures in each room. Compact fluorescent fixtures can be screwed into many existing lamps and ceiling fixtures. To prevent theft, many hotels are installing new fixtures with compact fluorescent lamps hardwired into the fixture.

- Consider purchasing Energy Star–labeled TVs and other energy-efficient appliances.

- Clean rooms with environmental cleaners to improve indoor air quality and reduce emissions of VOCs.

- Use placards in the room to inform your guests about your green efforts. Why not tell them a hotel can save 13.5 gallons of freshwater by choosing not to replace bath towels and linen daily?

- Use an opt-out approach to linen and towel reuse (this can save a 250-room hotel more than $15,000 per year).

- If a hotel adopts these and other measures every year, it would amount to savings of thousands of dollars. Consider also the gains for hotels that adopt and practice sustainable operations. In the case of Washington, D.C., it has been estimated that the hotel gained $800,000 of incremental group business as a result of having sustainable meeting and event management at the property.

▶ Check Your Knowledge

1. Describe the different types of reservations that guests make at hotels.

2. What is the role played by uniformed services?

3. Explain the responsibilities of an executive housekeeper.

Security/Loss Prevention

Providing guest protection and loss prevention is essential for any lodging establishment regardless of size. Violent crime is a growing problem, and protecting guests from bodily harm has been defined by the courts as a reasonable expectation from hotels. The security/loss division is responsible for maintaining security alarm systems and implementing procedures aimed at protecting the personal property of guests and employees and the hotel itself.

A comprehensive security plan must include the following elements:

Security Officers

- These officers make regular rounds of the hotel premises, including guest floors, corridors, public and private function rooms, parking areas, and offices.
- Duties involve observing suspicious behavior and taking appropriate action, investigating incidents, and cooperating with local law enforcement agencies.

Equipment

- Two-way radios between security staff are common.
- Closed-circuit television cameras are used in out-of-the-way corridors and doorways, as well as in food, liquor, and storage areas.
- Smoke detectors and fire alarms, which increase the safety of the guests, are a requirement in every part of the hotel by law.
- Electronic key cards offer superior room security. Key cards typically do not list the name of the hotel or the room number. So, if lost or stolen, the key is not easily traceable. In addition, most key card systems record every entry in and out of the room on the computer for further reference.

Safety Procedures

- Front desk agents help maintain security by not allowing guests to reenter their rooms once they have checked out. This prevents any loss of hotel property by guests.
- Security officers should be able to gain access to guest rooms, store rooms, and offices at all times.
- Security staff develop **catastrophe plans** to ensure staff and guest safety and to minimize direct and indirect costs from disaster. The catastrophe plan reviews insurance policies, analyzes physical facilities, and evaluates possible disaster scenarios, including whether they have a high or low probability of occurring. Possible disaster scenarios may include fires, bomb threats, earthquakes, floods, hurricanes, and blizzards. The well-prepared hotel develops formal policies to deal with any possible scenario and trains employees to implement chosen procedures should they become necessary.

Identification Procedures

- Identification cards with photographs should be issued to all employees.
- Name tags for employees who are likely to have contact with guests not only project a friendly image for the property, but are also useful for security reasons.

Trends in Hotel and Rooms Division Operations

- *Diversity of work force.* All the pundits are projecting a substantial increase in the number of women and minorities who will not only be taking hourly paid positions, but also supervising and management positions as well.

- *Increase in use of technology.* Reservations are being made by individuals over the Internet. Travel agents are able to make reservations at more properties. There is increasing simplification of the various PMSs and their interface with POS systems. In the guest room, increasing demand for high-speed Internet access, category 5 cables, and in some cases equipment itself is anticipated.

- *Continued quest for increases in productivity.* As pressure mounts from owners and management companies, hotel managers are looking for innovative ways to increase productivity and to measure productivity by sales per employee.

- *Increasing use of revenue management.* The techniques of revenue management will increasingly be used to increase profit by effective pricing of room inventory.

- *Greening of hotels and guest rooms.* Recycling and the use of environmentally friendly products, amenities, and biodegradable detergents will increase.

- *Security.* Guests continue to be concerned about personal security. Hotels are constantly working to improve guest security. For example, one hotel has instituted a women-only floor with concierge and security. Implementation of security measures will increase.

- *Diversity of the guest.* More women travelers are occupying hotel rooms. This is particularly a result of an increase in business travel.

- *Compliance with the ADA.* As a result of the Americans with Disabilities Act (ADA), all hotels must modify existing facilities and incorporate design features into new constructions that make areas accessible to persons with disabilities. All hotels are expected to have at least 4 percent of their parking space designated as "handicapped." These spaces must be wide enough for wheelchairs to be unloaded from a van. Guest rooms must be fitted with equipment that can be manipulated by persons with disabilities. Restrooms must be wide enough to accommodate wheelchairs. Ramps should be equipped with handrails, and meeting rooms must be equipped with special listening systems for those with hearing impairments.

- *Use of hotels' web sites.* Hotel companies will continue to try to persuade guests to book rooms using the hotel company web site rather than via an

Internet site such as Hotels.com because the hotel must pay about $20 for each room booking from such sites.

- *In-room technology.* Hotels are upgrading in-room technology.

Career Information

Hotel management is probably the most popular career choice among seniors who are graduating from hospitality educational programs. The reason for this popularity is tied to the elegant image of hotels and the prestige associated with being a general manager or vice president of a major lodging chain. Managing a hotel is a complex balancing act that involves keeping employees, guests, and owners satisfied while overseeing a myriad of departments, including reservations, front desk, housekeeping, maintenance, accounting, food and beverage, security, concierge, and sales. To be a GM, a person must understand all of the various functions of a hotel and how their interrelationship makes up the lodging environment. The first step down this career path is to get a job in a hotel while you are in college.

Once you become proficient in one area, volunteer to work in another. A solid foundation of broad-based experience in the hotel will be priceless when you start your lodging career. Some excellent areas to consider are the front desk, night audit, food and beverage, and maintenance. Another challenging but very important place to gain experience is in housekeeping. It has been said that if you can manage the housekeeping department, the rest of lodging management is easy. An internship with a large hotel chain property can also be a powerful learning experience. There is simply no substitute for being part of a team that operates a lodging property with several hundred rooms. You may hear about graduates being offered "direct placement" or "manager in training" (MIT) positions. (There are several name variations for these programs.) Direct placement means that when you graduate, you are offered a specific position at a property. An MIT program exposes you to several areas of the hotel over a period of time. Then you are given an assignment based on your performance during training. Neither one is better from a career standpoint.

Another important consideration of a lodging career is your wardrobe. In a hotel environment, people are judged based on their appearance. A conservative, professional image is a key to success. Clothes are the tools of the lodging professional's trade, and they are not inexpensive. Begin investing in clothes while you are in school. Buy what you can afford, but buy items of quality. Stay away from trendy or flashy clothes that will quickly be out of fashion. When you take a position, you can expect to work around fifty hours per week. The times you work may vary. You can expect to have a starting salary of between $30,000 and $34,000. Some hotel chains will assist with moving expenses and may even offer a one-time signing bonus. However, try not to focus too much on the money; instead, try to find a company that you feel comfortable with and that will allow you opportunities for advancement. Figure 12 shows a career path in lodging management.

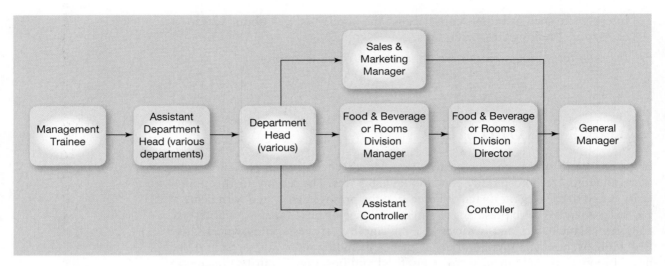

Figure 12 • A Career Path in Lodging Management.

Courtesy of Dr. Charlie Adams, Texas Tech University.

CASE STUDY

Checking Out a Guest

A guest walked up to the front desk agent in an upscale hotel, ready to check out. As she would usually do when checking out a guest, the agent asked the guest what his room number was. The guest was in a hurry and showed his anxiety by responding, "I stay in a hundred hotel rooms and you expect me to remember my room number?"

The agent then asked for the guest's name, to which he responded, "My name is Mr. Johnstein." After thanking him, the agent began to look for the guest's last name, but the name was not listed in the computer. Because the man had a heavy accent and the agent assumed that she had misunderstood him, she politely asked the guest to spell his last name. He answered, "What? Are you an idiot? The person who checked me in last night had no problem checking me in." Again, the agent looked on the computer to find the guest.

The guest, becoming even more frustrated, said, "I have a plane to catch and it is ridiculous that it has to take this long to check me out. I also need to fax these papers off, but I need to have them pho-tocopied first." The agent responded, "There is a business center at the end of the counter that will fax and photocopy what you need." The guest replied, "If I wanted your opinion, I would have asked you for it. Haven't you ever heard of customer service? Isn't this a five-star hotel? With your bad attitude, you should be working in a three-star hotel. I can't believe they let you work here at the front desk. Haven't you found my name yet?"

The agent, who was beginning to get upset, asked the guest again to spell out his full name. The guest only replied, "Here are my papers I want faxed if you are capable of faxing them." The agent reached to take the papers, and the guest shouted, "Don't grab them from my hand! You have a bad attitude, and if I had more time, I would talk to someone about getting you removed from your position to a hotel where they don't require such a level of customer service." The agent was very upset, but kept herself calm to prevent the guest from getting angrier.

The agent continued to provide service to the guest, sending the faxes and making the photocopies he had requested. Upon her return, the agent again asked the guest to repeat his last name because he had failed to spell it out. The guest replied by spelling out his name, "J-o-h-n-s-t-o-n-e." The agent was finally able to find his name on the computer and checked him out while he continued to verbally attack her. The agent finished by telling the guest to have a nice flight.

Discussion Questions

1. Is it appropriate to have the manager finish the checkout? Or should the front desk agent just take the heat?
2. Would you have handled the situation in the same manner?
3. What would you have done differently?

CASE STUDY

Overbooked: The Front-Office Perspective

Overbooking is an accepted hotel and airline practice. Many question the practice from various standpoints, including ethical and moral. Industry executives argue that there is nothing more perishable than a vacant room. If it is not used, there is no chance to regain lost revenue. Hotels need to protect themselves because potential guests frequently make reservations at more than one hotel or are delayed and, therefore, do not show up.

The percentage of no-shows varies by hotel and location but is often around 5 percent. In a 400-room hotel, that is 20 rooms, or an average loss of approximately $2,600 per night. Considering these figures, it is not surprising that hotels try to protect themselves by overbooking.

Hotels look carefully at bookings: Whom they are for, what rates they are paying, when they were made, whether they are for regular guests or from a major account (a corporation that uses the hotel frequently), and so on.

Jill Reynolds, the front-office manager at the Regency La Jolla, had known for some time that the 400-room hotel would be overbooked for this one night in October. She prepared to talk with the front-desk associates as they came on duty at 7:30 in the morning, knowing it would be a challenge to sell out without "walking" guests. Seldom does a hotel sell out before having to walk a few guests.

The hotel's policy and procedure on walking guests enables the front desk associates to call nearby hotels of a similar category to find out if they have rooms available to sell. If it is necessary to walk a guest, the associate explains to the guest that, regrettably, no rooms are available because of fewer departures than expected. The associate must explain that suitable accommodations have been reserved at a nearby hotel and that the hotel will pay for the room and transportation to and from the hotel. Usually, guests are understanding, especially when they realize that they are receiving a free room and free transportation.

On this particular day, the house count indicates that the hotel is overbooked by thirty rooms. Three or four nearby, comparable hotels had rooms available to sell in the morning. Besides walking guests, Jill considers other options—in particular "splitting" the fifteen suites with connecting parlors. If the guests in the suites do not need the parlor, it is then possible to gain a few more "rooms" to sell separately; however, rollaway beds must be placed in the rooms. Fortunately, eight parlors were available to sell.

Discussion Question

1. If you were in the same situation, what would you do?

301

CASE STUDY

Overbooked: The Housekeeping Perspective

It is no secret that in all hotels the director of housekeeping must be able to react quickly and efficiently to any unexpected circumstances that arise. Stephen Rodondi, executive housekeeper at the Regency in La Jolla, California, usually starts his workday at 8:00 A.M. with a department meeting. These morning meetings help him and the employees to visualize their goals for the day. On this particularly busy day, Rodondi arrives at work and is told that three housekeepers have called in sick. This is a serious challenge for the hotel because it is overbooked and has all its 400 rooms to service.

Discussion Question

1. What should Stephen do to maintain standards and ensure that all the guest rooms are serviced?

Source: Courtesy of Stephen Rodondi, Executive Housekeeper, Hyatt Regency, La Jolla, Ca.

Bob Weil, director of food and beverage at the Longboat Key Club and Resort, Sarasota, Florida, offers the following advice: "Be passionate about what you do and be in touch with the people you work with. I tour the property every day to get a feeling for the challenges our team may have—it's important to be in tune with what's going on." Another piece of advice is to never stop cooking and to maintain your fitness so that you can be a high-energy person. Students can expect many rewards in the hospitality business, but remember, it's a long journey, a process. You need to experience all levels in order to become a complete leader.

Summary

1. A big hotel is run by a general manager and an executive committee, which is represented by the key executives of all the major departments, such as rooms division, food and beverage, marketing, sales, and human resources.

2. The general manager represents the hotel and is responsible for its profitability and performance. Because of increased job consolidation, he or she also is expected to attract business and to empathize with the cultures of both guests and employees.

3. The rooms division department consists of front office, reservations, housekeeping, concierge, guest services, and communications.

4. The front desk, as the center of the hotel, sells rooms and maintains balanced guest accounts, which are completed daily by the night auditor. The front desk constantly must meet guests' needs by offering services such as mailing, faxing, and messages.

5. PMSs, centralized reservations, and yield management have enabled hotels to work more efficiently and to increase profitability and guest satisfaction.

6. The communications department, room service, and guest services (such as door attendants, bellpersons, and the concierge) are vital parts of the personality of a hotel.
7. Housekeeping is the largest department of the hotel. The executive housekeeper is in charge of inventory, cleaning, employees, and accident and loss prevention. The laundry may be cleaned directly in the hotel or by a hired laundry service.
8. The electronic room key and closed-circuit television cameras are basic measures provided to protect the guests and their property.

Key Words and Concepts

application service provider (ASP)
average daily rate (ADR)
call accounting systems (CAS)
catastrophe plans
central reservation office (CRO)
central reservation system (CRS)
city ledger
concierge
confirmed reservations
cost centers
daily report
Employee Right to Know
executive committee
global distribution systems (GDS)

guaranteed reservations
night auditor
Occupational Safety and Health Administration (OSHA)
productivity
property management systems (PMS)
revenue management
revenue centers
revenue per available room (REV PAR)
room occupancy percentage (ROP)
room rates
rooms division
uniformed staff
yield management

Review Questions

1. Briefly define the purpose of a hotel. Why is it important to empathize with the culture of guests?
2. List the main responsibilities of the front office manager.
3. How did Michelle Riesdorf become general manager of a Spring Hill Suites property?
4. What are the advantages and disadvantages of yield management?
5. Why is the concierge an essential part of the personality of a hotel?
6. Explain the importance of accident and loss prevention. What security measures are taken to protect guests and their property?

Internet Exercises

1. Organization: **Global Hyatt Corporation**
   Web site: **www.hyatt.com**
   Summary: Global Hyatt Corporation is a multibillion-dollar hotel management company. Together with Hyatt International, the company has about 8 percent of the hotel industry market share. Hyatt is recognized for its decentralized management approach, in which general managers are given a great deal of the management decision-making process. Click the "About Hyatt" tab, and click "Careers" under the "For Job Seekers" section. Then click on "mgmt training program" and take a look at the Management Training Program that Hyatt has to offer.

   (a) What is Hyatt's management training program?
   (b) What requisites must applicants meet to qualify for Hyatt's management training program?

2. Organization: **Hotel Jobs**
   Web site: **www.hoteljobs.com**
   Summary: Hoteljobs.com is a web site that offers information to recruiters, employers, and job seekers in the hospitality industry.

   (a) What different jobs are being offered under "Job Search" and which one, if any, interests you?
   (b) Post your résumé online.

Apply Your Knowledge

1. If you were on the executive committee of a hotel, what kinds of things would you be doing to ensure the success of the hotel?

2. Your hotel has 275 rooms. Last night 198 were occupied. What was the occupancy percentage?

Suggested Activities

1. Go to a hotel's web site and find the price of booking a room for a date of your choice. Then, go to one of the web sites (Hotels.com, Expedia, Travelocity, etc.) that "sell" hotel rooms and see how the price there compares with the price on the hotel's web site.

Endnotes

1. James E. McManemon, address to University of South Florida students, March 26, 2010.
2. Richard A. Wentzel, "Leaders of the Hospitality Industry or Hospitality Management," *An Introduction to the Industry*, 6th ed. (Dubuque, IA: Kendall/Hunt, 1991), 29.
3. Allen Brigid, "Ritz, César Jean (1850–1918)," in *Oxford Dictionary of National Biography*

(Oxford: Oxford University Press, May 2006), **www.oxforddnb.com** [site requires password], (accessed March 4, 2011).

4. F. Ashburner, "Escoffier, Georges Auguste (1846–1935)," *Oxford Dictionary of National Biography* (Oxford: Oxford University Press May 2006), **www.oxforddnb.com** [site requires password], (accessed March 4, 2011).

5. Donald E. Lundberg, *The Hotel and Restaurant Business*, 4th ed. (New York: Van Nostrand Reinhold, 1984), 33–34.

6. Personal conversation with Rollie Teves, July 20, 2007.

7. Personal correspondence with Jay R. Schrock, Ph.D., Dean, School of Hotel and Restaurant Management, University of South Florida, Sarasota-Manatee, January 18, 2011.

8. STR Global, *Products*, **http://www.strglobal.com/ Products/Product_Overview.aspx** (accessed March 3, 2011).

9. Personal conversation with Bruce Lockwood, March 16, 2006.

10. Susan Patel, *Triple Bottom Line and Eco-Efficiency: Where to Start?*, EcoGreenHotel, **www.ecogreenhotel. com/green_hotel_news_Triple-Bottom-Line-and-Eco-Efficiency.php** (accessed February 26, 2011).

11. Ibid.

12. "Green Hotel Certification Programs Snowball, Sparks Confusion," *Sustainable Travel*, **http://blog.sustainabletravel.com/green_hotel_ certification_prog_1.html** (accessed February 26, 2011).

13. Ibid.

14. New Hampshire Sustainable Lodging & Restaurant Program, Home Page, **www.nhslrp.org/** (accessed February 26, 2011).

15. Q Hotel and Spa, *Green Is Good*, **www.theqhotel.com/content.php?content_id=1**, (accessed February 26, 2011).

16. Pennsylvania Green Hotels & Motels, *Tourism and the Environment: Greening Your Hotel Operations*, **www.dep.state.pa.us/dep/deputate/ pollprev/industry/hotels/operations.htm** (accessed February 26, 2011).

Glossary

Application service provider (ASP)   Delivers a complete booking system tied to the hotel's inventory in real time via the Internet.

Average daily rate (ADR)   One of the key operating ratios that indicates the level of a hotel's performance. The ADR is calculated by dividing the dollar sales by the number of rooms rented.

Call accounting system (CAS)   A system that tracks guest room phone charges.

Catastrophe plan   A plan to maximize guest and property safety in the event of a disaster.

Central reservations office (CRO)   The central office of a lodging company, where reservations are processed.

Central reservations system (CRS)   A reservation system that is commonly used in large franchises to connect their reservation systems with one another; enables guests to call one phone number to reserve a room at any of the chain properties.

City ledger   A client whose company has established credit with a particular hotel. Charges are posted to the city ledger and accounts are sent once or twice monthly.

Concierge   A uniformed employee of a hotel who works at a desk in the lobby or on special concierge floors and answers questions, solves problems, and performs the services of a private secretary for the hotel's guests.

Confirmed reservation   A reservation made by a guest that is confirmed by the hotel for the dates they plan to stay.

Cost centers   Centers that cost money to operate and do not bring in revenue.

Daily report   A report prepared each day to provide essential performance information for a particular property to its management.

Employee right to know   Per U.S. Senate Bill 198, information about chemicals must be made available to all employees.

Executive committee   A committee of hotel executives from each of the major departments within the hotel; generally made up of the general manager, director of rooms division, food and beverage director, marketing and sales director, human resources director, accounting and/or finance director, and engineering director.

Global Distribution Systems (GDS)   A system that can distribute the product or service globally.

Guaranteed reservations   If rooms are available on guest demand, the hotel guarantees the guests rooms on those days.

Night auditor   The individual who verifies and balances guests' accounts.

Productivity   The amount of product, goods or services produced by employees.

Property management system (PMS)   A computerized system that integrates all systems used by a lodging property, such as reservations, front desk, housekeeping, food and beverage control, and accounting.

Revenue centers   Centers that produce revenue.

Revenue management   The management of revenue.

Revenue per available room (Rev par)   Total Rooms Revenue for Period divided by Total Rooms Available During a Period.

Room division The departments that make up the rooms division.

Room occupancy percentage (ROP) The number of rooms occupied divided by rooms available; a key operating ratio for hotels.

Room rates The various rates charged for hotel rooms.

Uniformed staff Front of the house staff.

Yield management The practice of analyzing past reservation patterns, room rates, cancellations, and no-shows in an attempt to maximize profits and occupancy rates and to set the most competitive room rates.

Photo Credits

Credits are listed in the order of appearance.

Tara Flake/Shutterstock

Angus Osborn/DK Images

Bonnie Kamin/PhotoEdit

akg-images/Newscom

Roberts Ratuts/Fotolia LLC

Dr. Charlie Adams Texas Tech University

Myrleen Ferguson-Cate/PhotoEdit, Inc.

MICROS

Denny Bhakta

Klehr & Churchill /Riser/Getty Images

stefanolunardi/Shutterstock

Rob Reichenfeld/DK Images

Managed Services

From Chapter 8 of *Introduction to Hospitality*, Sixth Edition. John R. Walker. Copyright © 2013 by Pearson Education, Inc. Published by Pearson.

Managed Services

OBJECTIVES

After reading and studying this text, you should be able to:

- Outline the different managed services segments.

- Describe the five factors that distinguish managed services operations from commercial ones.

- Explain the need for and trends in elementary and secondary school foodservice.

- Describe the complexities in college and university foodservice.

- Identify characteristics and trends in health care, business and industry, and leisure and recreation foodservices.

Overview

Managed services consist of foodservice and related operations, including the following:

- Airlines
- Military
- Elementary and secondary schools
- Colleges and universities
- Health care facilities
- Business and industry
- Leisure and recreation organizations
- Conference centers
- Airports
- Travel plazas

Companies and organizations such as educational or health care organizations decide if they want to operate their foodservice and related operations themselves or whether they want to contract them out to a managed services company. If they decide to operate their own foodservice, they may realize some cost savings, but if they lack the expertise, they may prefer to invite contractors to submit proposals. The company or organization can then invite contractors to make a presentation and to formally discuss and finalize all contractual details.

Several features distinguish managed services operations from **commercial foodservices** such as restaurants:

- In a restaurant, the challenge is to please the guest. In managed services, it is necessary to meet both the needs of the guest and the client (that is, the institution itself).

- In some operations, the guests may or may not have alternative dining options available to them and are a captive clientele. These guests may be eating at the foodservice operation only once or on a daily basis.

- Many managed operations are housed in host organizations that do not have foodservice as their primary business.

- Most managed services operations produce food in large-quantity batches for service and consumption within fixed time periods. For example, **batch cooking** means to produce a batch of food to serve at 11:30 A.M., another batch to serve at 12:15 P.M., and a third batch to serve at 12:45 P.M., rather than putting out all the food for the whole lunch period at 11:30 A.M. This gives the guests who come to eat later in the serving period as good a quality meal as those who came to eat earlier.

- The volume of business is more consistent and therefore easier to cater. Because it is easier to predict the number of meals and portion sizes, it is easier to plan, organize, produce, and serve meals; therefore, the atmosphere is less hurried than that of a restaurant. Weekends tend to be quieter than weekdays in managed services and, overall, the hours and benefits may be better than those of commercial restaurants.

A company or organization might contract its food- or other services for the following reasons:

- Financial
- Quality of program
- Recruitment of management and staff
- Expertise in management of service departments
- Resources available: people, programs, management systems, information systems
- Labor relations and other support
- Outsourcing of administrative functions[1]

Airlines and Airports

In-Flight and Airport Foodservice

When airlines do provide meals, foodservice either comes from their own *in-flight* business or they have the service provided by a contractor. In-flight food may be prepared in a factory mode at a facility close to but outside of the airport. In these cases, the food is prepared and packaged; then, it is transported to the departure gates for the appropriate flights. Once the food is loaded onto the aircraft, flight attendants take over serving the food and beverages to passengers.

In-flight foodservice is a complex logistical operation: The food must be able to withstand the transport conditions and the extended hot or cold holding period from the time it is prepared until the time it is served. If a food item is to be served hot, it must be able to rethermalize well on the plate. The meal should also look appetizing and taste good. Finally, all food and beverage items must be delivered on time and correctly to each departing aircraft.

Gate Gourmet is the largest in-flight food and related services provider, operating in twenty-eight countries on six continents from 122 flight kitchens and producing 250 million meals on average annually.[2] It is estimated that sales will exceed $2 billion, supported by more than 26,000 employees.

Another major player in the in-flight food service market is LSG Sky Chefs, headquartered in Neu-Isenburg, Germany. The LSG Sky Chefs group has the vision to "be the global leader in airline catering and the management of all in-flight service related processes."[3] LSG Sky Chefs consists of 130 companies with more than 200 customer service centers in 50 countries. In 2010, it produced about 460 million airline meals for more than 300 airlines worldwide.[4] The in-flight food and related services management operators plan the menus, develop the product specifications, and arrange the purchasing contracts. Each airline has a representative who oversees one or more locations and checks on the quality, quantity, and delivery times of all food and beverage items.

Airport restaurants from quick service to casual fine dining have seen an upswing in business as a result of the airlines cutting back on in-flight foodservice. Encounter is a restaurant at LAX (Los Angeles International Airport).

Airlines regard in-flight foodservice as an expense that needs to be controlled. To trim costs, most domestic airlines now sell snacks instead of meals on a number of short flights and even on flights that span main meal times. Both Gate Gourmet and Sky Chefs also now operate on-board retail solutions for most airlines.

International airlines try to stand out by offering superior food and beverages in hopes of attracting more passengers, especially the higher-paying business and first-class passenger. Others reduce or eliminate foodservice as a strategic decision to support lower fares. Because of the length of the flight, and the higher price paid for the ticket, international flights have better-quality food and beverage service.

On board, each aircraft has two or three categories of service, usually coach, business, and first class. First- and business-class passengers usually receive free beverages and upgraded meal items and service. These meals may consist of such items as fresh salmon or filet mignon; the rest of us get those "carry-on doggie-bags"!

A number of smaller regional and local foodservice operators contract to a variety of airlines at hundreds of airports. Most airports have caterers or foodservice contractors who compete for airline contracts. With several international and U.S. airlines all using U.S. airports, each airline must decide whether to use its own foodservice (if it has one) or to contract with one of several independent operators.

As airlines have decreased their in-flight foodservice, airport restaurants have picked up the business. Popular chain restaurants such as T.G.I. Friday's and Chili's are in several terminals, along with the quick-service restaurants such as McDonald's and Pizza Hut. These restaurants supplement airport foodservice offered by local restaurants.

▶ Check Your Knowledge

1. What are managed services?
2. Why would companies use contract management?

Military

Military foodservice is a large and important component of managed services. There are about 1.5 million soldiers, sailors, and aviators on active duty in the United States. Even with the military downsizing, foodservice sales top $6 billion per year. Base closings have prompted many military foodservice organizations to rethink services and concepts to better meet the needs of their personnel.

CORPORATE PROFILE

Sodexo

Sodexo, Inc., is a leading solutions company in North America, delivering on-site service solutions in corporate, education, health care, government, and remote site segments. Sodexo's mission is twofold: Improve the quality of daily life and contribute to the economic, social, and environmental development of the cities, regions, and countries in which it operates.

This company is also a member of the international Sodexo Alliance that was founded in 1966 by a Frenchman named Pierre Bellon with its first service provider in Marseille, France. Primarily serving schools, restaurants, and hospitals, the company soon became internationally successful by signing deals with Belgian foodservice contractors. In 1980, after considerable success in Europe, Africa, and the Middle East, Sodexo Alliance decided to expand its reach into North and South America. In 1997, the company joined with Universal Ogden Services, a leading U.S. remote-site service provider. The empire grew a year later when Sodexo Alliance and Marriott Management Services merged. The merger created a new company called Sodexo Marriott Services. Listed on the New York Stock Exchange, the new company became the market leader in food and management services in the United States. At that time, Sodexo Alliance was the biggest shareholder, holding 48.4 percent of shares on the company's capital. In 2001, however, Sodexo Alliance acquired 53 percent of the shares in Sodexo Marriott Services, which changed its name to simply Sodexo.

Today, Sodexo has more than 380,000 employees at 34,000 sites in 80 countries and serves 50 million consumers daily. In the United States, there are 120,000 employees. The goal of Sodexo is to improve the quality and life of customers and clients all over the United States and Canada. They offer outsourcing solutions to the health care, corporate, and education markets. This includes the following services: housekeeping, groundskeeping, foodservice, plant operation and maintenance, and integrated facilities management.

Sodexo's mission is to create and offer services that contribute to a more pleasant way of life for people wherever and whenever they come together. Its challenge is to continue to make its mission and values come alive through the way in which employees work together to serve the clients and customers. The values of Sodexo are service spirit, team spirit, and spirit of progress.

A leading provider of food and facilities management services in North America, Sodexo provides its services at more than 6,000 locations, including corporations, colleges and universities, health care organizations, and school districts. They are always looking to develop talent. Sodexo offers internships in foodservice and facilities management businesses as well as in staff positions such as finance, human resources, marketing, and sales. Sodexo believes that workforce diversity is essential to the company's growth and long-term success. By valuing and managing diversity at work, Sodexo can leverage the skills, knowledge, and abilities of all employees to increase employee, client, and customer satisfaction.

Sodexo has received numerous awards; among them are as follows: top ranked in the "services" category of 2010 Global Outsourcing; recognized as a Worldwise Supersector Leader for commitment to sustainable development; named one of the world's most ethical companies; number one of World's Most Admired Companies by Fortune Magazine and One of the best companies for Hourly Workers by *Working Mother* magazine.

Source: This feature draws on the following Sodexo web sites: Sodexo: *Identity & Key Figures,* http://www.sodexo.com/en/group/profile/key/figures.aspx (accessed November 8, 2011); Sodexo USA, About Us, http://www.sodexousa.com/usen/aboutus/aboutus.asp (accessed November 8, 2011).

Recent trends in military foodservice call for services such as officers' clubs to be contracted out to foodservice management companies. This change has reduced military costs because many of the officers' clubs lost money. The clubs now have moved the emphasis from fine dining to a more casual approach with family appeal. Many clubs are renovating their base concept even further, restyling according to theme concepts, such as sports or country western, for example. Other cost-saving measures include menu management, such as the use of a single menu for lunch and dinner (guests seldom eat both meals at the clubs). With proper plating techniques and portion size manipulation, a single menu (the same menu) can be created for lunch and dinner, meaning one inventory for both meals and less stock in general. To make this technique work successfully, the menu features several choices for appetizers, entrees, and desserts.

Another trend is the testing of prepared foods that can be reheated and served without much labor. Technological advances mean that field troops do not eat out of tin cans anymore; instead, they receive their food portions in plastic-and-foil pouches called meals ready-to-eat (MREs). Today, mobile field kitchens can be run by just two people, and bulk food supplies have been replaced by preportioned, precooked food packed in trays, which then are reheated in boiling water.

Feeding military personnel includes feeding troops and officers in clubs, dining halls, and military hospitals, as well as in the field. As both the budget and the numbers of personnel decrease, the military is downsizing by consolidating responsibilities. With fewer people to cook for, fewer cooks are required.

A model for such downsizing is the U.S. Marine Corps, which contracts out foodservice. With smaller numbers, they could not afford to take a marine away from training to work in the dining facilities without affecting military operations. Sodexo has the contract for the U.S. Marine Corps serves seven bases in fifty-five barracks, plus clubs and other related services. In addition, fast-food restaurants such as McDonald's and Burger King have opened on hundreds of bases; they are now installing Express Way kiosks on more bases. The fast-food restaurants on base offer further alternatives for military personnel on the move. One problem that may arise as a result of the downsizing and contracting out of military foodservice is that it is not likely that McDonald's could set up on the front line in a combat situation. The military will still have to do their own foodservice when it comes to mobilization.

Lately, military foodservice has been more innovative and creative in applying new ideas. For example, Naval Base San Diego Foodservice director Steve Hammel revaluated the base's system in terms of overall value, quality, quick service, and their packaging to enlisted personnel. He also looked at how to individualize the system for each base when each base has its own personality. Price points are also important, so the base has a $7.50 buffet and a fixed $5 lunch with different offerings every day.[5]

At another military operation in Fort Campbell, the cafeteria received a $10 million make-over and began a program of healthy eating. Out went the deep-fat fryer and in came rotisserie chicken, so now instead of selling 75 servings of fried chicken they sell 240 portions of rotisserie chicken.[6]

Smart Choices, created by VA Canteen Services, is a healthy choices menu approach that gives guests more healthy meal offerings. The campaign merges value, health, and wellness that offers a side salad, a bowl of soup, and a bottle of water totaling 235 calories or a sandwich, fruit, and a bottle of water totaling 340 calories. Interestingly, the calories, grams of fat, carbs, and protein are featured alongside the price on the receipt.[7]

Elementary and Secondary Schools

The United States government enacted the National School Lunch Act in 1946. The rationale was that if students received good meals, the military would have healthier recruits. In addition, such a program would make use of the surplus food that farmers produced.

Each day, millions of children are fed free or low-cost breakfast or lunch, or both, in approximately 101,000 schools to more than 31 million children each school day.[8] Many challenges currently face elementary and secondary school foodservice. One major challenge is to balance salability with good nutrition. Apart from cost and nutritional value, the broader social issue of the universal free meal arises. Proponents of the program maintain that better-nourished children have a better attention span, are less likely to be absent from school, and will stay in school longer. Offering free meals to all students also removes the poor-kid stigma from school lunch. Detractors from the universal program say that if we learned anything from the social programs that were implemented during the 1960s, it was that throwing money at problems is not always the best answer. Both sides agree that there is serious concern about what young students are eating. It's probably no surprise that the percentage of children who eat one serving or less of fruits and vegetables each day (excluding french fries) is as high as it is. These percentages are shown in Figure 1. One example of a school system "encouraging" a healthier meal program is in Texas, where

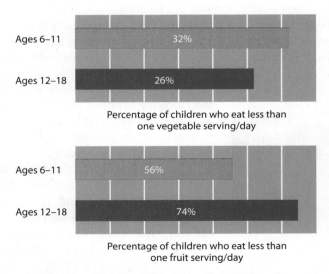

Figure 1 • Numbers of Servings of Fruit and Vegetables That Children Eat.

(*Source:* National Center Institute.)

fried chicken will no longer be a lunchtime staple and deep-fat frying is being eliminated. Instead, all potatoes, including french fries, must be oven baked and no food item can exceed 28 grams of fat. Fruits and vegetables, preferably fresh, must be offered every day for lunch and breakfast. Sodas will not be offered during the school day in middle school. The aim is to provide a healthy environment in which children can grow.[9]

The preparation and service of school foodservice meals varies. Some schools have on-site kitchens where the food is prepared and dining rooms where the food is served. Many large school districts operate a central commissary that prepares the meals and then distributes them among the schools in that district. A third option is for schools to purchase ready-to-serve meals that require only assembly at the school.

Schools may decide to participate in the **National School Lunch Program (NSLP)** or operate on their own. In reality, most schools have little choice because participating in the program means that federal funding is provided in the amount of approximately $2.72 per meal per student. Contract companies such as ARAMARK and Sodexo are introducing more flexibility in choices for students.

Meeting dietary guidelines is also an important issue. Much work has gone into establishing the nutritional requirements for children. It is difficult to achieve a balance between healthy food and costs, taking children's eating habits into account. Under the NSLP regulations, students must eat from what is commonly known as the type A menu. All the items in the type A menu must be offered to all children at every meal. The children have to select a minimum of three of the five meal components for the school to qualify for funding. However, U.S. Department of Agriculture (USDA) regulations have established limits on the amount of fat and saturated fat that can be offered: Fat should not exceed 30 percent of calories per week, and saturated fat was cut down to 10 percent of calories per week.

The government-funded NSLP, which pays in excess of $9.8 billion per year[10] for the meals given or sold at a discount to schoolchildren, is a huge potential market for fast-food chains. Chains are extremely eager to penetrate into the elementary and secondary school markets, even if it means a decrease in revenues. However, they believe that it is to their benefit to introduce Pizza Hut to young people very early—in other words, the aim is to build brand loyalty. For example, in Duluth, Minnesota, James Bruner, foodservice director for the city schools, was forced into offering branded pizza in several junior high and high schools. The local principals, hungry for new revenue, began offering Little Caesar's in direct competition to the cafeteria's frozen pizzas.

Taco Bell is in nearly 3,000 schools, Pizza Hut is in 4,500, and Subway is in 650. Domino's, McDonald's, Arby's, and others are well established in the market as well. Despite the positives, although it is not hard to convince the children, chains need to convince the adults. Much debate has arisen as to whether chains should enter the schools. Many parents feel that the school environment should provide a standard example of

Getting kids to eat proper food is a challenge.

what sound nutrition should be, and they believe that with fast food as an option, that will not be the case.

At a school lunch challenge at the American Culinary Federation (ACF) conference, chefs from around the country developed nutritious menus geared to wean children away from junk food to healthy foods. An 80-cent limit on the cost of raw ingredients was placed on the eleven finalists. Innovation and taste, as well as healthfulness, were the main criteria used to evaluate the winning entry: turkey taco salad, sausage pizza bagel, and stuffed potatoes.

Nutrition Education Programs

Nutrition education programs are now a required part of the nation's school lunch program. As a result of this program, children are learning to improve their eating habits, which, it is hoped, will continue for the rest of their lives. To support the program, nutritional education materials are used to decorate the dining room halls and tables. Perhaps the best example of this is the food guide called MyPlate developed by the Food and Nutrition Service of the USDA. Figure 2 shows the MyPlate food guide, which illustrates what to eat each day to follow a healthy diet.

Many schools are now developing unique ways to expose children to nutrition and proper eating guidelines. Planting a garden has sparked the interest of 1,500 elementary school students at Veterans Park Academy in Florida where students were involved with the planting of a vegetable garden as a result of a $10,000 grant. Students have increased their vegetable consumption as a result of their involvement with the program and have learned firsthand the value of good nutrition by participating in after-school cooking classes to learn how to prepare the vegetables they helped grow.[11]

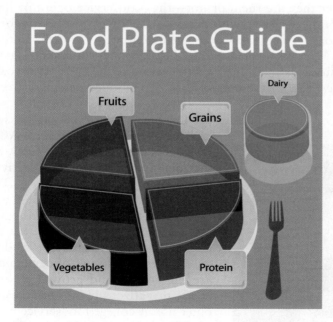

Figure 2 • The New MyPlate Healthy Eating Guide.

Colleges and Universities

College and university foodservice operations are complex and diverse. Among the various constituents of foodservice management are residence halls, sports concessions, conferences, cafeterias/student unions, faculty clubs, convenience stores, administrative catering, and outside catering.

On-campus dining is a challenge for foodservice managers because, as you well know, the clients live on campus and eat most of their meals at the campus dining facility. If the manager or contractor is not creative, students, staff, and faculty will quickly become bored with the sameness of the surroundings and menu offerings. Most campus dining is cafeteria style, offering cyclical menus that rotate every 10 or 14 days.

However, a college foodservice manager does have some advantages when compared with a restaurant manager. Budgeting is made easier because the on-campus students have already paid for their meals and their numbers are easy to forecast. When the payment is guaranteed and the guest count is predictable, planning and organizing staffing levels and food quantities are relatively easy and should ensure a reasonable profit margin. For instance, the **daily rate** is the amount of money required per day from each person to pay for the foodservice. Thus, if foodservice expenses for one semester of 98 days amount to $650,000 for an operation with 1,000 students eating, the daily rate is calculated as follows:

$$\frac{\$650,000 \div 98 \text{ days}}{1,000 \text{ students}} = \$6.63$$

College foodservice operations now offer a variety of meal plans for students. Under the old board plan, when students paid one fee for all meals each day—whether they ate them or not—the foodservice operator literally made a profit from the students who did not actually eat the meals for which they had paid. More typically now, students match their payments to the number of meals eaten: Monday through Friday, breakfast, lunch, dinner; dinner only; and prepaid credit cards that allow a student to use the card at any campus outlet and have the value of the food and beverage items deducted from his or her credit balance.

Leaders of the National Associations of College Auxiliary Services (NACAS), which represents 600 member institutes, have noticed that on-campus services and activities are undergoing continuous change.[12] The environment has become a critical part of policy and implementation that transcends parochial interests for those that best meet the needs of the institution and, ultimately, its students.

The driving forces of change on campuses are the advent and growth of branded concepts, privatization, campus cards, and computer use. A college foodservice manager today must have greater skills in retail marketing and

College foodservice.

INTRODUCING STEVE DOBROWOLSKI

Retail Operations Director for Dining Services, ARAMARK, University of South Florida

Steve began his career with ARAMARK at East Carolina University in 2000, as a shift manager for a small retail location. He quickly moved up to become the location manager of that operation and then became the assistant location manager of the largest dining hall on campus. He then became the location manager of that dining hall. In 2003, Steve transferred to New York University as the Assistant Food Service Director, managing many locations across the campus. In 2006, Steve was again promoted to Food Service Director when he transferred to the University of South Florida (USF). Most recently, in 2009, Steve was promoted to the Retail Operations Director at USF, managing all retail operations on campus.

Steve's major responsibilities are planning and managing high-volume, complex, multi-location foodservice operations at USF. Steve plans, directs, and controls all retail unit food-services and resources to meet operating and financial goals, client objectives, retail brand franchise relations, audits, and customer needs. He is also responsible for analyzing all financial reports for the retail operations, as well as reviewing all financial measurements with directors to ensure achievement of financial goals. In addition, Steve provides guidance and support in developing action plans to address areas requiring improvement and ensures compliance with ARAMARK Standard of Operations in all retail and catering operations. He interacts with USF clients daily and maintains effective client and customer relations at all levels within USF and USF dining services, including new building construction planning and renovations. He additionally regularly interfaces with ARAMARK's Regional Vice President, District Manager, Unit Directors, and their staff. Steve helps to ensure administration of human resources (HR) policies and interprets and ensures compliance with company policies such as safety, sanitation, and purchasing. Each week and month, Steve develops operational component forecasts and is able to explain any variances. Along with the Resident District Manager, Steve helps to define and hire for positions and roles for organization structure. In addition, he oversees the implementation and maintenance of new marketing and culinary concepts for retail locations.

There is no "typical" day for Steve as he oversees over 15 locations on the USF campus, in addition to the catering department for the university. A workweek usually involves meetings with various departments ranging from HR, marketing, finance, clients, catering events, customers, and his management team. In between all of these tasks, he also attends monthly meetings with students to allow them to voice their opinions and offer suggestions about the services on campus. Steve visits all of his operations often to review the notes from these meetings with the managers along with operational goals, successes, and opportunities. Steve is also the Labor Champion for the state of Florida. These duties include assisting other ARAMARK accounts with their labor management by finding efficiencies and opportunities and sharing best practices across the region. In his "spare time," on campus Steve has become known as "Mr. Fix-It," fixing equipment, lights, computers (he is also known as the IT guy) and anything else that may need his touch.

One of the most challenging responsibilities for Steve is being able to create new ideas and adapting our services daily to maintain a modern, innovative, and competitive edge in the ever-changing world of food.

Steve's favorite and most rewarding aspect of his job is that no day is ever the same. There is always something new and exciting happening. He also loves that he has opportunity to interact daily with so many great employees and customers and have the opportunity to positively influence their day!

merchandizing as students are given more discretion in how they may spend their money for food on campus.

Student Unions

As you know, the college student union offers a variety of managed services that caters to the needs of a diverse student body. Among the services offered are cafeteria foodservice, beverage services, branded quick-service restaurants, and take-out foodservice.

The cafeteria foodservice operation is often the "happening" place in the student union where students meet to socialize as well as to eat and drink. The cafeteria is generally open for breakfast, lunch, and dinner. Depending on the volume of business, the cafeteria may be closed during the nonmeal periods and weekends, and the cafeteria menu may or may not be the same as the residence foodservice facility. Offering a menu with a good price value is crucial to the successful operation of a campus cafeteria.

On campuses at which alcoholic beverage service is permitted, beverage services mainly focus on some form of a student pub where beer and perhaps wine and spirits may be offered. Not to be outdone, the faculty will undoubtedly have a lounge that also offers alcoholic beverages. Other beverages may be served at various outlets such as a food court or convenience store. Campus beverage service provides opportunities for foodservice operators to enhance profits.

In addition, many college campuses have welcomed branded, quick-service restaurants as a convenient way to satisfy the needs of a community on the go. Such an approach offers a win-win situation for colleges. The experience and brand recognition of chain restaurants such as Chick-fil-A, Moe's Southwest Grill, Au Bon Pain, Ben & Jerry's, Einstein Bros Bagels, Burger King, Smokehouse BBQ To Go, Starbucks, Beef 'O' Brady's, Pizza Hut, McDonald's, Subway, and Wendy's attract customers; the restaurants pay a fee, either to the foodservice management company or the university directly. Obviously, there is a danger that the quick-service restaurant may attract customers that the cafeteria might then lose, but competition tends to be good for all concerned. To create interest, an Iron Chef competition was held at the University of Missouri, where it gave students and chefs the opportunity to come up with innovative menu ideas, while creating a tighter knit campus community.[13]

Take-out foodservice is another convenience for the campus community. At times, students—and staff—do not want to prepare meals and are thankful for the opportunity to take meals with them. And it is not just during examination time that students, friends, and staff have a need for the take-out option. For example, tailgate parties prior to football and basketball games or concerts and other recreational/sporting events allow entrepreneurial foodservice operators to increase revenue and profits. The type of contract that a managed services operator signs varies depending on the size of the account. If the account is small, a fee generally is charged. With larger accounts, operators contract for a set percentage (usually about 5 percent) or a combination of a percentage and a bonus split. Figure 3 shows a typical college menu for the dining hall where students usually eat on campus.

WEEK 1

	MONDAY	TUESDAY	WEDNESDAY	THURSDAY	FRIDAY
Breakfast - Cold cereal, fruit and yogurt bar, toast, juices, milks, coffee, tea, hot chocolate and fresh fruit					
Bakery:	Quick Coffee Cake	Assorted Danish	Cinnamon Coffee Cake	Sticky Top Roll	Banana Nut Muffins
Hot Cereal:	Oatmeal	Malt-O-Meal	Cream of Wheat	Grits	Oatmeal
Entrees:	Buttermilk Pancakes	Waffles	French Toast	Oatmeal Pancakes	Waffles w/Peaches
	Scrambled Eggs	Scrambled Eggs	Scrambled Eggs	Scrambled Eggs	Scrambled Eggs
	Sausage Gravy	Egg O'Muffin w/Bacon	Ham & Cheese	Chorizo & Eggs	Egg Burrito
	& Biscuits	Hearty Fried Potatoes	Omelette	Cottage Fries	Home Fries
	Cottage Fries	Bacon	Hash Browns	Sausage Links	
Lunch - Salad Bar, Rice & Chili Bar, Cereal, Build-Your-Own-Sandwich Bar & Fresh Fruit					
Soup:	Beef Barley	Italian Minestrone	Chicken Gumbo	Chicken Noodle	New England Clam Chowder
Entrees:	Baked Seafood & Rice	Chicken Tortilla	Fishwich	Cheesy Mushroom	BBQ Ham Sandwich
	Grilled Ham & Cheese	Casserole	Spanish Macaroni	Burger	Ground Beef &
	Potato Salad	Patty Melt	Ranch Beans	Hamburger	Potato Pie
	Wax Beans	French Fries	Italian Green Beans	Grilled Cheese	Whipped Potatoes
	Mixed Vegetables	Hominy	Braised Carrots &	Onion Rings	Italian Green Beans
		Spinach	Celery	Carrots	Beets
				Oriental Veg. Blend	
Dessert:	Chocolate Pudding	Applesauce Cake	Peanut Butter	Coconut Cake	Vanilla Pudding
	Soft Serve Ice Cream	Soft Serve Ice Cream	Cookies		
Dinner - Salad Bar, Cereal, & Fresh Fruit (Tortillas served at Breakfast & Dinner)					
Soup:	Beef Barley	Italian Minestrone	Chicken Gumbo	Chicken Noodle	New England Clam Chowder
Entrees:	Oven Broiled Chicken	Beef Fajitas	Roast Turkey w/Gravy	Egg Roll Over Rice	Pizza! Pizza! Pizza!
	Grilled Liver & Onions	Fried Perch	Old Fashion Beef Stew	Grilled Pork Chop	Curly Fries
	Parsley Potatoes	Spanish Rice	Whipped Potatoes	Rice	Broccoli
	Corn	Asparagus	Corn Cobbettes	Beets	Mixed Vegetables
	Zucchini	Carrots	Brussel Sprouts	Cauliflower au Gratin	
Dessert:	Chocolate Chip	Spicy Whole	Chocolate Mayo	Peach Cobbler	Best Ever Cake
	Cookies	Wheat Bar	Cake		

Figure 3 • Sample College Menu.

(Courtesy of ARAMARK.)

As with all types of contract services, there are advantages and disadvantages. Here are both from a client's (that would be your college) perspective:

Advantages	Disadvantages
Experience in size and types of foodservice operations	
Use contracted department as a model for rest of institution	Potential for lost contracts, meaning foodservice contracts are generally for a period of five years, after which bids are requested for another contract. So, the operator must maintain the service and pricing that please the client (the college/university).
Variety of services	
Resource and support available	
Hold contractor to a higher level of performance	

Managing Managed Services[14]

Operating a large $24 million university campus foodservice operation with 32 managers and 680 hourly employees is exhilarating. Each university or college campus is somewhat different, so an operator is smart to become a part of the "living and learning" campus community and align with the university's goals. Also important is to seek input into many of the decisions made so that there is more of a buy-in by the campus community.

Each year, strategic planning and marketing sessions are held with each of the key operating divisions: residential, retail, concessions, and catering; then, financial budgets are completed by month and week for every operation and category. These figures are also updated monthly throughout the year.

The managed services operating ratios vary according to the type of operation, for example, labor costs, which range from the low teens to 50 percent. For residential and retail, labor costs are high and food costs are low, whereas for concessions, labor costs are low and food costs are high. Overall, a well-run operation makes a net profit of between 5 and 15 percent.

Communications are a vital part of a successful foodservice operation. Because there is so much going on, each director and manager has regular meetings to ensure everyone is on the same page. Many day-to-day operating decisions are made by supervisors, who, along with management, all use Outlook and newsletters to communicate electronically.

Foodservice directors spend about 75 percent of their time by following up and making sure that things are still happening the way they are intended to. The fact that foodservice directors need to spend so much time controlling underlines the importance of making good hires and setting clear and concise standards.

A foodservice manager's responsibilities in a small or midsize operation are frequently more extensive than those of managers of the larger operations.

CORPORATE PROFILE

ARAMARK

In the 1950s, Dave Davidson and Bill Fishman, both in the vending business, realized that they shared the same dreams and hopes of turning vending into a service and combining it with foodservice. And this they did—ARAMARK is the world's leading provider of quality managed services. It operates with 255,000 employees in all fifty states and in twenty-two foreign countries,[15] offering a very diversified and broad range of services to business of all sizes and to thousands of universities, hospitals, and municipal, state, and federal government facilities. Each day, they serve millions of people at more than 500,000 locations worldwide. ARAMARK's emphasis on the quality of service management was evident from the very beginning of its operations. ARAMARK entered new markets by researching the best-managed local companies, acquiring them, and persuading key managers to stay with the company.

The company's Business Purpose states that "We are a professional services organization dedicated to excellence."

- We develop and sustain our leadership position by engaging and supporting our most valuable differentiated asset: the competence, commitment and creativity of *our people*.

- We provide world-class *experiences*, *environments*, and *outcomes* for our clients and customers by developing relationships based on service excellence, partnership, and mutual understanding.

- We enable our clients to realize their *core mission*, and we will anticipate the needs and exceed the expectations of customers, by dedicating our skills in professional services—hospitality, food, facilities, and uniforms—to the goals and priorities of their institution.

- We create long-term value and capture the greatest opportunity for all ARAMARK shareholders— our people, clients, customers, communities, and shareholders—by delivering sustainable profitable growth in sales, earnings, and cash flow in a global company built on pride, integrity, and respect.

The focus on management skills at every level, especially the local one, gave ARAMARK an invaluable resource. In fact, with every acquisition, local managers were encouraged and rewarded for becoming multiskilled entrepreneurs. This approach to outsourcing is, put more simply, the ability of the company to take the best management skills and apply them to all the lines of business the company uses to diversify. Among ARAMARK operations are the following:

Parks and Destinations. ARAMARK manages food, lodging, hospitality, and support services at national parks and other recreational facilities that serve the general public.

Health Services. ARAMARK provides specialized management services for hospitals and medical services. It maintains hospital equipment valued at $5 billion and services 1,300 hospitals and senior living centers with 400,000 beds.

Colleges and Universities. A leading provider of dining facilities and conference center management to 1,000 colleges and universities. Specializing in residential dining, retail operations such as convenience stores, coffee kiosks, and late-night and branded restaurants.

(continued)

CORPORATE PROFILE *(continued)*

Conference Centers. ARAMARK manages 108 conference centers.

Convention Centers. ARAMARK offers full-service convention center operations at a number of diverse facilities across the country.

Correctional Institutions. ARAMARK Correctional Services provides a wide range of food, facility, and other customized support solutions to over 600 correctional facilities as well as over 1 million meals a day for state and municipal facilities.

Sports and Entertainment. ARAMARK offers services at recreational areas, cultural attractions, sports and entertainment venues, amphitheaters, parks, resorts, and tourists attractions.

School Districts. ARAMARK specializes in providing early-childhood and school-age education services to 4,000 schools to provide services to 7 million students.

Business and industry services. ARAMARK services millions of people annually at thousands of industry accounts, including delivering customized solutions to clients in business, industry, and government.

Uniform services. The company is America's largest provider of uniform services and work apparel for virtually all types of institutions. Millions of customers use uniform and work clothing services by ARAMARK.

ARAMARK has created an Innovation Center for corporate research, design, and product development resources. One interesting outcome is the design of a "cool" place for students to eat—it has a unique design with students in mind, different from the days of the old gym dining.

Joseph Neubauer, chairman and CEO, realizes this: "I am energized by the bright prospects for the journey ahead."

Source: Courtesy of ARAMARK.

This is because larger units have more people to whom certain functions can be delegated, such as human resources. For example, following are some of the responsibilities that the foodservice manager in a small or midsize operation might have in addition to strictly foodservice responsibilities:

Employee Relations
- Team development
- Rewards/recognition
- Drug alcohol abuse/prevention
- Positive work environment
- Coaching/facilitating versus directing

Human Resource Management
- Recruitment/training/evaluating
- Wage/salary administration
- Benefits administration

- Compliance with federal/state laws/EEOC (Equal Employment Opportunity)/Senate Bill 198
- Harassment/OSHA (Occupational Safety and Health Administration)
- Disciplinary actions/terminations
- Unemployment/wrongful disclosure

Financial/Budgeting
- Project budgets
- Actual versus projected budget monitoring (weekly)
- Controlling food cost, labor, expenses, and so on
- Record-keeping requirements/audit
- Monitoring accounts payable/receivable
- Billing/collecting
- Compliance with contracts
- Cash procedures/banking

Safety Administration
- Equipment training/orientation
- Controlling workers' compensation
- Monthly inspections/audits (federal/state/OSHA requirements/Senate Bill 198)

Safety Budget
- Work on the expensive injuries
- Reduce lost time frequency rate and injury frequency rate

Food Production/Service
- Menu/recipe development
- Menu mix versus competition
- Food waste/leftovers utilization
- Production records
- Production control
- Presentation/merchandising

Sanitation/Food-Borne Illness Prevention
- Food-borne illness (FBI) prevention
- Sanitation/cleaning schedule
- Proper food handling/storage
- Daily prevention/monitoring
- Monthly inspection
- Health department compliance

Purchasing/Recruiting

- Ordering/receiving/storage
- Food and beverage specifications/quality
- Inventory control
- Vendor relation/problems

Staff Training/Development

- On-the-job versus structured
- Safety/sanitation/food handling and so on
- Food preparation/presentation
- Guest service

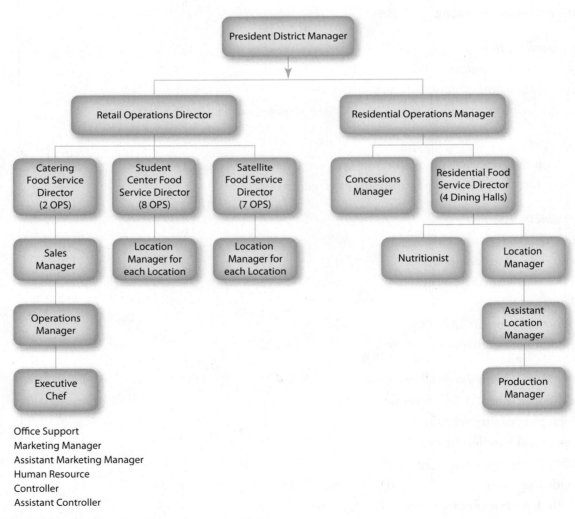

Office Support
Marketing Manager
Assistant Marketing Manager
Human Resource
Controller
Assistant Controller

Figure 3a • An Organization Chart for a Large University.

Sustainable Managed Services

Hospital foodservice directors often say that offering healthy choices in their cafeterias is a key department mission. But many operators are quick to add that they still offer the so-called unhealthy options to prevent a drop in participation and revenues. However, Raquel Frazier, food service director at La Rabida Children's Hospital in Chicago, did not have that luxury. She was mandated by the hospital's administration to make the cafeteria 100 percent healthy.[16] To meet new nutritional guidelines, food items could not exceed 450 calories, with ten grams of fat or three grams of saturated fat, and had to contain at least three grams of fiber. In addition, nutritional information for all items had to be posted on the menu and at the point of service. The outcome has been that most employees reported losing weight and keeping it off and leading a more healthy lifestyle.[17]

INTRODUCING REGYNALD G. WASHINGTON

Vice President and General Manager for Disney Regional Entertainment and Vice President of New Business Initiatives for Walt Disney Parks and Resorts

For a student majoring in hotel and restaurant management, being a general manager, president, or even chief executive officer in the food industry is a goal to be achieved. For Regynald G. Washington, not only has it been a goal reached, but a dream realized. His bright smile spells success. As a child growing up in a middle-income family in the town of Marathon in the Florida Keys, working was mandatory. At the early age of thirteen, he was introduced to the food industry. His first job consisted of waiting on and busing tables and doing other chores in the Indies Inn Resort and Yacht Club. He took this on as an exciting and new challenge.

For Regynald, attitude is everything. His positive attitude toward being the best that he can be was derived from a phrase his parents used to repeat to him: "A chip on your shoulder earns a lack of respect from colleagues, friends, and family." His great energy and pride in his work is what makes him stand out among many other leaders in the food industry. He has a quality and people-oriented mind that keeps him focused on any task he wishes to accomplish.

Regynald graduated from Florida International University with a degree in hotel and restaurant administration. He continued to work for Indies Inn Resort, but by this time he was running the food and beverage operation. This was the beginning of the long career road for Regynald G. Washington.

In the years that followed, Regynald worked as a restaurant general manager and at Concessions International, an airport food and beverage, duty free, gifts, and magazine organization in Atlanta. He was promoted to executive vice president in 1990. He then formed Washington Enterprises and developed Sylvia's Restaurant in Atlanta, which turned out to be very successful.

A few years later, though, a major entertainment company executive recruiter offered Washington an opportunity to join the new and creative food and beverage approach that the company was aiming to develop.

Regynald's secret to managing 2,500 employees and satisfying Epcot's customers is simply organization and care. Having organization and direction in your work eliminates stress and makes time for fun. Making sure that all the staff know what they are doing and that they are doing it well and serving guests hot food hot and cold food cold is all it takes. He uses a back-to-basics formula, which requires that everything go well, from making guests happy to proper staffing. Not only has his ambition and energy helped him climb

(continued)

INTRODUCING REGYNALD G. WASHINGTON (continued)

to the top, but he also has great concern for others and wants to help his employees learn new things and move forward in their careers. He is very well focused on quality and precision in anything and everything he does. One of his number one concerns is food safety.

To make sure everything is intact and going well, Regynald and his support team perform unannounced inspections every quarter. A specific food and beverage facility is concentrated on and fully evaluated for its table turns, guest service, food quality, and training programs. Specialists act as the guests and observe and report anything that seems less than perfect. Epcot executive chefs check the kitchen food as well as the menu. In-house sanitarians evaluate the level of sanitation at the facility. The goal of these inspections is to make sure nothing is less than perfect. Excellence is the goal for Regynald. He admires and respects the people who work with him and has ranked them as being the best food and beverage people.

Regynald is a frequent guest lecturer in educational forums and has served on the advisory boards of a number of universities for their hospitality management programs. His board service includes being a trustee of the National Restaurant Association Educational Foundation.

Regynald believes that he has achieved a lot and has had many successes during his career. His career is exciting and motivating and he has the opportunity to make a difference in people's lives every single day. This is what he always wanted and now he has it. He says, "My parents really wanted me to become a lawyer, physician, or architect. They didn't believe you could reach the top and do exciting things in the restaurant industry."

Source: This profile draws on Whit Smyth, "Regynald Washington, EPCOT's Chief of Food and Beverage, Says Pleasing Customers Is No Mickey Mouse," *Nation's Restaurant News* 33, (January 25, 1999): 28–30; personal correspondence with Regynald Washington, April 6, 2005.

A number of support staff positions offer career opportunities not only within managed services but also in all facets of hospitality operations and arrangements. They include sales, marketing, controller/audit, financial analysis, human resources, training and development, affirmative action/EEOC compliance, safety administration, procurement/distribution, technical services (recipes, menus, product testing), labor relations, and legal aspects.

A sample operating statement is shown in Figure 4. It shows a monthly statement for a college foodservice operation.

▶ Check Your Knowledge

1. In your own words, define in-flight foodservice.

2. What are some of the challenges faced by in-flight foodservice operators? What can be done to solve these problems?

3. Name the foodservice operations that constitute managed services.

4. How is each foodservice operation characterized?

5. In small groups, discuss the differences between the foodservice operations; then, share with the class.

DESCRIPTION		%	STUDENT UNION	%	TOTAL	%
SALES						
FOOD REGULAR	$ 951,178				$ 951,178	
FOOD SPECIAL FUNCTIONS	40,000				40,000	
PIZZA HUT EXPRESS			$ 100,000		100,000	
BANQUET & CATERING	200,000				200,000	
CONFERENCE	160,000				160,000	
BEER			80,000		80,000	
SNACK BAR			300,000		30,000	
A LA CARTE CAFE	60,000				60,000	
** TOTAL SALES	$ 1,411,178		$ 480,000	100.0%	$ 1,891,178	100.0%
PRODUCT COST						
BAKED GOODS	$ 9,420		$ 4,700		$ 14,120	
BEVERAGE	10,000		8,000		18,000	
MILK & ICE CREAM	11,982		2,819		14,801	
GROCERIES	131,000		49,420		180,420	
FROZEN FOOD	76,045		37,221		113,266	
MEAT, SEAFOOD, EGGS, & CHEESE	129,017		48,000		177,017	
PRODUCE	65,500		26,000		91,500	
MISCELLANEOUS					0	
COLD DRINK	0		0		0	
** TOTAL PRODUCT COST	$ 432,964		$ 176,160	36.7%	$ 609,124	32.2%
LABOR COST						
WAGES	$ 581,000		$ 154,000		$ 735,000	
LABOR—OTHER EMPLOYEES	101,500		545,000		156,000	
BENEFITS + PAYROLL TAXES	124,794		50,657		175,451	
MANAGEMENT BENEFITS	58,320		6,000		64,320	
WAGE ACCRUALS	0				0	
** TOTAL LABOR COST	$ 865,614		$ 265,157	55.2%	$ 1,130,771	59.8%
FOOD OPERATING COST-CONTROLLABLE						
CLEANING SUPPLIES	$ 24,000		$ 6,000		$ 30,000	
PAPER SUPPLIES	9,000		46,000		55,000	
EQUIPMENT RENTAL					0	
GUEST SUPPLIES					7,000	
PROMOTIONS	4,500		2,500		40,000	
SMALL EQUIPMENT	35,000		5,000		0	
BUSINESS DUES & MEMBERSHIP					3,000	
VEHICLE EXPENSE	3,000				4,300	
TELEPHONE	3,600		700		$ 22,000	
	$ 17,000		$ 5,000			

Figure 4 • An Operating Statement.

(continued)

Health Care Facilities

Health care managed services operations are remarkably complex because of the necessity of meeting the diverse needs of a delicate clientele. Health care managed services are provided to hospital patients, long-term care and assisted living residents, visitors, and employees. The service is given by tray, cafeteria, dining room, coffee shop, catering, and vending.

The challenge of health care managed services is to provide many special meal components to patients with very specific dietary requirements. Determining which meals need to go to which patients and ensuring that they reach their destinations

DESCRIPTION		%	STUDENT UNION	%	TOTAL	%
LAUNDRY & UNIFORMS					0	
MAINTENANCE & REPAIRS	$ 1,200		$ 200		$ 1,400	
FLOWERS	10,000		4,000		140,000	
TRAINING					0	
SPECIAL SERVICES	18,000		3,000		21,000	
MISCELLANEOUS						
** TOTAL CONTROLLABLE SUPPLIES	$ 125,300	8.9%	$ 72,400	15.1%	$ 197,700	10.5%
OPERATING COSTS- NONCONTROLLABLE						
AMORTIZATION & DEPRECIATION	$ 13,500		$ 7,000		$ 20,500	
INSURANCE	55,717		14,768		70,485	
MISCELLANEOUS EXPENSE	12,400		4,100		16,500	
ASSET RETIREMENTS					0	
RENT/COMMISSIONS	48,000		40,000		88,000	
PIZZA HUT ROYALTIES			7,000		7,000	
PIZZA HUT —						
LICENSING MARKETING			7,000		7,000	
TAXES, LICENSE & FEES	5,000		500		5,500	
VEHICLE —						
DEPRECIATION & EXPENSE	4,000				4,000	
ADMINISTRATION & SUPERVISION						
** TOTAL NONCONTROLLABLE COST	$ 138,617	9.8%	$ 80,368	16.7%	$ 218,985	11.6%
** TOTAL COST OF OPERATIONS	$ 1,562,495	110.7%	$ 594,085	123.8%	$ 2,156,580	114.0%
EXCESS OR (DEFICIT)	(151,317)	(10.7%)	(114,085)	(23.8)	(265,402)	(14.0%)
PARTICIPATION-CONTRACTOR						
*** NET EXCESS OR (DEFICIT)						
STATISTICS						
CUSTOMER COUNT						
HOURS WORKED						
AVERAGE FOOD- SALES/CUSTOMER						

Figure 4 • An Operating Statement. *(continued)*

involve especially challenging logistics. In addition to the patients, health care employees need to enjoy a nutritious meal in pleasant surroundings in a limited time (usually thirty minutes). Because employees typically work five days in a row, managers must be creative in the development of menus and meal themes.

The main focus of hospital foodservice is the **tray line**. Once all the requirements for special meals have been prepared by a registered dietitian, the line is set up and menus color coded for the various diets. The line begins with the tray, a mat, cutlery, napkin, salt and pepper, and perhaps a flower. As the tray moves along the line, various menu items are added according to the color code for the particular patient's diet. Naturally, each tray is double- and triple-checked, first at the end of the tray line and then on the hospital floor. The line generally goes floor by floor at a rate of about five trays a minute; at this rate, a large hospital with 600 beds can be served within a couple of hours. This is time consuming for the employees because three meals a day represent up to six hours of line time. Clearly, health care foodservice is very labor intensive, with labor accounting for about 55 to 66 percent of operating dollars. In an effort to keep costs down, many operators have increased the number of help-yourself food stations, buffets, salads, desserts, and topping bars. They also focus on increasing revenues through catering and retail innovations. Operators must also contend with the fact that food costs are not totally covered by Medicare.

Hospital foodservice has evolved to the point where the need for new revenue sources has changed the traditional patient and non-patient meal-service ratios at many institutions. This situation was imposed by the federal government when it narrowed the treatment-reimbursement criteria; originally 66 percent of a typical acute-care facility's foodservice budget went toward patients' meals, with the remainder allocated for feeding the employees and visitors. In the past few years, as cash sales have become more important, the 66/33 percent ratio has reversed.

Experts agree that because economic pressures will increase foodservice managers will need to use a more high-tech approach, incorporating labor-saving sous-vide and cook–chill methods. This segment of the industry, which currently is dominated by self-operated managed services, will continue to see contract specialists, such as Sodexo, Compass, and ARAMARK Services, increase their market share at the expense of self-operated health care managed services. One reason for this is that the larger contract companies have the economy of scale and a more sophisticated approach to quantity purchasing, menu management, and operating systems that help to reduce food and labor costs. A skilled independent foodservice operator has the advantage of being able to introduce changes immediately without having to support layers of regional and corporate employees.

The all-important tray line in health care foodservice.

Another trend in health care managed services is the arrival of the major quick-service chains. McDonald's, Pizza Hut Express, Burger King, and Dunkin' Donuts are just a few of the large companies that have joined forces with the contract managed services operators. Using branded quick-service leaders is a win-win situation for both the contract foodservice operator and the quick-service chain.

The chains benefit from long-term leases at very attractive rates compared with a restaurant site. Chains assess the staff size and patient and visitor count to determine the size of unit to install. Thus far, they have found that weekday lunches and dinners are good, but the numbers on weekends are disappointing.

In contrast, several hospitals are entering the pizza-delivery business: They hook up phone and fax ordering lines, and they hire part-time employees to deliver pizzas made on the premises. This ties in with the increasing emphasis on customer service. Patients' meals now feature "comfort foods," based on the concept that the simpler the food is, the better—hence, the resurgence of meat loaf, pot pies, meat and potatoes, and tuna salad, which contributes to customer satisfaction and makes patients feel at home and comfortable.

Some hospitals have adopted a "room service menu" concept for patients whose diets are not restricted. Here patients are often contacted before they arrive at the hospital so that the foodservice professionals may find out the likes and requests of future patients.

TECHNOLOGY SPOTLIGHT

Management by Exception

Cihan Cobanoglu, Ph.D., Dean, School of Hotel and Restaurant Management, University of South Florida, Sarasota-Manatee

While visiting industry trade shows and conferences over the past several years, I've noticed a growing number of business intelligence offerings that incorporate exception-based reporting tools into their solution. One simple reason for this trend is the large amount of data that is collected and maintained by hospitality organizations. Not only do hotels and restaurants store guest data, but they also store data related to their employees and other stakeholders, such as suppliers and vendors, blogs and bloggers, and review web sites.

For a long time, the challenge was to combine this data in a central location, mine it, and use it to predict the future. Data was often stored without any plans for further use, or it was used in isolation. Business intelligence tools have since emerged as a way to leverage this data to create a competitive advantage.

Exception-Based Approach

A traditional approach to data mining, and one that has had extreme success in bringing laser-focused insight to operations, is an enterprise-level, exception-based management and reporting solution. Exception-based reporting consolidates data from multiple end-points and systems across an enterprise and performs a rules-based analysis to provide exception reports to various stakeholders in the organization.

A key challenge in implementing a business intelligence and management-by-exception system is the integration of different systems. Following that is the importance of managing the rules that will create the exceptions. When too many noncritical exceptions are reported to management, their value will diminish, and over time those exceptions will not be taken seriously.

Solution Evolution

First-generation solutions focused on exceptions after the fact (that is, next business day). In most high-volume transaction-oriented environments like hospitality, managers receive exception-based information after the window of opportunity to affect an issue has already closed. In this scenario, the best that a manager can hope for is to view the exception report as a scorecard rather than a call to action.

Second-generation solutions focus on customized and real-time reporting. Mirus (**www.mirus.com**) offers a tool that allows users to create custom business rules based on data collected from the point of sale (POS). Another option, RealTime from Real Time Intelligence (www.jackbe.com), gathers information in the form of events and queries from property- and store-level systems, including the POS/PMS, access control, CCTV (closed-circuit TV), and facilities management, to processes this information constantly in real time against a sophisticated business-rules engine at the unit level.

The results of the analysis (the exceptions) are delivered to the appropriate person in real time. This intelligence enables management to affect a resolution before the issue becomes a statistic on tomorrow's report. Delivery may take the form of an SMS (Short Message Service) message to a cell phone, an e-mail to a PDA or standard inbox, telemetry displayed on a custom dashboard, or even a page or a phone call.

Practical Returns

Application of this technology delivers high returns in areas like labor management, compliance, loss prevention, service reparation, and information technology (IT) support. One simple advisory sent to a supervisor when any one of his or her employees is fifteen minutes away from entering overtime, coupled with metrics related to current and projected sales volume, check-ins/check-outs, or other similar information, can drastically reduce overtime and empower a manager to make informed decisions. This concept of targeted intelligence holds the promise of elevating the effectiveness of management by giving each manager, regardless of experience, the ability to perform with the experience of a seasoned colleague.

Implementing real-time exception-based reporting across the enterprise system is not easy or cheap. However, in an industry where profit margins are getting slimmer every year, an exception-based reporting system may pay for itself very quickly and help the company achieve a competitive advantage.

Business and Industry

Business and industry (B&I) managed services is one of the most dynamic segments of the managed services industry. In recent years, B&I foodservice has improved its image by becoming more colorful, with menus as interesting as commercial restaurants.

There are important terms to understand in B&I foodservice:

1. *Contractors*. **Contractors** are companies that operate foodservice for the client on a contractual basis. Most corporations contract with managed services companies because they are in manufacturing or some other service industry. Therefore, they engage professional managed services corporations to run their employee dining facilities.

2. *Self-operators*. **Self-operators** are companies that operate their own foodservice operations. In some cases, this is done because it is easier to control one's own operation; for example, it is easier to make changes to comply with special nutritional or other dietary requests.

A business and industry account of Sodexo.

An ARAMARK business and industry foodservice account.

3. *Liaison personnel.* **Liaison personnel** are responsible for translating corporate philosophy to the contractor and for overseeing the contractor to make certain that he or she abides by the terms of the contract.[18]

Contractors have approximately 80 percent of the B&I market. The remaining 20 percent is self-operated, but the trend is for more foodservice operations to be contracted out. The size of the B&I sector is approximately 30,000 units. To adapt to corporate downsizing and relocations, the B&I segment has offered foodservice in smaller units, rather than huge full-sized cafeterias. Another trend is the necessity for B&I foodservice to break even or, in some cases, make a profit. An interesting twist is the emergence of multitenant buildings, the occupants of which may all use a central facility. However, in today's turbulent business environment, there is a high vacancy rate in commercial office space. This translates into fewer guests for B&I operators in multitenant office buildings. As a result, some office buildings have leased space to commercial branded restaurants.

B&I managed services operators have responded to requests from corporate employees to offer more than the standard fast-food items of pizza and hamburgers; they want healthier food options offered, such as make-your-own sandwiches, salad bars, fresh fruit stations, and ethnic foods.

Most B&I managed services operators offer a number of types of service. The type of service is determined by the resources available: money, space, time, and expertise. Usually these resources are quite limited, which means that most operations use some form of cafeteria service.

B&I foodservice may be characterized in the following ways:

1. Full-service cafeteria with *straight line*, *scatter*, or *mobile systems*
2. *Limited-service cafeterias* offering parts of the full-service cafeteria, fast-food service, cart and mobile service, fewer dining rooms, and executive dining rooms

FOCUS ON MANAGED SERVICES

Mega-Event Management: The Olympics—Going for the Gold

Fred J. DeMicco, Professor and ARAMARK Chair, Department of Hotel, Restaurant and Institutional Management, University of Delaware, and Penn State Walter J. Conti Professor of HRIM

ARAMARK is a world leader in providing global managed services, including food, facility, and other support services. ARAMARK has leadership positions serving the business, education, health care, sports, entertainment, and recreation management segments. Related to sports, entertainment, and food service is "serving the world" at the Olympics.

ARAMARK has a long and rich history with the Olympic Games, dating back to 1968 when it served at the Mexico City Summer Games, the largest in history at the time. Since then, the company has managed services at more Olympic Games than any other company, earning its own "gold medal" performance at both the summer and winter games over the past four decades.

ARAMARK chefs and nutritionists develop a World Menu with more than 550 recipes designed to meet the needs of athletes from 200 different countries, with different ethnic and religious backgrounds and varying nutritional needs, to help them achieve their best during their Olympic performances.

For the third time, Dr. DeMicco is taking students to the Olympic Village to work for ARAMARK. In 1996, his students worked the Summer Games in Atlanta, and they traveled to Sydney to work in the 2000 Summer Games. With 1,500 different menu items available, twenty-four hours a day, the students will have their work cut out for them. Some of the stranger dishes that appeared on athletes' plates during the 2000 Sydney Olympics included kangaroo prosciutto, smoked emu, grilled mako shark, and goat vindaloo.

"The exposure to this type of event provides more learning than any other foodservice venture," Jerome Bill, of ARAMARK, says. "Usually a small city is built, operated for approximately thirty-three days, and then is taken down just as fast. The logistics are tremendous."

ARAMARK recruits and trains more than 6,500 persons to prepare and serve more than 5 million meals during the thirty-three days the Olympics and Para-Olympics take place. The grocery list for such an event is enormous. Some of the major ingredients that ARAMARK used included 576,000 eggs, 34,000 pounds of rice, 32,800 pounds of margarine, and 9,057 pounds of shredded cheddar cheese.

"Where else can you welcome 15,000 of the best in the world into your home for dinner? It is truly the ultimate display of blending one's background, classroom experience, and human nature into an unforgettable learning environment. Students learn more than just serving and cooking; they reach the brink of fully understanding the true meaning of hospitality," said Marc Bruno, MBA, ARAMARK.

The students were able to interact with elite athletes in the world in a fast-paced and constantly changing environment. They were able to be part of providing foodservice that met the unique cultural and nutritional needs of athletes from more than 200 countries. They went in every day knowing that their jobs were critical to each athlete's peak performance.

According to a student participant, "The Olympics allowed me to get an inside view of how a mega event was run, the problems that came up, and how they were overcome. Being in the Olympic Village introduced me to working with people of many different cultures. I am currently working for NBC Olympics in the Games Services department. I am really looking forward to being part of another Olympic Games."

▶ Check Your Knowledge

1. What roles other than those strictly related to foodservice does the foodservice manager perform?

2. Briefly explain some of the tasks the foodservice manager performs. What makes each task so important?

Managed Services Other Than Food

Many companies such as Sodexo have recognized the potential to increase their market opportunities by developing service capabilities beyond food. This also offers hospitality managers the opportunity to expand their career paths as well. Typically, hospitals, colleges, schools, and businesses outsource other service departments the same as they do food. Companies on the cutting edge are able to offer clients broader packages of services. These services often come under the area of facilities management[19] and offer the following services:

- Housekeeping/custodial/environment services
- Maintenance and engineering
- Grounds and landscaping
- Procurement and materials management
- Office and mail services
- Concierge services
- Patient transportation services (hospitals)

Many colleges and universities recognize that this is an area for career opportunities and are developing courses and programs surrounding the area of facilities management. Managers who work in the managed services segment of the industry have the advantage of learning about several disciplines. In doing so, they increase their career growth potential and can find career paths similar to those available in the lodging segment of the industry.

Leisure and Recreation

The leisure and recreation[20] segment of managed services may be the most unique and the most fun part of the foodservice industry in which to work.

Leisure and recreation foodservice operations include stadiums, arenas, theme parks, national parks, state parks, zoos, aquariums, and other venues where food and beverage are provided for large numbers of people. The customers are usually in a hurry, so the big challenge of the foodservice segment is to offer the product in a very short period of time. The average professional sporting event lasts for only two to three hours of time.

What makes this segment unique and fun is the opportunity to be part of a professional sporting event, a rock concert, a circus, or other event in a stadium or arena. There is also the choice of working in a national or state park and being part of the great outdoors. The roar of the crowd and the excitement of the event make this a very stimulating place to work. Imagine *getting paid* to see the Super Bowl versus *paying* to see the Super Bowl.

Stadium Points of Service

Leisure and recreation facilities usually have several points of service where food and beverage are provided. In the typical stadium, a vendor yells, "Here, get your hot dog here!" to the fans in the stands, while on the concourse other fans get their food and beverage from concession stands. These stands offer everything from branded—meaning well-known brands—foods to hot dogs and hamburgers to local cuisine. For example, in Philadelphia the cheesesteak sandwich is popular, whereas in Baltimore, crabcake sandwiches are favored by fans. Another place for people to get food is in a restaurant, which most stadiums have as a special area. In some cases, fans must be members of the restaurant; in other cases, fans can buy special tickets that provide them with access to this facility. These restaurants are like any other except that they provide unobstructed views of the playing area.

The other major point of service is the food and beverage offered in the premium seating areas known as superboxes, suites, and skyboxes. These premium seating areas are usually leased by corporations to entertain corporate guests and customers. In each of these areas, branded and gourmet food and beverage service is provided for the guests. These facilities are capable of holding thirty to forty guests and usually have an area where the food is set up buffet style and a seating area where the guests can see the sporting or other event. In a large, outdoor stadium, there could be as many as sixty or seventy of these superbox-type facilities. For stadium foodservices, more tickets are being placed on mobile devices to enter the stadium/arena; once in the stadium, there are promotions texted to fans, and GPS locations are used in stadiums for vendor ordering.

In summary, a large stadium or arena could have vendors in the stands, concession outlets, restaurants, and superboxes all going at once and serving upward of 60,000 to 70,000 fans. Feeding all these people takes tremendous planning and organization on the part of the foodservice department. The companies that have many of the contracts for stadiums and arenas are ARAMARK, Fine Host, Sodexo, Compass Group, and Delaware North.

Other Facilities

Besides stadiums and arenas, food and beverage service is provided in several other types of facilities by the same major managed service companies that service stadiums. Most of the U.S. national parks are contracted to these companies. These parks have hotels, restaurants, snack bars, gift shops, and a myriad of other service outlets where tourists can spend their money. In addition to parks, other venues where food and beverage are offered include zoos, aquariums, tennis tournaments such as the U.S. Open in New York, and professional golf tournaments. All these events involve big numbers of people. For example, a professional golf event, which lasts a week including practice time, will have upward of 25,000 spectators per day watching the pros play. Tournament events are similar to stadium and arena foodservice operations because they also include concession stands, food and beverage areas for the fans, and "corporate tents" for special catering and company guests.

Advantages and Disadvantages

A foodservice career in this segment has several advantages, which include the unique opportunity to see professional and amateur sporting events to your heart's delight; to hear the roar of the crowd; to be in rural, scenic areas and enjoy the great outdoors; to provide a diverse set of services for the guests or fans; and to have a set work schedule.

The disadvantages of this segment include very large crowds of people to serve in a short time; a work schedule of weekends, holidays, and nights; the chance to give only impersonal service; less opportunity to be creative with food; seasonal employment; and an on-season/off-season work schedule.

Leisure and recreation foodservice is a very exciting, unique part of the hospitality industry that offers employees very different opportunities from standard hotel and restaurant jobs. With the current trend toward building new stadiums and arenas around the country, this segment offers many new career openings.

Trends in Managed Services

- College and university foodservice managers face increasing challenges. *Restaurants and Institutions* magazine asked several managers to identify some of those challenges. In general, managers mentioned trying to balance rising costs with tighter dollars. Bill Rigan, foodservice center manager at Oklahoma State University, Stillwater, points out two main challenges: the reduction of revenues from board-plan sales and increased costs such as food and utilities. He dealt with these challenges by recognizing that because he could not change the utilities or hourly rates for employees, he would have to maximize purchasing potential. He also made optimal usage of "from scratch" cooking, convenience foods, and more efficient labor scheduling.

- Martha Willis, foodservice director at Tennessee Technological University, Cookesville, sees declining enrollment and a reduction in state funding as challenges. This translates to a cutback in services and more pressure to produce a bigger bottom line. Martha intends to achieve this by filling vacant full-time positions with part-time and student employees. The savings made by not paying full-time employee benefits can amount to 30 percent of a person's wage.

- Increased use of campus cards (declining balance or debit cards)

- Increased use of grab and go—and even room service, for instance—to dorms or offices and before sporting events

- Increased use of foodservice carts at vantage points to provide service to students who may not be able to reach the main buildings in time for refreshments before the next class

- Dueling demands for foodservice managers—from students who want more freshly prepared foods in convenient locations and from administrators who want more revenue from existing sources

- Twenty-four-hour foodservice for those clients who need round-the-clock service

- Increased business in health care and nursing homes. As the population ages, there is an increased need to provide services for this important and growing segment.

- Proliferation of branded concepts in all segments of managed services, including military, school and college, business and industry, health care, and airport

- Development of home meal replacement options in each segment of the managed services sector, as a way to increase revenue

- Increasing use of fresh product. People are more health conscious and want healthy produce.

- Increased use of "social media" to promote sales and to communicate with guests

- Foodservice offering more local and sustainable menu items and practices

CASE STUDY

Gas Leak

The kitchen at a major corporation's managed services business account includes several gas and electric stoves, ovens, broilers, steamers, grills, and other appliances. On average, the kitchen serves 500 lunches. At 10:15 A.M. on a Tuesday in December, a gas leak prompts the gas company to cut off the gas supply.

Discussion Question

1. What can be done to offer the best possible lunch food and service?

CASE STUDY

Chaos in the Kitchen

Jane is the foodservice director at an on-campus dining service that feeds 800 students per meal for breakfast, lunch, and dinner. Jane arrives at her office at 7:00 A.M. (half an hour before breakfast begins) only to find many problems.

After listening to her phone messages, she finds that her breakfast cashier and one of her two breakfast dishroom employees have called in sick. The cashier position is essential, and the second dishroom person is necessary at 8:15 A.M. when the students leave to go to their 8:30 A.M. classes.

(continued)

CASE STUDY (continued)

Then, the executive chef tells Jane that one of their two walk-in refrigerators is not working properly, so some of the food is above the safe temperature of 40°F.

The lead salad person later comes to her, saying that one of the three ice machines is not working. Hence, there will not be enough ice to ice down the salad bars and to use for cold beverages at lunch.

Last, the catering supervisor tells Jane that he has just found out that there was a misunderstanding with the bakery that supplies their upscale desserts. The desserts were requested by the president of the university for a luncheon he is having that day; however, because the employee at the bakery wrote the wrong delivery date, the desserts would not be delivered. This will cause the president to be angry.

Discussion Questions

1. How should Jane handle being short a cashier and a dishroom person at breakfast?

2. What should Jane do with the food in the defective refrigerator? Should the food that is measured to be above 40°F be saved?

3. What are Jane's options concerning the ice shortage?

4. How should Jane handle the president's function, knowing that the requested desserts have not been delivered?

5. If the special dessert cannot be purchased in time, how should the catering supervisor approach this situation when speaking with the president's office?

6. What can be done to ensure that mistakes, such as the one made by the bakery employee, do not happen again?

Summary

1. Managed services operations include segments such as airlines, military, schools and colleges, health care facilities, and businesses.
2. Food has become scarce on short and medium domestic flights. Most airlines have food prepared by a contractor, such as Dobbs International or Sky Chefs.
3. Service to the military includes feeding troops and officers in clubs, dining halls, and hospitals as well as out in the field. Direct vendor delivery, menu management, prepared foods, and fast-food chains located on the base have met new trends in military foodservice.
4. Schools are either equipped with on-site kitchens and dining rooms or receive food from a central commissary. They try to balance salability with good nutrition. Today, nutrition education is a required subject in school.
5. College and university managed services operations include residence halls, cafeterias, student unions, faculty clubs, convenience stores, and catering.
6. The responsibilities of a foodservice manager are very complex. He or she is in charge of employee relations, human resource management, budgeting, safety administration, sanitation, and inventory.
7. Health care managed services operations need to provide numerous special meals to patients with very specific dietary requirements and

nutritious meals in a limited time period for employees. The main areas of concern for health care managed services operations are tray lines and help-yourself food stations.

8. Business and industry managed services operations either operate with a full-service

cafeteria or limited-service cafeteria. The type of service is determined by money, space, and time available.

9. Leisure and recreation foodservice offers yet more career opportunities. It is often available at several points of service.

Key Words and Concepts

batch cooking
commercial foodservice
contractors
daily rate
liaison personnel

managed services
National School Lunch Program (NSLP)
nutrition education programs
self-operators
tray line

Review Questions

1. What are managed services operations?
2. List and explain features that distinguish managed services operations from commercial ones.
3. Describe the issues that schools are currently facing concerning school food service.
4. Explain the term *National School Lunch Program* (NSLP).

5. Identify recent trends in college foodservice management.
6. What are the pros and cons concerning fast-food chains on campus?
7. Briefly explain the complex challenges for health care managed services operations.

Internet Exercises

1. Organization: **ARAMARK**
   Web site: **www.aramark.com**
   Summary: ARAMARK is "a global leader in managed services" according to its web site. ARAMARK is an outsourcing company that provides services ranging from everyday catering to corporate apparel.
   (a) Click the "Careers" link. Go to ARAMARK's Web site and see what they are doing under the Social Responsibility heading.
   (b) What are some of the characteristics that make a star of the month?

2. Organization: **Sodexo**
   Web site: **www.sodexousa.com**
   Summary: Sodexo offers a full range of outsourcing solutions and is a leading food and facilities management services company in North America.
   (a) What corporate services does Sodexo offer?
   (b) Look at the current opportunities (at Sodexo or ARAMARK) within your area.

Apply Your Knowledge

1. From the sample operating statement (Figure 4), calculate the labor cost percentage by taking total labor cost and dividing by total sales × 100. Remember the formula:

$$\frac{\text{Cost}}{\text{Sales}} \times 100$$

2. Consider a retail operation at a local college where a grilled chicken combo, which consists of a grilled chicken breast, fries, and a 20-oz. soda, is on the menu. Find out the cost of the ingredients and write out everything needed for the combo, including its service. What is your cost price? How much would you charge customers for the item to make a reasonable profit?

Suggested Activity

Create a sample menu for a day at an elementary or high school. Then, compare your items to the MyPlate food guide and the recommended daily servings. How does your menu measure up?

Endnotes

1. Personal conversation with Susan Pillmeier, ARAMARK, and John Lee, Sodexo, July 28, 2005.
2. Gate Gourmet, *About Us*, www.gategourmet.com/gategourmet/index.php?option=com_content&view=article&id=377&Itemid=54 (accessed May 1, 2011).
3. LSG Sky Chefs, *About Us*, www.lsgskychefs.com/en/about-us.html (accessed November 8, 2011).
4. Ibid.
5. "Channeling the college environment: Viewing a military installation like a college campus can help foodservice enhance the retail experience," *Foodservice Director* (March 15, 2011): 6.
6. "Cafeteria boot camp: Fort Campbell's hospital cafeteria focuses on healthy dining after renovation," *Foodservice Director* (March 15, 2011): 8.
7. "Smart choices," *Foodservice Director* (April 15, 2011): 10.
8. United States Department of Agriculture, Food and Nutrition Service, *National School Lunch Program*, October 2011, www.fns.usda.gov/cnd/lunch/AboutLunch/NSLPFactSheet.pdf (accessed April 28, 2011).
9. Sahra Bahari, "Students can expect healthier selection," *Fort Worth Star-Telegram*, August 12, 2007.
10. United States Department of Agriculture, Food and Nutrition Service, *National School Lunch Program*, October 2011, www.fns.usda.gov/cnd/lunch/AboutLunch/NSLPFactSheet.pdf (accessed April 28, 2011).
11. "Teaching moments: School's garden spurs nutrition program for students," *Foodservice Director* (December 15, 2010): 8.
12. The National Association of College & University Food Services, *About NACUFS*, www.nacufs.org/about-nacufs-overview (accessed April 28, 2011).
13. "Smart choices," *Foodservice Director* (April 15, 2011): 1.
14. Based on an interview with Steve Dobrowolski, Retail Operations Director, ARAMARK, University of South Florida, April 27, 2011.
15. ARAMARK, *About ARAMARK*, www.aramark.com/aboutaramark/ (accessed April 28, 2010).
16. FSD Staff, "Environmental Awareness," *FoodService Director* 22(8), August 15, 2009, p. 58.
17. Ibid.
18. Personal correspondence with John Lee, director of college and external relations, Sodexho, September 13, 2005.
19. Ibid.
20. Courtesy of David Tucker.

Glossary

Contractor   A company that operates a foodservice for the client on a contractual basis.

Liaison personnel   Workers who are responsible for translating corporate philosophy for the contractor and for overseeing the contractor to be sure that he or she abides by the terms of the contract.

Managed services   Services that can be leased to professional management companies.

National School Lunch Program   The program that provides free lunches to students from a certain income level.

Nutrition education programs   Programs ensuring that food served in school cafeterias follows the nutrition standards set by government programs.

Self-operator   A company that manages its own foodservice operations.

Tray line   The line of trays in hospital meal preparation where items are added to the tray to complete the meal order.

Photo Credits

Credits are listed in the order of appearance.

Yakov Stavchansky/Fotolia LLC
Jamie Pham/Alamy
Sodexho
Monkey Business Images/Shutterstock
John T Takai/Shutterstock
Alamy Images Royalty Free

ARAMARK Educational Services, LLC
Regynald Washington
age fotostock/SuperStock
Sodexho
ARAMARK Educational Services, LLC
Frederick J. DeMicco

Recreation, Attractions, and Clubs

Recreation, Attractions, and Clubs

OBJECTIVES

After reading and studying this text, you should be able to:

- Discuss the relationship of recreation and leisure to wellness.

- Explain the origins and extent of government-sponsored recreation.

- Distinguish between commercial and noncommercial recreation.

- Name and describe various types of recreational clubs.

- Identify the major U.S. theme parks.

- Describe the operations of a country club.

Recreational activities include both active and passive activities. Passive activities include all kinds of sports—team and individual. Baseball, softball, football, basketball, volleyball, tennis, swimming, jogging, skiing, hiking, aerobics, rock climbing, and camping are all active forms of recreation. Passive recreational activities include reading, fishing, playing and listening to music, gardening, playing computer games, and watching television or movies. **Recreation** *is an integral part of our nation's total social, economic, and natural resource environment. It is a basic component of our lives and well-being.*[1]

Recreation, Leisure, and Wellness

As postindustrial society has become more complex, life has become more stressed. The need to develop the wholeness of the person has become increasingly important. Compared to a generation ago, the stress levels of business executives are much higher. The term *burnout*—and indeed the word *stress*—has become a part of our everyday vocabulary only in recent years. Recreation is all about creating a balance, a harmony in life that will maintain wellness and wholeness.

Recreation allows people to have fun together and to form lasting relationships built on the experiences they have enjoyed together. This recreational process is called *bonding*. Bonding is hard to describe, yet the experience of increased interpersonal feeling for friends or business associates as a result of a recreational pursuit is common. These relationships result in personal growth and development.

The word *recreation* implies the use of time in a manner designed for therapeutic refreshment of one's body or mind.[2] Recreation is synonymous with lifestyle and the development of a positive attitude. An example of this is the increased feeling of well-being experienced after a recreational activity. Some people make the mistake of trying to pursue happiness as a personal goal. It is not enough for a person to say, "I want to be happy; therefore, I will recreate." Nathaniel Hawthorne wrote in the midnineteenth century: "Happiness in this world, when it comes, comes incidentally. Make it the object of pursuit, and it leads us on a wild goose chase, and it is never attained. Follow some other object, and very possibly we may find that we have caught happiness without dreaming of it."[3]

Recreation is a process that seeks to establish a milieu conducive to the discovery and development of characteristics that can lead to happiness. Happiness and well-being, therefore, are incidental outcomes of recreation. Thus, happiness may be enhanced by the pursuit of recreational activities. Personal recreational goals are equally as important as any other business or personal goals. These goals might include running a mile in under six minutes or maintaining a baseball batting average above .300. The fact that a

Windsurfing is definitely an active recreational activity.

person sets and strives to achieve goals requires personal organization. This helps improve the quality of life.

Leisure is best described as time free from work, or discretionary time. Some recreation professionals use the words *leisure* and *recreation* interchangeably, while others define leisure as the "productive," "creative," or "contemplative" use of free time. History shows again and again a direct link between leisure and the advancement of civilization. Hard work alone leaves no time for becoming civilized. Ironically, however, the opportunity to be at leisure is the direct result of increased technological and productivity advancements.

Government-Sponsored Recreation

Hiking is a great exercise and an ideal way to get back to nature.

Various levels of government that constitute **government-sponsored recreation** are intertwined, yet distinct, in the parks, recreation, and leisure services. The founding fathers of America said it best when they affirmed the right to life, liberty, and the pursuit of happiness in the Declaration of Independence. Government raises revenue from income taxes, sales taxes, and property taxes. Additionally, government raises special revenue from recreation-related activities such as automobile and recreational vehicles, boats, motor fuels, **transient occupancy taxes (TOTs)** on hotel accommodations, state lotteries, and others. The monies are distributed among the various recreation- and leisure-related organizations at the federal, state/provincial, city, and town levels. Recreation and leisure activities are extremely varied, ranging from cultural pursuits such as museums, arts and crafts, music, theater, and dance to sports (individual and team), outdoor recreation, amusement parks, theme parks, community centers, playgrounds, libraries, and gardens. People select recreational pursuits based on their interests and capabilities.

Park and recreation leaders confront daunting challenges at a time when leisure and recreational resources are highly valued community assets. Yet, securing adequate funding for staff and services can be a juggling act.[4] The following are some of the issues with which recreation professionals must deal:

- Comprehensive recreation planning
- Land classification systems
- Federal revenue sharing
- Acquisition- and development-funding programs
- Land-use planning and zoning
- State and local financing
- Off-road vehicle impacts and policy
- Use of easements for recreation

- Designation of areas (such as wilderness, wild and scenic rivers, national trails, nature preserves)
- Differences in purposes and resources (of the numerous local, state/provincial, and federal agencies that control more than one-third of the nation's land, much of which is used for recreation)

National Parks in the United States

The prevailing image of a **national park** is one of grand natural playgrounds, such as Yellowstone National Park, but there is much more to parks than that.[5] The United States has designated 397 national park units throughout the country, including a rich diversity of places and settings. The **National Parks Service** was founded in 1916 by Congress to conserve park resources and to provide for their use by the public in a way that leaves them unimpaired for the enjoyment of future generations. In addition to the better-known parks such as Yellowstone and Yosemite, the Parks Service also manages many other heritage attractions, including the Freedom Trail in Boston, Independence Hall in Philadelphia, the Antietam National Battlefield in Sharpsburg, Maryland, and the USS *Arizona* Memorial at Pearl Harbor in Hawaii. The Parks Service is also charged with caring for myriad cultural artifacts, including ancient pottery, sailing vessels, colonial-period clothing, and Civil War documents.

The ever-expanding mandate of the Parks Service also calls for understanding and preserving the environment. It monitors the ecosystem from the Arctic tundra to coral atolls, researches the air and water quality around the nation, and participates in global studies on acid rain, climate change, and biological diversity. The idea of preserving exceptional lands for public use as national parks arose after the Civil War when America's receding wilderness left unique national resources vulnerable to exploitation. Recent years have seen phenomenal growth in the system, with three new areas created in the last twenty years. These include new kinds of parks, such as urban recreational areas, free-flowing rivers, long-distance trails, and historic sites honoring our nation's social achievements. The system's current roster of 397 areas covers more than 80 million acres of land, with individual areas ranging in size from the 13-million-acre Wrangell–St. Elias National Park and Preserve in Alaska to the Thaddeus Kosciuszko National Memorial (a Philadelphia row house commemorating a hero of the American Revolution), which covers two one-hundredths of an acre.

Annual visitation to the National Park system approaches 300 million visitors, who take advantage of the full range of services and programs.[6] The focus once placed on preserving the scenery of the most natural parks has shifted as the system has grown and changed. Today, emphasis is placed on preserving the vitality of each park's ecosystem and on the protection of unique or endangered plant and animal species.

The splendor of nature awaits us in our national parks.

National Park Management

The National Park Service is in the Department of the Interior and is overseen by a director who reports to the Secretary of the Interior. There are 397 National Parks divided into seven regions. The *Director* of the National Park Service establishes and approves service-wide natural resource policies and standards. The Director is ultimately responsible for establishing natural and cultural resource programs that conserve natural resources unimpaired for the enjoyment of future generations and for ensuring that such programs are in compliance with directives, policies, and laws.[7]

Each National Park has a superintendent, and the superintendent is responsible for understanding the park's resources and their condition. The superintendent is responsible for establishing and managing park backcountry-management programs and ensuring that they comply with directives, policies, and laws. The superintendent initiates the development of backcountry recreational use plans as necessary. The superintendent should coordinate the visitor use management plans with neighboring land managers as appropriate. Each superintendent with designated or eligible wilderness should designate a wilderness coordinator to review all activities ongoing in the wilderness.[8]

The National Park Service budget for 2011 is $3.14 billion, and it employs a staff of 21,501. Beyond these appropriated funds, the National Park Service is also authorized to collect and retain revenue from specified sources:[9]

- Recreation fees: approximately $190 million per year
- Park concessions franchise fees: approximately $60 million per year
- Filming and photography special use fees: approximately $1.2 million per year
- Additional funding comes from individual donations.

Managing a national park is a complex task that involves skilled professionals from many fields. Park management is not achieved by merely relying on experience and instincts. Whenever possible, it is based on solid scientific research, conducted not only by park staff, but by universities and independent researchers as well. Financial constraints are always an issue while managing our national parks.[10]

The Great Smoky Mountains National Park is the most visited of the National Parks, receiving about 9.5 million visitors a year. This park has the following main operating departments:

Ranger—rangers provide the chief response and visitor protection and are the sole law enforcement in the park. Rangers operate the camp grounds, perform search and rescue, and provide emergency medical services.

Resource Education—creates curriculum and delivers courses ranging from elementary students to adults and seniors. Known as "walks, talks, and tours," they cover pre-visitation to guided tours of the park.

Resource Management and Science—is responsible for the ongoing health of the natural and cultural resources.

Facility Management—responsible for a $2 billion infrastructure of roads, 350 nonhistoric buildings, and 72 bathrooms.

Administration—takes care of human resources, purchasing, contracts and property management.

Remember that the park service has the mission to conserve natural resources. This can prove very challenging, as nonnative pests and diseases threaten the biological diversity of the park, such as the case of the wolly adelgid, an aphid-like pest that kills hemlock trees. The Great Smoky Mountains National Park has about 75,000 acres of hemlock trees that are likely to be killed by these pests unless something can be found to stop the pest quickly.

Let's look at another National Park, Cape Lookout National Seashore. There are natural and cultural resources and numerous historic structures that are managed within the 56 miles of seashore. In all national parks, the need for efficient, innovative park management is especially important in order to protect the very best of this nation's rich heritage. And the law of the land dictates that, in turn, these resources, and the American public that owns them, deserve the very best that the National Park Service can give them.[11]

The National Park Service is required to maintain an up-to-date General Management Plan (GMP) for each unit of the park system. The purpose of each GMP is to ensure that the park has a clearly defined direction for asset preservation and visitor use. This foundation for decision-making is to be developed by an interdisciplinary team, in consultation with relevant offices within the Park Service, other federal and state agencies, interested parties, and the general public. The GMP should be based on use of scientific information related to existing and potential asset conditions, visitor experiences, environmental impacts, and relative costs of alternative courses of action. The GMP should take the long view, which may project many years into the future, when dealing with time frames. The plan should consider the park in its full ecological, scenic, and cultural contexts as a unit of the National Park Service and as part of a surrounding region.[12]

No two days are alike in the park service. On one day, a meth lab may be discovered; on another, a tornado may create havoc or visitors may get lost and need rescuing. Yet, every day at the Great Smoky Mountains National Park there are 8,000 visitors to take care of at the visitor center. Each visitor has questions ranging from "Where are the bathrooms?" to "Can I see a bear?"

Public Recreation and Parks Agencies

During the early part of the nineteenth century in the United States, the parks movement expanded rapidly as a responsibility of government and voluntary organizations. By the early 1900s, fourteen cities had made provisions for supervised play facilities, and the playground movement gained momentum. Private initiative and financial support were instrumental in convincing city government to provide tax dollars to build and maintain new play areas.

About the same time, municipal parks were created in a number of cities. Boston established the first metropolitan park system in 1892. In 1898, the New England Association of Park Superintendents (predecessor of the American

Institute of Park Executives) was established to bring together park superintendents and promote their professional concerns. Increasingly, the concept that city governments should provide recreation facilities, programs, and services became widely accepted. Golf courses, swimming pools, bathing beaches, picnic areas, winter sports facilities, game fields, and playgrounds were constructed.

▶ Check Your Knowledge

1. Name a few parks in the United States and in Canada. What are some characteristics that make the parks you named special?

2. Name your favorite park. Share with your classmates why it is your favorite.

Commercial Recreation—Attractions

Recreation management came of age in the 1920s and 1930s, when recreation and social programs were offered as a community service. Colleges and universities began offering degree programs in this area. Both public and private sector recreation management has grown rapidly since 1950.

Commercial recreation, often called eco- or adventure tourism, provides residents and visitors with access to an area's spectacular wilderness through a variety of guided outdoor activities. Specifically, commercial recreation is defined as outdoor recreational activities provided on a fee-for-service basis, with a focus on experiences associated with the natural environment.[13] Commercial recreation includes theme parks, attractions, and clubs.

Theme Parks

The idea of theme parks all began in the 1920s in Buena Park, California, with a small berry farm and tea room. As owner Walter Knott's restaurant business grew, different attractions were added to the site to keep waiting customers amused. After a gradual expansion, over eighty years after its humble beginnings, Knott's Berry Farm has become the largest independent theme park in the United States.

Today, Knott's Berry Farm is 150 acres of rides, attractions, live entertainment, historical exhibits, dining, and specialty shops. The park features six themes—Ghost Town, Indian Trails, Fiesta Village, the Boardwalk, Wild Water Wilderness, and Camp Snoopy, which is the official home of Snoopy and the Peanuts characters. In addition, the California Marketplace is located right outside the park, and offers fourteen unique shops and restaurants.

Knott's Berry Farm has truly been a great influence on the American theme park industry. Hundreds of parks, both independent and corporate

Street basketball is a great team sport.

A water park is an example of a single-themed park.

owned, started to develop following the birth of Knott's. Creator Walter Knott may have figured out why amusement parks became so popular so quickly. He was quoted as saying, "The more complex the world becomes, the more people turn to the past and the simple things in life. We [the amusement park operators] try to give them some of those things."[14] Even with the ever-increasing competition, Knott's continues to attract guests with its authentic historical artifacts, relaxed atmosphere, emphasis on learning, famous food, varied entertainment, innovative rides, and specialty shopping.[15]

Knott's Berry Farm is now owned and operated by Cedar Fair Entertainment Company.

Size and Scope of the Theme Park Industry

Visiting **theme parks** has always been a favorite tourist activity. Theme parks attempt to create an atmosphere of another place and time, and they usually emphasize one dominant theme around which architecture, landscape, rides, shows, foodservices, costumed personnel, and retailing are orchestrated. In this definition, the concept of *themes* is crucial to the operation of the parks, with rides, entertainment, and food all used to create several different environments.[16]

Theme parks and attractions vary according to theme, which might be historical, cultural, geographical, and so on. Some parks and attractions focus on a single theme, such as the marine zoological Sea World parks. Other parks and attractions focus on multiple themes, such as King's Island in Ohio, a family entertainment center divided into seven theme areas: International Street, Oktoberfest, Rivertown, Planet Snoopy, Coney Mall, Boomerang Bay, and Dinosaurs Alive. Another example is Great America in California, a 100-acre family entertainment center that evokes North America's past in five themes: Home Town Square, Yukon Territory, Yankee Harbor, Country Fair, and Orleans Place.

An abundance of theme parks are located throughout the United States. These parks have a variety of attractions, from animals and sea life to thrill rides and motion simulators. There are parks with educational themes and parks where people go simply to have a good time.

Many of the country's most well known parks are located in Florida. Walt Disney World, Sea World, Water Mania, Wet 'n Wild, and Universal Studios are just a few of the many parks located in Orlando. Busch Gardens and Adventure Island are both in Tampa.

Busch Gardens, located in both Tampa, Florida, and Williamsburg, Virginia, is perhaps the most well known of the animal-themed parks. Busch Gardens is like a zoo with a twist. It features equal amounts of thrill rides and animal attractions. Guests can take a train ride through the Serengeti Plains, where zebras and antelope run wild, hop aboard a giant tube ride through the Congo River rapids, or ride on one of the parks' many world-record-holding roller coasters.

Many cities in the United States are well known for their festivals, which bring in droves of vacationers year after year. One of the most well known is Mardi Gras (Fat Tuesday) in New Orleans. Mardi Gras began more than a hundred years ago as a carnival and has evolved into a world-renowned party. Mardi Gras takes place every year in February, the day before Ash Wednesday, the beginning of Lent. The days leading up to Fat Tuesday are filled with wild parades, costume contests, concerts, and overall partying. The famous Bourbon Street is the scene for most of the party-going crowd, and it is often too crowded even to walk around. Beads are big at Mardi Gras, and thousands are given out each year. The culture of New Orleans greatly adds to the festiveness of Mardi Gras, because traditional jazz and blues can always be heard on most street corners.

Orcas entertain the crowd at SeaWorld.

Another famous site of interest is the Grand Ole Opry in Nashville, Tennessee. The Grand Ole Opry is a live radio show in which country music guests are featured. Begun more than seventy-five years ago, the Grand Ole Opry is what made Nashville the "Music City." Since the Opry's start, Nashville created a theme park, Opryland (closed in 1997), and a hotel, the Opryland Resort. Famous musicians come from all over the world to showcase their talents, and tourists flock from everywhere to hear the sounds of the Opry and see the sites that Nashville has to offer.

Introducing Walt Disney: A Man with a Vision

In 1923, at the age of twenty-one, Walt Disney arrived in Los Angeles from Kansas City to start a new business. The first endeavor of Walt Disney and his brother Roy was a series of shorts (a brief film shown before a feature-length movie) called *Alice Comedies,* which featured a child actress playing with animated characters. Realizing that something new was needed to capture the audience, Walt Disney conjured up the concept of a mouse character. In 1927, Disney began a series called *Oswald the Lucky Rabbit.* It was well received by the public, but Disney lost the rights as a result of a dispute with his distributor.

Walt Disney.

Mickey and Minnie Mouse first appeared in *Steamboat Willie,* which also incorporated music and sound, on November 18, 1928. Huge audiences were ecstatic about the work of the Disney Brothers, who became overnight successes.

During the next few years, Walt and Roy made many Mickey Mouse films, which earned them enough to develop other projects, including full-length motion pictures in Technicolor.

According to Disney, "Disneyland really began when my two daughters were very young. Saturday was always Daddy's Day, and I would take them to the merry-go-round and sit on a bench eating peanuts while they rode. And sitting there alone, I felt there should be something built, some kind of family park where parents and children could have fun together."[17]

Walt's original dream was not easy to bring to reality. During the bleak war years, not only was much of his overseas market closed, but the steady stream of income that paid for innovation dried up. However, even during the bleak years, Walt never gave up. Instead, he was excited to learn of the public's interest in movie studios and the possibility of opening the studios to allow the public to visit the birthplace of Snow White, Pinocchio, and other Disney characters.

After its creation, Disneyland had its growing pains—larger-than-expected opening day crowds, long lines at the popular rides, and a cash flow that was so tight that the cashiers had to rush the admission money to the bank to make payroll. Fortunately, since those early days, Disneyland and the Disney characters have become a part of the American dream.

By the early 1960s, Walt had turned most of his attention from film to real estate. Because he was upset when cheap motels and souvenir shops popped up around Disneyland, for his next venture, Walt Disney World, he bought 27,500 acres around the park. The center of Walt Disney World was to be the Experimental Prototype Community of Tomorrow (Epcot). Regrettably, Epcot and Walt Disney World were his dying dreams; Walt Disney succumbed to cancer in 1966.

However, Walt's legacy carries on. The ensuing years since Walt's death have included phenomenal Disney successes with Epcot, movies, a TV station, the Disney Channel, Disney stores, and Disney's Hollywood Studios theme park (formerly Disney–MGM Studios). In April 1992, EuroDisneyland, now Disneyland Paris, opened near Paris. For a variety of reasons (location, cost, climate, and culture), it was initially a failure, until his Royal Highness Prince Al Waleed Bin Talal Bin Abdula of Saudi Arabia purchased 25 percent of the Disneyland Paris Resort.

Both Walt Disney World and Disneyland have excellent college programs that enable selected students to work during the summer months in a variety of hotel, foodservice, and related park positions. Disney has also introduced a faculty internship that allows faculty to intern in a similar variety of positions.

Walt Disney World is composed of four major theme parks: Magic Kingdom, Epcot, Disney's Animal Kingdom, and Disney's Hollywood Studios (formerly Disney–MGM Studios), with more than 100 attractions, 23 resort hotels themed as faraway lands, spectacular nighttime entertainment, and vast shopping, dining, and recreation facilities that cover thousands of acres in this tropical paradise.

Walt Disney World includes tennis courts, championship golf, marinas, swimming pools, jogging and bike trails, water skiing, and motor boating. The resort also offers a unique zoological park and bird sanctuary on Discovery Island in the middle of Bay Lake that is alive with birds, monkeys, and alligators; hundreds of restaurants, lounges, and food courts; a nightclub metropolis to please nearly any musical palate; a starry-eyed tribute to 1930s Hollywood; and even bass fishing. Walt Disney World is always full of new surprises: It now features an unusual water adventure park, a "snow-covered" mountain with a ski resort theme called Blizzard Beach.

The Disney hotels are architecturally exciting and offer a number of amenities. The fun-filled Disney's All-Star Sports Resort and Disney's colorful All-Star Music Resort are categorized as value-class hotels. Disney's Wilderness Lodge is one of the park's jewels, with its impressive tall-timber atrium lobby and rooms built around a Rocky Mountain–like geyser pool. In all, the park has a cast of thousands of hosts, hostesses, and entertainers famous for their warm smiles and commitment to making every night an especially good one for Disney guests.

There is more to enjoy than ever at Walt Disney World in Mickey's PhilharMagic, which incorporated new 3D movie technology in the Fantasyland area of the Magic Kingdom; Splash Mountain, a popular flume ride in Adventureland at the Magic Kingdom; Mission: SPACE, a motion simulator ride at Epcot that mimics what an astronaut experiences; and, at Disney's Hollywood Studios, the ultimate thriller, the Twilight Zone Tower of Terror.

Walt Disney World.

Magic Kingdom

The heart of Walt Disney World and its first famous theme park is the Magic Kingdom. It is a giant theatrical stage where guests become part of exciting Disney adventures. It is also the home of Mickey Mouse, Snow White, Peter Pan, Tom Sawyer, Davy Crockett, and the Swiss Family Robinson.

More than forty major shows and ride-through attractions, not to mention shops and unique dining facilities, fill its seven lands of imagination. Each land carries out its theme in fascinating detail—architecture, transportation, music, costumes, dining, shopping, and entertainment are designed to create a total atmosphere where guests can leave the ordinary world behind. The seven lands are as follows:[18]

Main Street USA Experience turn-of-the-century charm with horsedrawn trolley, horseless carriages, plenty of souvenir shops, a penny arcade, and a grand-circle tour of the park on the Walt Disney World Railroad.

Adventureland Explore exotic places with the Pirates of the Caribbean, the Jungle Cruise, the Swiss Family Treehouse, the Magic Carpets of Aladdin, and the Enchanted Tiki Room.

Frontierland Experience thrills on Splash Mountain and Big Thunder Mountain Railroad, musical fun in the Country Bear Jamboree, recreation in the Shooting Gallery, and adventure in the Tom Sawyer Island caves and its raft rides.

Liberty Square Go steamboating on the Rivers of America, find mystery in the Haunted Mansion, and view the impressive Hall of Presidents with the addition of President Barack Obama in a speaking role.

Fantasyland Cinderella Castle is the gateway to Fantasyland. Fantasyland is currently undergoing a major expansion centered around the Disney Princesses, with additional emphasis on the corresponding films' villains to attract the boys. Classic Fantasyland rides include Mickey's PhilharMagic, Peter Pan's Flight, Dumbo the Flying Elephant, Mad Tea Party, It's a Small World, Prince Charming Regal Carousel, and Winnie the Pooh.

The monorail zips through Walt Disney's Epcot Center in Orlando, Florida.

Tomorrowland Visit a sci-fi city of the future with the whirling Astro Orbiter, the shoot-em-up Buzz Lightyear's Space Ranger Spin, the interactive Monsters, Inc. Laugh Floor, the adventurous Stitch's Great Escape, the speedy Space Mountain, a new production of the Carousel of Progress, the Tomorrowland Speedway, and the elevated Tomorrowland Transit Authority.

Epcot

Epcot is a unique, permanent, and ever-changing world's fair with two major themes: Future World and World Showcase. Highlights include IllumiNations: Reflections of Earth, a nightly spectacle of fireworks, fountains, lasers, and classical music.

Future World shows an amazing exposition of technology for the near future for home, work, and play in Innoventions. The newest consumer products are continually added. Major pavilions exploring past, present, and future are shown in the Spaceship Earth story of communications (Spaceship Earth is the geosphere symbol of Epcot). The Universe of Energy giant dinosaurs help explain the origin and future of energy. There are also Mission: Space, which launches visitors into a simulated space adventure; Test Track, a high-speed vehicle-simulation ride; Journey into Imagination; The Land, with spectacular agricultural research and environmental growing areas, and the new simulation hang-gliding ride Soarin'; and The Seas with Nemo and Friends, which houses the world's second-largest indoor ocean with thousands of tropical sea creatures.[19]

Around the World Showcase Lagoon are pavilions where guests can see replicas of world-famous landmarks and sample the native foods, entertainment, and culture of eleven nations:[20]

Mexico Mexico's fiesta plaza and boat trip on Gran Fiesta Tour Starring the Three Caballeros, plus La Hacienda de San Angel for authentic Mexican cuisine

Norway Maelstrom, a thrilling Viking boat journey, and the Akershus restaurant

China Wonders of China Circle-Vision 360 film tours from the Great Wall to the Yangtze River, plus the Nine Dragons Restaurant

Germany An authentic Biergarten restaurant

Italy St. Mark's Square street players and Tutto Italia Ristorante

United States The American Adventure's stirring historical drama

Japan Re-creation of an Imperial Palace plus the Teppan Edo restaurant

Morocco Morocco's palatial Restaurant Marrakesh

France Impressions de France film tour of the French countryside, plus the Chefs de France and Bistro de Paris restaurants

United Kingdom Shakespearean street players, plus the Rose and Crown Dining Room pub

Canada O Canada, a Halifax-to-Vancouver Circle-Vision 360° tour

Each showcase has additional snack facilities and a variety of shops featuring arts, crafts, and merchandise from each nation.

Disney's Hollywood Studios

With fifty major shows, shops, restaurants, ride-through adventures, and backstage tours, Disney's Hollywood Studios (formerly Disney–MGM Studios) combines real working motion picture, animation, and television studios with exciting movie attractions. The newest adventure in the American Idol Experience, which puts guests center stage and under the spotlight. The famous Chinese Theater on Hollywood Boulevard houses the Great Movie Ride.

Other major attractions include the Tower of Terror, a stunning thirteen-story elevator fall; fast-paced adventure on the Rock 'n' Roller Coaster Starring Aerosmith; the Studio Backlot Tour of production facilities, Catastrophe Canyon, and New York Street; exciting shows at Indiana Jones Epic Stunt Spectacular and Muppet Vision 3D; plus a thrilling Star Wars adventure on Star Tours.

Especially entertaining for Disney fans is the Magic of Disney Animation, where guests can visit the Animation Academy and sit in on a class hosted by a Disney Animator. Favorite Disney films become entertaining stage presentations in the Voyage of the Little Mermaid theater and in Beauty and the Beast, a live, twenty-five-minute musical revue at Theater of the Stars. The best restaurants at Disney's Hollywood Studios include the Hollywood Brown Derby, 1950s Prime Time Cafe, Sci-Fi Dine-In Theater, and Mama Melrose's Ristorante Italiano.[21]

The Animal Kingdom is the newest edition to Walt Disney World. The Animal Kingdom focuses on nature and the animal world around us. Guests can go on time-traveling rides and come face to face with animals from the prehistoric past to the present. Shows are put on featuring Disney's most popular animal-based films, such as *Lion King* and *A Bug's Life*. Safari tours that bring guests up close and personal with live giraffes, elephants, and hippopotamuses are also offered at Animal Kingdom.

Crowds flock to the Disney's Hollywood Studios, Florida.

Walt Disney World's two water parks are Blizzard Beach and Typhoon Lagoon. Blizzard Beach has a unique ski-resort theme, while Typhoon Lagoon is based on the legend that a powerful storm swept through, leaving pools and rapids in its wake. Both parks offer a variety of slides, tube rides, pools, and moving rivers that drift throughout the parks.

All this and much more are what help make Walt Disney World the most popular destination resort in the world. Since its opening in 1971, millions of guests, including kings and celebrities from around the world and all eight U.S. presidents in office since the opening (excluding President Obama), have visited the parks. What causes the most comments from guests is the cleanliness, the friendliness of its cast, and the unbelievable attention to detail—a blend of showmanship and imagination that provides an endless variety of adventure and enjoyment.[22]

Universal Studios

Universal Studios Hollywood has been giving guided tours on its famous movie sets for almost forty years, and tens of thousands of people visit Universal every day.[23] Since its founding, Universal Studios has become the most formidable competitor facing the Walt Disney Company.

In Orlando, Florida, Universal Studios has enjoyed huge success, despite encroaching on the "kingdom" of Disney. In addition to its Hollywood and Orlando parks, Universal has since expanded into Singapore and Japan. Future locations are planned for Dubai, United Arab Emirates and Seoul, South Korea. One reason for Universal's success is its adaptation of movies into thrill rides; another is its commitment to guest participation. Guests get to help make sound effects and can participate in "stunts," making Universal Studios more than just a "look behind the scenes."

Universal Studios is also a good example of what is predicted to occur in the future regarding amusement and theme parks. It is offering more realistic thrill rides by combining new technologies and state-of-the-art equipment. Also, the company has realized that visitors tend to go to theme parks just because they happen to be in the area. By greatly expanding the experience, NBC Universal is hoping that its improvements will make travelers want to visit Universal Studios as a one-stop destination.

Let's take a closer look at the Universal theme parks:

Universal Studios Hollywood was the first Universal park and boasts the title of the world's largest movie studio and theme park. As part of the new studio tour, visitors are taken into the tomb of the Mummy, feel the hot breath of King Kong, experience a major earthquake, and are right in the middle of a Hollywood movie shoot. Afterward, guests can "chill" at the Universal CityWalk, a street that claims to offer the best in food, nightlife, shopping, and entertainment.

Universal Orlando Resort is a destination in itself, with two theme parks, several themed resorts, and a bustling CityWalk. In Universal Studios Florida, like in the Hollywood park, you can explore the exciting world of movie making. Its newest and most exciting park, Islands of Adventure, gives you the best in roller coasters and thrill rides, whereas Wet 'n Wild gives you the opportunity to enjoy a range of cool waterslides, among other things. If you're not already exhausted by the mere thought of it, why not check out CityWalk for some food, shopping, and a taste of the hottest nightlife in town. Myriads of venues, popular with tourists and locals alike, offer an amazing variety of cool bars, hot clubs, and live music.

Universal Studios Japan features eighteen rides and shows, some brand new and others old favorites, plus great dining and shopping.

Universal Studios Singapore is the newest addition and is located within Singapore's first integrated resort.[24]

TECHNOLOGY SPOTLIGHT

Use of Technology in Recreation, Attractions, and Clubs

Cihan Cobanoglu, Ph.D., Dean, School of Hotel and Restaurant Management, University of South Florida, Sarasota-Manatee

Depending on the size and amenities of an establishment, the following information technology systems can be used: call centers (for sales and customer service), point-of-sale systems (for retail distribution, food and beverage, rentals), and ticketing systems (for issuing tickets and passes). Besides these, there are some specific systems that can be implemented in the resorts and clubs.

Golf club property management systems would usually make the following functions available to users. The first is wide reservations options: online booking and group reservations. These systems usually can copy the guest's name on several tee times and thus help to save time on data entry. Another important function in golf clubs is tee-time management. This feature allows instant checking of tee-time availability to provide guests with a complete picture of what's available. Also, this module enables managing separate times and rates for different types of guests: public, member, twilight, and so forth. Besides this, club agents can relocate (drag and drop) one or multiple players from one tee time to another with ease. Some of the providers of club management software are Jonas Software, RTP, and CSI Software.

Radio-frequency identification (RFID) is rapidly entering the recreation and clubs niche of the hospitality industry. This is a technology that uses communication through radio waves for the purposes of tracking and identifying people or objects. RFID chips can be embedded in the guest cards or wristband. They enable authorization at the access points as well as retrieval of the guest's profile, picture, and membership privileges. The necessary components for this system are RFID chips and an antenna or "reader." The RFID antenna picks up a unique serial number from the microchip when a ticket, pass, or wristband with the RFID chip is presented. This technology helps to enhance fraud prevention on the management side and provides hands-free convenience on the guest side. RFID access systems have been widely used at European ski resorts, and now they are also spreading to the American market. In addition, RFID systems can have electronic "wallet" functionality. Often, RFID is implemented in beach resorts, where guests receive an opportunity to pay at different retail outlets without carrying an actual wallet. This provides the convenience of electronic payment to guests and encourages shopping. Moreover, RFID wristbands can be utilized at huge resorts and amusement parks in order to track children if they are lost.

Information kiosks appear often at large parks and resorts. Usually this technology allows park visitors to purchase park passes and other services on park grounds. Kiosks can be supplemented with digital displays that provide visitors with relevant information. These technologies optimize the use of parks' personnel, maximize the use of parks' resources, and ensure information is available to park visitors. These displays can digitally present pictures or event schedules of different parts of a resort or a park. This helps to attract guests to particular areas at the right time (for example, when there is an event taking place), as well as enables guests to plan a better recreation experience according to their interests.

SeaWorld Parks and Entertainment

SeaWorld Parks and Entertainment includes Busch Gardens and is a division of Blackstone Group. The animal parks not only offer guests from around the world the opportunity to see and experience the wonders of many marine and land animals, but they also have highly developed educational programs.

These programs reach millions of people a year—in the parks, on TV, and over the Internet—informing them on topics such as endangered animals, the environment, and the wonders of the ocean. In addition, SeaWorld Parks and Entertainment is active in the areas of conservation, research, and wildlife assistance worldwide.

The company is dedicated to preserving marine life. It uses innovative programs to research various wildlife dilemmas. It also participates in breeding, animal rescue, rehabilitation, and conservation efforts throughout the year. What SeaWorld Parks and Entertainment does for the preservation of animals is important to the existence of its theme parks because the research and rescue programs are subsidized through guest revenue. Also, each park offers unique shows and attractions that combine entertainment and education with a strong commitment to research and conservation.

Currently, SeaWorld Parks and Entertainment[25] runs the following parks in the United States:

SeaWorld The three SeaWorld parks are located in California (San Diego), Florida (Orlando), and Texas (San Antonio). Each park has various themes, marine and animal attractions, shows, rides, and educational exhibits. SeaWorld is based on the creatures of the sea. Guests can pet dolphins and other fish; watch shows featuring Shamu, the famous killer whale; and learn all about the mysteries of the sea. Several rides are also available at SeaWorld, and countless exhibits feature everything from stingrays to penguins.

Busch Gardens These theme parks, located in both Tampa, Florida, and Williamsburg, Virginia, feature exciting thrill rides and attractions in addition to large zoos and safari parks. The theme for the Williamsburg Park is the "Old Country." It re-creates the seventeenth-century charm of the Old World European atmosphere with a journey through nine authentically detailed European hamlets. "The Dark Continent" theme of Busch Gardens in Tampa has a distinctly African theme.

Adventure Island Also located in Tampa, Adventure Island is the only splash park in the Tampa Bay area. It is also the only water theme park on Florida's west coast featuring several unique water play areas and thrilling splash rides. The water park comprises more than twenty-five acres of fun-filled water rides, cafés, and shops.

Water Country USA Also located in Williamsburg, Water Country USA is the mid-Atlantic's largest water park, featuring state-of-the-art water rides and attractions, all set to a 1950s and 1960s surf theme, plus live entertainment, shopping, and restaurants.[26] Like Adventure Island, Water Country has an educational atmosphere to help guests, especially children, learn water safety techniques.

Aquatica Aquatica is a water park located in Orlando and operated as a companion to SeaWorld Orlando. The park is themed to the southern Pacific and features Australian- and New Zealand–based mascots. The park also features dolphins, which you ride by on one of the attractions.

Sesame Place This fourteen-acre park is located in Langhorne, Pennsylvania, and is dedicated totally to a Sesame Street theme. It was designed with the goal of stimulating children's natural curiosity to learn and explore, while building self-confidence as they interact with other children.

Discovery Cove Adjacent to Sea World in Orlando, Florida, Discovery Cove is where you can immerse yourself in adventure. It offers up-close encounters with dolphins and other exotic sea life. Guests can swim with dolphins and snorkel through a coral reef, tropical river, waterfalls, and an amazing freshwater lagoon, among other things.[27]

Exhilarating rides make theme parks more exciting to thrill seekers.

Hershey's

What does the name Hershey bring to mind?[28] It was at the 1893 World's Columbian Exposition in Chicago that Hershey first became fascinated with the art of chocolate. Then, Milton Hershey, a small-time candy manufacturer, decided he wanted to make chocolate to coat his caramels. He opened his new establishment in Lancaster, Pennsylvania, and named it the Hershey Chocolate Company. In the 1900s, the company started to produce mass quantities of milk chocolate, which resulted in immediate success. Soon after, Hershey decided that there was a need to increase his production facilities. He built a new factory on the farmland of south-central Pennsylvania in Derry Township. The following decades brought many product-line expansions. In 1968, the company was renamed the Hershey Foods Corporation. Today, the company is the leading manufacturer of chocolate, nonchocolate confectionery, and grocery products in North America.

In 1907, Milton Hershey opened Hershey Park as a leisure park for employees of Hershey's company. He wanted to create a place for his employees to relax and have some fun when they were not on the job. The park was small and simple, offering employees a place to picnic, canoe, and walk around the beautifully landscaped grounds. In 1908, the park started its soon-to-be huge expansion with the addition of a merry-go-round.

In the years to come, the park continued to add more rides and attractions. As the park continued to expand, the company decided to open the park's doors to the public. It became a small regional park with a pay-as-you-ride policy.

In 1971, the park underwent redevelopment to turn the small regional park into a large theme park. In addition, the company decided to add a one-time admission fee to eliminate the pay-as-you-ride policy and changed its name from Hershey Park to Hersheypark. Today, the park sits on more than 110 acres and is the home of more than sixty rides and attractions.

▶ Check Your Knowledge

1. What is Knott's Berry Farm?
2. Why did Walt Disney really create Disneyland?
3. Discuss your favorite theme park with your class. Explain why it is your favorite.

Regional Theme Parks

Just to show how varied the attractions industry is, consider the state of Florida and its attractions association. The Florida Attractions Association, founded in 1949, is a trade association representing 90-plus family-oriented attractions, including astronaut, historical, cultural, military, and scientific museums; botanical gardens; castles; collections of the unique and different; dinner entertainments; dolphin and marine parks; exhibitions of alligators, lions, monkeys, parrots, butterflies, and manatees; Native American villages; musical entertainment complexes; sightseeing trains, cruises, and boat tours; state parks; theme parks; towers; water parks; and zoological parks.

In addition to some of the larger theme parks mentioned in the preceding section, here are two others that cater to thousands of visitors each year. The Miami Seaquarium is a 38-acre tropical paradise, a place where dolphins walk on water, killer whales fly through the air, and endangered sea turtles and manatees find a safe haven.

There are eight different marine animal shows and an educational program that focuses on the mysteries of the sea even top marine scientists can't explain. In order to broaden its appeal and bring in additional revenue, the Miami Seaquarium has developed a company program for events and a schools and Scouts program to appeal to the youth market.

Marineland Dolphin Adventure in Miami began in 1938 in an effort to duplicate the variety of marine life as it exists in the wild for the purpose of making films. It was a hit with Hollywood and was used in a number of movies. Today, the park offers an array of dolphin adventures including opportunities to touch and feed the dolphins, to simulate being a trainer for the day, to make art with the dolphins, and take kayak tours in the local estuary.

Dollywood

In 1961, a small attraction with a Civil War theme called Rebel Railroad opened its doors to the public.[29] In the 1960s, the name Rebel Railroad was changed to Goldrush Junction, and the theme was changed to resemble the Wild West. This attraction is now known all across the world as Dollywood. The name came about in 1986 when Dolly Parton became a co-owner of the park. The park sits on 125 acres in the foothills of the Great Smoky Mountains in Pigeon Forge,

Tennessee. In addition to having all the rides of an amusement park, Dollywood is enriched by the culture of the Smoky Mountains. The park includes crafts such as blacksmithing, glass blowing, and wood carving. It also hosts several festivals, concerts, and musical events. Today, Dollywood brings in more than 2.5 million visitors every year and continues to be Tennessee's number one tourist attraction.[30]

Legoland

Legoland is a theme park partly owned by the Lego Group.[31] In 1968, Legoland, Billund, Denmark, opened and now has 1.6 million visitors annually. The parks are themed after—you guessed it—Legos, the brightly colored plastic bricks, gears, minifigures, and other pieces that are assembled to create models of almost anything. The parks are marketed toward young families. This is emphasized in the rides: All the parks have roller coasters that are not quite as extreme as the roller coasters found in other theme parks. Today there are five Legoland parks located in Windsor, England; Günzburg, Germany; Carlsbad, California; Billund, Denmark; and Winter Haven, Florida. Each park features a miniland, which is made up of millions of bricks that create models of landmarks and scenes from all around the world. The Windsor Legoland is one of Britain's most popular attractions, bringing 1.9 million visitors in 2010. The other parks (Californian, Danish, and German) all bring in approximately 1.4 million visitors annually. A majority interest in LegoLand's four theme parks is now owned by the Blackstore group, under its Merlin Entertainments brand.[32]

Gatorland

Gatorland is a 110-acre theme park and wildlife preserve located in Orlando, Florida.[33] It all started when Owen Godwin built an alligator pit in his backyard. After World War II, Godwin bought a sixteen-acre plot located off Florida's second-most-traveled highway. He decided that he wanted to build an attraction on his land that would provide a close-up view of Florida's animals in their native habitat. In 1949, Godwin opened the attraction's doors to the public under the name of the Florida Wildlife Institute, which he shortly after changed to the Snake Village and Alligator Farm. In 1954, Godwin once again changed the name of the attraction to its current name, Gatorland.

The 1960s brought growth to the tourism industry in Florida. As the industry grew, Gatorland continued to expand by adding a number of exhibits and attractions. Today, Gatorland features alligators, crocodiles, a breeding marsh, reptilian shows, a petting zoo, a swamp walk, educational programs, and train rides. In addition, it offers the following shows: Gator Jumparoo, which features alligators jumping four to five feet out of the water to retrieve food; Gator Wrestlin', an alligator wrestling show in which wranglers catch an alligator by hand; and Upclose Encounters, where visitors meet wildlife from around the globe. One of the oldest attractions in the area, Gatorland continues to be privately owned by Godwin's family.

Wet 'n Wild

Wet 'n Wild was founded by George Millay in Orlando, Florida, in 1977.[34] George Millay is also known as the creator of SeaWorld. Wet 'n Wild is considered the first major water park to be opened in the United States. Millay received the first Lifetime Achievement Award from the World Waterpark Association for creation of Wet 'n Wild. The association named him the official "Father of the Waterpark."

Today, Wet 'n Wild is a chain of water parks with locations in Florida and North Carolina. The Wet 'n Wild North Carolina located in Greensboro features more than thirty-six rides and attractions that are classified "from mild to wild." Wet 'n Wild Orlando also offers something for everyone. The rides fall into four categories: Thrill Rides, Multi Person Rides, Just For Kids, and Takin' It Easy. In 1998, Millay sold the Orlando Park to the Universal Studios Recreation Group.

Animal Attractions

Another sector that has been growing substantially is the one of animal attractions. Although they are usually not the main reason people visit a state or city, zoos, aquariums, and wild animal parks attract millions of visitors every year.

Zoos

Every kid's dream, and just as much fun for parents, zoos are one of those things that just don't seem to go out of style. They are forms of tourist attractions that people may visit when in a destination city such as New York, Chicago, or San Diego. Approximately 150 million people visit a U.S. zoo every year.[35] The first zoo in the United States was the Philadelphia Zoo, built in 1859. Even today, zoos are extremely popular in the United States and Canada, and almost every major city has one. In fact, the popularity of zoos was proven when the Walt Disney Company unveiled its Animal Kingdom as one way to combine the effects of visiting a zoo with the attractions of a theme park. Busch Gardens and SeaWorld also have similar parks.

Following are examples of two of the most popular and noteworthy American zoos.

San Diego Zoo, California

The San Diego Zoo attracts many tourists from across the country for a variety of reasons. It may be in part because of the favorable climate that allows the zoo to operate all year round. Also, the zoo has a large collection of animals, interactive programs, and educational programs for children.

The world-famous San Diego Zoo is located in historic Balboa Park in downtown San Diego, California. Founded in 1916 by Dr. Henry Wegeworth, the zoo's original collection totaled 50 animals. Today, it is home to over 4,000 animals of more than 800 different species. The zoo also features a prominent botanical collection with more than 700,000 exotic plants.[36] The zoo's breeding programs help not only to enhance the zoo, but also to provide hope for the survival of many endangered animals. The first baby panda ever born in captivity, Hua Mei, was born at the San Diego Zoo.[37]

The National Zoo

The National Zoological Park in Washington, D.C., is part of the respected Smithsonian Institution. More than 2,000 animals from nearly 400 species make their home in this zoo.[38] Among the rare animals featured at the National Zoo are a giant panda, komodo dragons, rare Sumatran tigers, and Asian elephants.

The National Zoo is located in a quiet residential area only minutes away from other Smithsonian museums, the Capitol, and the White House. It is not only a place to observe the behavior of certain animals, but also a place that works actively to educate visitors on conservation issues and the various interactions among living organisms. The National Zoo breeds endangered species and reintroduces the animals into their natural habitats. The zoo also participates in other visitor education programs and biological research.[39]

Aquariums

Aquariums are attractions that provide thrilling educational experiences to millions of tourists each year. They are also multi-million-dollar showpieces, displaying creatures vastly different from us who dwell on land. For example, each year, 1.6 million visitors pass through the doors of the National Aquarium in Baltimore.[40] This impressive aquarium seeks to stimulate public interest in and knowledge about the aquatic world, focusing on the beauty of these species in their natural environments. It uses only the most modern interpretative techniques to engage and get an emotional response from visitors. In fact, many visitors walk out with a desire to become more environmentally responsible.[41]

▶ Check Your Knowledge

1. What zoo is the oldest in the United States?
2. Name some rare animals you can find at the National Zoo.

Historic Places/Sites

Travelers and tourists have visited historic sites for thousands of years. The first sites visited in recorded history were the Seven Wonders of the ancient world, which included the Great Pyramid of Giza (Egypt), the Hanging Gardens of Babylon (modern-day Iraq), the Statue of Zeus at Olympia (Greece), the Temple of Artemis at Ephesus (modern-day Turkey), the Mausoleum at Halicarnassus (modern-day Turkey), the Colossus of Rhodes (Greece), and the Lighthouse of Alexandria (Egypt). Historic places, sites, and museums are a

The Great Pyramid of Giza, Egypt.

part of what is now called **heritage tourism**. Heritage tourism has gained prominence in recent years, particularly with baby boomers and older adults. These groups are less likely to engage in adventure tourism and usually prefer more passive activities. Tourists visiting historic places/sites and museums are interested in the national culture. The various historic attractions appeal to a broad spectrum of the community because they are diverse and located throughout the nation.

The National Park Service maintains properties listed in the National Register of Historic Places. The **National Register of Historic Places** is the United States' official list of districts, sites, buildings, structures, and objects worthy of preservation. The more than 85,000 listings represent significant icons of American culture, history, engineering, and architecture.[42] Historic sites include buildings that have been restored and that are now being used as private houses as well as hotels, inns, churches, libraries, galleries, and museums.

Because of declining funds, galleries, museums, and heritage sites have had to become creative in raising money. They have not only had to cover operating costs, but also cater to an increasing number of visitors. To self-generate revenues, they have had to become more entrepreneurial while continuing to meet their heritage preservation and educational goals. Revenue generation has often been achieved through an increased concentration on partnerships, promotions, and packages in which the sites team up with other operators in the tourism industry, such as tour companies, hotels, restaurants, and car rental companies.

Consider the following for a look at a few of the most important U.S. historical attractions:

- Monticello was the home of the famous statesman Thomas Jefferson, author of the Declaration of Independence, architect of American ideals as well as noble buildings, and father of the University of Virginia. The domed mansion of Monticello is set in the beautiful Virginia countryside and is well worth a visit.

- Alamo is a small mission in San Antonio, Texas, with a rich historical background. During Texas's fight for independence from Mexico, a vicious battle took place in this town. One hundred eighty-seven Texans held out for thirteen days in a group of fortified mission buildings against General Santa Anna's army of about 2,400 soldiers. The battle resulted in a tragic Texan defeat. Not long after that, Texans everywhere united in a rallying cry: "Remember the Alamo!"[43] And people still do.

- The French Quarter in New Orleans is an original part of the city, full of life and history. Unlike historic districts in many other cities, it is still growing and evolving, regardless of the recent natural disasters.

Locals constantly wrestle with the issue of balancing evolutionary changes with the need to preserve history. Visitors can have a great time when they visit during Mardi Gras.

- The Martin Luther King Jr. National Historic Site is located in the residential section of "Sweet Auburn," Atlanta. Two blocks west of the home is Ebenezer Baptist Church, the pastorate of King's grandfather and father. It was in these surroundings of home, church, and neighborhood that "M. L." experienced his childhood. Here, he learned about family and Christian love, segregation in the days of "Jim Crow" laws, diligence, and tolerance. This important site is a reminder of King's significant contribution to the civil rights movement.

- The Grand Ole Opry in Nashville, Tennessee, is a live radio show in which country music guests are featured. Started more than 75 years ago, The Grand Ole Opry is what made Nashville "Music City." Since the Opry's start, Nashville created a theme park, Opryland (now closed), and a hotel, the Opryland Resort. Famous musicians come from all over the world to showcase their talents, and tourists flock from everywhere to hear the sounds of the Opry and see the sites that Nashville has to offer.[44]

- The Freedom Trail is a walking tour through downtown Boston that passes 16 points of interest, plus other exhibits, monuments, and shrines just off the trail, some of which are a part of the Boston National Park. This interesting walk through a part of U.S. history includes both the State House and the Old South Meeting House. The Old South Meeting House was the site of many important town meetings concerning the British colonial rule, including those that sparked the Boston Tea Party. Today, there is a multimedia exhibition depicting the area's 300-year history. The building and two other restored structures today house a bustling marketplace of more than 100 specialty shops, restaurants, and bars. Paul Revere's house is the only seventeenth-century structure left in downtown Boston. It was from this house that the silversmith left for his historic ride on April 18, 1775. Another site on the Freedom Trail is the Bunker Hill Monument.

- The Liberty Bell is housed on Market Street in Philadelphia. The bell's inscription reads, "Proclaim liberty throughout all the land unto all the inhabitants thereof," which in fact is taken from the Bible, Leviticus 25:10. For many years, it was known as the State House bell. Its popularity rose when a group of abolitionists, remembering its inscription, adopted the bell as a symbol of their cause; they nicknamed it their liberty bell. In the late 1800s, the bell went on tour around the United States. This trip was an effort to show the war-torn country that there had been a time in history when they had fought and died for a common cause. In 1915, when the tour ended, the Liberty Bell, as it was then known, went home to Philadelphia, where it remains to this day. Throughout American history, the Liberty Bell has served as a simple reminder, a symbol of freedom, independence, and liberty, not just in the United States, but also all over the world.

► Check Your Knowledge

1. What were the first historic sites visited in recorded history?
2. Name some important U.S. historical attractions.

Museums

Some experts have speculated that people visit museums because of some innate fascination with the past and with diverse cultures. Nobody knows for sure, but it is a fact that the number of museums in the United States has more than quadrupled since 1950. There are many types of museums, including general, art, science and technology, natural history, history, and military. Someone has to manage these operations, and the more people that travel to experience them, the more career opportunities are available in the travel, hotel, and restaurant industries. Here are a couple of the big names in the museum sector.

The Smithsonian Institution

Established in 1846 by a man who never visited the United States, this well-known institution now holds almost 140 million artifacts, works of art, and specimens. It is composed of the following museums and galleries: the Anacostia Community Museum; the Arthur M. Sackler Gallery; the Cooper-Hewitt, National Design Museum; the Freer Gallery of Art; the Hirshhorn Museum and Sculpture Garden; the National Air and Space Museum; the National Museum of African American History and Culture; the National Museum of African Art; the National Museum of American History; the National Museum of Natural History; the National Museum of the American Indian; the National Portrait Gallery; the National Postal Museum; Smithsonian American Art Museum and its Renwick Gallery, and 9 research facilities in the United States and abroad, and 169 affiliate museums, as well as the National Zoo.[45] The institution's goal is to increase and diffuse knowledge, and it is also dedicated to public education, national service, and scholarship in the arts, sciences, and history.[46] Smithsonian museums attract approximately 24.2 million visitors annually, and entrance is free. The National Zoo attracts about 2.6 million visitors annually.[47] In addition to its museums and research facilities, parts of the Smithsonian collection can be viewed online at http://www.si.edu.

The Field Museum, Chicago

The Field Museum is a "unique institution of public learning that utilizes its collections, researchers, exhibits, and educational programs to increase public knowledge . . . of the world."[48] The museum, located in Chicago, takes on two issues that it reiterates time and time again in all of its exhibits and programs. These two issues are "balancing growth with responsible environmental stewardship" and the creation of "mutual respect and understanding among cultures."[49]

The museum was founded in 1893 as a place to house biological and anthropological collections for a world exposition. These types of objects continue to form the basis of the museum's collections. In addition, the museum conducts research in the areas of geology, paleontology, archaeology, and ethnography. Furthermore, the museum houses a world-class library collection consisting of more than 20 million items.[50]

Permanent exhibits at the Field Museum range from dinosaurs to minerals and gems, plants, animals, and cultural exhibits. Temporary exhibits are also displayed from time to time. One example of this is a program entitled "The Art of the Motorcycle." This exhibit discusses the motorcycle as a cultural icon and also its technological design.

Performance Arts

Have you ever wished that you could just take off and follow your favorite band on tour? Although some people do, most of us do not have the money or time to do so. However, that does not stop us from enjoying an occasional concert, musical, theater production, comedy show, and so forth when we are at home or on the road. However, these shows and productions are usually not the primary purpose of leisure travel, although in some circumstances they might be. In Orlando or Las Vegas, for example, certain shows have taken up permanent residence. The public knows this and therefore may take a trip to Orlando or Las Vegas at their convenience so that they may see a certain production. In places like New York City and London, stopping off to see a Broadway production or a concert may be an unplanned bonus.

Theaters once were immensely important. In a time before people had access to modern inventions like radio or television, books and theater were the only entertainment available. During the industrial era of the early 1900s, the importance of theaters began to wane somewhat as people became too busy juggling work and spending time with family. In addition, many people could not afford such luxuries. In modern times, however, the theater is again gaining importance. Old theaters from the vaudeville days are now being resurrected and reopened to the public—and the public is responding. Increasing numbers of people visit the theater or opera on weekends, holidays, or just for an evening out on the town. Theater is no longer attractive only to the upper classes; affordable prices make it reasonable entertainment for almost anyone.

Concerts, musicals, and comedy shows are also becoming increasingly affordable and are included in many people's vacations schedules. As we move up the hierarchy of needs, self-actualization becomes a greater motivation, and more and more people satisfy that need with a dose of culture and performing arts.

▶ Check Your Knowledge

1. What are the goals of the Smithsonian Institution?
2. Why are theaters, concerts, musicals, and comedy shows regaining importance?

Destinations

Some destinations are major attractions in themselves. For example, a trip to Europe might include visits to cities such as London, Paris, Rome, Athens, and Madrid or just focus on one country, where visitors enjoy not only the city but also the countryside. The following sections describe some of the world's most popular destinations.

Athens, Greece

Athens, the capital city of Greece, is one of the world's oldest cities—the cradle of Western civilization and the birthplace of democracy. Classical Athens was a powerful city-state, a center for the arts, learning, and philosophy, and home of Plato's Academy and Aristotle's Lyceum.[51] History abounds in Athens, as evidenced by the Parthenon—a temple to the Greek goddess Athena built in the fifth century B.C. on the Acropolis, a flat rock above the city. Today, Athens is a bustling city of more than 3 million—all of whom seem to be on the move, hence its notorious congestion.[52]

Of the millions of tourists who go to Greece, many, after visiting Athens, take a ferry boat ride to the famed Greek Islands in the Aegean Sea. Crete, the largest island, is rugged and mountainous with beautiful beaches and a reconstruction of King Minos's Palace, which is the largest Bronze Age archeological site on Crete, dating back to between 1700 and 1400 B.C. It was probably the ceremonial and political center of Minoan civilization and culture. The strikingly beautiful island of Santorini is a remaining part of the cone of an extinct volcano that erupted some 3,500 years ago. Some of the picturesque white buildings cling to the rim of the volcano and are among the most photographed in the world. The best way up to the town on top of the hill is by donkey ride. Mikonos is a trendy island with its famed windmills and fabulous beaches, some of them nude beaches. Other often-visited islands include Rhodes, with plenty of ruins, good beaches, and nightlife, and Corfu, off the west coast of Greece, with its lush vegetation due to higher rainfall than the other islands and its excellent beaches, museum, and nightlife—including a casino—making it a favorite of package tour groups.

London

London was once the center of an empire that included approximately one-quarter of the globe. The name suggests history, pageantry, royalty, theater, shopping, museums, music, fashion, and now even food. London has several interesting areas such as Chelsea and the River Thames and Hampstead on the hill with its quaint pubs and row houses. Trafalgar Square, named after the Battle of Trafalgar in which Nelson defeated the French, is where a statue of Lord Nelson stands atop a tall column. The four large lions that guard the statue were reputedly made from the cannons of the French fleet. Nearby is Piccadilly Circus, the core of the theater and nightlife district, along with neighboring Soho, which was a former royal park and favorite hunting ground of King Henry VIII. (In Old English, the word *so* means "wild boar or pig," and *ho* means "there.") There are many other fascinating areas such as London's East End, home of the Cockneys; the impressive buildings of the Houses of Parliament, with Big Ben, the clock tower; and of course, Buckingham Palace, the queen's London residence.

Outside London's popular tourist spots are Oxford, where travelers can visit the famous university; Stratford-upon-Avon, the birthplace of William Shakespeare, where travelers can visit the house in which Shakespeare was born in 1564 and can visit Ann Hathaway's cottage, where she lived before her marriage to Shakespeare; Bath, famous for its history of therapeutic heated springs; and Stonehenge, a complex of Neolithic and Bronze Age monuments whose purpose is mysterious and unknown. Bath is England's most elegant city known for its Georgian architecture and, of course, its baths that date back to Roman times and that are reputed to ease the pain of arthritis. Many visitors enjoy the English countryside ,with quaint villages and narrow winding roads and roundabouts. And visitors can always enjoy the British pubs.

Big Ben and Westminster Abbey make London a popular destination.

Paris

Paris is a city of beautiful buildings, boulevards, parks, markets, and restaurants and cafés. Paris is exciting! So, for tourists, what to see first is an often-asked question over morning coffee and croissants. There are city tours, but the best way to see the real Paris is on foot, especially if people want to avoid the hordes of other tourists. A tour could begin at the Eiffel Tower or the Notre Dame Cathedral, the Louvre or the Musée d'Orsay, or the Île de la Cité, or with simply with a stroll down the Champs-Elysées.

Paris began as a small island called Île de la Cité, in the middle of the River Seine. In time, Paris grew onto the Left Bank (Rive Gauche), where the University of the Sorbonne was founded. The university provided instruction in Latin, so it became known as the Quartier Latin, or Latin Quarter. The Latin Quarter has a Bohemian intellectual character with lots of small cafés and wine bars similar to Greenwich Village and Soho in New York. Nearby is Montparnasse, an area that is popular with today's artists and painters. On the Right Bank (Rive Droit) of the river Seine are many attractions; one favorite is the area of Montmartre, with the domes of Sacré-Coeur and the Place du Tertre. Just walking along the winding streets up to Sacré-Coeur gives visitors a feel of the special nature of Paris. Savoring the sights of the little markets with arrays of fresh fruits, vegetables, and flowers; catching the aromas wafting from the cafés; and seeing couples walking arm in arm in a way that only lovers do in Paris add to the ambiance that captivates all who go there and provide wonderful memories.

Rome

They say, "All roads lead to Rome." Rome, the Eternal City, also called the "Cradle of Civilization," is built on seven hills beside the Tiber River, with centuries of history that seem to exude from every building. Among the most visited sites are the Colosseum, the Pantheon, the Spanish Steps, Vatican City, and the Forum. The Colosseum is the ancient stadium where gladiators fought, Christians were martyred, other sports and games were played, and thousands of men fought with ferocious animals to amuse the crowds. The Pantheon, originally built in 27 B.C. as a temple to all the gods of ancient Rome, was destroyed by fire in A.D. 80, rebuilt in 126, and is likely the best preserved building of its era. The Spanish Steps, the widest steps in Europe, are situated between the Piazza di Spagna (Plaza of Spain) and the Piazza Trinità die Monti (The Holy See), the Episcopal jurisdiction of the Bishop of Rome, better known as the Pope. They are a popular hangout for tourists and residents. Vatican City is the smallest state in the world, with only 110 acres and a population of just over 800.[53] In this tiny area are St. Peter's Basilica, the Vatican Museums, and Michelangelo's *Creation*, painted on the ceiling of the Sistine Chapel, and his *Last Judgment*, on the wall behind the altar. The Roman Forum was the center of political, social, and economic life in imperial Rome, with temples, basilicas, and triumphal arches; it is the place where the Roman democratic government began. Several other interesting cities to visit in Italy include Venice, Naples, and Florence, along with the Tuscan countryside.

Managing Attractions

Managing attractions and theme parks has many similarities to managing any business. Theme park managers use the same main management functions (planning, including forecasting; organizing; decision making; and controlling).

Planning involves all types of planning that fall under two headings: strategic (long term) and tactical (short term). An example of strategic planning would be determining what kind of theme ride to build as the next major attraction or planning a new park in another country. An example of tactical planning would be forecasting the park's attendance for the next month so departments can staff correctly.

Organizing is getting everything arranged: who will do what, by whom, when, and where. For example, a theme park requires a structure to be organized for managing the process. The management team is assembled and given their assignments. Someone manages the reservations and admissions, the rides, the restaurants and foodservice, the gift shops, maintenance, marketing, human resources, and accounting and finance. Each department manager has daily, weekly, and monthly tasks that structure the organizing of the park to maximize operational efficiencies and effectiveness. Organization charts show who reports to whom and give a visual representation of the operation of the park.

Decision making can be quick and easy for the many programmed decisions—decisions that occur on a regular basis, allowing the decision to be handled with a "programmed" response. For example, when the inventory of an item falls below the reorder point, a programmed response is to order a predetermined quantity to bring the stock back up to par.

Another, more complicated type of decision making is nonprogrammed—which is nonrecurring and is caused by unusual circumstances. One example of a nonprogrammed decision is a situation with incomplete information—for example, which guest relations program or point-of-sale system to install.

The decision-making process consists of eight steps:[54]

1. Identification of the problem and definition of the problem
2. Identification of the decision criteria
3. Allocation of weights to the criteria
4. Development of alternatives
5. Analysis of alternatives
6. Selection of alternative
7. Implementation of alternative
8. Evaluation of decision effectiveness

Controlling is constantly checking to make sure that the results were what they should be. Was the actual revenue what was expected? Or, was it above or below expected, and by how much? What was the labor cost and how did it compare with the expected labor cost? Control examines performance results in all the key areas of operation.

Revenue comes from entrance ticket sales, parking, vending, retail program fees, food and beverage sales, and donations. There is a great variation among attractions. Some are for profit and others are nonprofit; however, both must operate with budgets. Many attractions obtain 70 percent of their revenue from ticket sales, approximately 15 percent income from retail, and another 15 percent from food and beverage sales. Many attractions are looking to attract new revenue by staging special events such as corporate events, Father's Day or Easter celebrations, or auto shows in the parking lot.

As managers of a business, attractions managers are also trying to stay ahead of the wave and keep on top of expenditures. They also try to retain the best employees during the slow season by cross-training them to do more than one job as the need arises. Because labor costs are the highest expense item, managers do their best to reduce labor costs by boosting the volunteer base in multiple areas.[55]

Attractions management is all about keeping the quality of product and guest service at the highest levels. It boils down to revenue minus expenses equal net profit.[56]

Clubs

Private clubs are places where members gather for social, recreational, professional, or fraternal reasons. Members enjoy bringing friends, family, and business guests to their club. Their club is like a second home, but with diverse facilities and staff to accommodate the occasion. Bringing guests to one's club can be more impressive than inviting them to one's home, and there is still a level of the same personal atmosphere as there would be if guests were invited home. Many of today's clubs are adaptations of their predecessors, mostly examples from England and Scotland. For example, the North American country club is largely patterned after the Royal and Ancient Golf Club of St. Andrews, Scotland, founded in 1758 and recognized as the birthplace of golf. Many

Big Island Country Club on Kona Coast of Hawaii.

business deals are negotiated on the golf course. A few years ago, country clubs were often considered to be bastions of the social elite.

Historically, the ambiance of these clubs attracted the affluent. The character of the clubs transcended generations. Member etiquette and mannerisms developed over years to a definable point by which members could recognize each other through subtleties, and those not possessing the desired qualities were not admitted.

Today there are more affluent people than ever, and their number continues to grow. The new rich are now targeted and recruited for a variety of new hybrid groups that also call themselves clubs. The newer clubs' cost of initiation and membership may be considerably less than some of the more established clubs. The stringent screening process and lengthy membership applications are now simplified, and cash is the key to admittance.

New clubs are born when a developer purchases a tract of land and builds a golf course with a clubhouse surrounded by homes or condominiums. The homes are sold and include a membership to the club. After all the homes are sold, the developer announces that the golf course and clubhouse will be sold to an investor who wishes to open it to the public. The homeowners rush to purchase the clubhouse and golf course to protect their investment. A board is formed, and the employees of the developer and all operations are usually transferred to and become the responsibility of the new owners or members.

Size and Scope of the Club Industry

There are a few thousand private clubs in North America, including both country and city clubs. When the total resources of all the clubs are considered, such as land, buildings, and equipment, along with thousands of employees and so forth, clubs have billions of dollars of economic impact.

Club Management

Club management is similar in many ways to hotel management, both of which have evolved in recent years. The general managers of clubs now assume the role of chief operating officer, and in some cases chief executive officer of the corporation. They may also have responsibility for management of the homeowners' association and all athletic facilities, including the golf courses. In addition, they are responsible for planning, forecasting and budgeting, human resources, food and beverage operations, facility management, and maintenance. The main difference between managing a club and managing a hotel is that with clubs the guests feel as if they are the owners (in many cases they are) and frequently behave as if they are the owners. Their emotional attachment to the facility is stronger than that of hotel guests who do not use hotels with the same frequency that members use clubs. Another difference is that most clubs do not offer sleeping accommodations.

CORPORATE PROFILE

ClubCorp

Founded in 1957, Dallas-based ClubCorp is the world leader in delivering premier golf, private club, and resort experiences. Internationally, ClubCorp owns or operates more than 150 golf and country clubs, business clubs, sports clubs, alumni clubs, and resorts in twenty-five states, the District of Columbia, and two foreign countries. ClubCorp has approximately $1.8 billion in assets. Among the company's nationally recognized golf properties are the Firestone Country Club in Akron, Ohio (site of the 2003–2005 World Golf Championships—Bridgestone Invitational) and Mission Hills Country Club in Rancho Mirage, California (home of the Kraft Nabisco Championship).

The more than forty business clubs and business and sports clubs include the Boston College Club; City Club on Bunker Hill in Los Angeles; Citrus Club in Orlando, Florida; Columbia Tower Club in Seattle; Metropolitan Club in Chicago; Tower Club in Dallas; and the City Club of Washington, D.C. The company's 14,000 employees serve the nearly 350,000 members of the ClubCorp properties.

ClubCorp is in the business of building relationships and enriching lives. The extraordinary private club environments nourish relationships old and new, as well as create a world of privacy, luxury, and relaxation where guests' every need is anticipated and every expectation exceeded. Crafting fine, private-club traditions for more than fifty years, ClubCorp has developed a signature philosophy of service that resonates with every encounter, every warm welcome, and every magic moment, joining to form the bedrock of all the clubs.

Each club has its own distinctive personality and takes pride in creating the perfect settings for casual gatherings with friends, business meetings, or formal celebrations. The clubs provide safe havens where members and their guests always are welcome. Whether looking for a country club experience or a professional retreat in which to conduct business affairs, ClubCorp's members are the beneficiaries of the ultimate in private club service and tradition.

ClubCorp clubs provide a variety of membership options and experiences for a range of lifestyle pursuits. In more than 150 private business and sports clubs, country clubs, golf courses, and resorts around the world, from Seattle to Mexico and from Boston to Beijing, ClubCorp provides for its members a haven of refuge, a home away from home, where every need is anticipated and every expectation surpassed.

Source: ClubCorp, *United States Securities and Exchange Commission Form 10-Q*, http://b2i.api.edgar-online.com/EFX_dll/EdgarPro.dll?FetchFilingHTML1?Session ID=MNp_Fy-6vHMBo-9&ID=8054747 (accessed November 15, 2011); and ClubCorp, *Company Profile*, http://www.clubcorp.com/About-ClubCorp/Company-Profile (accessed November 15, 2011).

Club members pay an initiation fee to belong to the club and annual membership dues thereafter. Some clubs also charge a set utilization fee, usually related to food and beverages, which is charged regardless of whether those services are used.

The Club Manager's Association of America (CMAA) is the professional organization to which many of the club managers belong. The association's goal is to advance the profession of club management by fulfilling the educational and related needs of the club managers. The association provides networking opportunities and fosters camaraderie among its member managers through meetings and conferences held locally and nationally. These gatherings keep managers abreast of current practices and procedures and new legislation. The general managers who join CMAA subscribe to a code of ethics.

Successful club general managers have adapted to their new and evolving environment. Some, however, have not, and sadly they have either gone bankrupt, as with Cyprus Run Country Club, which was sold at auction for just over $1 million, or gone from private to public. The successful clubs have added incentives, like becoming a member for a day or joining for the summer for only $500, to attract more members. Clubs in Florida and other southern states that attract "snowbirds"—seasonal visitors from the northern states—are offering special winter rates. For many clubs, the harsh economic climate has reduced membership, reducing revenue and making it more difficult to pay mortgages.

Most clubs have found creative ways of increasing revenue by including more items in the shops—not just golf or tennis clothing and clubs or racquets, but expanded merchandise such as jewelry, books, organic cookies, vitamins, and swim gear. In addition, clubs have expanded their offerings to include spas that offer Botox, facials, and cosmetic products. Clubs have extended their food and beverage offerings to make more money off events like weddings and social fund raisers such as the American Cancer Society and the Salvation Army. Additionally, revenue has been increased by letting high-end guests from local hotels pay handsomely for the privilege of playing the course.

Clubs are reducing expenses by paying about 40-percent-less property taxes and by trimming costly items like water for the golf course by using reclaimed water and by cutting back on the amount paid into employees' 401(k) retirement plans and by providing a fixed amount of $400 for a staff member and family per month for benefits.

Club Management Structure

The internal management structure of a club is governed by the corporation's articles of incorporation and bylaws. These establish election procedures, officer positions, a board of directors, and standing committees. Guidance and direction also are provided for each office and committee and how it will function. The general manager will usually provide an orientation for the new directors and information to help them in their new role. The members elect the officers and directors of the club. The officers represent the membership by establishing policies by which the club will operate. Many clubs and other organizations maintain continuity by having a succession of officers. The secretary becomes the vice president and the vice president becomes the president. In other cases, the person elected president is simply the person believed to be the most qualified to lead the club for that year. Regardless of who is elected president, the club's general manager must be able to work with that person and the other officers.

The president presides at all official meetings and is a leader in policymaking. The vice president is groomed for the role of president, which is usually eminent, and will in the absence of the president perform the presidential duties. If the club has more than one vice president, the titles *first*, *second*, *third*, and so on, may be used. Alternatively, vice presidents may be assigned to chair certain committees, such as membership. Board members usually chair one or more committees.

Committees play an important part in the club's activities. If the committees are effective, the operation of the club is more efficient. The term of committee

INTRODUCING EDWARD J. SHAUGHNESSY

General Manager, Belleair Country Club

For Ed Shaughnessy, working in a country club is not just a job but a passion. Clubs feature great recreational facilities, including some fabulous golf courses, gourmet dining, the finest entertainment, and clientele who are more like family than customers. Shaughnessy has worked for three prestigious clubs in his career. He began working in clubs at the tender age of fourteen as a busser. Shortly after graduating from high school, he accepted a full-time evening bar manager position at Sleepy Hollow Country Club in New York. He worked full time at night while attending college full time until he received his A.A.S. degree. Upon graduation, he was promoted to food and beverage manager, but continued his education, taking two or three courses every semester until he earned and received his B.B.A. He was subsequently promoted to assistant general manager.

After fourteen years at the same club and on his twenty-ninth birthday, he was offered and accepted the general manager's position at Belle Haven Country Club in Alexandria, Virginia. He began an active role in the National Capital Club Managers Association and was elected president. He continued his education and earned his Certified Club Manager (CCM) designation and his Certified Hospitality Educator (CHE) designation through the Club Managers Association of America (CMAA). He stayed at Belle Haven Country Club for eight years, but wanted to live closer to sunny beaches in a warmer climate.

An opportunity at the prestigious Belleair Country Club in Belleair, Florida, was brought to Shaughnessy's attention by John Sibbald, a top recruiter in the club industry, and in 1997 Ed Shaughnessy accepted the position of general manager/chief operating officer at the Belleair Country Club. He continued his education, earning his M.B.A. in International Hotel and Tourism Management from Schiller International University, where he now teaches a variety of hospitality-related courses. Shaughnessy is still active with the CMAA and serves on the Club Foundation Allocation Committee. This committee reviews scholarship and grant applications and recommends the awarding of funds to promote education. He also serves as the ethics chair for the Florida Chapter of the CMAA.

Shaughnessy believes that there are two stages in life—growth and decay—and that we are all in one of these stages. For him, to be in the growth stage is preferred in life. He believes we are all given the choice to change our environment, and he enjoys catering to those with the highest expectations. It appears that people will always recognize and be willing to pay for great value and quality. Meticulous attention to detail and proactively providing what customers desire before they have to ask is the key to success.

No two days are the same or predictable for a general manager. One day you could be developing a strategic plan, the next you may be invited to fly on a private Lear jet to see the Super Bowl. You have to make a conscious effort to balance work and family life. A general manager should remember that although you can enjoy many of the same privileges as the elite, you are still an employee and must always set an exemplary role as a professional. A general manager's people skills are very important, as well as having a comprehensive understanding of financial statements.

The challenge for the future is finding talented and service-oriented people who are needed to exceed the constantly increasing expectations of sophisticated and discriminating club members. Shaughnessy discovered some time ago that it may be necessary to grow one's own talent among his employees, and this gives him the confidence that he will be ready to serve his customers well. Shaughnessy has a high concern for the welfare of his loyal and dedicated employees. They could lose their jobs if the club is mismanaged. These people and their families count on him to operate the club efficiently. He also recognizes that he must take proactive steps to ensure the growth and success of his club. With two waterfront golf courses, a marina, and the amenities of a full-service country club, Ed Shaughnessy is taking steps to be sure he positions the club for continued success.

membership is specified, and committee meetings are conducted in accordance with Robert's Rules of Order, which are procedural guidelines on the correct way to conduct meetings. Standing committees include the following: house, membership, finance/budget, entertainment, golf, green tennis, pool, and long-range planning. The president may appoint additional committees to serve specific functions commonly referred to as ad hoc.

CMAA Code of Ethics

We believe the management of clubs is an honorable calling. It shall be incumbent upon club managers to be knowledgeable in the application of sound principles in the management of clubs, with ample opportunity to keep abreast of current practices and procedures. We are convinced that the Club Managers Association of America best represents these interests and, as members thereof subscribe to the following CODE OF ETHICS.

We will uphold the best traditions of club management through adherence to sound business principles. By our behavior and demeanor, we shall set an example for our employees and will assist our club officers to secure the utmost in efficient and successful club operations.

We will consistently promote the recognition and esteem of club management as a profession and conduct our personal and business affairs in a manner to reflect capability and integrity. We will always honor our contractual employment obligations.

We shall promote community and civic affairs by maintaining good relations with the public sector to the extent possible within the limits of our club's demands.

We will strive to advance our knowledge and abilities as club managers, and willingly share with other Association members the lessons of our experience and knowledge gained by supporting and participating in our local chapter and the National Association's educational meetings and seminars.

We will not permit ourselves to be subsidized or compromised by any interest doing business with our clubs.

We will refrain from initiating, directly or through an agent, any communications with a director, member, or employee of another club regarding its affairs without the prior knowledge of the manager thereof, if it has a manager.

We will advise the National Headquarters, whenever possible, regarding managerial openings at clubs that come to our attention. We will do all within our power to assist our fellow club managers in pursuit of their professional goals.

We shall not be deterred from compliance with the law, as it applies to our clubs. We shall provide our club officers and trustees with specifics of federal, state and local laws, statutes, and regulations to avoid punitive action and costly litigation.

We deem it our duty to report to local or national officers any willful violations of the CMAA CODE OF ETHICS.

Source: The author gratefully acknowledges the professional courtesy of the Club Managers Association of America.

The treasurer obviously must have some financial and accounting background because an integral part of his or her duties is to give advice on financial matters, such as employing external auditors, preparing budgets, and installing control systems. The general manager is responsible for all financial matters and usually signs or cosigns all checks.

It is the duty of the secretary to record the minutes of meetings and take care of club-related correspondence. In most cases, the general manager prepares the document for the secretary's signature. This position can be combined with that of treasurer, in which case the position is titled secretary–treasurer. The secretary may also serve on or chair certain committees.

The Club Managers Association of America (CMAA) has reexamined the role of club managers, and because of ever-increasing expectations, the role of the general manager has changed from the traditional managerial model to a leadership model. The new CMAA model is based on the premise that general managers or chief operating officers (COOs) are more responsible for operating assets and investments and club culture.

The basic level of competency required of a general manager or COO is management of club's operations, which includes private club management, food and beverage, accounting and financial management, human and professional resources, building and facilities management, external and governmental influences, management, marketing, and sports and recreation (see Figure 1).

The second tier of the model is mastering the skills of asset management. Today's general manager or COO must be able to manage the physical property, the financial well-being, and the human resources of the club. These facets of the manager's responsibilities are equally as important as managing the operations of the club.

The third and final tier of the new model is preserving and fostering the culture of the club, which can be defined as the club's traditions, history, governance, and vision. Many managers or COOs intrinsically perform this function; however, it is often an

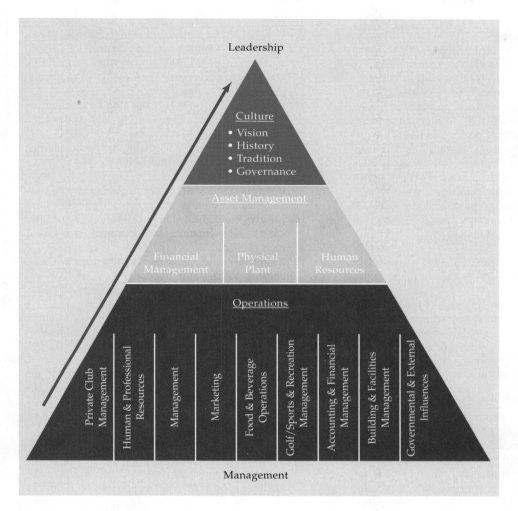

Leadership

Culture
- Vision
- History
- Tradition
- Governance

Asset Management

Financial Management | Physical Plant | Human Resources

Operations

Private Club Management | Human & Professional Resources | Management | Marketing | Food & Beverage Operations | Golf/Sports & Recreation Management | Accounting & Financial Management | Building & Facilities Management | Governmental & External Influences

Management

Figure 1 • Management to Leadership.

overlooked and underdeveloped quality. A job description for club manager is given in Figure 2. The club management competencies are shown in Figure 3. Additionally, you can see an example of the overall organization of a country club in Figure 4.

Types of Clubs

Country Clubs

Nearly all **country clubs** have one or more lounges and restaurants, and most have banquet facilities. Members and their guests enjoy these services and can be billed monthly. The banquet facilities are used for formal and informal parties, dinners, dances, weddings, and so on, by members and their personal guests. Some country clubs charge what might seem to be an excessive amount for the initiation fee—as much as $250,000 in some cases—to maintain exclusivity.

I. **Position:** General Manager

II. **Related Titles:** Club Manager; Club House Manager

III. **Job Summary:** Serves as chief operating officer of the club; manages all aspects of the club including its activities and the relationships between the club and its board of directors, members, guests, employees, community, government, and industry; coordinates and administers the club's policies as defined by its board of directors. Develops operating policies and procedures and directs the work of all department managers. Implements and monitors the budget, monitors the quality of the club's products and services, and ensures maximum member and guest satisfaction. Secures and protects the club's assets, including facilities and equipment

IV. **Job Tasks (Duties):**

1. Implements general policies established by the board of directors; directs their administration and execution

2. Plans, develops, and approves specific operational policies, programs, procedures, and methods in concert with general policies

3. Coordinates the development of the club's long-range and annual (business) plans

4. Develops, maintains, and administers a sound organizational plan; initiates improvements as necessary

5. Establishes a basic personnel policy; initiates and monitors policies relating to personnel actions and training and professional development programs

6. Maintains membership with the Club Managers Association of America and other professional associations. Attends conferences, workshops, and meetings to keep abreast of current information and developments in the field

7. Coordinates development of operating and capital budgets according to the budget calendar; monitors monthly and other financial statements for the club; takes effective corrective action as required

8. Coordinates and serves as ex-officio member of appropriate club committees

9. Welcomes new club members; meets and greets all club members as practical during their visits to the club

10. Provides advice and recommendations to the president and committees about construction, alterations, maintenance, materials, supplies, equipment, and services not provided in approved plans and/or budgets

11. Consistently ensures that the club is operated in accordance with all applicable local, state, and federal laws

12. Oversees the care and maintenance of all the club's physical assets and facilities

13. Coordinates the marketing and membership relations programs to promote the club's services and facilities to potential and present members

14. Ensures the highest standards for food, beverage, sports and recreation, entertainment, and other club services

15. Establishes and monitors compliance with purchasing policies and procedures

16. Reviews and initiates programs to provide members with a variety of popular events

17. Analyzes financial statements, manages cash flow, and establishes controls to safeguard funds; reviews income and costs relative to goals; takes corrective action as necessary

18. Works with subordinate department heads to schedule, supervise, and direct the work of all club employees

19. Attends meetings of the club's executive committee and board of directors

20. Participates in outside activities that are judged as appropriate and approved by the board of directors to enhance the prestige of the club; broadens the scope of the club's operation by fulfilling the public obligations of the club as a participating member of the community

V. **Reports to:** Club President and Board of Directors

VI. **Supervises:** Assistant General Manager (Club House Manager); Food and Beverage Director; Controller; Membership Director; Director of Human Resources; Director of Purchasing; Golf Professional (Director of Golf); Golf Course Superintendent; Tennis Professional; Athletic Director; Executive Secretary

Source: Club Managers Association of America.

Figure 2 • A Job Description for a Club Manager.

Source: The author gratefully acknowledges the professional courtesy of the Club Managers Association of America.

Country clubs have two or more types of membership. Full membership enables members to use all the facilities all the time. Social membership allows members only to use the social facilities: lounges, bars, restaurants, and so on, and perhaps the pool and tennis courts. Other forms of membership can include weekday and weekend memberships.

Private Club Management	***Accounting and Finance***	Contractors
History of Private Clubs	***in the Private Club***	Energy and Water Resource
Types of Private Clubs	Accounting and Finance Principles	Management
Membership Types	Uniform System of Accounts	Housekeeping
Bylaws	Financial Analysis	Security
Policy Formulation	Budgeting	Laundry
Board Relations	Cash Flow Forecasting	Lodging Operations
Chief Operating Officer Concept	Compensation and Benefit	
Committees	Administration	***External and Governmental***
Club Job Descriptions	Financing Capital Projects	***Influences***
Career Development	Audits	Legislative Influences
Golf Operations Management	Internal Revenue Service	Regulatory Agencies
Golf Course Management	Computers	Economic Theory
Tennis Operations Management	Business Office Organization	Labor Law
Swimming Pool Management	Long-Range Financial Planning	Internal Revenue Service
Yacht Facilities Management		Privacy
Fitness Center Management	***Human and Professional Resources***	Club Law
Locker Room Management	Employee Relations	Liquor Liability
Other Recreational Activities	Management Styles	Labor Unions
	Organizational Development	
Food and Beverage Operations	Balancing Job and Family	***Management and Marketing***
Sanitation	Responsibilities	Communication Skills
Menu Development	Time Management	Marketing Through In-House
Nutrition	Stress Management	Publications
Pricing Concepts	Labor Issues	Professional Image and Dress
Ordering/Receiving/Controls/Inventory	Leadership vs. Management	Effective Negotiation
Food and Beverage Trends		Member Contact Skills
Quality Service	***Building and Facilities Management***	Working with the Media
Creativity in Theme Functions	Preventive Maintenance	Marketing Strategies in a Private
Design and Equipment	Insurance and Risk Management	Club Environment
Food and Beverage Personnel	Clubhouse Remodeling and	
Wine List Development	Renovation	*Source:* Club Managers Association of
		America.

Figure 3 • The Club Management Competences.

Source: The author gratefully acknowledges the professional courtesy of the Club Managers Association of America.

City Clubs

City clubs are predominantly business oriented, although some have rules prohibiting the discussion of business and the reviewing of business-related documents in dining rooms. They vary in size, location, type of facility, and services offered. Some of the older, established clubs own their own buildings; others lease space. Clubs exist to cater to the wants and needs of members. Clubs in the city fall into the following categories:

- Professional
- Social
- Athletic
- Dining
- University

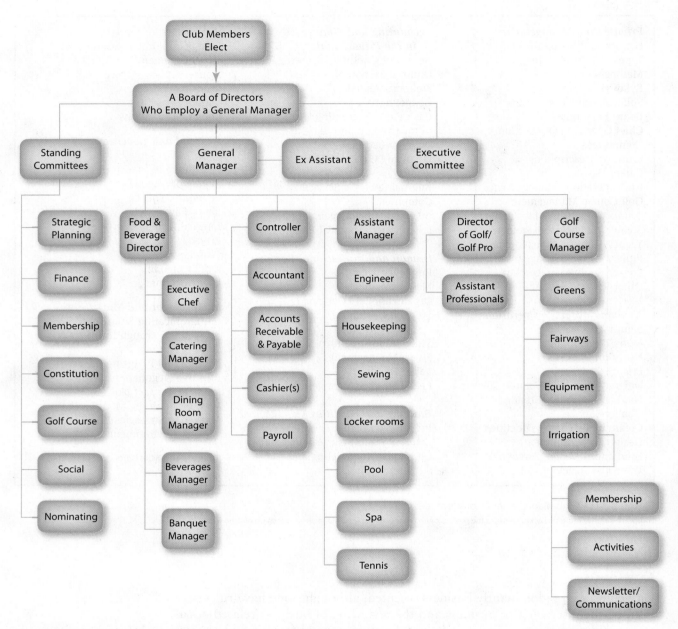

Figure 4 ● An Example of an Organizational Chart of a Country Club.

- Military
- Yachting
- Fraternal
- Proprietary

Professional clubs, as the name implies, are clubs for people in the same profession. The National Press Club in Washington, D.C., the Lawyers Club in New York City, and the Friars Club for actors and other theatrical people in Manhattan are good examples.

Social clubs allow members to enjoy one another's company; members represent many different professions, yet they have similar socioeconomic backgrounds. Social clubs are modeled after the famous men's social clubs in London, such as Boodles, St. James's, and White's. At these clubs, it is considered bad form to discuss business. Therefore, conversation and social interaction focus on companionship or entertainment unrelated to business.

The oldest social club in the United States is thought to be the Fish House in Philadelphia, founded in 1832. To ensure that the Fish House would always be socially oriented rather than business oriented, it was formed as a men's cooking club, with each member taking a turn preparing meals for the membership. Other social clubs exist in several major cities. The common denominator is that they all have upscale food and beverage offerings and club managers to manage them.

Athletic clubs give city workers and residents an opportunity to work out, swim, play squash and/or racquetball, and so on. Some of the downtown athletic clubs provide tennis courts and running tracks on the roof. Athletic clubs also have lounges, bars, and restaurants at which members may relax and interact socially. Some athletic clubs also have meeting rooms and even sleeping accommodations. The newest feature is known as the executive workout. This begins with a visit to the steam room, followed by a trip to the Jacuzzi, then sauna, a massage, and nap in the resting room before showering and returning to work.

Dining clubs are generally located in large city office buildings. Memberships are often given as an inducement to tenants who lease space in the office building. These clubs are always open for lunch and occasionally for dinner.

University clubs are private clubs for alumni. University clubs are generally located in the high-rent district and offer a variety of facilities and attractions focusing on food and beverage service.

Military clubs cater to both noncommissioned officers (NCOs) and enlisted officers. Military clubs offer similar facilities as do other clubs for recreation and entertainment and food and beverage offerings. Some military clubs are located on base. The largest membership club in the country is the Army Navy Country Club in Arlington, Virginia. The club has more than 6,000 members, 54 holes of golf, 2 clubhouses, and a host of other facilities. Many of the military clubs in recent years have given over their club management to civilians.

Yacht clubs provide members with moorage slips, where their boats are kept secure. In addition to moorage facilities, yacht clubs have lounge, bar, and dining facilities similar to other clubs. Yacht clubs are based on a sailing theme and attract members with various backgrounds who have sailing as a common interest.

Fraternal clubs include many special organizations, such as the Veterans of Foreign Wars, Elks, and Shriners. These organizations foster camaraderie and often assist charitable causes. They generally are less elaborate than are other clubs, but have bars and banquet rooms that can be used for various activities.

Proprietary clubs operate on a for-profit basis. They are owned by corporations or individuals; individuals wanting to become members purchase a membership, not a share in the club. Proprietary clubs became popular with the real estate boom in the 1970s and 1980s. As new housing developments were planned, clubs were included in several of the projects. Households pay a small initiation fee and monthly dues between $30 and $50, allowing the whole family to participate in a wide variety of recreational activities.

Clearly, the opportunities for recreation and leisure abound. The goal must be to achieve a harmony between work and leisure activities and to become truly professional in both giving and receiving these services. The next few years will see a substantial increase in the leisure and recreational industries.

FOCUS ON RECREATION

Hospitality and Recreation: Inextricably Intertwined

Bart Bartlett, Ph.D., Professor in Charge of Undergraduate Programs at Penn State University's School of Hospitality Management

Americans have more leisure time than ever before, and as leisure time has grown, leisure activities have evolved and grown as well. As this text points out, opportunities today for recreation and for careers in recreation management are vast and multifaceted. These include positions in commercial recreation (resorts, themed resorts, the ski industry), in noncommercial recreation (federal or state parks and community recreation), in clubs and sports venues, and in recreation with special populations.

In many situations, recreation and hospitality go hand in hand. When a ski trip incorporates recreation on the slopes with food and beverage services in the lodge or when a hotel guest uses the hotel's business services and the spa, recreation and hospitality are both involved. When a convention center hotel provides rooms, food, and beverage; coordinates meetings and breakout sessions; and also organizes recreation and group activities during the conference, hospitality and recreation begin to merge. In fact, because our guests' total experience often involves a combination of lodging, food and beverage, and recreation, we do not want to distinguish, but instead want to ensure guest satisfaction by seamlessly integrating these different elements into the total package.

As growth in leisure travel continues to outstrip growth in business travel, the growing leisure travel market will create an increasing emphasis on recreation as an integral part of hospitality. Furthermore, though hospitality and recreation may involve different emphases, the critical customer focus and customer service skills that we love about our industry are common to all aspects of hospitality and recreation.

Resorts and resort hotels are the prototypical combination of hospitality and recreation. A mega-resort such as Walt Disney World provides an ideal example of a venue that integrates hospitality and recreation skills and services. On a Disney vacation, a family may enjoy lodging and food and beverage services provided by hotel staff and management trained in hospitality, go into the park itself to enjoy attractions and shows arranged and managed by a recreation specialist, take a break to enjoy foodservice provided by a hospitality provider, and at the end of the day enjoy dinner provided by the hospitality staff and entertainment or dancing arranged by a recreation professional.

The golf industry provides other examples. At a typical golf club, the director of golf operations is primarily involved with managing recreation activities, including scheduling and supervising play, course maintenance, and the pro shop. The clubhouse manager, meanwhile, is responsible for hospitality functions, including food and beverage operations, catering events, and membership. If either were missing, the club simply could not meet guests' and members' overall expectations.

Finally, because cruise ships are essentially floating resort hotels with many features of land-based resorts, both hospitality and recreation are required. On a cruise ship, the purser and food and beverage manager are responsible for hospitality functions, while the cruise director provides recreation programming. Both are critical parts of the cruise experience, thus providing the all-around good time guests desire and deserve.

This text talks about recreation and the opportunities to apply your hospitality skills in recreation settings. Across the spectrum, from business travelers to family vacationers, from golfing outings to business banquets, from backcountry adventures to haute cuisine dining, from white-sand Caribbean beaches to black diamond ski slopes, customer service and a focus on customer satisfaction are constants, and both hospitality and recreation skills are critical to providing a memorable guest experience. The commonalities in settings, service, and focus on guest satisfaction indicate that hospitality and recreation are indeed inextricably intertwined!

Sustainable Golf Course Management

The golf course industry recognizes sustainability as it is referenced by the Environmental Protection Agency (EPA) and the United Nations, which indicates that it is "meeting the needs of the present without compromising the ability of future generations to meet their own needs."[57] In an effort to appear sustainable, some courses call themselves "green." This is vague. However, it is not vague to say that a course engages in water-quality protection through the responsible use of all inputs, such as nutrients and pesticides.

The EPA gives a basic rundown of sustainability at http://www.epa.gov/ sustainability/basicinfo.htm#sustainability. The Environmental Institute for Golf gives information on sustainable golf management practices (www.eifg.org). Sustainable practices include the following:

- Reducing energy use especially during the peak times (a utility company's bill is much higher for consumption during peak times).
- Holding departments accountable for their energy consumption budgets by breaking down the bills by departments.
- Recycling: from aluminum cans in the clubhouse to grass clippings on the course to motor oil from the golf carts.[58]

Golf course facilities are prime candidates for reducing or reusing waste: As landfill disposal costs rise, recycling becomes even more important. Golf courses can improve their sustainability by improving grass and plant selection and by using well water and organic fertilization.

► Check Your Knowledge

1. Name all the types of clubs discussed here and briefly describe their functions.
2. List the important duties of a club manager.
3. Describe the operations of a country club.

Noncommercial Recreation

Noncommercial recreation includes voluntary organizations, campus, armed forces, and employee recreation, as well as recreation for special populations.

Voluntary Organizations

Voluntary organizations are nongovernmental, nonprofit agencies, serving the public at large or selected elements with multiservice programs that often include a substantial element of recreational opportunity. The best-known voluntary organizations include the Boy Scouts, Girl Scouts, YMCA, YWCA, and YM–YWHA.

In the early 1900s, YMCAs began to offer sporting facilities and programs. The Ys, though nonprofit, were pioneers in basketball, swimming, and weight

A DAY IN THE LIFE OF CHRISTIE CHAPMAN

Beverage Cart Attendant, Tampa Palms Golf and Country Club

As a beverage car attendant for a golf and country club, my day starts out early at 7:30 A.M. I need to make sure I am prepared for my job, which happens to be supplying thirsty and hungry golfers on the course.

I work Tuesday through Sunday and will work additional hours or days on an as-needed basis. Organizations and other clubs often host golf tournaments at the club, and they will typically need at least one attendant for the duration of the tournament. I first start by stocking the beverage cart with beer, soda, Gatorade, liquor, and any pre-made sandwiches or snacks we offer on our menu. After I stock the cooler full of liquids and cold snacks, I have to cover everything with ice so that it will stay as cool as possible when I make my runs around the course. I also make coffee, as many golfers prefer a hot beverage during the cold mornings. This process should take no longer than an hour. I make sure I have everything I might need before I get out on the golf course, as it's often a long drive back to the clubhouse to stock up on a single item that a member or guest particularly wants.

I start the course off at Hole 18 and make my way back to Hole 1. This way, I am going against the flow of golfers, and they are more likely to need a snack or beverage a little further into their game. I stop at each group of golfers I come across to see if there is anything they need. If a member would like to purchase an item, I will either collect cash for their purchase or fill out a member ticket. The member tickets are for Tampa Palms Golf and Country Club members only, go straight to their private club account, and are billed at the end of each month. Many members golf frequently, and it is a part of my job to get to know not only the name of each member, but his or her most frequent order, member number, and so forth. If we are hosting an outside tournament, most of the golfers are not members, and therefore we require cash for all purchases made during the tournament if there are not already food and beverages provided to the golfers.

Throughout the day, especially on days with nice weather or holiday weekends, I will need to restock the cart. It's easier to restock when I'm keeping track in my head of what items are going quickest. For instance, if the last two groups of golfers each ordered Bud Lights and I haven't made a single coffee sale that morning, I'll know I don't need to make any more coffee and I'll need to stock up on Bud Lights. Even if only eight beers were purchased, the odds those two groups will be purchasing another round of Bud Lights is very likely.

At the end of my day, I unload all of my product from the cart into a fridge inside of the clubhouse. I ring in all of my member tickets, count the cash I've received, and type up an inventory sheet. The inventory sheets help me keep track of what is most popular and requested on the course, and track my sales and volume of distribution for my food and beverage director.

training. Later, commercial health clubs also began to evolve, offering men's and women's exercise. As the sports and fitness movement grew, clubs appealed to special interests. Now clubs can be classified as follows: figure salons, health clubs, bodybuilding gyms, tennis clubs, rowing clubs, swim clubs, racquetball centers, or multipurpose clubs.

A multipurpose club has more exclusive recreation programs than a health club does. Leagues, tournaments, and classes are common for racquet sports, and most clubs offer several types of fitness classes. Some innovative clubs offer automatic bank tellers, stock market quote services, computer matching for tennis competition, auto detailing, laundry and dry cleaning services, and wine-cellar storage.

Club revenue comes from membership fees, user fees, guest fees, food and beverage sales, facility rental, and so on. Human resources account for about 66 percent of expenses at most clubs.

It is amazing to realize that in the center of a city there may be several voluntary organizations, each serving a particular segment of the population. Richard Kraus writes that a study of the city of Toronto which examined various land uses and leisure programs in the city's core found the following organizations: a Boy's Club, a mission, the Center of the Metropolitan Association for the Retarded, a Catholic settlement house, a day care center, an Indian center, a YMCA and YWCA, a service center for working people, a Chinese center, a Ukrainian center, and several other organizations meeting special needs and interests. These were all in addition to public parks, recreation areas, and nineteen churches.

Campus, Armed Forces, and Employee Recreation

Campus Recreation

North America's colleges and universities provide a major setting for organized leisure and recreational programs with services involving millions of participants each year. The programs include involvement by campus recreation offices, intramural departments, student unions, residence staffs, or other sponsors. People spend much of their leisure time participating in a wide variety of organized recreational activities, such as aerobics, arts and crafts, the performing arts, camping, and sports. Recreation and fitness workers plan, organize, and direct these activities in local playgrounds and recreation areas, parks, community centers, health clubs, fitness centers, religious organizations, camps, theme parks, and tourist attractions. Increasingly, recreational and fitness workers also are found in workplaces, where they organize and direct leisure activities and athletic programs for employees of all ages.

The various recreational activities help in maintaining good morale on campus. Some use recreational activities such as sports or orchestras or theater companies as a means of gaining alumni support. Students look for an exciting and interesting social life. For this reason, colleges and universities offer a wide range of recreational and social activities that may vary from campus to campus.

Armed Forces Recreation

It is the official policy of the Department of Defense to provide a well-rounded welfare and recreational program for the physical, social, and mental well-being of its personnel. Each service sponsors recreational activities under the auspices of the Morale, Welfare, and Recreation Program (MWR), which is executed under the Installation Management Command. MWR activities are provided to all military personnel and civilian employees at all installations.

MWR programs include the following types of activities:

- Sports, including self-directed, competitive, instructional, and spectator programs
- Motion pictures
- Service clubs and entertainment
- Crafts and hobbies
- Youth activities for children of military families
- Special-interest groups such as aero, automotive, motorcycle, and power boat clubs, as well as hiking, skydiving, and rod and gun clubs
- Rest centers and recreation areas
- Open dining facilities
- Libraries

Recreation is perceived as an important part of the employee benefits package for military personnel, along with the G.I. Bill, medical services, commissaries, and exchanges.

Employee Recreation

Business and industry have realized the importance of promoting employee efficiency. Human resource experts have found that workers who spend their free time at constructive recreational activities have less absenteeism resulting from emotional tension, illness, excessive use of alcohol, and so on. Employee recreation programs may also be an incentive for a prospective employee to join a company. So, remember to ask for a signing bonus if you are a softball star and the company you are about to join wants to win the tournament!

In the United States and Canada, almost all the leading corporations have an employee recreation and wellness program. Some companies include recreation activities in their team-building and management-development programs.

Recreation for Special Populations

Recreation for special populations involves professionals and organizations who serve groups such as those with mental illness, mental retardation, or physical challenges. In recent years, there has been increased recognition of the need to provide recreational programs for special populations. These programs, developed for each of the special population groups, use therapeutic recreation as a form of treatment.

One sports program for people with disabilities that has received considerable attention in recent years is the Special Olympics, an international year-round program of physical fitness, sports training, and athletic competition for children and adults with intellectual disabilities. The program is unique because it accommodates competitors at all ability levels by assigning participants to competition divisions based on both age and actual performance.[59]

Today, the Special Olympics serves more than 1.4 million individuals in the United States and more than seventy other countries. Among the official sports are track and field events, swimming, diving, gymnastics, ice skating, basketball, volleyball, soccer, softball, floor hockey, bowling, Frisbee disk, downhill skiing, cross-country skiing, and wheelchair events. The National Parks and Recreation Association and numerous state and local agencies and societies work closely with the Special Olympics in promoting programs and sponsoring competitions.[60]

Trends in Recreation and Leisure

- An increase in all fitness activities
- A surge in travel and tourism
- In addition to a continuation of traditional recreation and leisure activities, a development of special programs targeted toward at-risk youths and latchkey children
- Several additional products in the commercial sector
- Additional learning and adventure opportunities for the elderly, such as Life Long Learning

Career Information

Theme Parks

The operation of a theme park includes countless occupations. SeaWorld Parks & Entertainment, Walt Disney Company, and others have excellent programs for employment during college. These programs provide information on career development. Upon graduation, careers may follow a number of paths. Graduates may start in any number of levels: operations management, marketing and sales, human resources, food service, planning and development, or information systems, to name but a few.

An internship is one of the best ways to get involved in the theme park industry. An internship provides valuable work experience and is a great way to learn more about various areas of the industry. Interns are very appealing to potential employers. If you are a college student who is interested in spending a summer working for one of America's premier companies, visit the Disney College Program web site at www.wdwcollegeprogram.com.

George Gonzalez, a theme park manager offers this advice:

Theme parks and attractions offer excellent career opportunities for hospitality graduates. Parks and attractions are generally organized by divisions and departments: rides, shows, animal attractions, up-close tours, special events, dining, gift shop, group events, education and classes, and animal attractions.

If you are interested in theme parks, it is a good idea to work at one during the school year and in the summer months. By gaining experience in any department, you gain an overall impression of the park and hopefully learn if a career in the theme park industry would be a good fit you. Good luck whichever career path you take.

Remember, someone has to run the Smithsonian museum and the national parks and Walt Disney World. All of these attractions have several departments, all with management ladders that can be climbed at varying speeds. Apart from the main attractions, there are careers in accounting, marketing, maintenance, and service, in addition to professional positions for entertainers, historians, and curators. Salary levels for graduates with experience is about $30,000, and for mid-level managers in the larger attractions, salary levels are about $80,000 to $120,000.[61]

Clubs

Club managers and hotel managers share many of the same responsibilities. They are in charge of preparing budgets and forecasting future sales; monitoring restaurants on the property and various internal departments, such as human resources; and making sure maintenance work is done properly. They are responsible for the overall well-being of the club. The CMAA (www.cmaa.org) gives club managers certification and other membership benefits, such as professional development and networking. Its web site is worth a visit.

Club management is different from hotel management in that guests at a club are members and feel like and sometimes behave like owners because they pay a lot of money to join the club. Because of this, many feel a stronger tie to the club and therefore expect a higher level of service.

Of the many types of clubs within the club management industry, the most predominant are golf, country, city, athletic, yacht. Country clubs are the most common. They are typically based on outdoor activities. Golf is the main draw, but other sports such as tennis and swimming are also popular. Some country clubs also offer their members a variety of classes and social activities. They typically have a lounge and/or restaurant on the property, as well. Country clubs can be private or semiprivate. If a country club is private, its facilities are only available to members; a semiprivate club offers some services to nonmembers. There is no one definite career path when it comes to club management. However, most people

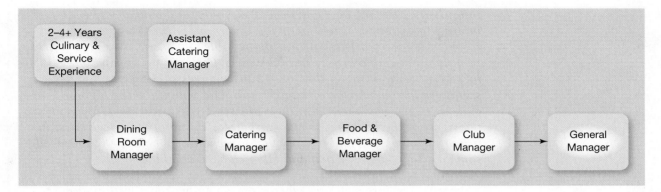

Figure 5 • A Career Path in Club Management.

make the transition to club manager from positions in kitchen or bar management (see Figure 5). It is rare that employees move from areas such as accounting to become club managers. Depending on the level of experience, one might start out as an assistant banquet or dining room manager and then progress to position as catering manager or assistant clubhouse manager. The next step occurs according to the amount of time in these positions, as well as the quality of the experience. For example, four to six years in a club that has gross income of $1.5 million in food and beverage sales would most likely lead to a club management position.

Club managers do not keep regular hours. They work long hours when the club is busy, and fewer hours when the club is slow. Club managers usually create their own schedules according to fluctuations in activity. On average, they typically work five or six days a week, 10 hours a day. Most entry-level club management positions have set salaries that range from $27,000 to $30,000. Entry-level positions are usually not subject to negotiation. Mid-level position salaries, however, can be negotiated until an agreeable sum is met. The actual salary depends on the amount of experience the employee has and the strength of his or her references. The best aspect of working as club manager is that the environment and facilities are usually top notch. Managers typically have access to the club's facilities and receive meals. ClubCorp is one of the largest corporate owners of clubs, operating more than 150 country clubs, business clubs, and golf resorts. Recent expansions in corporate ownership have made it slightly easier to enter the club management profession.

If you are serious about a career in club management, you should join the local student chapter of the CMAA. CMAA meetings are a great place for networking to find a summer job or an internship. The experience you gain during your collage tenure will provide you with the knowledge you need to begin your career in the recreation and leisure industries. Excellent opportunities for advancement come frequently. Club managers also often receive bonuses based on performance. These bonuses range from 5 to 15 percent of the manager's base salary of more than $100,000 annually. The highest paid country club manager makes about $1 million annually.

John Costello, country club general manager, offers this advice:

If you have an interest in country club management, get a job in a club, and then do an internship in one. The most likely area of initial employment is in the food and beverage department, with opportunities in dining rooms/

restaurants, catering, bars and beverage service, and culinary. The job and internship experiences will help you determine if the country club environment is for you. There is one big possible advantage over other types of hospitality employment: You have an opportunity to interact with club members over time rather than with transient guests. The general manager's six-figure income maybe of interest, too. Did you know the highest paid club manager gets about a million dollars a year? Yes, the GM [general manager] of the Palm Beach club earned $750,000 in 2006 (the latest information available) and by now that is reckoned to be $1,000,000. Well, someone has to manage that and other clubs. Good luck!"

The following are web sites where you can gather more information:

ClubCorp: www.clubcorp.com
Club Managers Association of America: www.cmaa.org
Club Management magazine: http://www.naylornetwork.com/mam-nxt/
National Parks Service: www.nps.gov
National Club Association: www.natlclub.org

CASE STUDY

Service Proposal for Guests

You recently joined the front desk of a nice resort hotel in New England, and your hotel manager has complimented you on your guest service ability. She has asked you to develop a walking/jogging trail for the guests.

Discussion Question

1. What would be some of the key elements to consider in developing a proposal for your hotel guests?

CASE STUDY

Overpopulation of National Parks

Our national parks are under serious threat from a number of sources, including congestion resulting from overvisitation, consequent environmental degradation, and pollution.

There are too many people and too many vehicles in the most popular national parks. Many visitors bring their city lifestyle, leaving garbage lying around, listening to loud music, and leaving the trails in worse shape.

Discussion Question

1. List the recommendations you have for the park superintendents to help save the parks.

Summary

1. Recreation is free time that people use to restore, rest, and relax their minds and bodies. Recreational activities can be passive or active, individual or group activities.
2. Recreational activities range from cultural pursuits such as museums or theaters, to sports or outdoor recreation such as amusement parks, community centers, playgrounds, and libraries. These services involve various levels of government.
3. National parks preserve exceptional lands for public use, emphasizing the protection of their ecosystems and endangered plant and animal species and honoring historical sites. Two of the best known of the current 397 parks in the United States include Yellowstone and Yosemite National Parks.
4. Today, city governments are increasingly expected to provide recreational facilities such as golf courses, swimming pools, picnic areas, and playgrounds as a community service.
5. Commercial recreation—for example, theme parks, clubs, and attractions—involves a profit for the supplier of the recreational activity.
6. Clubs are places where members gather for social, recreational, professional, or fraternal reasons. There are many different types of clubs such as country clubs and city clubs categorized according to the interests they represent to their members.
7. Noncommercial recreation includes governmental and nonprofit agencies, such as voluntary organization, campus, armed forces, and employee recreation, and recreation for special populations, such as the physically challenged.

Key Words and Concepts

city clubs
club management
commercial recreation
country clubs
government-sponsored recreation
heritage tourism
leisure
national park
National Parks Service

National Register of Historic Places
noncommercial recreation
recreation
recreation for special populations
recreation management
theme parks
transient occupancy tax (TOT)
voluntary organizations

Review Questions

1. Define recreation and its importance to human wellness. What factors affect an individual's decision to participate in recreational activities?
2. Describe the origin of government-sponsored recreation in consideration of the origin and purpose of national parks.
3. Briefly describe the difference between commercial and noncommercial recreation.
4. Briefly explain the purpose of a theme park and the purpose of clubs.
5. Explain the concept of recreation for special populations.

Internet Exercise

1. Organization: **Prestonwood Country Club**
   Web site: **www.prestonwoodcc.com**
   Summary: Prestonwood is a full-service country club that offers activities and fine food.

   (a) What kinds of activities are offered at the Prestonwood Country Club?
   (b) Parents may wish to take their kids on vacations. In these situations, what might this country club offer those kids?

Apply Your Knowledge

1. Create your own personal recreation goals and make a plan to reach them.

2. Describe the features of commercial versus noncommercial recreation.

Suggested Activities

1. On the Internet, research the history of Mardi Gras. Write a one-page description of the event and its cultural roots.

2. Look up your favorite theme park on the web. Think about what kind of position you would like to have at the park. If the site has job listings, tell whether any of them appeal to you.

Endnotes

1. Personal correspondence with Jay Sullivan, August 4, 2007.
2. Wikipedia, *Recreation*, http://en.wikipedia.org/wiki/recreation (November 15, 2011).
3. "Nathaniel Hawthorne," *BrainyQuote.com*, Xplore Inc. http://www.brainyquote.com/quotes/quotes/n/nathanielh163048.html (accessed November 15, 2011).
4. Peopleassets, *The PeopleAssets/California Park & Recreation Society Leadership Competency Profile*, www.peopleassets.net/cprs/reports/samplereport.htm (accessed November 15, 2011).
5. This section draws on information supplied by the National Parks Service.
6. Robert E. Manning, "Commons without Tragedy: Measuring and Managing Carrying Capacity in the National Parks," In *Natural Resource Year in Review—2006* (National Park Service, 2007): 13–14, http://www.nature.nps.gov/YearInReview/YIR2006/01_c.html (accessed November 15, 2011).
7. National Park Service, *Backcountry Recreation Management*, http://www.nature.nps.gov/Rm77/backcountry/roles.cfm (accessed May 10, 2011).
8. Ibid.
9. National Park Service, *Budget*, http://www.nps.gov/aboutus/budget.htm (accessed May 11, 2011).
10. National Park Service, *Cape Lookout National Seashore: Management*, http://www.nps.gov/calo/parkmgmt/index.htm (accessed May 10, 2011).
11. Ibid.
12. National Park Service, *General Management Planning Process: Frequently Asked Questions*, http://www.nps.gov/sero/planning/buis_gmp/buis_desc.htm (accessed May 10, 2011).
13. Wikipedia, *Recreation*, http://en.wikipedia.org/wiki/recreation (accessed November 15, 2011).
14. Personal correspondence with Knott's Berry Farm, April 2006.
15. Knott's Berry Farm, Inside the Park, http://www.knotts.com/public/park/index.cfm (accessed November 15, 2011).
16. Astrid Dorothea Ada Maria Kemperman, *Temporal Aspects of Theme Park Choice Behavior*, (Eindhoven University of Technology, 2000), http://alexandria.tue.nl/extra2/200013915.pdf (accessed November 15, 2011).
17. Todd D. MacCartney, *Excerpt from Walt Disney World Made Simple*, http://travelassist.com/mag/a12.

html (accessed November 15, 2011); Randy Bright, *Disneyland: Inside Story* (New York: Abraus, 1987), 33.

18. DIS, *Magic Kingdom*, http://www.wdwinfo.com/wdwinfo/guides/magickingdom/mkindex.htm (accessed November 15, 2011).

19. DIS, *Epcot—Future World*, http://www.wdwinfo.com/wdwinfo/guides/epcot/ep-futureworld.htm (accessed November 15, 2011).

20. DIS, *Epcot World Showcase*, http://www.wdwinfo.com/wdwinfo/guides/epcot/ep-worldshowcase.htm (accessed November 15, 2011).

21. DIS, *Disney's Hollywood Studios*, http://www.wdwinfo.com/wdwinfo/guides/mgm/st-overview.htm (accessed November 15, 2011).

22. Atlas Cruises and Tours, *Walt Disney World Vacation Packages*, www.atlastravelweb.com/waltdisneyworldpackages.shtml (site now discontinued).

23. Wikipedia, *Universal Studios Hollywood*, http://en.wikipedia.org/wiki/Universal_Studios_Hollywood (accessed November 18, 2007).

24. NBCUniversal, This Is NBCUniversal, http://www.nbcuni.com/corporate/about-us/ (accessed November 15, 2011).

25. Wikipedia, *SeaWorld Parks & Entertainment*, http://en.wikipedia.org/wiki/SeaWorld_Parks_%26_Entertainment (accessed November 15, 2011).

26. Water Country USA, *2011 Media Kit*, http://www.watercountryusa.com/AssetManagement/Assets/WIP/WC/2011%20WCUSA%20press%20kit.pdf (accessed November 15, 2011).

27. Discovery Cove, *Discover a Place beyond Words*, http://www.discoverycove.com/Explore/Discover.aspx (accessed November 15, 2011).

28. Hershey's, *Hershey's History*, http://www.thehersheycompany.com/about-hershey/our-story/hersheys-history.aspx (accessed November 15, 2011).

29. Dollywood, *About Dollywood*, http://www.dollywood.com/dollywood-q10143-c10132-About_Dollywood.aspx (accessed November 15, 2011).

30. Wikipedia, *Dollywood*, http://en.wikipedia.org/wiki/Dollywood (accessed November 15, 2011).

31. Wikipedia, *Legoland*, http://en.wikipedia.org/wiki/legoland (accessed November 15, 2011).

32. Ibid.

33. Gatorland, *History*, www.gatorland.com/history/history.html (accessed November 15, 2011).

34. Wikipedia, *Wet 'n Wild Orlando*, http://en.wikipedia.org/wiki/Wet_%27n_Wild_Orlando (accessed November 15, 2011).

35. Association of Zoos & Aquariums, *Home Page*, www.aza.org (accessed November 15, 2011).

36. San Diego Zoo, *About San Diego Zoo Global*, www.sandiegozoo.org/disclaimers/aboutus.html (accessed November 15, 2011).

37. San Diego Zoo, *Panda Baby Named in Zoo Ceremony*, www.sandiegozoo.org/news/panda_naming.html (accessed September 19, 2009).

38. Smithsonian National Zoological Park, *About Us*, http://nationalzoo.si.edu/aboutus/ (accessed September 19, 2009).

39. Ibid.

40. National Aquarium Baltimore, *Community Affairs*, www.aqua.org/communityaffairs.html (accessed September 19, 2009).

41. Ibid.

42. National Park Service, *National Register of Historic Places Program: About Us*, www.nps.gov/nr/about.htm (accessed September 19, 2009).

43. Wikipedia, *Battle of the Alamo*, http://en.wikipedia.org/wiki/Battle_of_the_Alamo (accessed November 15, 2011).

44. Opry.com, *Tour the Opry House*, http://www.opry.com/shows/TourTheOpryHouse.html (accessed November 15, 2011).

45. Smithsonian Institution, *About Us*, www.si.edu/about/ (accessed November 15, 2011).

46. Ibid.

47. Ibid.

48. Field Museum, *Mission Statement*, http://fieldmuseum.org/about/mission (accessed November 15, 2011).

49. Ibid.

50. Ibid.

51. Hellenic Ministry of Culture, *The Unification of the Archaeological Sites of Athens*, www.yppo.gr/4/e40.jsp?obj_id=90 (accessed January 20, 2009).

52. Wikipedia, *Athens*, http://en.wikipedia.org/wiki/Athens (accessed November 15, 2011).

53. Central Intelligence Agency: "Holy See (Vatican City)," *The World Factbook*, https://www.cia.gov/library/publications/the-world-factbook/geos/vt.html (accessed November 15, 2011).

54. John R. Walker, *Introduction to Hospitality Management*, 3rd ed. (Upper Saddle River, NJ: Pearson, 2010): 553–554.

55. Ibid.

56. Interview with Kurt Allen, General Manager, Marineland Dolphin Adventure, Miami, June 9, 2011.

57. Angela Nitz, "A Sustainable Term," *Club Management*, January/February 2010: 43, www.nxtbook.com/nxtbooks/naylor/MAMS0110/index.php?startpage=43&qs=sustainability#/42 (accessed November 15, 2011).

58. Angela Nitz, "Facility-wide Recycling: A Team Effort," *Club Management*, November/December 2009: 29, http://www.nxtbook.com/nxtbooks/naylor/MAMS0609/index.php?startpage=29&qs=sustainability#/28 (accessed November 15, 2004).

59. Special Olympics, *What We Do: Changing Attitudes*, http://www.specialolympics.org/changingattitudes.aspx (accessed November 15, 2011).

60. Special Olympics, "About Us," www.specialolympics.org/special+olympics+public+website/English/About_us/default.htm.

61. Interview with Bill Lupfer, CEO of the Florida Attractions Association, June 9, 2011.

Glossary

City clubs   Various clubs in cities.

Club management   The management of clubs.

Commercial recreation   For profit recreation.

Country clubs   Clubs that offer members golf and sometimes other sporting activities such as tennis and swimming along with games and social activities.

Government-sponsored recreation   Recreation paid for by government taxes; includes monies sent to cities for museums, libraries, and municipal golf courses.

Heritage tourism   Tourism the Involves or relates to heritage.

Leisure   Freedom from activities, especially time free from work or duties.

National park   A park belonging to the nation.

National Parks Service   The service that manages to National Parks.

Noncommercial recreation   Not for profit recreation.

Recreation   Refreshment of strength and spirits after work; a means of diversion.

Recreation for special populations   Recreation designed to accommodate persons with disabilities, for example the Special Olympics.

Theme park   A recreational park based on a particular setting or artistic interpretation; may operate with hundreds or thousands of acres of parkland and hundreds or thousands of employees.

Transient occupancy tax (TOT)   Tax paid by people staying in a city's hotels.

Voluntary organization   A nongovernmental, nonprofit agency serving the public.

Photo Credits

Credits are listed in order of appearance.

kavram/Shutterstock

svetlyachok/Shutterstock

Golden Pixels LLC/Shutterstock

Chee-Onn Leong/Shutterstock

Chris LeBoutillier/Shutterstock

Juriah Mosin/Shutterstock

Max Alexander/DK Images

Peter Carroll/Alamy

Jiawangkun/Dreamstime LLC

Bill Brooks/Alamy

mahout/Shutterstock

Kokhanchikov/Shutterstock

Manamana/Shutterstock

Nordic Photos/SuperStock

Dave Cannon/Stone/Getty Images

Edward J Shaughnessy

Bart Bartlett

Christie Chapman

Gaming Entertainment

From Chapter 11 of *Introduction to Hospitality,* Sixth Edition. John R. Walker. Copyright © 2013 by Pearson Education, Inc. Published by Pearson. All rights reserved.

Gaming Entertainment

OBJECTIVES

After reading and studying this text, you should be able to:

- Outline the history of modern casinos.

- Describe the various components of modern casino hotels.

- Explain how casinos have been integrated into larger hospitality operations.

- Appreciate the spread of casino gaming across the United States and throughout the world.

- Understand the basic principles of casino operations.

- Discuss the different positions within the gaming industry.

One of the most significant developments in the hospitality industry during the past three decades has been the astounding growth of the casino industry and its convergence with the lodging and hospitality industries. With its rapid expansion in North America and throughout the world, new opportunities have been created for hospitality careers within casino resorts.

The Casino Resort: A Hospitality Buffet

Today, **casino resorts** are among the most visible hospitality businesses in the world. Twenty of the thirty largest hotels in the world are casino resorts on the Las Vegas Strip.[1] Those aiming for careers in hospitality, even if they have no special interest in working on the gambling side of the operation, may find themselves considering a position in a resort that has a casino but also a full spread of lodging, food and beverage, entertainment, and retail offerings.

Even if you don't plan on working on the casino floor itself, a rudimentary understanding of the nature of gambling—and the specifics of casino gambling—is an essential tool for those who want to pursue careers in casino resorts. Today, many casino resort presidents and key executives have come up through the lodging or food and beverage side of operations; a solid understanding of what's happening in the casino—and how casino guests are different from other hospitality patrons—makes advancing through the ranks that much easier.

What Is Gambling?

In its broadest definition, **gambling** is the act of placing stakes on an unknown outcome with the possibility of securing a gain if the bettor guesses correctly.

To be considered gambling, an act must have three elements: something wagered (the bet), a randomizing event (the spin of slot reels or the flip of a card), and a payoff.

This broad definition of gambling includes many dissimilar activities: contests between animals (horse racing, cockfighting) and between humans (team and individual sports); lotteries; and games of chance played with cards, dice, and other randomizing elements. Some of the best-known games fall into the last category: Poker, blackjack, and baccarat are played with cards, and craps with dice. Slot machines, which were originally mechanical (but now electronic) devices that award prizes based on the

A themed gaming and slot machine area in a casino.

random stopping of reels, are also popular, and are typically the most-played games in most casinos today.

How do casinos make money from gambling? The answer lies in the kind of gambling they offer. There are two basic categories of gambling: **Social** gambling and **mercantile** (or commercial) gambling. Social gambling is conducted among individuals who bet against each other; mathematically, each player has the same chance of winning. Poker is a classic social game: Every player is drawing from the same deck and has the same opportunity to check, raise, or fold. Other social forms of gambling include dominoes and mah-jongg.

In mercantile or commercial gambling, players bet against "the house," a professional gambler or organization that accepts wagers from the general public. Mercantile games have a mathematical advantage for the casino, or a house edge that lets professionals profit from them while still offering fair games. All lotteries are mercantile games, and every game found on the casino floor is a mercantile game: There is a small guaranteed bias toward the house that, over time, ensures the casino will win more than it pays out.

The **house edge** is best explained by looking at the game of roulette, which features a wheel with thirty-eight slots numbered one to thirty-six, in addition to a single zero and a double zero. On each spin, a small ball falls into one of the thirty-eight slots. If you bet "straight up" on a number, you win thirty-five units for each one unit you bet. So if you bet one dollar straight on, you'd end up with thirty-six dollars: the one you staked, plus thirty-five more. Since the wheel has a one-in-thirty-eight chance of hitting any number, you should be paid off at a rate of 37:1, not 35:1. That extra two dollars is the house edge; it seems slight, but over time, it adds up.

The house edge is what makes casinos possible; without it, the only way to offer games of chance to the public that can generate an income would be to cheat. The house edge allows casinos to offer their customers honest games, fairly dealt, and still remain in business.

The game of poker is an interesting exception to the rule that all casino games have built-in house edges. Many casinos have poker rooms, in which players bet against each other using a table, cards, and dealer supplied by the house. The casino has no direct stake in the outcome of each hand, but instead takes a small percentage of each pot ("the rake") to defray the costs of operating the room. Though it is a popular game, poker makes little money for casinos (see Figure 1); casinos offer the game as an amenity for players who will also play straight-up mercantile games or for those who are visiting with slots or table games players.

This resort on the Las Vegas Strip models itself after New York City.

Game	# of Units	n Amount	Win %	Handle
Slot Machine	49,352	2,789,753	7.22%	38,639,238
Table Games	2,802	2,904,826	11.43%	25,414,051
Total Win		5,776,570	9.02%	64,053,289

Slots detail

Game	# of Units	n Amount	Win %	Handle
1 Cent	11,674	743,101	11.55%	6,433,775
5 Cent	1,948	72,254	9.16%	788,799
25 Cent	1,948	262,773	8.33%	3,154,538
1 Dollar	5,006	298,171	6.45%	4,622,806
Multi-Denom	22,576	1,233,092	6.04%	20,415,430

Table games detail

Game	# of Units	n Amount	Win %	Handle
Twenty-one	1,404	721,822	9.98%	7,232,685
Baccarat	241	1,181,967	11.03%	10,715,929
Craps	202	267,397	11.59%	2,307,135
Roulette	274	258,886	16.80%	1,540,988
3-Card Poker	126	96,159	29.05%	331,012
Mini-Bacc	89	62,424	8.34%	748,489
Car. Stud Poker	11	6,204	26.29%	23,598
Let It Ride	59	31,225	22.31%	139,960
Pai Gow	23	17,808	14.44%	123,324
Pai Gow Poker	115	58,006	19.85%	292,222
Keno	22	6,909	28.03%	24,649
Bingo	3	1,652	7.41%	22,294
Race Book	26	26,715	16.51%	161,811
Sports Book	37	69,338	5.11%	1,356,908
Poker tables	435	81,990 (rake only; no direct win)		

Figure 1 • Las Vegas Strip 2010 Gaming Win.

Win and Handle are in thousands of dollars.
Gaming Revenue Report, Nevada Gaming Control Board, December 2010.

The house edge is a theoretical number; it describes the amount of money wagered (handle) that the casino should keep over time. For tables and slots, casinos track the hold percentage to better understand how well the casino is performing.

To understand hold percentage, we need to understand two other terms: handle (or buy-in) and win. The **handle** is the total amount of money bet at a game. The **win** is the handle minus the money paid out on winning bets—essentially, what the casino keeps. The **hold percentage** is the percentage of the total handle that is retained as win. On slot machines, the hold percentage tracks very close to the theoretical house edge. On table games, however, it is usually considerably higher than the house edge.

Though the games offered in casinos have a statistical bias toward the house, they are still games of chance. In the short run, players can get lucky and walk away with the house's money. In small-stakes games this isn't a problem, since the sheer number of bets taken tends to drive the hold percentage toward its historically expected value (see Figure 2).

Games played for high stakes, such as baccarat, are different. Because there are large amounts of money being spread over fewer decisions, these games have a great deal of volatility; in a given month, the hold percentage for a baccarat game in single casino can fluctuate wildly (see Figure 3).

Casino Win Defined

Let's say you buy into a roulette game for $100 in $1 chips. You place 100 even-money bets, winning 94 and losing 6. In this case, the following are true:

The handle is $100.
The win is $6.
The winning percentage is 6 percent.

This is very close to the theoretical house edge of 5.26 percent. But if you continued playing for another 100 bets, you might lose another 6. In this case, the handle would still be $100, but the win would be $12, and the hold percentage 12 percent.

Theoretical hold versus actual 2010 win percentage for the Las Vegas Strip

Game	House Edge	Win %
Twenty-one	Approx 1%*	9.98%
Baccarat	1.15%	11.03%
Craps	1.4% (Pass line bet)	11.59%
Roulette	5.26%	16.80%

Figure 2 • House Edge versus Win Percentage.

Because there are several varieties of blackjack, it is difficult to provide a single 'house edge' for the game, but most games have a house edge near one percent. Gaming Revenue Report, Nevada Gaming Control Board, December 2010.

	Wheel of Fortune			Baccarat		
Month	Win	Drop	Hold	Win	Drop	Hold
Jan-07	91,717	195,126	47.00%	986,554	4,604,032	21.40%
Feb-07	92,750	188,835	49.12%	511,022	5,521,377	9.30%
Mar-07	99,949	194,208	51.46%	533,126	4,318,929	12.30%
Apr-07	88,537	182,643	48.48%	1,362,604	3,923,624	34.70%
May-07	74,434	183,663	40.53%	383,515	4,508,300	8.50%
Jun-07	85,933	176,311	48.74%	825,539	4,080,351	20.20%
Jul-07	84,886	208,992	40.62%	−406,421	4,718,282	−8.60%
Aug-07	93,739	214,358	43.73%	182,793	4,086,594	4.50%
Sep-07	55,157	155,184	35.54%	348,263	4,501,165	7.70%
Oct-07	52,935	149,538	35.40%	16,027	1,129,132	1.40%
Nov-07	77,557	173,000	44.83%	319,151	1,672,186	19.10%
Dec-07	80,646	164,742	48.95%	145,398	2,072,952	7.00%

Figure 3 • Wheel of Fortune versus Baccarat.

Results from two Atlantic City Casinos for 2007.
Monthly gross revenue returns, New Jersey Casino Control Commission.

As a manager of a casino resort, it is important that you have an appreciation of the nature of volatility. Just because the casino department is reporting a net loss for a shift does not necessarily mean that the department is inefficient or incompetent; it may just be an expression of volatility. Over time, gaming wins will tend towards their historical average.

Managers also need to understand that, because of volatility, casinos are not like other hospitality businesses. A typical hotel, running at 95-percent occupancy for the weekend and with full restaurant bookings, will certainly make a profit. Because of volatility, even a busy casino can end up in the red for a shift or even a weekend if one high-stakes player has a run of good luck.

Comps: A Usual Part of an Unusual Business

Volatility isn't the only aspect of the casino business that makes it different from most other hospitality businesses. **Comps** are another area that set casinos apart.

Comps are complimentary goods and services offered to casino patrons in order to attract their business. Comps are found in virtually every casino, and any casino guest of consequence has expectations of receiving comps. Unlike in other hospitality operations, where comps are given primarily as part of service recovery to compensate for a customer service failure or other miscue, comps are distributed as a usual part of a casino's operation.

The value of comps varies; generally speaking, higher-producing players are given higher-value comps. For example, a small-stakes slot player might receive an offer for a discounted or free buffet; a baccarat-playing high roller, betting $10,000 a hand for several hours, might receive a full RFB (room, food, beverage) comp, with all expenses in the casino's most lavish accommodations paid for. Casino guests might also receive comps for entertainment or other gifts. Many slots players receive cash back when they reach certain play thresholds.

Comps dramatically affect casino resort operations. As shown in Figure 4, a significant percentage of nongaming services are comped.

Casinos, with thousands of guests on any given day, rely on customer **loyalty programs** to track patron play. Patrons who wish to receive comps and other offers join the casino's player loyalty club (e.g., Caesars' Total Rewards, MGM Resorts' M life, Wynn Resorts' Red Card). Slot players insert

Department	Percentage of Comps
Rooms	24.6%
Restaurants	17.0%
Beverage	34.4%

Figure 4 • Las Vegas Strip Comps.

the card they receive into the machine they are playing; the card then tracks money played and won. Table games players have a pit manager swipe their card, tracking their time of play and average bet size.

Casinos use the information they gain about a player's gambling patterns to offer him or her comps, based both on theoretical wins by the player and his or her expected levels of play. Most loyalty programs have tiered rewards structures, giving patrons an incentive to play more and unlock more rewards.

Loyalty programs are an essential part of casino marketing; many guests base the money they spend gaming around where they receive the best comps, so good casino managers know they must send out good offers to qualified players. Casinos also use sophisticated software to monitor and deliver bonuses to slot patrons as they are playing on machines. Recently, some casinos have begun tracking and rewarding nongaming spending as well, a reflection of the broadening of the casino resort revenue stream.

Types of Casino Operations

There are several different kinds of casino operations, operating on vastly different scales. At one end of the spectrum is the Nevada-style gaming tavern, which is a typical bar and restaurant that has less than sixteen electronic gaming devices, usually bar-top video poker and slot machines. At the other is a fully-developed casino resort, with (on average) a 100,000-square-foot casino featuring thousands of slot machines and dozens of table games, approximately 3,000 hotel rooms, at least a dozen bars and restaurants, meeting and convention facilities, entertainment venues, retail shopping, and pool and spa facilities.

Between these two extremes, which are both found in Las Vegas, there are several other kinds of operations. Stand-alone casinos are not very common in the United States or elsewhere in the world. Where they are found, they usually consist of only slot machines; this type operation might be called a slot parlor. In Europe, the Middle East, Africa, and South America, casinos located in hotels might be extremely small and ancillary to the general hospitality operation.

In the United States, casinos on Indian reservation can take many forms, from bingo parlors in prefabricated buildings to fully functional casino resorts with lodging, dining, and entertainment that are indistinguishable from resorts on the Las Vegas Strip. Some states allow gambling only on riverboats, which originally cruised the waterways but today are usually "boat in a moat" operations that are permanently moored and connected almost seamlessly with a hotel and resort facility. Other states allow slot machines at racetracks (called "racinos"), and in some cases these have evolved to include hotel and resort operations as well. Finally, many cruise lines have casinos as part of the amenities available to guests on their ships.

FOCUS ON CASINO RESORTS

Casino Resorts and Hospitality

David G. Schwartz, Director, Center for Gaming Research, University of Nevada, Las Vegas

Casino resorts combine virtually every strand of the hospitality business. They've come a long way since the dusty saloons of frontier Nevada and the grimy illegal slot routes and bookmaking operations of American cities. Today, funded by mainstream capital, staffed by trained hospitality managers, and promoted globally, there is little that one can't find in a major casino resort.

It's important to note that casino resorts are so all-inclusive because it makes good economic sense. Originally, most revenues were generated on the casino floor. Yet, the nature of casino gambling—games that, over time, have a slight bias in favor of the house—demanded that casinos offer more than just gambling. To discourage spot play, in which a lucky player cashes out and leaves, casino resorts developed a number of attractions to lure and keep players near the casino. Lodging, food, beverage, and entertainment were offered as loss leaders to get players through the doors.

In the 1990s, following the opening of Steve Wynn's Mirage, the rules of the game changed. Though the old approach—offering loss leaders and focusing on gaming revenues—was profitable, there was more growth potential in a more balanced approach. Shifting the revenue center from exclusively gaming to also including rooms and particularly restaurants proved to be a lucrative decision. Guests got the chance to stay in more luxurious accommodations and sample a variety of dining experiences.

Now, major casino resorts earn most of their money from things other than gambling. But gambling is still central to their identity, and many high-value guests are primarily focused on gambling. Even if your job isn't directly on the gaming floor, it's important to remember that without gambling, the resort wouldn't exist.

At the same time, many smaller resorts still get most of their revenues from gambling, so managers of other departments may face an uphill battle for respect—and resources. If this is the case, it will be important to remind everyone that your department can help increase revenues, both by earning money itself and by contributing to an environment to which gamblers will flock.

At the end of the day, despite the sometimes obscure jargon and hard-to-figure-out gameplay, casino gambling is really no different from other hospitality operations: The idea is to help guests enjoy themselves. Guests pay for that privilege, and there are many other places where they can do so.

That's an important fact to remember: Today there are a wealth of choices for casino customers; any oversight or cut corner gives your customers an excuse to spend their money with your competition, who will gladly take it. A good casino manager, no matter what the department, will never lose sight of that fact, and will start and end each day with a single question: "What can I do to help my guests have a better time with us?" Anyone who can continue to come up with innovative but not budget-busting answers to this simple question will enjoy a long, successful career in the gaming and hospitality industry.

Components of Casino Resorts

The best example of the modern casino resort can be found on the Las Vegas Strip. These destination resorts are centered on casinos that have several types of games available:

- Slot machines
- Table games, including twenty-one (blackjack), craps, roulette, baccarat, and carnival games such as three-card poker
- Race and sports books, which accept wagers on horseracing and sporting events
- Poker rooms, where players bet against each other and where the house only keeps a portion of each pot

Gamblers playing poker at the Foxwoods Resort Casino in Mashantucket, Connecticut.

In most parts of the United States, slot machines produce the bulk of the revenue; on the Las Vegas Strip, due to high-stakes table play, it is closer to a 50/50 split (see Figure 1). Among table games, blackjack is most popular nationally, while on the Strip baccarat has recently become a favorite. In Macau casinos, nearly all revenue comes from high-stakes baccarat; slot machines are negligible.

Casino resorts also include the following components:

- Lodging (on average, 3,000 hotel rooms)
- Food and beverage outlets, ranging from fast food to gourmet eateries
- Entertainment venues, including lounges but also purpose-built theaters for Cirque du Soleil and similar spectaculars
- Retail shopping: Several casinos have shopping esplanades or even attached malls (Caesars Palace, Venetian, Planet Hollywood)
- Convention facilities, ranging from a few small rooms to the 1.9-million-square-foot Sands Expo Center at the Venetian/Palazzo
- Nightclubs, which are an increasingly lucrative part of the casino resort package
- Pool and spa facilities, which may be branded as "dayclubs" with DJ entertainment and bottle service available in cabanas

Casino resorts in other jurisdictions may have some, but not all, of these features. For example, outside of Nevada, sports betting is currently illegal, so those casinos will have, at most, a race book. Most casinos outside of Las Vegas, with a few notable exceptions, have smaller hotel and entertainment components.

> " The largest casino in the world is currently the Venetian Macao, with over 800 table games and 3,400 slot machines[2]. By contrast, the typical Las Vegas Strip casino has about 90 tables and 1,200 slot machines. "

> " People go to casinos and gamble for a variety of reasons, whether it's for fun, excitement, the possibility of hitting a jackpot, or just to feel challenged. "

Evolution of Gambling and Casinos

Gambling is among the oldest of human behaviors; archaeological evidence of gambling stretches back into prehistory, and purpose-built dice have been discovered at sites dating back to 7,000 years before the present. Gambling developed in nearly every ancient civilization of consequence and has been part of Western life since the days of Ancient Greece.

Casino resorts, as they are currently operated, are much younger, dating back only to 1941, though the casino industry has its antecedents in several earlier developments, both legal and illegal. Legal public gambling in casinos dates back to 1638, when the Grand Council of Venice awarded a franchise for a single legal casino in that city. Though that casino was closed in 1774, other European states—mostly small, resource-poor jurisdictions—also permitted gambling, usually as part of a larger spa complex; spas were Europe's first true tourist destination, and gambling was considered an essential part of many European spa communities. By 1872, however, casino-style gambling had been banned in all European countries save the tiny Mediterranean enclave of Monaco, whose Monte Carlo would grow wealthy on a decades-long monopoly.

In the United States, public gambling at cards and dice was legal intermittently during the nineteenth century in several states, including Louisiana, California, and Nevada, but by 1910 this kind of gambling—and playing at slot machines—had been outlawed everywhere in the United States. Both before and after the criminalization of all casino-style gambling, illegal gambling halls flourished in most of the major American cities.

Yet the tide soon turned toward legalization, at least in Nevada. When legislators authorized "wide open" commercial gambling there in 1931, the state was in the throes of the Great Depression. By allowing taverns and hotels to conduct games of chance, they hoped to increase tourism slightly. There was initially no state tax on gambling, and the economic impact was thought to be negligible. Reno and Las Vegas soon developed thriving downtown gambling districts, with small clubs offering slot machines and table games. These were usually simple, storefront operations with no real amenities.

The real creation of the modern casino came in 1941, with the opening of the **El Rancho Vegas**, the first casino resort on what would become the **Las Vegas Strip**. As a spa-like, self-contained destination with fine dining, entertainment, and gambling, the El Rancho Vegas appealed to casual tourists in a way that the smoky downtown gambling halls did not. Within a decade, a half-dozen other resorts joined the El Rancho Vegas, and the Las Vegas Strip was becoming a force.

These casinos were superior to gambling halls because, with rooms and a full range of amenities, they offered a diverse set of options for travelers–gamblers and nongamblers alike–and because they allowed casinos to keep visitors near the casino. Although in the short run the players might get lucky thanks to volatility, the longer they remained near the tables and slots, the more likely the casino was to end up with their money. Casinos in resorts therefore proved more profitable than stand-alone casinos, and they soon proliferated, particularly along the Strip.

By the mid-1950s, the casino resorts of the Las Vegas Strip had changed Nevada. Now numbering more than a dozen, they became an integral part of the state's economy. The legislature created a regulatory body, the Gaming Control Board, to oversee the industry, and the state began to rely on taxes extracted from casinos. With other development options failing to pan out, Nevada's casinos became the only game in town. The industry grew, and with the entrance of publicly traded corporations in the 1970s, it became more integrated into the national economic mainstream. The bulk of casinos were in Las Vegas; though Reno and Lake Tahoe remained key attractions in the north of the state, they failed to reinvent themselves, as Las Vegas did, in the face of new competition. As a result, by 2000, Las Vegas Strip casinos accounted for well over half of all state gambling revenues.

Others soon became interested in the potential of casino resorts for economic revitalization. In 1976, New Jersey voters legalized casino gambling in Atlantic City by referendum, and two years later the first legal casino on the East Coast opened. Within a few years, ten casinos were thriving in the city, helping to provide jobs, augment state revenues, and revitalize a formerly desolate resort town. Other states began exploring the possibilities of legalization, though they did so in far more restricted ways.

Riverboat gaming, which permitted games of chance only on boats, debuted in Iowa and Illinois in 1991, and soon spread throughout the Midwest and South, with a particularly robust presence in Mississippi. States like Colorado and South Dakota turned to "limited gambling" schemes, which like New Jersey confined casinos to particular towns, but also capped maximum bet sizes.

INTRODUCING STEPHEN A. WYNN

Chairman of the Board and CEO, Wynn Resorts

Casino developer Stephen A. Wynn is widely credited with transforming Las Vegas from a gambling venue for adults into a world-renowned resort and convention destination. As chairman of the board, president, and chief executive officer of Mirage Resorts, Mr. Wynn envisioned and built the Mirage, Treasure Island, and Bellagio—boldly conceived resorts that set progressively higher standards for quality, luxury, and entertainment. As chairman of the board and chief executive officer of Wynn Resorts, Limited, Mr. Wynn developed Wynn Las Vegas, among the world's preeminent luxury hotel resorts. Mr. Wynn also developed the Wynn Macau, a flagship Asian casino resort in Macau, where his company has been awarded a twenty-year concession by the Macau government.

Mr. Wynn began his career in 1967 as part owner, slot manager, and assistant credit manager of the Frontier Hotel. Between 1968 and 1972, he also owned and operated a wine and liquor importing company. But it was an entrepreneurial real estate deal with Howard Hughes in 1971 that produced sufficient profits for a major investment in the landmark Golden Nugget Casino. Once known only as a "gambling joint," he transformed the Golden Nugget into a Four-Diamond resort known for elegance and personal service. By 1973, at age thirty-one, Mr. Wynn controlled the property and began developing the Golden Nugget as a complete resort hotel. In 1978, Mr. Wynn used the profits from the Golden Nugget in Las Vegas to build the Golden Nugget Hotel and Casino on the Boardwalk in Atlantic City. The resort became

(continued)

INTRODUCING STEPHEN A. WYNN *(continued)*

known for its elegant facilities, television ads featuring Frank Sinatra, and its impressive lineup of superstar entertainment. From its opening in 1979 until its sale in 1986, the Atlantic City property dominated the market in revenues and profits despite its smaller size. In 1987, Mr. Wynn sold the Atlantic City Golden Nugget, which had cost $160 million, to Bally for $450 million and turned his creativity to developing the elegant Mirage Resort, which opened in 1989. With its imaginative erupting volcano and South Seas theme, the Mirage ignited a $12 billion building boom that catapulted Las Vegas to America's number-one tourist destination and fastest-growing city. In 1991, Golden Nugget Incorporated was renamed Mirage Resorts, Incorporated.

Following his staggering success at the Mirage, in 1993 Wynn opened Treasure Island, a Four-Diamond property with a romantic tropical theme indoors and a full-size pirate ship used in the daily reenactment of the Battle of Buccaneer Bay outdoors. He raised the bar again in 1998, when he opened the opulent $1.6 billion Bellagio, one of the world's most spectacular hotels. Visitors line the street in front of the hotel to watch the Dancing Waters, shooting fountains choreographed to music that "dance" on the hotel's 8.5-acre manmade lake. He then brought Mirage Resorts' standard of style to historic Biloxi, Mississippi, with the 1,835-room Beau Rivage, which blends Mediterranean beauty and Southern hospitality.

In June 2000, Mr. Wynn sold Mirage Resorts, Incorporated, to MGM for $6.6 billion and purchased Las Vegas's legendary Desert Inn Resort and Casino. The Desert Inn was closed in August 2000 and on that site Mr. Wynn began developing Wynn Las Vegas, a 2,700-room luxury destination resort that has inspired yet another wave of development on the Strip.

For every property he develops, Wynn is known for assembling a dream team of highly motivated employees who keep guestrooms and public spaces impeccable. His properties are always exceptional, drawing a commanding share of a demanding market and maintaining an exceptionally high occupancy. He is confident that both his projects and Las Vegas will continue to thrive.

Today, Mr. Wynn is active in the community and has received honorary doctorate degrees from the University of Nevada, Las Vegas, and Sierra Nevada College in northern Nevada. He is chairman of Utah's Moran Eye Institute; a trustee of his alma mater, the University of Pennsylvania; and a member of the board of the George Bush Presidential Library.

Source: Courtesy of Stephen A. Wynn.

In these years, the number of casinos in the United States has skyrocketed, as gambling halls on Indian reservations also became common. Indian gaming has its roots in the concept of tribal sovereignty, meaning that a tribe is not subject to the commercial restrictions of the state in which it is located. In the 1987 *Cabazon* decision, the Supreme Court affirmed that if a state allowed betting on bingo or card games, Indian tribes could offer these games without limits imposed by state regulators. The following year, the Indian Gaming Regulatory Act codified the rules under which Indian tribes could open "Las Vegas-style" casinos with slot machines and bank games: To do so, the tribes needed to sign a compact, or treaty, with the state in whose land the reservation sat. Frequently, these compacts specified fees that tribes would remit to state governments, often pegged to slot machine revenues, but states had no power to tax tribes; these payments were instead the result of negotiation. As of 2010, over 200 tribes in more than thirty states have some form of gambling operation, with combined annual revenues of more than $25 billion.

Casinos opened elsewhere, as well. Major cities like New Orleans and Detroit legalized a limited number of casinos within their borders, partly to spur tourism, partly to prevent the outflow of gambling dollars to neighboring jurisdictions. States like West Virginia and Delaware balked at authorizing new casino development but legalized slot machines at racetracks, businesses that came be to be known as racinos. The horseracing industry, which began to decline as track attendance fell in the 1970s, embraced the racino concept, and slot machines helped to stave off the demise of live racing in several states. In 2004, Pennsylvania authorized slot machines at racetracks, destination resorts, and urban slot parlors, signaling a further expansion of slot gaming. Gambling has proven to be a growth industry, even in areas of the country that have experienced an overall economic decline.

In addition, American-run casino operators have found that Asia is an even more lucrative market for casinos than the United States. Both Macau (concession awarded in 2002; first U.S.–owned casino opened in 2004) and Singapore (franchises awarded 2006; first U.S.–owned casino opened in 2010) have become casino powerhouses; since 2008, Macau's casino industry has become a leading gaming center with increasing revenues. See Figure 5 for a comparison of the revenues of the major gaming markets.

▶ Check Your Knowledge

1. Define the following:

    a. Handle

    b. Win

    c. House edge

    d. Hold percentage

    e. Volatility

2. Briefly describe why casino resorts are superior to stand-alone operations.

3. Explain the growth in casino gaming since the 1970s.

Year	Nevada	Las Vegas Strip	Atlantic City	Mississippi	Pennsylvania	Macau
2001	9,468,599	4,703,692	4,303,078	2,700,437	n/a	unkn
2002	9,447,660	4,654,808	4,381,406	2,717,258	n/a	2,772,500
2003	9,625,304	4,757,043	4,488,334	2,699,837	n/a	3,583,875
2004	10,562,247	5,333,508	4,806,698	2,776,970	n/a	5,172,250
2005	11,649,040	6,033,595	5,018,276	2,468,476	n/a	5,755,875
2006	12,622,044	6,688,903	5,217,613	2,570,883	31,567	7,077,875
2007	12,849,137	6,827,887	4,920,786	2,891,546	1,039,030	10,378,125
2008	11,599,124	6,126,292	4,544,961	2,721,139	1,615,565	13,596,500
2009	10,392,675	5,550,192	3,943,171	2,464,662	1,964,570	14,921,375
2010	10,404,731	5,776,570	3,565,047	2,389,779	2,486,408	23,542,875

Figure 5 • Comparative Revenues for Major Gaming Markets, 2001–2010.
All totals in thousands of dollars (U.S.)

Working in a Casino Resort

Students of the industry who understand the multidisciplinary needs of the casino business find five initial career tracks in hotel operations, food and beverage operations, casino operations, retail operations, and entertainment operations.

Hotel Operations

The career opportunities in gaming entertainment hotel operations are much like the career opportunities in the full-service hotel industry, with the exception that food and beverage can be a division of its own and not part of hotel operations. The rooms and guest services departments offer the most opportunities for students of hospitality management. Because gaming entertainment properties have hotels that are much larger than nongaming hotels, department heads have a larger number of supervisors reporting to them and more responsibilities. Reservations, front desk, housekeeping, valet parking, and guest services can all be very large departments with many employees.

Food and Beverage Operations

Gaming entertainment has a foundation of high-quality food and beverage service in a wide variety of styles and concepts. Some of the best foodservice operations in the hospitality industry are found in gaming entertainment operations. There are many career opportunities in restaurant management and the culinary arts. As with hotel operations, gaming entertainment properties are typically very large and contain numerous food and beverage outlets, including a number of restaurants, hotel room service, banquets and conventions, and retail outlets. Many establishments support gourmet, high-end signature restaurants. It is not unusual to find many more executive-level management positions in both front- and back-of-the-house food and beverage operations in gaming entertainment operations than in nongaming properties.

Casino Operations

Casino operations jobs fall into five functional areas. Gaming operations staff include slot machine technicians (approximately one technician for 40 machines), table-game dealers (approximately four dealers for each table game), and table-game supervisors. Casino service staff includes security, purchasing, and maintenance and facilities engineers. Marketing staff includes public relations, market research, and advertising professionals. Human resources staff includes employee relations, compensation, staffing, and training specialists. Finance and administration staff includes lawyers, accounts payable, audit, payroll, and income control specialists.[3]

The explosive growth of the gaming industry has increased the need for trained dealers skilled at working a variety of table games, including

blackjack, craps, roulette, poker, and **baccarat**. Through the use of textbooks and videotapes combined with hands-on training at a mock casino, future dealers learn the techniques and fine points of dealing at classes offered by both colleges and private schools.

Retail Operations

The increased emphasis on nongaming sources of revenues in gaming entertainment demands an expertise in all phases of retail operations, from store design and layout to product selection, merchandising, and sales control. Negotiating with concession subcontractors may also be a part of the overall retail activities. Retail operations often support the overall theme of the property and can often be a major source of revenue; however, retail management careers are often an overlooked career path in the gaming entertainment industry.

Entertainment Operations

Because of the increased competition, gaming entertainment companies are creating bigger and better production shows to turn their properties into destination attractions. Some production shows have climbed in the million of dollars range and require professional entertainment staffs to produce and manage them. Gaming entertainment properties often present live entertainment of all sorts, with headline acts drawing huge audiences.

Casino management is hierarchical. At the top of the management structure, a property president or general manager is in charge of day-to-day operations. Internal audit and surveillance departments report directly to the president or to the casino's board of directors, bypassing the management hierarchy because of their role in maintaining controls over cash and procedures in the casino.

Below the casino president are the vice presidents (sometimes called directors) of different divisions of the casino: the casino itself; hotel; food and beverage; entertainment; marketing (for casino guests); sales (typically directed toward business travel and group sales); retail; various support functions, including finance, which includes all casino cashiering operations; and security.

Within the casino, the vice president of gaming operations oversees a casino manager, who in turn oversees shift managers, one for each shift (day, swing, grave) of the casino's 24-hour day. The shift manager, in return, has authority over the managers on duty of each of the casino's departments, which may include slots, poker, keno, race and sports book, and casino hosts and marketing representatives, who work directly with high-value players, arranging comps and generally keeping them happy.

The slot department includes customer service representatives, who sign up players for the casino's loyalty program and technicians who keep the slot machines operational. Table games are organized into pits—clusters of about a dozen games—each run by a pit boss who reports directly to the casino shift manager. Below the pit boss, a floorperson oversees between two and four games, while one or more dealers staffs each table. The casino may have a high-limit room (also called a baccarat room) where high-stakes bets—as high as $50,000 per hand—are taken. The baccarat room frequently has its own manager who reports to the casino shift manager as well.

Other departments are managed similarly, with directors in charge of shift managers, who in turn oversee supervisors, who are then responsible for the performance of line employees.

The Mirage Effect

Since the 1990s, casino resorts on the Las Vegas Strip have seen their nongaming operations become much more central to their bottom line. In 1984, Strip casinos earned nearly 60 percent of their revenues from the casino itself; by 2008, that number had fallen below 40 percent.[4] In the 1990s, operators enlarged and upgraded their rooms. Originally merely places for gamblers to speak, rooms became attractions in and of themselves, at least partially because convention travelers were willing to pay higher premiums for better rooms. Rooms have become a major revenue center.

The rooms aren't the only part of the Strip that's become a money generator. This is because in addition to paying more for higher thread-count sheets and designer finishes, Strip visitors have eagerly opened their wallets for gourmet cuisine, delivered to them in celebrity chef eateries.

In 1992, Wolfgang Puck opened Spago in the Forum Shops at Caesars Palace. Puck, who had become famous with his restaurant of the same name on the Sunset Strip in Los Angeles, brought a different sensibility to Las Vegas eating. Spago at Caesars proved successful, and a cohort of established chefs from Paris, New York, and San Francisco followed Puck to Las Vegas, leading to an explosion of both gourmet-dining opportunities for patrons and an increase in restaurant revenues for casinos.

The cost of entertainment has gone up, too, as headliner concerts and installed shows (Cirque du Soleil alone has five) raised their production values and their prices. And with the growth of full-fledged shopping malls inside casinos, ranging from the Canal Shops at the Venetian to the Miracle Mile at Planet Hollywood, retail spending has climbed as well.

The ascendancy of nightclubs, ultra-lounges, and day clubs will further amplify the Mirage Effect. The nightclub trade, which skews to a demographic of 20- and 30-year-olds, represents a departure for Strip casinos, which traditionally considered 45-year-olds youngsters. Here, bottle service is the way of the future. Under this model, select patrons bypass the line and receive reserved tables along the dance floor in exchange for purchasing several bottles of liquor, at charges of up to $500 per bottle. By opening clubs and lounges along these lines, operators meet two objectives: They capture an extremely lucrative business, and they effectively orient new patrons to the casino.

Figure 6 shows the revenues generated by various aspects of casino resort operations.

	Daily Average	% of Total
Gaming	$557,792.48	38.70%
Rooms	$339,595.96	23.50%
Food	$222,101.89	15.40%
Beverage	$94,144.01	6.50%
Other	$228,523.55	15.80%
Total:	$1,442,157.89	100%

Casino Revenues

	Daily Average	% of Total
Tables	$252,092.10	45.20%
Slots	$282,030.71	50.60%
Poker	$11,932.21	2.10%
Race Book	$3,884.81	0.70%
Sports Book	$7,852.65	1.40%

Casino Expenses

	Daily Average	% of Revenues
Bad Debt	$14,706.78	2.60%
Comps	$156,541.94	28.10%
Gaming Taxes	$42,064.74	7.50%
Payroll	$105,581.73	18.90%
Total Expenses	$389,364.75	69.80%

Room Revenues and Occupancy

	Daily Average	% of Revenues
Sales	$256,201.04	75.40%
Comp Rooms	$83,394.91	24.60%
Available Rooms	3,089	
Rooms Occupied	2,781	
Rooms Payroll	$89,916	35.10%
Occupancy Rate	90.01%	

Number of Employees

Department	Per Casino
Casino	901
Rooms	751
Food	1,059
Beverage	291
G & A	507
Other	386
Total	3,894

> In fiscal 2010, 23 casinos in the Las Vegas Strip area produced gaming revenue of more than $72 million. The averages for several key financial statistics produce a picture of the statistically "average" Strip casino and give a good snapshot of the industry standard. All of the data is excerpted from the 2010 Nevada Gaming Abstract, published by the Nevada Gaming Control Board.

Figure 6 • The Average Strip Casino: Daily Revenues.

Sustainability in Gaming Entertainment

Sustainable initiatives are constantly gaining in popularity and prestige across the gaming industry. Gaming entertainment companies continue adapting their operations and practices to fit "green" standards. Many well-known companies in gaming entertainment are leading the way to establish sustainable initiatives as the standard practice in the industry, including Harrah's Entertainment, which operates Harrah's Resort, Caesars, and Bally's in Atlantic City, along with Delaware North, and Dover Downs Hotel & Casino.

One of the leading corporations in the gaming industry, Harrah's Entertainment Inc. has undertaken a sustainable initiative in several areas of operation, including energy, waste and water conservation, as well as climate control. Harrah's executives have urged their management teams to embrace a sustainable approach to their daily practices, designated "Code Green". This sustainable initiative involves the exchange of traditional incandescent lighting to a more resourceful energy conservative lighting, as well as ventilation controls in guest rooms, and throughout hotel and casino space in some of their larger properties. Select properties feature subsidized public transportation, habitat preservation fundraisers, recycling used oil, and composting waste products. Harrah's plans to continue the future implementation of sustainable practices in select properties throughout the country.[5]

Recently, gaming entertainment companies have begun implementing sustainable initiatives into the initial construction and development of new properties. Delaware North, a well-known player in gaming industry operations has recently built a new property in Daytona Beach, Florida, which complies with all the necessary standards required to be a Leadership in Engineering and Environmental Design (LEED) certified property. LEED employs a four tier rating system for buildings, based on the level of sustainability applied during property development, and maintained upon completion. The level of certification is based on the areas of "sustainable site development, water savings, energy efficiency, materials selection, and indoor environmental quality". The Daytona property received silver certification, which is the second tier of the rating system, which followed in the footsteps of their previous sustainable site developed in West Memphis, Arkansas in 2006.[6]

Hospitality Green LLC, an environmental consulting firm has taken on the task of creating a model for "green" standards that will set precedent for which existing and future initiatives will be measured. The company directed a property-wide assessment of Dover Downs Hotel & Casino's sustainable business practices in order to collect the necessary data required to provide an appropriate model. Dover Downs Hotel & Casino is one of the most noteworthy gaming and entertainment resorts in the Mid-Atlantic region. Currently, the AAA-four diamond property is working towards the objective of becoming the first certified "green" hotel in Delaware. In addition to the assessment of Dover Down's sustainable business practices, Hospitality Green will be conducting staff training in sustainable practices that can be implemented on a daily basis. This will ensure that Dover Down's employees are knowledgeable of proper standards and procedures, in order for the property to maintain "green" status.[7]

Career Information

The growth of the gaming industry has resulted in a variety of new job openings. People choose to work in the industry because it is known to place people first, whether they are employees or customers. The industry also has many opportunities for employees to learn new skills, which lead to growth and advancement in their careers.

Employees in the gaming industry may receive many tangible benefits. Most careers include impressive benefits packages and offer many career advancement opportunities. Casinos are known to hire from within, which gives current employees a greater chance to move into better positions over time. Because the gaming industry's positions are so varied, many educational and experiential backgrounds can be adapted to a specific casino's policies.

A variety of careers are specific to the gaming industry including dealer, slot attendant, marketing director, and casino surveillance. More opportunities are becoming available every day as new technology creates more openings. For example, systems such as MindPlay's Table Management System and IGT's EZpay technology and the introduction of advanced guest service technology will surely create new and exciting technical employment opportunities within the industry.

Although it may appear as if many gaming jobs have very specific qualifications, it is important not to focus too narrowly on one sector. Knowledge of all areas of the industry is essential for advancement. For example, today's casinos now rely on entertainment as well as gaming to bring in patrons. Therefore, an employee at such a casino also needs to have knowledge of the entertainment industry and of how casinos operate such events.

To get a job in the gaming industry, one must have very thorough knowledge of the legal, regulatory, and compliance issues related to daily operations in the casino. Broken laws can result in lawsuits and cost the company large sums of money. This can be avoided if all employees have the proper background knowledge.

Even though observing daily activity in a casino provides invaluable work experience, obtaining a college or graduate degree is also crucial. It is true that much of the necessary education can take place on the job; however, applicants who have received an outside education, as well as attended gaming certification programs, have a much better chance of standing out from their competition.

A general manager in the gaming industry earns a starting average annual salary of about $82,800. A casino operator begins at about $38,000, and marketing and sales employees start out at $55,000. Positions typically include full health benefits, yearly bonuses, and other compensation, depending on the casino.

TECHNOLOGY SPOTLIGHT

Technology Use in the Casino Industry

Cihan Cobanoglu, Ph.D., Dean, School of Hotel and Restaurant Management, University of South Florida, Sarasota-Manatee

Casinos are perhaps the heaviest users of technology in the hospitality industry. There are three main areas that should be considered in the casino information system: gaming technology, surveillance systems, and customer data mining.

Examples of gaming technology include slot machines and automated card shufflers. Slot machines were originally installed as an alternative to other games. They require minimal gambling knowledge and low bets (as low as one cent). Due to these factors, slot machines gained high popularity over time. The classic slot machine is configured of gears and levers. The handle mechanism that gets the system moving is connected to a metal shaft that supports the reels. A coin/bill detector identifies the payment and unlocks the brake so that the handle can move. When a game begins, the reels start moving and then are stopped by the breaking system. Special sensors built into the slot machine communicate the position of the reels to the payout system. However, technological advances have affected the way slot machines work. Most modern slot machines are computerized: The outcome of the game is being determined by a computer inside the machine. Now, the computer tells the reels where to stop. However, it does not mean that winning is impossible. Every round, the computer generates a random number (usually in the range from one to several billion), which determines where the reels will stop. All these numbers are generated in such a way that they have equal probability of hitting the jackpot.

Another important gaming technology is electronic card shufflers. This technology helps to shuffle card decks in seconds. The key point of using the technology is that it protects players from cheating. In contrast with the initial designs, modern devices are very small and convenient. Some of the main techniques of card shuffling include shelves (vertical carousels), ejectors, and mechanical fingers.

Computer surveillance systems are crucial for casino operations. Any casino can face such problems as intoxicated patrons, cheaters, thieves, and dishonest employees. Surveillance systems are necessary to ensure safety and minimize loss. Originally, surveillance systems were completely nonelectronic and were based on manager observations. However, technological advances of the previous decades enabled digital imaging technology, including facial recognition systems. Most modern versions of such systems are even capable of scanning the room in search of particular persons. Some of the vendors that provide surveillance systems are IQinVision, EZWATCH PRO, and CloseoutCCTV.com.

The casino industry is one of early adopters of data-mining techniques among all hospitality sectors. Data mining allows businesses to work with large volumes of information in order to identify unique useful patterns that can be helpful in decision making. To give an example, data mining was employed by Harrah's casinos to cluster the guests (based on demographics characteristics, preferences, loyalty points, etc.), classify them (e.g., to identify the customers with the high lifelong value), and establish association rules (e.g., if customers prefer a particular slot machine, are they all likely to be interested in any other type of a game?). The information generated by means of data mining helps to predict the value of the future guests by looking at existing ones and identifying patterns in their behavior. Having this information in hand enables managers to make important business decisions.

Figure 7 • A Career Path in the Gaming Industry.

Management careers can be very different, depending on your focus. If your interest is gaming management, it is important that you take courses in finance, law, human resources, management, and gambling. You also need to work in the gaming industry while in college, so that you can open doors for yourself through networking. Casinos still believe in promoting from within, and so you will have to work your way up the corporate ladder. You also need to understand that because of the continuous operation of a casino, your work schedule will vary. It is not uncommon to work several straight twelve-hour days, but the rewards for dedication and hard work can be very worthwhile: Casinos have many opportunities for advancement. Figure 7 shows an example of a career path in the gaming industry.

To see more of the types of jobs that are available in the gaming entertainment industry, go to **www.casinocareers.com/index.cfm**, where you can look up potential employers, available jobs, and areas of employment.

Trends in the Gaming Entertainment Industry

- Gaming entertainment is depending less on casino revenue and more on room, food and beverage, retail, and entertainment revenue for its profitability and growth.

- The gaming entertainment industry and lodging industry are converging as hotel room inventory is rapidly expanding in gaming entertainment properties.

- Gaming entertainment, along with the gaming industry as a whole, will continue to be scrutinized by government and public policymakers as to the net economic and social impact of its activities.

- As the gaming entertainment industry becomes more competitive, exceptional service quality will become an increasingly important competitive advantage for success.

- The gaming entertainment industry will continue to provide management opportunities for careers in the hospitality business.

CORPORATE PROFILE

Caesars Entertainment Inc.

Harrah's Entertainment was founded in 1937 by William F. Harrah as a small bingo parlor in Reno, Nevada. Today, Harrah's is the largest gaming company in the world, with a portfolio of forty-eight casinos totaling 4 million square feet of gaming, which it owns or manages in three countries under the Harrah's, Caesars, and Horseshoe brand names.[1] Harrah's has twenty-eight land-based and twelve riverboat or dockside casinos, plus golf courses and combination racetrack and casinos in several states, including Nevada, Louisiana, New Jersey, Mississippi, Kansas, and Missouri. Harrah's grew by new property development, expansions, and acquisitions, and it now employs some 85,000 people, with the vision that "each of our brands will be the overwhelming first choice for casino entertainment of its targeted customers."[2] Harrah's Entertainment is focused on building loyalty and value with its customers through a unique combination of guest service, excellent products, unsurpassed distribution, operational excellence, and technology leadership.[3] The marketing strategy is designed to appeal to those who are avid players, especially those who play in more than one market.[4]

[1] Yahoo! Finance, *HET (Harrah Entertainment Inc.)*, http://finance.yahoo.com/q/pr?s=het (April 21, 2011; site now discontinued).

[2] Harrah's Entertainment, www.harras.com/harrahs-corporate/about-us.html (April 21, 2011; site now discontinued).

[3] Harrah's Entertainment, *Name of Web Site,* www.harrahs.com/harrahs-corporate/index.html (June 4, 2009; site now discontinued).

[4] www.investords.com/cgi-bin/stocksymbol.cgi?ticker=het

[5] Arnold M. Knightly, "Deal closes: Harrah's now private," *Las vegas Review-Journal*, Jan. 29, 2008, as cited by http://en.wikipedia.org/wiki/Harrah%27s_Entertainment (accessed November 18, 2011).

[6] Wikinvest, *Harrah's Entertainment*, www.wikinvest.com/Harrah's_Entertainment (accessed November 18, 2011).

CASE STUDY

Negotiating with Convention Groups

Your convention sales department receives a call from a trip director for a large convention group. The group will use many function rooms for meetings during the day and will generate a substantial amount of convention services revenue. Likewise, the group's food and beverage needs are quite elaborate, so this will be good for the food and beverage department budget. However, the group is very sensitive concerning room price and is willing to negotiate the time of week for its three-night stay.

Discussion Question

1. What are the considerations that a gaming entertainment property must take into account when determining room rates for convention groups?

CASE STUDY

VIP

A frequent guest of the casino makes a last-minute decision to travel to your property for a weekend stay. The guest enjoys gambling as a leisure activity and is one of the casino's better customers. When he arrives at the casino, he is usually met by a casino host and is treated as a VIP due to his level of wagering at the blackjack tables. This guest is worth approximately $500,000 in casino win per year to the hotel. Due to his last-minute arrangements, however, the guest cannot notify a casino host that he is on his way to the hotel. Upon arriving, he finds a very busy registration desk. He must wait in line for twenty minutes, and when he tries to check in, he is told that the hotel is full. The front-desk clerk acts impatient when the guest says that he is a frequent customer. In a fit of frustration, the would-be guest leaves the hotel and makes a mental note that all casinos have similar odds at the blackjack table and that maybe another property will give him the respect he deserves.

Discussion Question

1. What systems or procedures could you institute to make sure this type of oversight does not happen in your property?

Summary

1. The casino industry is a growing international force that includes both gambling and more traditional hospitality elements.
2. To manage a casino resort, it is necessary to understand the relationship between the casino and other departments in the operation, as well as ways that casinos are different from other businesses.
3. Casino gambling is strictly regulated by state governments, and the integrity developed over time by these regulations is necessary for the survival of the industry.
4. Nongaming revenue is increasing as a percentage of total casino resort revenue, and nongaming parts of casino resorts are gaining in prominence.

Key Words and Concepts

Baccarat
Blackjack
Casino resort
Comp
Craps
Gambling

Handle
Hold percentage
Poker
Roulette
Win

Review Questions

1. Briefly describe the history of legalized gaming in the United States.
2. What defines a gaming entertainment business?
3. Explain the attraction of gaming entertainment to the destination of a tourist.
4. Why is it necessary for strict regulations to be in force on the casino floor?
5. How are hotel operations in a gaming entertainment business different from hotel operations in a nongaming environment?

Internet Exercises

1. Organization: **Wynn Las Vegas**
   Web site: **www.wynnlasvegas.com**
   Summary: Located on the Las Vegas Strip, the Wynn Las Vegas has a lot to offer. From gaming and concerts, to hosting some of the biggest conventions, the Wynn Las Vegas will certainly keep you busy.

   (a) What are some of the gaming features that attract customers to the Wynn Las Vegas?

   (b) What are the benefits to the different packages available?

2. Pick a casino in Las Vegas and look it up on the Internet. What does it offer that sets it apart from other casinos in Las Vegas and from other casinos in the United States? In what areas is it similar to other casinos?

Apply Your Knowledge

1. Name the major gaming entertainment hotels in Las Vegas.

2. Give examples of nongaming revenue.

Suggested Activity

1. Research careers in the gaming entertainment industry. Are there more opportunities than you realized? What careers in the industry interest you the most?

Endnotes

1. Insider Viewpoint of Las Vegas, 20 *Largest Hotels in the World*, http://www.insidervlv.com/hotelslargestworld.html (accessed November 18, 2011).
2. Wikipedia, *The Venetian Macao*, http://en.wikipedia.org/wiki/The_Venetian_Macao (accessed November 18, 2011).
3. www.harrahs.com/about_us/community_relations/IPImpacts.pdf
4. University of Nevada Las Vegas, *Annual Comparison: Revenue Statistics—Las Vegas Strip Casinos with Gaming Revenue over $1,000,000*, http://gaming.unlv.edu/abstract/lv_revenues.html (accessed November 18, 2011).
5. August, 2010. http://www.leonardoacademy.org/programs/standards/gaming/news.html. Retrieved on November 16, 2011.
6. http://www.delawarenorth.com/Gaming-Entertainment-Environmental-Management.aspx Retrieved on November 16, 2011.
7. October 17, 2011. http://www.4-traders.com/DOVER-DOWNS-GAMING-ENTE-12270/news/DOVER-DOWNS-GAMING-ENTERTAINMENT-INC-Dover-Downs-Hotel-Casino-reveals-details-of-innovative-sustaina-13845599/. Retrieved on November 16, 2011.

Glossary

Baccarat   A traditional table game in which the winning hand totals closest to nine.

Blackjack   A table game in which the winning hand is determined by whether the dealer or the player gets cards that add up to a number closest to or equal to 21 without going over.

Handle   The dollars wagered, or bet; often confused with *win*. Whenever a customer places a bet, the handle increases by the amount of the bet. The handle is not affected by the outcome of the bet.

Poker   A card game in which participants play against each other instead of the casino.

Roulette   A traditional table game in which a dealer spins a wheel and players wager on which number a small ball will fall.

Win   Dollars won by the gaming operation from its customers. The net spending of customers on gaming is called the *win*, also known as *gross gaming revenue (GGR)*.

Photo Credits

Credits are listed in order of appearance.

Meetings, Conventions, and Expositions

From Chapter 12 of *Introduction to Hospitality*, Sixth Edition. John R. Walker. Copyright © 2013 by Pearson Education, Inc. Published by Pearson. All rights reserved.

Meetings, Conventions, and Expositions

OBJECTIVES

After reading and studying this text, you should be able to:

- List the major players in the convention industry.

- Describe destination management companies.

- Describe the different aspects of being a meeting planner.

- Describe the different types of contractors.

- Explain the different types of meetings, conventions, and expositions.

- List the various venues for meetings, conventions, and expositions.

Development of the Meetings, Conventions, and Expositions Industry

People have gathered to attend **meetings, conventions,** and **expositions** since ancient times, mainly for social, sporting, political, or religious purposes. As cities became regional centers, the size and frequency of such activities increased, and various groups and associations set up regular expositions.

Associations go back many centuries to the Middle Ages and earlier. The guilds in Europe were created during the Middle Ages to secure proper wages and maintain work standards. In the United States, associations began at the beginning of the eighteenth century, when Rhode Island candle makers organized themselves.

Meetings, incentive travel, conventions, and **exhibitions (MICE)** represent a segment of the tourism industry that has grown in recent years. The MICE segment of the tourism industry is very profitable. Industry statistics point to the fact that the average MICE tourist spends about twice the amount of money that other tourists spend.

Size and Scope of the Industry

According to the American Society of Association Executives (ASAE), there are about 90,908 trade and professional associations[1]. The association business is big business. Associations spend billions holding thousands of meetings and conventions that attract millions of attendees.

The hospitality and tourism industries consist of a number of associations, including the following:

- American Hotel & Lodging Association (AH&LA)
- National Restaurant Association (NRA)
- American Culinary Federation
- International Association of Convention and Visitors Bureaus (IACVB)
- Hospitality Sales and Marketing Association International
- Association of Meeting Planners
- Club Managers Association of America
- Professional Convention Management Association

Associations are the main independent political force for industries such as hospitality, offering the following benefits:

- A voice in government/politics
- Marketing avenues
- Education

- Member services
- Networking

Thousands of associations hold annual conventions at various locations across North America and throughout the rest of the world. Some associations alternate their venues from east to central to west; others meet at fixed locations, such as the NRA show in Chicago or the AH&LA convention and show in New York City.

Associations have an elected board of directors and an elected president, vice president, treasurer, and secretary. Additional officers, such as a liaison person or a public relations person, may be elected according to the association's constitution.

Key Players in the Industry

The need to hold face-to-face meetings and attend conventions has grown into a multibillion-dollar industry. Many major and some smaller cities have convention centers with nearby hotels and restaurants.

The major players in the convention industry are **convention and visitors bureaus (CVBs)**, corporations, associations, meeting planners and their clients, convention centers, specialized services, and exhibitions. The wheel diagram in Figure 1 shows the types of clients that use convention centers by percentage utilization.

CVBs are major participants in the meetings, conventions, and expositions market. The IACVB describes a CVB as a not-for-profit umbrella organization

> " Meetings, conventions, and expositions provide attendees and personnel in specialized areas an opportunity to discuss important issues and new developments with their peers. "
>
> Laurel Ebert,
> The Boylston Convention Center,
> Boylston, Maryland.

> " Meetings provide managers the opportunity to give positive feedback to their employees, address employee concerns, and to emphasize projects and/or goals. "
>
> Lianne Wilhoitte,
> Wilhoitte & Associates,
> Baltimore, Maryland.

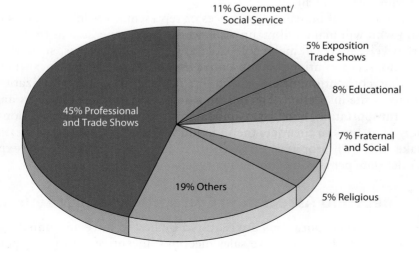

Convention Center Utilization by Market Sector

- 11% Government/Social Service
- 5% Exposition Trade Shows
- 8% Educational
- 7% Fraternal and Social
- 5% Religious
- 19% Others
- 45% Professional and Trade Shows

Figure 1 • Convention Center Clientele.

that represents an urban area and that tries to solicit business- or pleasure-seeking visitors. The CVB comprises a number of visitor industry organizations representing the various industry sectors:

- Transportation
- Hotels and motels
- Restaurants
- Attractions
- Suppliers

The bureau represents these local businesses by acting as the sales team for the city. A bureau has *five* primary responsibilities:

1. To enhance the image of tourism in the local/city area
2. To market the area and encourage people to visit and stay longer
3. To target and encourage selected associations and others to hold meetings, conventions, and expositions in the city
4. To assist associations and others with convention preparations and to give support during the convention
5. To encourage tourists to partake of the historic, cultural, and recreational opportunities the city or area has to offer

The outcome of these five responsibilities is for the city's tourist industry to increase revenues. Bureaus compete for business at trade shows, where interested visitor industry groups gather to do business. For example, a tour wholesaler who is promoting a tour will need to link up with hotels, restaurants, and attractions to package a vacation. Similarly, meeting planners are able to consider several locations and hotels by visiting a trade show. Bureaus generate leads (prospective clients) from a variety of sources. One source, associations, have national/international offices in Washington, D.C. (so that they can lobby the government), and Chicago.

A number of bureaus have offices or representatives in these cities or a sales team who will make follow-up visits to the leads generated at trade shows. Alternatively, they will make cold calls to potential prospects, such as major associations, corporations, and incentive houses. The sales manager will invite the meeting, convention, or exposition organizer to make a **familiarization (FAM) trip** for a site inspection. The bureau assesses the needs of the client and organizes transportation, hotel accommodations, restaurants, and attractions accordingly. The bureau then lets the individual properties and other organizations make their own proposals to the client. Figure 2 shows the average expenditure per delegate per stay by convention type.

Business and Association Conventions and Meetings

Publicly held corporations are required by law to have an annual shareholders' meeting. Most also have sales meetings, incentive trips (all-expenses paid trips for groups of employees that met or exceeded goals set for them), product

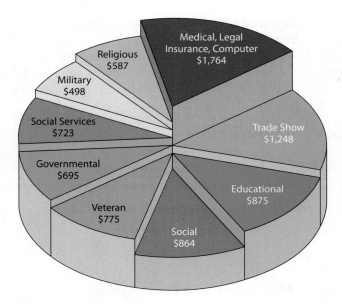

Average length of stay is 3.5 days.

Figure 2 • Average Expenditure per Delegate per Stay by Convention Type. The significance of these amounts is that given an attendance of several hundreds to thousands of guests, the economic impact quickly adds up and benefits the community in a variety of ways.

launches, focus groups, executive retreats, seminars and training sessions, and management meetings.

Corporations are big spenders, in part because they receive tax deductions on their meeting expenditures. When a corporation decides to hold a gathering, it determines what the budget will be, where the gathering will be held, and who will attend. Since the corporation typically pays for all expenses associated with attending the meeting, hotels, resorts, and convention centers compete for this lucrative business.[2] In the United States, almost 1.1 million corporate events are held annually, with a total attendance of 84 million. The total direct spending on these events is over $30 billion per year, with the average corporate event generating almost $550,000.[3] Corporations also arrange incentive trips—paying all expenses for a special vacation for the employee or customer and a significant other at a hotel, at a resort, or on a cruise ship.

Associations represent the interests of their members and gather at the state, regional, national, and international levels for professional industry–related reasons; for annual congresses, conventions, and conferences; and for scientific, educational, and training meetings.

Conventions are a major source of income for associations, as they charge attendees a registration fee and charge vendors for booth space (this gives vendors a chance to sell their products to attendees). Association conventions and meetings attract crowds ranging from hundreds to over 100,000, which only the larger convention facilities like New York, Orlando, Las Vegas, San Francisco, and Chicago can handle. The next level of convention facilities includes cities like Washington, D.C., San Diego, Dallas/Fort Worth, Miami, Boston, and Phoenix/Scottsdale.

The larger associations book their dates several years ahead, some in the same place at the same time of year; others move around the country. For example, the AH&LA holds its annual convention during the second week of November in New York City at the Javits Center, and the NRA holds its annual convention during the third week of May in Chicago at McCormick Place.

▶ Check Your Knowledge

1. According to the American Society of Association Executives (ASAE), how many associations operate at the national level in the United States?
2. What are the five primary responsibilities of a bureau?
3. What is the purpose of a familiarization (FAM) trip?

Destination Management Companies

A destination management company (DMC) is a service organization within the visitor industry that offers a host of programs and services to meet clients' needs. Initially, a destination management sales manager concentrates on selling the destination to meeting planners and performance improvement companies (incentive houses).

The needs of such groups may be as simple as an airport pickup or as involved as an international sales convention with theme parties. DMCs work closely with hotels; sometimes a DMC books rooms, and another time a hotel might request the DMC's expertise on organizing theme parties. Patricia Roscoe, chairperson of Patti Roscoe and Associates (PRA), says that meeting planners often have a choice of several destinations and might ask, "Why should I pick your destination?" The answer is that a DMC does everything, including airport greetings, transportation to the hotel, VIP check-in, arranging theme parties, sponsoring programs, organizing competitive sports events, and so on, depending on budget. Sales managers associated with DMCs obtain leads, which are potential clients, from the following sources:

- Hotels
- Trade shows
- CVBs
- Cold calls
- Incentive houses
- Meeting planners

Each sales manager has a staff or team, which can include the following:

- A special events manager, who will have expertise in sound, lighting, staging, and so on
- An accounts manager, who is an assistant to the sales manager

- A theme-events creative director

- An audiovisual specialist

- An operations manager, who coordinates everything, especially on-site arrangements, to ensure that what is sold actually happens

For example, Patti Roscoe's DMC organized meetings, accommodations, meals, beverages, and theme parties for 2,000 Ford Motor Company dealers in nine groups over three days for each group.

Roscoe also works closely with incentive houses, such as Carlson Marketing and Maritz Travel. These incentive houses approach a company and offer to set up incentive plans for companies' employees, including whatever it takes to motivate them. Once approved, Carlson contacts a DMC and asks for a program.

Meeting Planners

Meeting planners may be independent contractors who contract out their services to both associations and corporations as the need arises or they may be full-time employees of corporations or associations. In either case, meeting planners have interesting careers. According to the International Convention Management Association (ICMA), about 212,000 full- and part-time meeting planners work in the United States.

The professional meeting planner not only makes hotel and meeting bookings but also plans the meeting down to the last minute, always remembering to check to ensure that the services that have been contracted have been delivered. In recent years, the technical aspects of audiovisual and simultaneous translation equipment have added to the complexity of meeting planning. The meeting planner's role varies from meeting to meeting, but may include some or all of the following activities:

Premeeting Activities

- Estimate attendance

- Plan meeting agenda

- Establish meeting objectives

- Set meeting budget

- Select city location and hotel/convention site

- Negotiate contracts

- Plan exhibition

- Prepare exhibitor correspondence and packet

- Create marketing plan

- Plan travel to and from site

A meeting planner explains to clients how a meeting will take place.

- Arrange ground transportation
- Organize shipping
- Organize audiovisual needs

On-Site Activities

- Conduct pre-event briefings
- Prepare VIP plan
- Facilitate people movement
- Approve expenditures

Postmeeting Activities

- Debrief
- Evaluate
- Give recognition and appreciation
- Plan for next year

As you can see, this is quite a long list of activities that meeting planners handle for clients.

Service Contractors

Service contractors, *exposition service contractors*, *general contractors*, and *decorators* are all terms that have at one time or another referred to the individual responsible for providing all of the services needed to run the facilities for a trade show. Just as a meeting planner is able to multitask and satisfy all the demands in meeting planning, a general exposition contractor must be multitalented and equipped to serve all exhibit requirements and creative ideas.

The service contractor is hired by the exposition show manager or association meeting planner. The service contractor is a part of the facilities management team, and, to use the facility, the sponsor must use its service contractor. In other situations, the facility may have an exclusive contract with an outside contractor, and it may require all conventions and expositions to deal with this contractor. Today, there are Internet service companies that can take reservations, prepare lists, and provide all kinds of services via the Internet for meeting planners.

▶ Check Your Knowledge

1. What is a destination management company?
2. What are the primary responsibilities of professional meeting planners?

CORPORATE PROFILE

Hawai's Convention Center

The Hawai'i Convention Center (HCC) on the island of Oahu, Hawaii, is consistently recognized by meeting planners and conventioneers as the world's most desirable convention and meeting destination and has built its reputation around being a facility where business and *aloha* meet.

Hawaiian hospitality values are recognized as the most sophisticated and genuine in the world. To take advantage of this, the HCC offers each employee training in the Hawaii Institute of Hospitality, a program of the Native Hawaiian Hospitality Association (NaHHA). The seminar, headed by the Hawaii Institute of Hospitality, is just one element of a series of *Na Mea Ho'okipa* (Hawaiian hospitality) training for the staff at the center. More than teaching hospitality, *ho'okipa* advocates a personal behavior system based on Hawaiian values and a heightened "sense of place." "*Ho'okipa* is about understanding who we are and how we fit into this place, and the HCC has always had a fundamental sense of how it, as a viable economic powerhouse and ultimate host, fits successfully within Hawaii's cultural environment," says Peter Apo, director of the NaHHA.

Ho'okipa training also includes a novel approach to orienting staff to the concept of place, the most integral element of the visitor experience. A walking tour through historic Waikiki reiterates that it is not merely high rises and hotels, but one of the most sacred, culturally important places in Hawaii. The "Hawai'i Advantage" is a strategy to position the Convention Center and Hawaii as the world's most desirable convention and meeting destination. This advantage is channeled through various facets, each one an instrumental consideration for meeting planners. The premise is that Hawaii as a destination expounds on aspects including, but not exclusive to, location, productivity, competitive shipping, value of facility, destination appeal, industry support, and customer service in a way that no other destination can. And, of course, no other destination offers "business with aloha."

"The Hawai'i Advantage is a powerful concept that works on several levels; it distinguishes the HCC from other venues and is an initiative rooted in testimonials of past convention attendees," says Joe Davis, general manager of the HCC. "The Convention Center and Hawaii offers conventioneers an unmatched experience. Once we get them here for the first time, we know they will rebook," says Davis.

HCC highlights include the following:

- One million square feet of meeting facilities, including an exhibit hall, theaters, and expansive conference rooms

- Convention Television (CTV)—an exclusive service with the capability to broadcast convention information in 28,000 hotel rooms in Waikiki, as well as on screens within the convention center. CTV is an expedient way for organizations to reach out to conventioneers with its message, as well as to showcase sponsors, VIPs, and trade show participants.

- Designed with a "Hawaiian Sense of Place"—the Center captures the essence of the Hawaiian environment with a soaring, glass-front entry; a 70-foot misting waterfall; and mature palm trees

(continued)

CORPORATE PROFILE *(continued)*

- A $2 million Hawaiian art collection of unique pieces commissioned for specific locations within the building, and a rooftop outdoor function space complete with a tropical garden of native flora
- The center's state-of-the-art technical features include fiber-optic cabling, multilingual translation stations, satellite and microwave broadcast capability, and videoconferencing

The HCC's recent list of awards includes the following:

- Prime Site Award from *Facilities & Destinations* magazine
- Planners' Choice Award—Recognition for Excellence in the Hospitality Industry—*Meeting News* magazine
- Ranked as North America's most attractive convention center in the METROPOLL X study, Gerard Murphy & Associates

The HCC's web site (**http://www.hawaiiconvention.com/**) offers the following information:

The Las Vegas Convention and Visitors Authority (LVCVA) hosts hundreds of conventions attended by more than a million delegates. The LVCVA is organized in the followed way: State law establishes the number, appointment, and terms of the authority's board of directors. A twelve-member board provides guidance and establishes policies to accomplish the LVCVA mission.

Seven members are elected officials of the county, and each represents one of the incorporated cities therein; the remaining five members are nominated by the Las Vegas Chamber of Commerce, and each represents a different segment of the industry. The board is one of the most successful public/private partnerships in the country. Under the presidency of Manuel J. Cortez, the LVCVA and its board of directors have received numerous awards.

The LVCVA's organizational structure is shown in the accompanying diagram. The board of directors employs a president (executive) to serve as chief executive officer. Other members of the executive staff are vice president of marketing, vice president of operations, and vice president of facilities. The marketing division's first priority is to increase the number of visitors to Las Vegas and southern Nevada. The marketing division is composed of eight teams that specialize in various market segments to increase the number of visitors and convention attendance: marketing services, convention sales, tour and travel, corporate and incentive, international, wholesalers/special events, consumer advertising, and news bureau.

The marketing services team is responsible for providing visitor services including research, registration, convention housing, hotel/motel reservations, and visitor information. The research team tracks the dynamics of the Las Vegas and Clark Country tourism marketplace, along with the competitive gaming and tourism environment. The registration department coordinates and provides temporary help for conventions and trade shows being held in Las Vegas.

The housing division receives and processes hotel and motel housing forms from convention and trade show delegates, forwarding the reservations to participating hotels daily. The reservations department operates toll-free telephone lines, transferring the calls of travel agents, tourists, conventioneers, and special event attendees to hotel and motels within a requested location and price range.

The convention sales team coordinates convention sales efforts at the authority and contributes to the success of convention sales citywide by providing sales leads to the hotels. Sales managers travel throughout the United States and the world, meeting with association meeting planners to sell the benefits of holding conventions in Las Vegas. Members of the team also attend numerous conventions and trade shows, where they host or sponsor special events and functions to entice conventions and trade shows to Las Vegas.

Familiarization trips for travel agents are conducted by team members to generate enthusiasm and excitement around Las Vegas bookings. Travel agent presentations are also scheduled in both primary and selected secondary airline market cities. Similar events are also scheduled for Laughlin, which also advertises a 1-800 number for tourism information.

The corporate and incentive markets are traditionally considered the high end of the travel industry. These buyers are extremely sophisticated and value-conscious and are looking for the highest-quality facilities and amenities. Corporate and incentive team members attend various trade shows throughout the United States and Canada, as well as selected cities in Europe and Asia, promoting Las Vegas as a complete, value-oriented, flexible, and accessible resort destination for corporate meetings.

The operations division is divided into teams that are discussed in the following sections.

Finance

The finance division maintains a general accounting system for the authority to ensure accountability in compliance with legal provisions and in accordance with generally accepted accounting principles. Finance is composed of financial services, accounting, and payroll activities. Additional responsibilities include the preparation of the authority's annual financial report (CAFR) and the annual budget. The CAFR has received the Government Finance Officers Association (GFOA) Excellence in Financial Reporting Award a number of times in recent years.

Materials Management

Materials management supports the marketing, operations, and facilities divisions by providing for purchasing of materials, services, and goods needed to meet its goals and objectives. Materials management is responsible for the storage and distribution of various supply items through an extensive warehousing program, as well as through printing and mail distribution.

Security

The security division provides protection of the authority's property, equipment, employees, and convention attendees 24 hours a day, 365 days a year, and also oversees paid parking and fire safety functions. The team patrols both the convention center and Cashman Field properties and is trained in first-aid assistance. Several officers have been recognized by the authority board and convention organizations for providing life-saving measures to convention attendees.

Information Technology

The information technology division (ITD) is responsible for efficiently and effectively meeting the automation and information needs of the authority. The ITD sustains a staff of technically competent professionals to design, maintain, implement, and operate the systems necessary to support the goals of the authority.

The author gratefully acknowledges that this section draws on information given by the Las Vegas Convention and Visitors Authority.

TECHNOLOGY SPOTLIGHT

Meeting, Convention, and Exposition Technology

Cihan Cobanoglu, Ph.D., Dean, School of Hotel and Restaurant Management, University of South Florida, Sarasota-Manatee

Managing meetings, conventions, and expositions may be a challenging task. Technology comes to the rescue! There is software available in the market to help manage meetings, conventions, and expositions. One of the market leaders of this segment is Delphi by Newmarket International (**www.newmarketinc.com/products/delphi.aspx**). Some of the features of this software include the following:

- Providing forecast values that better estimate guestroom pickup, ensuring the desired mix between group and transient business

- Responding to Requests for Proposal (RFPs) from the software

- The ability to flag and determine which accounts should track transient production from the Property Management System

- Enhanced suite logic that enables guestroom configurations of suites for more accurate inventory reporting

- Customized guestroom security that lets you move guestrooms in and out of inventory for a specified period of time

- Configurable security settings that limit changes on key booking information

- Guestroom overblock controls that allow for specific room types to be overblocked while restricting other room types

- Simplified guestroom rate fields that drastically reduce time-consuming data entry

Similarly, there are online solutions for managing meetings. RegOnline (**http://www.regonline.com/**) offers online event management, registration, and planning software. This software allows anyone to create an event web site and allows registrants to self-register to the event. Additionally, it generates nametags and attendee lists.

With the advance of smartphones, a lot of conference and event-management applications were introduced for mobile phones such as iPhone and Droid. Some examples of these are as follows:

QuickMobile (www.quickmobile.com)—Features include full conference schedule, personal agenda building, area guide, search capabilities for attendees/speakers/exhibitors, integration with social media including Twitter/Facebook/Pathable, and messaging. QuickMobile builds apps for the iPhone, iPad, Blackberry, Android and mobile web, providing greater ease of use than companies that provide only mobile web versions.

Follow Me (www.core-apps.com)—Follow Me was the mobile app for the 2010 Consumer Electronic Show, one of the largest shows in the tradeshow industry. Features include a full conference schedule, personal agenda builder, maps, exhibit hall way-finding (you are a dot on the map), course notes/literature pickup, session alerts, Twitter integration, and sponsorship revenue sharing. Core-Apps also build native apps for the major smartphones (iPhone, Android, Blackberry) and mobile web for the rest.

SNIPP (www.snipp.com)—This application allows meeting planners to send text messages (SMS) to attendees. It is a low-cost, fast communication channel.

NearPod (www.nearpod.com)—NearPod creates iPod and iPad applications for surveys, data collection, prize giveaways, presentation tools, and metric tools with applications for meetings and trade shows.

Foursquare (www.foursquare.com) and Gowalla (www.gowalla.com)—These location-aware mobile applications allow people to check in at a location to network with others and to share with friends. Although originally used in restaurants, bars, and so forth, these applications are starting to be used for events.

Types of Meetings, Conventions, and Expositions

Meetings

Meetings are conferences, workshops, seminars, or other events designed to bring people together for the purpose of exchanging information. Meetings can take any one of the following forms:

- *Clinic.* A workshop-type educational experience in which attendees learn by doing. A clinic usually involves small groups interacting with each other on an individual basis.

- *Forum.* An assembly for the discussion of common concerns. Usually, experts in a given field take opposite sides of an issue in a panel discussion, with liberal opportunity for audience participation.

- *Seminar.* A lecture and a dialogue that allow participants to share experiences in a particular field. A seminar is guided by an expert discussion leader, and usually thirty or fewer persons participate.

- *Symposium.* An event at which a particular subject is discussed by experts and opinions are gathered.

- *Workshop.* A small group led by a facilitator or trainer. It generally includes exercises to enhance skills or develop knowledge in a specific topic.

The reason for having a meeting can range from the presentation of a new sales plan to a total quality management workshop. The purpose of meetings is to affect behavior. For example, as a result of attending a meeting, a person should know or be able to do certain things. Some outcomes are very specific; others may be less so. For instance, if a meeting were called to brainstorm new ideas, the outcome might be less concrete than for other types of meetings. The number of people attending a meeting can vary. Successful meetings require a great deal of careful planning and organization. Figure 3 shows convention delegates' spending in a convention city.

Meetings are set up according to the wishes of the client. The three main types of meeting setups are theater style, classroom style, and boardroom style:

- Theater style generally is intended for a large audience that does not need to make a lot of notes or refer to documents. This style usually consists of a raised platform and a lectern from which a presenter addresses the audience.

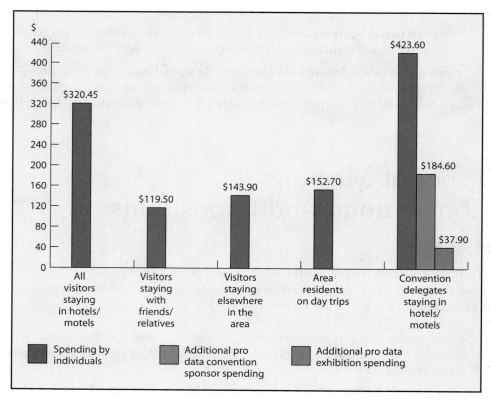

Figure 3 • Convention Delegates' Spending in a Convention City (San Francisco).
Source: J.R. Schrock.

- Classroom setups are used when the meeting format is more instructional and participants need to take detailed notes or refer to documents. A workshop-type meeting often uses this format.
- Boardroom setups are made for small numbers of people. The meeting takes place around one rectangular table.

Participants at an association meeting.

Association Meetings

Every year there are thousands of association meetings that spend millions of dollars sponsoring many types of meetings, including regional, special interest, education, and board meetings. The things that top the list of what an association meeting planner looks for when choosing a meeting destination include the availability of hotels and facilities, ease of transportation, distance from attendees, transportation costs, and food and beverage. Members attend association meetings voluntarily, so the hotel should work with meeting planners to make the destination seem as appealing as possible.

Associations used to be viewed as groups that held annual meetings and conventions with speeches, entertainment, an educational program, and social events. They have changed in activity and perception.

Conventions and Expositions

Conventions are generally larger meetings with some form of exposition or trade show included. A number of associations have one or more conventions per year. These conventions raise a large part of the association's budget. A typical convention follows a format like the following:

1. Welcome/registration
2. Introduction of the president
3. President's welcome speech, opening the convention
4. First keynote address by a featured speaker
5. Exposition booths open (equipment manufacturers and trade suppliers)
6. Several workshops or presentations on specific topics
7. Luncheon
8. More workshops and presentations
9. Demonstrations of special topics (e.g., culinary arts for a hospitality convention)
10. Vendors' private receptions
11. Dinner
12. Convention center closes

Figure 4 shows a convention event profile for a trade show.

Conventions are not always held in convention centers; in fact, the majority are held in large hotels over a three- to five-day period. The headquarters hotel is usually the one in which most of the activity takes place. Function space is allocated for registration, the convention, expositions, meals, and so on.

Expositions are events that bring together sellers of products and services at a location (usually a convention center) where they can show their products and services to a group of attendees at a convention or trade show. Exhibitors are an essential component of the industry because they pay to exhibit their products to the attendees. Exhibitors interact with attendees with the intention of making sales or establishing contacts and leads for follow-up. Expositions can take up several hundred thousand square feet of space, divided into booths for individual manufacturers or their representatives. In the hospitality industry, the two largest expositions are the AH&LA's conference, held in conjunction with the International Hotel/Motel & Restaurant Show (IHMRS; held annually in November at the Javits Center in New York), and the NRA's annual exposition held every May in Chicago. Both events are well worth attending.

Types of Associations

An association is an organized body that exhibits some variety of volunteer leadership structure, which may employ an activity or purpose that the leadership shares in common. The association is generally organized to promote and

San Diego
Convention Center Corporation
EVENT PROFILE

EVENT STATISTICS

Event Name:	San Diego Apartment Association Trade Show	ID:	9506059
Sales Person:	Joy Peacock	Initial Contact:	8/3/2005
Event Manager:	Trish A. Stiles	Move In Date:	6/22/2009
ConVis Contact:		Move In Day:	Wednesday
Food Person:		Move In Time:	6:01 am
Event Tech.:		First Event Date:	6/23/2009
Event Attend.:		First Event Day:	Thursday
Nature of Event:	LT Local Trade Show	Start Show Time:	6:01 am
Event Parameter:	60 San Diego Convention Center	End Show Time:	11:59 pm
Business Type 1:	41 Association	# of Event Days:	1
Business Type 2:	91 LOCAL	Move Out Date:	6/23/2009
Booking Status:	D Definite	Move Out Day:	Thursday
Rate Schedule:	III Public Show, Meetings and Location	Out Time:	11:59 pm
Open to Public:	No	Date Confirmed:	8/3/2005
Number of Sessions:	1	Attend per Sesn:	3000
Event Sold By:	F Facility (SDCCC)	Tot Room Nights:	15
Abbrev. Name:	/6/Apartment Assn	Public Release:	Yes
Est Bill Amount:	Rent - 6,060.00 Equip –	0.00 Food –	0.00
Last Changed On:	8/20/05 in: Comment Maintenance	By – Joy Peacock	

This Event has been in the facility before

CLIENT INFORMATION

Company: San Diego Apartment Assn, a non-profit Corporation
Contact Name: Ms. Leslie Cloud, Sales and Marketing Coord.
1011 Camino Del Rio South, Suite 200, San Diego, CA 92108
Telephone Number: (619) 297-1000
Fax Number: (619) 294-4510
Alternate Number: (619) 294-4510

ID: SDAA

Company: San Diego Apartment Assn, a non-profit Corporation
Alt Contact Name: Ms. Pamela A. Trimble, Finance & Operations Director
1011 Camino Del Rio South, Suite 200, San Diego, 92108
Telephone Number: (619) 297-1000
Fax Number: (619) 297-4510

EVENT LOCATIONS

ROOM	MOVE IN	IN USE	ED	MOVE OUT	BS	SEAT	RATE	EST. RENT	ATTEND
A	6/22/09 6:01 am	6/23/09	1	6/23/09 11:59 pm	D	E	III	6,060.00	5,000
AS	6/22/09 6:01 am	6/23/09	1	6/23/09 11:59 pm	D	E	III	0.00	10
R01	6/22/09 6:01 am	6/23/09	1	6/23/09 11:59 pm	D	T	III	0.00	450
R02	6/22/09 6:01 am	6/23/09	1	6/23/09 11:59 pm	D	T	III	0.00	350
R03	6/22/09 6:01 am	6/23/09	1	6/23/09 11:59 pm	D	T	III	0.00	280
R04	6/22/09 6:01 am	6/23/09	1	6/23/09 11:59 pm	D	T	III	0.00	280
R05	6/22/09 6:01 am	6/23/09	1	6/23/09 11:59 pm	D	T	III	0.00	460

FOOD SERVICES

ROOM	DATE	TIME	BS ATTEND	EST. COST FOOD SERVICE

There are No Food Services booked for this event

Figure 4 • Convention Event Profile for a Trade Show.

(Courtesy San Diego Convention Center.)

INTRODUCING JILL MORAN, CSEP

Principal and Owner, JS Moran, Special Event Planning & Management

In my life, there is no typical day. As the owner of a special event company, I provide a variety of services to corporate, nonprofit, and social clients. I must be able to communicate successfully with a client at one moment, a vendor at the next, and a prospect at another. My job also involves managing the growth of my company, hiring the right staff and vendors for projects, and getting each job done from start to finish in a professional and timely manner.

As a business owner, I am required to keep my eye on many facets of the company almost daily. Some areas are a must to attend to such as billing, scheduling, and marketing. The squeakiest wheel that gets the most grease, though, is the actual ongoing projects. Once a project is secured, the contracting, planning, and execution stages quickly follow after the initial handshake. These components of meeting and event planning can be time and energy consuming as the details are planned out and put into motion. Event details may involve researching, attending meetings, generating event documents, developing creative concepts and themes, securing vendors to satisfy event details, or executing an event. In the planning of any given event or conference, I may be required to attend off-site visits with vendors, venues, or clients as well as use the computer or telephone to facilitate the planning process. Visits to art supply, furniture, fabric stores, or storerooms of linen or décor vendors are also key elements as theme and design elements are worked on. Review of entertainment or speakers, planning of room layouts or trade show and exhibition space, or discussion with graphic artists also fits into the necessary details covered during the planning phase of an event.

A typical day may involve early computer time to work on production schedules, time lines, e-mails to vendors or clients, follow-up on contracts, or focused time spent on a new proposal. I find early morning (before 9 A.M.) or evening (after 8 P.M.) to be the best time for these activities. This is when I get the least telephone interruptions, and it is before or after scheduled appointments that would require my time out of the office. During the typical business day, phone calls, planning activities, and appointments occupy most of the day. If I am working on an international project, there is more flexibility with this because of the time differences.

While the execution phase of projects and events keeps me busy moment to moment, the strategic planning and business management of my company also demand attention. The challenge for me as the owner of a small business is to carve out time for the marketing and sales arm of the business—to take time to prospect for new business at the same time that I am in the execution phase of events, so that when one project comes to an end, another will be waiting in the wings. I do this by developing fresh marketing materials using photos or components of recent meetings and events; creating video or DVD–style materials to post on my web site or to send to clients; making calls to colleagues, prospects, or venues to say "hello" or touch base; and attending luncheons or visits with past clients to keep in touch. I also try to spend time getting a pulse on new markets to explore or niche areas to develop in my business. I typically subscribe to a wide variety of industry and professional magazines and try to end my day flipping through and tearing out articles that may be useful.

Sometimes I feel I eat, sleep, and live special events, and in many ways, I do. But work doesn't take up every moment of my life. As a mother and wife, I still try to create a fun, loving home for my family by cooking dinner almost every night and by walking daily with my husband and two dogs. These breaks during the day give me downtime and a chance to regroup. I am also active in the music ministry at my local church as a youth choir director, which offers me spiritual and community involvement. I also belong to a book group, which I often attend without finishing the book. There are only so many hours in the day, and I seem to use them up very quickly. But at the end of each day, I am always looking forward to the next!

Source: Courtesy of Jill Moran.

enhance that common interest, activity, or purpose. The association industry is significant in many respects—total employees, payroll, and membership—but in one area, it is the undisputed leader: It's the big spender when it comes to conventions and meetings. The following sections discuss different types of associations that participate in meetings, conventions, and expositions.

Historical Associations

Today's associations find their roots in historical times. Ancient Roman and Asian craftsmen formed associations for the betterment of their trade. The Middle Ages found associations in the form of guilds, which were created to ensure proper wages were received and to maintain work standards.

Types of Historical Associations

Trade Associations

A trade association is an industry trade group that is generally a public relations organization founded and funded by corporations that operate in a specific industry. Its purpose is generally to promote that industry through public relations (PR) activities such as advertising, education, political donation, political pressure, publishing, and astroturfing.[4]

Professional Association

A professional association is a professional body or organization, usually nonprofit, that exists to further a particular profession and to protect both the public interest and the interests of professionals.[5]

Medical and Scientific Associations

These associations are professional organizations for medical and scientific professionals. They are often based on their specific specialties and are usually national, often with subnational or regional affiliates. These associations usually offer conferences and continuing education. They often serve in capacities similar to trade unions and often take public policy stances on these issues.

Religious Organizations

Religious organizations include those groups of individuals who are part of churches, mosques, synagogues, and other spiritual or religious congregations. Religion has taken many forms in various cultures and individuals. These groups may come together in meeting places to further develop their faith, to become more aware of others who have the same faith, to organize and plan activities, to recognize their leaders, for fund-raising, and for a number of other reasons.

Government Organizations

There are thousands of government organizations in the United States made up of numerous public bodies and agencies. These types of organizations can range from federal, state, and local organizations. There are five basic types of local governments. Three of these are general-purpose governments; the remaining two include special-purpose local governments that fall into the category of school district governments and special district governments.

Types of Meetings

There are different types of meetings and purposes for having a meeting. Some of the types of meetings are annual meetings that are held by private or public companies, board and committee meetings, fund-raisers, and professional and technical meetings. The following sections describe some of the more popular types of meetings.

Annual Meetings

Annual meetings are meetings that are generally held every year by corporations or associations to inform their members of previous and future activities. In organizations run by volunteers or a paid committee, the annual meeting is generally the forum for the election of officers or representatives for the organization.

Board Meetings, Committee Meetings, Seminars and Workshops, Professional and Technical Meetings

Board meetings for corporations must be held annually, and most corporations hold meetings monthly or four times a year. Of course, not all are held in hotels, but some are, and that brings in additional revenue at the hotel. Committee meetings are generally held at the place of business and only occasionally are held in hotels. Seminars are frequently held in hotels, as are workshops and technical meetings. To meet these needs, hotels and convention centers have convention and meeting managers who go over the requirements and prepare proposals and event orders and budgets.

Corporate Meetings, Conventions, and Expositions

Meetings are mostly held by either the corporate or nonprofit industries. Both association and corporate meeting expenditures are in the billions of dollars each year. Corporations in various industries hold lots of meetings mostly for reasons of educating, training, decision making, research, sales, team building, the introduction of a new product, organization or reorganization, problem solving, and strategic planning. Corporate meetings may be held for the employees or for the general public. For employees of a company, a corporate meeting is a command performance. The major objective of corporate meeting planners is to ensure that the meetings are successful.

SMERF

Many participants in meetings are organized by either an association, a corporation, or **social, military, educational, religious, and fraternal groups (SMERF)**. Often, these groups are price conscious, because of the fact that the majority of the functions sponsored by these organizations are paid for by the individual, and sometimes the fees are not tax deductible. However, SMERF groups are flexible to ensure that their spending falls within the limits of their budgets; they are a good filler business during off-peak times.

The show floor of the Environmental Quality Trade Fair and Conference.

Incentive Meetings

The **incentive market** of MICE continues to experience rapid growth as meeting planners and travel agents organize incentive travel programs for corporate employees to reward them for reaching specific targets. Incentive trips generally vary from three to six days in length and can range from a moderate trip to an extremely lavish vacation for the employee and his or her partner. The most popular destination for incentive trips is Europe, followed closely by the Caribbean, Hawaii, Florida, and California. Because incentive travel serves as the reward for a unique subset of corporate group business, participants must perceive the destination and the hotel as something special. Climate, recreational facilities, and sightseeing opportunities are high on an incentive meeting planner's list of attributes for which to look.

▶ Check Your Knowledge

1. What are three different types of meetings described in this text and what is their purpose?
2. What is SMERF?

Meeting Planning

Meeting planning includes not only the planning but also the successful holding of the meeting and the postmeeting evaluations. As the following sections discuss, there are a number of topics and lots of details to consider. (See Figure 5.)

Needs Analysis

Before a meeting planner can start planning a meeting, a *needs analysis* is done to determine the purpose and desired outcome of a meeting. Once the necessity of the meeting has been established, the meeting planner can then work with the party to maximize the productivity of the meeting. The key to a productive meeting is a meeting agenda. The meeting agenda may not always fall under the responsibility of the meeting planner, but it is essential for the meeting planner to be closely involved with the written agenda and also with the core purpose of the agenda, which may be different from what is stated. For example, a nonprofit organization may hold a function to promote awareness of its objectives through a fun activity, but its hidden agenda is to raise funds for the organization.

The meeting agenda provides the framework for making *meeting objectives*. The meeting planner must know what the organization is trying to accomplish so as to be successful in the management of the meeting or conference. It is helpful for the meeting planner, regardless of what role he or she plays, to plan the meeting with the meeting objectives in mind. The meeting's objectives provide

SAN DIEGO CONVENTION CENTER

EVENT MANAGER

DEFINITION

Under moderate direction from the services manager, plans, directs, and supervises assigned events and represents services manager on assigned shifts.

KEY RESPONSIBILITIES

- Plans, coordinates, and supervises all phases of the events to include set ups, move ins and outs, and the activities themselves
- Prepares and disseminates set-up information to the proper departments well in advance of the activity, and ensures complete readiness of the facilities
- Responsible for arranging for all services needed by the tenant
- Coordinates facility staffing needs with appropriate departments
- Acts as a consultant to tenants and the liaison between in-house contractors and tenants
- Preserves facility's physical plant and ensures a safe environment by reviewing tenants plans; requests and makes certain they comply with facility, state, county, and city rules and regulations
- Prepares accounting paperwork of tenant charges, approves final billings, and assists with collection of same
- Resolves complaints, including operational problems and difficulties
- Assists in conducting surveys, gathering statistical information, and working on special projects as assigned by services manager
- Conducts tours of the facilities

MINIMUM REQUIREMENTS

- Bachelor's degree in hospitality management, business, or recreational management from a fully accredited university or college, plus two (2) years of experience in coordinating major conventions and trade shows
- Combination of related education/training and additional experience may substitute for bachelor's degree
- An excellent ability to manage both fiscal and human resources
- Knowledge in public relations; oral and written communications
- Experienced with audiovisual equipment

225 Broadway, Suite 710 • San Diego, CA 92102 • (619) 239-1989
FAX (619) 239-2030
Operated by the San Diego Convention Center Corporation

Figure 5 • An Event Manager's Job Description.

A DAY IN THE LIFE OF ALEXANDRA STOUT

Professional Meeting Planner

In most careers, organization and communication are two of the most important qualities to have. As a professional meeting planner, organization and communication defines what needs to be done on a daily basis. I work with different clients every day. No client is the same, and no client will have the same request as another, so being able to listen effectively to the wants and needs of an individual or group of individuals is what I focus on first. The second step is understanding the purpose the client has for their meeting or conference and organizing the details to carry out that purpose.

When I initially meet with a client, some know exactly what they need, and others only have an idea of what they need, which is often a challenge. For the clients who only have an idea, I must cover all aspects of their meeting by asking them what message they want to send. Once I reveal that message, I can ask additional questions that will assist in creating a successful meeting. For example, will there be guest speakers, food and/or beverages, accommodations, printed material, or special audiovisual equipment?

Company A is hosting three guest speakers at its annual conference. Who will be greeting the guests on the day of the meeting? Where will they be staying? How will they be arriving at the venue?

Clients that host larger meetings or conferences often have more detailed requests, as it is not a reoccurring event. Organizations like Company A that will have guest speakers attend will also have larger requests such as catered meals, blocked hotel rooms in the area or at the venue for the duration of the conference, and transportation to and from the airport and the venue location. Other organizations have monthly or bimonthly meetings, and their needs are the same from week to week. Company B plans on presenting a PowerPoint presentation during its monthly regional sales meeting, it will need a projector, screen, and appropriate audio and visual elements, as well as coffee and pitchers of water for its employees. Company B also asks for an assortment of fruit and breakfast pastries to be displayed by the coffee and water. Since Company B has its sales meeting on a monthly basis, its requests from month to month rarely change.

More recently, virtual meetings have been increasing in popularity. This option not only makes travel less demanding for members of an organization but is also more cost effective. "Go to" meetings allow a high volume of individuals to join a virtual conference through their computers. With a telephone, computer microphone, and speakers, everyone can communicate with one another, share ideas, and present information just the same as a conventional meeting.

By first listening and determining the purpose and impression the client wants to communicate to another organization, its own, or a group of individuals, I am then able to organize that message into a plan. Clients always have a message they want to get across; whether it be motivation to boost employee morale within a company or to make a lasting impression on a group of potential customers for a given product for sale, a meeting always has a purpose, and my job is to create and fulfill that request from start to finish.

the framework from which the meeting planner will set the budget, select the site and facility, and plan the overall meeting or convention.

Budget

Understanding clients and knowing their needs are both extremely important; however, the budget carries the most weight. Setting the *budget* for the meeting is more successful if the meeting planner is involved in the budget planning throughout and before making a finalized decision on how much to spend in each area. Setting the budget for the meeting is not a simple task. Knowing how much there is available to spend will help the meeting planner to better guide clients with parameters by which the event is designed. Budgets are planned for various activities and the amount of the budget needed fluctuates for different sites. Therefore, a working budget is necessary to be used as a guideline for making decisions for necessary changes. When changes in the budget are made, it is wise to communicate with the meeting planner these decisions so that the planning of activities is within budgetary constraints. Revenue and expenditure estimates must be accurate and be as thorough as possible to make certain that all possible expenditures are included in the budget prior to the event.

Income for a meeting, convention, or exposition comes from grants or contributions, event sponsor contributions, registration fees, exhibitor fees, company or organization sponsoring, advertising, and the sale of educational materials.

Expenses for a meeting, a convention, or an exposition could include, but are not limited to, rental fees; meeting planner fees; marketing expenses; printing and copying expenses; support supplies, such as office supplies and mailing; on-site and support staff; audiovisual equipment; speakers; signage; entertainment and recreational expenses; mementos for guests and attendees; tours; ground transportation; spousal programs; food and beverage; and on-site personnel.

Request for Proposal and Site Inspection and Selection

No matter how large or small a meeting, it is essential that clear meeting specifications are developed in the form of a written *request for proposal/quote (RFQ)*, rather than contacting hotels by telephone to get a quote. Many larger hotels and convention centers now have online submission forms available.

Several factors are evaluated when selecting a meeting site, including location and level of service, accessibility, hotel room availability, conference room availability, price, city, restaurant service and quality, personal safety, and local attractions. Convention centers and hotels provide meeting space and accommodations as well as food and beverage facilities and service. The convention center and a hotel team from each hotel capable of handling the meeting will attempt to impress the meeting planner. The hotel sales executive will send particulars of the hotel's meeting space and a selection of banquet menus and invite the meeting planner for a site inspection. During the site inspection, the meeting planner is shown all facets of the hotel, including the meeting rooms, guest sleeping rooms, the food and beverage outlets, and any special facility that may interest the planner or the client.

Negotiation with the Convention Center or Hotel

The meeting planner has several critical interactions with hotels, including negotiating the room blocks and rates. Escorting clients on site inspections gives the hotel an opportunity to show its level of facilities and service. The most important interaction is typically with the catering/banquet/conference department associates, especially the services manager, maître d', and captains; these frontline associates can make or break a meeting. For example, meeting planners often send boxes of meeting materials to hotels expecting the hotel to automatically know for which meeting they are intended. On more than one occasion, they have ended up in the hotel's main storeroom, much to the consternation of the meeting planner. Fortunately for most meeting planners, once they have taken care of a meeting one year, subsequent years typically are very similar.

Contracts

Once the meeting planner and the hotel or conference facility have agreed on all the requirements and costs, a contract is prepared and signed by the planner, the organization, and the hotel or convention center. The *contract* is a legal document that binds two or more parties. In the case of meetings, conventions, and expositions, a contract binds an association or organization and the hotel or convention center. The components that make up an enforceable contract include the following:

1. *An offer:* The offer simply states, in as precise a manner as possible, exactly what the offering party is willing to do, and what he or she expects in return. The offer may include specific instructions for how, where, when, and to whom the offer is made.

2. *Consideration:* The payment exchanged for the promise(s) contained in a contract. For a contract to be valid, consideration must flow both ways. For example, the consideration is for a convention center to provide services and use of its facilities in exchange for a consideration of a stated amount to be paid by the organization or host.

3. *Acceptance:* The unconditional agreement to the precise terms and conditions of an offer. The acceptance must mirror exactly the terms of the offer for the acceptance to make the contract valid. The best way to indicate acceptance of an offer is by agreeing to the offer in writing.[6]

Most important to be considered legally enforceable, a contract must be made by parties who are legally able to contract, and the activities specified in the contract must not be in violation of the law. Contracts should include clauses on "attrition and performance," meaning that the contract has a clause to protect the hotel or convention facility in the event that the organizer's numbers drop below an acceptable level. Because the space reserved is supposed to produce a certain amount of money, if the numbers drop, so does the money; unless there is a clause that says something like "there will be a guaranteed revenue of $$$ for the use of the room/space." The performance part of the clause means that a certain amount of food and beverage revenue will be charged for regardless of whether it is consumed.

Organizing and Preconference Meetings

The average lead time required for organizing a small meeting is about three to six months; larger meetings and conferences take much longer and are booked years in advance. Some meetings and conventions choose the same location each year and others move from city to city, usually from the East Coast to the Midwest or West Coast.

A preconference meeting.

Conference Event Order

A conference event order has all the information necessary for all department employees to be able to refer to for details of the setup (times and layout) and the conference itself (arrival, meal times and what food and beverages are to be served, and the cost of items so that the billing can be done). An example of a conference event order is given in Figure 6.

EVENT DOCUMENT
REVISED COPY

/6/SAN DIEGO INTERNATIONAL BOAT SHOW
Tuesday, January 4, 2005–Tuesday, January 11, 2005

SPACE: Combined Exhibit Halls AB, Hall A - How Manager's Office, Box Office by Hall A, Hall B –
Show Manager's Office, Mezzanine Room 12, Mezzanine Room 13, Mezzanine Rooms 14 A&B, AND
Mezzanine Rooms 15 A&B

CONTACT: Mr. Jeff Hancock
National Marine Manufacturers Association, Inc.
4901 Morena Blvd.
Suite 901
San Diego, CA 92117
Telephone Number: (619) 274-9924
Fax Number: (619) 274-6760
Decorator Co.:   Greyhound Exposition Services
Sales Person: Denise Simenstad
Event Manager: Jane Krause
Event Tech.:   Sylvia A. Harrison

SCHEDULE OF EVENTS:

Monday, January 3, 2005   5:00 am–6:00 pm   Combined Exhibit Halls AB
Service contractor move in GES,
Andy Quintena

Tuesday, January 4, 2005   8:00 am–6:00 pm   Combined Exhibit Halls AB
Service contractor move in GES,
Andy Quintena
12:00 pm–6:00 pm
Combined Exhibit Halls AB
Exhibitor move in

Wednesday, January 5, 2005   8:00 am–6:00 pm   Combined Exhibit Halls AB
Exhibitor move in
Est. attendance: 300

Thursday, January 6, 2005   8:00 am–12:00 pm   Combined Exhibit Halls AB
Exhibitor final move in
11:30 am–8:30 pm   Box Office by Hall A
OPEN: Ticket prices, Adults $6, Children 12 & under $3

Figure 6 • Conference Event Document.
(Courtesy of the San Diego Convention Center Corporation.)

FOCUS ON MARKETING

Meetings and Conventions Information Search

Amanda Alexander, M.S., Ph.D., Student

The meeting and conventions industry is one of the fastest growing sectors of the tourism and hospitality field, with expenditures in the billions of dollars and annual revenue growth. An event planner is responsible for organizing convention personnel and securing accommodations, transportation, guest speakers, food service, or equipment needs for the organization and production of an event. An event planner can act as a gatekeeper of information to his or her client, and therefore it is important that information is disseminated to the event planner and then the client. Understanding how event planners obtain their information is vital for the meeting and convention businesses.

Event planners can obtain information through various mediums including print, TV, radio, Internet, and word of mouth. The continuing advancement of Internet capabilities has allowed businesses to showcase their product or services in a way that hasn't been possible before, for example, through virtual tours of a property. Social media sites have changed how information is presented and how users can interact with other users to get personal experiences (virtual word of mouth) and reviews of a business. Applications on phones have allowed individuals to "check in" when they arrive at locations and then post this information on social media sites; this can create awareness of a business that otherwise may have not occurred. While many social media sites are driven by consumers, a business should monitor the site to ensure that negative comments are handled from a customer service perspective.

Even though the Internet offers many strategic opportunities, the medium that has been shown to be trusted and deemed most reliable by event planners is word of mouth. Word of mouth occurs when information is passed from one person to another. An individual will give attention to a source (another person) if the source is considered to be significant in making a decision. So how does a business ensure that event planners are receiving information via word of mouth? The following are a few tactics that will encourage word-of-mouth marketing to reach event planners:

- Making convention and visitors bureaus and destination management companies aware of your services and products through site visits and trials

- Having a sales member make cold calls to event planners and be available to meet one on one with event planners

- Creating a presence within organizations/associations such as the International Special Event Society (ISES) during meetings and annual conventions

- Following up after an event planner has used your business to find out what could have made the experience more positive (this will be an indication of what event planners are saying to others about your business)

Working in the meeting and conventions industry can be very exciting and rewarding, but to achieve success, whether an event planner or a business that offers services or products, knowing where and how to present information that leads to a decision is vital. As with all marketing tactics and strategies, the goal is to gain attention by the target market and create awareness of a product/service that is needed by the target market.

Postevent Meeting

A postevent meeting is held to evaluate the event—what went well and what should be improved for next time. Larger conferences have staff from the hotel or convention center where the event will be held the following year so that they can better prepare for the event when it is held at their facility.

Venues for Meetings, Conventions, and Expositions

Most of the time, meetings and functions are held in hotels, convention centers, city centers, conference centers, universities, corporate offices, or resorts, but more and more, meetings are housed in unique venues such as cruise ships and historical sites.

City Centers

City centers are good venues for some conferences because they are convenient to reach by air and ground transportation. There is plenty of action in a major city center; attractions range from cultural to scenic beauty. Most cities have a convention center and several hotels to accommodate guests.

Convention Centers

Convention centers throughout the world compete to host the largest exhibitions, which can be responsible for adding several million dollars in revenue to the local economy. Convention centers are huge facilities with parking, information services, business centers, and food and beverage facilities included.

Usually, convention centers are corporations owned by county, city, or state governments and are operated by a board of appointed representatives from the various groups having a vested interest in the successful operation of the center. The board appoints a president or general manager to run the center according to a predetermined mission, goals, and objectives.

Convention centers have a variety of expositions and meeting rooms to accommodate both large and small events. The centers generate revenue from the rental of space, which frequently is divided into booths (one booth is about 100 square feet). Large exhibits may take several booths' space. Additional revenue is generated by the sale of food and beverages, concession stand rentals, and vending machines. Many centers also have their own subcontractors to handle staging, construction, lighting, audiovisual, electrical, and communications.

In addition to the megaconvention centers, a number of prominent centers also contribute to the local, state, and national economies. One good example is the Rhode Island Convention Center. The $82 million center, representing the second largest public works project in the state's history, is located in the heart of downtown Providence, adjacent to the 14,500-seat Providence Civic Center. The 365,000-square-foot center offers a 100,000-square-foot main exhibit hall,

Denver, Colorado, Convention Center.

a 20,000-square-foot ballroom, eighteen meeting rooms, and a full-service kitchen that can produce 5,000 meals per day. The exhibit hall divides into four separate halls, and the facility features its own telephone system, allowing individualized billing. A special rotunda function room at the front of the building features glass walls that offer a panoramic view of downtown Providence for receptions of up to 365 people. Extensive use of glass on the façade of the center provides ample natural light throughout the entrance and prefunction areas.

Conference Centers

A conference center is a specially designed learning environment dedicated to hosting and supporting small- to medium-sized meetings, typically between twenty and fifty people.[7] The nature of a conference meeting is to promote a distraction-free learning environment. Conference centers are designed to encourage sharing of information in an inviting, comfortable atmosphere, and to focus sharply on meetings and what makes them effective. Although the groups that hold meetings in conference centers are typically small in terms of attendees, there are thousands of small meetings held every month. Increasingly, hotels are now going after executive meetings where expense is not a major issue.

Hotels and Resorts

Hotels and resorts offer a variety of locations from city center to destination resorts. Many hotels have ballrooms and other meeting rooms designed to accommodate groups of various sizes. Today, they all have web sites and offer meeting planners to help with the planning and organizing of conferences and meetings. Once the word gets out that a meeting planner is seeking a venue for a conference, there is plenty of competition among the hotels to get the business.

Cruise Ships

Meeting in a nontraditional facility can provide a unique and memorable experience for the meeting attendee. However, many of the challenges faced in traditional venues such as hotels and convention centers are also applicable to these facilities. In some cases, planning must begin much earlier for alternative meeting environments than with traditional facilities. A thorough understanding of goals and objectives, budget, and attendee profile of the meeting is essential to negotiate the best package possible. A cruise ship meeting is a uniquely different meeting setting and offers a number of advantages to the attendees such as discounts, complimentary meals, less outside distraction while at sea, entertainment, and visiting more than one destination while unpacking only once![8]

Colleges and Universities

More and more, alternative venues for meeting places include facilities such as colleges, universities, and their campuses. The paramount consideration in contemplating use of campus-based facilities is to know the nature of the target audience.[9] A certain knowledge and evaluation of the participants are inevitable and invaluable because, most of the time, the relative cost of campus-based meetings is less expensive than a medium-priced hotel.

Sustainable Meetings, Conventions, and Expositions

The meetings industry is becoming more responsible in its environmental stewardship, and it makes economic sense to do so. Companies that choose to do so are reporting higher gross margins, higher return on sales, higher return on assets, and a stronger cash flow within its own organization. Although there are some upfront costs with going green, the end result is generally a significant savings.[10]

Taking small steps to go green can make an enormous difference in a company's bottom line, as well as in the environment. Simply switching from bottled water to pitchers of water for attendees saved Oracle $1.5 million at its Open World event in San Francisco. Reusing name-badge holders saved another $500 in just one year. In addition to monetary savings to these groups, the amount of waste deposited into a landfill was dramatically reduced, just by making these small changes.

Convention centers are going green by reducing the heat, light, and power consumption. LEED (Leadership in Energy and Environmental Design) buildings require far less energy to air-condition the building, less electric lighting due to increased natural lighting, and less water consumption because of low-flow toilets and faucets that supply water when a sensor is triggered.

In an effort to encourage and support sustainability, various industry certifications have been introduced, including the Green Meeting Guide and the Certification in Green Meetings and Events (CGME). CGME is designed to help meeting planners organize meetings in a sustainable and socially responsible way. Additionally, there are carbon footprint calculators.

Career Information

Meetings, incentive travel, conventions, and expositions (the MICE segment) offer a broad range of career paths. Successful meeting planners are detail-oriented, organized people who not only plan and arrange meetings, but also negotiate hotel rooms and meeting space in hotels and convention centers.

Incentive travel careers include aspects of organizing high-end travel, hotels, restaurants, attractions, and entertainment. With big budgets, this can be an exciting career for those interested in a combination of travel and hotels in exotic locations.

Conventions and convention centers offer several career paths, from assistants to event managers to sales managers for a special type of account (e.g., associations) or territory. Senior sales managers are expected to book large conventions and expositions—yes, everyone has their quota. Event managers plan and organize the function/event with the client once the contract has been signed. Salaries range from $35,000 to $70,000 for both assistants on rise to sales or event managers. Careers are also possible in the companies that service the MICE segment.

Someone has to equip the convention center, get it ready for an exposition, and supply all the food and beverage items. Off-premise catering for special events also offers careers for creative people who like to come up with concepts and themes around which an event or function may be planned.

For all career paths, it is critical to gain experience in the areas of your interest. Ask people you respect to be your mentor. Ask questions! When you show enthusiasm, people will respond with more help and advice. Figure 7 illustrates a career path to becoming a meeting planner; Figure 8 shows an event manager's job description at a convention center.

John Moors, former administrator of the Tampa Convention Centre, offers the following advice: "The convention and meeting industry needs qualified candidates. Many come into the convention side of the industry with transferable skills from hotels and resorts with basic business principles. We hire personalities, not résumés. It does not take long to learn how to set up a meeting room. It does, however, take experience to learn how to lead people—this leadership aspect is very important. Get your degree! But remember, it's not only what you learn in the classroom, but also your demonstrated ability to stick to something and achieve it. So get into the industry and find a mentor. Good luck!"

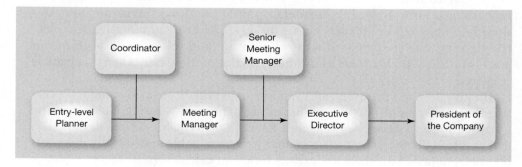

Figure 7 • A Career Path to Becoming a Top-Level Event Manager.

SAN DIEGO CONVENTION CENTER

EVENT MANAGER

DEFINITION

Under moderate direction from the services manager, plans, directs, and supervises assigned events and represents services manager on assigned shifts.

KEY RESPONSIBILITIES

- Plans, coordinates, and supervises all phases of the events to include set-ups, move ins and outs, and the activities themselves
- Prepares and disseminates set-up information to the proper departments well in advance of the activity, and ensures complete readiness of the facilities
- Responsible for arranging for all services needed by the tenant
- Coordinates facility staffing needs with appropriate departments
- Acts as a consultant to tenants and the liaison between in-house contractors and tenants
- Preserves facility's physical plant and ensures a safe environment by reviewing tenants' plans; requests and makes certain they comply with facility, state, county, and city rules and regulations
- Prepares accounting paperwork of tenant charges, approves final billings, and assists with collection of same
- Resolves complaints, including operational problems and difficulties
- Assists in conducting surveys, gathering statistical information, and working on special projects as assigned by services manager
- Conducts tours of the facilities

MINIMUM REQUIREMENTS

- Bachelor's degree in hospitality management, business, or recreational management from a fully accredited university or college, plus two (2) years of experience in coordinating major conventions and trade shows
- Combination of related education/training and additional experience may substitute for bachelor's degree
- An excellent ability to manage both fiscal and human resources
- Knowledge in public relations; oral and written communications
- Experienced with audiovisual equipment

225 Broadway, Suite 710 • San Diego, CA 92102 • (619) 239-1989
FAX (619) 239-2030
Operated by the San Diego Convention Center Corporation

Figure 8 • Event Manager's Job Description.

Trends in Meetings, Conventions, and Expositions

- More people are going abroad to attend meetings.
- Some international shows do not travel very well (i.e., agricultural machinery). Thus, organizations such as Bleinheim and Reed Exposition Group airlift components and create shows in other countries.
- Competitiveness has increased among all destinations. Convention centers will expand and new centers will come online.

- The industry needs to be more sophisticated. The need for fiber optics is present everywhere.

- Compared to a few years ago, large conventions are not as well attended, and regional conventions have more attendees.

CASE STUDY

Double-Booked

The convention bureau in a large and popular convention destination has jurisdiction over the convention center. A seasoned convention sales manager, who has worked for the bureau for seven years and produces more sales than any other sales manager, has rebooked a 2,000-person group for a three-day exposition in the convention center. The exposition is to take place two years from the booking date.

The client has a fifteen-year history of holding conventions, meetings, and expositions in this convention center and has always used the bureau to contract all space and services. In fact, the sales manager handling the account has worked with the client for seven of the fifteen years. The bureau considers this client a "preferred customer."

The convention group meeting planner also appears in a magazine ad giving a testimony of praise for the convention bureau, this particular sales manager, and the city as a destination for conventions.

Shortly after the meeting planner rebooks this convention with the bureau, the bureau changes sales administration personnel, not once, but three times. This creates a challenge for the sales manager in terms of producing contracts, client files, and event profiles, and in the recording and distribution of information. The preferred customer who rebooked has a contract, purchase orders for vendor services, a move-in and setup agenda, and an event profile, all supplied by the sales manager. The sales manager has copies of these documents as well. The two hotels where the group will be staying also have contracts for the VIP group.

As is the nature of this particular bureau, other sales managers have been booking and contracting space for the same time period as the group that rebooked. In fact, the exhibit hall has been double-booked, as have the breakout rooms for seminars, workshops, and food and beverage service. The groups that were contracted later are all first-time users of the facility.

This situation remains undetected until ten days prior to the groups' arrival. It is brought to the attention of the bureau and convention center only when the sales manager distributes a memo to schedule a precon-vention meeting with the meeting planner and all convention center staff.

Because of the administrative personnel changes, necessary information was not disseminated to key de-partments and key personnel. The convention center was never notified that space has been contracted for the preferred customer. The preferred customer has been told about this potentially catastrophic situation. Now there is a major problem to rectify.

Discussion Questions

1. Ultimately, who is responsible for decision making with regard to this situation?

2. What steps should be taken to remedy this situation?

3. Are there fair and ethical procedures to follow to provide space for the preferred customer? If so, what are they?

4. What measures, if any, should be taken in handling the seasoned sales manager?

5. What leverage does the meeting planner have to secure this and future business with the bureau?

6. What might the preferred customer do if it is denied space and usage of the convention center?

7. How can this situation be avoided in the future?

Summary

1. Conventions, meetings, and expositions serve social, political, sporting, or religious purposes. Associations offer benefits such as a political voice, education, marketing avenues, member services, and networking.
2. Meetings are events designed to bring people together for the purpose of exchanging information. Typical forms of meetings are conferences, workshops, seminars, forums, and symposiums.
3. Expositions bring together purveyors of products, equipment, and services in an environment in which they can demonstrate their products. Conventions are meetings that include some form of exposition or trade show.
4. Meeting planners contract out their services to associations and corporations. Their responsibilities include premeeting, on-site, and postmeeting activities.
5. The convention and visitors bureaus are nonprofit organizations that assess the needs of the client and organize transportation, hotel accommodations, restaurants, and attractions.
6. Convention centers are huge facilities, usually owned by the government, where meetings and expositions are held. Events at convention centers require a lot of up-front planning and careful event management. A contract that is based on the event profile and an event document is part of effective management.

Key Words and Concepts

associations
convention
convention and visitors bureaus (CVBs)
convention center
exposition
familiarization (FAM) trip
incentive market

meeting
meeting planner
meetings, incentive travel, conventions, and exhibitions (MICE)
social, military, educational, religious, and fraternal groups (SMERF)

Review Questions

1. What are associations and what is their purpose?
2. List the number of different people and organizations involved with meetings, conventions, and expositions.
3. List the primary sources of revenue and expenses involved in holding a meeting, a convention, and an exposition.
4. Describe the main types of meeting setups.
5. Explain the difference between an exposition and a convention.
6. List the duties of CVBs.
7. Describe the topics a meeting planner needs to deal with before, during, and after a meeting.

Internet Exercises

1. Organization: **Best of Boston**
Web site: **www.bestboston.com**
Summary: Best of Boston is an event-planning company that specializes in putting together packages for different events, such as conventions, corporate events, private parties, and weddings.

    (a) Explore this web site for events and list the different kinds of events this organization can organize.

    (b) After browsing the web site, discuss the importance of networking in the meetings, conventions, and expositions industry.

2. Organization: **M & C Online**
Web site: **www.meetings-conventions.com**
Summary: This excellent web site offers in-depth information on meetings and conventions from different perspectives, ranging from legal issues to unique themes and concepts.

    (a) Click the "Latest News" heading (it's on the left side of the page). What is the latest news?

    (b) Click "Current Issue" (at the top of the page), then "On the Cover" (on the left side near the top). See what the cover stories are, and then share your findings with your class.

Apply Your Knowledge

Make a master plan with all the steps necessary for holding a meeting or seminar on careers in hospitality management.

Suggested Activity

Contact meeting planners in your area, and, with permission of your professor, invite them to speak to the class about their work and how they do it.

Prepare questions in advance so that they may be given to the speaker ahead of time.

Endnotes

1. http://www.asaecenter.org/advocacy/ contentASAEOnly.cfm?ItemNumber=16341
2. George G. Fenich, *Meetings, Expositions, and Conventions: An Introduction to the Industry*, 3rd ed. (Upper Saddle River, NJ: Pearson, 2012), 23.
3. George G. Fenich, *Meetings, Expositions, and Conventions: An Introduction to the Industry*, 25.
4. Wikipedia, *Trade Association*, http://en.wikipedia.org/wiki/Trade_association (accessed November 21, 2011).
5. Wikipedia, *Professional Association*, http://en.wikipedia.org/wiki/Professional_association (accessed November 21, 2011).

6. Steven Barth, *Hospitality Law: Managing Issues in the Hospitality Industry* (Hoboken, NJ: John Wiley and Sons, 2006), 26–29.
7. Professional Convention Management Association, *Professional Meeting Management*, 4th ed. (Dubuque, IA: Kendall/Hunt, 2004), 557–561.
8. Professional Convention Management Association, *Professional Meeting Management*, 564–565.
9. Professional Convention Management Association, *Professional Meeting Management*, 552.
10. George G. Fenich, *Meetings, Expositions, and Conventions: An Introduction to the Industry*, 249.

Glossary

Convention   A generic term referring to any size business or professional meeting held in one specific location, which usually includes some form of trade show or exposition. Also refers to a group of delegates or members who assemble to accomplish a specific goal.

Convention center   A large meeting place.

Exposition   An event held mainly to promote informational exchanges among trade people. A large exhibition in which the presentation is the main attraction, as well as being a source of revenue for an exhibitor.

Familiarization (FAM) trip   A free or reduced-price trip given to travel agents, travel writers, or other intermediaries to promote destinations.

Meeting   A gathering of people for a common purpose.

Meeting planner   An individual who coordinates every detail of meetings and conventions.

Photo Credits

Credits are listed in order of appearance.

Yuri Arcurs/Shutterstock
Alexander Raths/Fotolia
Dorling Kindersley/Nigel Hicks/
   DK Images
Alan Keohane/Dorling Kindersley, Ltd
Dana White/PhotoEdit
Jill Moran

Bob Daemmrich/PhotoEdit
Alexandra Stout
Marcin Balcerzak/Shutterstock
Dr. Amanda Alexander, University
   of Missouri
Dean Allen Caron/Shutterstock

Special Events

From Chapter 13 of *Introduction to Hospitality*, Sixth Edition. John R. Walker. Copyright © 2013 by Pearson Education, Inc. Published by Pearson. All rights reserved.

Special Events

OBJECTIVES

After reading and studying this text, you should be able to:

- Define a special event.

- Describe what event planners do.

- Classify special events.

- Outline the skills and abilities required for event management.

- Identify the main professional organizations and associations involved with the special events industry.

*The **special events industry** is a dynamic, diverse field that has seen considerable growth and change over the past forty years. Today, the industry employs professionals who work together to provide a broad range of services to create what is termed a special event. But what is a special event? Dr. Joe J. Goldblatt, a leading academic and author in the special events field, distinguishes between daily events and special events in the following manner:*

Daily Events	Special Events	Examples of Special Events
Occur spontaneously	Are always planned	A convention
Do not arouse expectations	Always arouse expectations	A meeting
Usually occur without a reason	Are usually motivated by a reason for a celebration	A festival or wedding

*He uses these contributing factors to shape a definition of a special event: "A special event recognizes a unique moment in time with ceremony and ritual to satisfy specific needs."[1] The scope of this definition is very broad and encompasses many "moments." Special events include countless functions, such as **corporate seminars** and **workshops**, **conventions** and **trade shows**, **charity balls** and **fundraisers**, **fairs** and **festivals**, and **social functions** such as **weddings and holiday parties**. It is for this reason that the industry has seen such growth and presents so much potential for future careers and management opportunities.*

Food, clothing, and shelter are the accepted basic physical needs that humans require. Following those needs is an emotional need to celebrate, which has a direct impact on the human spirit. All societies celebrate—whether publicly or privately, as individuals or in groups. The need to celebrate has been recognized by corporations, public and government officials, associations, and individuals. This has contributed to the rapid growth of the special events industry with a wide range of possible employment opportunities. When you consider all of the planners, caterers, producers, event sites, and others that become part of the special event, you can imagine the potential for future careers and employment possibilities.

Event management is a newcomer in the hospitality industry compared with the hotel and restaurant industries. Yet as you will soon learn, special events is a field that doesn't have rigid boundaries. Closely related fields that may overlap include marketing, sales, catering, and entertainment. Future growth trends in special events management provide plenty of career opportunities in all hospitality sectors.

This text gives you an overview of the special events industry. You will learn about the various classifications of special events and where future career opportunities can be found. You will find information on the skills and abilities required to be successful in the field. Information on special events organizations, strategic event planning, and the future outlook of the industry will allow you to take a glimpse into this exciting, rewarding, and evolving field. As Frank Supovitz, Vice President of Special Events for the National Hockey League in New York, says, "The stakes have never been higher. Sponsors are savvier. Audiences are more demanding. And, event producers and managers are held accountable by their clients to meet their financial and marketing goals more than ever before. . . . So before the lights go down and the curtain rises, reach out for the experience and expertise in these pages . . . and explore the opportunities in special events management."[2]

Someone has to manage this incredible event, the Super Bowl.

What Event Planners Do

Event planning is a general term that refers to a career path in the growing field of special events. Its forecast includes a growing demand for current and future employment opportunities. Like several other professions, event planning came about to fill a gap—someone needed to be in charge of all the gatherings, meetings, conferences, and so on that were increasing in size, number, and spectacle among the business and leisure sectors. Corporate managers had to step away from their assignments to take on the additional challenges of planning conventions and conferences. Government officials and employees were displaced from their assignments to arrange recruitment fairs and military events. Consequently, whenever a special event was to be held, the planner became a person whose job description did not include "planning."

The title **event planner** was first introduced at hotels and convention centers. Event planners are responsible for planning an event, from start to finish. This includes setting the date and location, advertising the event, and providing refreshments or arranging catering services, speakers, or entertainment. Please keep in mind that this is a general list and will vary depending on the type, location, and nature of the event.

" Associations can be a valuable resource for students interested in a career in event management. Many offer scholarships and provide a great networking opportunity. "

Karen Harris

469

A VGM Career Book, *Opportunities in Event Planning Careers*, has the following to say about a good candidate: "In addition to good organizational skills, someone with a creative spirit, a flair for the dramatic, a sense of adventure, and a love of spectacle could expect to flourish in this field." Highlighted skills and characteristics of a future professional in this field include the following:

- Computer skills
- Willingness to travel
- Willingness to work a flexible schedule
- Experience in delegating
- Willingness to work long hours
- Negotiating skills
- Verbal and written communication skills
- Enthusiasm
- Project management skills

- Follow-through skills
- Ability to work with high-level executives
- Budgeting skills
- Ability to initiate and close sales
- Lots of patience
- Ability to handle multiple tasks simultaneously
- Ability to be a self-starter
- Ability to interact with other departments[3]

Event Management

Event management can be as small as planning an office outing, to something larger like organizing a music festival and as large as planning the Super Bowl or even the Olympics. Events can be one-off, annual (happening each year), or every four years, as for the Olympics. Things do not just happen by themselves; it takes a great deal of preparation to stage a successful event. To hold a successful event, the organizer should have a vision and leader/manager skills in the following key result areas: marketing, financial, operational, and legal. Getting good sponsorship is a big help. Sponsors provide money or in-kind contributions and receive recognition as sponsors of the event, including use or display of their logos in the event's promotion. Sponsors expect to get something in return for their sponsorship, so give them something tangible that will help their corporation or organization. Each year, thousands go to festivals and events of all kinds, and most, if not close to all, events receive some sponsorship, because it is too costly to stage an event without sponsorship.

Event management requires special skills in marketing and sales (to attract the business in the first place), planning (to ensure all details are covered and that everything will be ready on time), organization (to make sure all key staff know what to do, why, when, where, and how), financial (a budget needs to be made and kept to), human resources and motivation (the best people need to be selected and recruited, trained, and motivated), lots of patience, and attention to detail and endless checking on them. To gain business, event managers prepare a proposal for the client's approval and contract signature. There are some important how-tos in preparing an event proposal: Find out as much information as possible about the event (if it has been previously held) or what

> The art of networking will allow you to build a contact base that will help you succeed in the event industry.
>
> Karen Harris

470

the client really has in mind. Ask organizers, attendees, providers, and others what went right and what went wrong or what could be improved on next time the event is organized. Write the proposal in business English, no elaborate or florid language. Finally, do the numbers—nobody wants a surprise—do a pro-forma invoice so that the client will know the costs, and surprise the client by being on time and on budget.

An event can be costly to put on; in addition to advertising, there is a location charge, security costs, labor costs, and production costs (this may be food, beverage, and service, but also staging and decor). Usually, the event manager has a good estimate of the number of ticket sales expected. He or she then budgets the costs to include the entertainment and all other costs, leaving a reasonable profit.

Event management also takes place at convention centers and hotels, where event managers handle all the arrangements after the sales manager has completed the contract. The larger convention center events are planned years in advance. As stated earlier, the convention and visitors bureau is usually responsible for the booking of conventions more than eighteen months ahead. Obviously, both the convention and visitors bureau and the convention center marketing and sales teams work closely with each other. Once the booking becomes definite, the senior event manager assigns an event manager to work with the client throughout the sequence of pre-event, event, and postevent activities.

The booking manager is critical to the success of the event by booking the correct space and working with the organizers to help them save money by allocating only the space really needed and allowing the client to begin setting up on time. A contract is written based on the event profile. The event profile stipulates in writing all the client's requirements and gives all of the relevant information, such as which company will act as decorator/subcontractor to install carpets and set up the booths.

The contract requires careful preparation because it is a legal document and will guarantee certain provisions. For example, the contract may specify that the booths may only be cleaned by center personnel or that food may be prepared for samples only, not for retail. After the contract has been signed and returned by the client, the event manager will from time to time make follow-up calls until about six months before the event, when arrangements such as security, business services, and catering will be finalized. The event manager is the key contact between the center and the client. He or she will help the client by introducing approved subcontractors who are able to provide essential services.

Two weeks prior to the event, an event document is distributed to department heads. The event document contains all the detailed information that each department needs to know for the event to run smoothly. About ten days before the event, a WAG (week at a glance) meeting is held. The WAG meeting is one of the most important meetings at the convention center because it provides an opportunity to avoid problems—like two event groups arriving at the same time or additional security for concerts or politicians. About this same time, a preconvention or pre-expo meeting is held with expo managers and their contractors—shuttle bus managers, registration operators, exhibit floor managers, and so on. Once the setup begins, service contractors marshal the eighteen-wheeler trucks to unload the exhibits by using radio phones to call the trucks from a nearby depot. When the exhibits are in place, the exposition opens and the public is admitted.

The following sections discuss the stages in the event-planning process.

Research

The first stage of event planning is to answer the following simple questions:

1. Why should a special event be held?
2. Who should hold it?
3. Where should it be held?
4. What should the focus of the event be?
5. What outcomes are expected?

Once answers to these questions are available, you can move to the second stage of event planning.

Design

The second stage in the event-planning process can be both the most exciting and the most challenging. This stage allows freedom in creativity and the implementation of new ideas that support the objectives of the special event. The design process is a time when an event manager or team can brainstorm new innovative ideas or develop adaptations to previous events to make them better, grander, and more exciting for the attendees. The design process seeks to obtain original and fresh ideas that will create an event in which it's worth investing. The event may be a corporate meeting or it may be a beachside wedding, yet the design of the event will have a lasting impression on those who attend it.

Planning

Planning, the third stage in the event-planning process, is often led by the budget determined for the event. The planning process includes contracting out services and arranging all other activities that will become part of the event. The planning process may include the following tasks:

- Determine event budget
- Select the event site
- Select hotel accommodations
- Arrange transportation
- Negotiate contracts
- Arrange catering
- Arrange speaker, entertainment, music
- Organize audiovisual needs

- Create marketing plan for the event
- Prepare invitations or event packets

The type and size of the event will ultimately determine the steps required for the planning process. The information you learn about planning from your other courses and studies will help you if you choose to pursue a career in event management.

Coordination

The process of **coordination** can be compared to a director leading a band. The band may have rehearsed a piece of music countless times, and yet during a concert the director still has the ability to "direct" or control the performance. Similarly, the event manager engages in the process of coordinating the event as it unfolds. This may be a stressful time because of unforeseen problems that occur, or it may be a truly rewarding time with a flawless execution. Regardless, coordination of the event may involve decision-making skills and abilities as the event progresses.

Coordination also relates to the human resource aspect of the special event. Event managers are leaders who, through example, motivate others. As an event manager, you will engage in coordinating staff and/or volunteers to carry out the special event's planned objectives and goals. As mentioned earlier, empowering your staff will create a positive environment and will make your job of coordinating their efforts that much easier.

Evaluation

Evaluation should take place during each of the stages of the event-planning process and is a final step that can measure the success of the event in meeting the goals and objectives. If you take a look at the event-planning process diagram in Figure 1, you will notice that it is a continuous process. Outcomes are compared to expectations and variances investigated and corrected.

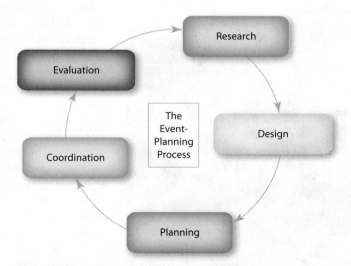

Figure 1 • Event-Planning Process Diagram.

Challenges and Tools for Event Planners and Managers

If you are at this point considering a professional career in event management, there are event-planning tools that you can use to your advantage as you pursue a career in this field. There are four primary challenges professional event managers face: time, finance, technology, and human resources.

Time management plays an important role in event planning, and it is an element that can be used effectively by budgeting your time the same way that you would your finances. Delegating tasks to the appropriate people, keeping accurate records and lists, preparing agendas before meetings, and focusing on what items deserve top priority are all examples of how to use time management effectively.

Financial management becomes important for an event planner when it becomes necessary for you to evaluate financial data, management fees, vendor fees, and so forth. This does not mean that you have to be a financial wizard; however, knowledge in this area will greatly enhance your opportunity to make profitable and sound decisions. There are resources that can be used in this area such as obtaining help or counsel from a financial professional and using technology that will help with event accounting.

Utilizing technology as a tool in event management can be a great opportunity to assist in the previous two areas. Software programs for word processing, financial management, and database management can help in daily tasks and event planning. Other technology products that are used by event professionals include laptop computers, cell phones, handheld devices, event management software, and the Internet.

The final tool relates to the effective management of your human resources. Empowering your employees is the key to success. As a manager and leader, you must train your employees and/or volunteers and give them the necessary information to perform their jobs. It is critical to select the right people, empower them, and develop their skills. This will ultimately help you succeed in accomplishing your goals. Empowering event staff can be used to allow them to make important decisions—successful events require many decisions to be made, and you as a manager will not have the time to make all of them. Empowering your team is the greatest tool you can use to become an effective leader and improve the performance of your staff.

Guests mingle at a charity event in Coral Gables, Florida.

▶ Check Your Knowledge

1. Give some examples to distinguish the differences between a daily event and a special event.
2. What are event planners responsible for?
3. Name the stages in the event-planning process.

Classifications of Special Events

The special events industry has been divided up into the following classifications:

- Corporate events (seminars, workshops, meetings, conferences)
- Association events (conventions, trade shows, meetings)
- Charity balls and fund-raising events
- Social functions (weddings, engagement parties, holiday functions)
- Fairs and festivals
- Concerts and sporting events

A poll taken from a wide variety of event professionals in the industry, *Event Solutions Black Book*, lists the following as the most popular types of event sites:

Hotel/resort	62.0 percent
Convention center	32.5 percent
Tent/structure	32.6 percent
Banquet hall	29.0 percent
Outdoors	21.8 percent
Corporate facility	28.4 percent
Museum/zoo/gardens	12.4 percent
Arena/stadium/theater	18.0 percent
Restaurant	16.1 percent
Private residence	22.8 percent
Club	16.7 percent[4]

With those figures in mind, take a closer look at the various classifications that make up this exciting industry. Each category has its own unique characteristics, rewards, and challenges. As a human resource specialist would say, "It's important to put the right person in the right position." This statement also holds true for special events. Any career selection, especially for a person seeking the management level, should look for the correct "fit." With such a vast array of options, you may find one that ignites your passion for the field, you may find several that are the wrong size before finding the right one, or you may decide that this is not the right match for your personality and goals. The following may help you to decide whether your future holds a professional career in the special events industry.

Corporate Events

Corporate events continue to lead the industry in terms of event business. About 80 percent of the event market is corporate events.

Corporate event managers are employed by the company to plan and execute the details of meetings for the corporation's employees, management, and owners. The growing use of special events in the corporate arena created the need for positions dedicated to the planning and management of them. The corporate event planners engage in the following management activities: They are involved in the planning and organizing of events, and they play a key leadership role. Additionally, the planner must possess the following skills: effective communication, ability to coordinate various activities, and attention to detail.

Corporate events include the following: annual meetings, sales meetings, new product launches, training meetings and workshops, management meetings, press meetings, incentive meetings, and awards ceremonies.

Corporate events benefit several sectors of the hospitality industry. For example, a client may hold an event at a major attraction like Sea World or a resort like The Breakers. Each corporate client can provide the hotel, restaurants, airlines, and other businesses in the destination's economy with tens of thousands of dollars. Corporate event planners will consider the factors most important to the attendees when using a hotel as part of the event, including corporate account rates for lodging, amenities such as fitness centers and business centers, airport transportation, and quick check-in and check-out at the hotel. Therefore, corporate event planners should have strong negotiating skills to book lodging and convention services as needed.

Association Events

There are more than 6,500 associations in the United States alone. The majority of the large association conventions are planned two to five years ahead of time, and the destination is a determining factor in the planning process. The American Medical Association and the American Dental Association are two of the most recognized examples of associations that hold large conventions. In the hospitality industry, the National Restaurant Association (NRA), the American Hotel & Lodging Association (AH&LA), and, at a global level,

Microsoft Chairman Bill Gates introduces Jay Leno at a corporate function.

the International Association of Convention and Visitors Bureaus are a few of the many associations that hold conventions. Associations account for millions in generated revenue. This stems from the millions of people who attend thousands of meetings and conventions. For example, the American Marketing Association holds more than twenty conferences annually, which generates approximately a million for each hotel.

Events relating to associations can range from a monthly luncheon at a private club or hotel to a yearly convention that may comprise an educational seminar(s) with an opportunity to network with other association members. Associations generally hire full-time paid planners to manage the yearly national membership meeting that is a requirement for most associations as part of their bylaws. Larger associations with greater financial resources often hire full-time meeting and convention management professionals who are involved in the large association events as well as other association events, including board meetings, educational seminars, membership meetings, professional meetings, and regional meetings.

Other opportunities for employment are widespread. They may include a position as a convention manager, a special events manager in a hotel, a conference manager, or a special events manager at a private club for the events held by local associations.

In the event-planning industry, professional associations have a great impact in contributing to the development of their members. Professional associations provide training, certification, networking, and assistance with business plans and other consulting services for their members.

Charity Balls and Fund-Raising Events

Charity balls and fund-raising events provide a unique opportunity for the event manager to work with the particular group or charity, and a theme is usually chosen for the event. The event manager is then responsible for selecting the location and coordinating all of the details that will determine the success of the event, which may include catering, entertainment, décor, lighting, floral arrangements, invitations, rentals, public relations, transportation, security, and technical support.

One of the key skills that a person entering this category must possess is the ability to plan the event on a set and often limited budget. Why is this skill so critical? These events are used to raise funds toward a set group or charity, and every dollar that is spent on the event is thereby one less dollar that could go toward the cause. Nevertheless, these events are expected to be extravagant—so a little creativity can go a long way in the planning and implementing of the theme. The event manager should also have strong negotiating skills to bargain with vendors on reduced rates or in some cases donated services or products. A smart planner will know how to market and sell the positive public relations that the event could provide to the vendors.

The demand for fund-raising event planners/managers is one that holds solid ground. To prove this point, *Opportunities in Event Planning Careers* quoted an in-house event planner as stating, "One of the major advantages of working for a nonprofit as an in-house planner for almost six years was that I never had to look for work. There were always new events to take on."[5]

Associations can be a valuable resource for students. Many offer scholarships and provide a great networking opportunity. I received a scholarship from the American Association of University Women and was therefore prompted to join as a student affiliate. Students interested in a career in event management can gain valuable experience by attending the meetings and, more importantly, becoming involved. Volunteering is rarely turned down!

Karen Harris

Volunteering is one of the best ways to gain experience in the event industry, and charity/fund-raising events provide a great opportunity. I recently had the opportunity to volunteer as a banquet server for the "Star Night Gala." More importantly, however, I was provided the opportunity to meet various people involved in the planning and to ask questions! Check your local paper for "upcoming events." In addition, I found a local Charity Register that provides a calendar of events for the upcoming year.

Volunteers are not paid. Not because they are worthless, but because they are priceless.

University of South Florida, Circle K International motto.

The ability to learn as a volunteer truly is priceless!

Karen Harris

Social Events

Social function planners or managers work on a broad variety of events. This category of special events includes the traditional wedding and party planners with which most of us are already familiar. This category of event planning includes weddings, engagement parties, birthday parties, anniversary parties, holiday parties, graduation parties, military events, and all other social gatherings or events. A social event planner/manager is usually responsible for selecting the venue, determining any themes and/or design schemes, ordering or planning decorations, arranging for catering and entertainment, and having invitations printed and mailed.

SMERF, which stands for social, military, educational, religious, and fraternal organizations, is a category of organizations that also falls into the category of social events. Individuals of these organizations often pay for the events, meaning the events are price sensitive. Needless to say, budgeting skills are important for those working with these groups.

Weddings are the most widely recognized social event. Wedding planners are a key player in the social event category. The title seems glamorous and has a certain perception that most of us will hold; yet the management involved in planning a wedding involves strict attention to detail. Don't forget that the planner is responsible for creating what is considered to be the most important day of a couple's life. "Realize this is a business," says Gerard J. Monaghan, president of the Association of Bridal Consultants. "A fun business to be sure, but a business nonetheless." Effective wedding planners will have contacts formed for a variety of services, such as venues like hotels, wedding locations, decorating, catering, bridal shops, musicians, photographers, florists, and so forth.

Today's weddings are more expensive than those of the past, and they are often longer. Weddings have become true "special events" because of the willingness of family and friends to travel longer distances to celebrate with the bride and groom. Many weddings today have become minivacations for those attending.

▶ Check Your Knowledge

1. What events continue to lead the industry in terms of event business?
2. When are the majority of large association conventions planned?
3. What are the key skills that a person entering the charity event category must possess?
4. What is SMERF?

Fairs and Festivals

The word *fair* is likely to evoke memories of cotton candy, funnel cakes, Ferris wheels, and other games. These memories are very important to why a fair is considered a special event, but the purpose of most fairs in the United

States is usually related to the agriculture industry. A professional staff chosen by an elected committee usually produces them. Fairs are generally held at the local, county, or state level.

Festivals are planned events that are often themed to the celebration's purpose. Cultures, anniversaries, holy days, and special occasions are commonly celebrated as a festival. Mardi Gras, for example, celebrates the beginning of Lent. Food and entertainment are greatly emphasized when planning a festival. **Festivals.com** is a site that allows you to search for festivals held throughout the world. The variety of festivals is astounding—art, music, sporting, literary, performing arts, air shows, science, and even children's festivals. The web site describes cultural festivals as "Magical parades. Fabulous feasts. Dizzying dancing. The spirit of celebration crosses languages, oceans, continents and cultures, as people revel in their heritages and communities."[6]

The following is a small sampling of festivals—some are commonly known, and others are surprising:

Oktoberfest

Mardi Gras

Biketoberfest

Hispanic Heritage Festival

Street Music Festival

American Dance Festival

Polar Bear Jumpoff Festival

Gilroy Garlic Festival

Bagelfest

One of the key strategies in planning special events for fairs and festivals is to determine the purpose of the event early on. It is important to analyze the "available manpower" in the form of both professionals and volunteers who will assist in staging the event. The **International Festival & Events Association (IFEA)** provides an opportunity for event managers from around the world to network and exchange ideas on how other festivals excel in sponsorship, marketing, fund-raising, operations, volunteer coordination, and management. The IFEA is highlighted later in the text.

Concerts and Sporting Events

Concert promoters are an alternative career choice relating to special events. For the purpose of this text, smaller concert and music events will be the focus. Woodstock, in 1969, was a large music festival that has been labeled as a transformational event—it transformed the participants and society. Many concerts are planned as fund-raisers, such as Live Aid, which raised millions of dollars to benefit starving people of Africa through a concert that included major rock performers. On a smaller scale, universities may provide a concert as a special event.

Opening ceremonies, halftime shows, and postgame shows for sporting events provide another "arena" an event manager can select as a career path. Shows such as these are highly visible because of the large number of sporting events that are televised. This provides a unique challenge for the event manager—to satisfy the millions of television viewers as well as those watching in the stadium (or whatever the venue may be).

Sporting events have historically been more popular than other forms of entertainment. This is probably because of our competitive nature and a desire to watch those who compete—a kind of flashback to the gladiator days of old. It is important to remember when planning special events in the sports environment that the primary attention should remain on the athletes and the competition. Therefore, the special event should be staged to add to and not subtract from the sport itself. Special events may even attract additional viewers and fans to the sport. The role of special events in the sports category has plenty of room for growth and expansion as professional sports become more and more competitive.

Sports entertainment is a field that will likely see considerable growth in the future. Just think, someone has to plan, organize, and run the halftime shows and the events before and after the game. A large audience awaits your Super Bowl–sized imagination, which can ensure that every sporting event is a winning experience for the most important player of all—the fan.

Mega Sporting Events

Mega sporting events are some of the biggest moneymakers in the industry. Both large and small communities embrace mega sporting events because of the positive economic impact. Activities in sports have brought forth tremendous economic impacts.

INTRODUCING SUZANNE BAILEY

Event Director

Suzanne graduated from Southern Utah University with a B.A. in Business Administration, Marketing, in 1996. Eager to get her career started, she accepted an entry-level position at Bowl Games of America (BGA), a student travel/special events production company that produces several NCAA bowl game halftime shows including the Orange Bowl (Miami, FL), Sugar Bowl (New Orleans, LA), Liberty Bowl (Memphis, TN), Alamo Bowl (San Antonio, TX), and the Gator Bowl (Jacksonville, FL). BGA recruits high school marching bands and dance groups to perform in the field shows along with guest stars. The students earn an opportunity to perform by excelling in competitions and working fund-raisers to pay for their three- to five-day trip. Within a year, Suzanne settled into the division of the company that interested her most—the tiny but growing dance division of BGA, BGA Performance, as an executive assistant.

Suzanne worked with the director of BGA Performance to create an entirely new marketing strategy, which eventually led to great success within the dance division. Rather than working with small high school dance groups exclusively, BGA Performance set up a commission system with large private dance competition companies, which would market the bowl game performance opportunities to their competition winners. This marketing strategy led to 300-percent growth in the first year.

Suzanne worked her way up the ladder to associate director and eventually director of BGA Performance. Her work changed dramatically with the seasons. During dance competition season, the marketing effort was immense—that was the time to make the big sales push. Every day, Suzanne created and sent hundreds of invitation packets to private dance competition companies and made as many sales phone calls as possible. She also reviewed audition tapes and selected dancers for the bowl game halftime shows. Once most of the dancers signed up for the bowl game they would perform in, Suzanne's work shifted to customer service and show production. A few months prior to each event, Suzanne traveled to each city with the dance directors and/or chaperones to give them a preview of what would happen during the event with their dancers.

Finally, the events took place. Suzanne became an event director during the actual events. Suzanne traveled to the destination city a few days before the dancers arrived to confirm with hotel group sales managers, caterers, rehearsal site workers, and bowl game executives. She met and directed her on-site staff (choreography team and event staff). The workdays of the events could be long and exhausting, full of excitement and anticipation. Much of the time was devoted to rehearsals, with some fun activities also included. Catered lunches, beach parties, and evening dinner/dance parties for the group at famous spots like Mardi Gras World in New Orleans are a few examples of some activities. The dancers enjoyed every minute of their week, including the long, hard rehearsals in the sun (or rain, or even snow, depending on the city). Game day (or show day) was always the most exciting of the days. After much hard work and preparation, the dancers went out on the field for their five minutes of fame. They performed, along with famous guest stars and the BGA–recruited marching bands, to a live stadium audience in the tens of thousands and often to a national television audience. This was when the position as director of BGA Performance really pays off. The excitement of the show outweighed all the frustrations and challenges of actually putting it all together. It was extremely rewarding to watch the young people have the time of their lives! For Suzanne, the next day was usually spent traveling to the next bowl game city and starting the process all over again.

After working on bowl game halftime shows for about six years, the 2002 Olympics came to Salt Lake City, Suzanne's hometown. Having worked with the dance choreographer and other directors of the Olympic Opening and Closing Ceremonies team for bowl game shows, she was offered a position as Senior Production Coordinator, Volunteer Cast, with the Ceremonies Production Team. She left her position at BGA Performance to work on the Olympic Ceremonies. The Olympic Opening Ceremony is truly the pinnacle of live productions. Suzanne helped manage a team of fifteen cast coordinators, who worked with more than 4,000 volunteer cast members and 200 production staff volunteers. Suzanne facilitated communication between choreographers, stage managers, the producers, and the cast. She managed all aspects of casting for the ceremonies, from recruitment to auditions to performer selection to the actual live performance. This was truly an opportunity of a lifetime for Suzanne. She enjoyed every minute of her work with the Ceremonies Production Team.

After the Olympics, Suzanne started her family and now accepts work as a subcontractor for specific events and shows. She enjoys tackling one project at a time according to her own schedule. The special events world is an exciting, exhausting, and fun place to work.

The *Olympic Games* is the hallmark of all sporting events, attracting more than 6 million people to the host city. That is a lot of people traveling, staying in hotels, eating in restaurants, and possibly looking at the host city's attractions. The Olympics is an international sporting event that takes place every two years, and it consists of both summer and winter games. The Olympics attract more people than any other sporting event, making it easy to see why the Olympics play an important role in the industry.

The *World Cup* features the best soccer teams in the world. It is an international competition that takes place every four years. However, the World Cup is an ongoing competition, as the qualifying rounds take place over the three years before the final rounds in which the championship is awarded. Close to one million people actually attend the World Cup, and millions more tune in via television or the Internet.

The *Super Bowl* is an annual competition between the two best American football teams. It is a tradition that the game is held on "Super Bowl Sunday," typically occurring in late January or early February. Over the years, this day has become a holiday to many Americans. Super Bowl is one of the most-watched U.S. TV broadcasts of the year and not just for the game. People also tune in to see the much-discussed commercials, on which millions of advertising dollars are spent. People also tune in to watch the halftime show, during which some of the most popular musical artists perform.

The *World Series* is the fight for the title of best baseball team in the United States. The series is played every year starting in October between the champions of the American League and National League and caps off the Major League Baseball (MLB) postseason. Today, the series winner is determined through a best-of-seven playoff. The winning team is awarded the World Series Trophy, and each player receives a World Series ring.

There are four major men's golf championships known as the *Majors*. The *Masters Tournament* is an annual gathering of the world's best golf players on the Augusta Golf Course. Champions of the Masters are automatically invited to play in the other three majors for the following five years, and earn a lifetime invitation to the Masters. The *U.S. Open Championship* is a men's open championship held in June of each year. The U.S. Open Championship is on the official schedule of the PGA Tour and the European Tour. The U.S. Open takes place on a variety of golf courses. The *British Open* is the oldest of the four major championships in men's golf. It is played annually on a links course (located in coastal areas causing frequent wind, on sandy soil, often amid dunes, with few water hazards and few if any trees). The *U.S. PGA Championship* is the final championship of the year, held in August. Champions of the PGA are also automatically invited to play in the other three majors for the next five years and are exempt from qualifying for the PGA Championship for life.

There are a number of boat races held on an annual basis. The *America's Cup* is perhaps the most famous of yachting races. In addition to the yacht races, it is also a test of boat design, sail design, fund-raising, and managing people. The races are held in a series that currently involves a best-of-nine series of match racing (a duel between two boats).

Cruise lines are also creating specialized sports cruises, enabling spectators and participants to enhance their skills, to meet professional athletes, to attend major events, and simply to immerse themselves in their favorite sports.

Where Do Event Planners Work?

- Hotels/resorts
- Private corporations
- Associations

- Caterers
- The government
- Private clubs
- Convention centers
- Bridal businesses
- Event production companies
- Nonprofit organizations
- Advertising agencies
- Self-employed

Required Skills and Abilities for Event Management

Special events management, like any other form of management, requires certain skills and abilities. The act of carrying out a successful event takes more than just an idea—it takes leadership, communication, project management, effective negotiating and delegating skills, the ability to work within a budget, the ability to multitask, enthusiasm, social skills, and even the ability to make contacts. The following sections will provide an overview of skills critical to effective event management.

Leadership Skills

As a leader, the event manager will wear many hats. The first is to inspire the staff and volunteers by providing valid reasons as to why they should want to assist in achieving the established goals for the event. In this role, the event manager will also act as a salesperson. The second hat represents the event manager's responsibility to provide tools for the staff and volunteers to achieve the goals. This includes training and coordination. The third hat the event manager will wear will be that of a coach. The event manager as a leader will act as mentor and provide a support system to build a team. Staff and volunteer motivation is an important factor for effective event management. Leadership ability is the number-one skill for successful event managers. The goal of an event manager is to become a leader who can direct a team of employees and/or volunteers who will respect, admire, and follow your direction to accomplish the established goals.

Effective event leadership can transform the people on your team. Empowering your event team to find their own solutions will benefit both the people and the event. It will allow the team members to create new opportunities for themselves and stimulate personal growth. For the event, empowerment will enable goals and objectives to be achieved quickly. Following are suggestions given by Dr. Joe Jeff Goldblatt, CSEP, for event leadership:

- Event leadership enables your team members to find the motivation to continue achieving the event goals and objectives.

- You cannot motivate others; they must motivate themselves by identifying clear personal goals and objectives.

- Volunteers are the lifeblood of most events. Recruiting, training, coordinating, and rewarding are critical to the success of this activity.

- The three styles of event leadership are democratic, autocratic, and laissez-faire. Each style may be used during the course of the event.

- Policies, procedures, and practices serve as the blueprint for event decision making.[7]

Ability to Communicate with Other Departments

The success of an event manager greatly depends on the ability of involved individuals to communicate effectively with one another. Communication can take different forms: oral, written, and electronic. It is very important for event managers to become effective communicators in order to maintain clear communications with all staff, volunteers, stakeholders, and other departments.

Written communications are an essential tool for record keeping and providing information to be mass distributed. Another way to communicate with other departments is through a meeting.

Delegating

One person cannot do everything, but managers seldom delegate enough. This contradiction is typical in the events business. The secret is to plan ahead of time and allow time for tasks to be delegated to others to help facilitate the smooth operation of an event. For successful delegation, a climate of trust and a positive working environment are needed. Also required is a committed associate who will complete the delegated task and who will communicate effectively throughout the process.

Project Management Skills

Event planning and management can be time consuming. Therefore, a good planner should have effective project management skills to be equipped to balance all of the elements of one event (or more if there are other events going on at the same time). Project management is the act of completing the project(s) on time and within budget. Project management is a perfect fit for the special events industry, where the entire event or components of an event can be managed as projects. Following are management tools by George G. Fenich that may be used to assist in event project management:

- Flow charts and graphs used for scheduling certain programs that will happen at the event. Look at any program of a meeting, and you will see start times and end times of a particular seminar, when the coffee break is to occur, when and where the lunch will be held, followed by the resumption of the meeting. A charting of the scheduling of the activities helps to guide your attendees and guests.

- Clearly defined work setup and breakdown schedules for the event. These provide the event manager with an opportunity to determine tasks that may have been overlooked in the initial planning process for the event.

- Policy statements will need to be developed to help guide in the decision-making process and the fulfilling of commitments. Some of the commitments would be to human resources, sponsorships, security, ticketing, volunteers, and even to paid personnel for the event.[8]

Meeting planners coordinating events during a meeting.

Negotiating Skills

Negotiation is the process by which a meeting planner and supplier (hotel representative, for example) reach an agreement on the terms and conditions that will govern their relationship before, during, and after a meeting, convention, exposition, or event. Effective negotiators will enter the negotiation with a good idea of what they want.

A seasoned negotiator gives the following tips:

- Do your homework. Develop a "game plan" of the outcomes sought, and prioritize your needs and wants. Learn as much about the other side's position as you can.

- Keep your eyes on the prize. Do not forget the outcome sought.

- Leave something on the table. It may provide an opportunity to come back later and renew the negotiations.

- Do not be the first one to make an offer. Letting the other person make the first move sets the outside parameters for the negotiation.

- Bluff, but do not lie.

- When there is a roadblock, find a more creative path. Thinking "outside the box" often leads to a solution.

- Timing is everything. Remember that time always works against the person who does not have it and that 90 percent of negotiation usually occurs in the last 10 percent of the time allocated.

- Listen, listen, listen . . . and do not get emotional. Letting emotions rule a negotiation will cause one to lose sight of what result is important.[9]

The planning and execution of a special event may involve the negotiation of several contracts. The most important is generally the one with the facility or event site. Contracts with other services may include destination management, entertainment, catering, temporary employees, security, and audiovisual equipment, to name a few. Event managers should keep the following two words in mind to strengthen their negotiating skills and position: information and flexibility.

A DAY IN THE LIFE OF TINA FORDE

Events Assistant at the Waldorf Astoria Orlando and Hilton Bonnet Creek

A day in the life of an events assistant is never the same. While I might be doing similar tasks on a day-to-day basis, everything is very different as you encounter each client. Each day is certainly an adventure, always leaving you thinking what will come next. This is an adventure I love.

As an events assistant at the Waldorf Astoria Orlando and Hilton Bonnet Creek, my first and most important task is to assist the events managers with anything they need. There are four managers whom I assist on a daily basis: Those managers are the Assistant Director of Events, two Senior Event Managers, and an Event Manager. I report to the Event Manager on a daily basis.

Through our meetings, my job is to help pre-plan any event that will be taking place at one of our sites. Once I understand what the event entails, I place all of the specifications, or "specs," the client has requested onto Banquet Event Orders, or BEOs. BEOs are like the road map for any event. The BEO will take you from point A to point B while ensuring the client's every request is fulfilled.

There are two types of BEOs: Food and Beverage, and Meeting. If I put together a food and beverage BEO, it would consist of every food item for each meeting, reception, break, or event that will be taking place. The banquet department will use this BEO information to know when, where, and what to set up for each event. Meeting BEOs will include information regarding the setup of the room, audio visual equipment, electric services, and any other specific needs the client has requested.

While working closely with the logistics of events, I also assist with transporting VIP clients that will be staying at one of our hotels. This includes arranging appropriate modes of transportation to and from airports and our hotels, fulfilling client requests, ensuring amenities provided meet the client's expectations, and other duties such as screening the client's telephone calls.

On a monthly basis, I also set up in-house meetings for both properties. Each department has monthly meetings, and it is my job to block times, block rooms, create the space, organize BEOs, and so forth. This also includes orientation for new employees; if Human Resource needs a space to introduce employees to the property and begin the training process, I must ensure that their needs are met for the space.

Because each event is never the same, communication and organization are the most important qualities to have when working as an events assistant. Clients may change their mind, something may not go as originally planned, and being able to adapt to situations while satisfying the client is the core of my job. If you can multitask, react quickly to situations that may become problematic, and balance working well with others and communicating effectively, you can become successful in this line of work.

I truly enjoy every aspect of being an events assistant. No day of work is the same, and being dedicated to what I love to do has helped me succeed with this job. My efforts as an assistant and the love for my career ensure that each event is as successful as the next.

Coordinating and Delegating Skills

The management of staff and volunteers involves coordinating their duties and job performance to enable you to accomplish the goals of the event. As the manager, you are responsible for assigning supervisors or group leaders to oversee the performance of the employees and/or volunteers. It is important to provide coaching and mentoring when working with staff and volunteers to arrive at the event's goals and objectives. When employees can see the purpose and value of their work as well as the outcomes of their work, they usually become more excited about achieving the goals and objectives.

Budgeting Skills

Budgeting is an activity that allows managers to plan the use of their financial resources. In the event industry, the event planner may be working with a fixed budget determined by an association, a SMERF group, or an individual (a wedding or an engagement). In other cases, the budget may be more flexible—a large corporation, for example, that has greater financial resources. Budgeting is a required skill in all hospitality fields, including the special events industry.

The financial history of previous identical or similar events, the general economy and your forecast of the future, and the income expenses you reasonably believe you can expect with the resources available are all factors to be considered in creating an event budget. Even though most event managers will view the budgeting aspect as the least interesting in their job, it is an area that should be carefully managed and is critical for success. The better you become in your budgeting skills, the more you will be able to use resources for other, "more creative" activities.

Ability to Multitask

Because of the nature of the business, an effective event manager should have the ability to multitask. During the planning and staging of the event, your ability to administrate, coordinate, market, and manage will be put to the test. Your job is ultimately to conduct and take control of whatever needs to be done to carry out your goals and objectives. You may encounter several problems arising at the same time, and an effective solution would be to delegate tasks accordingly.

Enthusiasm

In any hospitality field the risk of burnout is high and the work is demanding. At the same time, however, the rewards are great and so is the satisfaction when the event is a complete success. As perfectly stated by Norman Brinker, chairman of the board of Brinker International, "Find out what you love to do and you'll never work a day in your life. . . . Make work like play and play like hell!"[10] Enthusiasm and passion. Drive and determination. These are all qualities that will contribute to the success of an event manager/planner. As shown in the profile of Suzanne Bailey, the special events industry is an "exciting, exhausting, and fun place to work." For those with the right enthusiasm and passion, it can be a truly rewarding career path.

Effective Social Skills

Social skills are an important trait for any management position, including one in the special events industry. Social skills are critical in making those you do business with feel comfortable, in handling situations appropriately, and in eliminating barriers that get in the way of accomplishing your goals. Communication is a critical social skill as is another social skill—listening. Social etiquette is another skill that can make or break a career, and it is a practiced skill that can be acquired. Social etiquette is defined as exhibiting good manners established as acceptable to society and showing consideration for others. Professionals in the hospitality industry, including the special events field, must be proficient in proper social etiquette. Service is one of the largest products offered; therefore, social skills and etiquette are required to be successful. Proper social etiquette is required in planning special events, and correct social manners are key to business success.[11] Effective social skills are also critical to leading a motivated group of staff and/or volunteers. How well you communicate, coach, instruct, lead, and listen is a reflection of how well you will succeed as a manager.

Ability to Form Contacts

Many of us have heard the phrase, "It's not what you know, but who you know." Does this statement hold any value in the special events industry? It certainly does. An event may require various services, vendors, suppliers, or products. Here's how it works: An event planner prepares a specification of what is required and requests potential suppliers to submit their prices. The event planner then goes over this information with the client, and they make a decision as to who will provide the services. Over time, event planners quickly find out who is the best provider and therefore the one with whom they prefer to work.

▶ Check Your Knowledge

1. What does the International Festival & Events Association (IFEA) provide?
2. What is project management?
3. Define the process of negotiation.

Special Event Organizations

Like other hospitality industries, professional associations are a key contributor to the professional development of the special events field. Professional associations provide training and prestigious certification to their members, and membership provides an opportunity to network with other professionals in the field. Furthermore, associations can help members connect with vendors that provide products and services relating to special events.

66 We've all heard the term "networking" before. It is a practice worth the time and effort. Networking is one of the benefits of joining an association (explained in the next section). The art of networking will allow you to build a contact base that will help you succeed in the event industry. What would happen if your caterer backed out of a contract at the last minute? First of all, make sure you have a contract. Beyond that, having a strong contact base will allow you to plan for those "unexpected" occurrences that are bound to happen at some point in your career. 99

Karen Harris

CORPORATE PROFILE

International Special Events Society

Members of the International Special Events Society organize events like the Macy's Thanksgiving Day Parade

The **International Special Events Society (ISES)** was founded in 1987 and has grown to involve nearly 7,200 members who are active in forty-nine chapters around the world.[12] The organization includes professionals representing special events producers (from festivals to trade shows), caterers, decorators, florists, destination management companies, rental companies, special effects experts, audiovisual technicians, party and convention coordinators, hotel sales managers, specialty entertainers, and many others.

The ISES was founded with the objective to "foster enlightened performance through education while promoting ethical conduct. ISES works to join professionals to focus on the 'event as a whole' rather than its individual parts."[13] The organization has formed a solid network of peers that allows its members to produce quality events for their clients while benefiting from positive working relationships with other ISES members.

The ISES awards a designation of Certified Special Events Professional (CSEP), which is considered to be the benchmark of professional achievement in the special events industry. "It is earned through education, performance, experience, service to the industry, portfolio presentation and examination, and reflects a commitment to professional conduct and ethics,"[14] as stated by ISES. The program includes a self or group study program, point assessment of experience and service, application form, and exam.[15] Visit the ISES web site at **www.ises.com** for further information.

ISES Mission Statement

The mission of ISES is to educate, advance and promote the special events industry and its network of professionals along with related industries.

To that end, we strive to . . .

- Uphold the integrity of the special events profession to the general public through our "Principles of Professional Conduct and Ethics"
- Acquire and disseminate useful business information
- Foster a spirit of cooperation among members and other special events professionals
- Cultivate high standards of business practices[16]

Professional associations also provide their members with help in creating a business plan and other forms of consultation. Job banks and referral services are even provided by some associations. The following sections provide a brief overview of the key associations relating to the special events industry.

International Festivals & Events Association

The International Festivals & Events Association (IFEA) has provided fund-raising and modern developmental ideas to the special events industry for forty-five years. The IFEA began the program to enhance the level of festival management training and performance with a Certified Festival and Event Executive (CFEE) in 1983. Those seeking to achieve this distinguished title are committed to excellence in festival and event management, are using it as a tool for career advancement, and are in search of further knowledge. The organization currently has more than 2,000 plus professional members,[17] who are informed of industry developments through IFEA publications, seminars, an annual convention and trade show, and ongoing networking.[18]

"The CFEE Program is a four-part process based on festival and event management experience, achievements and knowledge. Enrolling in the program and fulfilling the requirements . . . is the first step. Completing the application is next. Successfully completing an oral interview with member(s) of the CFEE Commission is the third. After achieving the CFEE designation, the fourth step is to maintain the designation through continuing education and participation in the profession,"[19] according to an IFEA statement.

The benefits of joining this association and meeting the CFEE requirements include the ability to negotiate a better income or financial package, recognition by other industry professionals, and the inside knowledge that it provides for the festival industry. Visit the IFEA web site at **www.ifea.com** for further information.

Meeting Professionals International

Meeting Professionals International (MPI) is a Dallas-based association with nearly 19,000 members.[20] MPI believes that "as the global authority and resource for the $102.3 billion meeting and event industry, MPI empowers meeting professionals to increase their strategic value through education, clearly defined career pathways, and business growth opportunities." MPI offers professional development in two certification programs:

- Certified Meeting Professional (CMP)
- Certification in Meeting Management (CMM)

The CMP program is based on professional experience and academic examination. After gaining certification, the professional may use the CMP designation after his or her name on business cards, letterheads, and other printed items. Additionally, studies show that CMPs earn up to $10,000 more annually than non–CMPs.[21]

The CMM program is directed toward senior-level meeting professionals and provides an opportunity for continuing education, global certification and recognition, potential career advancement, and a networking base.[22] Visit the MPI web site at **www.mpiweb.org** for more information.

Hospitality Sales and Marketing Association International

Hospitality Sales and Marketing Association International (HSMAI) is the largest and most active travel industry sales and marketing membership organization in the world, with over 7,000 members in 47 chapters from 12 countries,[23] representing hotels and resorts, airlines, cruise lines, car rental agencies, theme parks and attractions, convention and visitors bureaus, destination management companies, reservations sales organizations, restaurants, golf and recreation sites, and much more. Membership is open to anyone involved in one of the sales, marketing, management, educational, planning, or reporting disciplines within the hospitality industry, including those involved in promoting, producing, or delivering support services to the travel, tourism, hospitality, convention, and meeting industries.[24]

HSMAI's mission is to be the leading source for sales and marketing information, knowledge, business development, and networking for professionals in tourism, travel, and hospitality.[25] HSMAI offers certification courses in Hospitality Sales Executive, Revenue Management, Sales Competencies, Hospitality Marketing Executive, and Hospitality Business Acumen.

Local Convention and Visitors Bureaus

A convention and visitors bureau (CVB) is a not-for-profit organization that is located in almost every city in the United States and Canada. Many other cities throughout the world also have a CVB or convention and visitors association (CVA). Simply stated, the CVB is an organization with the purpose of promoting tourism, meetings, and related business for its city. The CVB has three primary functions:

1. Encourage groups to hold meetings, conventions, and trade shows in the city or area it represents
2. Assist those groups with event preparations and during the event
3. Encourage tourists to visit the historic, cultural, and recreational opportunities the destination offers

The CVB does not engage in the actual planning or organizing of meetings, conventions, and other events. However, the CVB assists meeting planners and managers in several ways. First, it will provide information about the destination, area attractions, services, and facilities. Second, it provides an unbiased source of information to the planner. Finally, most of the services offered by the CVB are at no charge because they are funded through other sources, including hotel occupancy taxes and membership dues. Therefore, it can provide an array of services to event planners and managers. A sample of general services provided by a CVB include the following:

- CVBs act as a liaison between the planner and the community.
- CVBs can help meeting attendees maximize their free time through the creation of pre- and postconference activities, spouse tours, and special evening events.

- CVBs can provide hotel room counts and meeting space statistics.

- CVBs can help with event facility availability.

- CVBs are a network for transportation—shuttle service, ground transportation, and airline information.

- CVBs can assist with site inspections and familiarization tours.

- CVBs can provide speakers and local educational opportunities.

- CVBs can provide help in securing auxiliary services, production companies, catering, security, and so forth.

TECHNOLOGY SPOTLIGHT

GPS Drives Customers to Your Door

Cihan Cobanoglu, Ph.D., Dean, School of Hotel and Restaurant Management, University of South Florida, Sarasota-Manatee

On a trip to San Francisco, I had a meeting with a client that finished just before lunch time. Needless to say, I was hungry, and being in San Francisco, I knew I could find some interesting eateries. Instead of asking for recommendations at the front desk, I did something that I have been doing since the first day I bought my Garmin Nuvi 660 Global Positioning System (GPS). I left my hotel, turned it on, and was able to browse through a list of nearby restaurants, some of which I would never have found otherwise.

As the GPS guided me to a Turkish restaurant called Alaturka, a thought crossed my mind, one that I shared with the owner when I arrived: "Did you know that I found your restaurant using my GPS?" The owner had no idea.

But should he? My thoughts and the owner's inexperience with GPS led me to pursue a research study on the topic of U.S. consumer use of GPS with Dr. Silvia Ciccarelli of the University of Rome. Preliminary results are very promising for the hospitality industry.

Dashboard Results

As evidenced by the presence of GPS on the list of hot holiday items for 2007, a growing number of U.S. consumers are using GPS in their everyday lives. This is further supported by the study's findings: Only 33 percent of the U.S. consumers we polled had not used a GPS within the last 12 months, and only 4 percent did not know what a GPS was. Among those who had used a GPS within the last year (63 percent), 14 percent had rented or borrowed a GPS, 7 percent had a built-in GPS in their vehicle, 28 percent owned a portable/ dashboard GPS, and 5 percent had a phone with GPS capabilities.

The vast majority of consumers (94 percent) agree that a GPS makes life easier, and 84 percent indicate that they feel safer with a GPS. What's more, 11 percent even indicate that they cannot travel without a GPS. For many consumers, a GPS is a personal thing—approximately 30 percent name their GPS (e.g., Jack, Jill), while 34 percent talk to their GPS (e.g., "Good job, Jack!" or "OK, Jill, take me there!").

However, the most important and relevant finding for the hospitality industry is that 30 percent of respondents said that they travel more because of their GPS. More than half (55 percent) of consumers would like their GPS to suggest tourist attractions to them, and 42 percent think that a GPS could help them plan their vacation. Furthermore, 65 percent of consumers who used a GPS in the past 12 months found and ate in restaurants that they did not previously know of because of their GPS. When it comes to lodging, 51 percent found hotels this way, and 47 percent were able to find tourist attractions with the help of their GPS.

Marketing Opportunities

The increasing use of the GPS has not gone unnoticed. Recognizing the powerful marketing opportunity that a GPS offers, Dunkin' Brands inked a first-of-its-kind licensing agreement with GPS manufacturer Tom-Tom (**www.tomtom.com**). Under the terms of the agreement, users could download the Dunkin' Donuts and Baskin Robbins logos onto their devices as points of interest. The systems could also be programmed so that drivers were alerted as they approach a local Dunkin' Donuts or Baskin Robbins location.

GPS maker Garmin (**http://www.garmin.com/us/**) announced a partnership with MAD MAPS that will provide scenic reminders that traveling by car or motorcycle is more than simply reaching a destination.[26]

GPS: Here to Stay

If you haven't already noticed, the one take-away from this study should be that a GPS is a powerful marketing tool. These systems drive business to hospitality operations. Accordingly, hotels and restaurants need to contact GPS manufacturers to ensure that they are listed in GPS databases and that their listing provides the correct information for GPS users. Hospitality operators should also offer downloadable point-of-interest information on their web site so customers can input location information into their GPS. GPS is a tool that's here to stay, so don't get left behind.

Sustainability in Special Events

What drives hospitality and tourism companies to incorporate sustainability standards into their business practices and daily operations? What do these companies gain from employing Sustainability standards?

The recent increase in special event tourism has triggered the emergence of sustainable event standards. Britain has recently developed a system of standards for event management, which highlights policies and procedures necessary to implement sustainability. Event managers can use these standards as a benchmark for how to train employees on proper sustainable practices before, during, and after events. Currently in the U.S., ASTM International is creating a guide for sustainable event management called, "the New Guide for Standard Practice for the Evaluation and Selection of Destinations for Meetings, Events, Trade Show, and Conferences," which credits much of its content to the British system of standards.[27]

Sustainable event tourism refers to the implementation of practices and procedures which help conserve both the natural environment and the special event space. Special event tourism is one of the most lucrative and fastest growing segments of the tourism industry.[28] Special events are provided for a variety of reasons, which range from creating market demand for the host location as a desirable destination, generating publicity for the event's sponsors, achieving a specific purpose or goal, developing awareness of a particular cause or idea, etc.[29] Whatever the reason may be, special events play an important role in consumer's images, attitudes and perceptions of host destinations.[30] Because special events bring tourism to certain locations, it is the responsibility of the event host to employ sustainable practices, in order to preserve local resources and cultural interests.[31]

Sustainable event tourism not only provides environmental advantages, but financial returns as well. The organizations who are dedicated to incorporating sustainable programs into their business plans can expect to see the greatest return on investment as a result of cost reduction, revenue increase, etc.[32] Some practices that can result in financial gain include, conserving energy such as light spill from event and security lighting, turning off lights whenever they are not in use, utilizing low carbon fuels and renewable energy, ensuring appropriate waste and cleaning procedures are followed, utilizing low emission vehicles, reducing vehicle usage and increasing shared transportation.[33] Ultimately, the implementation of sustainable practices can increase the benefits of being in the special events business, as well as the excitement of actually hosting an event.

The Special Events Job Market

Becoming a special events consultant or an off-premise catering/event specialist requires a delicate balance of many skills. Experience gained from several avenues will propel you to the heights of success. As with any career, an "experience ladder" must be climbed.

First, allow yourself to gain all the experience you can in the food and beverage aspect of the hospitality industry. If time and resources permit, it is highly recommended that you gain knowledge from a culinary arts program. Second, experience gained as a banquet food server in a high-volume convention or resort hotel property is invaluable. Also, paying your dues as a guest service agent at a hotel front desk or as a concierge provides you with the opportunity to hone your customer service skills. Promote yourself to a banquet manager or a CSM (convention service coordinator), which provides the opportunity to learn and perfect organizational skills—to which end is the ability to multitask and deal with hundreds of details simultaneously. After all, the business of special events is the business of managing details.

The next step is obtaining a sales position. An excellent appointment to aspire to is an executive meeting manager, sometimes called a small meeting manager, in a convention or conference hotel. Here, you are responsible for booking small room blocks (usually twenty rooms or less), making meeting room arrangements, creating meal plans, and setting audiovisual requirements. On a small scale, hundreds of details are coordinated for several groups at any one time. From this position, you may laterally move to a catering sales position within a hotel.

Figure 2 • A Career Path for an Event Manager.

The catering sales position in a hotel will expose you to many different kinds of events: weddings, reunions, corporate events, holiday events, and social galas and balls. In this position, one either coordinates or has the opportunity to work with various vendors. This is where the florists, prop companies, lighting experts, entertainment agencies, rental companies, and audiovisual wizards come into play. Two to three years in this capacity grooms you for the next rung on the ladder.

Now, you can pursue several different angles: being promoted to a convention service manager within a hotel, moving into off-premise catering as a sales consultant, joining a production company, or perhaps affiliating yourself with a destination management company (DMC). Typically, without sales experience within a DMC, your first experience with them will be as an operations manager. Once proficient in this capacity, you then join the sales team.

After another two years creating and selling your heart out, you will be ready for the big leagues. The palette is now yours to paint your future. How about aspiring to be the next Super Bowl halftime creator and producer? Or perhaps creating the theme and schematics for the Olympics is in your future. Many avenues are available for exploring. Call on your marketing ideas, your business sense, your accounting skills, your aptitude for design, and your discriminating palette for creating unique entertaining and dining concepts. Continually educating yourself and discovering fresh ideas through adventurous experiences are essential to designing and selling special events. Don't forget to embark on as many internships as you can in the name of gaining knowledge and experience. Show your enthusiasm for what is different and unconventional. Know that creativity has no boundaries. Visualize the big picture and go for it! Figure 2 shows a career path for an event manager.

Trends in the Special Events Industry

- The special events industry is forecast to grow because clients want ever more spectacular events.

- Events are increasingly more complex, involving multimedia presentations, elaborate staging, and frequently upscale food and beverage service.

- Technology presents both an opportunity and a challenge—an opportunity in that it can facilitate event planning and management, and a challenge in that new software programs must be mastered.

CASE STUDY

Not Enough Space

Jessica is the event planner for a large convention center. A client has requested an exhibition that would not only bring excellent revenue but that is an annual event that several other convention centers would like to host.

Exhibitions typically take one or two days to set up, three or four days of exhibition, and one day to break down. Professional organizations handle each part of the setup and breakdown.

When Jessica checks the space available on the days requested for the exhibition, she notices that another exhibition is blocking part of the space needed by her client.

Discussion Question

1. What can Jessica do to get this exhibition to use the conventon center without inconveniencing either exhibition too much?

Summary

1. Special events differ from daily events, which occur spontaneously, do not arouse expectations, and usually occur without reason, in that they recognize a unique moment in time with ceremony and ritual to satisfy specific needs and are always planned.

2. The special events industry is a growing field that will provide many professional career opportunities in event management and planning.

3. Special events planners and managers have filled a need that was first introduced at hotels and convention centers. They are responsible for planning the event from start to finish.

4. The special events industry can be grouped into several smaller classifications, including corporate events, association events, charity balls and fund-raising events, social functions, fairs and festivals, and concert and sporting events.

5. The event-planning process includes the following steps: research, design, planning, coordination, and evaluation.

6. Special events planners can work in a variety of settings. They range from hotels/resorts, convention centers, and private clubs to self-employment.

7. Critical skills and abilities required for a career in special events management include leadership skills, effective communication, project management skills, negotiating skills, coordinating and delegating skills, budgeting skills, multitasking abilities, enthusiasm, effective social skills, and the ability to form contacts.

8. The special events industry has its own selection of professional associations that offer certification, continuing education, and networking to their members. The International Special Events Society (ISES), International Festivals & Events Association (IFEA), and Meeting Professionals International (MPI) are three of the largest and most recognized professional associations in the field. Local convention and visitors bureaus (CVBs) are organizations that can be valuable

resources to the special events industry. A CVB has the purpose of promoting tourism, meetings, and related business for its city.

9. The management of time and finances, along with technology and human resources are event-planning tools that can be utilized to your advantage as you pursue a career in this field.

10. The special events industry does not have rigid boundaries. Closely related fields that may overlap include catering, marketing, sales, and entertainment.

Key Words and Concepts

charity balls
conventions
coordination
corporate events
corporate seminars
event planner
event planning
fairs and festivals

International Festival & Events Association (IFEA)
International Special Events Society (ISES)
Meeting Professionals International (MPI)
social functions
special events industry
trade shows
weddings and holiday parties
workshops

Review Questions

1. What do event planners do?
2. What are the challenges for event planners and managers?
3. Describe three of the classifications of special events.
4. Explain the skills and abilities required for event management.

Internet Exercises

1. Organization: **International Special Events Society (ISES)**
   Web site: **www.ises.com**
   Click on "Learn." Look for ISES Eventworld under "Education & Programs" and see what an ISES Eventworld can do for professional development and who should attend.

2. Organization: Meeting Professionals International
   http://careers.mpiweb.org/c/search. cfm?site_id=8168
   Go to "Career Development," click on "Career Connections," and check out a couple of good jobs.

Apply Your Knowledge

Make a plan for a local event in your area. List all the headings and formulate a budget.

Suggested Activity

Attend a special event and write a brief report on the event and its planning and organization.

Endnotes

1. Joe J. Goldblatt, *Special Events: Best Practices in Modern Event Management*, 2nd ed. (New York: John Wiley and Sons, 1997), 2; Joe J. Goldblatt, *Special Events: The Art and Science of Celebration* (New York: Von Nostrand Reinhold, 1990), 1–2.

2. Frank Supovitz, "Foreword," in Joe J. Goldblatt, *Special Events: Best Practices in Modern Event Management*, 2nd ed. (New York: John Wiley and Sons, 1997), iv.

3. Blythe Cameson, *Opportunities in Event Planning Careers* (New York: McGraw-Hill, 2002), 4–7.

4. Event Solutions, *2004 Black Book* (Tempe, AZ: Event Publishing, 2004), 22

5. Blythe Cameson, *Opportunities in Event Planning Careers*, 115.

6. Festivals.com, *Culture*, www.festivals.com/culture/ (accessed November 27, 2011).

7. Goldblatt, *Special Events: Best Practices in Modern Event Management*, 129–139.

8. George G. Fenich, *Meetings, Expositions, Events, and Conventions: An Introduction to the Industry* (Upper Saddle River, NJ: Pearson Education, 2005), 181–182.

9. Fenich, *Meetings, Expositions, Events, and Conventions*, 366.

10. Norman Brinker, presentation to the National Restaurant Association, May 14, 1994.

11. Judy Allen, *Event Planning Ethics and Etiquette: A Principled Approach to the Business of Special Event Management* (Etobicoke, Ontario, Canada: John Wiley and Sons, 2003), 79.

12. International Special Events Society (ISES), *ISES 2010–2011 Fact Sheet*, www.ises.com/portals/0/About_ISES.pdf (accessed November 27, 2011).

13. Ibid.

14. International Special Events Society, *Learn*, http://www.ises.com/Learn/tabid/78/Default.aspx (accessed November 27, 2011).

15. International Special Events Society (ISES), *Certified Special Events Professional (CSEP)*, http://isesew.vtcus.com/CSEP/index.aspx (November 27, 2011)

16. International Special Events Society (ISES), *ISES Vision and Mission*, www.ises.com/MediaCenter/ISESVisionandMission/tabid/92/Default.aspx (accessed November 27, 2011).

17. http://www.ifea.com/joomla1_5/index.php

18. International Festivals & Events Association (IFEA), *About the IFEA*, http://www.ifea.com/joomla1_5/index.php (accessed November 30, 2011).

19. http://www.ifea.com/joomla1_5/index.php

20. http://www.mpiweb.org/Portal/Research/BusinessBarometer/download (retrieved November 30, 2001).

21. Cameson, *Opportunities in Event Planning Careers*, 36–41.

22. Meeting Professionals International, *CMM: Certification in Meeting Management*, www.mpiweb.org/Education/CMM (accessed November 27, 2011).

23. Hospitality Sales and Marketing Association International (HSMAI), *About HSMAI*, www.hsmai.org/GlobalAbout.cfm (accessed November 27, 2011).

24. Hospitality Sales and Marketing Association International (HSMAI), *HSMAI Information*, www.hsmai.org/Mission.cfm (accessed June 8, 2011).

25. Hospitality Sales and Marketing Association International (HSMAI), *About HSMAI*, www.hsmai.org/GlobalAbout.cfm (accessed November 27, 2011).

26. http://www8.garmin.com/pressroom/corporate/102907.html

27. O'Connor, M.C. (July 8, 2010). On the Agenda: Sustainable Event Standards. http://www.triplepundit.com/2010/07/on-the-agenda-sustainable-event-standards/. Retrieved on November 17, 2011.

28. Reid, S., & Arcodia, C. (2002). Understanding the role of stakeholders in event management.

29. Turney, Michael. (2009). Special events generate publicity but are they effective public relations. http://www.nku.edu/~turney/prclass/sections/special_events.html. Retrieved on November 17, 2011.

30. Chalip, L., Green, C., & Hill, B. (2003). Effects of sport media on destination image and intentions to visit. *Journal of Sport Management*, 17, 214–234.

31. Okech, Roselyne N. (2011). Promoting sustainable festival events tourism: a case study of Lamu Kenya. *Worldwide Hospitality and Tourism Themes*. Vol. 3 No. 3.

32. Beer, Mitchell. (November 14, 2011). Commentary: New Green Standards Help Make Sustainability Sustainable. http://meetingsnet.com/green_meetings/commentary_beer_new_green_standards_1114/?YM_MID=1272883&YM_RID=operations@meetingstrategiesworldwide.com. Retrieved on November 17, 2011.

33. http://www.london2012.com/documents/locog-publications/london-2012-sustainability-events-guidelines.pdf. Retrieved on November 17, 2011.

Glossary

Charity ball A gala dinner-dance event whose purpose is to raise funds toward a group or charity.

Convention A generic term referring to any size business or professional meeting held in one specific location, which usually includes some form of trade show or exposition. Also refers to a group of delegates or members who assemble to accomplish a specific goal.

Corporate events Annual meetings, sales meetings, new product launches, training meetings, workshops, management meetings, press meetings, incentive meetings, and awards ceremonies.

Corporate seminar A corporate meeting whose purpose is to exchange ideas; a conference.

Event planner An individual who is responsible for planning an event from start to finish. Duties include setting the date and location; advertising the event; and providing refreshments or arranging catering services; and arranging speakers and/or entertainment.

Event planning A general term that refers to a career path in the growing field of special events.

Fairs and festivals Planned events that are often themed to the celebration's purpose.

Fund-raiser An event whose purpose is to raise funds for a group or charity.

International Festivals & Events Association An organization that provides an opportunity for event managers from around the world to network and exchange ideas on how other festivals excel in sponsorship, marketing, fund-raising, operations, volunteer coordination, and management.

Social functions Events that include weddings, engagement parties, and holiday functions.

Special events industry An industry that employs professionals who work together to provide a broad range of services to create what is termed a *special event*.

Trade show Generally, a large display of products and services available for purchase, promoting information exchange among trade people. Trade shows frequently take place in convention centers where space is rented in blocks of 10 square feet. Also called *exposition*.

Weddings and holiday parties Of all social gatherings, weddings are the most widely recognized social event.

Workshop A usually brief, intensive educational program conducted by a facilitator or a trainer, designed for a relatively small group of people, that focuses especially on techniques and skills in a particular field. Emphasizes interaction and exchange of information among a relatively small number of participants.

Photo Credits

Leadership and Management

From Chapter 14 of *Introduction to Hospitality,* Sixth Edition. John R. Walker. Copyright © 2013 by Pearson Education, Inc. Published by Pearson. All rights reserved.

Leadership and Management

Leadership

Our fascination with **leadership** goes back many centuries. Lately, however, it has come into prominence in the hospitality, tourism, and other industries as these industries strive for perfection in the delivery of services and products in an increasingly competitive environment. Leaders can and do make a difference when measuring a company's success.

One person working alone can accomplish few tasks or goals. You have probably already experienced being part of a group that had good leadership. It might have been with a school, social, sporting, church, or other group in which the leader made a difference. The reverse might also be true: You may have been in a group with ineffective leadership. Few groups can accomplish much without an individual who acts as an effective leader. The leader can and often does have a significant influence on the group and its direction.

Characteristics and Practices of Leaders

So, what are the ingredients that result in leadership excellence? If you look at the military for examples of leadership excellence, you see that leaders can be identified by certain characteristics. For example, the *U.S. Guidebook for Marines* lists the following leadership traits:

- Courage
- Decisiveness
- Dependability
- Endurance
- Enthusiasm
- Initiative
- Unselfishness
- Integrity
- Judgment
- Justice
- Knowledge
- Loyalty
- Tact

A Marine officer would likely choose integrity as the most important trait. Integrity has been defined as "doing something right even though no one may be aware of it."

In addition to these leadership traits, the following identifiable practices are common to leaders:

1. *Challenge the process.* Be active, not passive; search for opportunities; experiment and take risks.
2. *Inspire a shared vision.* Create a vision; envision the future; enlist others.
3. *Enable others to act.* Do not act alone; foster collaboration; strengthen others.
4. *Model the way.* Plan; set examples; strive for small wins.
5. *Encourage the heart.* Share the passion; recognize individual contributions; celebrate accomplishments.

Definitions of Leadership

Because of the complexities of leadership, the different types of leadership, and individual perceptions of leaders, *leadership* has several definitions. Many definitions share commonalities, but there are also differences. In terms of hospitality leadership, the definition "Leading is the process by which a person with vision is able to influence the activities and outcomes of others in a desired way" is appropriate.

Leaders know what they want and why they want it—and they are able to communicate those desires to others to gain their cooperation and support. Leadership theory and practice has evolved over time to a point where current industry practitioners may be identified as transactional or transformational leaders.[1]

INTRODUCING HORST SCHULZE

West Paces Hotel Group

Horst Schulze is a legendary leader in the hospitality industry and one of the most influential hospitality industry leaders of our time. His vision helped reshape concepts of guest service throughout the hospitality and service industries.

Mr. Schulze grew up in a small village in Germany, and he was eleven years old when he told his parents that he wanted to work in a hotel. When he was fourteen, his parents took him to the finest hotel in the region, where they had an "audience" with the general manager—it lasted ten minutes, and he didn't speak to him again for the next two years! Everyone, including young Schulze's mother, the general manager, and the restaurant maître d', told him how important the guests were, so with knees shaking, young Schulze found himself in the restaurant working as a busser. The maître d' made a favorable impression on the young man because he was respected by both guests and staff alike. So, when Horst had to do an essay for his hotel school (he attended hotel school on Wednesdays), he chose the title, "We Are Ladies and Gentlemen Serving Ladies and Gentlemen." He kept the essay because it was the only A he received, but that A also became the foundation of his philosophy to create service excellence.

Mr. Schulze now speaks on guest service to thousands every year, graciously sharing with others his knowledge and experience. He says that there are three aspects of service[2]:

1. Service should be defect free.
2. Service should be timely.
3. People should care.

It is the caring piece that is service. The guest relationship begins when a guest perceives that he or she has contacted you, and the human contact should begin with a warm welcome. Mr. Schulze adds that all hospitality businesses should be doing four things[3]:

1. Keeping guests equals loyalty, meaning guests trust you and are happy to form a relationship with you.
2. Find new guests.

(continued)

INTRODUCING HORST SCHULZE (continued)

3. Get as much money as you can from the guest without losing him or her.
4. Create efficiencies.

Mr. Schulze also worked with Hyatt Hotels and Hilton Hotels. After joining the Ritz-Carlton as a charter member and vice president of operations in 1983, Mr. Schulze was instrumental in creating the operating and service standards that have become world famous. He was appointed executive vice president in 1987, and president and chief operating officer (COO) in 1988. Under his leadership, the group was awarded the Malcolm Baldrige National Quality Award in both 1992 and 1999; it was the first and only hotel company to win even one such award. In 2002, Mr. Schulze, along with several former Ritz-Carlton executives, formed the West Paces Hotel Group to create and operate branded hotels in several distinctive market segments. The canon of the company is as follows: "The West Paces Hotel Group is in business to create value and unparalleled results for our owners by creating products which fulfill individual customer expectations."[4]

They offer significant opportunities within three profiles[5]:

1. Ultra-luxury hotel properties in gateway cities and spectacular resort destinations
2. Luxury hotel accommodations for frequent travelers
3. Management of select independent hotel properties

West Paces has hotels and resorts under two brands: Solis and Capella. They can be viewed at **http://www.capellahotelgroup.com/?corp**.

Transactional Leadership

Transactional leadership is viewed as a process by which a leader is able to bring about desired actions from others by using certain behaviors, rewards, or incentives. In essence, an exchange or transaction takes place between leader and follower. Figure 1 shows the transactional leadership model. This figure illustrates the coming together of the leader, the situation, and the followers. A hotel general manager who pressures the food and beverage director to achieve certain goals in exchange for a bonus is an example of someone practicing transactional leadership.

Transformational Leadership

Leadership involves looking for ways to bring about longer-term, higher-order changes in follower behavior. This brings us to transformational leadership. The term **transformational leadership** is used to describe the process of eliciting performance above and beyond normal expectations. A transformational leader

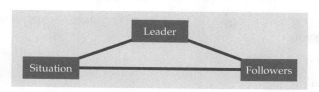

Figure 1 • Transactional Leadership Model.

is one who inspires others to reach beyond themselves and do more than they originally thought possible; this is accomplished by raising their commitment to a shared vision of the future.

Transformational leaders practice a hands-on philosophy, not in terms of performing the day-to-day tasks of subordinates, but in developing and encouraging their followers individually. Transformational leadership involves three important factors:

1. Charisma
2. Individual consideration
3. Intellectual stimulation

Of course, it is also possible to be a charismatic transformational leader as well as a transactional leader. Although this does involve a measurable amount of effort, these leaders are guaranteed to rake in success throughout their careers.

Examples of Excellence in Leadership

Dr. Martin Luther King Jr. was one of the most charismatic transformational leaders in history. King dedicated his life to achieving rights for all citizens through nonviolent methods. His dream of how society could be was shared by millions of Americans. In 1964, Dr. King won the Nobel Peace Prize.

Another transformational leader is Herb Kelleher, the co-founder, Chairman Emeritus, and former CEO of Southwest Airlines. He was able to inspire his followers to pursue his corporate vision and reach beyond themselves to give Southwest Airlines that something extra that set it apart from its competitors.

Kelleher recognizes that the company does not exist merely for the gratification of its employees. He knows that Southwest Airlines must perform and must be profitable. However, he believes strongly that valuing individuals for themselves is the best way to attain exceptional performance. Passengers who fly Southwest Airlines may have seen Herb Kelleher because he travels frequently and previously was likely to be found serving drinks, fluffing pillows, or just wandering up and down the aisle, talking to passengers. The success of Southwest and the enthusiasm of its employees indicate that Herb Kelleher achieved his goal of weaving together individual and corporate interests so that all members of the Southwest family benefit. Kelleher is a great transformational leader who is able to lead by visioning, inspiring, empowering, and communicating.[6]

In their fascinating book *Lessons in Leadership: Perspectives for Hospitality Industry Success*, Bill Fisher, former president and CEO of the American Hotel & Lodging Association and current Darden Eminent Scholar in Restaurant Management at the University of Central Florida,

Martin Luther King Jr., one of the most charismatic transformational leaders of the twentieth century, giving his famous "I Have a Dream" speech.

and Charles Bernstein, an editor of *Nation's Restaurant News*, interviewed more than 100 industry leaders and asked each to give advice in an up-close-and-personal manner. Here is an example of the leaders' answers: "Experience is a hard teacher. It gives the test first, and then you learn the lesson[7]."

Richard P. Mayer, former chairman and CEO of Kentucky Fried Chicken and president of General Foods Corporation, says that the key traits and factors he looks for in assessing talent include the following:

- Established personal goals
- The drive and ambition to attain those goals, tempered and strengthened with integrity
- Proven analytical and communications skills
- Superior interpersonal capabilities
- A sense of humor
- An awareness and appreciation of the world beyond his or her business specialty
- Receptivity to ideas (no matter the source)
- A genuine, deep commitment to the growth and profitability of the business

Success has as many meanings as there are people to ponder it. One concept of success is to couple one's personal and family interests, dreams, and aspirations with a business or professional career such that they complement and fortify each other. Another aspect of leadership is the ability to motivate others in a hospitality working environment; decision making is also essential. These are discussed later in the text.

FOCUS ON LEADERSHIP

Leadership—The Basis for Management

William Fisher, Darden Eminent Scholar in Restaurant Management, Author and Former Executive Vice President of the National Restaurant Association and the American Hotel & Lodging Association

The concept and practice of leadership as it applies to management carries a fascination and attraction for most people. We all like to think we have some leadership qualities, and we strive to develop them. We look at leaders in all walks of life, seeking to identify which qualities, traits, and skills they possess so that we can emulate them. A fundamental question remains: What is the essence of leadership that results in successful management as opposed to failed management? At least part of the answer can be found within the word itself:

1. *Loyalty.* Leadership starts with a loyalty quadrant: Loyalty to one's organization and its mission, loyalty to organizational superiors, loyalty to subordinates, and loyalty to oneself. Loyalty is multidirectional, running up and down in the organization. When everyone practices it, loyalty bonds occur, which drives high morale.

Loyalty to oneself is based on maintaining a sound body, mind, and spirit so that one is always "riding the top of the wave" in service to others.

2. *Excellence.* Leaders know that excellence is a value, not an object. They strive for both excellence and success. Excellence is the measurement you make of yourself in assessing what you do and how well you do it; success is an external perception that others have of you.

3. *Assertiveness.* Leaders possess a mental and physical intensity that causes them to seek control, take command, assume the mantle of responsibility, and focus on the objective(s). Leaders do not evidence self-doubt, as they are comfortable within themselves that what they are doing is right, which, in turn, gives them the courage to take action.

4. *Dedication.* Leaders are dedicated in mind, body, and spirit to their organization and to achievement. They are action oriented, not passive, and prefer purposeful activity to the status quo. They possess an aura or charisma that sets them apart from others with whom they interact, always working in the best interest of their organization.

5. *Enthusiasm.* Leaders are their own best cheerleaders on behalf of their organization and people. They exude enthusiasm and instill it in others to the point of contagion. Their style may be one of poise, stability, clear vision, and articulate speech, but their bristling enthusiasm undergirds their every waking moment.

6. *Risk management.* Leaders realize that risk taking is part of their management position. They manage risk, rather than letting it manage them, knowing full well that there are no guaranteed outcomes, no foregone conclusions, no preordained results when one is dealing with the future. Nonetheless, they measure risk, adapt to it, control it, and surmount it.

7. *Strength.* Leaders possess an inner fiber of stamina, fortitude, and vibrancy that gives them a mental toughness, causing them to withstand interruption, crises, and unforeseen circumstances that would slow down or immobilize most people. Leaders become all the more energized in the face of surprises.

8. *Honor.* Leaders understand they will leave a legacy, be it good, bad, or indifferent. True leaders recognize that all their relationships and actions are based on the highest standard of honor and integrity. They do the right things correctly, shun short-term, improper expediency, and set the example for others with high-mindedness, professional bearing, and unassailable character.

9. *Inspiration.* Leaders don't exist without followers. People will follow leaders who inspire them to reach beyond the normal and ordinary to new levels of accomplishment, new heights of well-being, and new platforms for individual, organizational, and societal good. Inspiration is what distinguishes a leader from a mere position holder, as the leader can touch the hearts, minds, and souls of others.

10. *Performance.* At the end of the day, leader/managers rise or fall on the most critical of all measurements: their performance. Results come first, but the ways in which results are achieved are also crucial to sustaining a leader's role. Many dictators don't last despite results, and many charismatics don't last despite personal charm.

These ten elements together spell LEADERSHIP! Always remember, if you want to develop a leadership quality, act as though you already possess it!

Demands Placed on Leaders

Demands on a leader in the hospitality industry include those made by owners, the corporate office, guests, employees, regulatory agencies, and competitors (Figure 2). In response to many demands, the leader must balance two additional forces: how much energy to expend on getting results and how much to expend on relationships (Figure 3).

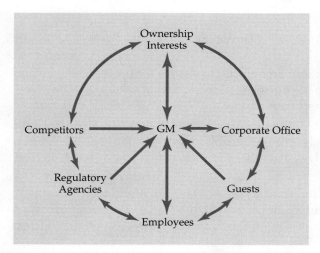

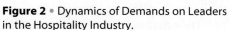

Figure 2 • Dynamics of Demands on Leaders in the Hospitality Industry.

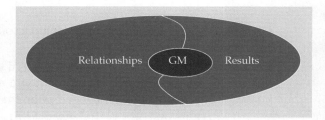

Figure 3 • Amount of Energy the Leader Needs to Spend on Getting Results and Maintaining Relationships.

Applied social scientists such as Peter Drucker, powerful industry leaders such as Bill Marriott, and public service leaders such as former New York mayor Rudolph Giuliani all seem to have common traits, among which are the following:

1. High ego strength
2. Ability to think strategically
3. Orietation toward the future
4. A belief in certain fundamental principles of human behavior
5. Strong connections that they do not hesitate to display
6. Political astuteness
7. Ability to use power both for efficiency and for the larger good of the organization

Leaders vary in their values, managerial styles, and priorities. Peter Drucker, the renowned management scholar, author, and consultant of many years, has discussed with hundreds of leaders their roles, goals, and performance. These discussions took place with leaders of large and small organizations, with for-profit and volunteer organizations. Interestingly, Drucker observes the following:

All the leaders I have encountered—both those I worked with and those I watched—realized:

1. The only definition of a leader is someone who has followers. Some people are thinkers. Some are prophets. Both roles are important and badly needed. But without followers, there can be no leaders.
2. An effective leader is not someone who is loved or admired. She or he is someone whose followers do the right things. Popularity is not leadership. Results are.

3. Leaders are highly visible. They therefore set examples.

4. Leadership is not about rank, privileges, titles, or money. It is about responsibility.[8]

Drucker adds that regardless of their enormous diversity with respect to personality, style, abilities, and interests, effective leaders all behave in much the same way:

1. They did not start out with the question "What do I want?" They started out asking, "What needs to be done?"

2. Then they asked, "What can and should I do to make a difference?" This has to be something that both needs to be done and fits the leader's strengths and the way he or she is most effective.

3. They constantly asked, "What are the organization's mission and goals? What constitutes performance and results in this organization?"

4. They were extremely tolerant of diversity in people and did not look for carbon copies of themselves. It rarely even occurred to them to ask, "Do I like or dislike this person?" But they were totally—fiendishly—intolerant when it came to a person's performance, standards, and values.

5. They were not afraid of strength in their associates. They gloried in it. Whether they had heard of it or not, their motto was the one Andrew Carnegie wanted to have put on his tombstone: "Here lies a man who attracted better people into his service than he was himself."[9]

6. One way or another, they submitted themselves to the mirror test—that is, they made sure the person they saw in the mirror in the morning was the kind of person they wanted to be, respect, and believe in. This way they fortified themselves against the leader's greatest temptations—to do things that are popular rather than right and to do petty, mean, sleazy things.[10]

Finally, these leaders were not preachers; they were doers.

The most effective leaders share a number of skills, and these skills are always related to dealing with employees. The following suggestions outline an approach to becoming a hospitality industry leader rather than just a manager:

- *Be decisive.* Hospitality industry leaders are confronted with dozens of decisions every day. Obviously, you should use your best judgment to resolve the decisions that come to roost at your doorstep. As a boss, make the decisions that best meet both your objectives and your ethics, and then make your decisions known.

- *Follow through.* Never promise what you can't deliver, and never build false hopes among your employees. Once expectations are dashed, respect for and the reputation of the boss are shot.

- *Select the best.* A boss, good or bad, is carried forward by the work of his or her subordinates. One key to being a good boss is to hire the people who have the best potential to do what you need them to do. Take the time and effort to screen, interview, and assess the people who have not only the skills that you require, but also the needed values.

- *Empower employees.* Give people the authority to interact with the customer. The more important people feel, the better they work.

- *Enhance career development.* Good bosses recognize that most of their people want to improve themselves. However, career development is a two-edged sword: If we take the initiative to train and develop our people properly, then the competition is likely to hire them. The only way a boss can prevent the loss of productive workers looking for career development is to provide opportunities for growth within the organization and to maintain an empowering work environment.

CORPORATE PROFILE

The Ritz-Carlton Hotel Company: A Commitment to Excellence and Quality Service Worldwide

The Ritz-Carlton Hotel Company was officially organized in the summer of 1983, although the Ritz-Carlton history and tradition long precede that date. Indeed, this tradition has entered our language: To be "ritzy" or "putting on the ritz" denotes doing something with class. With the purchase of the Ritz-Carlton Boston and the acquisition of the exclusive rights to use the name came a rich heritage.

The legacy of the Ritz-Carlton begins with the celebrated hotelier Cesar Ritz, the "king of hoteliers and hotelier to kings." Cesar Ritz's philosophy of service and innovations redefined the luxury hotel experience in Europe through his management of the Ritz Paris and the Carlton in London. The Ritz-Carlton Boston revolutionized hospitality in the United States by creating luxury in a hotel setting.

Cesar Ritz died in 1918, but his wife Marie continued the expansion of hotels bearing his name. In the United States, the Ritz-Carlton Investing Company was established by Albert Keller, who bought and franchised the name. In 1927, the Ritz-Carlton Boston was opened by Edward N. Wyner, a Boston real estate developer, with room rates of $15 per night. Because of the reputation of Ritz in Europe and the cosmopolitan society in Boston, Wyner knew the Ritz-Carlton name would secure immediate success.

Fast-forward to 1983, when William B. Johnson acquired the rights to establish the Ritz-Carlton Hotel Company. The company now operates seventy-seven hotels worldwide.[1] Further expansion plans are included for Africa, Asia, the Caribbean, the Middle East, and the Americas.[2]

The Ritz-Carlton Hotel Company was named the winner of the prestigious Malcolm Baldrige National Quality Award in 1992 and again in 1999. The Ritz-Carlton is the only hospitality organization ever to have

[1]The Ritz-Carlton, *Fact Sheet*, http://corporate.ritzcarlton.com/en/Press/FactSheet.htm (accessed November 28, 2011).
[2]The Ritz-Carlton, *Future Opening*, http://www.ritzcarlton.com/en/Locations/Upcoming.htm (accessed November 28, 2011).

won this coveted honor for quality management, given by the U.S. Department of Commerce. Seven categories make up the award criteria: leadership, strategic planning, customer and market focus, information and analysis, human resources focus, process management, and business results. At the Ritz-Carlton, a focus on these criteria has resulted in higher employee and customer satisfaction, and increased productivity and market share. Perhaps most significant is increased profitability.

Horst Schultze, founding president and CEO, whose vision and leadership was the driving force behind the success in obtaining the Malcolm Baldrige Awards. Since joining the company, Herve Humler has been responsible for the successful opening of several hotels. This expansion continues with seven hotels and resorts slated for opening over the next decade. The Ritz-Carlton Residences and the Ritz-Carlton Club were also successfully developed and launched under Cooper's tenure.

Committed employees rank as the most essential element to Ritz-Carlton's success. All employees are schooled and carry a pocket-sized card stating the company's Gold Standards, which include a credo, motto, three steps of service, and twenty Ritz-Carlton basics. Each employee is expected to understand and adhere to these standards, which describe processes for solving problems that guests may have as well as detailed grooming, housekeeping, and safety and efficiency standards. "We are Ladies and Gentlemen serving Ladies and Gentlemen" is the motto of the Ritz-Carlton, exemplifying anticipatory service provided by all staff members. "Every employee has the business plan of the Ritz-Carlton—constantly reinforcing that guest satisfaction is our highest mission," says Hulmer.

The company has quickly grown a collection of the finest hotels around the world. Several of these hotels are historic landmarks, following a commitment of the company to preserving architecturally important buildings. Some examples are the Ritz-Carlton New York, Central Park; the Ritz-Carlton, San Francisco; the Ritz-Carlton, Philadelphia; the Ritz-Carlton, New Orleans; and the Ritz-Carlton, Huntington Hotel & Spa. Each property is designed to be a comfortable haven for travelers and a social center for the community. The architecture and artwork are carefully selected to complement the hotel's environment. "We go to great lengths to capture the spirit of a hotel and its locale," says Cooper. "This creates a subtle balance and celebrates a gracious, relaxed lifestyle. The Ritz-Carlton is warm, relaxed yet refined; a most comfortable home away from home." The Ritz-Carlton Hotel Company is now owned and operated by Marriott International.

In recent years, the role of the hotel general manager (GM) has changed from that of being a congenial host, knowledgeable about the niceties of hotelmanship, to that of a multigroup pleaser. Guests, employees, owners, and community should all not only be satisfied but be delighted with the operation's performance.

Many GMs are so bogged down with meetings, reports, and "putting out fires" that they hardly have any time to spend with guests. One GM who makes time for guests is Richard Riley, GM of the fabulous Shangri-La Hotel Makati in Manila, the Philippines. Richard extends an invitation for guests to visit with him in the hotel lobby between 5:00 and 7:00 P.M. every Thursday. As GM of a luxury Caribbean resort in Barbados, West Indies, the author of this book personally greeted every guest to the property. Obviously, there is a difference between a small resort and a large city hotel. Resort guests stay for at least two, sometimes four, weeks in high season, so they need individual attention.

TECHNOLOGY SPOTLIGHT

Use of Social Networking Tools in the Hospitality Industry

Cihan Cobanoglu, Ph.D., Dean, School of Hotel and Restaurant Management, University of South Florida, Sarasota-Manatee

One of the most significant recent advances in consumer-based information technology is the introduction, and extremely fast adoption, of social networking tools. Today there are more than 800 million active users on Facebook, according to the site, with its popular "friending" approach to making connections. On any given day, 50 percent of these users log into their accounts. More than 250 million photos are uploaded daily; more than 350 million active users access Facebook through a mobile device; and more than 70 languages are used on the site.[1]

In the business arena, thousands, if not millions, local businesses have active pages on Facebook and those pages have created billions of fans combined. Twitter, with its 140-character "tweeting" approach to getting the word out, is powerful in its own right, with an estimated 32.1 million users in 2009, a growth of nearly 2,000 percent over the 1.6 million users in 2008.

Marketing rules used to dictate that a happy customer would tell three friends about your establishment and an angry customer would tell eleven friends. This is no longer the case; in both instances, whether happy or displeased, customers can easily reach tens if not hundreds of contacts. Given the vastness of social media connections and networks, this can quickly multiply into thousands or more potential customers with word-of-mouth insight into your products and service.

Hotels and Restaurants in the Fray

Many hotel and restaurant operators are aware that social media tools can and should be leveraged for their businesses, but they struggle to identify specific return on investment. In fact, according to Hospitality Technology's 12th annual Restaurant Technology Study, although nearly one-half of restaurants recognize that there is value in Twitter as a marketing tool, only one-third of restaurant operators use it. There exist, however, many successful examples of hotels using social networking sites to generate awareness and additional revenue opportunities. As of press time, Seattle's Hotel 1000, as a single property, has about 3,083 Facebook fans, and Excalibur Hotel and Casino in Las Vegas has more than 60,397. Hilton Hotels has more than 128,436, and Sheraton Hotels has more than 108,173 fans, while Olive Garden Restaurants has more than 1,891,748 fans.

While the size of the fan base is important, the true value is in the interaction. A quick scan of these Facebook pages shows two factors for success: First, they have personality and build emotional connections, and second, people respond and interact on these pages.

Strategies for Success

Social networking tools can be used for more than connecting to external customers. Companies also use these tools to find employees and to solicit feedback from current and potential customers on menu items, decorations, room design, and more. They can even be used as a venue to prompt customers to suggest new menu items. If encouraged properly, employees can be ambassadors of your company in their own social networks.

---

[1]Facebook, *Statistics*, http://www.facebook.com/press/info.php?statistics (accessed November 28, 2011).

One creative example of a hotel's use of social networking to boost guest participation is demonstrated by Pod Hotel New York's own social networking site, The Pod Culture message board. When guests make reservations online, they are invited to become a member of the Pod Community. There, they can choose a log-in and password and participate in an array of forums: Drink with Me, Eat with Me, Shop with Me, Go Out with Me, and so forth.

Though social networking tools are powerful, they must be well planned and carefully implemented to avoid pitfalls. If you ask for customers' opinions, listen to them. What's more, managing social networking tools will take time. For this reason, each company should assign personnel to the task of monitoring and regularly updating its social networks. Some hotel companies are recruiting managers dedicated to online services and e-commerce initiatives. Many are combining this responsibility with a revenue, marketing, or front office manager.

My recommendation to all hotels and restaurants would be to connect to their guests, employees, families, and vendors through different social networking tools. If you are not doing this already, you are behind the curve.

▶ Check Your Knowledge

1. What three factors does transformational leadership involve?
2. Define *leadership*.
3. Describe some examples of leadership.
4. Explain the demands placed on leaders.

Hospitality Management

Managers plan, organize, make decisions, communicate, motivate, and control the efforts of a group to accomplish predetermined goals. Management also establishes the direction the organization will take. Sometimes this is done with the help of employees or outside consultants, such as marketing research specialists. Managers obtain the necessary resources for the goals to be accomplished, and then they supervise and monitor group and individual progress toward goal accomplishment.

Managers, such as presidents and CEOs, who are responsible for the entire company, tend to focus most of their time on strategic planning and the organization's mission. They also spend time organizing and controlling the activities of the corporation. Most top managers do not get involved in the day-to-day aspects of the operation. These duties and responsibilities fall to the middle and supervisory management. In hospitality lingo, one would not expect Bill Marriott to pull a shift behind the bar at the local Marriott hotel. Although capable, his time and expertise are better used in shaping the company's future. Thus, although the head bartender and Bill Marriott may both be considered management, they require slightly different skills to be effective and efficient managers.

What Is Management?

Management is simply what managers do: plan, organize, make decisions, communicate, motivate, and control. *Management* is defined as "coordinating and overseeing the activities of others so that their activities are completed efficiently and effectively."[11] In looking at this statement, you can see that the functions of management and working with and through the work of others are ongoing. Additionally, management involves getting efficient and effective results.

Efficiency is getting the most done with the fewest number of inputs. Managers work with scarce resources: money, people, time, and equipment. You can imagine the rush in the kitchen to be ready for a meal service. But it's not enough

A DAY IN THE LIFE OF STEPHANIE SUMMERALL

Director of Sales and Marketing, Intercontinental Hotels Group

"Choose a job you love and you will never have to work a day in your life." Well, this quote could not be further from the truth, yet those of us who have chosen to work in the amazing field of hospitality would never consider making a move! There is something indescribable about being invited into the lives of a family planning a 50th wedding anniversary, a young bride obsessing over every last detail, a Fortune 500 company organizing its annual investors conference, and a political campaign trying to capture the perfect setting to deliver its message. It's a wonderfully infectious environment and one worth every ounce of hard work.

I began my career working as Director of Member Relations at Mission Hills Country Club in Palm Springs, California, a position that I was nowhere near ready to take on. Thankfully, I had the wonderful fortune of working with a fantastically talented team of professionals and from them I learned the skill needed to cultivate strong business relationships, I learned how to get creative when things didn't go as planned, and I became as resilient, as this field requires you to be in order to achieve success. Four years later in December 2004, I moved to London and, with a great deal of luck, managed to receive the most glamorous position imaginable, Senior Sales Manager for Claridge's, The Berkeley, and The Connaught, three of the most prestigious hotels in the world.

Being in sales is the most rewarding, but can also be the most illusory, of hospitality jobs. To many, being in the sales department means having a very cushy job. After all, we do enter through the front doors and are seen entertaining over lunches and cocktail receptions, but what isn't so obvious are the hours of researching new businesses, countless hours of telephone calls to qualify possible leads, and the pressure of exceeding revenue numbers that are set each month, each quarter, each year. I believe a close comparison can be made between sales and childbirth: Once it all comes together and you are holding a beautifully signed deal in your hands and your client is happy and smiling at you, you quickly forget about the heartache that came along the way . . . what a blessing it is! Although most of us chose this field because we have a desire to serve people and work creatively, it is a business like any other. I feel Mr. Henry Ford said it best, "A business absolutely devoted to service will have only one worry about profits. They will be embarrassingly large."[12] During these recent economic times, it is amazing the swing of successful hotels and those in financial struggle. They aren't located in different cities, they aren't vastly different in size, they are evenly matched in product, but they are indescribably different in their service delivery.

to just be efficient; management is also about being effective. **Effectiveness** is "doing the right thing." As an example, cooks do the right thing when they cook the food correctly according to the recipe and have it ready when needed.

Who Are Managers?

The changing nature of organizations and work has, in many hospitality organizations, blurred the lines of distinction between managers and nonmanagerial employees. Many traditional jobs now include managerial activities, especially when teams are used. For instance, team members often develop plans, make decisions, and monitor their own performance. This is the case with total quality management.

So, how do we define who managers are? A manager is someone who works with and manages others' activities to accomplish organizational goals in an efficient and effective way. Managers are often classified into three levels: **frontline managers** are the lowest-level managers; they manage the work of line employees. They may also be called supervisors. A front-office supervisor, for example, takes charge of a shift and supervises the guest service agents on the shift.

Middle managers are akin to department heads; they fall between frontline managers and top management. They are responsible for short- to medium-range plans, and they establish goals and objectives to meet these goals. They manage the work of frontline managers.

Top managers are responsible for making medium- to long-range plans and for establishing goals and strategies to meet those goals. Figure 4 shows the three levels of management plus nonmanagerial employees.

Key Management Functions

The key management functions are planning, organizing, decision making, communicating, human resources and motivating, and controlling. These management functions are not conducted in isolation; rather, they are interdependent and frequently happen simultaneously or at least overlap. Figure 5 shows the key management functions leading to goal accomplishment.

Hospitality companies exist to serve a particular purpose, and someone has to determine the vision, mission, and strategies to reach or exceed the goals. That someone is management. The **planning** function involves setting the company's goals and developing plans to meet or exceed those goals. Once plans are complete, **organizing** is undertaken to decide what needs to be done, who will

Top Managers
Middle Managers
Front-line Managers
Nonmanagerial Associates

Figure 4 • Three Levels of Management Plus Nonmanagerial Associates.

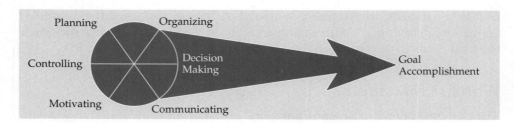

Figure 5 • Key Management Functions Leading to Goal Accomplishment.

do it, how the tasks will be grouped, who reports to whom, and who makes decisions.

Decision making is a key management function. The success of all hospitality companies, whether large, multinational corporations or sole proprietorships, depends on the quality of the decision making. Decision making includes determining the vision, mission, goals, and objectives of the company. Decision making also includes scheduling employees, determining what to put on the menu, and responding to guest needs.

Communication with and motivation of individuals and groups are required to get the job done. **Human resources and motivating** involves attracting and retaining the best employees and keeping morale high.

Controlling is the final management function that brings everything full circle. After the goals are set and the plans formulated, management then organizes, communicates, and motivates the resources required to complete the job. Controlling includes the setting of standards and comparing actual results with these standards. If significant deviations are seen, they are investigated and corrective action is taken to get performance back on target. This scientific process of monitoring, comparing, and correcting is the controlling function and is necessary to ensure that there are no surprises and that no one is guessing what should be done.

Managerial Skills

In addition to the management functions of forecasting, planning, organizing, communicating, motivating, and controlling, managers also need other major skills: conceptual, interpersonal, and technical.

Conceptual skills enable top managers to view the corporation as a complete entity and yet understand how it is split into departments to achieve specific goals. Conceptual skills allow a top manager to view the entire corporation, especially the interdependence of the various departments.

Managers need to lead, influence, communicate, supervise, coach, and evaluate employees' performances. This necessitates a high level of interpersonal human skills. The abilities to build teams and work with others are human skills that successful managers need to cultivate.

Managers need to have the technical skills required to understand and use modern techniques, methods, equipment, and procedures. These skills are more important for lower levels of management. As a manager rises through the

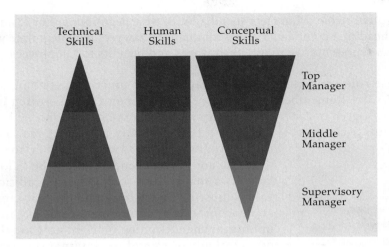

Figure 6 • Management Skill Areas Required by Management Level.

ranks, the need for technical skills decreases and the need for conceptual skills increases.

You next need to realize the critical importance of the corporate philosophy, culture, and values, and of a corporation's mission, goals, and objectives. Figure 6 shows the degree of managerial skills required by top managers, middle managers, and supervisory managers.

The Manager's Changing Role

Managers may still have subordinates, but today's successful manager takes more of a team leader/coach approach. There are, of course, other ways to "slice and dice" what managers do. For example, managers don't just plan, organize, make decisions, communicate, motivate, and control. They wear a variety of hats, including the following:

- *Figurehead role.* Every manager spends some time performing ceremonial duties. For example, the president of a corporation might have to greet important business guests or clients or represent the corporation by attending dinners.

- *Leader role.* Every manager should be a leader, coaching, motivating, and encouraging employees.

- *Liaison role.* Managers spend a lot of time in contact with people in other departments both within the organization and externally. An example would be the sales manager liaising with the rooms division director.

- *Spokesperson role.* The manager is often the spokesperson for the organization. For example, a manager may host a college class visit to the property.

- *Negotiator role.* Managers spend a lot of time negotiating. For example, the head of a company along with qualified lawyers may negotiate with a union representative to establish wages and benefits for employees.

These roles, together with the management functions, encompass what managers do. Remember, managers need to be many things—often in quick succession—even to the point of wearing two or more hats at once.

Twenty-first-century managers face not only a more demanding and increasingly complex world, but also a more dynamic and interdependent one. The "global village" is a reality, and sociocultural traditions and values must be understood and diversity respected and encouraged by future managers. The two most important changes going on right now are the technological advances and the internationalization of hospitality and tourism. The extent to which you as a future **leader/manager** can master these events and functions will determine your future.

The manager's role is not only internal but also external. For instance, a manager must be responsive to market needs and income generation. Managers must continually strive to be innovative by realizing efficiencies in their respective areas of responsibility through process improvement—for example, by determining how to reduce long check-in lines at airports and hotels. Some companies use innovative and creative ways to streamline the check-in procedures to make the process a more worthwhile experience for the guests. Disney, for instance, uses the creative approach of sending Mickey and the gang to entertain the guests while they stand in line.

A General Manager's Survival Kit

Ali Kasiki is a top-level manager at the Peninsula Beverly Hills, California. He holds the title of managing director and is involved in creating and implementing broad and comprehensive changes that affect the entire organization. Ali offers his list of tips:

- Know yourself, your own core competencies, and your values.
- Hire a seasoned management team.
- Build barriers of entry; that is, make yourself indispensable.
- Be very flexible.

You, Too, Are a Manager

Your classmates have just voted you to be the leader/manager of the summer study-abroad trip to France. None of you knows much about France or how to get there, what to do when you get there, and so on. Where would you start? (Resist the temptation to delegate the whole trip to a travel agent, please.)

You might start by thinking through what you need to do in terms of planning, organizing, deciding, communicating, motivating, and controlling. What sort of plans will you need? Among other things, you'll need to plan the dates your group will be leaving and returning, the cities and towns you'll visit, the airline you'll take there and back, how the group will get around France, and where you'll stay when you're there. As you can imagine, plans like these are very important: You would not want to arrive at Orly Airport with a group of friends who are depending on you and not know what to do next.

Realizing how much work is involved—and that you cannot do it all and still maintain good grades—you get help. You divide up the work and create an organization by asking someone to check airline schedules and prices, another person to check hotel prices, and someone else to research the sights to see and the transportation needs. However, the job won't get done with the group members simply working by themselves. Each person requires guidance and coordination from you: The person making the airline bookings can't confirm the bookings unless she knows in what city and airport the trip will originate. Similarly, the person making the hotel arrangements can't make any firm bookings until he knows what cities are being visited. To improve communications, you could set up regular meetings, with e-mail updates between meetings. Leadership and motivation could be a challenge because two of the group members do not get along well. So, ensuring that everyone stays focused and positive will be a challenge.

Of course, you'll have to make sure the whole project remains in control. If something can go wrong, it often will, and that's certainly the case when groups of people are traveling together. Everything needs to be double-checked. In other words, managing is something managers do almost every day, often without even knowing it.

Source: Adapted from Gary Dessler, *A Framework for Management* (Upper Saddle River, NJ: Prentice Hall, 2002) 8.

- Get close to your guests and owners to define reality versus perception.
- Show leadership, from both the top and the bottom.
- Delegate. There is no way you can survive without delegation.
- Appeal to trends.
- Trust your instincts.
- Take risks and change the ground rules.
- Don't become overconfident.
- Look successful, or people will think you're not.
- Manage the future—it is the best thing you can do. Bring the future to the present.[13]

Sustainable Leadership

Sustainable leadership is individual leadership that benefits the long-term good of society by positively influencing people, creating change, and demonstrating values that support the highest principles of society.[14]

The United Nations has developed a blueprint for Corporate Sustainability Leadership. The blueprint has four parts under the following headings:[15]

1. Global Compact
   a. Full coverage and Integration across principals
   b. Robust management policies and procedures
   c. Mainstreaming into corporate functions and business units
   d. Value chain implementation

2. Tracking action in support of broader UN goals and issues
   a. Core business contributions to UN goals and issues
   b. Strategic social investments and philanthropy
   c. Advocacy and public policy engagement
   d. Partnership and collective action

3. Engaging with UN global compact
   a. Local network and subsidiary engagement
   b. Global and local networking groups
   c. Issue-based and sector indicatives
   d. Promotion and support of the UN global compact

4. The cross-cutting components
   a. CEO commitment and leadership
   b. Broad adoption and oversight
   c. Stakeholder engagement
   d. Transparency and disclosure

Many business leaders, including hospitality ones, are becoming increasingly more concerned about sustainability. Not only are they concerned about the environment but also social responsibility. Leaders and managers need to steer the organization on a path of sustainability for all associates to follow.

If leaders stress the importance of sustainability then others will follow. Sustainability does not happen by itself; it needs leaders to promote it. From cities that do not allow styrofoam food containers to reducing water, paper, and electric consumption it all comes together when leaders focus on sustainability in all the key result areas of their operations.

Distinction Between Leadership and Management

Managing is the formal process in which organizational objectives are achieved through the efforts of subordinates. *Leading* is the process by which a person with vision is able to influence the behavior of others in some desired way. Although managers have power by virtue of the positions they hold, organizations seek managers who are leaders by virtue of their personalities, their experience, and so on. The differences between management and leadership can be illustrated as follows:

Managers

- Work in the system
- React
- Control risks
- Enforce organizational rules
- Seek and then follow direction
- Control people by pushing them in the right direction
- Coordinate effort

Leaders

- Work on the system
- Create opportunities
- Seek opportunities
- Change organizational rules
- Provide a vision to believe in and strategic alignment
- Motivate people by satisfying basic human needs
- Inspire achievement and energize people[16]

▶ Check Your Knowledge

1. What is management and what are the three management skill areas?

2. Explain levels of management.

3. Describe the key management functions.

4. What is the distinction between leadership and management?

Ethics

Ethics is a set of moral principles and values that people use to answer questions about right and wrong. Because ethics is also about our personal value system, there are people with value systems different from ours. Where did the value system originate? What happens if one value system is different from another? Fortunately, certain universal guiding principles are agreed on by virtually all religions, cultures, and societies. The foundation of all principles is that all people's rights are important and should not be violated. This belief is central to civilized societies; without it, chaos would reign.

Today, people have few moral absolutes; they decide situationally whether it is acceptable to steal, lie, or drink and drive. They seem to think that whatever is right is what works best for the individual. In a country blessed with so many diverse cultures, you might think it is impossible to identify common standards of ethical behavior. However, among sources from many different times and places, such as the Bible, Aristotle's *Ethics*, William Shakespeare's *King Lear*, the Koran, and the *Analects* of Confucius, you'll find the following basic moral values: integrity, respect for human life, self-control, honesty, and courage. Cruelty is wrong. All the world's major religions support a version of the Golden Rule: Do unto others as you would have them do unto you.[17]

In the foreword to *Ethics in Hospitality Management*, edited by Stephen S. J. Hall,[18] Dean Emeritus of Cornell University, Robert A. Beck poses this question: "Is overbooking hotel rooms and airline seats ethical? How does one compare the legal responsibilities of the innkeeper and the airline manager to the moral obligation?" He also asks, What is a fair or reasonable wage? A fair or reasonable return on investment? Is it fair or ethical to underpay employees for the benefit of investors?

English Common Law, on which American law is based, left such decisions to the "reasonable man." A judge would ask the jury, "Was this the act of a reasonable man?" Interestingly, what is considered ethical in one country may not be in another. For instance, in some countries, it is considered normal to bargain for room rates; in others, bargaining would be considered bad form.

Ethics and morals have become an integral part of hospitality decisions, from employment (equal opportunity and affirmative action) to truth in menus. Many corporations and businesses have developed a code of ethics that all employees use to make decisions. This became necessary because too many managers were making decisions without regard for the impact of such decisions on others. Stephen Hall is one of the pioneers of ethics in hospitality; he has developed a code of ethics for the hospitality and tourism industry, as follows:

1. We acknowledge ethics and morality as inseparable elements of doing business and will test every decision against the highest standards of honesty, legality, fairness, impunity, and conscience.

2. We will conduct ourselves personally and collectively at all times so as to bring credit to the hospitality and tourism industry.

3. We will concentrate our time, energy, and resources on the improvement of our own products and services and we will not denigrate our competition in the pursuit of our success.

4. We will treat all guests equally regardless of race, religion, nationality, creed, or sex.

5. We will deliver all standards of service and product with total consistency to every guest.

6. We will provide a totally safe and sanitary environment at all times for every guest and employee.

7. We will strive constantly, in words, actions, and deeds, to develop and maintain the highest level of trust, honesty, and understanding among guests, clients, employees, employers, and the public at large.

8. We will provide every employee at every level all the knowledge, training, equipment, and motivation required to perform his or her tasks according to our published standards.

9. We will guarantee that every employee at every level will have the same opportunity to perform, advance, and be evaluated against the same standard as all employees engaged in the same or similar tasks.

10. We will actively and consciously work to protect and preserve our natural environment and natural resources in all that we do.

11. We will seek a fair and honest profit, no more, no less.[19]

As you can see, it is vitally important for future hospitality and tourism professionals to abide by this code. The following sections present some ethical dilemmas in hospitality. What do you think about them?

Ethical Dilemmas in Hospitality

Previously, certain actions may not have been considered ethical, but management often looked the other way. A few scenarios follow that are not seen as ethical today and are against most companies' ethical policies:

1. As catering manager of a large banquet operation, the flowers for the hotel are booked through your office. The account is worth $15,000 per month.

A florist offers you a 10-percent kickback to book the account with him. Given that your colleague at a sister hotel in the same company receives a good bonus and you do not, despite having a better financial result, do you accept the kickback? If so, with whom do you share it?

2. As purchasing agent for a major hospitality organization, you are responsible for purchasing $5 million worth of perishable and nonperishable items. To get your business, a supplier, whose quality and price are similar to others, offers you a new automobile. Do you accept?

3. An order has come from the corporate office that guests from a certain part of the world may only be accepted if the reservation is taken from the embassy of the countries. One Sunday afternoon, you are duty manager and several limos with people from "that part of the world" request rooms for several weeks. You decline, even though there are available rooms. They even offer you a personal envelope, which they say contains $1,000. How do you feel about declining their request?

Trends in Leadership and Management

- Many leaders will be leading a more diverse group of associates.
- Many entry-level employees will not have basic job skills.
- There will be an increasing need for training.
- There will be a need to create leaders out of line managers.
- Leaders will need to manage sales revenue all the way to the bottom line.
- Independent business units will be established to make their own profit, or that department will be subcontracted out.
- Instead of keeping a person on payroll for a function that is only needed occasionally, that service will be outsourced to specialists.
- The amount of full-time employees will be cut and more part-time employees will be hired to avoid paying benefits.
- Keeping up with technological advances and their benefits will be an increasing challenge.
- Social and environmental issues will continue to increase in importance.
- A greater emphasis will be placed on ethics.

CASE STUDY

Performance Standards

Charles and Nancy both apply for the assistant front-office manager position at a 300-room upscale hotel. Charles has worked for a total of eight years in three different hotels and has been with this hotel for three months as a front-office associate. Initially, he had a lot of enthusiasm. Lately, however, he has been dressing a bit sloppily and his figures, cash, and reports have been inaccurate. In addition, he is occasionally rattled by demanding guests.

Nancy recently graduated from college with honors, with a degree in hospitality management. While attending college, she worked part-time as a front desk associate at a budget motel. Nancy does not have a lot of experience working in a hotel or in customer service in general, but she is quite knowledgeable as a result of her studies and is eager to begin her career.

It appears that Charles would be considered a prime candidate for the office manager position because of his extensive experience in other hotels and his knowledge of the hotel's culture. In view of his recent performance, however, the rooms division manager will need to sit down with Charles to review his future career development track.

Discussion Questions

1. What are the qualifications for the job that should be considered for both applicants?
2. How should the discussion between the rooms division manager and Charles be handled? Make specific recommendations for the rooms division manager.
3. Who would be the better person for the job? Why?

CASE STUDY

Reluctant to Change

You have just been appointed assistant manager at an old, established, but busy, New York restaurant. Your employees respond to your suggested changes with "We have always done it this way." The employees really do not know any other way of doing things.

Discussion Question

1. How should you handle this situation?

Summary

1. Leadership is defined as the process by which a person is able to influence the activities and outcomes of others in a desired way.
2. Contemporary leadership includes transactional and transformational types of leadership.
3. Increased demands placed on hospitality leaders include ownership, corporate, regulatory, employee, environmental, and social interests. Leaders must balance results and relationships.
4. Managing is the process of coordinating work activities so that they are completed efficiently and effectively with and through other people.
5. Leaders, according to Peter Drucker, realize four things and behave in much the same way.
   a. A leader is someone who has followers— some people are thinkers, and some are prophets.
   b. An effective leader is not someone who is loved or admired, but rather someone whose followers do the right things. Popularity is not leadership; results are.
   c. Leaders are highly visible. Leaders set examples.
   d. Leadership is not about rank, privileges, titles, or money. It is about responsibility.
6. There are six key management functions: planning, organizing, decision making, communicating, motivating, and controlling. However, in addition to these functions, managers occasionally have to fill roles such as figurehead, leader, spokesperson, and negotiator.
7. The difference between management and leadership is that the former is the formal process in which organization objectives are achieved through the efforts of subordinates, and the latter is the process by which a person with vision is able to influence the behavior of others in some desired way.

Key Words and Concepts

communication
controlling
decision making
effectiveness
efficiency
ethics
frontline managers
human resources and motivating
leader/manager

leadership
management
managing
middle managers
organizing
planning
top managers
transactional leadership
transformational leadership

Review Questions

1. What kind of leader/manager will you be?
2. Give examples of the management functions as they apply to the hospitality industry.
3. Discuss the changing role of managers.
4. Define leadership and name the essential qualities of a good leader.
5. Distinguish between transactional and transformational leadership.

Internet Exercises

1. Organization: **WetFeet.com**
   Web site: **www.wetfeet.com**
   Summary: WetFeet.com is an organization dedicated to helping you make smarter career decisions. WetFeet.com provides inside understanding of jobs and careers for both job seekers and recruiters. By all means, take the time to check this one out! Click on "Careers & Industries" at the bottom of the page and scroll down to "General Management" under "Careers." Answer the following questions.

   (a) What are the requirements for becoming a GM, and what tips does WetFeet.com have to offer?

   (b) The "General Management" section illustrates several attributes that managers have in common. In groups, list these attributes and discuss their significance.

2. Organization: **American Management Association**
   Web site: **www.amanet.org**
   Summary: The American Management Association (AMA), a practitioner-based organization, offers a wide range of management development programs for managers and organizations.
   Find the section titled "Articles and White Papers." Choose two current reports on leadership. Read through these and make a bullet list of the key information. Then, write a description of how this information might affect the way a hospitality manager plans, organizes, makes decisions, communicates, motivates, and controls.

3. Organization: **Ritz-Carlton Hotel Company**
   Web site: **http://corporate.ritzcarlton.com/en/ Default.htm**
   Summary: Ritz-Carlton hotels are known for their superior luxury and service in the hospitality industry. This particular Web exercise illustrates how Ritz-Carlton maintains its culture of service excellence. Take a look at the Ritz-Carlton Leadership Center. Click on "Leadership Center." Now answer the following questions:

   (a) What kinds of courses does the Leadership Center offer?

   (b) **What are the seven habits of highly effective people?**

Apply Your Knowledge

Your resort has management vacancies for the following positions: executive chef, executive housekeeper, and front-office manager. List the traits and characteristics that you consider essential and desirable for these positions.

Suggested Activity

Think of someone you admire as a leader. Make a list of the qualities that make him or her a good leader.

Endnotes

1. For a more detailed review of the many leadership theories, consult one of the many texts on the topic.
2. Horst Schultz, Presentation to the University of South Florida School of Hotel and Restaurant Management, March 26, 2005.
3. Ibid.
4. West Paces Hotel Group, *Philosophy*, http://www.capellahotelgroup.com/?corp (accessed November 26, 2011).
5. West Paces Hotel Group, *Home Page*, http://www.capellahotelgroup.com/?corp (accessed November 26, 2011).
6. Jay R. Schrock, Presentation to University of South Florida students and faculty, May 2, 2005.
7. Vernon Saunders Law, Major League Baseball player. http://www.boardofwisdom.com/default.asp?topic=10 05&listname=Learning retrieved Jaunary 1, 2012.
8. Adapted from Peter F. Drucker, "Foreword," in *The Leader of the Future*, ed. F. Hesselbein, et al., xii–xiii (San Francisco: Josey-Bass, 1996).
9. George Ambler, "Peter Drucker on Effective Leadership," *The Practice of Leadership*, Aug. 6, 2006, http://www.thepracticeofleadership.net/ peter-drucker-on-effective-leadership (accessed November 27, 2011).
10. Drucker, "Foreword," ix.
11. Stephen P. Robbins and Mary Coulter, Management 9th ed., Pearson, Upper Saddle River, NJ: 2007. P. 7.
12. BrainyQuote, *Henry Ford Quotes*, http://www.brainyquote.com/quotes/quotes/h/ henryford151873.html (accessed November 28, 2011).
13. Personal correspondence with Ali Kasiki, August 4, 2005.
14. http://www.highlandconsultinggroupinc.com/ programs/sustainable.html retrieved November 17, 2001.
15. http://www.unglobalcompact.org/docs/news_ events/8.1/Blueprint.pdf retrieved on November 19, 2011.
16. Vadim Kotelnikov, *Ten3 Business e-Coach*, version 2005a, http://www.1000ventures.com/business_guide/ crosscuttings/e_coach.html.
17. Religious Tolerance, *Shared Belief in the "Golden Rule" (a/k.a. Ethics of Reciprocity)*, http://www.religioustolerance.org/reciproc.htm (accessed November 28, 2011).
18. Stephen S. Hall, ed., *Ethics in Hospitality Management: A Book of Readings* (East Lansing, MI: Educational Institute, American Hotel & Lodging Association, 1992), 75.
19. Hall, *Ethics in Hospitality Management*, 108.

Glossary

Control   The provision of information to management for decision-making purposes. The process of monitoring activities to ensure that they are being accomplished as planned and of correcting any significant deviations.

Effectiveness   Completing activities so that organizational goals are attained; also referred to as "doing the right things" or "getting things done."

Efficiency   Getting the most output from the smallest amount of inputs; also referred to as "doing things right" or "getting things done well."

Ethics   The study of standards of conduct and moral judgment; also, the standards of correct conduct.

Frontline manager/supervisor   A low-level manager who manages the work of line employees and has guest contact.

Leader-manager   An individual whose duties combine the functions of leadership and management.

Leadership   The influence of one person over another to work willingly toward a predetermined objective.

Management   The process of coordinating work activities so that an organization's objectives are achieved efficiently and effectively with and through other people.

Middle manager   A manager between the first-line level and the top level of the organization who manages the work of first-line managers.

Planning   The process of defining the organization's goals, establishing an overall strategy for achieving those goals, and developing a comprehensive set of plans to integrate and coordinate organizational work.

Top manager   A manager at or near the top level of the organization who is responsible for making organization-wide decisions and establishing the goals and plans that affect the entire organization.

Transactional leadership   A type of leadership that focuses on accomplishing the tasks at hand and on maintaining good working relationships by exchanging promises of rewards for performance.

Transformational leadership   A type of leadership that involves influencing major changes in the attitudes and assumptions of organization members and building commitment for the organization's mission, objectives, and strategies.

Photo Credits

Tourism

Tourism

OBJECTIVES

After reading and studying this chapter, you should be able to:

- Define tourism.
- Outline the important international and domestic tourism organizations.
- Describe the economic impact of tourism.
- Identify promoters of tourism.
- List reasons why people travel.
- Describe the sociocultural impact of tourism.
- Describe ecotourism.

Highlights of Tourism

It is difficult to determine when tourism began because, centuries ago, very few people traveled for pleasure or business as they do today. We do know the following:

- In the fourth century B.C. (before Christ), work started on the Great Wall of China and continued for centuries until the1600s. Although not exactly a tourist destination or attraction back then, it certainly is today.

- In 776 B.C., athletic games were held on the plain of Olympia in Greece (the modern Olympic Games were inspired by these games), and presumably people traveled there to participate or to watch.

- The Romans liked to visit the Bay of Naples, so they built a road there from Rome in 312 A.D. (*anno Domini*, after Christ). The road was 100 miles long and took four days by litter to get there (in which a nobleperson sat on a platform and was carried by some unfortunate servants).

- Religious pilgrimages to Rome and the Holy Land (now Israel) began in the 1200s, so inns sprang up to feed and accommodate the pilgrims.

- Marco Polo became the first noted European business traveler as he pioneered trade routes from Europe to China from 1275 to 1292, staying at primitive inns called *khans* along the way.

- In the 1600s, during the age of horse-drawn coach travel in England, posthouses were set up to feed and shelter travelers and change the teams of horses every few miles. The journey from London to Bristol took three days—it now takes less than three hours by rail.

- In 1841, Thomas Cook organized a group tour for 570 people to a religious meeting in England.

- Cruising began in the 1840s with the Cunard Lines crossing the Atlantic between England and North America.

- In the 1840s, the Peninsula and Oriental Steam Navigation Company (P&O) cruised the Mediterranean.

- In the 1850s, Monaco (a principality in the south of France) decided to cure its economic woes by becoming a winter haven for the rich as a health resort and a casino.

- During the age of the grand tour, from 1880 through the 1930s, wealthy Europeans toured Europe as a part of their education.

- Rail travel began in the 1800s.

- Auto travel began in the 1900s.

- Air travel began in the 1900s.

- American Airlines introduced its first transcontinental flight between New York and Los Angeles in 1959.

- In 1970, the Boeing 747 began flying 450 passengers at a time across the Atlantic and Pacific Oceans.

- In the 1970s, ecotourism and sustainable tourism became important topics.

- In the 1980s, cruising became popular.

- In 1986, the United States established the Visa Waiver Program to eliminate unnecessary barriers to travel to the United States. Currently, thirty-six countries are part of the program.

- In the 2000s, tourism temporarily declined as a result of the September 11 attacks, severe acute respiratory syndrome (SARS), bird flu, and war. However, tourism is projected to grow at a rate of between 3.0 and 3.5 percent a year, according to the World Travel & Tourism Council.[1]

- In 2008, there were over 922 million international tourist arrivals, but as a result of the 2007–2010 recession, tourism was down 4 percent in 2009. However, it was expected to rise in 2010–2012.[2]

International tourism arrivals grew by almost 5 percent in the first half of 2011, consolidating the nearly 7-percent growth rate from 2010.[3]

What Is Tourism?

Tourism is a dynamic, evolving, consumer-driven force and is the world's largest industry, or collection of industries, when all its interrelated components are placed under one umbrella: tourism, travel; lodging; conventions, expositions, meetings, and events; restaurants and managed services; assembly, destination, and event management; and recreation. Tourism plays a foundational role in framing the various services that hospitality companies perform.

The leading international organization in the field of travel and tourism, the **World Tourism Organization (UNWTO)** is vested by the United Nations with a central and decisive role in promoting the development of responsible, sustainable, and universally accessible tourism, with the aim of contributing to economic development, international understanding, peace, prosperity, and universal respect for and observance of human rights and fundamental freedoms. In pursuing this aim, the organization pays particular attention to the interests of the developing countries in the field of tourism. The UNWTO's definition of tourism is, "Tourism comprises the activities of persons traveling to and staying in places outside their usual environment for not more than one consecutive year for leisure, business, and other purposes."[4]

The UNWTO plays a catalytic role in promoting technology transfers and international cooperation, stimulating and developing public–private-sector partnerships, and encouraging the implementation of the Global Code of Ethics for Tourism. The UNWTO is dedicated to ensuring that member countries, tourist destinations, and businesses maximize the positive economic, social, and cultural effects of tourism and fully reap its benefits, while minimizing its negative social and environmental impacts. Francesco Frangialli, secretary-general of the UNWTO from 1998 to 2008, writes:

The Global Code of Ethics for Tourism sets a frame of reference for the responsible and sustainable development of world tourism. It draws inspiration from many similar declarations and industry codes that have come before and it adds new thinking that reflects our changing society at the beginning of the 21st century.

With international tourism forecast to reach 1.6 billion arrivals by 2020, members of the World Tourism Organization believe that the Global Code of Ethics for Tourism is needed to help minimize the negative impacts of tourism on the environment and on cultural heritage while maximizing the benefits for residents of tourism destinations. The Global Code of Ethics for Tourism is intended to be a living document. Read it. Circulate it widely. Participate in its implementation. Only with your cooperation can we safeguard the future of the tourism industry and expand the sector's contribution to economic prosperity, peace and understanding among all the nations of the world.[5]

Through tourism, the UNWTO aims to stimulate economic growth and job creation, to provide incentives for protecting the environment and cultural heritage, and to promote peace, prosperity, and respect for human rights. Membership includes 154 countries, 7 territories, and some 400 affiliate members representing the private sector, educational institutions, tourism associations, and local tourism authorities.[6] Unfortunately, the United States is not a member, but it may soon be.

The UNWTO and the World Travel and Tourism Council (WTTC) declare the travel and tourism industry to have the following characteristics:

- A 24-hour-a-day, 7-day-week, 52-week-a-year economic driver
- Total contribution to world gross domestic product (GDP) of 9.1 percent
- Employer of 259 million people, or 8.8 percent of the global workforce, and is expected to be responsible for about 1 in 10 jobs by 2021[7]
- Leading producer of tax revenues

Given declining manufacturing and agricultural industries, and in many countries the consequent rise in unemployment, world leaders should turn to the service industries for real strategic employment gains. For many developing nations, tourism represents a large percentage of gross national product and a way of gaining a positive balance of trade with other nations.

Waikiki Beach is a popular tourist destination.

▶ Check Your Knowledge

1. What role does the UNWTO play in the tourism industry?
2. Describe the characteristics of tourism.
3. How is tourism sometimes categorized?

Benefits of Tourism

Tourism is firmly established as the number-one industry in many countries and the fastest-growing economic sector in terms of foreign exchange earnings and job creation. International tourism is the world's largest export earner and an important factor in the balance of payments of most nations.

Tourism has become one of the world's most important sources of employment. It stimulates enormous investment in infrastructure, most of which helps to improve the living conditions of residents as well as tourists. It provides governments with substantial tax revenues. Most new tourism jobs and businesses are created in the developing countries, helping to equalize economic opportunities and keep rural residents from moving to overcrowded cities. Intercultural awareness and personal friendships fostered through tourism are powerful forces for improving international understanding and contributing to peace among all the nations of the world.

The UNWTO encourages governments, in partnership with the private sector, local authorities, and nongovernmental organizations, to play a vital role in tourism. The UNWTO helps countries throughout the world to maximize the positive impacts of tourism, while minimizing its possible negative consequences on the environment and societies.[8] Tourism is a collection of industries, or segments, that when combined, form the world's largest industry. Tourism offers the greatest global employment prospects. This trend is caused by the following factors:

1. The opening of borders: Despite security concerns, we can travel to more countries now than ten years ago. The United States has a Visa Waiver Program with thirty-six European countries, meaning citizens of these countries with machine-readable passports do not require a visa to visit the United States.

2. An increase in disposable income and vacation taking

3. Reasonably affordable airfares

4. An increase in the number of people with more time and money to travel

5. More people with the urge to travel

According to the WTTC—the industry's business leaders' forum—tourism and travel generate, directly and indirectly, 9.1 percent of global GDP, investment, and employment.[9] The industry is forecast to grow strongly in real terms during the next ten years. This means growth in jobs in the United States and abroad.

Long-Term Prospects: Tourism 2020 Vision[10]

Despite the terrorist attacks and a weak economic recovery, the long-term prospects for tourism appear to be good. *Tourism: 2020 Vision* is the UNWTO's long-term forecast and assessment of the development of tourism for the first twenty years of the new millennium. An essential outcome of the *Tourism: 2020 Vision* is quantitative forecasts covering a twenty-five-year period, with 1995 as the base year and forecasts for 2000, 2010, and 2020 (Figure 1).

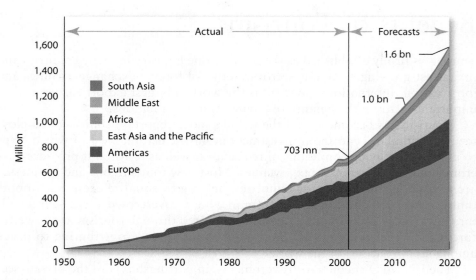

Figure 1 • Actual and Forecast Tourism Arrivals, 1950–2020.
(© UNWTO, 9284403211)

UNWTO's *Tourism Toward 2030* forecasts that international arrivals will hit 1.8 billion by the year 2030.

The total tourist arrivals by region show that by 2020 the top three receiving regions will be Europe (717 million tourists), East Asia and the Pacific (397 million), and the Americas (282 million), followed by Africa, the Middle East, and South Asia.

The fact that tourism is expected to grow rapidly presents both tremendous opportunities and challenges. The good news is the variety of exciting career prospects for today's hospitality and tourism graduates. Tourism, although a mature industry, is a young profession. Careful management of tourism and travel will be necessary to avoid repercussions and negativism toward the "pesky" tourist, which is already happening to some extent in Europe, where the sheer number of tourists overwhelms attractions and facilities.

There is an **interdependency** between the various segments of tourism, travel, lodging, foodservice, and recreation. Hotel guests need to travel to reach the hotel. They eat in nearby restaurants and visit attractions. Each segment is, to an extent, dependent on another for business.

The Five Ages of Tourism

The historical development of tourism has been divided into five distinct ages (or periods),[11] four of which paralleled the advent of a new means of transportation:

Pre–Industrial Revolution (prior to 1840)

The railway age

The automobile age

The jet aircraft age

The cruise ship age

Pre–Industrial Revolution

As early as 5,000 years ago, some ancient Egyptians sailed up and down the Nile River to visit and construct the pyramids. Probably the first journey ever made for the purposes of peace and tourism was made by Queen Hatshepsut to the Land of Punt (believed to be on the east coast of Africa) in 1480 B.C. Descriptions of this tour have been recorded on the walls of the temple of Deir el-Bahri at Luxor.[12] These texts and bas-reliefs are among the world's rarest artworks and are universally admired for their wondrous beauty and artistic qualities. The Colossi of Memnon at Thebes have on their pedestals the names of Greek tourists of the fifth century B.C.[13] The Phoenicians were among the first real travelers in any modern sense. In both the Mediterranean and the Orient (now called Southeast Asia), travel was motivated by trade. Later, the Roman Empire provided safe passage for travelers via a vast road system that stretched from Egypt to Britain. Wealthy Romans traveled to Egypt and Greece, to baths, shrines, and seaside resorts.[14] The Romans were as curious as are today's tourists. They visited the attractions of their time, trekking to Greek temples and places where Alexander the Great slept, Socrates lived, Ajax committed suicide, and Achilles was buried and to the pyramids, the Sphinx, and the Valley of the Kings—just as today's tourists do.[15] The excavated ruins of the Roman town Pompeii, which was buried by the volcanic eruption of Mount Vesuvius, revealed some twenty-plus restaurants, taverns, and inns that tourists visit even today.

The Hall of Supreme Harmony in Beijing's Forbidden City.

The earliest Olympic Games for which we still have written records were held in 776 B.C. (though it is generally believed that the games had been going on for many years before that).[16] Thus, sports have been a motivation for tourism for a long time.

Travel in the Middle Ages was mostly for religious or trade reasons. People made pilgrimages to various shrines: Muslims to Mecca and Christians to Jerusalem and Rome. The Crusades (which began in 1095 and lasted for the next two hundred years) stimulated a cultural exchange that was in part responsible for the Renaissance.

Marco Polo (1254–1324) traveled the Silk Road, which was anything but a road as we know it, from Venice to Beijing, China. He was the first European to journey all the way across Asia to Beijing, and his journey, which lasted twenty-four years, and the tales from it became the most well-known travelogue in the Western world.[17]

Marco Polo's father and uncle had traveled extensively in Asia before Marco joined them. The journey was both difficult and dangerous (excerpts of Marco's account can be read at several Marco Polo web sites). One time, to make sure the Polo brothers would be given every assistance on their travels, Kublai Khan presented them with a golden tablet (or *paiza*, in Chinese, *gerege*, in Mongolian) a foot long and three inches wide and inscribed with the words "By the strength of the eternal Heaven, holy be the Khan's name. Let him that pays him not reverence be killed." The golden tablet was a special VIP passport, authorizing the travelers to receive throughout the Great Khan's dominions such horses, lodging, food, and guides as they required.[18] This was an early form of passport.

▶ Check Your Knowledge

1. Describe the benefits of tourism.
2. How many arrivals are forecast for 2020?
3. What are the five ages of tourism?

Rail, Automobile, and Coach Travel

Changes in the technology of travel have had widespread implications for society. In the United States, rail travel influenced the building of towns and cities, caused hotels to be built near rail depots, and opened up the West, among other things. Likewise, auto travel produced the motel and a network of highways, and the commercial jet created destination resorts in formerly remote and exotic locations, made the rental car business a necessity, and changed the way we look at geography. Although long-distance travel has always been fairly comfortable for the wealthy, it was not until the development of the railroad in the 1830s that travel became comfortable and cheap enough to be within reach of the masses.

Traveling by Train

Coast to coast, the United States has a lot of land with a fair share of mountains, canyons, forests, deserts, rivers, and other natural barriers to travel. One of the main factors that led to the development of railroads in the United States was the need to move goods and people from one region of the country to another. Farmed goods needed to be transported to industrial areas, and people wanted a quicker route to the West, especially after the discovery of gold in California. Those who already lived at the frontier wanted the same conveniences as their neighbors in the East, such as efficient postal service.

The train made mass travel possible for everyone. Long-distance travel became both cheaper and faster, making the horse and ship seem like "overpriced snails." The vast rail networks across North America, Asia, Australia, and Europe made the train station a central part of nearly every community. Naturally, entrepreneurs soon built hotels conveniently close to train stations.

Although hugely important and popular for many years, the popularity of rail travel started to decline as early as the 1920s. Why did people stop using the train? For two main reasons: the bus and the car. In addition, the Great Depression of the 1930s certainly deterred travelers. Although World War II brought a new surge in passenger numbers, people were seldom traveling for pleasure, and at the close of the war, the decline continued. Automobiles were again available, and people had the money to buy them. By 1960, airplanes had taken over much of the long-distance travel market, further reducing the importance of the train.

Facing a possible collapse of passenger rail services, the U.S. Congress passed the Rail Passenger Service Act in 1970 (amended in 2001). Shortly after, the National Railroad Passenger Corporation began operation as a semipublic corporation established to operate intercity passenger trains, a move in the direction of semi-nationalization of U.S. railroads. The corporation is known today as Amtrak.

The aerodynamic Amtrak ACELA train speeding along between Washington, D.C., and New York City reaches its destination in 2 hours 45 minutes.

Rail Travel Abroad

While the United States tries to rejuvenate rail travel under the direction of Amtrak, rail service in other parts of the industrialized world is far ahead in progress. Taking the train makes good sense in densely populated areas such as those in Western Europe and parts of Asia, and high-speed networks are already well developed, often drawing most of the traffic that formerly went by air. One good example is the Eurostar, connecting the United Kingdom with mainland Europe via the thirty-one-mile-long underwater Channel Tunnel. France's TGV (Trains à Grande Vitesse) trains are perhaps the best known of them all, serving more than 150 cities in France and Europe, and traveling at about 186 mph (although they have the capacity of running at 250 mph). The TGV's most spectacular feature is the smoothness of the ride: It is like sitting in your armchair at home. Because of their importance, all trains—high speed or not—run frequently and on time. Fares are generally reasonable, and service levels are high.

Japan's Shinkansen, the bullet train system, makes the 550-mile run between Tokyo and Osaka in 3 hours and 10 minutes, down from the former rail time of 18 hours. In addition, it provides a ride so smooth that a passenger can rest a coffee cup on the windowsill and not a drop will spill, just like on the TGV.

Do you dream of exploring Europe? As a student, you have probably heard of the famous Eurail Pass. Several European nations have banded together to offer non-European visitors unlimited first-class rail service for a reduced lump-sum. However, if you want to use the Eurail Pass, be sure to purchase a pass before you leave home because not all types of passes are available in Europe and the ones that are cost on average 20 percent when bought in Europe. When visiting Europe, you can choose to travel in one country, in a few selected ones, or in all with Eurail Pass; it's up to you to choose between the different passes available. In other parts of the world, Australia offers the Australpass, India the Indrail Pass, Canada the Canrail Pass, and Canada and the United States the

North American Rail Pass. The new rail line in China linking Beijing to Nepal is of interest because it is one of the longest and highest rail lines in the world, and, according to some, it is going to dilute the Tibetan culture. This is one of the dilemmas of tourism: Travel and tourism can bring an economic and social development, yet it can also damage local cultures and environments.

TECHNOLOGY SPOTLIGHT

Use of the Internet for Travel

Cihan Cobanoglu, Ph.D., Dean, School of Hotel and Restaurant Management, University of South Florida, Sarasota-Manatee

Advances in information technology have made a significant impact on all parties involved in tourism industry: tourism organization, travelers, transportation companies, and travel destinations.

Development of the Internet and online booking systems has drastically changed travel agents' operations. From working with huge price catalogs, calling for seats and room availability, and faxing reservations, travel agents have moved to online reservation systems that allow convenient access to information and instant updates. All these became available due to the invention of Global Distribution Systems (GDSs). Originally, these systems were developed by airline companies to enable bookings among different airline companies. Later, they were also extended to hotels and car-rental companies. The most popular GDSs are Amadeus, Sabre, Galileo, Worldspan, and Travel Sky (a new GDS that is emerging in China). For example, more than 30,000 travel agents use Sabre and nearly 75,000 use Amadeus. GDSs provide travel agents with rapid search, booking, and confirmation facilities for airline, hotel, and car-hire products. In hospitality, GDSs are dependent on modern hotel Central Reservation Systems (CRSs), which provide full details of hotel properties, locations, room types, availability, prices, and booking conditions. If a hotel wants to make its inventory available to numerous customers and travel agents all around the world, it needs to interface its CRS to one (or several) GDSs. This interface can be done by means of a switch company, for example, Pegasus Solutions. The Internet also gave rise to online travel agencies (OTAs) such as Expedia and Travelocity. OTAs are an electronic overlay of GDSs. These sites may focus on travel reviews, online bookings, and providing relevant information to customers. There are three major OTA business models: merchant (net rate, for example, Expedia), agency (commission, for example, Booking.com), and opaque (for example, Priceline.com).

The development of information technology has greatly enhanced travelers' experience by increasing their access to information, their awareness, and the travel options available to them. Previously, travelers used to be dependent on travel agents in their search for vacation places and decision-making process. However, the extensive resources of the Internet today allow every traveler to be a travel agent on his or her own. On the Web, travelers can find information about millions of hotels, destinations, and things to do all over the world. Review web sites (for example, Tripadvisor.com) provide firsthand evaluation of hotels, destination, and attractions through the recording of people's experiences. These web sites have become one of the key forces in travel decision-making.

Airline companies have also greatly developed and improved their electronic systems in order to improve operations and customer service. As mentioned earlier, airlines were the initiators of the GDSs. Airline companies also developed comprehensive reservation systems that allow customers to create their accounts, select seating, and check in online, as well as customer relationship management (CRM) and loyalty systems. Recently, airlines introduced a new initiative by implementing electronic boarding passes. This pass is sent to a smartphone or personal digital assistant (PDA) of a traveler and does not require any printouts. This system is already available in select airports around the United States.

Traveling by Car

The internal combustion engine automobile was invented in Germany but quickly became America's obsession. In 1895, there were about 300 "horseless carriages" of one kind or another in the United States, including gasoline buggies, electric cars, and steam cars. In 1914, Henry Ford began making the Model T on the first modern assembly line, making the car available to many more Americans because of its lower cost. Even during the Great Depression, almost two-thirds of American families had automobiles. Henry Ford's development of the assembly line and construction of good, solid roads helped make the automobile the symbol of American life that it is today.

Rental cars offer business and leisure travelers the convenience of fly–drive or drive-only to facilitate tourists' needs.

The auto changed the American way of life, especially in the leisure area, creating and satisfying people's urge to travel. The automobile remains the most convenient and rapid form of transportation for short and medium distances. Without question, it has made Americans the most mobile people in history and has given them options not otherwise possible. Whereas many Europeans ride their bikes or use the bus or train to get to school or work, Americans cannot seem to function without their cars. In fact, it is not uncommon for an American to drive 20,000 miles a year.

Road trips are a must for most Americans—college students, families, and retirees alike. Travel by car is by far the largest of all segments in the ground transportation sector of the travel and tourism industry. It is no wonder, then, that the highways and byways of the United States and Canada play such important roles in tourism. The advantages of car travel are that the car brings you to places that are otherwise inaccessible. Mountain resorts, ski destinations, dude ranches, and remote beaches are just a few examples. This travel generates millions of dollars, and in certain places the local economy depends on the car tourist.

Rental Cars

Some 5,000 rental car companies operate in the United States. Waiting at nearly every sizable airport in the world are several highly competitive rental car agencies, a significant segment of the travel/tourism business. About 75 percent of their sales take place at airport counters that are leased from the airport, the cost of which is passed on to the customer. The larger companies do 50 percent or more of their business with large corporate accounts, accounts that receive sizable discounts under contract. The hurried business traveler is likely to rent a car, speed out of the airport, do his or her business in a day or two, return to the airport, and hop on a plane to return home. The pleasure traveler, however, is more likely to rent a small car for a week or more. This group constitutes about 30 percent of the rental car market. The top-five rental car companies in the United States are Hertz, Avis, Enterprise, National, and Budget. The agencies maintain approximately 625,000 rental cars that are usually new and are sold after six months to reduce maintenance costs and help avoid breakdowns.

Traveling by Bus

Although scheduled bus routes aren't as competitive as scheduled service for airlines, buses still play an important role in the travel and tourism industry, especially with regards to charter and tour services. Some bus companies even offer services such as destination management, incentive programs, and planning of meetings, events, and conferences. Some companies to check out are Gray Line Worldwide, Contiki Tours, and Canadian Tours International.

The major reasons for selecting the bus over other modes of travel are convenience and economy. Many passengers are adventurous college students from the United States and abroad or senior citizens, both with limited funds but plenty of time on their hands. Most people don't choose bus travel for long trips, however, because a flight is much quicker and often just as economical. However, in places such as the heavily populated northeast corridor, regular bus service between most sizable communities in New England and New York often makes it easier and safer for travelers to ride the bus than to drive their cars into the city. Anyone who has experienced New York City traffic will probably agree.

Another reason why buses are popular is because they allow the leisure traveler to sit back, relax, and enjoy the scenery. In addition, they are hassle free and provide an opportunity to make new friends and stop along the way. Long-distance buses offer a variety of amenities similar to an airplane, with an extra benefit of almost door-to-door service! Buses travel to small and large communities, bringing with them tourist dollars and thus a boost to the local economy.

Types of Bus Service

In addition to routes between towns and cities, bus travel includes local route service, charter service, tour service, special services, commuter service, airport service, and urban and rapid transit service. The largest and most recognized of all of the specialized travel services is Gray Line. Founded in 1910, Gray Line is a franchise operation based in Colorado. The company assembles package tours and customized tours, arranges rail and air transfers, and even provides meeting and convention services. Its major service, however, is sightseeing trips by bus. When a traveler arrives at a destination and wishes to see the town and the major tourist attractions, Gray Line is usually ready to serve. The 150-member organization carries about 28 million passengers a year at more than 200 destinations. Their trips are widely diversified, such as "around-the-town" in Paris and "around-the-country" in Thailand. In the United States, Gray Line's biggest market is Los Angeles, followed by San Francisco and then Manhattan.

▶ Check Your Knowledge

1. In what locations does rail travel make the most sense?

2. What is the future of rail travel?

3. Who are the major users of buses?

Airlines

Air travel has made it possible to build great resorts on remote islands, it has fostered multinational enterprises, and it has broadened the horizons of hundreds of millions of people. Without the airplane, most resort destinations would have been virtually impossible to build. The number of international travelers would be far fewer because of the time, money, and difficulty involved in travel. The airplane makes travel easier and more convenient because even the most remote location is just a few hours away by plane, and reasonable airfares make it possible for more people to travel by air.

Air transport has become an integral factor in the travel and tourism industry. Hotels, car rental agencies, and even cruise lines depend heavily on airplanes for profits. For instance, lower airfares result in more passengers and hence a higher occupancy at hotels. Whole towns and cities can and do benefit from this concept by receiving more taxes from tourists, which leads to better public facilities, better schools, and even lower local and property taxes.

In the United States, there are, at any one time, about 5,500 airplanes in the skies.[19] By 2012, total passenger traffic between the United States and the rest of the world is projected to reach 1 billion flights annually. In recent years, the airline has become the preferred means of travel for the long haul. The jet aircraft has made previously inaccessible places such as Bali, Boracay, and Bangkok easily accessible, for a reasonable price. Today millions of Americans travel within the United States and abroad, and millions more visit the United States because of air travel.

Over the past few years—with the exception of Southwest, AirTran, and JetBlue—major U.S. airlines have lost billions of dollars. One reason is competition from low-cost domestic and international airlines.

Since the economic recession, business travelers continue to spend less, and airlines' pension, fuel, and security costs have risen. The major airlines have laid off employees, delayed delivery of new jets, and closed some hubs, reservations, and maintenance centers in an effort to reduce costs. Several of the major U.S. airlines have been and are in financial trouble, so they are charging an additional fuel surcharge on tickets and charging for checked bags, food, beverages, and selected seats just so that they can stay in the air. Other strategies are needed to keep airlines viable.

For example, in efforts to promote passenger loyalty and operating effectiveness, the major U.S. airlines have formed strategic alliances with partner airlines to provide passengers with easier ticket purchases and transportation to destinations in countries not served by U.S. airlines. Many of the world's major airlines are grouped with either Star Alliance, Sky Team, or One World. Sky Team

American Airlines and its eleven One World partner airlines go just about anywhere. The One World partners include British Airways, Cathy Pacific Airways, and Japan Airlines.

includes Delta Air Lines from the United States, Aeroflot from Russia, Aeromexico, Air Europa from Spain, Air France, Alitalia from Italy, China Airlines, China Southern, KLM from the Netherlands, Korean Air from South Korea, and others. Alliances of this nature will allow airlines access to each other's feeder markets and to resources that will enable them to compete in what will ultimately be a worldwide deregulation. A *feeder market* is a market that provides the source—in this case, passengers for the particular destination. Ultimately, any major European airline without a strategic alliance in the United States will only limit its own horizons and lose market share. Airlines have merged or taken over others to increase their scope of operations and reduce costs in an effort to stay competitive. Delta acquired Northwest Airlines and Continental was acquired by United.

Another example is Southwest Airlines. Southwest operates more efficiently than the competition does despite the fact that its workforce is unionized. Southwest gets more flight time from its pilots than does American Airlines—672 hours a year versus 371—and racks up 60 percent more passenger miles per flight attendant. These efficiencies have resulted in annual profits for thirty consecutive years as a result of Southwest's dedication to a low-cost, high-customer-satisfaction strategy.

Carriers such as Southwest, AirTran, and JetBlue have lower operating costs because they use only one type of aircraft, fly point to point, and offer a no-frills service. Their lower fares have forced many larger airlines to retreat.

To reduce losses brought about by deregulation and high labor, pension plan, and fuel costs, major carriers have eliminated unprofitable routes, often those serving smaller cities. New airlines began operating shuttle services between the smaller cities and the nearest larger or hub city. This created the hub-and-spoke system (see Figure 2).

The Hub-and-Spoke System

To remain efficient and cost effective, major U.S. airlines have adopted a **hub-and-spoke system**, which enables passengers to travel from one smaller city to another smaller city via a hub or even two hubs. Similarly, passengers may originate their

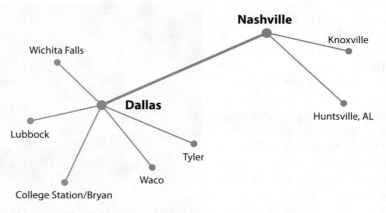

Figure 2 • The Hub-and-Spoke System.

travel from a small city and use the hub to reach connecting flights to destinations throughout the world.

The hub-and-spoke system has two main benefits: (1) Airlines can service more cities at a lower cost, and (2) airlines can maximize passenger loads from small cities, thereby saving fuel. The airlines have also used deregulation to their advantage to save money whenever possible, for instance, by cutting nonprofitable routes from some smaller cities.

New Airplanes

Boeing's first new airplane model in several years, the Dreamliner 787, takes advantage of huge advances made in aviation technology in the past decade and is capable of flying long-haul routes using up to 20 percent less fuel than today's similar-sized airplanes. Up to 50 percent of the primary structure of the plane, including the fuselage and wing, is made of components such as carbon fiber, which reduces the weight of the plane.[20]

Able to fly up to 9,700 miles without refueling, the Boeing 787 Dreamliner could easily manage a flight between New York and Moscow, Manila, or Sao Paulo or between Boston and Athens. Richard Aboulafia, chief analyst with Teal Group, comments, "If you look at it from an airline standpoint: you don't have a choice. If you don't have a 787-class aircraft and your competitor does, he can under price you and out-profit you."[21]

Boeing's competitor, Airbus, makes the Airbus A380. The giant double-decker Airbus A380 can carry up to 500 passengers for a distance of up to 8,000 miles. Singapore Airlines flew the first commercial flight of this aircraft in October 2007 between Singapore and Sydney, Australia.

Components of Airline Profit and Loss

Have you ever wondered why air travel is so expensive? You might find some answers in this section, where we look at the different costs included when you buy an air ticket. Airlines have both fixed and variable costs. *Fixed costs* are constant and do not change regardless of the amount of business. Examples are the lease of airplanes, the maintenance of airline-owned or leased terminals, interest on borrowed money, insurance, and pensions. *Variable costs* tend to rise and fall with the volume of sales or the number of flights. They include wages and salaries, advertising and promotion, fuel costs, passenger food and drink, and landing fees.

The biggest single cost for airline operations is labor, which is typically 30 to 45 percent of total operating

The new Boeing 787 Dreamliner is able to fly up to 9,700 miles without refueling.

costs. Senior pilots for airlines such as United and Delta can receive as much as $150,000 or more a year.[22] The median salary for a flight attendant is $56,000 or more a year, plus benefits.[23] Additionally, landing and takeoff charges charged to airlines by airports can add up to thousands of dollars per plane, depending on the airport and time of day. Passenger servicing costs such as reservations, ticketing, food, baggage handling, and an amount for additional security and fuel must also be accounted for in the ticket price. Once a schedule is set and the break-even point is reached, selling tickets to extra passengers produces large profits for airlines. Being able to offer just the right amount of discount tickets that are needed to fill a plane then becomes highly important. Capacity control is one yield-management technique for maximizing sales income by lowering the price of seats according to expected demand.

The Load Factor

A key statistic in analyzing an airline's profitability is the **load factor**, which means the percentage of seats filled on all flights, including planes being flown empty to be in position for the next day's schedule. The load factor, like the occupancy rate of a hotel, is an indicator of efficient or inefficient use. The current U.S. commercial air carrier load factor is usually around 79.74 percent. [24] The break-even point, the point at which carriers neither lose money nor make a profit, is likely to be unique on any given flight. This point is determined by the rate structure in effect, the length of the flight, the time spent on the ground, and other costs such as wages and salaries. An airline with a long-haul high-density route—for example, from New York to Los Angeles—has a decided cost advantage over another airlines' short-haul, low-density routes. The cost of flying a plane is sharply reduced once it reaches cruising altitude. A short flight thus costs more per mile than a long one does because a greater proportion of flight time and fuel is consumed in climbing to and descending from the cruising altitude.

In busy airports such as Atlanta, O'Hare, Los Angeles, and Kennedy, planes may spend much time waiting to take off or land. Every minute's wait adds dollars to personnel, fuel, and other costs. To keep costs down, the airlines have shifted to newer two-engine planes such as the Boeing 767, which enables them to reduce fuel consumption by as much as 30 percent. Aircraft have also reconfigured seat arrangements to include more seats, but this results in seats that are smaller and have less leg room for passengers. Claustrophobic? You'd better travel business class! A few years ago, American Airlines removed some rows of seats to give more leg room by spacing the remaining seats farther apart. This has proven to be a popular decision, and many others have followed.

Cruise Ships

More than 200 cruise lines offer a variety of wonderful vacations, from a Carnival cruise to freighters that carry only a few passengers. Travelers associate a certain romance with cruising to exotic locations and being pampered all day.

Being on a cruise ship is like being on a floating resort. For example, the *Diamond Princess* is a "Super Love Boat," weighing in at 116,000 tons with 18 decks and costing $400 million to build. This ship is longer than two football fields and is capable of carrying up to 2,670 passengers.[25] Cruise ship accommodations range from luxurious suites to cabins that are even smaller than most hotel rooms. Attractions and distractions range from early morning workouts to fabulous meals and nightlife consisting of dancing, cabarets, and sometimes casinos. Day life might involve relaxation, visits to the hair salon or spa, organized games, or simply reclining in a deck chair by the pool. Nonstop entertainment includes language lessons, charm classes, port-of-call briefings, cooking, dances, bridge, table tennis, shuffleboard, and more.

The cruise market has increased dramatically in recent years. About 9.0 million Americans cruise each year. Rates vary from a starting point of about $95 per person per day on Carnival Cruise Lines to $850 on the *Seabourn Yachts*. Rates typically are quoted per diem (per day) and are cruise-only figures based on double occupancy. Some 215 ships provide lake and river cruises, but most cruises are oceangoing. Casual ships cater to young couples, singles, and families with children. At the other end of the spectrum, ships that appeal to the upscale crowd draw a mature clientele that prefers a more sedate atmosphere, low-key entertainment, and dressing up for dinner. The spectacular new ships with multideck atriums and razzle-dazzle entertainment cater to the tourist market who have a median income of $50,000 a year.

Carnival Cruise Lines is the most financially successful of the cruise lines, netting about 20 percent of cruise sales. It targets adults between the ages of twenty-five and fifty-four and expects to attract millions of passengers with its spectacular atriums and round-the-clock activities. Its largest income, other than the fare itself, is from beverage service. Casino income is also high, and its casinos are the largest afloat. Carnival hopes that passengers will enjoy buying drinks and putting quarters, or preferably dollars, into the shipboard slot machines. They also hope their passengers will not mind their small cabins because the activities on the ship occupy passengers' waking hours and much of the night.

In 2009 alone, about 13.5 million passengers vacationed on a ship. As of Fall 2008, approximately 17 percent of the U.S. population target market had taken a cruise, but millions more intended to cruise in the next few years.[26] Many passengers are remarkably loyal to one particular vessel; as many as half of the passengers on a cruise may be repeat guests. Most cruise ships sail under foreign flags because they were built abroad for the following reasons:[27]

Take a Princess cruise for a dream vacation.

1. U.S. labor costs for ships, officers, and crew, in addition to maritime unions, are too high to compete in the world market.

2. U.S. ships are not permitted to operate casino-type gambling.

3. Many foreign shipyards are government subsidized to keep workers employed, thereby lowering construction costs.

A DAY IN THE LIFE OF RICHARD SPACEY

Cruise Director, Royal Caribbean International

Voyager of the Seas, one of the largest and most innovative cruise ships ever built, has a total guest capacity of 3,700, with 1,200 crew members. *Voyager of the Seas* is truly a revolution in the cruising industry. A virtual city in itself, she features the world's first floating ice-skating rink, a rock-climbing wall, an inline skating track, and the largest and most technically advanced theater afloat. There is a four-story Royal Promenade shopping and entertainment boulevard spanning the length of the ship that acts as a hub for the ship's vast array of activities and entertainment. Cruise director Richard Spacey was instrumental in implementing the unique entertainment and activities program aboard with the help of a support staff of 130 people. What follows is an account of a day in the life of the cruise director of one of the largest cruise ships in the world.

Monday—First Day at Sea

7:30–8:30 A.M. Yesterday we embarked 3,650 guests in Miami and headed for our first port of call, Labadee, our own private island on the coast of Hispaniola. Before most of the guests are up for the day, I plan and submit our daily activities schedule for the rest of the voyage to our hotel director for his approval. All of the cruise director's staff management team have submitted their reports after our staff meeting at embarkation yesterday. The assistant cruise director, who also submits the payroll and overtime hours for my approval, schedules the twelve activities staff for the week. Our cruise programs administrator says that three couples were married in the wedding chapel yesterday, and they are included in the 108 couples that have chosen to spend their honeymoon with us. A special party will be held later on in the week to celebrate this happy occasion. The youth activities manager reports that there are more than 600 children aboard, ranging in age from three to seventeen. The youth activities manager and her team of thirteen are responsible for providing age-appropriate activities for our junior cruisers. We offer a special deck and pool area/arcade for children in addition to our extensive youth facilities, which include a teen disco.

A large part of our business is group and incentive business. The group coordinator appropriates lounges and facilities for these special group events under the auspices of the cruise director. There will be seminars, group meetings, presentations, and cocktail parties. We have a state-of-the-art conference center/executive boardroom/screening room in addition to a large convention facility named "Studio B," which doubles as the ice rink. A retractable floor over the ice rink makes this a great space for large conventions. The shore excursion manager reports that tour sales are good for this voyage among the fifty land-based excursions that we offer. All of this information is consolidated into a report to the hotel director that is submitted on a daily basis.

8:45–9:30 A.M. Hotel director's meeting. All of the division heads in the Hotel Department meet to discuss the daily operation of this floating hotel. Today's agenda includes a monthly safety meeting. Each division head presents his or her monthly report on safety and environmental protection. Hospitality and the safety of our guests and crew are our top priorities.

9:45 A.M. The start of my public duties. I give a daily announcement and rundown of all the activities and entertainment happenings around the ship.

10:00 A.M. Morning walk-around. Time to kick off the first session of Jackpot Bingo for the week. On my way through the promenade, I encounter our interactive performers hamming it up with our guests.

10:30 A.M. The Studio B ice rink is busy with guests skating at our first All Skate session. There are several sessions throughout the day. The ice-skating cast (ten individuals) are responsible for running the sessions as well as skating in our Ice Show.

11:00 A.M. Time to change out of my day uniform into a business suit and put on stage makeup for the taping of our onboard talk and information show, "Voyager Live." I produce this segment from the Royal Promenade. We have three video programmers and an interactive TV technician. Interactive TV allows our guests to order room service, excursions, and movies with the click of a button in the privacy of their staterooms.

12:00 noon Noon lunch with the staff in the Officers and Staff Dining Room.

1:00 P.M. Change out of the business suit into shorts and a Polo shirt to emcee the Belly Flop Competition at 1:30 P.M. poolside. This is always a popular event among our guests. It gets quite a few laughs. This is followed by horse racing, cruising style. We pick six jockeys who move six wooden horses by a roll of the dice. The betting is fierce as the guests cheer their favorite horses on. I become the track announcer for three races and the horse auctioneer. Today we auction off the six horses for our Voyager Derby later in the week. The horses go to the highest bidder, and then the "owners" run them in a race later in the week for all the money. The six horses go for $2,100. A nice pot for one lucky winner.

2:30 P.M. I stop by the Sports Court to check out the action. The sports court is full of families enjoying our Family Hour activities with the youth staff. We offer a nine-hole miniature golf course, a golf driving simulator, full-court basketball/volleyball, inline skating, table tennis, and a rock-climbing wall that rises up the smokestack 200 feet above sea level—the best view in the Caribbean. By the end of the day, 125 people will have climbed the wall.

3:00–4:30 P.M. POWER-NAP TIME. The day will not end until about 12:30 A.M. Being "on stage" and available practically twenty-four hours a day can take its toll. This nap will carry me through until the end of the evening.

6:00 P.M. Back to the office to catch up on e-mail and general administrative business. It is also time to work on budget and revenue forecasting for the upcoming year.

7:30 P.M. Off to the Royal Promenade deck to mingle with the guests at the Welcome Aboard reception. The captain gives his welcome speech, and then we send the guests off to their dinner or the show at 8:30 P.M.

8:30 P.M. Meet in the Champagne Bar with the hotel director before dinner. Tonight we will entertain guests who are on their fiftieth cruise and also a representative from an insurance company who is thinking of booking 700 guests on a future cruise with us.

9:00 P.M. On my way to the dining room, I introduce our production show in the La Scala Theater for the main-seating guests.

10:45 P.M. After dessert, I introduce the show for second-seating guests and watch the show for quality control.

11:45 P.M. After the show finishes, I do a final walk around the lounges on the ship with my assistant. Karaoke has just finished in one of the secondary lounges and we have music playing everywhere. We have thirty-five musicians comprising several bands featuring all varieties of music (string quartet, jazz ensemble, piano bar, Calypso, Latin, Top 40). The disco is lively with singles' night tonight, and there are a few couples enjoying light jazz in the Jazz Club.

12:30 A.M. A full day. Definitely a far cry from Julie on the *Love Boat*! Time for bed because I have to be on the gangway at 8:00 A.M. to welcome our guests to Labadee.

In addition, cruise ships sail under foreign flags (called flags of convenience) because registering these ships in countries such as Panama, the Bahamas, and Liberia means fewer and more lax regulations and little or no taxation.

Employment opportunities for Americans are mainly confined to sales, marketing, and other U.S. shore-based activities, such as reservations and supplies. Onboard, Americans sometimes occupy certain positions, such as cruise director and purser.

The reasons that few Americans work onboard cruise ships are because the ships are at sea for months at a time with just a few hours in port. The hours are long and the conditions for the crew are not likely to be acceptable to most Americans. No, you don't get your own cabin! Still interested? Try **www.crewunlimited.com**.

The Cruise Market

There are marked differences between the segments of the cruise industry:

Mass Market—Generally, people with incomes in the $35,000 to $74,000 range, interested in an average cost per person of between $95 and $195 per day, depending on the location and size of the cabin

Middle Market—Generally, people with incomes in the $75,000 to $99,000 range, interested in an average cost per person of $175 to $350 per day. These ships are capable of accommodating 750 to 1,000 passengers. The middle-market ships are stylish and comfortable, with each vessel having its own personality that caters to a variety of different guests. Among the cruise lines in the middle market are Princess Cruises, Norwegian Cruise Lines, Royal Caribbean, Holland America Lines, Windstar Cruises, Cunard Lines, and Celebrity Cruises.

Luxury Market—Generally, people with incomes higher than $100,000, interested in an average cost per person of more than $400 per day. In this market, the ships tend to be smaller, averaging about 700 passengers, with superior appointments and service. What constitutes a luxury cruise is partly a matter of individual judgment, partly a matter of advertising and public relations. The ships that received the top accolades from travel industry writers and others who assign such ranks cater only to the top 5 percent of North American income groups. Currently, the ships considered to be in the very top category are *Seabourn Spirit*, *Seabourn Legend*, *Seabourn Pride*, *Crystal Cruises Crystal Harmony*, *Radisson Diamond*, and *Silversea Silver Wind*. These six-star vessels have sophisticated cuisine, excellent service, far-reaching and imaginative itineraries, and highly satisfying overall cruise experiences.

The rising demand for cruising means larger ships with resort-like design, numerous activities, and amenities such as "virtual golf," pizzerias, and caviar bars. Significant growth opportunities still exist for the industry. With only about 10 percent of the cruise market tapped and with an estimated market potential of billions, the cruise industry is assured of a bright future.

▶ Check Your Knowledge

1. Why are the major U.S. airlines struggling financially?
2. Why do most cruise ships sail under foreign flags?
3. Describe the cruise market.

An Exciting Destination

Now, let's visit one of the world's most popular and exciting cities.

Think of the excitement of planning a trip to the city of Paris, which is for many the most fabulous city in the world. Known as the City of Light, it is also one of the most romantic cities. Paris is a city of beautiful buildings, boulevards, parks, markets, and restaurants and cafés. Paris has excitement. So, for tourists, what to see first is an often-asked question over morning coffee and, of course, a croissant. There are city tours, but the best way to see Paris is on foot, especially if you want to avoid the hordes of tourists hovering around the popular attractions! Take your pick from the many places of interest: You could begin with the Eiffel Tower or the Notre Dame Cathedral, the Louvre or the Musée d'Orsay, the Île de la Cité, or simply a stroll down the Champs-Elysées.

Paris began as a small village on an island called the Île de la Cité, in the middle of the river Seine. In time, Paris grew onto the Left Bank (Rive Gauche) where the University of the Sorbonne was founded, which gave instruction in Latin—thus, it became known as the Quartier Latin, or Latin Quarter. The Latin Quarter has a Bohemian intellectual character with lots of small cafés and wine bars similar to Greenwich Village and Soho in New York. Nearby is Montparnasse, an area that is popular with today's artists and painters. On the Right Bank (Rive Droit) of the river Seine are many attractions; one favorite is the area of Montmartre, with the diminutive St. Pierre Church, the domes of Sacré-Coeur, and the Place du Tertre. Just walking along the winding streets up to Sacré-Coeur gives one a feel of the special nature of Paris. Savoring the sights of the little markets with arrays of fresh fruits, vegetables, and flowers; catching the aromas wafting out from the cafés; and seeing couples walking arm in arm in a way that only lovers in Paris do add to the ambiance that captivates all who go there and provide wonderful memories.

Close-up, Sacré-Coeur is a magnificent building in gleaming white. It towers over Paris, with its five bulb-like domes resembling a Byzantine church. The view from there, one of the highest parts of Paris, is spectacular, especially at sunset.

Notre-Dame Cathedral is the most famous Gothic cathedral in the world. The thirteenth-century cathedral is adorned with

The Sacré-Coeur in Paris.

The River Seine and the Eiffel Tower at night.

ornate stone carvings depicting the Virgin Mary, signs of the Zodiac, the Last Judgment, Vices and Virtues, Christ and His Apostles, and Christ in Triumph after the Resurrection. A portal above these and other stone carvings are the gargoyles immortalized in Victor Hugo's *The Hunchback of Notre Dame* as Quasimodo's den.

The Eiffel Tower was built more than 100 years ago for a World's Fair and has become one of the most recognizable buildings in the world and a symbol of Paris. On a clear day, you can see for up to forty miles at the top of the tower.

Of the many fashionable boulevards and avenues, the Avenue des Champs-Elysées, the main boulevard of Paris, stands out as one of the most grand. The Arc de Triomphe commemorates Napoleon's victories and houses.

The Louvre, the former residence of King Louis XIV, is the world's largest palace and largest museum. It is here that priceless works of art are displayed for public view. The *Mona Lisa* and *Venus de Milo* are the star attractions of extensive collections of Chinese, Egyptian, Greek, Roman, French, and European art, sculpture, and ceramics. In the courtyard of the Louvre is the controversial Plexiglas pyramid that was built to ease overcrowding at the entrance—but perhaps in part because of its striking contrast with the palace, the lines of museum visitors are now even longer than they were before. Other museums in Paris house collections of the best works of art by the greatest painters the world has known. They represent various periods of art throughout the centuries.

The Economic Impact of Tourism

The World Travel and Tourism Council, a Brussels-based organization, suggests that the revenue from travel and tourism will be $1.850 billion (2.8 percent of GDP) in 2011 and will rise by 4.2 percent per year.[28] The total contribution of travel and tourism to GDP, including its wider economic impacts, is forecast to be $9,226.9 billion (9.6 percent) by 2021. Total contribution of travel and tourism to employment, including jobs indirectly supported by the industry, is forecasted to rise to 323,826,000 jobs (9.7 percent) by 2021.[29]

Tourism accounts for 7.72 million jobs in the United States. The United States is second to France in the number of tourists (59.7 million) but first in tourism revenues (see Figure 3).

World international arrivals, according to the UNWTO, will reach 1.8 billion by 2030, more than triple the 475 million people who traveled abroad in 1992. Nearly every state publishes its own tourism economic impact study

International Tourism Receipts
(US $ billion)

Rank		2009
1	United States	93.9
2	Spain	53.2
3	France	49.4
4	Italy	40.2
5	China	39.7
6	Germany	34.7
7	United Kingdom	30.0
8	Australia	25.6
9	Turkey	21.3
10	Austria	19.4

Source: World Tourism Organization (WTO)©.

Figure 3 • World's Top Ten Tourism Earners. Notice that China now features prominently as a leading tourism nation.
(© UNWTO, 9284403211)

indicating billions of dollars in tourism revenue. The Tourism Industry Association's annual *Tourism Work for America Report*[30] indicates that travel and tourism are one of the nation's leading sectors. Statistics include the following:[31]

- International travelers spend about $134.4 billion on travel-related expenses (for example, lodging, food, entertainment) in the United States annually.

- There are 7.72 million people are directly employed in the travel industry, making travel and tourism the nation's second largest employer after health services.

- Travel generates more than $100 billion a year in tax receipts. If it were not for tourism, each U.S. household would have to pay about $1,000 more per year in taxes.

- Spending by international visitors in the United States is about $31 billion more than travel-related spending by Americans outside the United States.

- Approximately 59.7 million international travelers visit the United States each year.

- Just a small percentage increase in the world market would mean millions more visitors, which would create thousands of jobs and contribute billions of dollars in new tax revenue.

By employing approximately one out of every ten workers, travel and tourism is the world's largest employer and is the world's largest industry grouping.

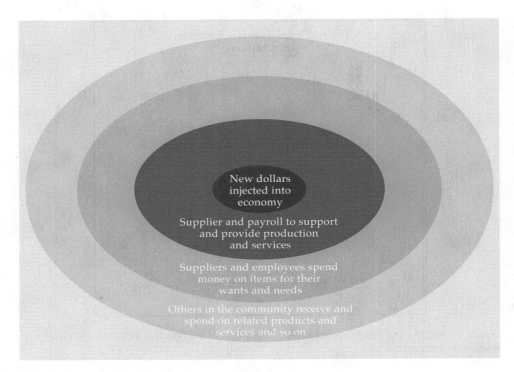

Figure 4 • The Multiplier Effect.

The Multiplier Effect

Tourists bring new money into the economy of the place they are visiting, and this has effects beyond the original expenditures. When a tourist spends money to travel, to stay in a hotel, or to eat in a restaurant, that money is recycled by those businesses to purchase more goods, thereby generating further use of the money. In addition, employees of businesses who serve tourists spend a higher proportion of their money locally on various goods and services. This chain reaction, called the **multiplier effect**, continues until there is a leakage, meaning that money is used to purchase something from outside the area. Figure 4 illustrates the multiplier effect.

In most economic impact studies to date, developed economies have a multiplier effect of between 1.5 and 2.0.[32] This means that the original money spent is used again in the community between 1.5 and 2.0 times. If tourism-related businesses spend more money on locally produced goods and services, it benefits the local economy.

Promoters of Tourism

The **Pacific Area Travel Association (PATA)** represents thirty-four countries in the Pacific and Asia that have united behind common goals: excellence in travel and tourism growth. PATA's accomplishments include shaping the future of travel in the Asia/Pacific region; it has had a remarkable record of success with research, development, education, and marketing.

Many countries have a minister of tourism, which is a cabinet-level position that can advocate tourism development, marketing, and management through the national tourism organization (NTO). Unfortunately, the United States does not have even a senior-level government official for tourism. Instead, an organization known as the Travel Industry of America (TIA) is the main body for the promotion and development of tourism in the United States. It speaks for the common interests and concerns of all components of the U.S. travel industry. Its mission is to benefit the entire U.S. travel industry by unifying its goals, coordinating private sector efforts to encourage and promote travel to and within the United States, monitoring government policies that affect travel and tourism, and supporting research and analysis in areas vital to the industry. Established in 1941, TIA's membership represents more than 2,000 travel-related businesses, associations, and local, regional, and state travel-promotion agencies.

State offices of tourism promote places of interest, such as Faneuil Hall and Quincy Market in Boston.

State Offices of Tourism

In the United States, the next level of organizations concerned with tourism are the state offices of tourism. These offices are charged by their legislative bodies with the orderly growth and development of tourism within the state. They promote information programs, advertising, publicity, and research on the recreation and tourism attractions in the state.

City-Level Offices of Tourism and Convention Centers

Cities have also realized the importance of the "new money" that tourism brings. Many cities have established **convention and visitors bureaus (CVBs)**, whose main function is to attract and retain visitors to the city. The CVBs are staffed by representatives of the city's attractions, restaurants, hotels and motels, and transportation system. These bureaus are largely funded by the transient occupancy tax (TOT) that is charged to hotel guests. In most cities, the TOT ranges from 8 to 18 percent. The balance of funding comes from membership dues and promotional activities. In recent years, convention centers have sprung up in a number of large and several smaller cities. Spurred on by expectations of economic and social gain, cities operate both CVBs and convention centers.

National Offices of Tourism

National offices of tourism (NOTs) seek to improve the economy of the country they represent by increasing the number of visitors and consequently their spending in the country. Connected to this function is the responsibility to oversee and ensure that hotels, transport systems, tour operators, and tour guides maintain high standards in the care and consideration of the tourist. The main activities of NOTs are as follows:

- Publicizing the country
- Assisting and advising certain types of travelers
- Creating demand for certain destinations
- Supplying information
- Ensuring that the destination is up to expectations
- Advertising[33]

Tour Operators

Tour operators promote tours and trips that they plan and organize. A *tour* is a trip taken by an individual or group of people who travel together with a professional tour manager/escort and follow a preplanned itinerary. Most tours include travel, accommodations, meals, land transportation, and sightseeing. The tour operator negotiates discounted travel, accommodation, meals, and sightseeing and then adds a markup before advertising the package. Tour operators also offer **vacation packages** to people traveling alone. Vacation packages include a combination of two or more travel services—hotel, car rental, and air transportation—offered at a package price. Most vacation packages offer a choice of components and options, allowing the client to customize his or her package to personal interests and budget.

Travel Agencies

A *travel agent* is a middleperson who acts as a travel counselor and sells travel services on behalf of airlines, cruise lines, rail and bus transportation companies, hotels, and auto rental companies. Agents may sell individual parts of the overall system or several elements, such as air and cruise tickets. The agent acts as a broker, bringing together the client (buyer) and the supplier (seller). Agents have quick access to schedules, fares, and advice for clients about various destinations.

The American Society of Travel Agents (ASTA) is the world's largest travel trade association, with more than 20,000 members in more than 165 countries. Agents use computer reservation systems (CRSs) to access service availability and make bookings. In the United States, the main vendors of CRSs are Amadeus, Sabre, Travel Sky, Worldspan, and Galileo.

A travel agent is more than a ticket seller. Agents serve their clients in the following ways:

- Arranging transportation by air, sea, rail, bus, car rental, and so on
- Preparing individual itineraries, personally escorted tours, group tours, and prepared package tours
- Arranging for hotel, motel, and resort accommodations; meals; sightseeing tours; transfers of passengers and luggage between terminals and hotels; and

special features such as tickets for music festivals, the theater, and so forth

- Handling and advising on many details involved with travel, such as insurance, foreign currency exchange, documentary requirements, and immunizations and other inoculations needed

- Using professional know-how and experience (for example, schedules of air, train, and bus connections, rates of hotels, quality of accommodations)

- Arranging reservations for special-interest activities, such as group tours, conventions, business travel, gourmet tours, and sporting trips

Travel agents have knowledge of destinations and can make air, ground, and hotel reservations for clients to visit popular destinations such as Venice, Italy.

However, the travel business has changed, resulting in a sharp decline in the number of travel agents, because there is less need for the traditional travel agent in the age of the Internet. Internet travel services such as Travelocity and Expedia have changed the way we book travel. As you know, it is quick and easy to go online and select travel dates, times, and fares. In fact, tourism services are among the top online purchases. As consumers, we can shop for the best price and most convenient schedule and purchase electronic tickets by entering our credit card numbers and billing information over a secure connection.

Tour Wholesalers and Consolidators

Tour suppliers provide the package components for tour operators via the services of hotels, attractions, restaurants, airlines, cruise lines, railroads, and sightseeing, which are packaged into a tour that is sold through a sales channel to the public.[34] Tour wholesaling came into prominence years ago because airlines had vacant seats, which, like hotel rooms, are perishable. Airlines naturally wanted to sell as many seats as possible and found that they could sell blocks of seats to wholesalers close to departure dates. These tickets are for specific destinations around which tour wholesalers build a tour. Wholesalers then sell their tours directly through retail agents.

Consolidators work closely with airlines to purchase discounted seats that they then sell to consumers for a price that is generally about 20 percent lower than the price offered by airlines or an online service company such as Travelocity. For example, the price of a consolidator's fare for a round trip to Bali from New York is $975, but the airline or Travelocity fare can be double that. So, consolidators are the place to call or e-mail when you are interested in booking an airfare.

Destination Management Companies

A destination management company (DMC) is a service organization in the visitor industry that offers a host of programs and services to meet clients' needs. Initially, a destination management sales manager concentrates on selling the

INTRODUCING PATTI ROSCOE

Chairperson, Patti Roscoe and Associates (PRA) and Roscoe/Coltrell, Inc. (RCI)

Patricia L. Roscoe landed in California in 1966, charmed by the beautiful San Diego sun compared to the cold winters in Buffalo, New York, her hometown. She was a young, brilliant middle manager who was to face the challenges of a time when women were expected to become either nurses or teachers. She became involved with the hotel industry, working for a large private resort hotel, the Vacation Village. Those were years to be remembered. She gained a very thorough knowledge of southern California tourism, as well as the inherent mechanisms of the industry. With the unforgettable help and guidance of her manager, she began to lay the foundations of her future career as a very successful leader in the field. The outstanding skills that she learned are, in fact, the very basis of her many accomplishments.

The list of her awards and honors is astounding: the prestigious CITE (Certified Incentive Travel Executive) distinction, the San Diego Woman of Accomplishment, and San Diego's Allied Member of the Year. The U.S. Small Business Administration gave her the Wonder Woman Award for her outstanding achievements in the field, and the San Diego Convention and Visitors Bureau has conferred on her the prestigious RCA Lubach Award for her contributions to the industry.

She is also extremely involved in civic and tourism organizations, including the Rotary Club, the American Lung Association of San Diego and Imperial Counties, and the San Diego Convention and Visitors Bureau.

The key to her success perhaps lies in her remarkable skill for interacting with people. It is the human resources, in fact, that represent the major strength of PRA. Its employees are experienced, dedicated, and service oriented. But what makes them so efficient is their dedication to working together as a team. Patti Roscoe guides, inspires, and motivates the teams. She is a self-admitted "softy," a creative and emotional leader who enjoys training her employees and following their growth step by step, to eventually give them the power of initiative they deserve, as a tool to encourage their creativity and originality. She constantly seeks to balance the concept of teamwork with the individual goals and private lives of her employees. It is through the achievement of such a balance that a profitable, healthy community is preserved. PRA is a bit more than a community, however: It is a family, and just like a mother, Patti's formula is discipline and love. At the same time, Patti's leading efforts are aimed at training her employees to think outside of the box, and to keep their views as broad as possible, which is the only way to rise above the commonplace, the rhetorical, and the trivial, to escape provincialism, and thus become unique individuals.

That's how the magic is done. PRA excels in creating "something that becomes exclusively yours—that has never been done before." PRA is decentralized into service teams to foster an entrepreneurial environment in which initiative and creativity can be boosted to the fullest. Therefore, PRA staff design personalized, unique events to give their customers an unforgettable time.

Since its opening in 1981, PRA has become one of the most successful destination management companies in the country, providing personal, caring service characterized by flexibility and creativity.

destination to meeting planners and performance improvement companies (incentive houses).

The needs of such groups may be as simple as an airport pickup or as involved as hosting an international sales convention with theme parties. DMCs work closely with hotels; sometimes DMCs book rooms, and other times hotels request the DMC's know-how on organizing theme parties.

Patricia Roscoe, chairperson of Patti Roscoe and Associates (PRA), says that meeting planners often have a choice of several destinations and might ask, "Why should I pick your destination?" The answer is that a DMC does everything, including providing airport greetings, transportation to the hotel, and VIP check-in; organizing theme parties; sponsoring programs; organizing competitive sports events, and so on, depending on the budget.

Sales managers associated with DMCs obtain leads, which are potential clients, from the following sources:

- Hotels
- Trade shows
- CVBs
- Cold calls
- Incentive houses
- Meeting planners

Each sales manager has a staff or team that includes people in the following positions:

- Special events manager, who has expertise in sound, lighting, staging, and so on
- Accounts manager, who is an assistant to the sales manager
- Operations manager, who coordinates everything, especially on-site arrangements, to ensure that what is sold actually happens

For example, Patti Roscoe's DMC organized meetings, accommodations, meals, beverages, and theme parties for 2,000 Ford Motor Company dealers in nine groups over three days per group.

Roscoe also works closely with incentive houses, such as Carlson Marketing or Maritz Travel. These incentive houses approach a company and offer to evaluate and set up incentive plans for the sales team, including whatever it takes to motivate them. Once approved, Carlson contacts a DMC and asks for a program.

In conclusion, thousands of companies and associations hold meetings and conventions all over the country. Many of these organizations use the services of professional meeting planners, who in turn seek out suitable destinations for the meetings and conventions. Some larger hotels and resorts now have a destination management department to handle all the arrangements for groups and conventions.

▶ Check Your Knowledge

1. Describe the economic impact of tourism.
2. Is it better to have a higher or lower multiplier effect and why?
3. Describe the promoters of tourism.

Business Travel

In recent years, business travel has declined due to[35] the general economic climate; in addition, increases in airfares, incidences in terrorism, and businesses reducing their travel budgets have negatively affected business travel.

Yet, a good percentage of the guests who check into upscale hotels around the world are traveling for business reasons. Much **business travel** is hard work, whether it is travel in one's own automobile or in the luxury of a first-class seat aboard an airplane. A good portion of business travel, however, is mixed with pleasure.

Counted as business travelers are those who travel for business purposes, such as for meetings; all kinds of sales, including corporate, regional, product, and others; conventions; trade shows and expositions; and combinations of more than one of these purposes. In the United States, meetings and conventions alone attract millions of people annually. Sometimes the distinction between business and leisure travel becomes blurred. If a convention attendee in Atlanta decides to stay on for a few days after the conference, is this person to be considered a business or leisure traveler? Business travelers, when compared to leisure travelers, tend to be younger, spend more money, travel farther, and travel in smaller groups, but they do not stay as long as leisure travelers do.

Beaches at the Cote d'Azur in southern France may be standing room only.

Social and Cultural Impact of Tourism

From a social and cultural perspective, tourism can have both positive and negative impacts on communities. Undoubtedly, tourism has made significant contributions to international understanding. World tourism organizations recognize that tourism is a means of enhancing international understanding, peace, prosperity, and universal respect for and observance of human rights and fundamental freedom for all without distinction as to race, sex, language, or religion. Tourism can be a very interesting sociocultural phenomenon. Seeing how others live is an interest of many tourists, and the exchange of sociocultural values and activities is rewarding.

Provided that the number of tourists is manageable and that they respect the host community's sociocultural norms and values, tourism provides an opportunity for a number of social interactions. A London pub or a New York café are examples of good places for social interaction. Similarly, depending on the reason for the tourist visit, myriad opportunities are available to interact both socially and culturally with local people. Even a visit to another part of the United States can be both socially and culturally stimulating. For example, New Orleans has a very diverse social and cultural heritage. Over the years, the city has been occupied by the Spanish, French, British, and Americans, so the food, music, dance, and social norms are unique to the area. The competitiveness of international destinations is based on attributes such as service quality, value for the price, safety, security, entertainment, weather, infrastructure, and natural environment.[36] Political stability is also important in determining the desirability of a destination for international tourism. Imagine the feelings of an employee in a developing country who earns perhaps $5 per day when he or she sees wealthy tourists flaunting money, jewelry, and an unobtainable lifestyle.

CORPORATE PROFILE

G Adventures

If you are tired of the one-week-in-the-Florida-sun vacation and want to do something exciting and off the beaten path, then G Adventures is the perfect company to turn to. They provide more than 1,000 small group experiences, safaris, and expeditions on all seven continents, to more than 100,000 travelers a year. This year, approximately 1.5 million more people are expected to visit their web site, some of them to change their lives forever.

G Adventure's CEO Bruce Poon Tip has been honored with the Entrepreneur of the Year Award, sponsored by NASDAQ, Ernst & Young, and the National Post. G Adventures has also been named one of Canada's 50 best managed companies and top 100 employers. Furthermore, they have greatly helped to improve the conditions in the many countries they visit.

Their philosophy, "The Freedom of Independent Travel with the Security of a Group," has been practiced since the start. They respect their travelers as individuals, and there is no requirement to be athletic to embark on one of their trips. The only thing needed is to have the spirit of adventure and the desire to experience a world totally different from what you are accustomed to.

In addition, the concept of responsible tourism is very important to G Adventures; the company employees interact with the local population, striving to leave behind only footprints. Their commitment is to support local people and communities and to protect the environment in which they travel. To that end, G Adventures developed Planeterra—the G Adventures Foundation that gives back to the people and communities that its passengers visit on their trips.

G Adventures hires people in different departments, including Operations, Product, Sales and Marketing, Finance, Human Resources, and Tour Leading. G Adventures employs more than 1,350 staff worldwide. All current postings can be found under the career section of their web site.

Maybe the most obvious choice for you is the position of G Adventures tour leader, which G Adventures calls Chief Experience Officers (CEOs). In this position, your main task is to make people's holiday dreams come true and make sure all travelers have an enjoyable time abroad.

As a CEO, most of the time the local hostel where you spend the night is your home, and your office is your backpack. On your way to work, you might have to hike the Inca Trail or canoe down the Amazon River.

(continued)

CORPORATE PROFILE (continued)

If you are interested in meeting and really interacting with people from different cultures, and like to show your passion to travelers of different backgrounds, ages, and interests, this is the perfect job for you.

Some of the requirements to work as a CEO include fluency in English and Spanish, a passion for travel, a love for Latin America (which is their main area of operations), and excellent people skills. No matter what happens and how bad your day has been, you always have to be the happy and helpful leader. Additional skills needed include awareness of, and commitment to, sustainable tourism, both environmentally and culturally, as well commitment to an eighteen-month contract. It takes time to become the perfect adventure tour leader, and once you have learned it, the company may decide to renew your contract. You also need to be resourceful, which here means being able to solve any kind of problem that might arise, expected or unexpected. Because of the nature of the work, you also need to have good health, first-aid certification, and an average level of computer literacy (Internet/e-mail/Microsoft Word/Microsoft Excel). If you have seen the world, or want to see it, in a truly interactive way, and you have leadership skills and are adventurous and brave, then this might be the perfect job for you. Why not give it a try?

Note: To apply to be a tour leader, you must complete the online application form found on the web site.

Just imagine what will happen when another 500 million people become tourists by virtue of increasing standards of living and the ability of more people to obtain passports. Currently, only about 37 percent of the U.S. population have passports, although that may increase because everyone returning to the United States from Mexico and Canada must now have a passport.[37] The population of eastern Europe and the new rich of the Pacific Rim countries will substantially add to the potential number of tourists.

Ecotourism

Ecotourism is focused more on individual values; it is "tourism with a conscience," sharing many of the same aspirations as sustainable tourism (described next). The International Ecotourism Society (TIES) defines *ecotourism* as "responsible travel to natural areas that conserves the environment and improves the well-being of local people."[38] This means that those who implement and participate in ecotourism activities should respect the following principles:

- Minimize impact.
- Build environmental and cultural awareness and respect.
- Provide positive experiences for both visitors and hosts.
- Provide direct financial benefits for conservation.
- Provide financial benefits and empowerment for local people.
- Raise sensitivity to host countries' political, environmental, and social climate.
- Support international human rights and labor agreements.[39]

Most ecotourism destinations can be found in developing countries with natural surroundings and plentiful flora and fauna. Places such as deserts, tropical rain forests, coral reefs, and ice glaciers are prime locations. Also important in ecotourism is the presence of a culture that is unique. The focus of ecotourism is to provide tourists with new knowledge about a certain natural area and the culture that is found in it, along with a little bit of adventure. As for the local inhabitants, ecotourism aims to help improve the local economy and conservation efforts. All parties are to gain a new appreciation for nature and people.

Generally, most of the more popular ecotourism destinations are located in underdeveloped and developing countries. As vacationers become more adventurous and visit remote, exotic places, they are participating in activities that should affect nature, host communities, and themselves in a positive manner. And because of the growing interests of travelers, many developed countries are following the trend and developing ecotourism programs. Ecotourism can be a main source of worldwide promotion of sustainable development geared toward tourists and communities in all countries.

Thus far, ecotourism projects tend to be developed on a small scale. It is much easier to control such sites, particularly because of limits that are normally set on the community, the local tourism business, and the tourists. Limitations may include strict control of the amount of water and electricity used, more stringent recycling measures, regulation of park and market hours, and more important, and caps on the number of visitors to a certain location at one time and the size of the business. Another reason ecotourism projects are kept small is to allow more in-depth tours and educational opportunities.

Sustainable Tourism

The increasing number of tourists visiting destinations has heightened concerns about the environment, physical resources of the place, and sociocultural degradation. The response of tourism officials has been to propose that all tourism be sustainable. The concept of **sustainable tourism** places a broad-based obligation on society, especially those involved in making tourism policy, planning for development, and harmonizing tourism and tourism development by improving the quality of a place's environment and physical and sociocultural resources. According to the UNWTO definition, sustainable tourism refers to the environmental, economic, and sociocultural aspects of tourism development, with the establishment of a suitable balance between these three dimensions to guarantee its long-term sustainability.[40]

The United Nations Environment Program (UNEP) says that sustainability principles refer to the environmental, economic, and sociocultural aspects of tourism. Sustainable

The Great Barrier Reef off the coast of Australia is one of the World Heritage sites.

tourism should (1) make optimal use of environmental resources that constitute a key element in tourism development; (2) respect the sociocultural authenticity of host communities, conserve their built and living cultural heritage and traditional values, and contribute to intercultural understanding and tolerance; and (3) ensure viable, long-term economic operations, providing socioeconomic benefits to all stakeholders that are fairly distributed, including stable employment and income-earning opportunities and social services to host communities, and contributing to poverty alleviation.

The two key factors are community-based tourism and quality tourism. Community-based tourism ensures that a majority of the benefits go to locals and not to outsiders. Quality tourism basically offers tourists "good value for their money." This also serves as a protection of local natural resources and as an attraction to the kinds of tourists who will respect the local environment and society. All tourism should be sustainable, but the problem is that all too frequently it is not.

Let's look around the world and see how the concept of sustainable tourism is applied. Europe has been criticized for lack of sustainability, but apart from the congested areas of, for example, London, Rome, and Paris, there are plenty of destinations focusing on sustainable tourism. In particular, tours to explore the ancient ruins, architecture, and cultures of Turkey and Greece are popular choices. Also, the largely untouched nature and distinctive culture of the Scandinavian countries are growing in recognition and importance.

If you want to explore Asia, join an ecotour to the snow-capped Himalayas in Nepal or the sultry jungles of Thailand. More and more places, such as Malaysia, Thailand, and the Philippines, are developing their tourism programs based on environmental conservation and protection. Looking for Shangri-la? The former hidden kingdom of the Hunza Valley in Pakistan has been opened for ecotourism, allowing a select number of tourists to see the 700-year-old Hunza Fort and village. The project has been internationally acclaimed as an outstanding example of sustainable tourism.

More adventures await you in Africa, where the tourism industry, especially ecotourism, has been growing tremendously over the past years. The most popular activity is the safari, which lets you get up close and personal with exotic wildlife such as elephants, gazelles, lions, tigers, cheetahs, and countless others. Kenya is an important destination for safaris, as are Tanzania, South Africa, Botswana, and Malawi.

Australia is home to an impressive variety of eco-friendly places. The Great Barrier Reef is perhaps the most famous spot. The "Leave No Trace" program, originally an American initiative, ensures that visitors to the reef act in a responsible manner. As a visitor to the Great Barrier Reef, you can enjoy activities such as snorkeling, fishing, diving, hiking, camping, and much more with many certified eco-friendly companies. Another area that is subject to increasing interest and attention is the massive glaciers of Antarctica.

These days, many regions of the world are designating their attractions as ecotourism sites. Vacationers are becoming more adventurous and are visiting remote, exotic places. They are participating in activities that hopefully affect nature, host communities, as well as themselves, in a positive manner.

From Yellowstone National Park in the United States to the Mayan ruins of Tikal in Guatemala, from the Amazon River in Brazil to the vast safari lands

FOCUS ON TOURISM

Ann-Marie Weldon, Johnson & Wales University, Charlotte, North Carolina

Think of the last vacation you took, or the one you are planning now. Where have you gone or where are you going? Is it somewhere exotic or is it close to home? How are you going to get there? Will you be flying, driving, or taking the train? Where are you going to stay? Are you going to a hotel, to a resort, or on a cruise ship? What will you do once you are there? Will you explore a new city, go to a museum, hang glide, visit a nature preserve, see a ball game, or visit an amusement park? What about the business traveler? Where are their business meetings? How about members of an association? Where is their convention or conference? Many people think tourism is just for the big cities or someplace they dream about visiting. As people travel, for either business or pleasure, they touch all the aspects of the hospitality industry. Tourism is what drives the need for hotels, resorts, cruise lines, restaurants, airlines, recreation, theme parks, and entertainment—in your home town or around the world.

The World Tourism Organization (UNWTO) report *Tourism: 2020 Vision*, which you learned about in this chapter, forecasts "that international arrivals are expected to reach nearly 1.6 billion by the year 2020" and "of these worldwide arrivals in 2020, 1.2 billion will be intraregional." This information may not mean anything to you right now, but each of the 1.6 billion people that are expected to travel will need a place to stay, eat, and experience something new. This indicates opportunities for new hotels, food and beverage outlets, places to hold meetings or conventions, and activities to keep guests busy. This will also provide employment potential in the traditional as well as the creative sense. We tend to forget the impact tourism has on our industry and what that means to our economy. Even in tough economic times, people still travel, though maybe not as far as they would otherwise. But they will need a way to get where they want to go and a place to stay, food to eat, and things to do once they get there.

Remember that each segment of the hospitality industry is interconnected with each other and depends on tourism—people traveling, experiencing, and exploring. Happy travels on your exciting new adventure in hospitality!

of Kenya, from the snow-capped Himalayas in Nepal to the sultry jungles of Thailand, from the Great Barrier Reef in Australia to the massive ice glaciers in Antarctica, it seems that sustainable tourism is taking place in all corners of the world. Quite frankly, some sort of ecotourism activity is happening in almost every country.

Cultural, Heritage, Nature, and Volunteer Tourism

Tourism has developed to the point that there are now several special-interest areas. *Culture* and *heritage* are "our legacies from the past, what we live with today, and what we pass on to future generations. Our cultures and natural heritages are irreplaceable sources of life and inspiration."[41] The **United Nations Educational, Scientific, and Cultural Organization (UNESCO)** has designated a number of World Heritage Sites worthy of protection and preservation because of the outstanding value to humanity of their natural and cultural heritage. There are nineteen U.S. sites on the World Heritage List, among them the Statue of Liberty and the Grand Canyon. Other places as unique and diverse as the wilds of East Africa's Serengeti, the pyramids of Egypt, the Great Barrier Reef in Australia, and the Baroque cathedrals of Latin America are also on the list. What makes the concept of world heritage exceptional is its universal application. World Heritage Sites belong to all the peoples of the world, no matter where they call home.[42]

Various examples of cultural tourism, heritage tourism, nature tourism, and volunteer tourism are as follows:

Cultural tourism. These trips are motivated by interest in cultural events such as feasts or festivals or activities such as theater, history, arts and sciences, museums, architecture, and religion. An example of **cultural tourism** is a visit to the Polynesian Center in Hawaii where you will find information on and examples of the lifestyles, songs, dance, costumes, and architecture of seven Pacific islands: Fiji, New Zealand, Marquesas, Samoa, Tahiti, Tonga, and Hawaii.

Heritage tourism. This type of tourism is motivated by historic preservation—a combination of the natural, cultural, and architectural environment. An example of heritage tourism is a visit to the Alamo in Texas, a former battlefield that attracts 3 million visitors a year.

Nature tourism. These trips are motivated by nature, such as a visit to a national park. In recent years, aging baby boomers have increasingly become interested in nature tourism and include nature attractions as a part of or a reason for their trip. (Notice that there are some similarities among these tourism areas of special interest.)

Culinary tourism. Gastronomic tours of Europe and Asia in places like Florence, Italy, and Bangkok, Thailand, have an appeal to the "foodies" among us. If not the main reason for a trip, culinary adventures are certainly a contributing reason, and the appeal is growing stronger with the advent of such programs as Anthony Bourdain's "No Reservations."

Volunteer tourism. **Volunteer tourism** provides travelers with an alternative to standard commercial vacation options. A major attraction for those who volunteer for overseas aid projects is the opportunity to travel safely and cheaply. While volunteers provide material benefits for the host community in exchange for shelter, both have the opportunity to experience each other's cultural differences. Dr. Stephen Wearing of the University of Technology in Sidney, Australia, and author of a book on volunteer tourism says:

The growth of eco-tourism, which grew out of the Green movement, proves people want an alternative, and volunteer tourism offers a similarly enriching experience.

While volunteers provide material benefits for the host community in exchange for shelter, both have the opportunity to experience each other's cultural difference.[43]

Dr. Wearing believes volunteer tourism will rival the popularity of ecotourism this decade.

Trends in Tourism and Travel

- Ecotourism, sustainable tourism, and heritage tourism will continue to grow in importance.
- Globally, the number of tourist arrivals will continue to increase by about 4 percent per year, soon topping 1 billion.
- Governments will increasingly recognize the importance of tourism not only as an economic force, but also as a sociacultural force of growing significance.
- More bilateral treaties are being signed, which will make it easier for tourists to obtain visas to visit other countries.
- The promotion and development of tourism will move even more from the public sector (government) to the private sector (involved industry segments).
- Technology will continue to advance, allowing even more information to be available more quickly to more places around the world.
- Marketing partnerships and corporate alliances will continue to increase.
- Employment prospects will continue to improve.
- Ticketless air travel will continue to increase.
- Travel and tourism bookings via the Internet will continue to increase rapidly.
- As an ever-increasing number of tourists visit destinations, managing these destinations will continue to be a challenge.
- Low-cost, no-frills airlines, such as Jet Blue, AirTran, ATA, and, of course, Southwest, will continue to gain an increased market share at the expense of the six main U.S. airlines.
- Airlines will try to entice travelers to book their trips via the airline's web site rather than through Expedia and similar sites.
- Automatic airport check-ins will become more popular.
- The cruise industry will continue to expand.
- There will be more alternative cruises.
- There will be increased concern for the health and safety of travel and tourism.
- Nature, culinary, and volunteer tourism will continue to increase.

CASE STUDY

Congratulations! You have just been appointed to your city's council. You discover that a hot topic soon to be presented to the council is the construction of a convention center. Your initial research shows that several midsized cities are considering the convention center as a way to increase economic activity, including job creation. The challenge these cities face is how to finance the convention center; projected costs are $100 million. Voters may resist a ballot to increase local taxes (either property or sales), but there is still the transient occupancy tax (TOT)—that is, taxes paid by people staying in local hotels—to consider. However, that tax is already earmarked for various local charities, and as we all know, good politicians want to get reelected, so voting against several worthy causes would not be popular. How can the center be financed and built? The city could float a bond on the market or could raise the TOT, but that might dissuade some groups from coming to your city because other cities have lower TOTs.

What would you do? What information do you need in order to decide whether to support or oppose the convention center?

Summary

1. Tourism can be defined as the idea of attracting, accommodating, and pleasing groups or individuals traveling for pleasure or business. It is categorized by geography, ownership, function, industry, and travel motive.

2. Tourism involves international interaction and, therefore, government regulation. Several organizations, such as the World Tourism Organization, promote environmental protection, tourism development, immigration, and cultural and social aspects of tourism.

3. Tourism is a collection of industries that, when combined, form the world's largest industry and employer. It affects other industry sectors, such as public transportation, foodservice, lodging, entertainment, and recreation. In addition, tourism produces secondary impacts on businesses that are affected indirectly, which is known as the multiplier effect.

4. Travel agencies, tour operators, travel managers, wholesalers, national offices of tourism, and destination management companies serve as middlepersons between a country and its visitors.

5. Physical needs, the desire to experience other cultures, and an interest in meeting new people are some of the motives of travelers. Because of flexible work hours, early retirement, and the easy accessibility of traveling, tourism is constantly growing.

6. From a social and cultural perspective, tourism can further international understanding and economically improve poorer countries. However, it can also disturb a culture by presenting it with mass tourism and the destruction of natural sites. A trend in avoiding tourism pollution is ecotourism.

7. Business travel has increased in recent years as a result of the growth of convention centers in several cities. As a result, business travelers have given a boost to hotels, restaurants, and auto rental companies. The number of female business travelers is rising as well.

8. Ecotourism is tourism with a conscience, or responsible travel to natural areas that conserves the environment and improves the well-being of the local people.

9. The concept of sustainable tourism places a broad-based obligation on society, especially those involved with tourism policy, planning, and development.

Key Words and Concepts

business travel
convention and visitors bureaus (CVBs)
cultural tourism
ecotourism
hub-and-spoke system
interdependency
load factor
multiplier effect

Pacific Area Travel Association (PATA)
sustainable tourism
tourism
United Nations Educational, Scientific, and
Cultural Organization (UNESCO)
vacation package
volunteer tourism
World Tourism Organization (UNWTO)

Review Questions

1. Give a broad definition of tourism and explain why people are motivated to travel.
2. Give a brief explanation of the economic impact of tourism. Name two organizations that influence or further the economic impact of tourism.
3. Choose a career in the tourism business and give a brief overview of what your responsibilities would be.
4. Discuss the positive and negative impacts that tourism can have on a country in relation to tourism pollution and ecotourism.

Internet Exercises

1. Organization: **World Tourism Organization (UNWTO)**
Web site: **www.world-tourism.org/**
Summary: The UNWTO is the only intergovernmental organization that serves in the field of travel and tourism and is a global forum for tourism policy and issues. It has about 154 member countries and 7 territories. Its mission is to promote and develop tourism as a significant means of fostering international peace and understanding, economic development, and international trade.
    (a) How much is spent on international tourism?
    (b) What does the *Tourism: 2020 Vision* predict?

2. Organization: **World Travel and Tourism Council**
Web site: **www.wttc.org**
Summary: The World Travel and Tourism Council is the forum for business leaders in the travel and tourism industry. With chief executives of some 100 of the world's leading travel and tourism companies as its members, the WTTC has a unique mandate and overview on all matters related to travel and tourism.
    (a) What is your opinion of the "Blueprint for New Tourism"?

Apply Your Knowledge

1. Analyze your family's and friends' recent or upcoming travel plans and compare them with the examples in the text for reasons why people travel.

2. Suggest some ecotourism activities for your community.
3. How would you promote or improve tourism in your community?

Suggested Activities

1. Go online and get prices for an airline round-trip ticket between two cities for a flight that is as follows:
   (a) More than 60 days out
   (b) 30–59 days out
   (c) 15–29 days out
   (d) 7–14 days out
   (e) for tomorrow
2. Compare the prices and share the results with your class.

Endnotes

1. World Travel & Tourism Council, *Travel & Tourism 2011*, www.wttc.org/site_media/uploads/downloads/traveltourism2011.pdf (accessed November 13, 2011).
2. World Tourism Organization (UNWTO), "In Focus: Transport," *UNTO World Tourism Barometer* 7 (June 2009), 42–46.
3. World Tourism Organization (UNWTO), *Press Release: Healthy Growth of International Tourism in First Half of 2011*, September 7, 2011, http://media.unwto.org/en/press-release/2011-09-07/healthy-growth-international-tourism-first-half-2011 (accessed November 14, 2011).
4. World Tourism Organization (UNWTO), Understanding Tourism: Basic Glossary, http://media.unwto.org/en/content/understanding-tourism-basic-glossary (accessed November 14, 2011).
5. World Tourism Organization, *Ethics and Social Dimensions or Tourism: Background*, http://ethics.unwto.org/en/content/background (accessed November 13, 2011).
6. World Tourism Organization (UNWTO), *About UNWTO*, http://unwto.org/en/about/unwto (accessed April 18, 2011).
7. World Travel & Tourism Council, *World: Key Facts at a Glance*, www.wttc.org/research/economic-impact-research/regional-reports/world/ (accessed November 14, 2011).
8. World Tourism Organization (UNWTO), *About UNWTO*, http://unwto.org/en/about/unwto (accessed November 14, 2011).
9. World Travel & Tourism Council, *World: Key Facts at a Glance*, www.wttc.org/research/economic-impact-research/regional-reports/world/ (accessed November 14, 2011).
10. World Tourism Organization (UNWTO), *Tourism: 2020 Vision* (Madrid: UNWTO, 1999).
11. Charles R. Goeldner and J. R. Brent Ritchie, *Tourism: Principles and Practices*, 9th ed. (New York: John Wiley and Sons, 2003), 42–48.
12. Goeldner and Ritchie, *Tourism: Principles and Practices*, 43.
13. Ibid.
14. Donald E. Lundberg, *The Tourist Business*, 6th ed. (New York: Van Nostrand Reinhold, 1990), 16.
15. Lundberg, *The Tourist Business*, 17.

16. N. S. Gill, "101 on the Ancient Olympic Games," *About.com*, http://ancienthistory.about.com/cs/olympics/a/aa021798.htm (accessed April 6, 2011).

17. Silk Road Foundation, *Marco Polo and His Travels*, www.silk-road.com/artl/marcopolo.shtml (accessed April 6, 2011).

18. Ibid.

19. Federal Aviation Administration, *Air Traffic: NextGen Briefing*, http://www.faa.gov/air_traffic/briefing/ (accessed November 14, 2011).

20. "Boeing Unveils Ambitious 787 Dreamliner Passenger Jet," *Philippine Star*, July 10, 2007, B8.

21. Ibid.

22. Salary.com, *Salary Wizard: Captain/Pilot in Command (Large Jet)*, http://swz.salary.com/SalaryWizard/Captain-Pilot-in-Command-Large-Jet-Salary-Details.aspx (accessed November 14, 2011).

23. Salary.com, *Salary Wizard: Flight Attendant*, http://swz.salary.com/SalaryWizard/Flight-Attendant-Salary-Details.aspx (accessed November 14, 2011).

24. Wikinvest, *Wiki Analysis: Industry-Specific Metrics*, www.wikinvest.com/industry/airlines (accessed April 13, 2001).

25. Princess Cruises, *Diamond Princess*, www.princess.com/learn/ships/di/index.html (accessed November 14, 2011); and Fran Golden, *Diamond Princess Review*, Cruise Critic, www.cruisecritic.com/reviews/review.cfm?shipID=296 (accessed November 14, 2011).

26. Bob Sharak, "Cruise Vacations Are Hot Even if the Economy's Not," *Travel Marketing Decisions*, Fall 2008: 3.

27. www.cruising.org/press/overview%202006/2.cfm

28. World Travel & Tourism Council, *Economic Impact Research*, http://www.wttc.org/eng/Tourism_Research/Economic_Research/ (accessed April 13, 2011).

29. Ibid.

30. www.world_tourism.org/market_research/facts

31. World Travel & Tourism Council, *Economic Impact Research*, http://www.wttc.org/eng/Tourism_Research/Economic_Research/ (accessed April 15, 2011).

32. Personal conversation with Dr. Greg A. Dunn Vice President, Y Partnership, April 12, 2011.

33. Personal correspondence with Karen Smith and Claudia Green, June 28, 2005.

34. NTA, *Home Page*, http://ntaonline.com (accessed November 14, 2011).

35. Personal correspondence with Edward Inskeep, June 4, 2007.

36. Personal conversation with Dr. Greg A. Dunn, September 14, 2007.

37. The Expeditioner, *How Many Americans Have a Passport?* http://www.theexpeditioner.com/2010/02/17/how-many-americans-have-a-passport-2/ (accessed April 16, 2011).

38. International Ecotourism Society (TIES), *What Is Ecotourism?* http://www.ecotourism.org/site/c.orLQKXPCLmF/b.4835303/k.BEB9/What_is_Ecotourism__The_International_Ecotourism_Society.htm (accessed November 14, 2011).

39. Ibid.

40. World Tourism Organization, *Sustainable Development of Tourism: Definition*, http://sdt.unwto.org/en/content/about-us-5 (accessed November 14, 2011).

41. http://whc.unesco.org/en/about/ retrieved November 16, 2011.

42. United Nations Educational, Scientific, and Cultural Organization, *World Heritage*, whc.unesco.org/en/about (accessed November 14, 2011).

43. University of Technology, Sydney, *Volunteer Tourism Beckons*, www.uts.edu.au/new/releases/2002/January/22.html (accessed April 18, 2011).

ndex